THE OXFORD
HISTORY OF
ANCIENT
EGYPT

Ian Shaw is a Lecturer in Egyptian Archaeology at the University of Liverpool. He studied Archaeology and Egyptology at Cambridge University, gaining a Ph.D. on the archaeological remains at Tell el-Amarna. He later undertook research into Egyptian quarrying and mining sites as a British Academy Research Fellow at New Hall, Cambridge. His other publications include *Ancient Egyptian Warfare and Weapons* (1992), *The British Museum Dictionary of Ancient Egypt* (1995), *The Dictionary of Archaeology* (1999), *Ancient Egyptian Materials and Technology* (2000), and *Ancient Egypt: A Very Short Introduction* (forthcoming).

THE OXFORD
HISTORY OF
ANCIENT
EGYPT

Edited by

IAN SHAW

OXFORD

UNIVERSITY PRESS

OXFORD

UNIVERSITY PRESS

Great Clarendon Street, Oxford OX2 6DP

Oxford University Press is a department of the University of Oxford.
It furthers the University's objective of excellence in research, scholarship,
and education by publishing worldwide in

Oxford New York

Auckland Bangkok Buenos Aires Cape Town Chennai
Dar es Salaam Delhi Hong Kong Istanbul Karachi Kolkata
Kuala Lumpur Madrid Melbourne Mexico City Mumbai Nairobi
São Paulo Shanghai Taipei Tokyo Toronto

Oxford is a registered trade mark of Oxford University Press
in the UK and in certain other countries

Published in the United States
by Oxford University Press Inc., New York

British Library Cataloguing in Publication Data

Data available

Library of Congress Cataloging in Publication Data

Data available

ISBN 0-19-280293-3 (Pbk)

10 9 8 7 6

ISBN 0-19-815034-2 (Hbk)

10 9 8 7 6

Printed in China

Frontispiece: faience plaque showing a king (perhaps Iuput II)
as a child-god emerging from a lotus.

PREFACE

This book describes the emergence and development of the distinctive civilization of the ancient Egyptians, from their prehistoric origins to their incorporation into the Roman empire. In 1961 Alan Gardiner's *Egypt of the Pharaohs* presented a fresh and detailed view of Egyptian history, based on the textual and archaeological data then available. Gardiner's history was largely concerned with the activities of kings, governments, and high officials through the centuries, from the beginning of the pharaonic period until the arrival of the Ptolemies. The *Oxford History of Ancient Egypt*, however, is concerned not only with political change but also with social and economic developments, processes of religious and ideological change, and trends in material culture, whether in the form of architectural styles, techniques of mummification, or the fabrics of ceramics. This more wide-ranging historical picture draws on the new types of evidence that have become available as archaeologists have begun to survey and excavate types of sites that were previously neglected.

Each chapter describes and analyses a particular phase in ancient Egyptian history. The contributors outline the principal sequence of political events, traces of which have survived to varying degrees in the textual record. However, against this backdrop of the rise and fall of ruling dynasties, they also examine the cultural and social patterns, including stylistic developments in art and literature. This allows them to compare and contrast purely political phases with archaeological and anthropological evidence ranging from the changing styles of pottery to human mortality rates. Each contributor seeks to explore not only *which* aspects of culture change at different points in time, but also *why* some change more rapidly than others or remain surprisingly stable at times of political disruption. A major influence on all of the chapters, however, is the patchiness of the archaeological record, which means that some sites and periods can be viewed through a huge number of different types of sources, while others can be only tentatively reconstructed, because of a lack of certain kinds of evidence (through poor preservation, inadequate excavation, or a combination of both). Because each of the periods in Egyptian history is no more or less than the sum of its archaeological and textual parts, the individual chapters in this history are direct reflections of such abundance or inadequacy, and the differences in authors' style, emphasis, and content can largely be traced back to the nature of the evidence with which they are dealing.

Although the sequence of chapters takes the form of a relatively straightforward historical progression from the Palaeolithic to the Roman period, the various sections incorporate critical approachs to each of the phases, sometimes questioning whether they deserve to be regarded as discrete chronological units, or whether there are broader trends in material culture that transcend (or even conflict with) the perceived political framework. It has been pointed out, for instance, that the decreasing size of royal pyramid complexes after the 4th Dynasty need not be evidence of a decline in royal power, as most historians have tended to assume, but might, on the contrary, indicate a more efficient use of resources in the late Old Kingdom and First Intermediate Period.

The pace of change in such aspects of Egyptian culture as monumental architecture, funerary beliefs, and ethnicity was not necessarily tied to the rate of political change. Each of the authors of this history has set out to elucidate the underlying patterns of social and political change and to describe, with due regard to the dangers of archaeological and textual distortion and bias, the changing face of Egyptian culture, from the biographical details of individuals to the social and economic factors that shaped the lives of the population as a whole.

Ian Shaw

School of Archaeology, Classics and Oriental Studies
The University of Liverpool
31 January 2000

ACKNOWLEDGEMENTS

I am most grateful to Hilary O'Shea, Senior Editor for Ancient History at Oxford University Press, and Georga Godwin, Assistant Editor, for their help in the production of this book. I would also like to thank Cathie Bryan for her translation of Chapter 3, and Meg Davies for compiling the Index.

Janine Bourriau would like to thank Manfred Bietak, Irmgard Hein, and David Aston for generously allowing her to draw on unpublished information on the current excavations at the site of Avaris (Tell el-Dab'a).

Alan Lloyd would like to record his thanks to Dr M. A. Leahy, Dr Dorothy Thompson, and Professor F. W. Walbank, who read draft versions of his chapters and offered many valuable comments.

CONTENTS

LIST OF COLOUR PLATES

LIST OF MAPS AND PLANS

LIST OF CONTRIBUTORS

IAN SHAW   University of Liverpool

STAN HENDRICKX   Provinciale Hogeschool Limburg (Hasselt)

PIERRE VERMEERSCH   Katholieke Universiteit, Leuven

BÉATRIX MIDANT-REYNES   Centre National de Recherches
Scientifiques, Paris

KATHRYN BARD   Boston University, Massachusetts

JAROMIR MALEK   Griffith Institute, Oxford

STEPHEN SEIDLMAYER   Berlin-Brandenburgische Akademie der
Wissenschaften

GAE CALLENDER   Macquarie University, Australia

JANINE BOURRIAU   McDonald Institute, Cambridge

BETSY BRYAN   Johns Hopkins University, Baltimore

JACOBUS VAN DIJK   Rijksuniversität, Groningen

JOHN TAYLOR   British Museum, London

ALAN LLOYD   University of Wales, Swansea

DAVID PEACOCK   University of Southampton

1 INTRODUCTION

CHRONOLOGIES AND CULTURAL CHANGE IN EGYPT

IAN SHAW

All history is clearly reliant on some form of chronological framework, and a great deal of time has been spent on the construction of such dating systems for ancient Egypt. Ever since the first Western-style history of Egypt was written by an Egyptian priest called Manetho in the third century BC, the 'pharaonic period', from c.3100 to 332 BC, has been divided into a number of periods known as 'dynasties', each consisting of a sequence of rulers, usually united by such factors as kinship or the location of their principal royal residence. This essentially political approach has served very well over the years as a way of dividing up Egyptian chronology into a series of convenient blocks, each with its own distinctive characteristics. It is, however, becoming increasingly difficult to reconcile this politically based chronology with the social and cultural changes revealed by excavations since the 1960s.

Chronology

As Egyptian historical and archaeological data have expanded and diversified, it has become apparent that Manetho's system—simple, durable, and convenient though it is—often strains to contain the many new chronological trends and currents that can be perceived outside the simple passing of the throne from one group of individuals to another. Some of the new work shows that at many points in time Egypt was far less culturally unified and centralized than was previously assumed, with cultural and political changes taking place at different speeds in the various regions. Other analyses show that short-term political events, which have often tended to be regarded as the paramount factors in history, may often be less historically significant than the gradual processes of socio-economic change that can transform the cultural landscape more over-whelmingly in the long term. As the long 'pre-Dynastic' periods of Egyptian prehistory have begun to be understood in terms of cultural rather than politi-cal developments, so the Dynastic Period (as well as the Ptolemaic and Roman periods) has begun to be understood not only in terms of the traditional sequence of individual kings and ruling families but also in terms of such fac-tors as the types of fabric being used for pottery, and the painted decoration applied to wooden coffins.

Modern Egyptologists' chronologies of ancient Egypt combine three basic approaches. First, there are 'relative' dating methods, such as stratigraphic exca-vation, or the 'sequence dating' of artefacts, which was invented by Flinders Petrie in 1899. In the late twentieth century, as archaeologists have developed a more subtle understanding of the ways in which the materials and design of different types of Egyptian artefacts (particularly ceramics) changed over time, it has become possible to apply forms of seriation to many different types of object. Thus Harco Willems's seriation of Middle Kingdom coffins, for in-stance, has provided a better understanding of cultural changes in the various provinces of 11th–13th Dynasty Egypt, complementing the information already available about national political change during the same period.

Secondly, there are so-called absolute chronologies, based on calendrical and astronomical records obtained from ancient texts. Thirdly, there are 'radio-metric' methods (the most commonly used examples of which are radiocarbon dating and thermoluminescence), by means of which particular types of arte-facts or organic remains can be assigned dates in terms of the measurement of radioactive decay or accumulation.

Radiocarbon Dating and Egyptian Chronology

The relationship between the calendrical and radiometric chronological sys-tems has been relatively ambivalent over the years. Since the late 1940s, when a series of Egyptian artefacts were used as a benchmark in order to assess the reli-ability of the newly invented radiocarbon dating technique, a consensus has emerged that the two systems are broadly in line. The major problem, however, is that the traditional calendrical system of dating, whatever its failings, virtu-ally always has a smaller margin of error than radiocarbon dates, which are nec-essarily quoted in terms of a broad band of dates (that is, one or two standard deviations), never capable of pinpointing the construction of a building or the making of an artefact to a specific year (or even a specific decade). Certainly the advent of dendrochronological calibration curves—allowing the spans of radiocarbon years to be converted into actual calendar years—represents a sig-nificant improvement in terms of accuracy. However, the vagaries of the curve and the continued need to take into account associated error mean that dates must still be quoted as a range of possibilities rather than one specific year.

The prehistory of Egypt, on the other hand, has benefited greatly from the application of radiometric dating, since it was previously reliant on relative dating methods (see Chapters 2 and 3). The radiometric techniques have made it possible not only to place Petrie's 'sequence dates' within a framework of absolute dates (however imprecise), but also to push Egyptian chronology back into the earlier Neolithic and Palaeolithic periods.

From Prehistory to History: Late Predynastic Artefacts and the Palermo Stone

There are only a small number of artefacts from the late Predynastic Period that can be used as historical sources, documenting the transition into full unified statehood. These are funerary stelae, votive palettes, ceremonial maceheads, and small labels (of wood, ivory, or bone) originally attached to items of élite funerary equipment. In the case of the stelae, palettes, and maceheads, it was clearly the intention that they should commemorate many different kinds of royal act,

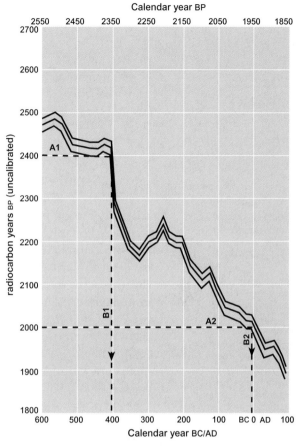

whether the King's own death and burial or his act of devotion to one of the gods or goddesses. Some of the smaller, earlier labels (particularly those recently excavated from the late Predynastic 'royal tomb' U-j at Abydos, see Chapter 4) are simply records of the nature or origins of the grave goods to which they were attached, but some of the later labels, from the Early Dynastic royal graves at Abydos, employ a similar repertoire of depictions of royal acts in order to assign the items in question to a particular date in the reign of a specific king.

If the purpose of this mobiliary art of the late fourth and early third millennia BC was to label, commemorate, and date, then their decoration has to be seen in terms of the desire to communicate the 'context' of the object in terms of event and ritual. Nick Millet has particularly demonstrated this in his analysis of the Narmer macehead, which was part of a group of late Predynastic and early pharaonic votive items (including the Narmer palette and Scorpion macehead) excavated by Quibell and Green in the temple precinct at Hierakonpolis. The analysis of the scenes and texts on these objects is complicated by our modern need to be able to distinguish between event and ritual. But the ancient Egyptians show little inclination to distinguish consistently between the two,

In order to convert radiocarbon dates into real calendar dates, they have to be 'calibrated' with the use of a dendrochronological (tree-ring) curve. Radiocarbon dates can be converted into ranges of calendar dates. The central line of the curve shows the mean estimate of the age, while the two outer lines show the extent of the probable error on the date (at one 'standard deviation'). It is possible to use a diagram of this type to produce a rough calibration, but more precise results can be achieved with the use of widely available computer software.

These scenes carved on the ceremonial macehead of King Narmer from the temple of Hierakonpolis, *c.*3100 BC, include a ceremonial appearance of the king, wearing the Red Crown and seated on a stepped throne dias, shaded by a canopy. In front of him are a seated figure in a carrying chair, rows of bearded men (Asiatics?), and animals captured in a military campaign. The prisoners were evidently paraded between two rows of three cairns.

and indeed it might be argued that Egyptian ideology during the pharaonic period—particularly in so far as it related to the kingship—was reliant on the maintenance of some degree of confusion between real happenings and purely ritual or magical acts.

In terms of the palettes and maceheads, the Canadian Egyptologist Donald Redford suggests that there must have been a need to commemorate the unique events of the unification at the end of the third millennium BC, but that these events were 'commemorated' rather than 'narrated'. This distinction is a crucial one: we cannot expect to disentangle 'historical' events from scenes that are commemorative rather than descriptive—or, at least, if we do so we may often be misled.

One of the most important historical sources for the Early Dynastic Period (3000–2686 BC) and the Old Kingdom (2686–2160 BC) is the Palermo Stone, part of a 5th Dynasty basalt stele (*c.*2400 BC) inscribed on both sides with royal annals stretching back to the mythical prehistoric rulers. The main fragment has been known since 1866 and is currently in the collection of the Palermo Archaeological Museum, Sicily, although there are also further pieces in the Egyptian Museum, Cairo, and the Petrie Museum, London. The slab must originally have been about 2.1 m. long and 0.6 m. wide, but most of it is now missing, and there is no surviving information about its provenance. This document—along with the 'day-books', the annals and 'king-lists' inscribed on temple walls, and the papyri held in temple and palace archives—was doubtless the kind of document that Manetho consulted when he was compiling his history or *Aegyptiaca*.

The text of the Palermo Stone enumerates the annals of the kings of Lower Egypt, beginning with the many thousands of years that were assumed to have been taken up by mythological rulers, until the time of the god Horus, who is said to have given the throne to the human king Menes. Human rulers are then listed up to the 5th Dynasty. The text is divided into a series of horizontal registers divided by vertical lines that curve in at the top, apparently in imitation of the hieroglyph for regnal year (*renpet*), thus indicating the memorable events of individual years in each king's reign. The situation is slightly confused by the fact that the dates cited in the Palermo Stone appear to refer to the number of biennial cattle censuses (*hesbet*) rather than to the number of years that the king had reigned; therefore the number of 'years' in the date may well have to be doubled to find out the actual number of regnal years.

The types of event that are recorded on the Palermo Stone are cult ceremonies, taxation, sculpture, building, and warfare—that is, precisely the type of phenomena that are recorded on the protodynastic ivory and ebony labels from Abydos, Saqqara, and various other early historical sites. The introduction of the *renpet* sign on the labels, in the reign of Djet, makes this comparison even closer. There are two differences, however: first, the labels include clerical information, while the Palermo Stone does not, and, secondly, the Palermo Stone includes records of the Nile inundation, whereas the labels do not. Both of these types of information seem to have occupied the same physical part of the document's format—that is, the bottom of the record. Redford suggests that this shows that the Old Kingdom *genut* (the royal annals that are assumed to have existed at this date, but have

not survived except in the form of the Palermo Stone) were concerned with hydraulic/climatic change, which, with its crucial agricultural and economic consequences, was potentially the most important aspect of change as far as the reputation of each individual king was concerned. This kind of hydraulic information would, however, have perhaps been regarded as irrelevant to the function of the labels attached to funerary equipment.

This inscribed fragment of a basalt slab is the largest surviving section of the 5th Dynasty king-list known as the Palermo Stone. It is inscribed with the names of rulers stretching from the Old Kingdom back into the semi-mythological times that were believed to precede the Dynastic Period. The rows of compartments, containing inscriptions summarizing the main events of a particular year, are each separated by the hieroglyph *renpet*, signifying a regnal year.

King-Lists, Royal Titles, and the Divine Kingship

Apart from the Palermo Stone, the basic sources used by Egyptologists to construct the traditional chronology of political change in Egypt are Manetho's history (which, unfortunately, has survived only in the form of excerpts compiled by the later authors Josephus, Africanus, Eusebius, and George Syncellus), the so-called king-lists, dated records of astronomical observations, textual and artistic documents (such as reliefs and stelae) bearing descriptions apparently referring to historical events, genealogical information, and synchronisms with

In this 'king-list', on a wall in the temple of Sety I at Abydos, c.1300 BC, Sety and the young prince Rameses (the future Rameses II) bring offerings to the list of names of kings written out in a continuous sequence from the 1st to the 19th Dynasty. Certain kings' names (and sometimes whole dynasties) were omitted from the list when the priests at Abydos regarded them as illegitimate.

non-Egyptian sources, such as the Assyrian king-lists. For the 28th–30th Dynasties, the Demotic Chronicle serves as a unique early Ptolemaic source concerning political events in this last phase of the Late Period, compensating to some extent for the dearth of historical information provided by the papyri and monuments of this date (as well as the fact that Manetho gives only the names and reign lengths of the kings). Wilhelm Spiegelberg and Janet Johnson have shown that careful translation and interpretation of the 'oracular statements' in this pseudo-prophetic document can shed new light not only on the events of the period (such as the suspected co-regency between Nectanebo I and his son

Tachos) but also on the ideological and political context of the fourth century BC.

Like most other ancient peoples, the ancient Egyptians dated important political and religious events not according to the number of years that had elapsed since a single fixed point in history (such as the birth of Christ in the modern Western calendar), but in terms of the years since the accession of each current king (regnal years). Dates were, therefore, recorded in the following typical format: 'day 2 of the first month of the season *peret* in the fifth year of Nebmaatra (Amenhotep III)'. It is important to be aware of the fact that, for the

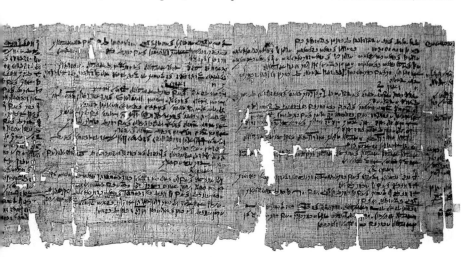

This is the first page of the Demotic Chronicle (Papyrus 215 in the Bibliothèque National, Paris), *c*.300 BC, an early Ptolemaic document consisting of a list of pseudo-prophecies that can be used to reconstruct one particular ancient version of Late Period history.

Egyptians, the reign of each new king represented a new beginning, not merely philosophically but practically, given the fact that dates were expressed in such terms. This means that there would probably have been a psychological tendency to regard each new reign as a fresh point of origin: every king was, therefore, essentially reworking the same universal myths of kingship within the events of his own time.

One important aspect of the Egyptian kingship throughout the pharaonic period was the existence of a number of different names for each individual ruler. By the Middle Kingdom, each king held five names (the so-called fivefold titulary), each of which encapsulated a particular aspect of the kingship: three of them stressed his role as a god, while the other two emphasized the supposed division of Egypt into two unified lands. The birth name (or *nomen*), such as Rameses or Mentuhotep, introduced by the title 'son of Ra', was the only one to be given to the pharaoh as soon as he was born. It was also usually the last name given in inscriptions identifying the king by his whole sequence of names and titles. The other four names—Horus, *nebty* ('he of the two ladies'), (Horus of) Gold, and *nesu-bit* ('he of the sedge and the bee')—were given to him at the time of his installation on the throne, and their components may sometimes convey something of the ideology or intentions of the king in question. As far as the rulers of Dynasty 0 and the beginning of the Early Dynastic Period were

The mummified head of Rameses II still preserves the king's distinctive facial features. Although nearly all of the royal tombs in the Valley of the Kings were thoroughly robbed in ancient times, the mummies of most of the New Kingdom rulers survived, because they were deliberately gathered together into two secret caches by Theban priests in the early first millennium BC.

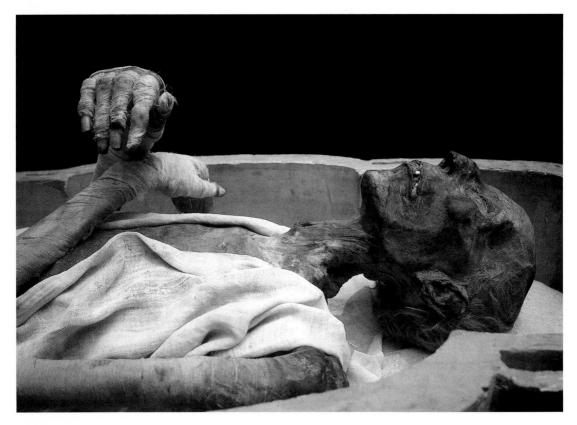

concerned, we know only their 'Horus names', typically written inside a *serekh* frame (a kind of diagram of the palace gateway), upon which a Horus-falcon was perched. It was the late 1st Dynasty ruler Anedjib (*c.*2900 BC) who was the first to hold a *nesu-bit* name (Merpabia), but it was not until the reign of Sneferu, 2613–2589 BC, in the 4th Dynasty, that this name was first framed by the familiar cartouche shape (an encircling loop that perhaps signified the infinite extent of the royal domain).

The title *nesu-bit* has often been translated as 'King of Upper and Lower Egypt', but it actually has a much more complex and significant meaning. *Nesu* seems to be intended to refer to the unchanging divine king (almost the kingship itself), while the word *bit* describes the current ephemeral holder of the kingship: the one individual king in power at a specific point in time. Each king was, therefore, a combination of the divine and the mortal, the *nesu* and the *bit*, in the same way that the living king was linked with Horus, and the dead kings, the royal ancestors, were associated with Horus' father Osiris. It was primarily because of the Egyptians' sense of each of their kings as incarnations of Horus and Osiris that the tradition of the worship of divine royal ancestors developed. This convention, whereby the current ruler made obeisance to his predecessors, is the reason for the creation of the so-called king-lists, which were lists of royal names mainly recorded on the walls of tombs and temples (most notably the 19th Dynasty temples of Sety I and Rameses II at Abydos), but also in the form of papyri, only one example of which survives (the so-called Turin Canon), or remote desert rock carvings, as with the list at the Wadi Hammamat siltstone quarries in the Eastern Desert. The continuity and stability of the kingship were preserved by making offerings to all those kings of the past who were regarded as legitimate rulers, just as we see Sety I doing in his cult temple at Abydos. It is usually presumed that king-lists were among the sources used by Manetho in compiling his history.

The Turin Canon, a Ramessid papyrus dating to the thirteenth century BC, is the most informative of the Egyptian king-lists. From the Second Intermediate Period (1650–1550 BC), it stretched back with reasonable accuracy to the reign of the 1st Dynasty ruler Menes (*c.*3000 BC), and even beyond that into a mythical prehistoric time when the gods ruled over Egypt. Each king's reign was recorded in terms of years, months, and days. It also provides some support for Manetho's system of dynasties by incorporating a break at the end of the 5th Dynasty (see Chapter 5).

The king-lists were not concerned so much with history as with ancestor worship: the past is presented as a combination of the general and the individual, and the constancy and universality of the kingship are celebrated through the listing of specific individual holders of the royal titulary. In his commentary on *Herodotus Book II*, Alan Lloyd writes, 'Since all historical study involves general and particular, attempting to place particular phenomena against a background of general principle or law, there is always a tension between the two, and this tension is resolved in Egypt overwhelmingly in favour of the latter.' The conflict between the general and the particular is undoubtedly an important factor in ancient Egyptian chronology and history. The texts and artefacts that form the basis of Egyptian history usually convey information that is either general (mythological or ritualistic) or particular (historical), and the trick in constructing a historical narrative is to distinguish as clearly as possible between these types of information, taking into account the Egyptians' tendency to blur the boundaries between the two.

The Swiss Egyptologist Erik Hornung describes Egyptian history as a kind of 'celebration' of both continuity and change. Just as the living king could be regarded as synonymous with the falcon-god Horus, so his individual subjects (from at least the First Intermediate Period onwards) eventually came to identify themselves with the god Osiris after their deaths. In other words, the Egyptians were used to the idea of portraying human individuals as combinations of the general and the particular. Their own sense of history therefore comprised both the specific and the universal in equal measure.

The Role of Astronomy in Traditional Egyptian Chronology

The task of the modern historian of ancient Egypt is usually to attempt to tie together all the strands of evidence in the form of individuals' biographies on the walls of tombs, lists of kings on temple walls, stratigraphic evidence of archaeological excavations, and a whole range of other pieces of information. In the pharaonic, Ptolemaic, and Roman periods, the 'traditional' absolute chronologies tend to rely on complex webs of textual references, combining such elements as names, dates, and genealogical information into an overall historical framework that is more reliable in some periods than in others. The so-called intermediate periods have proved to be particularly awkward phases, partly because there was often more than one ruler or dynasty reigning simultaneously in different parts of the country. The surviving records of observations of the heliacal rising of the dog-star Sirius serve both as the linchpin of the reconstruction of the Egyptian calendar and its essential link with the chronology as a whole.

The goddess Sopdet, known as Sothis in the Graeco-Roman period (332 BC–AD 395), was the personification of the 'dog-star', which the Greeks called Seirios (Sirius). She was usually represented as a woman with a star poised on her head, although the earliest depiction, on an ivory tablet of the 1st Dynasty king Djer (c.3000 BC) from Abydos, appears to show her as a seated cow with a plant between her horns. Since a depiction of a plant is used as the ideogram meaning 'year' in the pharaonic writing system, the Egyptians may have already been correlating the rising of the dog-star with the beginning of the solar year, even in the early third millennium BC. Along with her husband Sah (Orion) and her son Soped, Sopdet was part of a triad that paralleled the family of Osiris, Isis, and Horus. She was therefore described in the Pyramid Texts as having united with Osiris to give birth to the morning star.

In terms of the Egyptian calendar, Sopdet was the most important of the stars or constellations known as decans, and the 'Sothic rising' coincided with the beginning of the solar year only once every 1,460 years (or, more accurately, 1,456 years). We know that this rare synchronization of the heliacal rising of Sopdet with the beginning of the Egyptian civil year (or 'wandering year', as it is sometimes described, given that it gradually falls behind the solar year at a rate of about a day every four years) took place in AD 139, during the reign of the Roman emperor Antoninus Pius, because the event was commemorated by the issue of a special coin at Alexandria. There would have been earlier heliacal risings in 1321–1317 BC and 2781–2777 BC, and the period that elapsed between each such rising is known as a Sothic cycle.

Two Egyptian textual records of Sothic risings (dating to the reigns of Senusret III and Amenhotep I) form the basis of the conventional chronology of Egypt, which, in turn, influences that of the whole Mediterranean region. These two documents are a 12th Dynasty letter from the site of Lahun, written on day 16, month 4, of the second season in year 7 of the reign of Senusret III, and an 18th Dynasty Theban medical papyrus (Papyrus Ebers), written on day 9, month 3, of the third season of year 9 in the reign of Amenhotep I. By assigning absolute dates to each of these documents (1872 BC for the Lahun rising in year 7 of Senusret III, and 1541 BC for the Ebers rising in regnal year 9 of Amenhotep I), Egyptologists have been able to extrapolate a set of absolute dates for the whole of the pharaonic period, on the basis of records of the lengths of reign of the other kings of the Middle and New kingdoms.

It is not possible, however, to be totally confident of the absolute dates cited above, since the precise dating is dependent on our knowledge of the location (or locations) where the astronomical observations were made. It used to be assumed—without any real evidence—that such observations were made at Memphis or perhaps Thebes, but Detlef Franke and Rolf Krauss have argued that they were all made at Elephantine. William Ward, on the other hand, suggested that they are all more likely to have been separate local observations, which would have resulted in a time lag in terms of the various 'national' religious festivals (that is, both the observations and the corresponding festivals may actually have taken place at different times and in different parts of the country). This continuing uncertainty means that our astronomical linchpins are in reality somewhat floating, although it should be noted that the differences between the 'high' and 'low' chronologies (based largely on assumptions concerning different observation points) are usually only a few decades at most.

Co-Regencies

One of the peculiarities of Egyptian chronology, provoking both confusion and debate, is the concept of the 'co-regency', a modern term applied to the periods during which two kings were simultaneously ruling, usually consisting of an overlap of several years between the end of one sole reign and the beginning of the next. This system may have been used, from at least as early as the Middle Kingdom, in order to ensure that the transfer of power took place with the minimum of disruption and instability. It would also have enabled the chosen successor to gain experience in the administration before his predecessor died.

It seems, however, that the dating systems during co-regencies may have differed from one period to another. Thus 12th Dynasty co-regents may have each used separate regnal dates, so that overlaps occurred between the kings' reigns, producing examples of so-called double dates, when both dating systems were used to date a single monument (see Chapter 7). In the New Kingdom, there are no certain instances of double dates, therefore a different system seems to have been used. In the reigns of Thutmose III 1479–1425 BC and Hatshepsut 1473–1458 BC, for instance, year dates appear to have been counted with reference to Hatshepsut's accession, as if Hatshepsut had become ruler at the same time as Thutmose III. It is a moot point as to whether separate dates were used by two kings during the possible co-regencies of Thutmose III–Amenhotep II and Amenhotep III–Amenhotep IV. The arguments for and against a co-regency between the two latter kings have been carefully reviewed by Donald Redford and later by William Murnane. However, there is still considerable controversy over the question of which co-regencies actually took place and how long they lasted. There are also some scholars (including Gae Callender in Chapter 7 of this volume) who argue that co-regencies may never have occurred at all.

'Dark Ages' and Other Chronological Problems

Some of the problems encountered in Egyptian chronology have already been mentioned, such as the potential confusion of links between astronomical observations and specific dates, the uncertainty as to which co-regencies (if any) actually occurred, and the assumption that the Egyptians of the pharaonic period and later continually dated events according to an artificial 'wandering' civil year of 365 days, which was rarely synchronized with the real solar year.

There are also, of course, a number of other Egyptian historical problems, ranging from unreliability of sources (for example, Manetho's history, given that we neither know his sources nor have his original text) and frequent uncertainty regarding lengths of kings' reigns (for example, the Turin Canon says that Senusret II and III have reigns of nineteen and thirty-nine years respectively, whereas their highest recorded regnal years on documents that are actually contemporary with their reigns are only six and nineteen).

Egypt, like other cultures, has periods in history that are more or less documented than others, and it is primarily this patchiness in the survival of archaeological and textual records from different dates that has led to the assumption that there were 'intermediate periods', when the political and social stability of the pharaonic period appeared to have been temporarily damaged. Thus, those periods of political and cultural continuity described as the Old, Middle, and New kingdoms were each thought to be followed by 'dark ages', when the country became disunited and weakened by conflict (either civil war between provinces or invasion by foreigners). This scenario was both denied and bolstered by Manetho's history. First, Manetho created a misleading air of continuity in the succession of kings and dynasties through his assumption that only one king could occupy the throne of Egypt at any one time. Secondly, his descriptions of some of the dynasties corresponding to the times of the intermediate periods suggest that the kingship was changing hands with alarming rapidity.

The study of the Third Intermediate Period has become one of the most controversial areas of Egyptian history, particularly during the 1990s, when it has been subjected to intensive study by a number of different scholars. Three areas of investigation have blossomed. First, several aspects of the culture of the period (for example, ceramics and funerary equipment) have been analysed in terms of changes in such factors as style and materials. Secondly, anthropological, iconographic, and linguistic studies have been undertaken with regard to the 'Libyan' ethnic identity of many of the 21st–24th Dynasty rulers. Thirdly, and most crucially from the point of view of the history of the pharaonic period as a whole, it was argued by a small number of scholars that the period of 400 years occupied by the Third Intermediate Period (and numerous other, roughly contemporaneous, 'dark ages' elsewhere in the Near East and the Mediterranean) may have been artificially inflated by historians. They suggested that the New Kingdom might have ended not in the eleventh century but in the eighth century BC, leaving a much smaller gap of about 150 years between the end of the 20th Dynasty and the beginning of the Late Period. Such a view, however, has been widely dismissed, not only because Egyptologists, Assyriologists, and Aegeanists have been able to refute many of the individual textual and archaeological arguments for chronological change, but also, more significantly, because the scientific dating systems (that is, radiocarbon and dendrochronology) almost always provide solid independent support for the conventional chronology. Indeed, the irrelevance of such tinkering with the conventional chronological framework, given the overwhelming and increasing significance of scientific dates, has been memorably described by the classical archaeologist Anthony Snodgrass as 'a bit like a detailed scheme for reorganizing the East German economy, produced in 1989 or early 1990'.

On a more cultural, rather than chronological level, the significance of the most basic historical divisions (that is, the distinctions between the Predynastic, pharaonic, Ptolemaic, and Roman periods) have begun to be questioned. On the one hand, the results of excavations during the 1980s and 1990s in the cemeteries of Umm el-Qaʿab (at Abydos) suggest that before the 1st Dynasty there was also a Dynasty 0 stretching back for some unknown period into the fourth millennium BC. This means that, at the very least, the last one or two centuries of the 'Predynastic' were probably in many respects politically and socially 'Dynastic'. Conversely, the increasing realization that Naqada III pottery types were still widely used in the Early Dynastic Period shows that certain cultural aspects of the Predynastic Period continued on into the pharaonic period (see Chapter 4).

Whereas there are definite political breaks between the pharaonic and Ptolemaic periods, and between the Ptolemaic and Roman periods, the gradually increasing archaeological data from the two latter periods have begun to create a situation where the process of cultural change may be seen to be less sudden than the purely political records suggest. Thus it is apparent that there are aspects of the ideology and material culture of the Ptolemaic Period that remain virtually unaltered by political upheavals. Instead of the arrival of Alexander the Great and his general Ptolemy representing a great watershed in Egyptian history, it might well be argued that, although there were certainly a number of significant *political* changes between the mid-first millennium BC and the mid-first millennium AD, these took place amid comparatively leisurely processes of social and economic change. Significant elements of the pharaonic civilization may have survived relatively intact for several millennia, only undergoing a full combination of *cultural and political* transformation at the beginning of the Islamic Period in AD 641.

Historical Change and Material Culture

There has been an enormous growth in the study of Egyptian pottery in the late twentieth century, both in terms of the quantity of sherds being analysed (from a wide variety of types of site) and in terms of the range of scientific techniques now being used to extract more information from ceramics. Inevitably the improvement in our understanding of this prolific aspect of Egyptian material culture has had an impact on the chronological framework. The excavation of part of the city of Memphis (the site of Kom Rabi'a) in the 1980s provides a good instance of the ways in which more sophisticated approaches to pottery have enabled the overall process of cultural change to be better understood.

Pottery vessels can be arranged in terms of relative date by such traditional techniques as seriation of cemetery material and the analysis of large quantities of stratified material at domestic or religious sites, but they can also be given fairly precise absolute dates either by the conventional method of association with inscribed or artistic material (particularly in tombs) or by the use of such scientific techniques as thermoluminescence dating. Some scholars have begun to study the ways in which vessel and fabric types change over the course of time. Thus, the form of pottery bread moulds, for instance, underwent a dramatic change at the end of the Old Kingdom, but it is not yet clear whether the source of this change lies in the social, economic, or technological spheres of life, or whether it is merely the result of a change in 'fashion'. Such analyses show that processes of change in material culture took place for a whole variety of reasons, only some of which were linked to the political changes that tend to dominate conventional views of Egyptian history. This is not to deny the many connections between political and cultural change, such as the correlation between centralized production of pottery in the Old Kingdom and resurgence of local pottery types during the more politically fragmented First Intermediate Period (and then the renewed homogenization of pottery during the more unified 12th Dynasty).

In the study of certain phases of Egyptian history, such as the emergence of the unified state at the beginning of the pharaonic period or the decline and demise of the Old Kingdom, scholars have sometimes examined numerous environmental and cultural factors in order to explain sudden important political changes. One of the problems with this *selective* attention to non-political historical trends, however, is the fact that we still know so little about environmental and cultural change during periods of stability and prosperity, such as the Old and Middle kingdoms, that it is much more difficult to interpret these factors at times of political crisis. The increased study of pottery vessels and other common artefacts (as well as environmental factors such as climate and agriculture) are beginning to create the basis for more holistic versions of Egyptian history, in which political narratives are viewed within the context of long-term processes of cultural change.

This painted relief fragment from an unknown 18th Dynasty Theban private tomb, *c.*1400 BC, shows a carpenter working with an adze. Such paintings and reliefs depicting scenes from daily life provide evidence of social history throughout the Dynastic Period.

Egyptian 'History'

Art and texts throughout the pharaonic period continued to maintain the Predynastic and Early Dynastic tension between recording and commemorating, which might be characterized as the distinction between, on the one hand, the utilitarian labels attached to grave goods, and, on the other hand, such ceremonial votive items as palettes and maceheads, described above. We know that the purpose of the early funerary labels was to use history as a means of dating particular things, and that the purpose of such mobiliary art as the palettes and maceheads—as well as of stelae and temple reliefs in the pharaonic period—was not to record historical events but primarily to use them as a means of commemorating universal acts undertaken by specific rulers or by royal officials.

In the mortuary temple of Rameses III at Medinet Habu there is a scene in which the Libyan chieftain Meshesher is brought into the presence of the king.

This is obviously intended to be a record of the surrender of a particularly important foreign individual, whose personal humiliation encapsulates the defeat of his people, but to the left-hand side we can also see the careful assembling and counting of a pile of Libyans' hands—this alerts us to one of the ways in which the scene differs from a more modern Western historical tableau. It is part of a relief in a mortuary temple and as such it is fulfilling the king's piety to the gods. Just as private individuals in the New Kingdom inscribed 'autobiographical' texts on the walls of their tomb chapels to remind the gods of their piety and beneficence, so the reliefs in royal mortuary temples were intended to symbolize a kind of accounting procedure, a visual quantification of the success achieved by the king both for and through the gods.

The Egyptian sense of history is one in which rituals and real events are inseparable—the vocabulary of Egyptian art and text very often makes no real distinction between the real and the ideal. Thus the events of history and myth were all regarded as part of a process of assessment, whereby the king demonstrated that he was preserving Maat, or harmony, on behalf of the deities. Even when an Egyptian monument appears to be simply commemorating a specific event in history, it is often interpreting that event as an act that is simultaneously mythological, ritualistic, and economic.

2 PREHISTORY

FROM THE PALAEOLITHIC
TO THE BADARIAN CULTURE
(*c.*700,000–4000 BC)

STAN HENDRICKX AND PIERRE VERMEERSCH

It has become a truism that ancient Egypt was a gift of the Nile because the river's flooding brought new life into the valley in the late summer of every year. Egypt was, therefore, essentially a rich oasis amid the very extensive expanse of the Sahara. This, however, has not always been the case: the very earliest inhabitants of Egypt lived in a different kind of environment. First, the climate was not always as arid as it is now (modern Upper Egypt being one of the most arid regions in the world), oscillating instead between the present hyperaridity and a dry sahelian condition. Secondly, the river itself was not always a meandering river in a wide floodplain, with its late summer high floods. During some periods, the Nile was either reduced to a series of independent ephemeral wadi basins or had a generally low discharge, choked by its own huge floodplain deposits. It brought its rich alluvia into Egypt only when its headwaters reached back to Ethiopia. Finally, although the river clearly brought life to Egypt, it has also brought about the erosion of older archaeological deposits—we should, therefore, not be surprised to find that only very scarce remains from the earliest occupation have been preserved.

Because of its geographical position, Egypt certainly served as an important conduit for early humans migrating from East Africa towards the rest of the Old World. We know that early *Homo erectus* left Africa and arrived in Israel as early as 1.8 million years ago. There is, therefore, no reason to doubt that small bands of *Homo erectus* visited and probably stayed in the Nile Valley. Unfortunately, only very sparse evidence of this event is available and, worse still, it cannot be dated, because circumstantial evidence is also very poor. In some Early and Middle Pleistocene deposits, isolated choppers, chopping tools, and flakes,

Facing: painted pottery female figurines of the Naqada II period sometimes have small bird-like faces and curved arms raised above their heads, similar to the figures depicted on roughly contemporary painted pottery vessels.

Facing, inset: an unusual pottery head, dating to the late 5th millennium BC, was excavated at the large Neolithic settlement of Merimda Beni Salama in the western Delta. There are traces of ochre still visible on the face, suggesting that it was originally painted, while a deep hole under the chin may be an indication that it was originally attached to a post.

similar to those associated with early hominids in East Africa, have been recovered in gravel quarries at Abbassiya, as well as in Theban gravel deposits. However, most of these published 'artefacts' are probably not of human origin and all of them are from secondary deposits.

The Lower Palaeolithic

Many Lower Palaeolithic artefacts, including numerous handaxes of Acheulean type, have been found in and on local gravel deposits. No human bones have been found in Egypt in association with this Acheulean phase, but *Homo erectus* can probably be assumed to have been the maker of these artefacts. Misunderstanding of the desert geomorphology has led many researchers to believe that the Acheulean can be correlated with a Nile terrace chronology, but this is unfortunately not the case. We can presume, however, that *Homo erectus* at least passed by regularly and left his handaxes at numerous sites. Pedimentation and fluviatile erosion led to the dispersal of most of the handaxes and their related artefacts. It is, therefore, not exceptional to find Acheulean handaxes on the present surface of the desert areas in the Nile Valley. In the early twentieth century, the hills over which a path leads from Deir el-Medina to the Valley of the Kings, overlooking the western side of Luxor, were particularly popular for 'collecting' handaxes; although these stray finds cannot be dated, they are probably all that remain, after intensive erosion, of large Acheulean sites. At some locations, such as Nag Ahmed el-Khalifa, near Abydos, it has proved possible to observe that artefacts remained grouped together, even when they were no longer in their original context. There, and in other parts of the Qena region, such handaxe concentrations occur on top of the first clay deposits that attest the connection of the river Nile with its headwaters in Ethiopia. We presume that the age of those concentrations should be set at about 400,000–300,000 BP, but this is only a guess. In order to document the Acheulean occupation properly, we would need more information about such factors as the original spatial distribution and the associated faunal remains.

Our knowledge of prehistoric Nubia is comparatively well documented as a result of the rescue excavations carried out in the 1960s, before most of the area was flooded by Lake Nasser. Acheulean handaxe concentrations occurred mainly on 'inselbergs' (eroded hilltops), where it was possible to extract a good raw material: ferruginous sandstone. Since such sites remained exposed on the surface for many hundred thousands of years, we should not expect any remains to have survived apart from lithics. Even in the case of the lithics, we have only limited information and no secure means of dating except by typological approaches. According to these typologies, the sites can be assigned to Early, Middle, and Late Acheulean respectively. It is remarkable that cleavers, so characteristic for the rest of Africa, are lacking in the assemblages, suggesting that, in Acheulean times, Nubia probably constituted a particular province, an original enclave, in Africa.

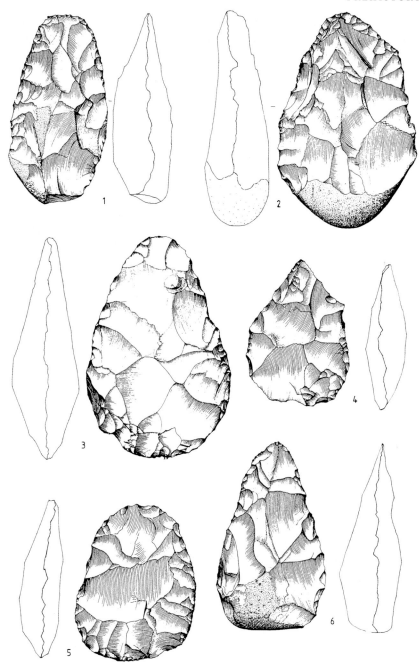

These Lower Palaeolithic handaxes from Nag Ahmed el-Khalifa, near Abydos, are typical of the earliest phase of tool use in the Nile Valley, *c*.400,000–300,000 BP (before present).

In the Western Desert, several Final Acheulean sites are known, especially at the oases of Kharga and Dakhla and at Bir Sahara and Bir Tarfawi. These sites are located on the scarps surrounding the oases, but the most important finds are associated with fossil springs in the floor of the oasis depressions or in the playa deposits. All of these sites are clearly related to wetter conditions, when life as hunter-gatherers was possible. Most of the known sites are in a bad state of preservation, but it has been suggested that ancient channels in the Western Desert, discovered by radar from the space shuttle, are rich in well-preserved Acheulean sites, none of which has yet been excavated.

The Middle Palaeolithic

The picture that emerges for the Egyptian Middle Palaeolithic is rather complex. It originated in the Late Acheulean, when handaxes became associated with bifacial foliates and a typical Nubian knapping method. Such assemblages may date from before 250,000 BP. The fate of sites with such assemblages is similar to that of the Acheulean: all over the desert one can collect scattered artefacts which once belonged together in a site that is now destroyed. Judging from the high number of such artefacts, it is tempting to assume that the population density was relatively high.

As in many areas of the Old World, the Egyptian Middle Palaeolithic is characterized by the introduction of the Levallois method, a special technique designed to produce flakes and blades of fixed dimensions from a flint nodule. In addition to the classical Levallois approach, the Nubian Levallois knapping method was introduced for the production of pointed flakes. In the Egyptian Middle Palaeolithic, several artefactual 'entities' can be distinguished. The chronology is still unclear, but research, especially in the Western Desert and in

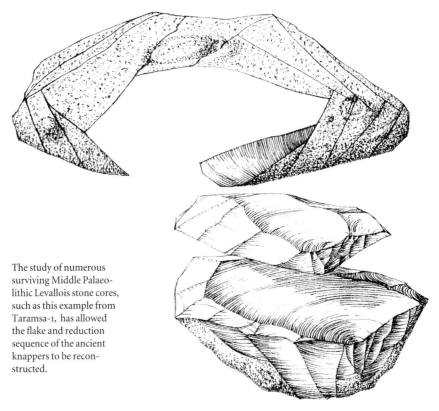

The study of numerous surviving Middle Palaeolithic Levallois stone cores, such as this example from Taramsa-1, has allowed the flake and reduction sequence of the ancient knappers to be reconstructed.

Artefactual entry	Date
Upper Palaeolithic	24,000–50,000(?) BP
Transitional group with the Taramsan	50,000–70,000 BP
Late Middle Palaeolithic with Halfan and Safahan	70,000–80,000 BP
Mid-Middle Palaeolithic with Khormusan, Denticulate Mousterian, Egyptian Group K, Egyptian Group N, Nubian Mousterian, and Saharan Mousterian	80,000–150,000 BP
Early Middle Palaeolithic with Nubian Middle Palaeolithic	150,000–250,000 BP

A tentative chronological scheme for the various artefactual entities of the Egyptian Middle Palaeolithic period (c.250,000–24,000 BP)

the Qena area, provides some clues. We can tentatively propose the scheme shown in the figure above.

The Nubian Middle Palaeolithic is characterized by the Nubian Levallois technique and by bifacial foliates and pedunculates. It is mainly known from Nubia, where several sites have been discovered. Although it is certainly also present in Egypt, no well-preserved sites have yet been found there. Lastly, important information has been disclosed in relation to the mid-Middle Palaeolithic. At Bir Tarfawi and Bir Sahara in the Western Desert, numerous well-preserved sites from the Saharan Mousterian were excavated. It is clear that sites in this area were accessible only during wet phases, which should probably be regarded as short spells punctuating a mainly dry climate.

During most periods of occupation, there were permanent lakes in the Western Desert, or, in some intervals, seasonal playas, fed by local rainfall of up to 500 mm. per annum. In some phases the lakes could be more than 7 m. deep. The area was abandoned during the periods of hyperaridity that separated the lacustrine events. Side-scrapers, points, and denticulates are the best-represented tools. The lake and playa environments were probably rich in floral resources that could easily be exploited, but unfortunately there is no archaeological evidence available. The fauna apparently exploited by people at this date consist of hare, porcupine, and wild cat, at one end of the size spectrum, and buffalo, rhinoceros, and giraffe, at the other end. Small gazelles, mainly the dorcas species, dominate the assemblage. The presence of such animals suggests that selective—perhaps seasonal—hunting of small gazelles was combined with more opportunistic meat procurement from bigger game.

The apparent differences in content among sites in different settings may reflect variations in activities carried out at the sites. Sites embedded in fossil hydromorphic soils, characterized by low artefact densities, indicate limited use, probably comprising several brief phases and these only during very dry

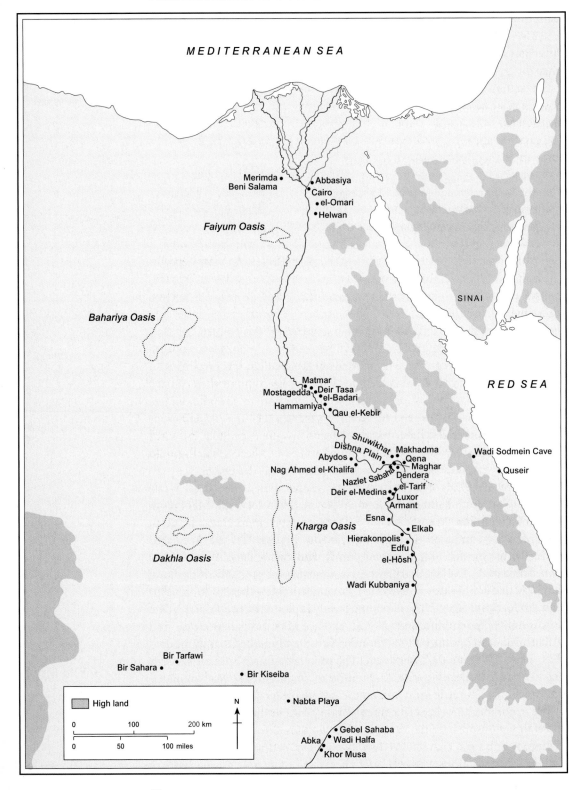

MEDITERRANEAN SEA

Merimda
Beni Salama
Abbasiya
Cairo
el-Omari
Helwan

Faiyum Oasis

SINAI

Bahariya Oasis

RED SEA

Matmar
Deir Tasa
Mostagedda
el-Badari
Hammamiya
Qau el-Kebir

Shuwikhat
Dishna Plain
Makhadma
Qena
Wadi Sodmein Cave
Abydos
Maghar
Nag Ahmed el-Khalifa
Quseir
Dendera
Nazlet Sabaha
el-Tarif
Deir el-Medina
Luxor
Armant

Esna

Kharga Oasis
Elkab
Hierakonpolis
Edfu
el-Hôsh

Dakhla Oasis

Wadi Kubbaniya

Bir Tarfawi
Bir Sahara
Bir Kiseiba

High land
N

Nabta Playa

0   100   200 km

0   50   100 miles

Gebel Sahaba
Abka
Wadi Halfa
Khor Musa

years. Sites embedded in beach sands were accessible for a greater part of the year, but probably not during the season of highest water, presumably in summer. Sites associated with dry lake bottoms reflect unusually arid episodes when the lakes dried up and their beds were exposed.

Excavations in the Sodmein cave near Quseir in the Red Sea mountains disclosed similar wet conditions during part of the mid-Middle Palaeolithic, with the presence of crocodile, elephant, buffalo, kudu, and other large mammals. The cave was apparently visited over a long period but always for a short time. Sometimes, large hearths were utilized.

A comparable way of life may have existed in the Nile Valley, but no sites from the floodplain have yet been disclosed. On the other hand, the Nile Valley has furnished us with many sites that document the extraction of raw material. Sites that are contemporaneous with the Western Desert occupation occur at Nazlet Khater and Taramsa, where mid-Middle Palaeolithic groups were in search of raw material, mainly comprising chert cobbles from terrace deposits. These groups differ in terms of the knapping methods they used: Egyptian group K utilized the classical Levallois method, in addition to flake production from single and double platform cores, while Egyptian group N frequently used the Nubian Levallois method. Tools are always rare at such quarrying sites, because the artefacts produced at such sites were meant to be exported to the living sites, which were probably situated on the Nile floodplain. Unfortunately, such floodplain sites have probably been covered by recent alluvia and remain unknown.

Late Middle Palaeolithic material, along with Halfan and Safahan (Levallois Idfuan) artefacts, has been recovered from extraction sites, such as Nazlet Safaha, near Qena, as well as from living sites near Edfu. The Halfan industry, however, was mainly restricted to Nubia. In comparison with the earlier mid-Middle Palaeolithic, the Nubian Levallois technique was disappearing, and, in addition to flake and blade production from single and double platform cores, only an evolved classical Levallois was utilized for production of thin Levallois flakes. At living sites, burins, notches, and denticulates were being used. Meanwhile, the climate had again become arid to hyperarid and continued to be such. The evolution of the climate changed the living conditions completely, in that food resources were now almost entirely restricted to the floodplain. This climatic development must have obliged people living in the Sahara to leave the area, resulting in a concentration of human population in the Nile Valley.

During the last period of the Middle Palaeolithic (the Taramsan) there was a clear tendency towards blade production from large cores, where, instead of obtaining a few Levallois flakes from each individual core, a virtually continuous process of blade production made it possible to create a large number of blades from each core. At Taramsa-1, an impressive extraction and production site of this date near Qena, it can be observed that there was increasing interest in blade production, a system that was later to be generalized during the Upper Palaeolithic. Similar assemblages have been identified in the Negev, where the

Facing: Map of Egypt showing the principal Palaeolithic, Neolithic, and Badarian sites.

transition from Levallois flaking to blade production has been documented at the site of Boker Tachtit, around 45,000 BP. A burial of an 'anatomically modern' child at Taramsa-1 is associated with the late Middle Palaeolithic. This burial is probably the oldest grave that has so far been identified in Africa.

The techniques employed at the extraction sites were simple but well adapted to the natural chert occurrences. The chert cobbles were removed from the terrace deposits by means of open-trench and pit systems with a maximum depth of about 1.7 m. Only the uppermost part of the cobble terrace was mined, and the pits and trenches are characterized by a very irregular planimetry, with many tentacles and bulges. They have vertical walls with only minor undercutting, and their widths vary from about 1 m. to nearly 2 m. Since the chert cobble deposit was not consolidated, only simple extraction tools were required. Depressions in the trenches were often used as workshops for the fabrication of Levallois products. Extraction was very extensive and, in the region of Qena, affected areas covered many square kilometres. The search for good-quality chert and the use of specialized tool production demonstrate the complex organization of the inhabitants of the Nile Valley at that time. It also indicates that Middle Palaeolithic humans were not only capable of tridimensional reasoning but also had developed a knowledge of geology and geomorphology.

If the 'out-of-Africa' theory of human origins is true (and it is still contested by some good anthropologists), anatomically modern *Homo sapiens* should have passed through the Nile valley on its way out of East Africa to Asia. However, it remains unclear as to whether archaeological data can confirm that there were similarities between the Middle Palaeolithic in Egypt and in southwest Asia. Finally, it is to be noted that the Aterian industry, which is so important for the rest of North Africa, is present only in some oases in the Western Desert.

The Upper Palaeolithic

Upper Palaeolithic sites are rare in Egypt. The oldest site of this date is Nazlet Khater-4 in Middle Egypt, where chert was extracted not only by trenches and mining pits (with a maximum depth of 2 m.) but also by underground galleries starting from the trench walls or from the bottom of a pit. In this manner, underground galleries covering an area of more than 10 sq. m. were obtained. Hearths found in the fill of the trenches where flaking activities took place suggest that mining activities were spread over a long period extending from about 35,000 to 30,000 BP, which would make Nazlet Khater-4 one of the oldest examples of underground mining activity in the world. The lithic assemblage from Nazlet Khater-4 no longer showed any trace of the Levallois technique. Production aimed at obtaining simple blades from single platform cores. Among tools, some end-scrapers, burins, and denticulates but also some bifacial foliates and bifacial axes occur. As no other such sites have been disclosed in Egypt, it is difficult to establish its importance for the evolution of Egyptian prehistory.

This body of a child, excavated in 1994 at Taramsa-1, near the temple of Hathor, at Dendera, is the earliest Egyptian so far identified, dating to c.55,000 BP.

Next to the mine, and obviously in association with it, excavators revealed a grave in which the deceased was buried lying on his back with a bifacial axe next to his head.

The next oldest phase, after Nazlet Khater-4, was the Shuwikhatian industry, which is attested at several sites in the neighbourhood of Qena and Esna. The type site Shuwikhat-1 has been dated to around 25,000 BP. The study of the environment and the animal remains shows that the site, which was located within the floodplain at that time, functioned as a hunting and fishing camp. It is possible that the Shuwikhatian is contemporaneous with a short wetter spell, but this climatic change was not important enough to bring about the repopulating of the Western Desert, which remained devoid of human occupation. The Shuwikhatian is characterized by robust blades obtained from opposed platform cores. Most common tools are denticulated blades, end-scrapers, and burins.

Within the framework of North Africa and south-west Asia, the Upper Palaeolithic of Egypt seems to be rather insular, although it is possible that there were some connections with the Dabban industry of Cyrenaica and the Ahmarian of southern Israel and Jordan.

The Late Palaeolithic

In contrast to the Upper Palaeolithic Period, many Late Palaeolithic sites have been found in Upper Egypt, dating between 21,000 and 12,000 BP. The climate remained hyperarid, as it had been during the Upper Palaeolithic, but the river Nile had begun to contain less water and more clays because of aridity in its headwaters and because of important erosion activity due to the late glacial coldness affecting the highlands of Ethiopia. These clays were deposited in the

The excavations of Upper Palaeolithic chert quarries at the site of Nazlet Khater-4, in Middle Egypt, have provided evidence of gradually evolving quarrying techniques, including trenches, pits, and galleries, dating from *c.*35,000–30,000 BP.

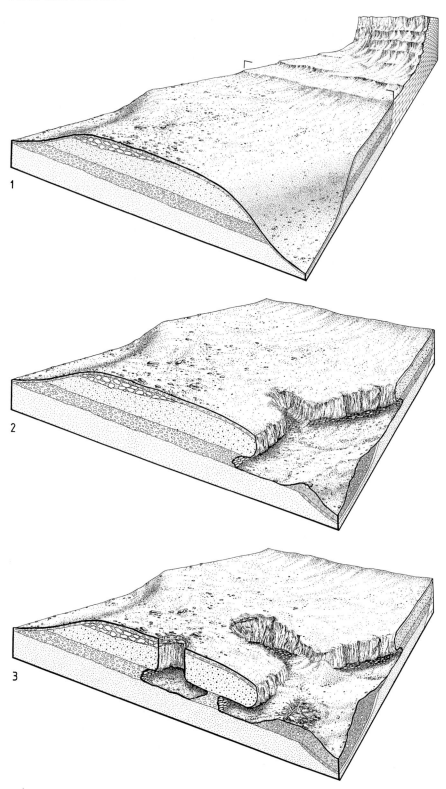

Nile Valley, filling it in Upper Egypt with thick alluvia and resulting in a flood-plain that, in Nubia, was 25–30 m. higher than the modern one. No Late Palae-olithic sites have been recorded in Lower and Middle Egypt, apparently because this part of the Nile Valley was more deeply cut, due to a very low water level in the Mediterranean Sea, a little more than 100 m. below the present level. This resulted in regressive erosion along the Nile, creating a surface that has been covered by more recent alluvia, concealing the sites from archaeologists.

There is great typological variety among Late Palaeolithic sites, and, because of our limited knowledge of the Upper Palaeolithic, it is difficult to determine the origins of the Late Palaeolithic. Among the different groups, the Fakhurian (21,000–19,500 BP) and the Kubbaniyan (19,000–17,000 BP) are the oldest. Al-though the Kubbaniyan was defined at Wadi Kubbaniya, near Aswan, sites have also been found near Esna and Edfu. At Wadi Kubbaniya, the Fakhurian and Kubbaniyan sites occur in three different physiographic settings, all of which are related to a temporary lake barred yearly after the Nile flood inundation by a dune in the mouth of the wadi. After the size of the dune became so significant

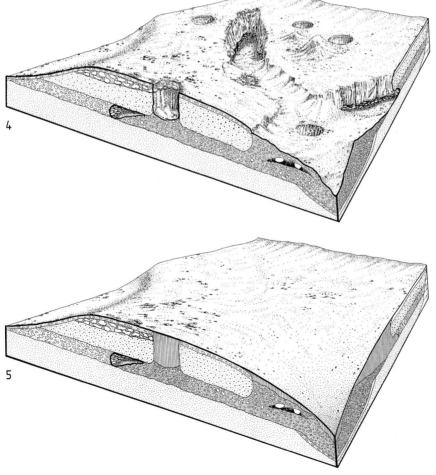

27

In the Late Palaeolithic, *c*.13,000 BP, the mouth of the Wadi Kubbaniya was blocked by a dune barrier, thus causing the formation of a temporary lake each year, when the annual flood waters receded. Eventually the entire wadi was permanently closed off by the dune, and the lake became a focus for seasonal exploitation by small groups of hunter-gatherers.

that the entire wadi was blocked, the lake was fed by the water table, thus creating an extremely favourable environment for hunter-gatherers. Some of the sites are situated on a dunefield that was occasionally flooded by the Nile; others are located on a flat silty plain of the wadi floor in front of the dunes; and finally there are sites on hillocks of fossil dunes in the flat area near the wadi mouth, which were surrounded by water during the period of inundation.

Most sites at Wadi Kubbaniya are the result of repeated use by small groups of people, perhaps several times a year, over a long period. The floral remains clearly reflect seasonality. Many edible plants, such as club-rush, camomile, and nut-grass tubers, must have been part of the diet. The presence of nut-grass tubers is particularly remarkable, since these would have had to have been thoroughly ground up in order to remove the toxins and break up the fibres. This might well explain the large number of grinding stones found at Wadi Kubbaniya. At Kubbaniyan and other Late Palaeolithic sites, fish were caught seasonally in large quantities, forming the major source of animal protein. One annual fishing season is indicated by an overwhelming frequency of catfish, indicating massive catches of spawning catfish, which appear with the rising floods of July and August. A second fishing season is characterized by the high frequency of surviving remains of yearling and adult *Tilapia* and numerous catfish. This spectrum suggests that fish were gathered in October or November in the shallow pools that remained after the inundation. In addition to fishing, hunting for hartebeest, wild cattle, and dorcas gazelle was an important aspect of the subsistence pattern. Lithics mainly consisted of bladelets obtained from opposed platform cores.

Four major tool classes are well represented in the Fakhurian. Backed bladelets, some with Ouchtata retouch, are the most frequent, followed by retouched pieces, perforators, notches, and denticulates. End-scrapers are present but less frequent, while truncations and burins are rare and generally poorly made. The tool inventory of the Kubbaniyan is characterized by a predominance of backed bladelets, often with a non-invasive nibbling retouch, representing up to 80 per cent of all tools.

The kill-butchery camp site E71K12 near Esna belongs to the Fakhurian or is closely related to it. This site, which consists of a dune hollow in which a seasonal pond was fed by the rising groundwater during the summer floods, attracted animals that were driven from the floodplain by the rising water. This resulted in ideal hunting circumstances. There were three major prey animals: hartebeest, wild cattle, and gazelle. This site most probably represents the basic manner of subsistence during the late flood and the early post-flood period.

A distinctive feature of the Ballanan–Silsilian industry (16,000–15,000 BP) is debitage from single and opposed platform cores. Tools comprise backed bladelets and truncated bladelets. There was frequent use of the microburin technique, an innovation also found in the Negev and southern Israel and Jordan. While well-made burins are quite common, Ouchtata-retouch and geometric microliths are rare, while end-scrapers are never common.

Climatic changes by the end of the last Ice Age resulted in unusually high Nile water discharges around 13,000–12,000 BP, creating exceptionally high floods. This 'Wild Nile' stage was caused by climatic conditions in sub-Saharan Africa, but in Egypt itself there was no local rainfall. One site that was out of reach of the catastrophic inundations of the Wild Nile was Makhadma-4, an example of the Afian industry (12,900–12,300 BP), located about 6 m. above the modern floodplain, a little to the north of Qena. It was on the desert fringe, in a flat embayment resulting from the joining of different wadi bottoms, and its rich array of fish remains includes 68 per cent *Tilapia* and 30 per cent *Clarias*, the rest consisting of *Barbus*, *Synodontis*, and *Lates*. The high amount of *Tilapia* and the small size of both *Tilapia* and *Clarias* indicate that fishing must have been practised rather late within the post-flood season. The fish must have been caught in shallow basins through which the fishers were able to wade. The small size of the fish also suggests that sophisticated tackle, such as thrust baskets, nets, and scoop baskets, were used. The fish that were caught in large quantities were probably not all intended for immediate consumption, and the fact that the site includes pits containing a large amount of charcoal suggests that fish were being deliberately preserved by smoking. The expansion of the site demonstrates that the locality was repeatedly used over a long period.

The Isnan industry has been attested on several sites between Wadi Kubbaniya and the Dishna plain. The assemblage is characterized by rough knapping techniques, resulting in thick and wide flakes, and the tool inventory is largely dominated by end-scrapers on flakes. At the site of Makhadma-2, fishing for *Clarias* seems to have been the economic basis. The occupation dates to 12,300 BP and therefore coincides with the Wild Nile floods.

The Qadan industry, between the second cataract and southern Egypt, is a microlithic flake assemblage, but its interest lies primarily in the fact that it is associated with three cemeteries. The most important is the cemetery at Gebel Sahaba, where fifty-nine skeletons were excavated. Each of them was in a semi-contracted position on the left side of the body, with the head to the east, facing south. The graves are simple pits, covered with slabs of sandstone, and the associated lithic material can be attributed to the final phase of the Qadan, around 12,000 BP. Out of the fifty-nine individuals, twenty-four showed signs of a violent death attested either by many chert points embedded in the bones (and even inside the skull) or by the presence of severe cut marks on the bones. The existence of multiple burials (including a group of up to eight bodies in one grave) confirms the picture of violence. Since women and children represent about 50 per cent of this population, it is most probable that the Gebel Sahaba cemetery represents an exceptionally dramatic event. It has been suggested that this may have been a consequence of the increasingly difficult conditions of living caused by the Wild Nile and the subsequent cutting down of the Nile into its former floodplain. A smaller cemetery, almost opposite Gebel Sahaba on the other side of the Nile, where such 'projectiles' were entirely absent from the bodies, shows that death was not always caused by violence at this date.

The chronological position of the Sebilian industry is not clear, despite the fact that it is the most widespread Late Palaeolithic industry, occurring from the second cataract to the north of the Qena bend. The Sebilian lithic technology is characterized by the manufacture of large flakes and a preference for quartzitic sandstones or volcanic rocks as raw material. This is completely incompatible with the lithic tradition of the other Late Palaeolithic industries. The Sebilian might, therefore, represent intrusive groups from the south, moving northwards along the Nile.

Before leaving the Late Palaeolithic it is necessary to mention that there may already have been rock art in the Nile Valley at this remote date. At Abka, near the second cataract, in Sudanese Nubia, a possible instance of Late Palaeolithic rock art has been identified at 'site XXXII'. In Egypt proper, there are also a few rock-art sites that appear to be pre-Neolithic in date. Among the most remarkable drawings are the fish traps represented at el-Hôsh, south of Edfu. The plan of these labyrinth fish fences consists of a complicated layout of curvilinear shapes leading to mushroom-shaped ends, which functioned as the actual traps. This type of fishing in shallow waters would fit well with the observations concerning massive fishing at Late Palaeolithic sites, such as Makhadma-4.

Many of the Late Palaeolithic human skeletons in the Gebel Sahaba cemetery, *c.*12,000 BP, had pieces of chert embedded in their bones, suggesting that they may have met violent ends, perhaps as a result of conflict between different groups at a time of unusually unfavourable environmental conditions.

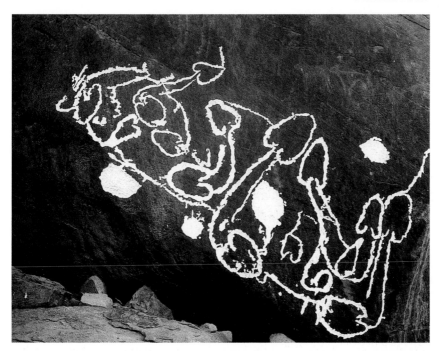

A set of Late Palaeolithic (?) rock drawings at el-Hôsh, south of Edfu, are thought to represent early fish traps.

After the Late Palaeolithic, there was a hiatus in the occupation of the Nile Valley. No human presence has been attested in Egypt between 11,000 and 8000 BP, apart from a group of very small Arkinian sites (around 9400 BP) in the region of the second cataract. It has been suggested that the attested down-cutting of the Nile during this period, with a reduced floodplain as a consequence, had a detrimental effect on the environmental conditions. Although this environmental change undoubtedly took place, it seems highly unlikely that the Nile Valley was entirely deserted at this date. It is more likely that the sites are simply covered by modern alluvial deposits, considering a narrowing of the floodplain and the normal location of sites on the fringe of the low desert.

Saharan Neolithic/Ceramic

The Western Desert was abandoned towards the end of the Middle Palaeolithic, and people returned there only in about 9300 BC, as a result of the Holocene wet phase. Because there was no human presence immediately before the Early Neolithic, and because the area was also uninhabited after this period, the conditions of archaeological preservation are very good. Since the annual rainfall in the early Holocene was still only about 100–200 mm. (all of which probably fell during a brief summer season), only desert-adapted animals such as the hare and the gazelle could live there. Nevertheless, this meant an enormous amelioration of living conditions in comparison with the Upper and Late Palaeolithic. The amount of rainfall was not continuous and arid intervals are most important for chronological differentiation. The rainfall is a result of the northward shift of the monsoon belt; therefore human occupation in the Western Desert started from the south. The settlers came most probably from the Nile Valley, an idea that is primarily based on the absence of other possibilities, but seems to be confirmed by similarities with the lithic technology of sites in the Nubian Nile Valley.

In Egypt, the earliest 'Neolithic' cultures emerged in the Western Desert. It should, however, be made clear from the outset that agriculture has not yet been attested for the Saharan Neolithic. This culture has been identified as Neolithic purely on the basis of the evidence for cattle herding. The Saharan Neolithic is, therefore, completely different from the Neolithic culture that emerged at about the same time in Israel, where the phrase 'Neolithic economy' is a synonym for the process whereby agriculture was introduced and later joined by animal domestication. Most probably, the Neolithization process that occurred in Egypt was completely independent from that in Israel. Because of the absence of agriculture and the presence of some ceramics, it has been suggested that the term 'Ceramic' should be applied to this Saharan culture, as opposed to 'Neolithic'.

Two main periods can be distinguished: the Early Neolithic (8800–6800 BC), and a more recent period consisting of Middle (6500–5100 BC) and Late Neolithic (5100–4700 BC). For the Early Neolithic, the most complete information comes from sites near Nabta Playa and Bir Kiseiba. Most sites are small, short-term camps of hunter-gatherers. Larger sites are always located in the lower parts of playa basins. Although these sites were apparently used for longer periods, they too were seasonally abandoned, since the lower parts of the playa basins were seasonally flooded. Sedentism was not yet known.

Lithics are characterized by numerous backed bladelets (often pointed) and some rare geometrics, as well as tools produced with the microburin technique. Every faunal collection of any size includes a few bones of cattle, which, according to the excavators, were domesticated (although this interpretation is not generally accepted), since it seems unlikely that cattle would have been able to survive without human aid in an arid environment that otherwise supports only desert-adapted animals. It is particularly significant that the fauna includes no remains of hartebeest, an animal that often occurs in the same ecological niche as wild cattle. It therefore seems most plausible that pastoralists were keeping wild cattle in an environment where the cattle would not have been able to survive by themselves. Before 7500 BC, it is possible that people and cattle came into the desert only during and after the summer rains, which coincide with the period of inundation of the Nile Valley, during which it would have been difficult to find herding facilities. After 7500 BC, the digging of wells is attested at Bir Kiseiba and other sites. Some of the wells have a shallow side basin for watering animals. The paucity of cattle bones indicates that the animals were not used for meat production but mainly for protein in the form of milk and blood. In this manner, while humans helped cattle to survive in the Western Desert, the animals permitted people to live in this difficult environment. As well as keeping cattle, these people were hunting local wild animals, predominantly hare and gazelle.

It is presumed that the stone-grinding equipment found at nearly all sites from the beginning of the Early Neolithic was used for processing harvested wild plant foods, but the plants themselves have only been recovered at site E-75-6 at Nabta Playa. Among them are wild grasses, *Ziziphus* fruits, and wild sorghum.

All Early Neolithic sites, even the earliest, have yielded potsherds, albeit in very small numbers. The vessels had very simple shapes, but they were carefully made and fired, and all of them were decorated. Usually the entire surface of the vessel was filled with lines and points, often created by comb or cord impressions, and the general appearance of the vessels was probably imitating basketry. Ostrich eggshells, used as containers for water, were far more common than pottery vessels. The relative dearth of potsherds suggests that pottery was not being used regularly in daily life. It is not possible to determine the exact function of the pottery, but it obviously must have had great social significance and—because of the decoration—probably also symbolic meanings. It seems beyond doubt that these ceramics were an independent, African invention.

Site E-75-6 (around 7000 BC) is one of the most interesting Early Neolithic localities at Nabta Playa. This drainage basin received enough water to store large quantities of subsurface water, which could be reached with wells during the dry season. The site consists of three or four rows of huts, probably each representing different shore lines of the lake, accompanied by bell-shaped storage pits and wells. It is not possible to estimate the number of huts that were contemporaneously in use. Despite its size, this was not a permanent settlement.

It was during the Middle and Late Neolithic periods (6600–5100 and 5100–4700 BC respectively) that the human occupation of the Western Desert reached its peak. Sites of this date are very numerous, and, although most of them are small, there are also some very large ones. Structures are more common than before, including wells, slab-lined houses, and evidence for wattle-and-daub constructions. The large settlements, near the playa lakes, probably represent permanent settlements, while the smaller ones are more likely to derive from task forces of herdsmen who set out from the large sites to drive their animals across

The Late Neolithic settlement remains at Nabta Playa, in the Western Desert, *c.*5100–4700 BC, represent the peak of population in this region.

the grassland after the summer rains. The presence of shells proves that there was contact with both the Nile Valley and the Red Sea, but it is likely that the people themselves remained in the desert all year round. As in the Early Neolithic, domestic cattle were kept as living sources of protein, but, despite the fact that sheep and goat also appear for the first time during this period (about 5600 BC), most meat was still obtained from wild animals. Again it is usually assumed that a large variety of wild plants was consumed at this date.

In the Middle Neolithic there was a dramatic shift in lithic technology. Blade production was no longer so prevalent, and instead there was a gradual introduction of bifacial flaking for foliates and concave-based arrowheads. Geometrics, except lunates, were rare. At Late Neolithic sites, basin-type grinding stones are common. Ground and polished stone celts, palettes, and ornaments are also present in assemblages of this date: together with side-blow flakes, they are considered characteristic of the period. Ceramics before 5100 BC fall within the 'Saharo-Sudanese' or 'Khartoum' tradition, similar to the Early Neolithic ceramics, although the decoration tends to consist of more complicated patterns. Somewhat before 4900 BC, this type of pottery disappeared somewhat abruptly and was replaced by burnished and smoothed (occasionally black-topped) pottery at Nabta Playa and Bir Kiseiba. The reason for this sudden transition is by no means obvious, but its occurrence in the Western Desert is of great importance for our understanding of the origin of the Predynastic cultures in the Nile Valley.

At Nabta Playa, a remarkable megalithic complex has been discovered adjacent to an exceptionally large Late Neolithic site. It consists of three parts: an alignment of 10 large (2 × 3 m.) stones, a circle of small upright slabs (almost 4 m. in diameter), and two slab-covered tumuli, one of which had an underlying chamber containing the remains of a long-horned bull. Small alignments of megaliths have also been observed elsewhere in the Nabta Basin. Although their function is not obvious, these megalithic constructions clearly represent public 'architecture' and therefore refer to increasing social complexity.

In the Dakhla Oasis, several archaeological units have been distinguished, and the main phases are known as Masara, Bashendi, and Sheikh Muftah. The Masara phase is contemporaneous with (and similar to) the Early Neolithic of Nabta Playa and Bir Kiseiba. The Middle and Late Neolithic Bashendi and Sheikh Muftah cultures continued into dynastic times. These two Neolithic cultures are characterized by contrasting types of settlement, with Sheikh Muftah sites situated in close correlation with lake sediments and Bashendi sites being located just outside the oasis proper. It has been suggested that two different types of occupation may be represented. Thus the Sheikh Muftah sites might represent full-time oasis-dwellers, while the Bashendi sites might have belonged to periodic visitors, probably nomadic pastoralists. Starting in about 5400 BC, people relied heavily on their flocks and herds of domesticated animals (imported from the Levant and mainly consisting of goats), while still undertaking some hunting.

The lithic technology of the Bashendi culture is similar to that of the Middle and Late Neolithic, with the addition of a variety of arrowheads, often bifacially retouched. From a little before 4900 BC, burnished and smoothed pottery, somewhat similar to fragments of vessels found at Nabta Playa and Bir Kiseiba, was produced at Bashendi sites, while black-topped pottery occurs occasionally at sites in the Dakhla Oasis. In the south-east corner of Dakhla, various stone-built structures are present; it remains unclear how typical this oasis was for the whole of the Western Desert, but it obviously contains the strongest cultural parallels with the Nile Valley.

After 4900 BC and especially from 4400 BC onwards, the desert became less and less inhabitable because of the onset of the arid climate that continues up to the present day. However, a few select areas were still occupied in historic times.

The Nile Valley Epipalaeolithic

From 7000 BC onwards, human groups are again present in the Nile Valley, but the number of Epipalaeolithic sites is very limited, and they have only been discovered in exceptional circumstances because they are normally covered by flood plain deposits. Thus, only two cultures—the Elkabian and the Qarunian—can be distinguished. During the Epipalaeolithic, there was a continuation of the Palaeolithic style of subsistence, based on hunting, fishing, and gathering.

At Elkab, a few small Epipalaeolithic sites, dating to about 7000–6700 BC, have been found in an exceptionally good state of preservation because they are located within the far more recent Dynastic-Period enclosure wall. The sites were located on the beach of a silting-up Nile branch, the occupations having taken place after the floodplain inundations. The Epipalaeolithic fishing practices were more highly developed than those of the Late Palaeolithic. Indeed, fishing took place not only in the receding high waters but also in the main channel of the Nile, which suggests that by this date the people must have been using boats with a reasonable degree of stability. Because of the more humid climate, hunting for aurochs, dorcas gazelle, and barbary sheep was possible in the wadi area. The Elkabian industry is microlithic, including a large number of microburins. It is readily comparable with the Early Neolithic of the Western Desert. The presence of numerous grinding stones cannot be used as evidence for plant processing, because red pigment was still visible on a number of them. The presence of an Elkabian occupation in the Tree Shelter site at Wadi Sodmein, near Quseir in the Eastern Desert, suggests that the Elkabians should be viewed as nomadic hunters, following east–west routes with wintertime fishing and hunting in the Nile Valley and exploitation of the desert during the wet summer.

The Qarunian is a renaming of the Faiyum B culture (attributed by Caton-Thompson to the Mesolithic). Qarunian sites, originally located on high ground overlooking the Proto-Moeris Lake (which dates to about 7050 BC), have been identified in the area north and west of the present Faiyum lake. The Holocene history of the lake is characterized by a number of fluctuations, which are of the utmost importance for the understanding of the history of occupation around the lake. In the Qarunian phase, fishing conditions were exceptionally good in the shallow waters of the lake and it comes as no surprise that fish provided the basis of subsistence for groups living in this region. In addition, hunting and food gathering were practised. The Qarunian industry is also microlithic and fits in with the general technological context of the Elkabian and the Early Neolithic of the Western Desert. A single burial is known for the Qarunian. The body of a woman aged about 40 was buried in a slightly contracted position, on the left side, head to the east, facing south. Her physical characteristics are far more modern than the Late Palaeolithic Mechtoids from Gebel Sahaba.

The presence of microlithic industries in the neighbourhood of Helwan has been known since the nineteenth century, showing similarities with the Pre-Pottery Neolithic from the Levant, but the real significance of these industries cannot be determined because of the poor information available. In the Eastern Desert, in the Red Sea mountains, there are also Neolithic settlements. According to the evidence from Sodmein Cave near Quseir, these settlers would have introduced domesticated sheep/goat during the first half of the sixth millennium BC.

The Nile Valley Neolithic

In the Nile Valley, no other traces have been found of the people that dwelled in the Eastern and Western Desert, except for the Elkabian and Qarunian cultures. There is no indication of any shift towards agriculture, which was already well established in the Levant from about 8500 BC onwards. The Egyptian population seems to have continued their traditional way of life, based on fishing, hunting, and gathering. Unfortunately, we have no information on human population in the Nile Valley for the period between 7000 and 5400 BC.

The Tarifian culture is known from a small site at el-Tarif, in the Theban necropolis, and from another one in the neighbourhood of Armant. It is a ceramic phase of a local Epipalaeolithic culture, which, however, remains unknown. It shows no connection with the later Naqada culture, and its relation with the Badarian culture is also unclear, although apparently the lithic industries show no close links. The Tarifian is characterized by a flake industry, with, on the one hand, a small microlithic component referring to the Epipalaeolithic and on the other hand some bifacial pieces announcing Neolithic technology. Pottery, mainly organic tempered, is restricted to a number of small fragments. Traces of agriculture or animal breeding are lacking. No remains of structures have been found and the settlement at el-Tarif is presumed to have been similar to Final Palaeolithic camps.

The Faiyumian culture, which is identical to Caton-Thompson's Faiyum A culture, starts in about 5450 BC and disappears around 4400 BC. Technological and typological differences between the Qarunian and the Faiyumian are so significant that there can be no question of the Faiyumian having developed out of the Qarunian. The Faiyumian lithic technology is clearly related to that of the Late Neolithic in the Western Desert. People were living along the ancient beach of lake Faiyum, and the most important remains found so far are groups of storage pits for grain, often lined with matting. For the first time in Egypt, agriculture, most probably introduced from the Levant, is clearly the basis of subsistence. Six-row barley and emmer wheat were grown and probably also flax. Because the storage pits are in groups, it is supposed that agriculture was practised on a community basis. One storage area consists of 109 silos, with diameters between 30 and 150 cm., and a depth between 30 and 90 cm., which obviously represents a major storage capacity. Besides agriculture, animal husbandry was certainly important, with evidence of the presence of sheep/goat, cattle, and pigs. Fishing also remained basic to the economy.

Faiyumian pottery is coarsely made and fashioned into simple shapes. A limited number of pieces were red coated and burnished, but no decorated pottery has been found. The lithic industry is a flake industry with a minor bifacial component. Links with distant places, presumably indirect, have been inferred from seashells of both Mediterranean and Red Sea species, as well as cosmetic palettes of Nubian diorite and beads of green feldspar, but no copper has been found.

The large settlement of Merimda Beni Salama is situated on a low terrace at the edge of the western Nile Delta. The settlement debris has an average depth of 2.5 m. and consists of five levels, corresponding to three main cultural stages. These span a long period between 5000 and 4100 BC. Level I, labelled *Urschicht*, is clearly different from the more recent stages, and is characterized by ceramics without temper, both polished and unpolished; decoration consisting of a herringbone pattern is typical of this ceramic phase (but neverthless rare). Level I lithics are characterized by a flake technology and the presence of numerous end-scrapers as well as bifacial retouched tools. The settlement remains of this level are restricted to hearths and possible remains of flimsy shelters. The economy was probably a mixture of agriculture, animal husbandry (sheep, cattle, and pig) related to the Levant, but also fishing and hunting. Radiocarbon analysis suggests a date at about 4800 BC, although this estimate is considered by the excavator of the site to be too recent. Ceramics

Many Faiyumian (Late Neolithic) storage pits, dating to the 6th and 5th millennia BC, were excavated by Gertrude Caton-Thompson in the Faiyum region; this one (Silo 51) still contained a sickle *in situ*.

with herringbone pattern decorations have also been found in recent excavations at Sodmein Cave, near Quseir.

There was probably a break in occupation between levels I and II at Merimda. Level II, known as the *Mittleren Merimdekultur* and considered by the excavator to be related to Saharo-Sudanese cultures, is marked by a denser occupation of the site, with simple oval dwellings of wood and wickerwork, well-developed hearths, storage jars sunk in the clay floors, and large clay-coated baskets in accessory pits serving as granaries. Contracted burials were also located among the dwellings. Ceramics are radically different from the previous period because they are straw tempered, but the shapes were still simple. Nearly half of the pottery was polished, and none of it appears to have been decorated. The lithic industry is predominantly bifacial. Concave-base arrowheads appear for the first time at Merimda. A large number of artefacts in bone, ivory, and shell have been found, and three-barbed harpoons are typical. Agriculture continues as the basic economic activity, but, judging from the number of bones, cattle become more important, while fishing and hunting are both still well attested. No radiocarbon dates are available, but a date between 5500 and 4500 BC has been suggested by the excavator.

Levels III–V are called *Jüngeren Merimdekultur*, and correspond to the phase identified as 'classic' Merimda culture by the site's first excavator in the early twentieth century. The settlement at this date consisted of a large village of mud dwellings, huts, and work spaces. Well-made oval houses were laid out densely along narrow streets. The buildings are between 1.5 and 3 m. wide, with floors dug into the ground to a depth of about 40 cm., and walls made of straw-tempered mud and mud clods; they were roofed with light materials such as branches and reeds. Within the houses, hearths, grinding stones, sunken water jars, and holes once containing pottery were discovered, indicating a variety of domestic activities carried out indoors. Granaries were associated with individual dwellings, demonstrating that the family units had probably become more or less economically independent. In general, it can be concluded that settlement organization at Merimda certainly represents a 'formal' organization of village life. Contracted burials in shallow oval pits are located among the houses. Remarkably, hardly any grave goods were included. Both the absence of grave goods and the location of burials within the settlement are aspects of funerary protocol that appear to contrast sharply with Upper Egyptian burial customs. However, it seems likely—given the limited number of graves (less than 200), the restricted presence of adult males, and the occurrence of stratigraphic confusions—that only children and adolescents were buried within the settlement, which is also well known for Upper Egypt, while the adults were buried in areas that were only later occupied by houses. It is however to be supposed that the majority of the cemeteries remain at present indiscovered.

The ceramic evolution shows a tendency towards closed shapes, with half the repertoire comprising large rough vessels. Polishing is used for decorative effects, and during this period polished pottery becomes dark red/black. The bifacial chert technology is improved, compared to the previous phase of occupation at Merimda. Implements made from bone, ivory, and shell remain frequent. Most remarkable, however, are a small number of figurines, one of which is a roughly cylindrical head of a human figure, covered with small holes that evidently served for the application of hair and a beard. The shape of the holes seems to indicate that feathers were used for the imitation of hair and beard. The head must originally have been fixed to a wooden body, which makes it the oldest human representation yet known from Egypt. According to the excavator, this most recent period at Merimda would be equivalent to the Faiyumian. However, this is only partially confirmed by radiocarbon dating, according to which the *Jüngeren Merimdekultur* is to be assigned to the period between 4600 and 4100 BC, and would therefore be contemporaneous only with the second half of the Faiyumian.

Still in Lower Egypt, several sites in the neighbourhood of Wadi Hof–Helwan consist of separated settlements and cemeteries. They represent a Neolithic culture that has been called the el-Omari culture, after its discoverer, Amin el-Omari. It dates to about 4600–4350 BC and is therefore contemporaneous with the *Jüngeren Merimdekultur*. In the settlements, mainly pits have been found, used for storage or the dumping of refuse. Associated constructions could not be described exactly, but were certainly very light. Cemeteries developed in settlement areas that were no longer in use. All graves are pit burials, with contracted bodies, ideally preferentially to the south, lying on their left.

The el-Omari pottery always has an organic temper; the shapes are very simple and many vessels are polished, often with a red coating. The lithic industry shows the same improvement of the bifacial technique as at Merimda II–V. Agriculture and animal husbandry (goat/sheep, cattle, pigs) are the base of subsistence, but fishing was particularly important at el-Omari. Desert hunting, on the contrary, was hardly practised at all.

The presence of domesticated goats from about 5900 BC, in both the Western and Eastern deserts, is astonishing when compared to the age of their presence in the Nile Valley, where they did not appear until some five centuries later.

The Badarian culture

The Badarian culture, which is the earliest attestation of agriculture in Upper Egypt, was first identified in the region el-Badari, near Sohag. A large number of mainly small sites near the villages of Qau el-Kebir, Hammamiya, Mostagedda, and Matmar yielded a total of about 600 graves and forty poorly documented settlements.

The chronological position of the Badarian culture is still the subject of some debate. Its relative chronological position in relation to the more recent Naqada culture was established some time ago through excavation at the stratified site of North Spur Hammamiya, and, according to a number of thermoluminescence dates, the culture might already have existed by about 5000 BC.

Facing: a small number of clay and ivory female figurines have survived at Badarian sites, *c.*4400–4000 BC. This example, carved from hippopotamus ivory, comes from a grave at the site of el-Badari itself.

However, it can only be definitely confirmed to have spanned the period around 4400–4000 BC.

The existence of a still earlier culture, called the Tasian, has been claimed. This culture would have been characterized by the presence of round-based caliciform beakers with incised designs filled with white pigment, which are also known from contexts of similar date in Neolithic Sudan. However, the existence of the Tasian as a chronologically or culturally separated unit has never been demonstrated beyond doubt. Although most scholars consider the Tasian to be simply part of the Badarian culture, it has also been argued that the Tasian represents the continuation of a Lower Egyptian tradition, which would be the immediate predecessor of the Naqada I culture. This, however, seems rather implausible, first because similarities with the Lower Egyptian Neolithic cultures are not convincing, and, secondly, because of the Tasian's obvious ceramic links with the Sudan. If the Tasian must be considered as a separate cultural entity, then it might represent a nomadic culture with a Sudanese background, which interacted with the Badarian culture.

Despite the existence of some excavated settlement sites, the Badarian culture is mainly known from cemeteries in the low desert. All graves are simple pit burials, often incorporating a mat on which the body was placed. Bodies are normally in a loosely contracted position, on the left side, head to the south, looking west. Graves of very young children are lacking. There is sufficient evidence to show that these were buried within the settlement, or rather within parts of the settlements that were no longer used. Analysis of Badarian grave goods demonstrates an unequal distribution of wealth. In addition, the wealthier graves tend to be separated in one part of the cemetery. This clearly indicates social stratification, which still seems limited at this point in Egyptian prehistory, but which became increasingly important throughout the subsequent Naqada Period.

The most characteristic pottery vessels of the Badarian culture are the so-called rippled bowls, the surface of which is slightly undulating, as a result of combing and polishing the clay.

The pottery that accompanies the dead in their graves is the most characteristic element of the Badarian culture. All pottery is made by hand, from Nile silts, which, except for the very fine wares, always has a very fine organic temper. This very characteristic temper is always finer than that used for the so-called rough ware during the Naqada Period. For their best products, the Badarian potters spared no efforts in refining the clay and obtaining very thin walls, which have never been equalled in any

subsequent period of the Egyptian past. Pottery shapes are simple, mainly comprising cups and bowls with direct rims and rounded base. A significant proportion of the vessels are black topped, but they generally have a more brownish surface than the Naqada I black-topped pottery. Red slip, with which the Naqada I black-topped pottery is covered, is far more exceptional for the Badarian. The most characteristic element of the Badarian pottery is the 'rippled surface' that is present on the finest pottery, meaning that the surface has been combed with an instrument and afterwards polished, resulting in a very decorative effect. Carinated vessels are also considered highly characteristic of the culture, but decorated pottery is rare: occasionally, incised, white-filled, geometrical motifs have been applied, perhaps imitating basketry.

The lithic industry is mainly known from settlement sites, although the finest examples have been found in graves. It is principally a flake and blade industry, to which a limited number of remarkable bifacial worked tools are added. Predominant tools are end-scrapers, perforators, and retouched pieces. Bifacial tools consist mainly of axes, bifacial sickles, and concave-base arrowheads. It should also be noted that the characteristic side-blow flakes were also present in the Western Desert.

Other products of the Badarian culture include such personal items as hairpins, combs, bracelets, and beads in bone and ivory. The repertoire of greywacke cosmetic palettes was at this date limited to long rectangular or oval shapes, but they would later become very characteristic aspects of the Naqada culture, when they were produced in a great variety of shapes. A few clay and ivory female statuettes have been found, varying immensely in style from fairly realistic examples to others that are highly stylized. It should also be noted that hammered copper was present in limited quantities.

For a long time it was thought that the Badarian culture remained restricted to the Badari region. However, characteristic Badarian finds have also been made much further to the south, at Mahgar Dendera, Armant, Elkab, and Hierakonpolis, and also to the east, in the Wadi Hammamat.

Originally, the Badarian culture was considered a chronologically separate unit, out of which the Naqada culture developed. However, the situation is certainly far more complex. For instance, the Naqada I period seems to be poorly represented in the Badari region; therefore, it has been suggested that the Badarian was largely contemporary with the Naqada I culture in the area to the south of the Badari region. However, since a limited

41

number of Badarian or Badarian-related artefacts have also been discovered south of Badari, it might instead be argued that the Badarian culture was present between at least the Badari region and Hierakonpolis. Unfortunately most of these finds are very limited in number, and a comparison with the lithic industry or the settlement ceramics from the Badari area is in most cases impossible or has not yet been published. The Badarian culture may, therefore, have been characterized by regional differences, the unit in the Badari region itself being the only one that has so far been properly investigated or attested. On the other hand, a more or less 'uniform' Badarian culture may have been represented over the whole area between Badari and Hierakonpolis, but, since the development of the Naqada culture took place more to the south, it seems quite possible that the Badarian survived for a longer time in the Badari region itself.

The origins of the Badarian are equally problematic, having been sought in all directions. For a long time the Badarian was considered to have emerged from the south, because it was thought that the Badarians had 'poor knowledge' of chert, which would show that they came from the non-calcareous part of Egypt to the south; on the other hand, the origins of agriculture and animal husbandry were assumed to lie in the Near East. The theory that the Badarian originated in the south is, however, no longer accepted. The selection of chert is perfectly logical for the Badarian lithic technology, which seems to show links with the Late Neolithic from the Western Desert. Rippled pottery, one of the most characteristic features of the Badarian, probably developed from burnished and smudged pottery, which is present both in late Sahara Neolithic sites and from Merimda in the north down to the Khartoum Neolithic sites in the south. Rippled pottery may thus have been a local development of a Saharan tradition.

It seems obvious that the Badarian culture did not appear from a single source, although the Western Desert was probably the predominant one. On the other hand, the provenance of domesticated plants remains controversial: an origin in the Levant, via the Lower Egyptian Faiyum and Merimda cultures, might be possible.

Evidence from Badarian settlements shows that the economy of the culture was primarily based on agriculture and husbandry. Among the contents of storage facilities, wheat, barley, lentils, and tubers have been found. A number of circular constructions at Hammamiya, previously identified as houses, most probably represent small animal enclosures. In some of them, 20–30 cm. thick layers of sheep or goat droppings have been found. Furthermore, fishing was certainly very important, and may have been the principal economic activity during certain periods of the year. Hunting, on the other hand, was apparently only of marginal importance.

Settlement sites in the Badari region show a pattern of small villages or hamlets, which seem to have moved horizontally after fairly short periods of occupation. Storage pits and vessels are the most obvious features in these sites, which is, of course, partially due to their preferential preservation. The constructions are all very light and seem in most cases to have been temporary. Indeed, it is quite possible that the settlements on low desert spurs that are attested in the Badari region are only marginal outliers or seasonal encampments. On that basis, the larger, permanent settlements would have been closer to the floodplain and would have long ago either been washed away by the Nile or covered with alluvium, thus remaining unknown.

The temporary character of Badarian settlements is confirmed at Mahgar Dendera, about 150 km. to the south of Badari. The site was seasonally used from the end of the low-water season onwards, at the moment when the harvest was finished and when areas of land suitable for herding had to be looked for along the Nile, within the alluvial plain. Besides herding, the second economic activity at Mahgar Dendera was fishing, which was practised in the main channel of the Nile, while it was at its lowest level. At Mahgar Dendera, the alluvial plain is very small; therefore, the site is both close to the Nile and out of reach of the inundation, allowing people to stay at the same place when the inundation started and even at its highest point. During this period, when the living conditions reached an annual low, a part of the flock, mainly young males, seems to have been butchered. People had left Mahgar Dendera before the alluvial plain became fordable, because at that time they had to start working the fields, which cannot have been situated at Mahgar Dendera because of the limited floodplain.

Only limited information is available concerning the foreign contacts of the Badarian culture. Relations with the Red Sea are attested through the presence of Red Sea shells in graves, while copper ore may have come from the Eastern Desert or, less likely, the Sinai. The latter was also considered the source of turquoise, but recently the identification of turquoise from Badarian contexts was shown to be erroneous. If there were occasional contacts between the Badari region and the Sinai, they most probably passed through the Eastern Desert rather than Lower Egypt, where there appear to be no indications of the Badarian culture. This possibility of Badari–Sinai links through the Eastern Desert may eventually be confirmed by reported finds from the Wadi Hammamat, which unfortunately are still not fully published.

3 THE NAQADA PERIOD

(*c.*4000–3200 BC)

BÉATRIX MIDANT-REYNES

The second major phase of the Predynastic Period—the Naqada culture—derives its name from the site of Naqada, in Upper Egypt, where in 1892 Flinders Petrie uncovered a vast cemetery of more than 3000 graves. Petrie, struck at once by the unusual nature of these burials, compared with those previously known in Egypt, mistakenly ascribed them to a group of foreign invaders. This group was supposed to have continued in existence until the end of the Old Kingdom, and it was even suggested that they might have been responsible for its decline.

Archaeologists in Egypt had grown used to monumental funerary architecture, but the humble Naqada burials consisted of little more than the body of the deceased in foetal position, wrapped in an animal skin, sometimes covered by a mat, and most often deposited in a simple pit hollowed out of the sand. None of the offerings accompanying the deceased corresponded to the usual hallmarks of pharaonic civilization, as it was recognized in Petrie's day. The pottery vessels of black-topped polished red ware, zoomorphic schist palettes, combs and spoons of bone or ivory, and flint knives and other artefacts together constituted a peculiar type of assemblage. Jacques de Morgan was the first to suggest that these might be the remains of a *prehistoric* population. Petrie then set about testing de Morgan's assumption scientifically; eventually, after excavating thousands of other graves from comparable sites, he was able to establish the first chronology of Predynastic Egypt. Petrie must, therefore, undoubtedly be regarded as the father of Egyptian prehistory.

Facing: map of Egypt showing the principal sites of the Naqada I and II phases.

Chronology and Geography

Having established that the graves were Predynastic, the next task was to organize the considerable quantity of material uncovered, and to place the newly defined Predynastic culture within a chronological framework. Using the pottery from 900 graves in the cemeteries of Hiw and Abadiya, Petrie devised a method of seriation that formed the basis for a system of 'sequence dates', in which the new categories of pottery were defined according to the form and decoration of the vessels. Petrie reached the intuitive hypothesis that wavy-handled pots evolved gradually from globular vessels with clearly moulded functional handles towards cylindrical forms on which the handles were merely decorative. The 'sequence-dates' chronology was initially organized around this concept of evolution in wavy-handled design.

A table of fifty sequence dates resulted, numbered from 30 onwards, in order to leave space for earlier cultures that had not yet been discovered. This turned out to be a wise precaution, given that Brunton's excavations at Badari would later result in the identification of the Badarian Period, the first stage of the Upper Egyptian Predynastic (see Chapter 2). The lengths of the individual phases represented by each of these sequence dates were uncertain, and the only link with any absolute date was that between SD 79–80 and the accession of King Menes at the beginning of the 1st Dynasty, which was assumed to have taken place in c.3000 BC.

The sequence dates were grouped into three periods. First, there was the Amratian (or Naqada I), from the type site of el-Amra, containing styles SD 30–38; this phase corresponds to the maximum

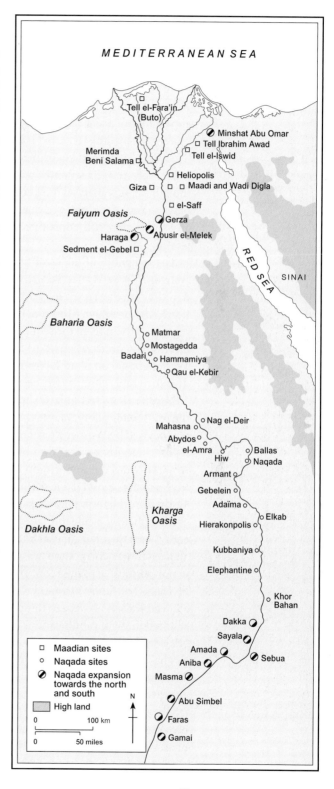

45

development of the black-topped red ware and of vessels with painted white decorative motifs on a polished red body. Secondly, there was the Gerzean (or Naqada II), from el-Gerza, containing styles SD 39–60 and characterized by the appearance of pottery with wavy handles, coarse utilitarian ware, and decorations comprising brown paint on a cream background. Finally, there was Naqada III, representing the final phase of SD 61–80, which was marked by the appearance of a so-called late style, whose forms were already evoking Dynastic pottery. According to Petrie, it was during the Naqada III phase that an Asiatic 'New Race' arrived in Egypt, bringing with it the seeds of pharaonic civilization.

Scholars have frequently praised Petrie's relative dating system, and, although various analyses have corrected it and improved its precision, the three basic phases of the late Predynastic have never been fundamentally questioned, and today they still constitute the loom upon which Egyptian prehistory is woven.

The reliability of the ceramics corpus is fundamental to the validity of the system. In 1942 Walter Federn, a Viennese exile to the USA, exposed certain flaws in Petrie's corpus. In order to classify the vessels from de Morgan's collection in the Brooklyn Museum, he was obliged to revise Petrie's groups, removing two of them from the sequence. It was Federn who introduced a factor that had been ignored by Petrie: the *fabric* of the vessels. It also became apparent that a system based on material from Upper Egyptian cemeteries was not necessarily transferable either to the necropolises of the north or to those of Nubia.

In spite of its recognized shortcomings, Petrie's work nevertheless formed the sole means of organizing the Predynastic into cultural phases until the system devised by Werner Kaiser in the 1960s, which even then could not actually replace it. Kaiser seriated the pottery of 170 tombs from cemeteries 1400–1500 of Armant using the publication of the site made by Robert Mond and Oliver Myers in the 1930s. His work showed that there was also a 'horizontal' chronology in the cemetery. The black-topped red ware abounded in the southern part of the cemetery, while the 'late' forms were concentrated towards the northern end. A very detailed analysis of the classification, still based on Petrie's corpus, allowed him to correct and fine-tune the sequence-dating system. Petrie's three major periods were thus confirmed, but refined by the addition of eleven subdivisions (or *Stufen*) from Ia to IIIb. In 1989 Stan Hendrickx's doctoral thesis allowed Kaiser's system to be applied to all of the Naqadan sites in Egypt. This resulted in slight modifications, particularly to the transitional phases between Naqada I and II.

The other important progress in Predynastic chronology has involved advances in absolute dating. Both Petrie's sequence dates and Kaiser's *Stufen* constitute relative dating systems; they have a *terminus ante quem* of *c.*3000 BC (the presumed date for the unification of Egypt), but they cannot in themselves provide any absolute date for the beginnings and ends of each of the Naqada phases and subdivisions. The necessary links to an absolute chronology were made possible in the second half of the twentieth century by the development of methods of dating based on the analysis of physical and chemical phenomena. As far as the Egyptian Predynastic is concerned, thermoluminescence (TL) and radiocarbon (C-14) dating are the most important of these scientific methods.

Libby tested the accuracy of the radiocarbon dating system on material from the Faiyum region, and since then the testing of samples for dating has been sufficiently systematic to enable the construction of a fairly precise chronological framework, in which Petrie's three great phases have come to take their place. The first Naqada phase (Amratian) lies between 4000 and 3500 BC, followed by the second phase (Gerzean), from 3500 to 3200 BC, and the final Predynastic phase runs from 3200 to 3000 BC.

The geographical locations of Naqada I sites all lie within Upper Egypt, from Matmar in the north to Kubbaniya and Khor Bahan in the south. This situation changes, however, in the Naqada II culture, which is particularly characterized by a process of expansion: emerging from its southern nucleus, it diffuses northwards as far as the eastern edge of the Delta, and also southwards, where it comes into direct contact with the Nubian 'A Group'.

Naqada I (Amratian)

Petrie and Quibell uncovered several thousand Predynastic graves between them (15,000 for the whole Predynastic Period). As a result, our knowledge of the period was—for over a century—based almost entirely on funerary remains.

In broad terms, the Amratian is not different from the earlier Badarian culture. The burial rituals and the types of funerary offerings are so similar that one wonders if the latter does not constitute an older, regional version of the former.

In general, the Amratian dead were buried in simple oval pits in a contracted position, lying on the left side with the head pointing south, looking towards the west. A mat was placed on the ground below the deceased, and sometimes the head rested on a pillow of straw or leather. Another mat or the skin of an animal, usually goat or gazelle, covered or enclosed the deceased and most of the time covered the offerings as well. The surviving remains of clothing suggest that the usual apparel worn by the dead was a sort of fabric loincloth or a hide loincloth trimmed with fabric. Although simple burials of single individuals were in the majority, multiple burials were also fairly frequent, most notably involving a woman (possibly the mother) and a newborn infant. Compared with the previous period, larger burial places appeared, provided with coffins of wood or clay, and more lavishly equipped. Although plundered, the Amratian tombs of Hierakonpolis are remarkable for their rectangular form and unusual size (the largest being 2.50 m. × 1.80 m.). In two instances, the inclusion of magnificent disc-shaped porphyry maceheads probably indicates the burials of powerful individuals. The Amratian culture particularly differs from the

Badarian in terms of the diversity of types of grave goods and consequent signs of hierarchy, and Hierakonpolis was clearly already an important site from the point of view of such diversification.

The differences between the Badarian and Amratian cultures can be seen above all in changes in material culture. The black-topped red ware gradually became less common, and this trend would eventually lead to its total disappearance at the end of the Predynastic. The rippling effect on the surface of the pottery became rarer, as did black-polished pottery. At the same time, however, red-polished pottery continued to flourish in a variety of forms, often incorporating different styles of surface decoration. The best-decorated examples feature sculpture in the round and white painted designs comprising geometrical, animal, and vegetal motifs. These constitute the beginnings of an iconography that would eventually lie at the core of pharaonic civilization.

The fauna represented on the vessels are essentially riverine, such as hippopotami, crocodiles, lizards, and flamingoes, but there were also scorpions, gazelles, giraffes, ichneumons, and bovids. The bovids are rendered schematically, thus making their precise identification difficult. Sometimes a boat might also be depicted, prefiguring the leitmotif of the Naqada II phase. Human figures, although at this date unobtrusive, were nevertheless present in the Amratian version of the universe. Such figures, however, were represented schematically, each with a small round head on a triangular torso terminating in thin hips and standing on stick legs, often without feet. The arms were represented only when the figure was engaged in some activity.

The depictions involving human figures can be divided into two types: the first—and most frequent—is the hunt, and the second is the victorious warrior.

Facing, above: some of the graves at Naqada II sites contained multiple inhumations, as in the case of this double burial at the cemetery of Adaïma, near Hierakonpolis.

Facing, below: the Naqada II cosmetic palettes tended to be carved into simple geometric shapes, but the earlier Naqada I examples are often either decorated with incised animal figures or carved into zoomorphic forms, as in the case of this 19-centimetre-long fish-shaped example from Tomb S218 at Adaïma.

The rim of this pottery vessel, dating to the Naqada I phase, is decorated with five three-dimensional hippopotamus figures. Such riverine motifs are typical of the decoration of vessels at this stage of the Predynastic Period.

A good example of the hunt is shown on a Naqada I vessel in the Pushkin Museum of Fine Arts, Moscow (the 'Moscow bowl'). This scene comprises a person holding a bow in his left hand, while in his right he controls four greyhounds on a leash. This is the very image of the hunter, with the king wearing the tail of an animal at his belt, that can still be seen several centuries later on the so-called Hunter's Palette or on the Gebel el-Arak knife handle (the former now in the British Museum and the latter in the Louvre), and indeed continued to be a powerful image until the end of the pharaonic period.

The theme of the victorious warrior occurs on the elongated body of a Naqada I vessel in the collection of the Petrie Museum, University College London. The depiction comprises two human figures among plant motifs; the larger figure, with stalks or plumes fastened in his hair, lifts his arms above his head, while his virility is unequivocally marked by a penis or penis sheath. Interlaced ribbons descending from between his legs may represent decorated cloth. A white line emerges from the larger figure's chest and wraps around the neck of the second figure, a much smaller person with long hair. A swelling on the back of the smaller figure could represent bound arms. Despite a clear pelvic protuberance, the sexuality of the smaller figure remains ambiguous; if it were feminine, this would justify the small size. A similar scene decorates an identical vessel in the Brussels Museum, as well as one of the same material excavated in the 1990s by German archaeologists at Abydos. The prevalence of the bound figure, and the absence or obstruction of the arms of small persons, strongly suggest the imagery of the conqueror and the vanquished. This early theme of domination appears to be the prototype of traditional scenes of victory in the pharaonic period. It is interesting to note that, as early as the Naqada I phase, the dual theme of hunting and war—always understood to be victorious—is established, implying the existence of a group of hunter-warriors already invested with an aura of power.

The graves and the funerary offerings indicate not so much increasing hierarchization as a tendency towards social diversity in the Naqada I culture. The offerings in this phase appeared initially to be intended simply to mark the identity of the deceased. It is not until the Naqada II phase (and even more so Naqada III) that larger accumulations of funerary artefacts are clearly in evidence.

The funerary statuettes are particularly significant. Both men and women are represented standing, more rarely seated, with emphasis on the primary sexual characteristics. Only a few of the thousands of excavated tombs contained such statuettes, and usually they occurred only singly, groups of two or three in one tomb being comparatively rare. The maximum number found in a

One of the most distinctive features of the Naqada I culture was the painted pottery vessel. This hunting scene executed in white pigment on a red-polished vessel (the 'Moscow bowl') appears to show someone grasping a bow in one hand and the leashes of four dogs in the other.

Facing: the Narmer Palette, c.3000 BC, is regarded as the most recent and most elaborate in a sequence of ceremonial palettes decorated with relief carvings, which were probably dedicated as royal votive gifts at early Egyptian temples.

Two of the carved male figurines with triangular beards (and sometimes also Phrygian-style caps), which are usually found at the ends of tusks or throwsticks. First found in Naqada I, they continued to be produced in the Naqada II, with the beards perhaps already being a symbol of male power.

single burial was a set of sixteen figurines. Based on an analysis of the other offerings, the tombs that contained multiple statuettes were not particularly rich in other respects, and such small sculpted figures were sometimes the sole funerary offering. Could these be the tombs of sculptors? Whatever their significance, the presence of these objects indicates greater exclusivity than wealth as determined by sheer quantity of grave goods. The use of copper and flint knives as funerary offerings raises the same kind of question during the Naqada II phase.

The more or less schematically rendered heads of bearded men seem to constitute another new category of human representation in Naqada I, which was to be further developed in Naqada II. Found on small throwsticks of carved ivory or on the tips of hippopotamus or elephant tusks, the one repeated feature of these representations is the presence of a triangular beard, often balanced by a sort of 'phrygian' cap pierced by a suspension hole. Unlike women, men were no longer being solely identified by their primary sexual characteristics, but by a secondary sexual characteristic and the social status that this conferred on them. The beard was evidently a symbol of power, and, in the form of the ceremonial 'false beard', it later became strictly reserved for the chins of kings and gods.

Another symbol of power that characterizes the Naqada I phase is the disc-shaped macehead, usually carved from a hard stone, but sometimes also occurring in softer materials such as limestone, terracotta, or even unfired pottery, and occasionally provided with a haft. It was during this phase that techniques of working both hard and soft stones (including greywacke, granite, porphyry, diorite, breccia, limestone, and Egyptian alabaster) began to be developed, and this craftsmanship would eventually ensure that the Egyptian culture became the 'civilization of stone' *par excellence*. Greywacke cosmetic palettes constituted the item of choice for funerary equipment during the Amratian. Their shapes became increasingly diverse, ranging from a simple oval shape, sometimes incised with figures of animals, to complete zoomorphs, including fish, tortoises, hippopotami, gazelles, elephants, and birds (although the range of beasts depicted on the painted vessels was nevertheless much greater).

Two typical stone artefacts from the Naqada I phase are disc-shaped maceheads and 'fish-tail lanceheads' or daggers. Disc-shaped maceheads (*left*) were later replaced by pear-shaped types, while the lanceheads (*below*) eventually developed into the *pesesh-kef* instruments used in the Old Kingdom for the ritual of the Opening of the Mouth.

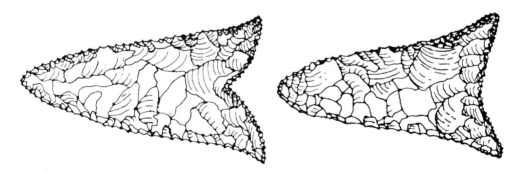

The production of bone and ivory objects, including punches, needles, awls, combs, and spoons, extended—and improved upon—the repertoire of the preceding Badarian culture. Not many worked stone tools have been found in Naqada I graves, but the rarity of such finds was equalled by their quality. These delicate and long bifacially flaked blades, some as much as 40 cm. long, were regularly serrated. Their most unusual feature was that they had all been polished *before* retouching. This process was also used on beautiful daggers with bifurcated blades, which look ahead to the Old Kingdom forked instruments known as *pesesh-kef* used in the Opening of the Mouth funerary ceremony.

Glazed steatite, already known in the Badarian period, continued in use. The first attempts at crafting Egyptian faience appear to date from the Naqada I phase, whereby a nucleus of crushed quartz was shaped into the desired form and coated with a natron-based glaze coloured by metallic oxides.

Metalwork shows few differences from the Badarian period, apart from an extension of the repertoire, including such artefacts as pins, harpoons, beads, looped pins for attachment, and bracelets, often executed in hammer-worked native copper. The tips of bifurcated spears from a tomb in el-Mahasna, which imitate worked-stone specimens, evoke comparison with the techniques of metal production employed by their northern neighbours at Maadi (see below).

The picture derived from the analysis of the tombs and their contents is of a structured and diversified society, with a tendency towards hierarchical organization, in which the major traits of pharaonic civilization can already be seen in embryonic form.

Compared with the significant remains of the world of the dead, the surviving traces of Naqada I settlement are poor, not only because too few sites of this type have been preserved but also because of the nature of Predynastic land-use practices. Since the buildings making up the settlements were essentially constructed from a mixture of mud and organic materials (such as wood, reed, and palm), they have not survived well, and the work invested by the archaeologist would have to be considerable to yield even a minimum of data. Among the vestiges of subdivided huts made from beaten earth (which are not even definitely known to be dwellings) are hearths and post-holes. The zones of habitation are indicated by deposits of organic material dozens of centimetres thick. The sole surviving built structure has been excavated at Hierakonpolis, where the American team uncovered a burnt man-made structure consisting of an oven and a rectangular house partially enclosed by a wall, measuring 4.00 × 3.50 m. Although it is possible that such houses may have been present at all Nile Valley settlements of this date, it should be borne in mind that Hierakonpolis may well have been unusual—it had been an important site from an early date, and from this time onwards it was the centre of an élite group, judging from its large-scale graves.

One of the results of the lack of excavated settlements is an imprecise knowledge of the Naqada I economy. The domesticated animal species represented among the grave goods include goats, sheep, bovids, and pigs, which have survived either in the form of food offerings or as small statuettes modelled in clay. As far as wild fauna were concerned, gazelles and fish appear to have been plentiful.

Barley and wheat were cultivated, as were peas and tares, the fruits from the jujube, and a possible ancestor of the watermelon.

Naqada II (Gerzean)

During the second phase of the Naqada culture, fundamental changes took place. These developments, however, took place not at the margins of the culture but in its Amratian heartland; in essence, they can be regarded as an evolution rather than a sudden break. The Naqada II phase was characterized primarily by expansion, as the Gerzean culture extended from its source at Naqada northwards towards the Delta (Minshat Abu Omar) and southwards as far as Nubia.

There was a distinct acceleration of the funerary trend first seen in the Amratian, whereby a few individuals were buried in larger, more elaborate tombs containing richer and more abundant offerings. Cemetery T at Naqada and Tomb 100 (the so-called Painted Tomb) at Hierakonpolis are good examples of this overall trend.

Gerzean cemeteries comprise a wide range of grave types, ranging from small oval or round pits, poorly provided with offerings, to burials in pottery vessels and the construction of rectangular pits subdivided by mud-brick partitions, with specific compartments for offerings. There were coffins of wood and air-dried pottery, as well as the first indications of the wrapping of the body in strips of linen. Early 'mummification' of this type is attested in a double tomb at Adaïma, an Upper Egyptian site near Hierakonpolis, excavated since 1990 by the French Archaeological Institute at Cairo. The Naqada II burials generally remained simple, but multiple burials, containing up to five individuals, became more common. Funerary rituals appear to have become more complex, sometimes involving dismemberment of the body, a practice that was not attested in the preceding phase. In Tomb T5 at Naqada, a series of long bones and five crania were arranged along the tomb walls, and at Adaïma there are some examples of skulls detached from their torsos. The possibility of human

Tomb 100 at Hierakonpolis is the only Predynastic painted tomb that has so far been found. Dated by its Naqada IIc material, it must have belonged to a powerful member of the Hierakonpolitan élite. The motifs in the wall-painting are similar to those on Gerzean painted pottery vessels, such as large river-boats and the image of the 'conquering hero', the latter becoming one of the most characteristic icons of late Predynastic mobiliary art, such as the sculpted ivory handle of the Gebel el-Arak knife.

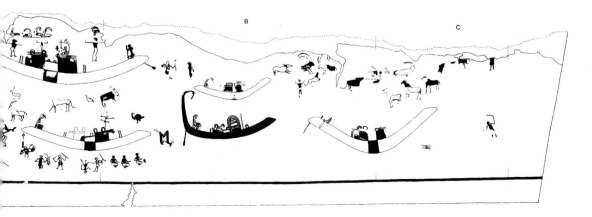

sacrifice was noted by Petrie at Naqada, and two cases of throat slitting followed by decapitation have been identified at Adaïma. Although sparse and scattered, this possible evidence for self-sacrifice could be an early prelude to the mass human sacrifices around the Early Dynastic royal tombs at Abydos, which represented a turning point in the emergence of the Egyptian kingship of the Dynastic Period.

Two new types of pottery make their appearance: first, 'rough' pottery, which has been found in tombs dating to this phase but was later found in domestic contexts, and, secondly, 'marl ware', which was fashioned partly in a calcareous clay derived from the desert wadis rather than the Nile Valley. The marl pottery, sometimes decorated with ochre-brown paintings on a cream ground, replaces the white-painted red ware of the Naqada I phase. There are two types of motifs: geometrical (consisting of triangles, chevrons, spirals, check patterns, and wavy lines) and representational. The repertoire is limited to about ten elements, combined according to a system of symbolic representation that is still not properly understood.

The predominant motif in the representational art of the phase is the boat; its omnipresence reflects the importance of the river, not only as the provider of fish and wild fowl but also as the principal channel of communication that was to be indispensable to the northward and southward expansion of the Naqada culture. It was by boat that raw materials were obtained, such as ivory, gold, ebony, incense, and skins of wild cats from the south, and copper, oils, stone, and seashells from the north and east, mostly destined for an élite whose social position was becoming increasingly distinct from the rest of the population. In these depictions, the boat represents both a mode of travel and a status symbol. It is clear, however, that from this date onwards the Nile, flowing from the north to the south, had also been transformed into a mythical river on which the first gods sailed. The links between the human and cosmic orders were already being established.

During the Naqada II phase, there was considerable development in techniques of stoneworking: various limestones, alabasters, marbles, serpentine, basalt, breccia, gneiss, diorite, and gabbro were being discovered and exploited all along the Nile Valley as well as in the desert, particularly at Wadi Hammamat. The increasing skills in the carving of stone vessels prepared the way for the great achievements of pharaonic stone architecture. The ripple-flaked knives of this period are among the most accomplished examples of the working of flint anywhere in the world.

Cosmetic palettes became fewer in number, evolving towards simple rectangular and rhomboidal shapes, but at the same time they began to be decorated with reliefs, starting a line of development towards the narrative-style decorated palettes of the Naqada III phase. The disc-shaped macehead of the Amratian period was replaced by the pear-shaped type, two examples of which had already appeared at an earlier date in the Neolithic settlement of Merimda Beni Salama. By the Naqada II phase the macehead had become mysteriously

This figurative scene on a Naqada II beige pottery vessel consists of several of the basic motifs of the period: a human figure, animals, and a boat with cabins and a standard.

charged as a symbol of power, and in the pharaonic period it was the weapon characteristically held by the victorious king.

Copper working intensified, no longer being limited to small objects but gradually beginning to produce artefacts that were substitutes for stone objects, such as axes, blades, bracelets, and rings. Alongside developments in copper production there was also a growth in the use of gold and silver, and the evidence at sites such as Adaïma suggests that the increased attraction of metal might well account for much of the tomb robbery during the Predynastic Period.

The picture of Naqada II society that is thus revealed is a blueprint for the development of a class of artisans who were specialized in the service of the élite.

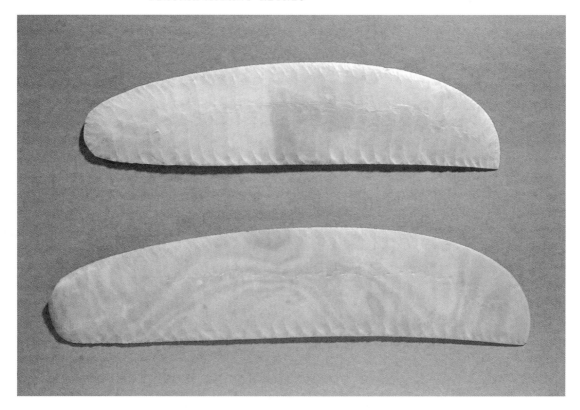

Ripple-flaked flint knives, entirely polished as well as being worked on one face, are typical of the Naqada II phase. The undulating retouches ('ripple flaking') were created by pressure exerted on the edges of the blade with the help of a special tool probably made from copper. The high level of craftsmanship involved in the production of such knives represents one of the great peaks of flint knapping in Egypt and elsewhere.

This fact has two implications: first, there had to be an economy that was capable of supporting groups of non-self-sufficient craftsmen, at least during a part of the year, and, secondly, there must have been urban centres that brought together the clients, the workshops, the apprentice craftsmen, and the facilities for commercial exchange.

This process of cultural development was always tied closely to the Nile. As Michael Hoffman showed in his interpretation of the Predynastic remains at Hierakonpolis, settlement clustered near the river, which supported the cultivated land, where simple artificial irrigation techniques could take advantage of the annual flood. The entire Nile Valley was covered by a string of villages, which are often known simply because of their surviving cemeteries. We have evidence for different species of barley and wheat, flax, various fruits (such as water-melon and dates), and vegetables. As in the preceding phase, cattle, goats, sheep, and pigs comprise the domestic livestock. Among the domesticates, the dog enjoyed special status, judging from its burials within the settlement of Adaïma. Fish also played an important role in diet, but the hunting of large riverine and desert mammals (such as hippopotami, gazelle, and lions) gradually became more socially restricted until it became the prerogative of the dominant élite groups.

Three large centres arose in Upper Egypt: Naqada, the 'gold town' at the mouth of Wadi Hammamat; Hierakonpolis, further to the south; and Abydos, where the necropolis of the first pharaohs was to be located. Two large residential zones were uncovered at Naqada by Petrie and Quibell in 1895: the 'South Town' (in the central part of the site) and the 'North Town'. The South Town incorporates a large rectangular mud-brick structure measuring 50 × 30 m., which may possibly be the remains of a temple or a royal residence. To the south of this large structure, a group of rectangular houses and an enclosure wall can be made out. These two elements, the rectangular house and the enclosure wall, are typical of the emerging towns of Naqada II. There may be a shortage of primary archaeological evidence of settlements at this date, yet two artefacts from funerary contexts help to compensate for this defficiency. The first is a terracotta model house from a Gerzean grave at el-Amra (British Museum). An Amratian tomb from Abadiya has provided a second model (Oxford, Ashmolean) representing a crenellated wall, behind which two people are standing; the Amratian date of the second model suggests that dwellings of this type began to be used at a relatively early date.

Northern Cultures (including the Maadian Complex)

The Maadian cultural complex of about a dozen sites has only recently been brought to light. These sites include the excavated cemetery and settlement complex at Maadi itself, a suburb of modern Cairo. The Maadian culture appeared during the second part of Naqada I and continued until Naqada IIc/d, when it was eclipsed by the spread of the Naqada II culture, exemplified by the cemeteries of el-Gerza, Haraga, Abusir el-Melek, and Minshat Abu Omar.

The earliest Neolithic sites have been discovered in this part of the Nile Valley, in the Faiyum region and at Merimda Beni Salama and el-Omari (see Chapter 2), and it is these sites that represent the tradition from which the Maadian material culture emerged. Maadian culture differs in all its characteristics from sites of similar date in Upper Egypt. In a reversal of the situation at the sites of the Naqada culture, cemeteries were much less prominent in the archaeological record, and most of our knowledge derives instead from settlements.

At Maadi, the Predynastic remains cover nearly 18 ha., including the cemetery. In the first half of the twentieth century an area of about 40,000 sq. m. was excavated. The depth of archaeological deposits is almost 2 m., including heaps of refuse preserved *in situ*, the stratigraphy of which is complex. The excavated structures show that there were three types of settlement remains, one of which is unique in an Egyptian context, strongly reminiscent of the settlements at Beersheba in southern Palestine. It involves houses excavated from the living rock in the form of large ovals measuring 3 × 5 m. in area and up to 3 m. in depth, each of which was entered via an excavated passageway; the walls of one of these subterranean houses were faced with stone and dried Nile-silt mud bricks, but this is the only known instance of the use of mud brick at Maadi. The presence of hearths, half-buried jars, and domestic debris suggests that these were genuine permanent habitations. The other types of domestic structures at Maadi are already well attested elsewhere in Egypt: first, a form of oval hut accompanied by external hearths and half-buried storage jars, and, secondly, a rectangular style of house in which narrow foundation trenches are all that remain of walls that were presumably made from plant material.

In general, Maadian pottery is globular with a broad, flat base, a more or less narrow neck, and flared rims, partially fashioned from alluvial clay. They are rarely decorated, except sometimes with incised marks applied after firing. It is interesting to note that the oldest strata at the late Predynastic sites of Buto (Tell el-Fara‘in), Tell el-Iswid, and Tell Ibrahim Awad include sherds decorated with impressions that are reminiscent of Saharo-Sudanese pottery. Links with Upper Egypt, dating back to the period before the Maadian culture, are indicated by the presence of sherds from imported vessels of black-topped red ware, which mingle with their pale imitations made locally at Maadi. Conversely, the commercial links with Early Bronze Age Palestine account for the presence of distinctive footed ceramics, with neck, mouth, and handles decorated *en mamelons*, made from a calcareous clay fabric, which contained imported products (oils, wines, resins). Maadian culture was thus a kind of cultural crossroads, subject to the influences of the Western Desert (perhaps an extremely early association), the Near East, and the emerging kinglets of Naqada to the south.

Palestinian influence is also clearly discernible in the worked flint of the Maadian culture. In contrast to the local flint industry essentially employing pressure-flake technology, the Maadian assemblages also include large circular scrapers knapped from large nodules with smooth surfaces, which are well known throughout the Near East. Beautiful edged blades with rectilinear ribbing, known as 'Canaanite blades', also appear at Maadian sites; these were to develop into the pharaonic-period 'razors' (actually double scrapers) that were elements of royal funerary equipment until the end of the Old Kingdom, sometimes polished and sometimes reproduced in copper and even gold. The bifacial pieces, few in number, include projectile points, daggers, and sickle blades. The latter were products of the local tradition (Faiyum bifacial sickles) and were gradually replaced by a Near Eastern style of sickle mounted on a blade.

The comparative rareness of greywacke cosmetic palettes imported from Upper Egypt is presumably an indication of their limited availability and therefore the luxury nature of the object. The more numerous limestone palettes, on the other hand, show signs of wear that indicate their regular daily use. Hard stone maceheads are of the disc-shaped type characteristic of the Amratian and early Gerzean cultures.

Apart from several combs imported from Upper Egypt, objects in polished bone and ivory include the traditional repertoire of needles, harpoons, punches, and awls. Catfish darts, consisting of the first spine of the pectoral and dorsal fins, are found in great number, particularly in jars that were probably stockpiled for export.

There are many indications of Maadi's involvement in intercultural contacts and commerce. In this regard, the role of copper is particularly significant.

Metallic objects seem to have been particularly common at Maadi. Not only are there simple pieces such as needles or harpoons, but also rods, spatulas, and axes. These forms of artefacts were made from stone in the Faiyum and Merimda cultures, but at Maadi they were made from metal. This situation is paralleled in Palestine during the same period, where polished stone axes totally disappear and are replaced with metal versions, albeit using different techniques from those at Maadi. This substitution of metal for stone cannot be mere coincidence, but must be the result of a process of technological progress that is an indication (and a direct result) of the genuine symbiosis between the two regions. Large quantities of copper ore have also been found at Maadi, which under analysis reveal a probable provenance in the region of Timna or Fenan, both of which are copper-mining sites in Wadi Arabah, at the southeastern corner of the Sinai peninsula. However, rather than the ore being processed at Maadi itself, it was perhaps imported primarily for processing into cosmetics, and the initial processing must have been undertaken near the mines themselves.

Despite the involvement of the Maadian people in a network of contacts with the Near East, their culture was above all pastoral-agricultural and sedentary. There are few traces of wild fauna to counterbalance the enormous quantity of domesticated animals (pigs, oxen, goats, sheep) that, apart from the dog, comprised the basic meat diet of the community. The donkey doubtless served as transport for the merchandise. Kilos of grain found in jars and in storage pits include wheat and barley (*Triticum monococcum, Triticum dicoccum, Triticum aestivum, Triticum spelta, Hordeum vulgare*) as well as pulses such as lentils and peas.

Compared with the good evidence of agricultural activity at Maadi, the interment of the deceased was relatively unobtrusive, indicating a community that had perhaps undergone little social change since the Neolithic and was evidently lacking in stratification or hierarchy. A total of 600 Maadian tombs has been recovered, as opposed to more than 15,000 Predynastic graves in the south. Geographical and geological factors contribute to this imbalance: the northern cemeteries, located in areas prone to heavy flooding, might well have been buried in thick layers of Nile silt. This, however, does not explain everything, because there is also a contrast in the quality and quantity of funerary equipment in the north, compared with the Upper Egyptian situation. The Lower Egyptian graves are characterized by extreme simplicity, comprising basic oval pits with the deceased placed in a foetal position, shrouded in a mat or in fabric, and accompanied by only one or two pottery vessels or sometimes even nothing at all.

However, as we review the development of the Northern Cultures (consisting of three phases roughly corresponding to the cemeteries of Maadi, Wadi Digla, and Heliopolis), certain tombs appear better equipped than others, without ever displaying conspicuous luxury like that found in Upper Egypt. Nevertheless, a gradual tendency towards social stratification can be discerned,

Some of the pottery vessels of the Naqada II phase (*above left*) bear painted scenes of boats and riverine vegetation, presumably indicating that the Nile was already a fundamental aspect of Egyptian life. Others (*above right*) are decorated with scenes of ostriches, game, and schematic ranges of hills, evoking, in contrast, the landscape and fauna of the desert.

and it is possible that the mixing of the graves of dogs and gazelles with those of humans is part of this process of social change. The final phase of the Maadian culture, represented by the earliest stratigraphic layers at Buto, is equivalent to the middle of the Naqada II phase (levels IIc–d).

At the exceptional site of Buto, there are seven successive archaeological strata in which the transition between the Maadian phases and the overlapping protodynastic can be observed. During this transition, there is a perceptible increase in Naqada pottery styles, while the Maadian pottery progressively disappears. Thus the end of the Maadian culture was not an abrupt phenomenon, as the site of Maadi would suggest, but was instead a process of cultural assimilation. It is probable that, with its fluvial and maritime location, Buto was well placed for important trade, and perhaps also incorporated a palace for local rulers. While the archaeological data from Buto are less startling than the remains at Naqada, there was a comparable process of cultural development here which led, in the same way, to increased social complexity, eventually producing a society characterized by its own beliefs, rites, myths, and ideologies. This was the necessary precondition for the next great step forward in the history of Egypt, which took place in the Naqada III and Early Dynastic periods.

4 THE EMERGENCE OF THE EGYPTIAN STATE

(*c.*3200–2686 BC)

KATHRYN A. BARD

The Naqada III phase, *c.*3200–3000 BC, is the last phase of the Predynastic Period, according to Kaiser's revision of Petrie's sequence dates. It was during this period that Egypt was first unified into a large territorial state, and the political consolidation that laid the foundations for the Early Dynastic state of the 1st and 2nd Dynasties must also have occurred then. In the latter part of this phase there is evidence of kings preceding those of the 1st Dynasty, in what is now called 'Dynasty 0'. They were buried at Abydos near the royal cemetery of the 1st Dynasty. On the Palermo Stone, a late 5th Dynasty king-list (see Chapter 1), the presence of names and figures of seated kings in compartments in the broken top part of the list suggests that the Egyptians believed that there had been rulers preceding those of the 1st Dynasty. There is considerable debate, however, regarding such factors as the precise nature of the process of unification, the date when it took place, and the question of the origins of Dynasty 0.

State Formation and Unification

From the Naqada II phase onwards, highly differentiated burials are found in cemeteries in Upper Egypt (but not in Lower Egypt). Élite burials in these cemeteries contained large quantities of grave goods, sometimes made from exotic materials such as gold and lapis lazuli. These burials are symbolic of an increasingly hierarchical society, probably representing the earliest processes of competition and the aggrandizement of local polities in Upper Egypt, as economic interaction and long-distance trade developed. Control of the distribution of exotic raw materials and the production of prestigious craft goods would have reinforced the power of chiefs in Predynastic centres, and such goods were important status symbols. Despite a lack of archaeological evidence, it seems likely that the larger Predynastic towns in Upper Egypt were becoming centres of craft production. Some of these centres also became walled settlements, like the South Town at Naqada, documented by Petrie.

The core area of the Naqada culture was in Upper Egypt, but, in the Naqada II phase, sites of the Naqada culture began to be established in northern Egypt for the first time. Petrie excavated a Naqada II cemetery at el-Gerza in the Faiyum region, from which he derived the term Gerzean (Naqada II) for his middle Predynastic phase. Somewhat later, Naqada culture burials are found much further north, at the Delta site of Minshat Abu Omar. Such evidence suggests the gradual northward movement of peoples from Upper Egypt in Naqada II times.

Since the major Upper Egyptian sites were located near the Eastern Desert, from which gold and various kinds of stone used for beads, carved vessels, and other craft goods were obtained, they were much richer in natural resources than Lower Egyptian sites: the ancient name of Naqada is Nubt ('[city] of gold') and it is no coincidence that the largest Predynastic cemetery is located there. As cereal agriculture was practised with increasing success on the floodplain of Upper Egypt, surpluses accrued and could be exchanged for craft goods, the production of which was becoming increasingly specialized. Possibly the first southerners to go north were traders, and as the economic interaction increased they may have been followed by colonists. There is no archaeological evidence to demonstrate the northward movement of people (as opposed to artefacts), but if such migration occurred it seems more likely to have been a peaceful expansion rather than a military invasion, at least in the early stages.

A motivating factor for the expansion of the Naqada culture into northern Egypt might have been the desire to gain direct control over the lucrative trade with other regions in the eastern Mediterranean, which had developed earlier in the fourth millennium BC. But the development of the technology to construct large boats was also the key to control and communication on the Nile and large-scale exchange. Timber (cedar) for the construction of such boats did not grow in Egypt, but came from the area of the Levant now occupied by Lebanon.

As the discussion of the Maadian culture in Chapter 3 indicates, Lower Egypt was not a cultural vacuum in the fourth millennium BC, and eventually Naqada expansion would probably have met with some resistance. The archaeological evidence in the north, however, demonstrates only the eventual replacement of the Maadian culture. At Maadi itself, occupation came to an end in the Naqada IIc/d phase, while stratigraphic evidence at sites in the northern Delta, such as Buto, Tell Ibrahim Awad, Tell el-Rub'a, and Tell el-Farkha, demonstrates that there were earlier strata containing only Maadian and local wares, but above these were strata comprising only ceramics of the Naqada III culture and the later forms of the 1st Dynasty. At Tell el-Farkha a transitional layer of aeolian sand between such strata suggests the abandonment of the settlement by the local population for unknown reasons (intimidation?) and the later reoccupation of the site in Dynasty 0 by people of the Naqada culture, which by then had spread throughout Egypt.

By the end of the Naqada II phase (c.3200 BC) or early Naqada III, the indigenous material culture of Lower Egypt had disappeared and was replaced by artefacts (especially pottery wares) deriving from Upper Egypt and the Naqada culture. This archaeological evidence has sometimes been interpreted as an indication of the political unification of Egypt by this time, but the material evidence does not necessarily imply (unified) political organization and a number of alternative socio-economic factors might be proposed to explain this change. Given that the evidence from the élite burials in three major Predynastic centres in Upper Egypt (Naqada, Abydos, Hierakonpolis) suggests separate (and possibly competing) centres or polities during the Naqada II phase, the first unification of Upper Egyptian polities probably took place in early Naqada III times, either as a result of a series of alliances or through warfare (or perhaps through a combination of both), followed by the political unification of the north and south and the emergence of Dynasty 0 towards the end of Naqada III.

Naqada III burials in the largest Predynastic cemetery at Naqada and the élite Cemetery T are impoverished compared to the earlier Naqada II burials at this site. More than 6 km. south of these cemeteries, two large niched mud-brick tombs and a cemetery with Early Dynastic graves were excavated at the end of the nineteenth century by Jacques de Morgan. The location of this cemetery and the sudden appearance of a new style of 'royal' burial at the end of Naqada III, together with the more impoverished (earlier) burials in the cemeteries far

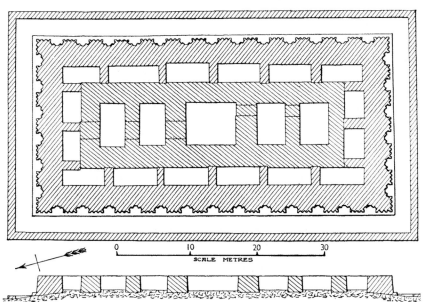

A few Early Dynastic palace-façade style mud-brick tombs were excavated at Naqada by Jacques de Morgan in the late nineteenth century, including this one, attributed to Queen Neithhotep of the 1st Dynasty, c.3000 BC. The rectangles in the centre of the plan indicate that the burial chambers were incorporated into the superstructure at ground level.

Inscribed labels—the earliest known examples of Egyptian writing—have been excavated from the multi-room burial of a powerful late Predynastic individual buried in tomb U-j at Abydos, c.3150 BC. These labels have provided insights into the early development of hieroglyphs, the invention of which probably preceded political unification.

to the north, all suggest a break with the polity centred at South Town (located only 150 m. north-east of the large Predynastic cemetery), probably coinciding with the absorption of the Naqada polity into a larger one.

In contrast, in the Umm el-Qaʿab region of Abydos the graves in one area (Cemeteries U and B and the 'royal cemetery') evolved from fairly undifferentiated burials in early Naqada times, to an élite cemetery in late Naqada II, and finally to the burial place of the kings of Dynasty 0 and the 1st Dynasty. One Naqada III tomb, U-j, dating to c.3150 BC, consisted of twelve rooms covering an overall area of 66.4 sq. m. Although robbed, it contained many artefacts in bone and ivory, a great deal of Egyptian pottery, and about 400 imported jars from Palestine that may possibly have contained wine. The 150 small labels found in this tomb are inscribed with what appear to be the earliest known hieroglyphs. According to the excavator, Günter Dreyer, traces of a wooden shrine in the burial chamber and an ivory model sceptre demonstrate that this was the tomb of a ruler, possibly King Scorpion, whose estates may be listed on a number of labels. This ruler, however, probably reigned in the thirty-first century BC.

Excavations at 'Locality 6' in Hierakonpolis, 2.5 km. up the Great Wadi, revealed several large tombs, each measuring up to 22.75 sq. m. in floor area and containing Naqada III ware. Tomb 11, although looted, still contained beads in carnelian, garnet, turquoise, faience, gold, and silver; fragments of artefacts in lapis lazuli and ivory, obsidian, and crystal blades; and a wooden bed with carved bulls' feet. Such a rich burial suggests that élite individuals of considerable means were being buried at Hierakonpolis, but that they were still not of the same class as the rulers at Abydos.

Whereas Naqada was politically insignificant in the Early Dynastic Period, Abydos was the most important centre for the cult of the dead king, and Hierakonpolis remained an important cult centre associated with the god Horus, symbolic of the living king. In a late Predynastic power struggle in Upper Egypt, it is possible that the Naqada polity was vanquished, whereas rulers whose power base was originally at Abydos went on to control the entire country, perhaps in alliance with less powerful élite groups (the so-called Followers of Horus) at Hierakonpolis, who were nonetheless in a strategic position because of valued raw materials coming from the south.

The final unification of Upper and Lower Egypt may have been achieved through one or more military conquests in the north, but there is not much evidence for this apart from scenes with symbolically military content carved on a number of ceremonial palettes dated stylistically to the late Predynastic (Naqada III/Dynasty 0), such as the fragmented Tjehenu (Libyan), Battlefield, and Bull palettes. The interpretation of such scenes is problematic, because these artefacts are without known provenances and the fragmented scenes are symbolic of conflict without specifying real historical events.

Fortunately, three important artefacts with carved scenes relevant to this period were excavated at Hierakonpolis: the Macehead of King Scorpion, and the Palette and Macehead of King Narmer. All three of these ceremonial objects were found in or near the area described as the 'main deposit' by J. E. Quibell and F. W. Green when they excavated the temple of Horus at Hierakonpolis. They were possibly royal donations to the temple and suggest that Hierakonpolis was still an important centre at the end of the Naqada III phase. While the unification of Upper and Lower Egypt is too specific an interpretation for the scenes on the Narmer Palette, the scenes illustrate dead enemies and vanquished peoples and/or settlements. Scenes and signs on the Narmer Macehead represent war captives and booty, and conquered peoples are also represented on the Scorpion Macehead. Such scenes suggest that warfare played a role at some point in the forging of the early state in Egypt. Even if there is no evidence of destruction layers of Naqada III date at settlement sites in the Delta, warfare could still have implemented the consolidation of this early state and its expansion into Lower Nubia and southern Palestine, which occurred in the early 1st Dynasty.

From Petrie onwards, it was regularly suggested that, despite the evidence of Predynastic cultures, Egyptian civilization of the 1st Dynasty appeared suddenly and must therefore have been introduced by an invading foreign 'race'. Since the 1970s, however, excavations at Abydos and Hierakonpolis have clearly demonstrated the indigenous, Upper Egyptian roots of early civilization in Egypt. While there is certainly evidence of foreign *contact* in the fourth millennium BC, this was not in the form of a military invasion.

Ceramics from excavated strata at sites in northern Egypt and southern Palestine now make it possible to coordinate specific cultural periods in the two regions, and demonstrate continuing contact as the Maadi culture in the north was replaced by the Naqada culture. While the Naqada IIb phase corresponds

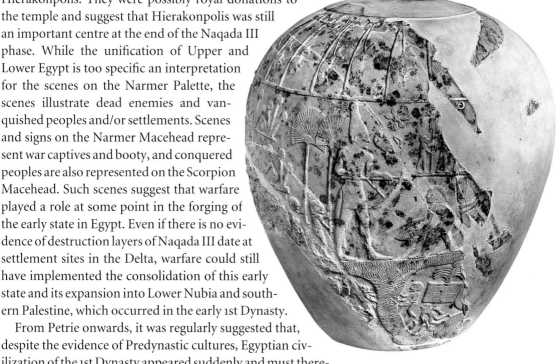

The macehead of King Scorpion dating to the end of the Naqada III phase, c.3000 BC, was found in the temple of Horus at Hierakonpolis, along with many other Early Dynastic votive objects. It appears to depict an early ruler ceremonially wielding a hoe, perhaps inaugurating some form of early irrigation project.

to the Early Bronze Age (EBA) Ia phase in Palestine, Naqada II c–d and Naqada III/Dynasty o were evidently contemporaneous with the EBA Ib culture. Contact between northern Egypt and Palestine at this time was overland, as evidence in the northern Sinai demonstrates. Between Qantar and Raphia, about 250 early settlements have been located by the North Sinai Expedition of Ben Gurion University, with 80 per cent of the ceramics of Egyptian wares dating to Naqada II–III and Dynasty o. The settlement pattern consists of a few larger core sites interspersed with seasonal encampments and way stations.

Israeli archaeologists suggest that this evidence represents a commercial network established and controlled by the Egyptians as early as EBA Ia, and that this network was a major factor in the rise of the urban settlements found later in Palestine in EBA II. Naomi Porat's technological study of ceramics from EBA sites in southern Palestine clearly demonstrates that in EBA Ib strata many of the pottery vessels used for food preparation were probably manufactured by Egyptian potters using Egyptian technology but local Palestinian clays. In EBA Ib strata there are also many storage jars made from Nile silt and marl wares, which must have been imported from Egypt. Not only did the Egyptians establish camps and way stations in the northern Sinai, but the ceramic evidence also suggests that they established a highly organized network of settlements in southern Palestine where an Egyptian population was in residence.

The importance of the Delta for Egyptian contact with south-west Asia is also suggested by enigmatic evidence from Buto. In strata of the Lower Egyptian Predynastic culture at this site, two unexpected types of ceramics were found by Thomas von der Way in the late 1980s: clay 'nails' and a so-called *Grubenkopfnagel* (a tapering cone with a concave burnished end) that resemble artefacts used in the Mesopotamian Uruk culture to decorate temple façades. Von der Way suggests that contact with the Uruk culture network may have taken place via northern Syria, as the earliest Predynastic stratum at Buto was found to contain sherds decorated with whitish stripes characteristic of the Syrian 'Amuq F ware. The clay nails and the *Grubenkopfnagel* are not associated with any (mud-brick) architecture in the Predynastic levels, which might be expected if von der Way's interpretation were correct, but the ongoing excavations at Buto may yet provide more data on connections between the Delta and south-west Asia in the fourth millennium BC.

Both imported and Egyptian-made cylinder seals, an artefact type unquestionably invented in Mesopotamia, are found in a few élite graves of the Naqada II and III phases. Beads and small artefacts in lapis lazuli, which could only have come from Afghanistan, are first found in Upper Egyptian Predynastic graves. Mesopotamian motifs also appear in Upper Egypt (and Lower Nubia), including the motif of the *héros dompteur* (a victorious human figure between two lions/beasts), painted on the wall of Tomb 100 at Hierakonpolis, which dates to Naqada II. Other typically Mesopotamian motifs, such as the niched palace façade and high-prowed boats, are also found on Naqada II and III artefacts and also in the rock art. The styles of these motifs are more characteristic of the glyptic art of Susa in south-west Iran than of the Uruk culture, and the fact that such artefacts are not found in Lower Egypt has raised the possibility of some southern route of contact between Susa and Upper Egypt, the nature of which is unknown at present.

In Lower Nubia there are numerous burials of the A-Group culture (which was roughly contemporaneous with the Naqada culture), and these contain many Naqada craft goods. The A-Group wares are very distinct from the Naqada ones, and Egyptian products were probably obtained through trade and exchange. It has been suggested by Bruce Williams that the élite A-Group Cemetery L at Qustul in Lower Nubia represents Nubian rulers who conquered and unified Egypt, founding the early pharaonic state, but most scholars do not agree with this hypothesis. The model that may best explain the archaeological evidence is one of accelerated contact between the cultures of Upper Egypt and Lower Nubia in later Predynastic times. Luxury raw materials, such as ivory, ebony, incense, and exotic animal skins, all greatly desired in Egypt in Dynastic times, largely came from further south in Africa, passing through Nubia. Some A-Group chiefs must, therefore, have benefited economically from the trade in raw materials, as is clearly evident from the rich burials excavated at Qustul and Sayala, but the kind of socio-political complexity attested in Upper Egypt at that date is unlikely to have occurred in Nubia. The floodplain of the Nile is much narrower in Lower Nubia than in Upper Egypt, and Lower Nubia simply did not have the agricultural potential to support greater concentrations of population and full-time specialists such as craftsmen and government administrators. The fact that the material culture of the Naqada culture was later found in northern Egypt with no Nubian elements would also seem to argue against any Nubian origin for the unified Egyptian state.

The Early 1st Dynasty State

By c.3000 BC, the Early Dynastic state had emerged in Egypt, controlling much of the Nile Valley from the Delta to the first cataract at Aswan, a distance of over 1000 km. along the Nile. While the presence of the Naqada culture is clearly evident in the Delta in later Naqada II and Naqada III times, the extension of Egyptian political control southwards during the 1st Dynasty is demonstrated by the remains of a fortress on the highest point of the shore on Elephantine Island, a region that had been occupied by A-Group peoples in Predynastic times. With the 1st Dynasty, the focus of development shifted from south to north, and the early Egyptian state was a centrally controlled polity ruled by a (god-)king from the Memphis region.

What is truly unique about the early state in Egypt is the integration of rule over an extensive geographic region, in contrast to contemporaneous polities in Nubia, Mesopotamia, and Syria–Palestine. Although there is certainly evidence of foreign contact in the fourth millennium BC, the Early Dynastic state that emerged in Egypt was unique and indigenous in character. It is likely that a common language, or dialects of that language, facilitated political unification, but nothing is really known about the spoken language, while early writing preserves specialized information that is of a very cursory nature at this point in cultural development.

One result of the expansion of Naqada culture throughout northern Egypt would have been a greatly elaborated (state) administration, and by the beginning of the 1st Dynasty this was managed in part by early writing, used on sealings and tags affixed to state goods. Archaeological evidence for state control consists of the names of 1st Dynasty kings (*serekh*s) on pots, sealings, labels (originally attached to containers), and other artefacts found at major Early Dynastic sites in Egypt. Such evidence also suggests that a state taxation system was already in place in the early dynasties.

At Memphis the earliest archaeological strata that have so far been excavated date to the First Intermediate Period, and strata from the Early Dynastic city may be buried under much alluvium. Further west, drill cores taken by David Jeffreys have revealed both Old Kingdom and Early Dynastic pottery. Graves and tombs, however, are found in this region from the 1st Dynasty onwards; therefore it is likely that the city was founded around then. Tombs of high officials have been found at nearby North Saqqara, and officials of all levels were buried at other sites in the Memphite region. Such funerary evidence suggests that the Memphis region was the administrative centre of the state and also indicates that the early Egyptian state was highly stratified in its social organization.

In the south, Abydos remained the most important cult centre, and it has been suggested that in the 1st Dynasty the smaller Predynastic settlements, which have left more ephemeral archaeological evidence, were replaced by one town constructed in mud brick at Abydos. The kings of the 1st Dynasty were buried at Abydos, another indication of the Upper Egyptian origins of this state. From the very beginning of the Dynastic Period the institution of kingship was a strong and powerful one and would remain so throughout the major historical periods. Nowhere else in the ancient Near East at this early date was kingship so important and central to control of the early state.

Other towns must have developed or been founded as administrative centres of the state throughout Egypt, but the spatial organization of communities was not like that in contemporaneous southern Mesopotamia, where huge cities were organized around large cult centres. On the other hand, neither was early Egypt a 'civilization without cities', as was once suggested. Egyptian towns and cities may have been more loosely organized spatially than Mesopotamian ones, and the royal residence is known to have shifted in location. Owing to a number of factors, towns and cities in ancient Egypt have not been well preserved, or are deeply buried under alluvium or modern settlements and thus cannot be excavated. Nevertheless, some archaeological evidence for the earliest towns has survived. At Hierakonpolis, an elaborately niched mud-brick façade within the town (Kom el-Ahmar) has been interpreted as the gateway to a 'palace', possibly an administrative centre of the early state. At Buto, in the Delta, a rectangular mud-brick building dating to the early 1st Dynasty, which was constructed above earlier layers of Naqada II and III and Dynasty 0, may be the remains of a temple within the town.

Most ancient Egyptians in the Early Dynastic Period (and all later periods), however, were farmers living in small villages. Cereal agriculture was the economic base of the ancient Egyptian state. Throughout the fourth millennium BC, villages became increasingly dependent on the cultivation of emmer wheat and barley, which was incredibly successful in the environment of the Nile floodplain in Egypt.

By the Early Dynastic Period, simple basin irrigation may have been practised, thus extending the amount of land under cultivation and producing increased yields. Unlike practically any other irrigation system in the world, salinization did not occur in Egypt, because the annual Nile flood flushed out the salts. Given that rainfall by this time was negligible, the annual flooding provided the necessary moisture at the right time of year—July and August—so that the wheat could be sown in September after the flooding receded. The species of wheat that were introduced into Egypt matured during the winter months and could be harvested before spring, when the return of high temperatures and drought might otherwise have killed the crops. Huge agricultural surpluses were possible in this environment, and when such surpluses were controlled by the state they could support the flowering of Egyptian civilization that is seen in the 1st Dynasty.

The Royal Cemetery at Abydos

The nature of early Egyptian civilization was expressed primarily through monumental architecture, especially the royal tombs and funerary enclosures at Abydos, and the large tombs of high officials at North Saqqara. Formal art styles, which are characteristically Egyptian, also emerged in the Naqada III/Dynasty 0 and Early Dynastic periods. What is characteristically Egyptian in the monumental architecture and commemorative art (such as the Narmer Palette) is reflective of full-time craftsmen and artisans supported by the crown. Artefacts redolent of the highest quality of craftsmanship are found in royal and élite tombs of the period. Examples include a steatite disk inlaid with an Egyptian alabaster carved scene of two hounds hunting gazelles (from Tomb 3035 at Saqqara), and bracelets with beads of gold, turquoise, amethyst, and lapis lazuli (from King Djer's tomb at Abydos). A similarly high standard of craftsmanship may be observed in the ebony and ivory artefacts and the copper tools and vessels found in the élite tombs, all of which were reflective of court sponsorship. The presence of copper artefacts in the tombs was probably the result of royal expeditions to copper mines in the Eastern Desert and/or increased trade with copper-mining regions in the Negev/Sinai, as well as the expansion of copper working in Egypt.

Each of the Early Dynastic royal tombs at Abydos was originally provided with a pair of carved stone funerary stelae. This example, excavated by Amélineau, is certainly the most elegant surviving one, bearing a single serpent hieroglyph representing the 'Horus name' of the 1st Dynasty ruler Djet.

Although it was previously thought that the 1st Dynasty rulers were buried at North Saqqara, where Bryan Emery excavated the large mud-brick superstructures with elaborately niched façades, it is now thought by most scholars that these tombs belonged to 1st and 2nd Dynasty high officials while the royal cemetery in the Umm el-Qaʿab area at Abydos is the burial place of their kings. Only at Abydos is there a small number of large tombs that correspond to the kings (and one queen) of this dynasty, and only at Abydos are there the remains of the funerary enclosures for all but one of the rulers of this dynasty, as has been demonstrated by David O'Connor's excavations during the 1980s and 1990s.

What is clearly evident in the Abydos royal cemetery is the ideology of kingship, as symbolized in the mortuary cult. The development of monumental architecture symbolized a political order on a new scale, with a state religion headed by a god-king to legitimize the new political order. Through ideology and its symbolic material form in tombs, widely held beliefs concerning death came to reflect the hierarchical social organization of the living and the state controlled by the king—a politically motivated transformation of the belief system with direct consequences in the socio-economic system. The king was accorded the most elaborate burial, which was symbolic of his role as mediator between the powers of the netherworld and his deceased subjects, and a belief in an earthly and cosmic order would have provided a certain amount of social cohesion for the Early Dynastic state.

Seven tomb complexes of the 1st Dynasty were first excavated by Émile Amélineau in the 1890s and then re-excavated more carefully by Petrie. These belong to the following kings: Djer, Djet, Den, Anedjib, Semerkhet, and Qaʿa, as well as Queen Merneith, who may have been the mother of Den and perhaps also regent during the earlier part of his reign. Not only had these tombs been plundered, but there is evidence that they had been intentionally burned. In the Middle Kingdom the tombs were excavated and rebuilt for the cult of Osiris, and Djer's tomb was converted into a cenotaph for the god. Given such a history, it is remarkable that the work of Petrie in 1899–1901 and the excavations undertaken by the German Archaeological Institute since the 1970s have enabled the appearance of the early tombs to be reconstructed. Although only subterranean chambers of mud brick remain, the tombs would originally have been roofed and may have been covered by a mound of sand before which stone stelae carved with the royal name (several of which have survived) would probably have been placed. Rows of subsidiary graves surrounded each royal tomb.

In the area to the north-east of the royal cemetery, called Cemetery B, is the tomb complex of Aha, now conventionally listed as the first

king of this dynasty. Also in Cemetery B are tombs that have been identified by Werner Kaiser as those of the last three kings of Dynasty 0: Iri-Hor, Ka, and Narmer. These tombs consist of double chambers, whereas the tomb complex of Aha is made up of several separate chambers built in three stages with a number of subsidiary burials to the north-east. Although looted, a new dimension in burial can clearly be seen in Aha's tomb complex: traces of large wooden shrines are found in three chambers and thirty-three subsidiary burials contained the remains of young males, 20–25 years old, who had probably been killed when the king was buried. Near one of these subsidiary graves were the remains of the burials of at least seven young lions.

The 1st Dynasty tomb of Qa'a at Abydos, *c.*2900 BC, was one of several Early Dynastic tombs that were re-excavated in the 1990s by the German Archaeological Institute, revealing many small artefacts and architectural details that had been overlooked by Flinders Petrie in the late nineteenth century.

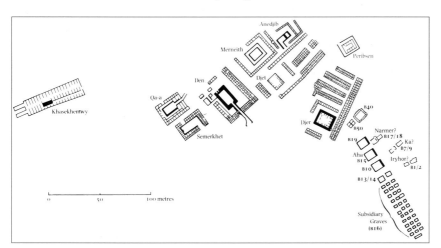

Plan of the Early Dynastic royal cemetery and Cemetery B at Umm el-Qa'ab, Abydos. On the left-hand side is the latest tomb in the group (that of the 2nd Dynasty ruler, Khasekhemwy) and at the bottom right is a row of much smaller tombs dated to Dynasty 0 and the beginning of the 1st Dynasty.

71

All of the other 1st Dynasty royal burials at Abydos have subsidiary burials in wooden coffins. This is the only period in ancient Egypt when humans were sacrificed for royal burials. Nancy Lovell, who has examined the skeletons from some of these subsidiary burials, suggests that their teeth show evidence of death by strangulation. Perhaps officials, priests, retainers, and women from the royal household were all sacrificed to serve their king in the afterlife. Crude stelae carved with the names of the deceased accompany many of these burials, which are found with grave goods, such as pots, stone vessels, copper tools, and ivory artefacts. Dwarfs (who may perhaps have been employed to amuse the king) and dogs that may have been hounds or pets have also been found in these graves. The tomb of Djer has the most subsidiary burials (338), and in general the later royal burials have fewer ones. For unknown reasons, the practice seems to have been discontinued after the 1st Dynasty, and in later times small servant statues and then *shabtis* (funerary figurines) may have become more acceptable substitutes.

All of the 1st Dynasty tombs at Abydos contained wooden shrines where the actual burial was located. The tomb complex of Djer is the largest, covering an area of 70 × 40 m. (including the subsidiary burials in rows). The royal burial was located in the centre of a mud-brick-lined chamber, measuring 18 × 17 m. (306 sq. m. in floor area) and 2.6 m. deep, with short walls perpendicular to three sides of the burial chamber, forming separate storage chambers. Although this tomb was later converted into a shrine for the god Osiris, Petrie still found a linen-wrapped arm with bracelets that apparently derived from the original burial; the arm itself no longer survives, but the jewellery is in the Egyptian Museum, Cairo.

By the reign of Den, in the middle of the 1st Dynasty, a major innovation can be seen in the design of the royal tombs: the addition of a staircase. This made it possible for the entire tomb, including the roofing, to be built during the king's lifetime, and would have facilitated the construction work in a very deep pit. In the middle of the staircase was a wooden door, and beyond this, at the entrance to the burial chamber, was a portcullis to block grave robbers. The tomb and 136 subsidiary burials cover about 53 × 40 m., and the burial chamber itself is 15 × 9 m. in area and 6 m. deep. The tomb's design and decoration are the most elaborate at Abydos: the floor of the burial chamber was paved in slabs of red and black granite from Aswan, which is the earliest known use of this very hard stone on a large scale. A small room to the south-west, with its own small staircase, may have been an early *serdab* (a chamber where statues of the deceased were placed). Excavations by the German Institute in the debris from earlier excavations indicate that grave goods would have included many pots with seal impressions, stone vessels, inscribed labels, and other carved artefacts in ivory and ebony, as well as inlays from boxes or furniture. To the south of the tomb chamber the unusually long subsidiary chambers contained many jars, probably originally containing wine.

In a later royal burial belonging to Semerkhet, Petrie found the entrance ramp (not a staircase as in Den's tomb) saturated up to 'three feet' deep with aromatic oil. Almost 5,000 years after the burial, the scent was still so strong that it permeated the entire tomb. In the tomb belonging to the last king of the 1st Dynasty, Qaʿa, thirty inscribed labels describing the delivery of oil were found during re-excavation by the German Archaeological Institute. Most likely these oils were imported from Syria–Palestine, and may have been made from berries or resins of trees found there. The presence of such huge quantities of oil in Semerkhet's tomb (perhaps in the course of his funeral ceremony) certainly suggests very large-scale foreign trade controlled by the crown and indicates the importance of such luxury goods for royal burials.

The royal tombs at Abydos are located in the low desert (Umm el-Qaʿab). To the north-east of them, closer to the edge of the cultivation, are the funerary enclosures, called 'fortresses' by earlier excavators, where the cults of each king may have been perpetuated by priests and other personnel after the burial in the royal tomb, as was the custom in later royal mortuary complexes. The best-preserved funerary enclosure, now known as the Shunet el-Zebib, belonged to Khasekhemwy of the 2nd Dynasty. Its niched inner walls are still preserved up to a height of 10–11 m., enclosing an area of about 124 × 56 m. In 1988 O'Connor discovered a large mound of sand and gravel covered with mud brick, approximately square in plan, within the enclosure. This mound was located more or less in the same area as the Step Pyramid of King Djoser's funerary complex at Saqqara in the 3rd Dynasty (which began as a low 'mastaba' structure and only in its fourth stage was expanded to a stepped structure). Both Khasekhemwy's and Djoser's complexes were surrounded by huge niched enclosure walls, with only one entrance on the south-east.

Djoser's complex was constructed 40–50 years after Khasekhemwy's, and the mound at the Shunet el-Zebib may possibly be evidence for a 'proto-pyramid' structure or mound. It is not known if mounds were constructed in the earlier 1st Dynasty funerary enclosures at Abydos, but this seems likely. Thus, at Abydos the evolution of the royal mortuary cult and its monumental form can clearly be seen. By the 3rd Dynasty, the royal funerary cult came to reflect a new order of royal power, deploying vast resources and labour for the construction of the earliest monument in the world built entirely in stone.

In the early 1990s, twelve 'boat burials' were discovered by O'Connor to the south-east of Djer's funerary enclosure and just outside the north-east outer wall of Khasekhemwy's. These burials consist of pits that contained wooden

Excavations in the vicinity of the Early Dynastic 'funerary enclosures' at Abydos have revealed 'boat burials' (pits containing wooden hulls) similar to those from the burials of high officials at Saqqara and Helwan.

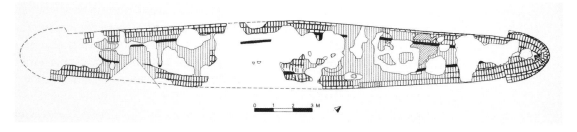

0 1 2 3 M

hulls of boats 18–21 m. long but only about 50 cm. high. Mud bricks had been placed within the hulls and built up around the outside, forming structures up to 27.4 m. in length. The pottery associated with the boats is all Early Dynastic in date, but it is not known at present if the boats date to the 1st or 2nd Dynasty. They all seem to have been created at the same time, and possibly more boat burials will be discovered when excavations are extended in this area.

Smaller boat burials have been found associated with the Early Dynastic tombs of high officials at Saqqara and Helwan. The most famous Old Kingdom examples are the two undisturbed boats associated with Khufu's pyramid at Giza. The purpose of these boat burials is unknown: possibly the boats were actually used in a funerary ceremony or they may have been symbolically buried for the journey in the afterlife. The examples at Abydos are the earliest evidence of an association between boats and the royal mortuary cult.

The Abydos evidence demonstrates the huge expenditure of the state on the mortuary complexes—both tombs and funerary enclosures—of the 1st dynasty kings. These rulers had control over vast assets, including craft products from royal workshops, exotic goods, and raw materials imported in huge quantities from abroad, and probably also conscripted labour (as well as individuals who could be sacrificed for burial with the king). The paramount role of the king is certainly expressed in these monuments, and the symbols of the royal mortuary cult which evolved at Abydos were to become further elaborated in the pyramid complexes of the Old and Middle Kingdoms.

The Tombs of High Officials at North Saqqara and Elsewhere

At North Saqqara there are some very impressive tombs of high officials of the 1st Dynasty, although none is on the scale of the combined monuments (tomb and funerary enclosure) which the 1st Dynasty kings built at Abydos. Some of the North Saqqara tombs are very substantial, and the elaborately niched mud-brick superstructures (missing in the royal burials at Abydos) are truly impressive. The North Saqqara tombs were much better preserved than the Abydos royal tombs; when they were excavated, some of the niched façades still retained evidence of painted geometric designs and the burial chambers still had wooden floors. A number of the North Saqqara tombs were also accompanied by rows of subsidiary burials, but there are fewer of these than in the royal cemetery at Abydos.

It is possible that the North Saqqara tombs combined in one structure the two monumental symbols of status at Abydos: a subterranean tomb and an above-ground niched enclosure. For example, Tomb 3357, which dates to the reign of Aha at the beginning of the 1st Dynasty, is an elaborately niched super-structure surrounded by two mud-brick walls, measuring 48.2 × 22 m. in area. The substructure is divided by mud-brick walls into five large chambers, roofed with timbers, while the superstructure contains twenty-seven additional chambers for more grave goods. To the north of this is a so-called model estate with

small-scale rooms, three granary-like structures, a mud-brick boat grave, and traces of a garden. The hundreds of pottery vessels found in this tomb are inscribed with the king's name and information about their contents. Although the owner of the tomb is unknown, he must have been one of the most important officials of the kingdom, as indicated not only by the size of the superstructure and its contents but also by the additional structures and the boat burial.

In the course of time, the design of these Saqqara tombs became even more elaborate, with a more complex arrangement of chambers, both subterranean and within the superstructure or the enclosure walls. As at Abydos, staircases down into the tomb were introduced at North Saqqara. Two tombs constructed later in the 1st Dynasty were designed with low, rectangular stepped superstructures of mud brick, which were later surrounded by niched walls. Emery thought that Djoser's Step Pyramid evolved from these two stepped structures, but it is more likely that the elements of the first pyramid complex derive from the funerary enclosures and royal tombs at Abydos.

Although large tombs with niched façades have been recorded at other sites

The tombs of many high officials of the Early Dynastic Period were located at the north-eastern end of the Saqqara necropolis. This view along one side of tomb 3507 at Saqqara shows its unusual stepped mud-brick tumulus, which may have been a forerunner of the 3rd Dynasty step pyramids.

(Tarkhan, Giza, and Naqada), the largest number—and those that are largest in size—are concentrated at North Saqqara. What is found at North Saqqara in the 1st Dynasty, then, is evidence of an official class of a large state. These tombs would also have been the most important monuments of the state in the north and thus were symbolic of the centralized state ruled very effectively by the king and his administrators. That huge quantities of craft goods were going out of circulation in the economy and into tombs is indicative of the wealth of this early state, which was shared by a number of officials.

Clearly, the mortuary cult was also of great importance to non-royalty, and the elements of royal burials were emulated in more modest form in the exclusive cemetery at North Saqqara. Apart from the subsidiary burials (of retainers or servants?), there is no evidence from the 1st Dynasty at North Saqqara of smaller burials of middle and lower officials; they were buried elsewhere—for instance, in the cemetery near the village of Abusir. The North Saqqara cemetery is on a prominent limestone ridge overlooking the valley, and the presence of large, elaborately niched superstructures would have been very impressive symbols of status seen by the other classes of officials at Memphis.

Smaller tombs and simple pit graves dating to the 1st Dynasty are found throughout Egypt, which is evidence not only of social stratification but also of the importance of the mortuary cult for all classes. The simplest burials of this period are pits excavated in the low desert, such as those in the 'Fort Cemetery' at Hierakonpolis. These burials are without coffins and grave goods consist mostly of a few pots. Higher status burials were larger and supplied with a greater variety and quantity of grave goods. Sometimes such burials were lined with wood or mud brick and provided with roofs, as in the case of the graves that Petrie excavated at Tarkhan. A more elaborate grave of this type was found at Minshat Abu Omar in the Delta, where the burial pit was partitioned by mud-brick walls into two or three rooms and contained up to 125 items of funerary equipment; the largest of these graves measures 4.9 × 3.25 m. Tombs with mud-brick superstructures, such as those that George Reisner excavated in Cemetery 1500 at Nag el-Deir, are found in both Upper and Lower Egypt. Superstructures of this type, which were sometimes niched, covered a simple burial pit or more elaborate substructures with one to five rooms. In such tombs, the contracted body was found in a wooden or ceramic coffin and a great variety of grave goods accompanied the burial.

Given that most of the archaeological evidence for the 1st Dynasty is mortuary, inferences about socio-political and economic organization are mostly drawn from these data. As tells in the Delta continue to be excavated, however, more early settlement data from this period will become available. From the present evidence, a pattern can be discerned that points to the establishment of many new settlements and their associated cemeteries on both banks of the Nile in the Memphis region, as the socio-economic centre shifted to the north by the 1st Dynasty. New sites also emerged in the eastern Delta, undoubtedly connected to increasing trade and other ventures abroad.

Expansion of the Early State into Southern Palestine and Nubia

In Dynasty 0 and the early 1st Dynasty there is evidence of Egyptian expansion into Lower Nubia and a continued Egyptian presence in the northern Sinai and southern Palestine. The Egyptian presence in southern Palestine did not last to the end of the Early Dynastic Period, but with Egyptian penetration into Nubia the indigenous A-Group culture came to an end later in the 1st Dynasty.

The source of A-Group wealth was the trade in exotic raw materials coming from southern regions through Nubia to Upper Egypt. With the unification of Egypt into a large territorial state, the Crown most likely wanted to control this trade more directly, which resulted in Egyptian military incursions in Lower Nubia. A late Predynastic scene carved on a rock at Gebel Sheikh Suliman near Wadi Halfa suggests some kind of military victory by the Egyptians, and a Nubian campaign may possibly be depicted on an ebony label from Abydos. With the display of force by the Egyptians, A-Group peoples may simply have left Lower Nubia and gone elsewhere (to the south or desert regions), and there is no evidence of indigenous peoples living in Lower Nubia until the C-Group culture, beginning in the late Old Kingdom. How Egypt controlled Lower Nubia in the Early Dynastic Period is unknown. Evidence of an Egyptian installation has been found at Buhen North, with strata which possibly date as early as the 2nd Dynasty. More secure dating at Buhen, however, is provided by seals of kings of the 4th and 5th Dynasties, and it is uncertain if there were permanent Egyptian forts or administrative/trading centres in Nubia in the Early Dynastic Period.

Fortified cities found in the north and south of Palestine have been dated to the EBA II period, which corresponds to the 1st Dynasty, a connection that depends on evidence excavated by Petrie in two royal tombs at Abydos (those of Den and Semerkhet). Petrie found sherds of an imported ware bearing painted designs, which he interpreted as 'Aegean'. This pottery has been called 'Abydos Ware', and is now known to derive from the EBA II culture of southern Palestine. In stratum III at the site of Ain Besor in southern Palestine, ninety fragments of seal impressions of Egyptian kings have been found associated with a small mud-brick building and ceramics that are mainly Egyptian, including many fragments of bread moulds. The seal impressions are made from local clay and evidently belonged to royal officials of the 1st Dynasty. Four kings' names are attested (Djer, Den, Anedjib, and probably Semerkhet), and the ceramics and seal impressions suggest state-organized trade directed by Egyptian officials residing at this settlement for most of the 1st Dynasty. Alan Schulman, who identified the seal impressions, thinks that the site operated as an Egyptian border-control checkpoint, which would have been an early prototype for those described in two papyri dating to the Ramessid Period. Such evidence in southern Palestine is missing during the 2nd Dynasty, however, and active overland contact may have been broken off by then, as the sea trade with the Lebanon intensified. As raw materials from this region (wood, oils, and

Facing: one of the most famous Dynasty 0 artefacts, the Narmer Palette, was excavated from the so-called Main Deposit at Hierakonpolis, *c.*3000 BC. This side shows King Narmer wearing the White Crown and smiting a captive foreigner held by the hawk-god Horus.

resins from coniferous trees) were imported in increasing quantities, which could perhaps only have been conveyed by sea, the land route to Palestine may have been gradually bypassed. It is probably significant that the earliest inscriptional evidence of an Egyptian king at the Lebanese site of Byblos belongs to the reign of Khasekhemwy, the last ruler of the 2nd Dynasty.

The Invention and Use of Writing

Depending on when the early state in Egypt emerged, the earliest known use of writing (in Tomb U-j at Abydos) may predate political unification of the north and south. Certainly by Dynasty 0, writing was used by scribes and artisans of the Egyptian state. Although some scholars believe that the Egyptian writing system was invented in the late fourth millennium BC, with stimulus from Mesopotamia, where the earliest writing is found, the two writing systems are so different that it seems more likely that they are both the result of independent invention.

The earliest codification of signs probably occurred in Naqada III/Dynasty 0. Like Egyptian writing in the Dynastic Period, these early hieroglyphs consist of elements of ideographic and phonetic signs. Specific decipherments of many of the Early Dynastic inscriptions, however, remain uncertain. The use of writing by the early state in Egypt has a royal context, and was an innovation of great importance to this state. Just as a royal style of art developed as a court-centred institution following the unification, so did writing. The early state used writing in two contexts: for economic and administrative purposes, and in royal art.

The economic function of writing must have developed as more resources of the state came under royal control. Hieroglyphs appear on royal seal

Many of the Early Dynastic tombs at Abydos and Saqqara contained labels that are assumed to have originally been connected with items of funerary equipment. This ebony label is decorated with a scene portraying the race undertaken by King Den (*c.*2950 BC) in the course of his *sed*-festival (royal jubilee).

impressions, labels, and potmarks to identify goods and materials marshalled for and by the state, as well as on seals of officials of the state. Titles of owners of these goods and places of origin are also sometimes recorded.

Beginning in Dynasty 0, royal *serekh*s are first seen. The *serekh* is the earliest format of the king's name in hieroglyphs, comprising phonetic signs, placed inside a 'palace-façade' design that was surmounted by the image of a falcon. *Serekh*s are found inscribed or painted on jars and labels and impressed on jar sealings. Such containers were probably storage jars, for agricultural products collected by the state (perhaps as taxation), and some of these goods were traded or exported abroad through the northern Sinai to southern Palestine.

From this economic use of writing it can be inferred that there was already a functioning administrative system by Dynasty 0. Early in the 1st Dynasty, a more complex message of identification developed, and a combination of hieroglyphs and graphic art is found on labels. In the absence of texts composed of signs ordered in a format by grammar, which are not known until later, the information conveyed on labels, especially those arranged in registers, is probably to be read as a text (a year name) containing historical information. Donald Redford has suggested that the context of this information on royal labels is an annals system. The addition of the year sign by the middle of the 1st Dynasty represents a more specific system for recording regnal years than on earlier labels.

The second use of early writing was on royal commemorative art, such as the Narmer Palette. Hieroglyphs identify specific persons and possibly places in representational scenes that are symbolic of the king's legitimacy to rule. In such scenes, the king is depicted in roles, both real and symbolic, based on a new ideology: the institution of Egyptian kingship. Numerical signs, such as those on the Narmer Macehead, represent captured booty and prisoners, and are probably greatly exaggerated, as is so often the case in later Egyptian historical texts.

The iconography of power is clearly seen within the context of such royal art and includes the use of several important conventions. The king and his officials are shown in the special dress of their offices, while their conquered enemies wear next to nothing. A hierarchy of social classes is also evident, from the large-sized king, who is followed by his smaller sandal-bearer, to his even smaller officials, to the smallest figures of conquered enemies, farmers, and servants. The king is frequently depicted trampling on his enemies, in visual puns. The early Egyptian signs do not replicate the information conveyed in the scenes, but serve as name labels for places and persons.

Part of the problem of understanding how writing developed in Early Dynastic Egypt is connected both with the types of artefacts on which early writing appears and with their archaeological contexts. Most examples of early writing are associated with the funerary cult and are not records of economic activities from settlements. Thus the early labels inscribed with hieroglyphs have been found in royal and élite tombs. From the royal cemetery at Abydos are stelae

Facing: the Narmer Palette. This side shows the king (this time in the Red crown) and various officials reviewing the decapitated corpses of the dead.

Several fragments of statues of the fertility-god Min were excavated by Flinders Petrie at Koptos. Probably dating to Dynasty 0 or 1 (*c.*3100–3000 BC), these earliest colossal figures are assumed to have stood in the temple courtyard.

with the kings' names in *serekh*s and smaller inscribed stelae associated with the subsidiary burials. The one funerary stele with a longer text, from the late 1st Dynasty tomb of Merka at Saqqara, is simply a list of his titles. The early state probably kept economic records of some sort to facilitate its economic and administrative control, but there is only indirect evidence of this in the form of inscribed labels.

Early Dynastic Cult Centres

Some of the inscribed labels from the 1st Dynasty bear scenes with structures that are temples or shrines, such as the walled compound for the goddess Neith in the top register of a wooden label from Aha's tomb at Abydos. Early writing also appears on some of the small votive artefacts that were probably offerings or donations to cult centres. Early Dynastic carved stone vessels were sometimes inscribed, and signs on some of these suggest that they may have come from cult centres. A number of such stone vessels may have been usurped from cult centre(s) of gods and buried in Djoser's Step Pyramid at Saqqara. Such evidence points to the existence of cult temples outside the royal mortuary cult in the Early Dynastic Period, but there is very little archaeological evidence of such architecture.

Perhaps the most impressive examples of early temple art are the three colossal limestone figures of a fertility god (Min?) that Petrie excavated at Koptos. One restored figure in the Ashmolean Museum is over 4 m. high. Stylistically, the colossi seem to date either to Dynasty 0 or the early 1st Dynasty. Buried in a deep deposit beneath the floor of the later temple of Isis and Min were figurines (possibly votive items) that are now thought to date to the Old Kingdom, but there are also potsherds that are clearly from late Predynastic (Naqada) wares. Such evidence strongly suggests the existence of a temple or shrine at this location since Predynastic times. Given the huge size of the colossi, they were probably placed in a temple courtyard, although no remains of any early structures were found. The quarrying, transport, carving, and erection of such large pieces of stone imply large-scale (community) organization for renovating and furnishing a cult centre. Given that such expenditure of energy is much more evident in the royal mortuary cult of the 1st Dynasty, the association of the Koptos colossi with a cult centre is remarkable.

During the 1980s and 1990s, German Archaeological

Institute excavations on Elephantine Island at the first cataract revealed the remains of a shrine dating to the Early Dynastic period, a fortress built during the 1st Dynasty, and a large fortified wall encompassing the town in the 2nd Dynasty. What cult was practised at this early shrine cannot be identified, but it was located beneath an 18th-Dynasty stone temple of the goddess Satet. The early shrine is very simple, consisting only of some mud-brick structures less than 8 m. wide nestled into a natural niche formed by granite boulders. Hundreds of small votive artefacts, mainly comprising human and animal faience figurines, were excavated beneath the 18th-Dynasty temple. Many of these date to

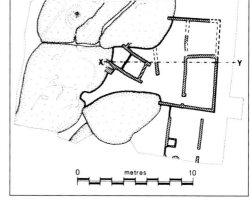

the Old Kingdom, but some are Early Dynastic, including a fragment of a small statue of a seated king with a sign that has been identified as Djer's name. Such a concentration of so many votive figurines made over the course of six dynasties (c.800 years) suggests a craft workshop associated with this temple where worshippers and/or petitioners could obtain such artefacts to leave during their visits.

The excavations of the German Archaeological Institute at Elephantine have revealed the plan of an Early Dynastic shrine beneath the later 18th Dynasty temple of the goddess Satet.

Similar figurines have been also found in deposits at Abydos, beneath an Old Kingdom structure that has been identified either as a temple of the god Khenti-amentiu or a ka-chapel of the 6th Dynasty ruler Pepy II. Probably some of these figurines derive from an Early Dynastic temple. At Hierakonpolis, more animal figurines in faience, fired clay, and stone, which belong stylistically to the late Predynastic and Early Dynastic, have been found in Quibell and Green's 'Main Deposit,' beneath a later temple. The same archaeological context (near the Main Deposit) produced the Scorpion Macehead, the Narmer Palette, and the Narmer Macehead, as well as another ceremonial palette (the Two Dog Palette) which appears to be stylistically earlier than that of Narmer, a number of small ivories inscribed with the names of Narmer and Den, two statues of King Khasekhemwy of the 2nd Dynasty, and inscribed stone vessels made during his reign. Structural evidence for an early temple is found in the same area, where a low oval revetment of sandstone blocks, about 42 × 48 m., encased a mound of sterile sand that had been brought to the site from the desert. This structure was made sometime between the late Predynastic period and the 3rd Dynasty; it was located within a walled enclosure, which O'Connor has suggested was a temple compound similar in design to Khasekhemwy's funerary enclosure and mound at Abydos.

If O'Connor is correct, the main Early Dynastic cult temples at Abydos, Hierakonpolis, and Elephantine have not yet been located and excavated, but what evidence there is points to the existence of cult temple compounds within towns. Such temples served a different function from those associated with the funerary complexes, which were located outside the towns. The architectural evidence of Early Dynastic Egyptian cults (of unknown deities) is much less

84

impressive than the contemporaneous remains of temples in southern Mesopotamia. Nevertheless, town cult centres in Early Dynastic Egypt may have
served to integrate society in towns and nomes in a shared belief system that was
perhaps of more immediate significance to the lives of the local peoples than the
mortuary cults in royal and élite cemeteries.

The 2nd Dynasty State

There is much less evidence for the kings of the 2nd Dynasty than those of the
1st Dynasty until the last two reigns (Peribsen and Khasekhemwy). Given what
is known about the early Old Kingdom in the 3rd Dynasty, the 2nd Dynasty
must have been a time when the economic and political foundations were put
in place for the strongly centralized state, which developed with truly vast
resources. Such a major transition, however, cannot be demonstrated from the
archaeological evidence for the 2nd Dynasty.

In 1991–2 the tomb of the last king of the 1st Dynasty, Qaʿa, was re-excavated
at Abydos by the German Archaeological Institute, and seal impressions of
Hetepsekhemwy, the first king of the 2nd Dynasty, were found in it.
The German archaeologists have interpreted this find as evidence that
Hetepsekhemwy completed the tomb of his predecessor and that there was no
break in the dynastic succession. Where the early kings of the 2nd Dynasty were
buried is uncertain, however, as there is no evidence of their tombs at Abydos.
The only 2nd Dynasty monuments at Abydos are two tombs and two funerary
enclosures that belonged to Peribsen and Khasekhemwy. There is also a large
niched enclosure known as the 'Fort' at Hierakonpolis, by the entrance to the
Great Wadi, which has been dated to the reign of Khasekhemwy by an inscribed
stone jamb. The existence of this sole structure at Hierakonpolis cannot be
explained, and it is unclear whether it was a second royal funerary enclosure for
Khasekhemwy.

At Saqqara two enormous series of underground galleries, each over 100 m.
long, have been found south of Djoser's Step Pyramid complex. Associated
with these galleries are seal impressions of the first three kings of the 2nd
Dynasty (Hetepsekhemwy, Raneb, and Nynetjer), whose names are also listed
on the shoulder of a granite statue of a 2nd Dynasty priest called Hetepdief
(found at nearby Mitrahina and now in the Egyptian Museum, Cairo). The
superstructures of these Saqqara tombs are entirely gone, but it is possible that
two of the kings of this dynasty were buried there. Two sets of underground
galleries have also been found beneath the north court of the Step Pyramid
complex, and may have been created for royal burials of the 2nd Dynasty.
When Djoser's monument was constructed in the 3rd Dynasty, the superstructures of the two earlier tombs would have had to be removed. Such a reconstruction of events is not impossible, given that huge quantities of stone vessels
from the 1st and 2nd Dynasties, presumably usurped from earlier mortuary
complexes and/or cult centres, were found beneath Djoser's complex.

The tomb of Peribsen (perhaps also known as Horus-Sekhemib) in the royal cemetery at Abydos is fairly small (16.1 × 12.8 m.). The central burial chamber is made of mud brick, unlike the 1st Dynasty royal burial chambers, which were lined with wood. When the name Peribsen is written in a *serekh*, it is surmounted not by the usual Horus falcon (as the Sekhemib name is) but by the Seth animal, a hound- or jackal-like creature with a wide, straight tail. This dramatic change in the format of the royal name has been interpreted as representing some kind of rebellion, which was squashed or reconciled by the last king of the dynasty, Khasekhemwy, whose name appears in *serekh*s surmounted by both the Horus falcon and the Seth animal. Such a conflict may be symbolized in Egyptian mythology, as in the case of the literary tale *The Contendings of Horus and Seth*. Whether mythologies, which are known from much later texts, and symbols in the *serekh*s of two kings of the late 2nd Dynasty represent actual historical reality is uncertain. An epithet of Khasekhemwy's from seal impressions, 'the Two Lords are at peace in him', however, lends support to the theory that he resolved some internal conflict, if 'Two Lords' can be taken to refer to Horus and Seth (and their followers).

The last tomb constructed in the royal cemetery at Abydos is that of Khasekhemwy, who was known as 'Khasekhem' earlier in his reign. It is much larger than Peribsen's, and its design is different, comprising one long gallery, 68 m. long and 39.4 m. at its widest point, divided into fifty-eight rooms with a central burial chamber made of quarried limestone. The constructed burial chamber, measuring about 8.6 × 3 m. and preserved to a height of 1.8 m., is the earliest known large-scale construction in stone. Although most of the contents were removed by Amélineau, they were well recorded, and Petrie discusses them in his 1901 publication. The funerary equipment includes huge quantities of copper tools and vessels, stone vessels (some with gold covers), flint tools, and pottery vessels filled with grain and fruit. Petrie also describes small glazed artefacts, carnelian beads, model tools, basketwork, and a great quantity of sealings. Given the large number of storerooms in this tomb, it could certainly have held more grave goods than all the 1st Dynasty tombs in this cemetery.

High officials of the state continued to be buried at North Saqqara in the 2nd Dynasty. Near the pyramid of the 5th Dynasty ruler Unas, Quibell excavated five large subterranean gallery tombs, carved into the limestone bedrock, and he suggested that they represented a kind of house for the afterlife, with men's and women's quarters, a 'master bedroom' for the burial, and even bathrooms with latrines. The largest of the five, Tomb 2302, consisted of twenty-seven rooms beneath a mud-brick superstructure, covering an area of 58.0 × 32.6 m. The superstructures of these 2nd Dynasty tombs were no longer elaborately niched on all four sides as in the 1st Dynasty, but were designed with only two niches on the east side, perhaps indicating places where offerings could be left by priests or family members after the burial (a design feature that would later be found in private tombs throughout the Old Kingdom).

The plans of the 2nd Dynasty élite tombs clearly evolved from the 1st Dynasty high officials' tombs at North Saqqara. Because the Saqqara plateau was made up of good quality limestone, these 2nd Dynasty tombs were designed with rooms for funerary goods that were excavated deep in the bedrock, where the storage rooms may have been better protected from grave robbing than when they had been located in the superstructure. The later 2nd-Dynasty tombs at Saqqara, which probably belonged to middle-level officials, are similar in design to standard Old Kingdom *mastaba*-tombs, consisting of a vertical shaft excavated in the bedrock leading to a walled-off burial chamber. Above the shaft and chamber was a small mud-brick superstructure with two niches on the eastern side.

At Helwan, on the east bank of the Nile, excavations have revealed over 10,000 graves dating from Naqada III to the 1st and 2nd Dynasties, and probably the early Old Kingdom. These tombs were somewhat modest in size and belonged to middle-level officials. A distinctive feature of a number of the 2nd Dynasty tombs at Helwan was the presence of a stele set in the tomb's ceiling, which was carved with a seated representation of the tomb owner, as well as his name, titles, and the so-called offering formula.

Short wooden coffins for contracted burials, which had been found only in élite tombs in the 1st Dynasty, became much more common in 2nd Dynasty graves such as those at Helwan. At Saqqara, Emery and Quibell found 2nd Dynasty corpses wrapped in linen bandages soaked in resin, early evidence of some attempt to preserve the actual body before mummification techniques had been worked out. Such measures were necessitated by burial in a coffin, as opposed to Predynastic burials, in which the body was naturally dehydrated by the warm sand in a pit in the desert. The increased use of wood and resin in middle-status burials of the 2nd Dynasty probably also points to greatly increased contact and trade with the Lebanese region at this time.

Conclusions

The architecture, art, and associated beliefs of the early Old Kingdom clearly evolved from forms of the Early Dynastic period. What is seen in the Step Pyramid complex of Djoser is a transformation of the Early Dynastic tombs into the first monument in the world made entirely of stone—on a truly huge scale. While this monument is also symbolic of the enormous control exercised by the Crown, such power must have been developing incrementally throughout the 1st and 2nd Dynasties, following the unification of the large territorial state in Naqada III and Dynasty 0.

The Early Dynastic Period was a time of consolidation of the enormous gains of unification, which could easily have failed, when a state bureaucracy was successfully organized and expanded to bring the entire country under royal control. This was done through taxation, to support the Crown and its projects on a grand scale, including expeditions for goods and materials to the Sinai, Palestine, the Lebanon, Lower Nubia, and the Eastern Desert. Conscription must presumably also have been practised in order to build the large royal mortuary monuments and to supply soldiers for military expeditions. The use of early writing no doubt facilitated such state organization.

There were obvious rewards for those who were bureaucrats of the state, as the early cemeteries on both sides of the river in the Memphis region clearly attest. Belief in the benefits of a mortuary cult, where huge quantities of goods were constantly going out of circulation in the economy, was a cohesive factor that helped to integrate this society in both the north and south. In the early dynasties, when the Crown began to exert enormous control over land, resources, and labour, the ideology of the god-king legitimized such control and became increasingly powerful as a unifying belief system.

The flowering of early civilization in Egypt was the result of major transformations both in socio-political and economic organization and ideology. That such transformations were successful in the Early Dynastic Period is truly remarkable, given that contemporaneous polities elsewhere in the Near East were much smaller in territory and population. That this state was successful for a very long time—a total of about 800 years until the end of the Old Kingdom—is in part due to the enormous potential of cereal agriculture on the Nile floodplain, but it is also a result of Egyptian organizational skills and the strongly developed institution of kingship.

5 THE OLD KINGDOM

(*c*.2686–2160 BC)

JAROMIR MALEK

The term 'Old Kingdom' was imposed on Egyptian chronology by nineteenth-century historians and its connotations can be misleading. It reflects an approach to the periodicity of history about which we may now entertain serious reservations. The ancient Egyptians never used it and would have found the difference between the Early Dynastic Period (3000–2686 BC) and the Old Kingdom (2686–2160 BC) rather difficult to grasp. The last king of the Early Dynastic Period and the first rulers of the Old Kingdom were, it seems, all related to Queen Nimaathap, who was described as mother of the king's children under Khasekhemwy and as 'mother of the king of Upper and Lower Egypt' under Djoser 2667–2648 BC. For the Egyptians even more important was the fact that the place of the royal residence did not change, but remained at White Wall (Ineb-hedj), on the west bank of the Nile south of modern Cairo.

However, the Egyptians were aware of, and acknowledged, the revolutionary contribution made by King Djoser's builders to royal funerary architecture. Large state-organized building projects exerted an immediate and profound effect on Egyptian economy and society. For us, this is the main justification of a division between the Early Dynastic Period and the Old Kingdom, although it is signalled by progress in architecture rather than personal royal changes.

Chronological Considerations and the Main Characteristics of the Period

Thanks to the information provided by a Ramessid king-list written on a papyrus in the Museo Egizio in Turin, the so-called Turin Canon, there are remarkably few weak links in the order and dating of Old Kingdom rulers. Among the chronologically significant kings, only the reigns of Menkaura

Facing: map of Egypt showing the principal sites of the
Old Kingdom.

(2532–2503 BC, but perhaps less) and Neferirkara (2475–2455 BC, but this is almost certainly too long) present more serious difficulties. We have no safe dates based on contemporary astronomical observation, and calculations made for other periods may change the relative position of the Old Kingdom in the chronological scheme of ancient Egyptian history. The degree of reliability with which we credit ancient sources and our understanding of the Egyptian dating system are also important. On the whole, however, it seems that 2686 BC as the beginning of the reign of Nebka (the first ruler in Manetho's 3rd Dynasty, although his position in the dynasty has recently been challenged) is secure within a margin of error of about twenty-five years.

The end of the period, about five and a half centuries later, is more obscure, but the ancient Egyptians and modern historians are in broad agreement on its characteristics. For the Egyptians, the transfer of the royal residence away from Memphis was represented by a sharp division in their king-lists. As this approximately coincided with profound political, economic, and cultural changes in Egyptian society, it is convenient to follow their example. All the same, the lack of accurate chronological indicators is daunting, and the degree of uncertainty is such that much of the often lively polemic is, in the present state of our knowledge, purely academic.

Although the division of Egyptian kings into dynasties (royal ruling houses), introduced by the Ptolemaic historian Manetho in the third century BC is generally followed, its weaknesses have rarely been exposed more convincingly than in the case of the Old Kingdom. We can establish contemporary reasons for nearly all dynastic breaks, but more often than not it would be difficult to defend them as sound historical criteria or discontinuity in the line of kings. Nevertheless, in the absence of a radical alternative, Manetho's system provides a convenient chronological scheme that avoids the more fluid absolute dates (in years BC).

During the Old Kingdom Egypt experienced a long and uninterrupted period of economic prosperity and political stability, in continuation of the Early Dynastic Period. It rapidly grew into a centrally organized state ruled by a king believed to be endowed with qualified supernatural powers. It was administered by a literate élite selected at least partly on merit. Egypt enjoyed almost complete self-sufficency and safety within its natural borders; no external rivals threatened its dominance of the north-eastern corner of Africa and the immediately adjacent areas of Western Asia. Advances in religious ideas were reflected in breathtaking achievements in arts and architecture.

Large-Scale Building Projects as Catalysts of Change

King Djoser, known from his monuments as Netjerikhet (his Horus and *nebty* names), is one of the most famous rulers in Egyptian history. On the Turin Canon, his name is preceded by a rubric in red ink. As late as the reign of Ptolemy V Epiphanes (205–180 BC), nearly 2,500 years later, the Famine Stele on the island of Sehel, in the first-cataract region, still bore testimony to his image as a paragon of a wise and pious ruler (*djoser* means 'holy', 'sacred'). Although the stele was a tendentious and spuriously historic text put out by the priests of the local god Khnum, its importance lies in the late awareness of Djoser that it conveys rather than in the historicity of the events it records.

The annals preserved on the Palermo Stone record the construction of a stone building called Men-netjeret either in the reign of Khasekhemwy, the last ruler of the 2nd Dynasty, or Djoser's predecessor, Nebka (2686–2667 BC). We learn nothing more about the building although there is a good chance that this is the structure known as Gisr el-Mudir at North Saqqara, to the south-west of Djoser's pyramid. However, it hardly got beyond the initial stages and so the credit for the first successfully completed large stone building in the world, the Step Pyramid, goes to Djoser.

The superstructure of Djoser's tomb is the result of six variants of the plan adopted in turn as the full potential of the new building material was being realized. Before Nebka and Djoser, stone had been used only in a limited way for elements of brick-built tombs. The final structure is a pyramid of six steps, with a ground plan of 140 × 118 m. and a height of 60 m. It stands within an enclosure measuring some 545 × 277 m., the walls of which probably imitated the façade of the royal palace. The king's body was laid to rest in a chamber constructed beneath the pyramid, below ground level. While for us this new architectural form ushered in a new historical period, it also contains a clear link with the past. In its initial design it was a mastaba of a rectangular ground plan, a typical royal tomb of the Early Dynastic period.

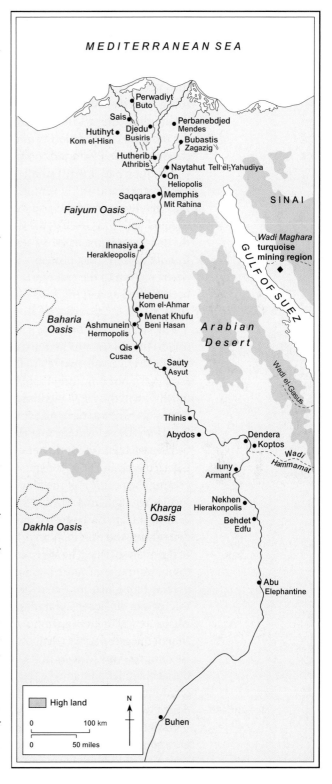

A remarkable feature of the enclosure is a large open court and a complex of shrines and other buildings, the replicas in stone of structures that would have been built in perishable materials for *sed*-festivals (royal jubilees) in the king's lifetime. Here Djoser hoped to continue to celebrate—during his afterlife—such periodic occasions in which his energy and powers, and so his ability to rule effectively, would be renewed. In the southern part of the enclosure, there is a building (the so-called South Tomb) that imitates the underground parts of the pyramid. Its function is unclear, but it may be compared to the satellite pyramids in later pyramid complexes.

Tradition had it that Imhotep (Greek form: Imouthes) was the architect of Djoser's pyramid and inventor of building in stone. Later he was deified and regarded as a son of the god Ptah and the patron of scribes and physicians, equated with the Greek god Asklepios. His historicity has been confirmed by the discovery of the base of a statue of Djoser that also bears Imhotep's name. Imhotep's tomb was probably located at Saqqara, perhaps at the edge of the desert plateau to the east of the pyramid of his royal master, but it has not yet been located and so offers one of the most exciting prospects for future field-work.

The fact that Imhotep was a high priest of Heliopolis is a pointer to the early importance of the sun-god Ra (or Ra-Atum). The royal residence and Egypt's administrative centre were situated in the area where the god Ptah was the chief local deity, but it is likely that Heliopolis (Egyptian Iunu, Biblical On), to the north-east of the Old Kingdom capital and on the east bank of the Nile (now a Cairo suburb), was recognized as the country's religious capital early in the Old Kingdom. Djoser was the first ruler to dedicate a small shrine there.

The striving for monumental grandeur appropriate to a royal burial can be detected early in Djoser's reign; it reflected the prevailing view at the time concerning the position of the king in Egyptian society. This view may have been further strengthened when it found an ideal means of expression in funerary architecture. In the course of the next two centuries the approach was explored to its limits, and this, in its turn, became a powerful catalyst in the development of Egyptian society. The step pyramid was now adopted as the norm for a royal tomb, but none of those planned by Djoser's successors was completed. The pyramid intended for Sekhemkhet (2648–2640 BC) was begun to the south-west of that of Djoser and its design was even more ambitious. A graffito on the enclosure wall mentions Imhotep, who may still have been active. The owner-ship of the pyramid was deduced from the presence of Sekhemkhet's name on clay impressions of seals in its underground rooms. Although the pyramid's burial chamber contained a sealed sarcophagus carved from Egyptian alabaster, this was found to be empty, and it is clear that the superstructure was abandoned when it reached a height of about 7 m.

A similarly unfinished structure at Zawiyet el-Aryan, to the north of Saqqara, is assigned with some probability, though without certainty, to Khaba (2640–2637 BC). The short duration of the reigns of these two kings (only six years each) was almost certainly to blame for their failure to complete the pyramids. Little can be said with any confidence about the family relationships between the kings of the 3rd Dynasty, but the first two, Nebka and Djoser, may have been brothers.

The 4th Dynasty (2613–2494 BC)

In the reign of King Sneferu (Horus Nebmaat, 2613-2589 BC) the external form of the royal tomb changed to that of a true pyramid. This might be regarded as a straightforward architectural development if it were not for other profound changes that occurred at the same time. New elements were added to the overall plan, and together they now formed a pyramid complex. A new orientation was applied to its plan (the main axis of the complex was now from east to west, while previously the north–south direction predominated). The pyramid temple that served as the focus of the funerary cult was built against the eastern face of the pyramid (that of Djoser is to the north). It was linked by a causeway to a valley temple, close to the edge of the cultivated area further to the east, which provided a monumental entrance to the whole complex. A small satellite pyramid was placed near the southern face of the pyramid proper. These architectural innovations must have resulted directly from changes in the doctrine concerning the king's afterlife. It seems that the earlier astronomically oriented star concepts were gradually being modified by the incorporation of ideas centred around the sun-god Ra. Although textual evidence is lacking, already at this early stage beliefs concerning Osiris were probably also beginning to influence Egyptian concepts of the afterlife.

Sneferu, probably as the result of planning that went wrong rather than by choice, had two pyramids constructed at Dahshur, to the south of Saqqara. The first is the southern Rhomboidal (or Bent) Pyramid, where the angle of the sloping sides was altered some two-thirds up its height after structural flaws had been discovered during its construction. The other is the northern Red Pyramid (named from the colour of the limestone blocks used in the core of the structure), in which Sneferu was buried. He may also have started, and towards the end of his reign completed, a third structure at Meidum, still further south. Visitors who came to see it in the 18th Dynasty, some 1,200 years later, made it quite clear in their graffiti that they thought it belonged to Sneferu. It is possible that it was originally conceived as a step pyramid for Sneferu's predecessor Huni (more correctly known as Nysuteh, and perhaps also to be equated with Horus Qahedjet, 2637–2613 BC), but such a substantial contribution to the pyramid of one's predecessor would be unique in Egyptian history. Sneferu's later reputation as a benign ruler may owe much to the etymology of his name, in that *snefer* can be translated as 'to make beautiful'.

The sheer volume of material involved in Sneferu's building activities was greater than that of any other ruler in the Old Kingdom. The Turin Canon puts the length of his reign at twenty-four years, although stonemasons' graffiti

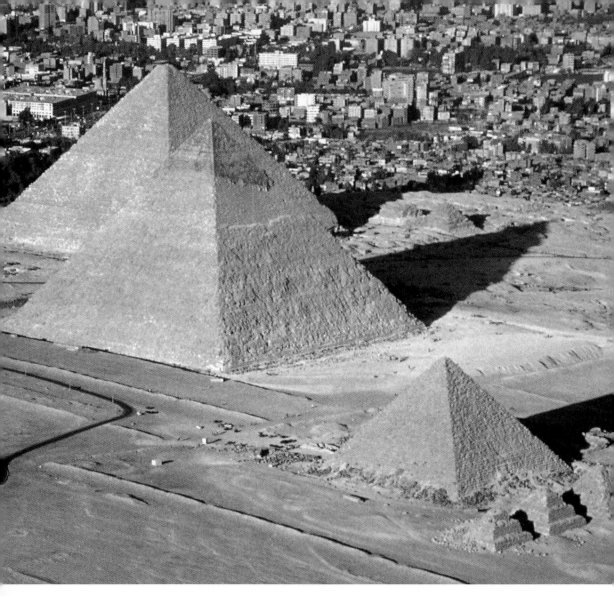

View of the 4th Dynasty pyramids at Giza, seen from the south-west. The pyramids (*c.*2589–2503 BC) are those of (from the foreground) Menkaura, Khafra, and Khufu.

found on the blocks inside his northern (and later) pyramid at Dahshur may suggest a longer reign. The problem could easily be solved if it could be shown that the eponymous occasions of a census that were used for dating purposes (the year was of the *n*th census or it was the year after the *n*th census), and that are known to have been regularly biennial during the Early Dynastic Period, now became more frequent (less regular) occasions. The contemporary dating system probably required annals or similar records to which one could refer in order to calculate dates accurately.

Manetho began a new dynasty, his 4th, with Sneferu. It seems that once again architectural changes provided the criterion for a dynastic division. The perfection of pyramid design and construction reached its peak under Sneferu's son and successor, Khufu (Herodotus' Cheops, Horus Medjedu, 2589–2566 BC), whose full name was Khnum-khufu, meaning 'the god Khnum protects me'. Khnum was the local god of Elephantine, near the first Nile cataract, but the reason for the king's name is not known. Information about the reign and the king himself is remarkably meagre. He must have been a middle-aged man when he ascended the throne, but this did not affect the planning of his grandiose funerary monument. The Great Pyramid at Giza, with a ground plan of 230 sq. m. and a height of 146.5 m., is the largest in Egypt. Unusually, the burial chamber is situated in the core of the pyramid, and not below or on ground level. The plan was changed in the course of the construction, but more recent thinking suggests that the design of the superstructure may have been foreseen at the outset. The usually quoted figure of some 2,300,000 building blocks averaging about 2.5 tons that were required may be approximate, but probably not far off the mark. The valley and pyramid temples and the causeway were originally decorated in low raised relief with scenes that conveyed the ideas of the Egyptian kingship and recorded in anticipation certain events that the king hoped to enjoy in afterlife, such as *sed*-festivals. The reliefs are, unfortunately, almost completely lost.

A dismantled boat, some 43.4 m. long and built mainly of cedarwood, discovered in a pit near the southern face of the pyramid, has been successfully excavated and restored. Another such boat still lies in another pit nearby, but is not as well preserved. It seems likely that these craft were intended to be used by the deceased king in his journeys across the sky in the company of gods. Two more large boat-shaped pits were cut in the rock against the eastern face of the pyramid, and a fifth is situated near the upper end of the causeway.

Three pyramids that contained the burials of Khufu's queens are lined up to the east of the pyramid. A cache with objects belonging to Khufu's mother Hetepheres was also discovered to the east of the pyramid. It was undisturbed and contained some remarkable examples of furniture, but the body of Hetepheres was not present. A settlement of priests and craftsmen connected with the king's funerary cult probably grew up near the valley temples of most pyramids. Khufu's valley temple is located under the houses of the densely populated modern village of Nazlet el-Simman, below the desert plateau, but conditions are too difficult for a full excavation.

The man ultimately responsible for the successful completion of the project before the end of Khufu's twenty-three-year reign was his vizier Hemiunu, who was buried in a huge *mastaba*-tomb in the cemetery to the west of the pyramid of his royal master. Hemiunu's father, Prince Nefermaat, was King Sneferu's vizier and may have organized the building of Sneferu's pyramids. The two family lines, of the kings and their viziers, ran parallel here for at least two generations. The pyramid's date and its function as a tomb are in no doubt, despite the fact that the king's body and all funerary equipment fell victim to tomb-robbers and disappeared without a trace. However, its enormous size, the astonishing mathematical properties of its design, and the perfection and accuracy of its construction still invite unscientific explanations. It may have been the scale of the pyramid that contributed to Khufu's later reputation as a heartless despot, hinted at in Egyptian literature and reported by Herodotus.

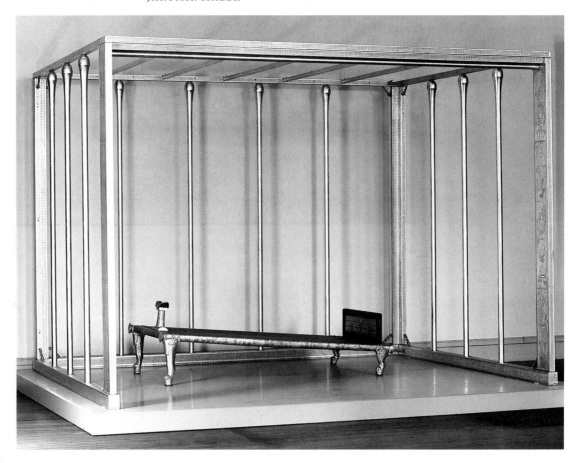

Numerous items of furniture were found in the unplundered cache of Queen Hetepheres (mother of the 4th Dynasty ruler Khufu, c.2589–2566 BC), which was discovered to the east of her son's pyramid at Giza.

Facing: the huge 4th Dynasty wooden funerary boat of Khufu at Giza was found in a pit beside the southern face of his pyramid; its state of preservation was so good that it has been reconstructed by modern conservators.

The long reigns of Huni, Sneferu, and Khufu and the large number of royal offspring complicated royal succession. One of them, Khufu's son Hardjedef, is known from several Egyptian sources. His tomb has been located at Giza, to the east of the pyramid of his father. Hardjedef achieved fame as a wise man and supposedly author of a literary work known as *The Instructions of Hardjedef*, which continued to be read, transmitted down on papyri, throughout the rest of Egyptian history. Kawab, the eldest son of Khufu by his chief queen, Mertiotes, predeceased his father, and so the Egyptian throne passed on to another of Khufu's sons, probably by a minor queen.

The pyramid of Khufu's immediate successor, Djedefra (Horus Kheper, 2566–2558 BC), was started at Abu Rawash, to the north-west of Giza. Another pyramid, at Zawiyet el-Aryan, south of Giza, belongs to a king whose name, although attested several times in masons' graffiti, remains uncertain (readings such as Nebka, Baka, Khnumka, Wehemka, and others have been suggested). Even his place in the 4th Dynasty is disputed. Djedefra was the first to use the epithet 'son of the god Ra' and incorporate the name Ra into his own. Both pyramids were abandoned in the early stages of their construction (although, it seems, both were used for the intended burial).

96

King Khafra (Chephren of Herodotus, Horus Weserib, 2558–2532 BC), whose name may alternatively have been pronounced Rakhaef, was another son of Khufu. He and his son Menkaura (Mycerinus of Herodotus, Horus Kakhet, 2532–2503 BC) built their pyramids at Giza. Their plans, measurements, and the choice of building material differed from those of Khufu and show further development of ideas associated with such monuments. The ground plan (side 214.5 m.) and the height (143.5 m.) of Khafra's pyramid make it the second largest in Egypt, and a judicious choice of location, on somewhat higher ground than the pyramid of Khufu, gives the impression that it is its equal.

Khafra's pyramid complex contains a feature not repeated elsewhere, a huge guardian statue to the north of the valley temple, close to the causeway ascending to the pyramid temple and the pyramid. It is a human-headed lion couchant now known as the Great Sphinx (a Greek term that may derive from the Egyptian phrase *shesep-ankh*: 'living image'). Its size, some 72 m. long and 20 m. tall, makes it the largest statue in the ancient world. The Sphinx was not worshipped in its own right until early in the 18th Dynasty, when it came to be regarded as the image of a local form of the god Horus (Horemakhet, Greek Harmachis, Horus on the Horizon). In front of it, though apparently unconnected with it, was a building constructed according to an unusual plan, with an open court, and this is interpreted as an early sun-temple. The designation 'son of Ra' now became a standard part of the royal titulary and both Khafra and Menkaura followed Djedefra's example in incorporating the name of the sungod into their own.

The pyramid of Menkaura shows extensive use of granite, a more prestigious building material than limestone, but it was built on a smaller scale (side 105 m. and 65.5 m. in height), suggesting that the striving for sheer size had passed its peak. It is a precursor of the smaller and less painstakingly constructed pyramids of the 5th and 6th Dynasties. The Giza pyramids display a clear relationship in the layout of the site, but this is more likely due to the techniques used in the initial surveying than to an overall plan conceived at the outset. A theory according to which the positions of the pyramids at Giza reflect the stars of Orion in the sky is unlikely to be correct.

The pyramid complex of Menkaura was apparently hastily completed by his son and successor, Shepseskaf (Horus Shepseskhet, 2503–2498 BC). He was the only ruler of the Old Kingdom who abandoned the pyramidal form, instead constructing a huge sarcophagus-shaped *mastaba* at South Saqqara, the base of which measured 100 by 72 m. The monument is known as Mastabat el-Fara'un. Khentkawes, probably a queen of Menkaura, had a similar tomb at Giza, but a small pyramid complex was also constructed for her at Abusir. The significance of Shepseskaf's move away from a pyramid towards a sarcophagus-shaped tomb escapes us, and it is tempting to regard it as a sign of religious uncertainty, if not crisis. The Turin Canon inserts a reign of two years after Shepseskaf, but the name of the king is lost (perhaps he is Manetho's Thamphthis) and it has not yet been possible to confirm it from contemporary monuments. It seems,

Facing, above: the 3rd Dynasty Step Pyramid enclosure of Djoser at Saqqara included a *sed*-festival complex along the east side of the pyramid. In the foreground here are restored parts of the dummy chapels that lined the sides of the festival court.

Facing, below: one of the earliest painted private tombs of the Old Kingdom is the late 3rd or early 4th Dynasty *mastaba*-tomb of Nefermaat and Itet at Meidum, bearing this classic depiction of a group of geese, the details of their feathers clearly and accurately delineated.

therefore, that all of the 4th Dynasty kings were Sneferu's descendants. The idea of the son burying his father and succeeding him was ubiquitous in Egypt, but this was not an absolute precondition for royal succession and did not automatically confer such a right.

The precise location of White Wall (Ineb-hedj), the capital of Egypt traditionally founded by King Menes at the beginning of Egyptian history, has not yet been established. It may have been near the modern village of Abusir, in the Nile Valley approximately to the north-east of the pyramid of Djoser. The reasons for the choice of Zawiyet el-Aryan, Meidum, Dahshur, Saqqara, Giza, and Abu Rawash for the siting of the pyramids of the 3rd and 4th Dynasties are far from clear. The location of the royal palaces and the availability of a suitable building site near the pyramid of the King's predecessor may have played a part in the decision.

Kingship and the Afterlife

For a modern mind, especially one that no longer knows profound religious experience and deep faith, it is not easy to understand the reasons for such huge and seemingly wasteful projects as the building of pyramids. This lack of understanding is reflected in the large number of esoteric theories about their purpose and origin. The profusion of these views is helped by an almost complete reticence on the subject by Egyptian texts.

In ancient Egypt, the king enjoyed a special position as a mediator between the gods and people, an interface between divine and human, who was responsible to both. His Horus name identified him with the hawk-god (of whom he was a manifestation), and his *nebty* ('two ladies') name related him to the two tutelary goddesses of Egypt, Nekhbet and Wadjet. He shared the designation *netjer* with the gods, but it was usually qualified as *netjer nefer*, junior god (although this could also be understood as perfect god). From the reign of Khafra onwards, one of his names was introduced

Above: this greywacke statue of King Menkaura and Queen Khamerernebty II is one of the number of magnificent royal group statues excavated from the western end of the king's valley temple at Giza.

Facing: the Great Sphinx at Giza is the largest surviving statue from the ancient world. Situated next to the causeway and valley temple of Khafra, *c.*2558–2532 BC, its original significance is uncertain, but by the 18th Dynasty it had begun to be worshipped as a local variant of the god Horus.

99

by the title 'son of Ra'. The king had been chosen and approved by the gods and after his death he retired into their company. Contact with the gods, achieved through ritual, was his prerogative, although for practical purposes the more mundane elements were delegated to priests. For the people of Egypt, their king was a guarantor of the continued orderly running of their world: the regular change of the seasons, the return of the annual inundation of the Nile, and the predictable movements of the heavenly bodies, but also safety from the threatening forces of nature as well as enemies outside Egypt's borders. The king's efficacy in fulfilling these responsibilities was therefore of paramount importance for the well-being of every Egyptian. Internal dissent was minimal, and

This limestone sculpture of the head of a woman is one of about thirty so-called 'reserve heads' from Old Kingdom private *mastaba*-tombs in the Memphite necropolis (mainly at Giza and primarily from the reigns of Khufu and Khafra in the 4th Dynasty). The heads were placed in the burial chamber close to the corpse, whereas other Old Kingdom private statues were usually placed either in the chapel or in the *serdab*.

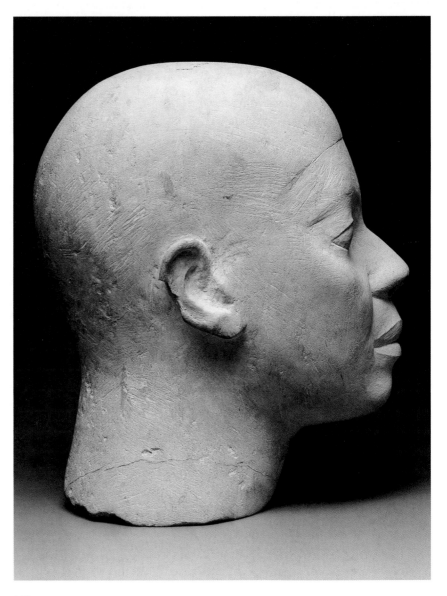

support for the system was genuine and widespread. Coercive state mechanisms, such as police, were conspicuous by their absence; people were tied to the land and control over every individual was exercised by local communities who were closed to newcomers.

The king's role did not end with his death: for his contemporaries who were buried in the vicinity of his pyramid and for those involved in his funerary cult their relationship with the king continued for ever. It was, therefore, in everybody's interests to safeguard the king's position and status after his death as much as in his lifetime. At this period of Egyptian history, monumentality was an important way of expressing such a concept. Given the degree of economic prosperity enjoyed by the country, the availability of labour-force resources, and the high standard of management, there is no need to doubt that the Egyptians were perfectly capable of successfully completing pyramid projects. To look for extraneous motives and forces behind them is futile and unnecessary.

The tombs of the members of the royal family, priests, and officials of the 3rd Dynasty were separated from the exclusive areas with the royal pyramids. Almost all of these tombs continued to be built in mud brick, although early examples of private *mastaba*-tombs in stone may exist at Saqqara. However, in the 4th Dynasty such tombs, now stone-built, surrounded the pyramids, as if the tombs themselves were part of the complexes (and this, indeed, is how they may have been perceived). Because many of them were gifts from the king and made by royal craftsmen and artists, the volume of royal building activities was even larger than suggested by the pyramids alone. Extensive fields of *mastaba*-tombs built according to an overall plan, separated by streets intersecting at right angles, are unique to the 4th Dynasty and are especially known from around the pyramid at Meidum, Sneferu's northern pyramid at Dahshur, and Khufu's pyramid at Giza. We must not forget that most of the evidence used in our reconstruction of the history of the Old Kingdom derives from funerary contexts and so carries a possibility of being biased; Old Kingdom settlements have rarely been preserved or excavated (the towns at Elephantine and Ayn Asil being unusual survivals). The state of technology can be deduced from the projects in which it was applied, but detailed information is lacking. So, for example, only post-Old Kingdom sources make it quite clear that the pyramid-builders did not use wheeled vehicles (although the wheel was known).

The Old Kingdom Economy and Administration

The enormous volume of construction work carried out during the two centuries when the kings of Manetho's 3rd and 4th Dynasties held sway had a profound effect on the country's economy and society. It would be wrong to underestimate the considerable effort and expertise required in the construction of large brick-built *mastaba*-tombs of the Early Dynastic Period, but pyramid construction in stone elevated such enterprises onto a completely different plane. The number of professional builders required must have been

Facing: the late 5th Dynasty *mastaba*-tomb of Ptahhotep at Saqqara includes a depiction of the inspection of cattle, perhaps for taxation purposes.

large, especially if one takes into account all those involved in the quarrying and transport of stone blocks, the construction of approach ramps needed by the builders, and all the logistics, such as provision of food, water, and other necessities, the maintenance of tools and many other related tasks.

The Egyptian economy was not based on slave labour. Even if one allows for much of the work to have been carried out at the time when the annual inundation made it impossible to work in the fields, a large section of the labour force required for pyramid building had to be diverted from agricultural tasks and food production. This must have exerted considerable pressure on the existing resources and provided powerful stimuli for efforts to increase agricultural production, to improve the administration of the country, to develop an efficient way of collecting taxes, and to look for additional sources of revenue and manpower abroad.

Demands on Egyptian agricultural production changed dramatically with the inauguration of pyramid building because of the need to support those who had been removed from food production. The consumption and expectations of those who joined the managerial élite increased in line with their new status. However, agricultural techniques remained the same. The state's main contribution was organizational, including such acts as the prevention of local famines by bringing in surplus resources from elsewhere, the lessening of the effects of major calamities (such as low inundations), the elimination of damaging local conflicts by providing arbitration, and the improvement of security. Irrigation works were the responsibility of local administrators, and the attempts to increase agricultural production focused on expanding cultivated land for which the state was able to provide labour forces and other resources.

This went hand in hand with the need for a better administrative organization of the country and a more efficient way of collecting taxes. The existing major centres of population, often royal estates, now became capitals of administrative districts (nomes), with the strategically placed capital of the country, at the vertex of the Delta, providing the equilibrium between Upper Egypt (*ta shemau*) in the south, and Lower Egypt (*ta mehu*) in the north. Old Kingdom cities are, however, overlaid by later settlements and, especially in the Delta, they often lie below the present water-table. These early settlements are therefore archaeologically practically unknown; even the capital of Egypt has not yet been excavated, and towns such as Elephantine, or Ayn Asil in the Dakhla Oasis, are exceptional. The earlier semi-autonomous village communities now lost their independence and privately owned land practically disappeared, all replaced by royal estates. The earlier rudimentary census was transformed into an all-embracing fiscal system.

Egypt during much of the Old Kingdom was a centrally planned and administered state, headed by a king who was the theoretical owner of all its resources and whose powers were practically absolute. He was able to commandeer people, to impose compulsory labour, to extract taxes, and to lay claim to any resources of the land at will, although in practical terms this was tempered by a

This early 5th Dynasty statue of a seated scribal official from his tomb at Saqqara is perhaps the most effective portrayal of the serenity and power of the Old Kingdom Egyptian bureaucrat.

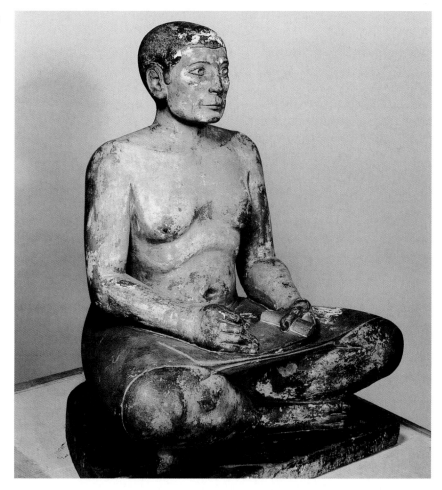

number of restrictions. During the 3rd and 4th Dynasties, many of the top officials of state were members of the royal family, in direct continuation of the system of government of the Early Dynastic Period. Their authority derived from their close links with the king. The highest office was that of a vizier (the word conventionally used to translate the Egyptian term *tjaty*), who was responsible for overseeing the running of all state departments, excluding the religious affairs. It was under the kings of the 4th Dynasty that a whole series of royal princes held the vizierate with spectacular success.

Titles of various officials represent a major source of information on Egyptian administration. Explicit, detailed texts, such as that of the early 4th Dynasty official Metjen, were exceptional. The intensity of state control over every individual now increased dramatically and the number of officials at all levels of administration grew in a corresponding fashion. A consequence of this was that a bureaucratic career was open to competent literate newcomers not related to the royal family. These officials were remunerated for their services in several different ways, but the most significant was an *ex officio* lease of state (royal) land, usually estates settled with their cultivators. Such estates produced practically all that their personnel needed—internal trade at this economic level was limited to opportunist bartering—and the *ex officio* remuneration was their surplus produce. This land reverted, at least in theory, to the king after the official's term of office expired and so could be assigned as remuneration of another official. In an economic system that did not know money it was a very effective way of paying salaries of officials, but it also represented a significant erosion of the king's resources.

Royal Funerary Cults

The effect of pyramid building did not stop with the completion of the structure itself. Each pyramid complex was the focus of the cult of a deceased king that was meant to continue indefinitely. Its aim was to provide for the king's needs and, less directly, those of his dependents—that is, members of his family and his officials and priests buried in the tombs nearby. The primary benefactor was the king himself, who, in his lifetime, endowed his pyramid establishment with land or made arrangements for contributions from the state treasury. The cult arrangements involved presentations of offerings, although it is likely that only a small part of the produce available to these establishments ended on their altars and offering tables (and even this was probably not wasted but recycled, being either consumed by the temple personnel or redistributed more widely). Most of it was used to support priests and officials involved in the funerary cult, and craftsmen living in the pyramid town, or else it was redirected to support funerary cults in non-royal tombs. This was a distinctive ancient Egyptian way of redistributing the national produce, and its benefits trickled down through all the strata of Egyptian society. However, land donations made to pyramid establishments were protected for ever by royal decrees that made them permanent and inalienable, and the result was a gradual reduction of the king's economic power.

Arrangements for the royal funerary cult were made even in the provinces. Sneferu's cult may have focused on a number of small step pyramids, each with a ground plan of *c.*20 sq. m., at least seven of which are known (at Elephantine, Edfu, el-Kula, Ombos, Abydos, el-Seila, and Zawiyet el-Mayitin). Only one of them, at el-Seila, can be dated with precision to the reign of Sneferu by a stele and a statue.

Large building projects also provided stimuli for expeditions that were sent abroad to secure mineral and other resources not available in Egypt itself. These were state organized: no other form of long-distance trade was known before the 6th Dynasty. The names of Djoser, Sekhemkhet, Sneferu, and Khufu are attested in rock inscriptions at the turquoise and copper mines of Wadi Maghara in the Sinai peninsula. Djoser may have been preceded there by Nebka, if this is the same king as Horus Sanakht. The Palermo Stone contains a record of forty ships that brought wood from an unnamed region abroad in the

reign of Sneferu. The names of both Khufu and Djedefra were inscribed in the gneiss quarries deep in the Nubian Western Desert, 65 km. to the north-west of Abu Simbel. Greywacke and siltstone for the making of statues came from Wadi Hammamat, between Koptos (modern Qift) and the Red Sea. Commerce or diplomacy probably explain the presence of Egyptian objects at Byblos, north of Beirut, in the reigns of Khufu, Khafra, and Menkaura, and also at Tell Mardikh (Ebla) in Syria, in the time of Khafra.

No serious threat to Egypt from abroad existed during the 3rd and 4th Dynasties. Military campaigns in foreign countries, especially in Nubia and Libya, must be perceived as exploitation of the neighbouring areas in search of ready resources. It was one of the main duties of the Egyptian king to subjugate Egypt's external enemies, and the kingship doctrine and *realpolitik* here conveniently coincided. Most evidence comes from the reign of Sneferu, but this probably was not unique, only better documented. Such crude forms of external policy seem to have been particularly common during the 4th Dynasty when the country's economy was probably stretched to its limits. Nubia was the destination of a large expedition sent by Sneferu in search of such resources as human captives and herds of cattle, as well as raw materials, including wood. The Palermo Stone records a booty of 7,000 captives and 200,000 head of cattle. These campaigns destroyed local settlements and depopulated Lower Nubia (between the 1st and 2nd Nile cataracts), apparently resulting in the disappearance of the local culture known as the A Group (see Chapter 4). During the 4th Dynasty, a southern settlement was established at Buhen, in the second-cataract area.

Monumental building provided unprecedented opportunities for artists, especially those making statues and carving reliefs. The experience in small-scale working in stone acquired during the preceding periods was turned to large-scale sculpture, with brilliant results. Royal pyramid complexes were provided with statues, mostly of the king, sometimes accompanied by deities. Although for us their aesthetic qualities are so striking, these works of art were, in the first instance, functional. Thus, the earliest preserved large royal statue, that of Djoser, was found in his pyramid temple at Saqqara. It was placed in his *serdab* ('statue-room', from the Arabic word for cellar), at the northern side of the pyramid, and was intended as a secondary manifestation of the king's *ka* (spirit), after the body itself. A similar motive must be ascribed to tomb statues made for private individuals.

The number of royal statues set up in temples increased during the 4th Dynasty. The gneiss statue of Khafra, protected by a hawk (perched on the back of his throne as a manifestation of the god Horus, with whom the king was identified), is a masterpiece that was often imitated in later periods, but never equalled. Statues of gods were also presented to the temples of local deities, but hardly any of these have survived.

The temples and causeways associated with pyramids were decorated in superb raised relief, and the same was true of the chapels of many tombs from

Facing: several seated statues of King Khafra, *c.*2558–2532 BC, with the hawk-god Horus clasping the back of his head, were found in his valley temple at Giza. Each was carved from a single block of gneiss, but this is the only one to have survived largely intact.

the mid-4th Dynasty. These reliefs were not mere decoration but expressed concepts such as kingship in royal monuments, or fulfilment of needs in the afterlife in non-royal tombs, and their inclusion in temples and tombs guaranteed their perpetuity. The wooden niche stelae from the tomb of Djoser's official Hesyra at Saqqara (now in the Egyptian Museum, Cairo) display a high standard of relief decoration at a remarkably early period. These reliefs were created by the same artists who worked on royal monuments and, like the tombs and their statues, were royal gifts.

The hieroglyphic script now became a fully developed system employed for monumental purposes. Its cursive counterpart, called hieratic by Egyptologists, was used for writing on papyrus, but finds of such documents dating from before the 5th Dynasty remain extremely scarce.

Sun-Temples and the Ascendancy of the God Ra

Until quite recently, the rise of Manetho's 5th Dynasty used to be described in terms of a literary text set out in Papyrus Westcar. This is an incompletely preserved collection of stories, probably compiled during the Middle Kingdom and written down a little later. The Arabian Nights setting is the court of King Khufu, where royal princes entertain their fretful father by stories. Prince Hardjedef's narrative foretells the birth of triplets, the future kings Userkaf, Sahura, and Neferirkara, to Radjedet, the wife of a priest of the god Ra at Sakhbu (in the Delta) as the result of her union with the sun-god. To Khufu's sorrow, these children are destined to replace his own descendants on the throne of Egypt. The beginning of Manetho's new Dynasty, the 5th, appears to be linked to a major change in Egyptian religion and, as Papyrus Westcar shows, the division may reflect ancient Egyptian tradition.

The first king of the new Dynasty was Userkaf (Horus Irmaet, 2494–2487 BC), whose name is of the same pattern as that of the last (or perhaps penultimate) king of the 4th Dynasty, Shepseskaf. It has been suggested that Userkaf was a grandson of Djedefra, but, although there were undoubtedly some family links between him and the rulers of the 4th Dynasty, their precise nature is uncertain. We know nothing about the history of Userkaf's reign and there is no contemporary evidence to support the version of events given in Papyrus Westcar.

The main surviving architectural achievement of Userkaf's reign was the building of a temple specifically dedicated to the sun-god Ra. This was the beginning of a trend; six of the first seven kings of Manetho's 5th Dynasty (Userkaf, Sahura, Neferirkara, Raneferef, Nyuserra, and Menkauhor) built such temples in the next eighty years. The names of these temples are known from the titularies of their priests, but only two have so far been located and excavated, those of Userkaf and Nyuserra. The sun-temple built by Userkaf is at Abusir, north of Saqqara (although it seems that current excavations confirm the view that the division between Saqqara and Abusir has been created by modern archaeologists and was not felt to exist in antiquity).

Userkaf's pyramid is at North Saqqara, close to the north-eastern corner of Djoser's enclosure. A substantial re-evaluation of rigid monumentality had taken place by this time, judging from the pyramid's small size (side 73.5 m. and height 49 m.), the less painstaking method of construction, and the evident willingness to improvise (the main pyramid temple is, unusually, set against the *southern* face of the pyramid, perhaps in order not to interfere with an already existing structure). Userkaf, whose reign lasted for only seven years, may have come to the throne as an old man.

The building of sun-temples was the outcome of a gradual rise in importance of the sun-god. Ra now became Egypt's closest equivalent to a state god. Each king built a new sun-temple and their proximity to the pyramid complexes, as well as their similarity to the royal funerary monuments in plan, suggest that they were built for the afterlife rather than the present. A sun-temple consisted of a valley temple linked by a causeway to the upper temple. The main feature of the upper temple was a massive pedestal with an obelisk, a symbol of the sun-god. An altar was placed in a court open to the sun. There were no wall reliefs in Userkaf's construction, the earliest of the sun-temples, but in Nyuserra's they were extensive. On the one hand, they emphasized the sun-god's role as the ultimate giver of life and the moving force in nature, and, on the other, they established the king's place in the eternal cycle of events by showing his periodic celebration of the *sed*-festivals. A large mud-brick replica of a barque of the sun-god was built nearby. The temples were, therefore, personal monuments to each king's continued relationship with the sun-god in the afterlife. Like pyramid complexes, sun-temples were endowed with land, received donations in kind on festival days, and had their own personnel.

The 5th Dynasty

The explanation of the origins of the 5th Dynasty given in Papyrus Westcar can be confronted by evidence contemporary with the reigns of Sahura and Neferirkara. Queen Khentkawes is identified by a unique title in her *mastaba*-tomb at Giza: 'mother of the two kings of Upper and Lower Egypt'. The same title is known from her pyramid (recently discovered by Czech archaeologists), which is situated next to Neferirkara's pyramid at Abusir. If the Giza Khentkawes and the Abusir Khentkawes are the same person, the two sons referred to in her title were Sahura (Horus Nebkhau, 2487–2475 BC) and Neferirkara (Kakai, Horus Userkhau, 2475–2455 BC), and Papyrus Westcar is partly correct. The pyramids of these two kings are at Abusir, as are the pyramids of all the kings who built sun-temples (and probably also that of Shepseskara, 2455–2448 BC). The causeway linking the valley and pyramid temples of Sahura's pyramid complex was decorated with very accomplished reliefs which anticipated the better-known reliefs of King Unas (2375–2345 BC). These Abusir kings form a closely knit group and their monuments display many similarities.

The pyramid temple of Neferirkara has yielded the most important group of

Many Old Kingdom hieratic papyri have been found among the pyramid complexes at Abusir, enabling some of the administrative, economic, and religious practices of the late Old Kingdom to be reconstructed.

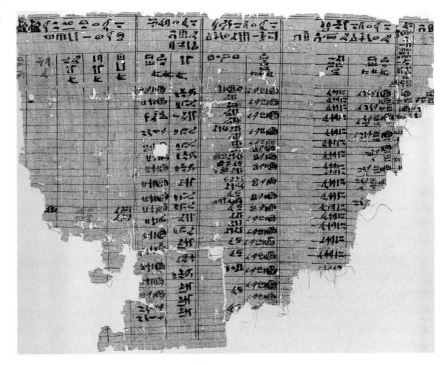

administrative papyri known from the Old Kingdom. These documents throw light on the day-to-day running of the pyramid establishment and include detailed records of produce delivered to it, lists of priests on duty, inventories of temple equipment, and letters. The pyramid complex, however, was left unfinished and its valley temple and causeway were later incorporated by Nyuserra into his own pyramid complex.

King Shepseskara (Horus Sekhemkhau, 2455–2448 BC) is the most ephemeral of the Abusir group, and no textual or archaeological evidence for his sun-temple has yet been found. This is probably due to the brevity of his reign. That of King Raneferef (Isi, Horus Neferkhau, 2448–2445 BC) was even shorter. Although his pyramid did not progress beyond its lowermost courses, the pyramid temple has recently produced papyri comparable to those found in the temple of Neferirkara.

The sun-temple of King Nyuserra (Iny, Horus Setibtawy, 2445–2421 BC) is at Abu Ghurab, north of Abusir. The last king who built a sun-temple was Menkauhor (Ikauhor, Horus Menkhau, 2421–2414 BC). His pyramid has not yet been located, but the tombs of its priests and other indications suggest that it may be concealed by the sand somewhere at southern Abusir or North Saqqara.

The most striking development in Egyptian administration during this period was the withdrawal of members of the royal family from the highest offices. Another noteworthy feature was the skilful way in which sun-temples were incorporated into the country's economic system. Some of the appointments to the priesthood in sun-temples were purely nominal and made in order to entitle their holder to benefits derived from such offices; these may have included temple land leased *ex officio*. The same was true of appointments to the personnel of pyramid establishments. There was no glaring contradiction between the demands of the world of the gods and the dead, and the needs of the living. One could well visualize a system where most of the national product would, in theory, be earmarked for the needs of the deceased kings, their sun-temples, and shrines of the local gods, but would, in fact, be used to support most of the Egyptian population.

Religious beliefs of the ancient Egyptians were locally diverse and socially stratified. Practically every area of Egypt had its local god, which for its inhabitants was the most important deity, and the elevation of Ra to the level of state god had little effect on this. If anything, the annals show that the kings now began to pay even greater attention to local deities in all parts of the country by making donations, often of land, to their shrines, or exempting them from taxes and forced labour.

Expeditions continued to be dispatched to the traditional places outside Egypt, especially to bring turquoise and copper from Wadi Maghara (Sahura, Nyuserra, Menkauhor) and Wadi Kharit (Sahura) in the Sinai, and gneiss from the quarries north-west of Abu Simbel (Sahura and Nyuserra). During the reign of Sahura and Nyuserra, there is a reference to an expedition to procure exotic goods (malachite, myrrh, and electrum, an alloy of gold and silver) from Punt, an African country somewhere between the upper reaches of the Nile and the Somali coast. Contacts with Byblos were maintained (Sahura, Nyuserra, Neferirkara). The discovery of objects bearing the names of several 5th Dynasty kings at the site of Dorak, near the Sea of Marmara, remains ambiguous.

During the 5th Dynasty there was an increase in the number of priests and officials who were able to secure tombs by their own effort. Some of these *mastaba*s are among the largest and best decorated in the Old Kingdom, as in the case of the tombs of Ty (Saqqara) and Ptahshepses (Abusir), both probably of the reign of Nyuserra. Many of them are located in provincial cemeteries rather than in the vicinity of the royal pyramids. Such loosening of the dependence on royal favour was, inevitably, accompanied by a corresponding variety in the forms and artistic quality of statues and reliefs. 'Autobiographical' texts that appeared in these tombs provide new insights into contemporary society. Most of them consisted of conventional phrases and less usual topics often concerned with the tomb-owner's relationship to the king. These trends were to continue throughout the rest of the Old Kingdom.

The Kings of the Pyramid Texts

The portents of change were in the wind after the death of Menkauhor, but the nuances of the process escape us. A degree of standardization and rationalization pervaded royal building activities. Menkauhor's successors did not build sun-temples, although the position of the sun-god Ra remained unaffected.

The long reign of King Djedkara (Isesi, Horus Djedkhau, 2414–2375 BC) links the Abusir group of kings with those who followed. Some of his officials were buried in the Abusir necropolis, and so attest to continuity rather than a break, but the king's pyramid is at southern Saqqara. Its modest measurements (side 78.5 sq. m., height 52.5 m.) were, with the exception of his immediate successor Unas, adopted by all the remaining major rulers of the Old Kingdom (Teti, Pepy I, Merenra, and Pepy II). *The Maxims of Ptahhotep*, a major literary work of the Old Kingdom, which summarizes the rules of conduct of a successful official, is ascribed to the vizier of Djedkara.

The reign of King Unas (Horus Wadj-tawy, 2375–2345 BC) was also a long one. His pyramid is at the south-western corner of Djoser's enclosure, but it is even smaller than that of his predecessor. Its long causeway, stretching for nearly 700 m., was originally decorated with remarkable scenes, now very fragmentary, which surpass the stereotyped means of expression of Egyptian kingship, or at least convey it in a novel way. They include records of events in Unas's reign, such as transport of columns from the granite quarries at Aswan to the king's pyramid complex. But the main innovation of Unas's pyramid, and one that was to be characteristic of the remaining pyramids of the Old Kingdom (including some of the queens), was the first appearance of the Pyramid Texts inscribed on the walls of its burial chamber and other parts of its interior. The Pyramid Texts represent the earliest large religious composition

The late 5th Dynasty pyramid of Unas, *c.*2375–2345 BC, at Saqqara was the first to have Pyramid Texts (sets of magical utterances connected with the king's survival in the afterlife) inscribed on the walls of its inner chambers.

known from ancient Egypt; some of their elements were created well before the reign of Unas and map out the development of Egyptian religious thought from Predynastic times. The deceased King Unas is identified with the gods Ra and Osiris and referred to as Osiris Unas. The Osirian religious doctrine is by far the most important in the Pyramid Texts, but ideas associated with the sun-god are also important, as well as the remains of star-oriented concepts and some others, probably even older. However, the complexity of the Pyramid Texts makes interpretation of individual spells difficult, and understanding of their mutual relationship is especially hard. The reason for their inclusion inside the pyramid was to provide the deceased king with texts that were regarded as essential for his survival and well-being in afterlife. Their mere presence was probably deemed sufficient to make them effective. While the distribution of the Pyramid Texts within the structure is not accidental, it is unlikely that they are connected with such a transient event as a funeral.

The belief that after death the deceased entered the kingdom of the god Osiris now became widespread. Osiris, originally a local deity in the Eastern Delta, was a chthonic (linked to the earth) local god associated with agriculture and annually recurring events in nature. He was probably an ideal choice for the universal god of the dead, given that the myths concerning his resurrection mirrored the revitalization of Egyptian soil after the annual flood receded (which used to happen until the building of a dam at Aswan at the beginning of this century and the High Dam in the 1960s). The early stages of the development of the cult of Osiris are far from clear. He was an appropriate counterpart for the sun-god Ra and his rise to prominence may have been caused by corresponding considerations. Our written records are, however, inadequate to establish exactly when this happened. In their tombs, deceased persons are described as *imakhu* ('honoured') by Osiris: in other words, their needs in afterlife were satisfied because of their association with him. The concept of *imakhu* (which can also be translated as 'being provided for') was an expression of a remarkable moral dictum that ran through all levels of Egyptian society and that corrected the extreme cases of social inequality: it was the duty of a more influential and richer person to take care of the poor and socially disadvantaged in the same way as the head of a family was responsible for all of its members.

The 6th Dynasty

According to Manetho, the reign of Unas concluded the 5th Dynasty, and the next king, Teti (Horus Seheteptawy, 2345–2323 BC), ushered in the 6th Dynasty. We have no definite information on the personal relationship between Teti and his predecessors, but his chief wife Iput was probably Unas's daughter. Teti's vizier Kagemni began his career under Djedkara and Unas. However, the Turin Canon also inserts a break at this point followed by a total for the kings between Menes (the first king of the 1st Dynasty) and Unas (the figure is now lost). This gives us some food for thought, because the criterion for such divisions in the

This small statue from Hierakonpolis is one of a pair of copper figures dating to the reign of Pepy I (*c*.2321–2287 BC), whom they probably portray. This is the appearance of the statue before its recent cleaning and restoration.

Turin Canon invariably was the change of location of the capital and royal residence.

The original capital at White Wall, founded at the beginning of the 1st Dynasty, was probably gradually replaced in importance by the more populated suburbs further to the south, approximately to the east of Teti's pyramid. Djed-isut, the name of this part of the city, derived from the name of Teti's pyramid and its pyramid town. The royal palaces of Djedkara and Pepy I (and possibly also that of Unas) may, however, have already been transferred further south, away from the squalor, noise, and smell of a crowded city, to places in the valley east of the present South Saqqara and separated from Djed-isut by a lake. This would, at least, explain the choice of South Saqqara as the site for the pyramids of Djedkara and Pepy I.

In a development that paralled that near the pyramid of Teti, the adjacent settlement took its name Mennefer (Greek Memphis) from the name of Pepy I's pyramid and its pyramid town. This may have already at the end of the Old Kingdom become physically linked with the settlements around the temple of the god Ptah further to the east, and the city in its entirety began to be known as Mennefer. So the site of the royal residence and of the city itself may have changed at the end of the 5th or early in the 6th Dynasty and this may explain the division in the Turin Canon, later reflected in Manetho's account (Pepy I's father Teti was included in the new line of rulers). But here we are entering a realm of speculation and only future fieldwork will show how much of it is justified.

Teti may have been followed by King Userkara (2323–2321 BC), although his existence can be disputed. Some confusion may be due to the fact that Pepy I (Horus Merytawy, 2321–2287 BC), the son of Teti and Queen Iput, was called Nefersahor in the first part of his reign. This was his 'prenomen' or 'throne name', received at his coronation, preceded by the title *nesu-bit* ('he of the sedge and bee') and enclosed in an oval cartouche. Later he changed it to Meryra. The 'nomen' or 'birth name', Pepy (the number that conventionally follows is ours, and was never used by the ancient Egyptians), predated his accession to the throne; it was introduced by the title *sa Ra* ('son of the god Ra') and was also written in a cartouche.

Egypt's internal situation now began to change. The king's position remained theoretically unaffected, but there can be no doubt that difficulties appeared. This impression can be only partly explained by the increase in the volume and quality of information that allows us a deeper insight into Egyptian society, beyond the monolithically monumental and largely formal façade of the earlier periods. The king's person was no longer untouchable: a biographical text of Weni, a high court official, mentions an unsuccessful plot against Pepy I inspired by one of his queens late in his reign. Her name is not given, but marriage politics were known: in his declining years, the king married two sisters, both called Ankhnes-meryra ('King Meryra [Pepy I] lives for her'). Their father Khui was an influential official at Abydos. These were dramatic events, but the growth of power and influence of local administrators (especially in Upper Egypt, further away from the capital) and the corresponding weakening of the royal authority may have had less dramatic, but potentially much more serious, consequences. A new office of 'overseer of Upper Egypt' was created late in the 5th Dynasty.

The kings of the 6th Dynasty built extensively, constructing shrines of local gods all over Egypt, but these fell victim to later rebuilding or have not yet been excavated. Upper Egyptian temples, such as those of Khenti-amentiu at Abydos, Min at Koptos, Hathor at Dendera, Horus at Hierakonpolis, and Satet at Elephantine, were especially favoured. Donations made to these temples and exemptions from taxes and compulsory service granted to them multiplied.

The pyramid temples of the late 5th and 6th Dynasties include scenes that appear so convincing that one might be tempted to take them at face value. So, for example, a scene showing the submission of Libyan chiefs during the reign of Pepy II is a close copy of such a representation in the temples of Sahura, Nyuserra, and Pepy I (and, some 1,500 years later, it was repeated in the temple of King Taharqo at Kawa, in Sudan). These scenes were standard expressions of the achievements of the ideal king and as such bore little resemblance to reality. Their inclusion in the temples guaranteed their continuity. The same explanation may be given to the scenes of ships returning from an expedition to Asia and a raid on the nomads of Palestine, depicted in the causeway of Unas. However, other sources show that similar events did take place. The already mentioned Weni describes repeated large-scale military actions against the Aamu of the Syro-Palestinian region. In spite of the way these were presented, they were preventative or punitive raids rather than defensive campaigns.

The exploitation of mineral resources in the deserts outside Egypt continued. Turquoise and copper continued to be mined at Wadi Maghara in the Sinai (Djedkara, Pepy I and II), Egyptian alabaster at Hatnub (Teti, Merenra, Pepy I and II), greywacke and siltstone in the Wadi Hammamat (Pepy I, Merenra) in the Eastern Desert, and gneiss in the quarries north-west of Abu Simbel (Djedkara). Expeditions were sent to Punt by Djedkara, and commercial and diplomatic contacts were maintained with Byblos (Djedkara, Unas, Teti, Pepy I and II, and Merenra), and also with Ebla (Pepy I).

Nubia became particularly important during the later 6th Dynasty and attempts were made to improve navigation in the first-cataract region in the time of Merenra. The area now began to receive an influx of new settlers (the so-called Nubian C Group) from further south, between the 3rd and 4th cataracts, with the centre at Kerma. There were occasional clashes with these people as Egypt tried to prevent a potential threat to its economic interests and its security. Caravan expeditions across the Nubian territory (the lands of Wawat, Irtjet, Satju, and Iam) were organized by administrators of the southernmost Egyptian nome at Elephantine, such as Harkhuf, Pepynakht Heqaib, and Sabni. African luxury goods that reached Egypt this way included incense, hard wood (ebony), animal skins, and ivory, but also dancing dwarfs and exotic animals. The employment of Nubians, especially in border police units and as mercenaries in military expeditions, dates from this period onwards.

The Western Desert was criss-crossed by caravan routes. One of them left the Nile in the area of Abydos for the Kharga Oasis and then proceeded southwards along the track now known as Darb el-Arbain (Arabic: 'forty-day route') to the Selima Oasis. Another departed from Kharga westwards, to the Dakhla Oasis, where an important settlement thrived at Ayn Asil, near modern Balat, especially during the reign of Pepy II.

The Decline of the Old Kingdom

Pepy I was succeeded by two of his sons, first by Merenra (fully Merenra-nemtyemsaf, Horus Ankh-khau, 2287–2278 BC), and then by Pepy II (Horus Netjerkhau, 2278–2184 BC). Both of them came to the throne very young and both built their pyramids at South Saqqara. Pepy II's reign of some ninety-four years (he inherited the throne at the age of 6) was the longest in ancient Egypt, but its second half probably was rather ineffective, as the forces that had been insidiously eroding the theoretical foundations of the Egyptian state became apparent. The ensuing crisis was inevitable, because its seeds were contained in the system itself. It was, in the first instance, ideological, because the king whose economic power had been greatly weakened could no longer perform the role assigned to him by the doctrine of Egyptian kingship. The consequences of this for the whole of Egyptian society were serious; the *ex officio* system of remuneration no longer functioned satisfactorily and the fiscal system was probably on the verge of collapse.

Some offices became, in effect, hereditary and were kept in the same family for several generations. In Middle and Upper Egypt, rock-cut tombs at sites such as Sedment, Dishasha, Kom el-Ahmar Sawaris, Sheikh Said, Meir, Deir el-Gebrawi, Akhmim (el-Hawawish), el-Hagarsa, el-Qasr wa 'l-Saiyad, Elkab, and Aswan (Qubbet el-Hawa) testify to the aspirations of the local administrators, now would-be semi-independent local rulers. We know less about the corresponding cemeteries in the Delta, although sites such as Heliopolis, Kom el-Hish, and Mendes prove that they existed. The proximity of the capital may have made any moves towards increased autonomy more difficult, but the main reason for the lack of evidence is local geography and geology. Old Kingdom levels are close to or below the current water table and this makes excavations very difficult. We know much more about the local administrators of

Dakhla Oasis who lived in the settlement of Ayn Asil and were buried in large *mastaba*-tombs in the local cemetery (Qilat el-Dabba).

Centralized government all but ceased to exist, and the advantages of a unified state were lost. The situation was further aggravated by climatic factors, especially a series of low Niles and a decline in precipitation that affected areas adjacent to the Nile Valley and produced pressure on Egypt's border areas by nomadic inhabitants. The fact that many potential royal successors were waiting in the wings after Pepy II's exceptionally long reign probably contributed to the chaotic situation that followed.

Pepy II was succeeded by Merenra II (Nemtyemsaf), Queen Nitiqret (2184–2181 BC), and some seventeen or more ephemeral kings who represent Manetho's 7th and 8th Dynasties. His dynastic separations are hard to explain except as accidental divisions in the lists. Most of these rulers are little more than names for us, but several of them are known from the protective decrees issued for the temple of Min at Koptos. Qakara Iby is the only one whose small pyramid (side 31.5 sq. m.) has been found at South Saqqara. So it was mainly the Memphite residence and the theoretical claim to the whole of Egypt that linked these kinglets with the giant kings of the earlier Old Kingdom. The Turin Canon's grand total of 955 years that separated Menes, at the beginning of the 1st Dynasty, from the last of these ephemeral rulers, concludes the line of Memphite kings and the period described by us as the Old Kingdom.

6 THE FIRST INTERMEDIATE PERIOD

(*c*.2160–2055 BC)

STEPHAN SEIDLMAYER

Egyptologists traditionally distinguish between the major periods of pharaonic history on the basis of the political state of the country. 'Kingdoms'—defined as times of political unity and strong, centralized government—alternate with 'intermediate periods', which are in contrast characterized by the rivalries of local rulers in their claims for power. In the case of the First Intermediate Period, the long line of kings who had ruled the country from Memphis ended with the last pharaohs of the 8th Dynasty. After the 8th Dynasty power was held by a succession of rulers originating from Herakleopolis Magna, which was located in northern Middle Egypt, near the entrance to the Faiyum. These kings appear as both the 9th and 10th Dynasties in Manetho's history, having been mistakenly subdivided in the course of the transmission of the original king-list (see Chapter 1 for a discussion of Manetho's *Aegyptiaca*).

The shift of the royal residence from Memphis to Herakleopolis was evidently regarded by the ancient Egyptians as a major break. This is suggested by the fact that the compilers of the 19th Dynasty Turin Canon inserted a grand total for the earlier part of Egyptian history after the list of 8th Dynasty rulers. In addition, the king-list in the temple of Seti I at Abydos gives no royal names for the period between the 8th Dynasty and the beginning of the Middle Kingdom.

In fact, the Herakleopolitans never wielded control over southern Upper Egypt. Here, in the course of prolonged struggles between local magnates, a family of Theban nomarchs established itself as the leading force, assumed the titles of royalty, and duly appeared in the annals of pharaonic kingship as the

11th Dynasty. From this moment onwards, two competing states confronted each other within the territory of Egypt, until, terminating an era of intermittent war, the Theban king Nebhepetra Mentuhotep II managed to defeat his Herakleopolitan opponent and reunite the country under Theban control, thus inaugurating the Middle Kingdom. This chapter therefore deals with the period between the end of the 8th Dynasty and the reign of Nebhepetra Mentuhotep II.

Chronological Problems

We are comparatively well informed concerning the second part of the First Intermediate Period—the phase of competition between Herakleopolitans and Thebans, which lasted for some 90 to 110 years. However, the earlier part of the period—the phase of Herakleopolitan rule before the advent of the 11th Dynasty—is rather less clear. There is a dearth of information of immediate chronological value because of the loss of most of the names of the Herakleopolitans and of all information concerning the lengths of their reigns in the Turin Canon, and because of the unsatisfactory state of archaeological research in northern Middle Egypt and the Delta, the heartlands of the Herakleopolitan kingdom. Because of the scarcity of data directly relating to the Herakleopolitans, it was even at one stage proposed that there must have been no period during which Herakleopolitans were (at least nominally) the sole rulers, and that they must have been entirely coeval with the 11th Dynasty. This is impossible, however, since we know of prominent individuals and important political events that can be placed only in the period between the 8th and 11th Dynasties.

Detailed studies of the succession of holders of important administrative and priestly posts in several towns of Upper Egypt, as well as studies of developments in the archaeological material, strongly suggest that this interval between the 8th and 11th Dynasties occupied a fairly long span of time, probably amounting to some three or four generations. In addition, the figure that Manetho reports as the length of his 10th Dynasty can be interpreted to support an estimate of nearly two centuries for the whole of the First Intermediate Period, an assessment that would also be in perfect agreement with the prosopographical and archaeological evidence.

The Nature of the First Intermediate Period

The First Intermediate Period, however, was not just a time of disorder in terms of the succession to the throne of Egypt; it was also a period of crisis and of new developments, both of which deeply affected the whole of Egyptian society and culture. This point can be appreciated as soon as we turn to the evidence of the monuments. The Old Kingdom mortuary complexes of the kings and the highest officials in the cemeteries of the capital, Memphis, play a prominent part in shaping our ideas of the Egyptian state. This series of spectacular buildings came to a halt after the reign of Pepy II, and they were revived only by Men-tuhotep II with his mortuary temple at Deir el-Bahri in western Thebes.

To match this state of affairs, the upper chronological limit of the First Inter-mediate Period is sometimes raised to include the three decades during which the last kings of the Memphite line after Pepy II still held power. While taking liberties with the scheme whereby Egyptian history is divided into dynasties, this approach is not wholly unjustified. In fact, large-scale building may be understood as good evidence not only for the nature of the core institutions of the state but also for the fact that they were still actually functioning. The glar-ing gap in the monumental record during the First Intermediate Period there-fore suggests that the social system had become fragmented, both in its political organization and in its cultural patterns.

It is equally apparent, however, that the First Intermediate Period archaeo-logical and epigraphic data indicate the existence of a thriving culture among the poorer levels of society, as well as vigorous social development in the provincial towns of Upper Egypt. Rather than being an outright collapse of Egyptian society and culture as a whole, the First Intermediate Period was char-acterized by an important, though temporary, shift in its centres of activity and dynamism.

To understand both the crisis of the pharaonic state and the processes that ultimately led to the re-establishment of a unified political organization on a new basis, it is crucial to investigate the ways in which political institutions were rooted in society. Much of Egyptian history tends to concentrate on the royal residence, the kings, and 'court culture', but in writing the history of the First Intermediate Period it is necessary to focus instead on provincial towns and on the people themselves, who make up the most basic elements of society.

The Capital and the Provinces

The pharaonic state originally emerged as a centralized system. From the earli-est times, its key institutions—the king and his court—were firmly installed in the capital. The social élite was also concentrated there, as well as the adminis-trative expertise and the control of the traditions of high culture. In addition, the installations of state religion, and the cult of the king and his divine ances-tors, were located in the immediate vicinity of the capital. The administration of the country was controlled by royal emissaries, who were put in charge of extensive sections of the Nile Valley. Although these administrators were deal-ing with the provinces, they still retained their attachment to the royal resi-dence and continued to regard themselves as members of the élite society of the capital. Until well into the 5th Dynasty, nothing of the cultural achievements that attest to the grandeur of the Old Kingdom was to be seen outside the Mem-phite region. There was a vast chasm of social and cultural inequality between the country and its rulers.

However, a profound change in the system began to appear in the 5th

Dynasty and was completely in place by the end of the 6th. From this period onwards, provincial administrators were appointed for single nomes and took up permanent residence in their districts. As in other branches of the administration, members of the same family frequently succeeded each other in office. Although this political move was probably intended to enhance the efficiency of the provincial administration, it was to have far-reaching and unforeseen consequences. In the first place, it meant a change in the socio-economic patterns that lay at the heart of the system. Originally, economic resources were concentrated at the royal residence and redistributed to the beneficiaries by the central administration. Now, however, the nobles residing in the provinces were able to gain direct access to the products of the country. The opposition between the centre and the provinces began to act as a differentiating factor within the formerly homogeneous élite group of officials.

The provincial aristocracy was eager to ensure that its way of life was on a par with the style of the royal court. This is evident in the decorated monumental tombs that began to appear in the cemeteries of the regional centres throughout the country. Iconographic patterns, textual models, religious and ritualistic knowledge flowed from the stock of court culture to the periphery. In addition, the king himself provided specialist craftsmen, ritualists trained at the residence, and costly goods to maintain and strengthen the bonds of loyalty between the provincial aristocrats and the court. These tombs, however, are only the tip of the iceberg; in fact, the various provincial élites and their staff acted as separate centres within the political organization, sustaining specialist professionals and keeping a growing amount of local production for use within the provinces themselves (rather than allowing it to be exploited by the royal court), thus leading to a change in the social and economic patterns of the provinces. Rural Egypt became economically richer and culturally more complex.

The Provincial Milieu

The transformation of the culture and economy of the provinces affected the whole of society. This process can be followed in profound changes in the archaeological record, which were rooted in the 6th Dynasty, and which reached their climax in the earlier half of the First Intermediate Period. Again we have to turn to the cemeteries for essential data—partly because of the unfortunate lack of excavated settlements of this period, but mainly because of the inherent significance of the remains of funerary culture.

If we compare the situation in the earlier Old Kingdom with that in the late Old Kingdom and the First Intermediate Period, a change in the quantity of graves becomes immediately obvious. For the later period, many more cemeteries are known, and, whenever a particular region has been explored systematically, there is a marked increase in the number of tombs. To explain this phenomenon, two factors must be taken into account. First, the increase in

Facing: the development
of medium-sized pottery
vessels during the First
Intermediate Period (illustrated for Upper and Lower
Egypt in the upper section of
the diagram) clearly reflects
the impact of the new technique of throwing vessels on
a potter's wheel. An early
example of this device is
depicted in the 5th Dynasty
tomb of Ti at Saqqara (bottom right). In the case of the
earlier, high-shouldered
vessels, a large area of the
surface had to be scraped
manually into shape, a task
that was considerably less
cumbersome in the case of
the later, sagging shapes
(bottom left). Nevertheless,
in Lower Egypt, the traditional, high-shouldered
model was retained
throughout the First
Intermediate Period.

tombs clearly attests to demographic growth during the Old Kingdom, and probably the most influential factors for change were rooted in the local settings themselves, where population growth was probably accompanied and accentuated by the development of more intensive and more efficient uses of the available agrarian resources. Secondly, during the late Old Kingdom and the First Intermediate Period, ordinary tombs became considerably larger and burials began to be provided with much better grave goods. Not only have such tombs been more easily identified and dated (because of their greater size and more varied contents), but they have also attracted more excavators. In fact, provincial cemeteries of the first part of the Old Kingdom had a reputation, among earlier archaeologists, for not repaying the labour of excavation.

Like the appearance of decorated monumental tombs in Upper Egypt, the increase in numbers of graves in the provincial cemeteries therefore reflects, to an important degree, a change in the social pattern of consumption. This phenomenon seems particularly obvious in the funerary record, but it was not restricted to this sphere. In fact, the most valuable objects that become most abundant and widely represented in the graves of the early First Intermediate Period—cosmetic stone vessels, ornaments and amulets of gemstones, and even gold—were everyday items of daily life, rather than being specially made for funerary use. It seems clear, therefore, that the provinces enjoyed favourable economic conditions during the late Old Kingdom and the First Intermediate Period.

The distribution of the cemeteries can also provide some indications of settlement patterns. The landscape was dotted with villages, while the sites of the nome capitals are marked not only by the groups of rock tombs or monumental mastaba-tombs belonging to the provincial aristocracy, but also by very extensive cemeteries of ordinary townspeople. The tombs of the urban population do not differ, in principle, from those of the villagers; however, they are often larger and better equipped. An urbanized structure, therefore, dominated the provincial settlement pattern not only politically and socially but also demographically and economically.

Changes in Styles and Shapes as Signs of Cultural and Social Development

The period that followed the close of the Old Kingdom brought about fundamental changes in material culture. In fact, during the First Intermediate Period, almost all artefacts took on a different appearance. We can review a few of the most significant aspects of this process.

From an archaeologist's point of view, pottery is clearly the most important type of artefact. Since the Early Dynastic Period and throughout the Old Kingdom, the repertoire of containers had been dominated, morphologically, by ovoid shapes: the point of maximum extension almost always lay slightly above the middle of the vessel. During the First Intermediate Period, this style was

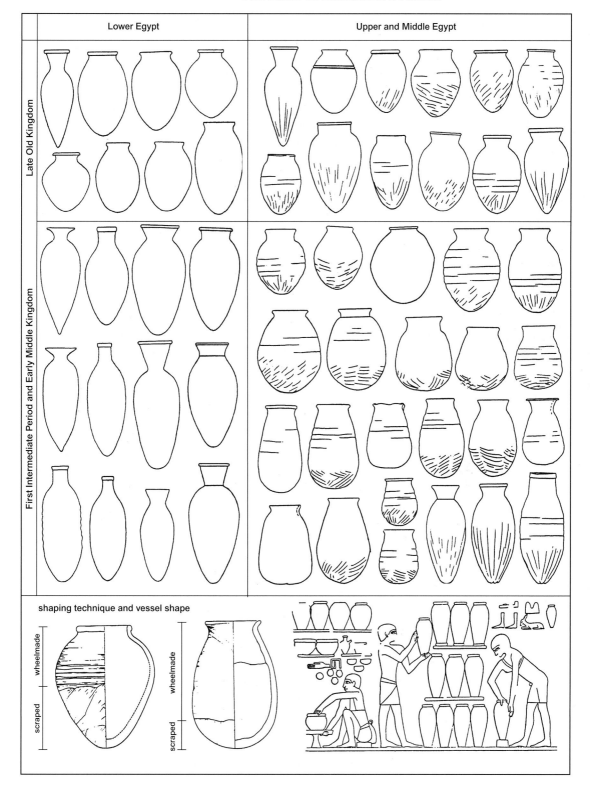

quickly abandoned. Now, baglike or even droplike sagging shapes were made. It is not difficult to identify the driving force behind this process. Clearly, the aim was to adapt vessel shapes in order to take advantage of the capabilities of the potter's wheel. In the case of ovoid containers, a large part of the outer surface had to be scraped into shape manually after throwing. In the case of bag-shaped vessels, the amount of work necessary could be reduced considerably. It seems significant, however, that this process took place only some 200 years after the first introduction of the potter's wheel to Egyptian workshops during the 5th Dynasty. It was apparently only with the emergence of the First Intermediate Period that people were prepared to dispose of traditional models and give preference to more efficient modes of production.

Furthermore, a whole range of new object classes became popular in provincial burials during the First Intermediate Period. In the Old Kingdom, the grave goods of poorer burials had been chosen entirely from among the types of objects used in daily life, but in the First Intermediate Period objects began to be made exclusively for funerary use. Crudely made wooden figures of offering bearers, boats, even whole workshop scenes, are good instances of this trend. Another example is the appearance and increasing use of coloured masks made from gypsum and linen (cartonnage) to cover the heads of the mummified bodies. It also became increasingly common to use simple slab stelae as a means of marking the offering place in the superstructure of small *mastaba*-tombs or in the chapels of simple rock tombs.

The appearance of these objects indicates that both the demand and the means available in the provincial towns were sufficient to support an area of craftsmanship specializing in 'non-functional' products. Even more important, however, is the fact that the prototypes of these types of object have their origins in Old Kingdom élite culture. The model funerary figures of people engaged in fundamental tasks can be traced back directly to the repertoire of scenes from daily life depicted in Old Kingdom *mastaba*-tomb decoration. It appears that by the First Intermediate Period those factors that had previously inhibited cultural communication between different social strata now ceased to operate.

Passing on the traditions of élite culture to a wider circle of users went hand in hand with a marked loss of

During the First Intermediate Period the heads of many mummies began to be covered with coloured cartonnage masks, such as this example from the cemetery at Sedment.

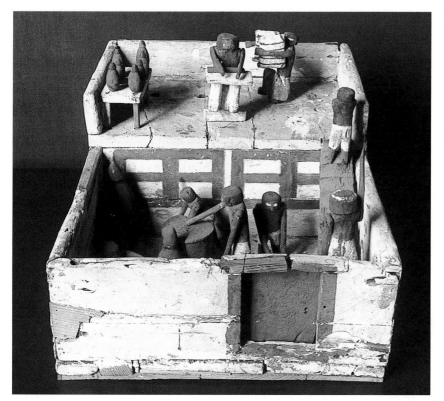

The private tombs of the First Intermediate Period began to include types of objects that were made specifically for funerary use, such as models of offering bearers and sometimes entire workshop scenes. This wooden granary is a typical example of such 'funerary models'.

artistic quality. Not infrequently even iconographic patterns were misunderstood and formulaic inscriptions misconstrued. While the provincial art of the First Intermediate Period often exhibits an astonishing degree of originality and creativity (as will become plain later in this chapter), there is no way of denying that many pieces are simply ugly and incompetently made. This aspect, in particular, has caught the attention of historians and was taken as a sign of overall cultural decline during the First Intermediate Period. However obvious the latter interpretation may seem, to assume that this was simply a period of cultural decay would be to overlook two important processes: first, the assimilation of cultural models developed in Old Kingdom court culture on a nationwide basis, and, second, the emergence of mass consumption.

Religious Ideas

Some of the changes in material culture are indicative of developments in religious beliefs and ritual practices, as in the case of the introduction of mummy masks. However, the most important body of evidence for belief systems in provincial society during the First Intermediate Period and the Middle Kingdom is the vast corpus of Coffin Texts, which were magical and liturgical spells inscribed principally onto the sides of wooden coffins. While it is obvious that the bulk of the evidence for these texts dates to the Middle Kingdom, there are a few instances that show that they had already emerged during the First Intermediate Period. The textual origins of the Coffin Texts are still a matter of much debate, in terms of both date and geographical origin. Clearly, the corpus of royal Pyramid Texts of the Old Kingdom, which were sometimes inscribed onto the coffins along with the Coffin Texts, provided important models, but the Coffin Texts themselves included crucial new material and fresh concepts.

There are only a few surviving examples of Coffin Texts from the First Intermediate Period, and ownership of inscribed coffins always remained restricted to the uppermost level of provincial society. Sometimes, however, it seems possible to connect ideas explicitly featured in the Coffin Texts with aspects of the archaeological record. Only then does the great antiquity and popularity of some of these concepts become apparent. This observation lends support to the notion that it was the provincial setting of the First Intermediate Period that played a significant role in the origins of the Coffin Texts and contributed to its conceptual content.

One series of Coffin Text spells was designed to 'assemble a man's family in the realm of the dead'. The range of persons envisaged is extensive; the texts mention not only close relatives but also servants, followers, and friends. The same desire makes itself felt in the development of tomb types as early as the 6th Dynasty. Egyptian tombs were originally built to house only one burial, but by the late Old Kingdom extensive multi-chambered *mastaba*-tombs were sometimes constructed, providing space for a whole family or even an extended family in the sense defined above. The architecture of the tombs provides evidence for ranking within these groups, in that some shafts are deeper and some chambers larger than others, thus providing for more sumptuous burials. In fact, wherever the burials themselves are preserved, both aspects of this new situation—the size of the family groups involved and the inequality between persons within these groups—are particularly prominent, since chambers were often used for successive multiple burials on a regular basis.

The burial customs of the First Intermediate Period therefore emphasize the crucial importance of interpersonal relations on a primary level of social organization. This strain of religious thought closely reflects the role that extended families played as the basic units of social organization. The funerary spells in question emphasize the authority wielded by the head of the family over its members, but also stress the fact that he was able to shelter them from outside demands. Thus the family, as a unit of solidarity and collective responsibility, was acting as an interface between the higher levels of social and political organization. Thanks to this role, the extended family also appears as a recognized institution in juridical texts of the 6th to 8th Dynasties.

Regional Style and Identity

One of the most intriguing aspects of First Intermediate Period archaeology is the stylistic variation between different regions. While the differences between the pottery styles of northern and southern Egypt are certainly clear-cut, matters are less straightforward with regard to differences between pottery in different regions within Upper Egypt or regional variations in terms of other types of artefacts. In fact, some types of objects appear to have been more affected by regional variation than others, and it seems that Egyptian material culture in general was not broken up into a series of unconnected local variants.

There is one aspect of regional variation, however, that seems to be of particular significance. Throughout the Old Kingdom, the architecture of *mastaba*-tombs in Upper Egypt followed uniform patterns and a continuous course of development. But during the 6th Dynasty and the First Intermediate Period, distinctive local traditions of tomb construction arose. Examples of such local architectural styles include the Theban *saff*-tombs (discussed below) and the *mastaba*-tombs with niched façades and long, sloping access corridors leading to subterranean chambers, which have been found at Dendera.

These local types are so different from the principal architectural styles of earlier periods that the change can hardly be explained simply in terms of the development of local workshop traditions. Instead, it seems likely that these architectural innovations were deliberately introduced by the local élites in order to express their own regional identities.

Society and Government

Even this short survey of the archaeological material provides ample evidence that far-reaching change occurred in the provinces during the late Old Kingdom and the First Intermediate Period. In the present state of research, the meanings of many of the archaeological phenomena discussed (and the mechanisms that produced them) are still poorly understood. Even our present knowledge, however, strongly suggests that internal forces of change and powerful external influences (particularly the impact of Old Kingdom provincial politics) conspired to produce greater cultural, economic, and social complexity throughout the country.

These developments inevitably affected the political system: tensions between the centre and the provinces now gained greater importance, and the provincial nobility in particular—occupying a crucial position between the court and the local groups—won new options for independent action, and, at the same time, had to mediate between competing interests. This situation raises the question of the ways in which the organization and ideology of government were adapted to the social and cultural conditions in the country at large. During the Old Kingdom, provincial districts were usually (though not always) run by a two-tiered administration. 'Overseers of priests' of the local cults were important because of the role played by their temples as nodes in the network of economic administration, but the leading office was that of 'great overlord of the nome' (often translated as 'nomarch').

It is important to realize, however, that the end of the Old Kingdom was not

Facing: the early 4th Dynasty limestone funerary statues of Rahotep and Nofret, found in their *mastaba*-tomb at Meidum, still bear most of their original painted decoration.

brought about by the increasing power of the great families of nomarchs. In fact, new lines of local magnates appeared during the First Intermediate Period. It is, therefore, likely that the Old Kingdom aristocracy—despite the degree to which they contributed, as a social group, to the process of change in the political structure of the country—nevertheless remained dependent on their links with the Crown. By tracing these new developments we can gain insights into the relationships between social conditions and political developments during the First Intermediate Period.

The Case of Ankhtifi: Crisis, Care, and Power

Ankhtifi, a nomarch of the 3rd and 2nd Upper Egyptian nomes during the earlier part of the Herakleopolitan period, embodies the new type of local ruler that emerged during the First Intermediate Period. His autobiographical text, inscribed on the pillars of his rock tomb near el-Moʿalla (some 30 km. south of Thebes), is one of the most spectacular examples of its genre to survive from ancient Egypt. It provides the ideal guide to the great issues of the time, and compellingly evokes the political atmosphere of southern Upper Egypt during the First Intermediate Period.

The tomb of Ankhtifi at el-Moʿalla, rightly famous for the biographical inscription of its owner, also provides splendid examples of First Intermediate Period art. The traditional scene showing Ankhtifi spearing fish illustrates the artist's predilection for the use of light green and for patterns of alternating colours. Unexpected, though pleasing, is the way in which a number of different fish are arranged in the free space in front of Ankhtifi's figure, omitting any indication of water. Another deviation from Old Kingdom conventions is the absence of the thicket of papyrus plants that would usually form the background to this scene.

As 'great overlord of the nomes of Edfu and Hierakonpolis' and 'overseer of priests', Ankhtifi simultaneously held key positions in both the religious and secular wings of the Old Kingdom provincial administration. In fact, this combination of offices was typical for the largely independent local rulers during the First Intermediate Period. The two key events in Ankhtifi's political career were his intervention in order to pacify and reorganize the nome of Edfu, and his military expedition against the Theban nome, where his opponents, a coalition of the Theban and Koptite nomes, actually refused to give battle. All this was essentially small-scale politics, and, reading between the lines, he was probably not even particularly successful. It is notable, for instance, that there are no known successors to Ankhtifi in his role as semi-independent ruler of the southernmost nomes. Nevertheless, his inscription proclaims his glory without a trace of false modesty:

His Excellency, the overseer of priests, overseer of desert-countries, overseer of mercenaries, great overlord of the nomes of Edfu and Hierakonpolis, Ankhtifi, the brave, he says: 'I was the beginning and the end (i.e. the climax) of mankind, since nobody like

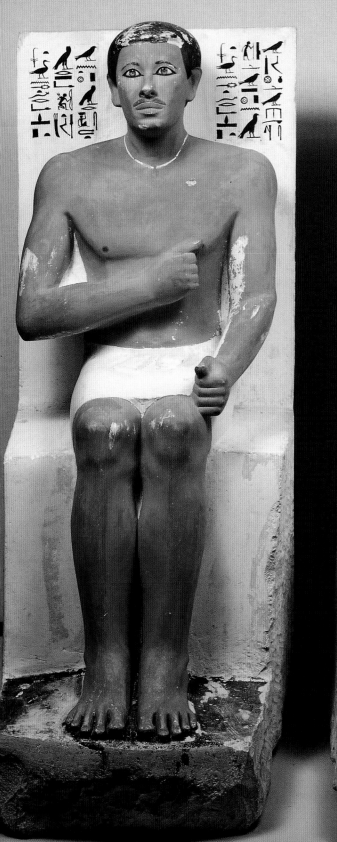

myself existed before nor will he exist; nobody like myself was ever born nor will he be born. I surpassed the feats of the ancestors, and coming generations will not be able to equal me in any of my feats within this million of years.

I gave bread to the hungry and clothing to the naked; I anointed those who had no cosmetic oil; I gave sandals to the barefooted; I gave a wife to him who had no wife. I took care of the towns of Hefat [i.e. el-Moʿalla] and Hor-mer in every [situation of crisis, when] the sky was clouded and the earth [was parched (?) and when everybody died] of hunger on this sandbank of Apophis. The south came with its people and the north with its children; they brought finest oil in exchange for the barley which was given to them. My barley went upstream until it reached Lower Nubia and downstream until it reached the Abydene nome. All of Upper Egypt was dying of hunger and people were eating their children, but I did not allow anybody to die of hunger in this nome . . . I cared for the house of Elephantine and for the town of Iat-negen in these years after Hefat and Hor-mer had been satisfied. . . . I was like a (sheltering) mountain for Hefat and like a cool shadow for Hor-mer.' Ankhtifi said: 'The whole country has become like locusts going upstream and downstream (in search of food); but never did I allow anybody in need to go from this nome to another one. I am the hero without equal.'

Economic crisis is one of the great issues in the texts of the time. Local magnates were accustomed to boasting that they managed to feed their own towns while the rest of the country was starving. These accounts have tended to make a considerable impression on modern readers, with the result that famines and economic crisis are often regarded as an essential hallmark of the period. It has even been argued that the dire consequences of repeated failures of the Nile flood, caused by climatic change, were responsible for the end of the Old Kingdom. There can be no doubt that these texts indeed relate to fact. This becomes obvious when references to famine occur in less grandiose contexts. An employee of a Koptite 'overseer of priests', for instance, relates: 'I stood in the doorway of his excellency the overseer of priests Djefy handing out grain to (the inhabitants of) this entire town to support it in the painful years of famine.'

It remains to be carefully considered, however, to what extent this situation was really specific to the First Intermediate Period. In fact, independent evidence confirming climatic change during the First Intermediate Period is lacking. Instead, the available data seem to suggest that the 'Neolithic Wet Phase' had already ended during the Old Kingdom, bringing drier climatic conditions in the adjacent desert areas in particular, as well as encouraging a general process of adaptation to lower levels of annual Nile flooding. These environmental changes showed no signs of affecting the development of pharaonic civilization at that date, thus calling into question any supposed connections with the First Intermediate Period. Recent archaeological observations from Elephantine even seem to indicate that Egypt was experiencing flood levels slightly above average during the First Intermediate Period.

Considering the long-term regularities and variations of the flood of the Nile, it seems clear that the spectre of famine due to Nile failure in individual years must have haunted the Egyptians to greater or lesser degrees throughout

Facing, above: the wall decoration of the First Intermediate Period tomb chapel of Iti at Gebelein includes a scene in which cattle are slaughtered.

Facing, below: the crudely executed First Intermediate Period painted stele of a Nubian mercenary from his tomb at Gebelein shows the deceased receiving offerings from his family.

all periods of Egyptian history. To understand the prominence of this issue in the texts of the First Intermediate Period, it is therefore necessary to place it in a wider literary context.

The introductory phrase that forms the basis for Ankhtifi's account is a very traditional one. It is actually one of the stock phrases of the autobiographical texts of Old Kingdom officials, asserting their moral integrity. During the First Intermediate Period, the principle of caring for the weak was greatly elaborated. At this time the great men were prepared to step in whenever and wherever need might arise in society, through economic problems, political crises, or individual misfortunes. The provincial rulers were not merely sheltering and supporting a few people (as a father might shelter and support the members of his family) but taking responsibility for the whole of society, whether the population of their home town or that of the nome or nomes they ruled. The message is clear: people would be helpless without their rulers. Left on their own, they would simply not be able to face the hazards of life. It goes without saying that this beneficent role of the ruler was indissociable from his right to obeisance and his authority—thus Ankhtifi points out, 'on whomsoever I laid my hand—no harm could approach him, because my reasoning was so expert and my plans were so excellent. But every ignorant person, every wretch who opposed me—I retaliated against him for his deeds.'

In the First Intermediate Period, crises had evidently become socially significant as contexts in which personal power and social dependence could be legitimized, and this observation probably helps a good deal in explaining why the issue of famine and sustenance was so important to local magnates at that time.

Competition and Armed Conflict

During the Old Kingdom, the local administrators were obliged to organize the military service of the people under their jurisdiction and to lead such troops on aggressive and peaceful missions into the regions adjoining the Nile Valley. As early as the 6th Dynasty, foreign mercenaries—particularly Nubians—were already being recruited into the Egyptian army. During the First Intermediate Period, the use of local troops and the military experience of the local governors therefore emerged as decisive forces in their struggle for ascendancy. Thus Ankhtifi declares:

I was one who found the solution when it was lacking, thanks to my vigorous plans; one with commanding words and untroubled mind on the day when the nomes allied together (to wage war). I am the hero without equal; one who spoke freely while people were silent on the day when fear was spread and Upper Egypt did not dare to speak . . . As long as this army of Hefat is calm, the whole land is calm; but if one steps on (its) tail like (that of) a crocodile, then the north and south of this whole land are trembling (with fear). . . . I sailed downstream with my strong and trustworthy troops and moored on the west bank of the Theban nome . . . and my trustworthy troops searched for battle throughout the west of the Theban nome, but nobody dared to come out through fear of them. Then I sailed downstream again and moored on the east bank of the Theban nome... and his [probably Ankhtifi's opponent's] walls were besieged since he had locked the gates through fear of these strong and trustworthy troops. They became a search party looking for battle throughout the west and the east of the Theban nome, but nobody dared to come out through fear of them.

It was not really new for an official to claim authority over more than one nome. At the end of the 5th Dynasty, for example, the kings had established the office of 'overseer of Upper Egypt' to supervise the administrators of the individual Upper Egyptian nomes. During the First Intermediate Period, there are also documented instances of officials who were responsible for a larger territory, such as Abihu, who governed the nomes of Abydos, Diospolis Parva, and Dendera in the early Herakleopolitan period. Thus there was nothing unusual about Ankhtifi's double nomarchy or even his claim to military supremacy as far south as Elephantine.

The narrative of Ankhtifi's wars, however, makes it plain that, by this time, the king was not being mentioned even nominally as an authority who could control the distribution of power between local rulers. It is important to realize that this situation implies a radical change in mentality. In the closed political system of the Old Kingdom, the king had been the sole source of legitimate authority. All actions of the officials relied on his command, and he judged and rewarded their merits. When the power of kingship faded, however, a more open situation emerged. Now, local rulers could act in accordance with their own aims. They had to rely on their own power bases; they had to defend their positions in competition with others; and they also gained a new awareness of their own achievements, which is such a prominent feature of Ankhtifi's inscriptions.

Gods, Politics, and the Rhetoric of Power

On the walls of Ankhtifi's tomb, the king (one of the 9th–10th Dynasty Herakleopolitan rulers) is mentioned only once in a short label appended to one of the wall paintings: 'May Horus grant a (good) Nile flood to his son Neferkara.' It is significant that in this instance an appeal is being made to the king in his sacred role as a mediator between human society and the forces of nature. His political role, however, has evidently been taken over by other authorities:

The god Horus fetched me to the nome of Edfu for life, prosperity and health to re-establish it... In fact, Horus wished to re-establish it, and therefore he fetched me to re-establish it. I found the domain of (the administrator) Khuu like a swampy estate neglected by its keeper, in a condition of civil strife and under the lead of a wretch. Now I caused a man to embrace (even) those who had killed his father or brother in order to re-establish the nome of Edfu.

In Ankhtifi's texts, it is not the king but Horus, the god of Edfu, who appears as the supreme authority guiding political action. This concept is not unique in First Intermediate Period inscriptions. Even the reunification of Egypt under Mentuhotep II (2055–2004 BC) was described in similar terms as a result of intervention by Montu, the great god of the Theban nome: 'A good beginning came about when Montu gave both lands to King Nebhepetra (Mentuhotep II)' (on the Abydos stele of an overseer of the treasury, Meru in the time of Mentuhotep II).

This ideology rested on solid foundations, given that local rulers usually acted as 'overseers of priests', which secured them a privileged role in the cult of the gods. Ankhtifi himself is depicted in a scene in his tomb supervising one of the great festivals of his local god Hemen, and the earliest mention of the temple of Amun of Karnak derives from a stele of a Theban overseer of priests who claims to have taken care of it in years of famine.

From earliest times, provincial temples were both administrative centres and foci of the personal loyalty of the local population, and it seems likely that the priesthoods attached to these temples formed the core group of an early provincial élite. In a way, provincial cults may be understood as symbolic representations of collective identity. Therefore, during the First Intermediate Period, god and town often appear side by side in phrases referring to social embeddedness. People say, 'I was one beloved by his town and praised by his god', and curses directed against transgressors threaten that 'his local god shall despise him and his townspeople (or sometimes "his family group") shall despise him'. By integrating their personal authority with that wielded by the local cults, provincial magnates therefore managed to link their power with one of the moral foundations of local society.

The intriguing subject matter of Ankhtifi's inscription should, however, not be allowed to eclipse its merits as literature. It is a composition of unusual brilliance, abounding in original and striking expressions. Similar qualities may be found in the painted decoration of his tomb and indeed generally in the art of Upper Egypt during the First Intermediate Period. The Upper Egyptian painters of this time no longer conformed to Old Kingdom court conventions. Their style is angular, even bizarre at times, and boldly expressive. Having freed themselves from outdated models, they created a whole range of new scenes: files of soldiers and hunters, mercenaries engaged in battle, and religious festivals. In addition, they introduced new pictures of everyday occupations, such as spinning and weaving, and updated age-old scenes to tie in

The tomb of Setka, a governor of the Aswan area in the Herakleopolitan period, is situated in the necropolis of Qubbet el-Hawa. Its painted decoration abounds in original motifs. In one scene, a group of Nubian archers is shown engaged in battle; they are characterized by their dark-coloured skin and by their national costume, wearing feathers in their hair and coloured kilts. Similar kilts, made of leather with decorative coloured beads sewn onto them, are attested in burials of the so-called C-Group population in Lower Nubia.

with the latest cultural and technological developments. Far from being a period of cultural decline, these turbulent years witnessed an upsurge of outstanding creativity, adapting and developing the existing media of literary and pictorial expression to correspond to a new range of social experiences.

This process of change also indicates that the élite of the First Intermediate Period felt the need to communicate new social developments; when government could no longer rely on the simple imposition of power, its foundations had to be made explicit. Ankhtifi's text may, therefore, be read as a speech concerning the necessity of government and the benefits of strong rule. It is also notable how closely these ideals—to which Ankhtifi so persuasively appeals—link up with the underpinnings of local social organization and provincial traditions.

The 'Theban Ascendancy' and the Necropolis of el-Tarif

During the Old Kingdom, Thebes, the capital of the 4th nome of Upper Egypt, had been a third-rate provincial town. However, during the early Herakleopolitan period, a series of overseers of priests in charge of the local affairs is known from funerary stelae recovered from the extensive cemetery of el-Tarif, on the west bank immediately opposite Karnak temple. This series of officials was succeeded by a nomarch Intef, who combined (as Ankhtifi had done) the post of 'great overlord of the Theban nome' with that of 'overseer of priests'. In addition, however, he claimed the titles of 'the king's confidant at the narrow gateway of the south [i.e. Elephantine]' and 'great overlord of Upper Egypt'. Since an inscription referring to this Intef was found in the cemetery of Dendera (the capital of the 6th nome of Upper Egypt), it seems fair to assume that his authority was recognized far beyond the confines of his native province.

This nomarch Intef is in all probability identical with a certain 'Intef the Great, born of Iku', who was named in contemporary inscriptions and to whom even the early Middle Kingdom ruler Senusret I (1956–1911 BC) dedicated a statue in the temple of Karnak. Furthermore, this man is described as 'count Intef', the ancestor of the Theban 11th Dynasty, in the king-list inscribed on the walls of Thutmose III's 'chapel of royal ancestors' in Karnak. Only his immediate successor, Mentuhotep I, however, was designated as a king in later tradition, although the Horus name assigned to him, namely Tepy-a (literally 'the ancestor'), clearly betrays this as posthumous fiction. Contemporary epigraphic sources are lacking both for Mentuhotep I and for his son, Sehertawy Intef I (2125–2112 BC), but the latter's tomb is still the most prominent landmark in the necropolis of el-Tarif, serving as the sole surviving monument to the power and the grandeur of the earliest Theban kings.

In the necropolis of el-Tarif, a special type of rock tomb developed during the First Intermediate Period, apparently as an adaptation to the local topography. For the smaller tombs of private individuals, a broad court was sunk into the strata of gravel and marl of the low desert terrace. In the rear face of this court, a portico with a row of heavy, square pillars formed the façade of the tomb, and this row of pillars gave rise to the modern designation of the architectural type as a *saff*-tomb (*saff* being Arabic for 'row'). A short, narrow corridor in the centre of the façade led to the tomb chapel, which also contained the burial shaft leading down to the tomb.

King Intef I chose to build for himself a *saff*-tomb of gigantic dimensions. The court of the Saff Dawaba, as it is called today, was sunk into the ground as a huge rectangle, 300 m. long and 54 m. wide; 400,000 cu. m. of gravel and soft rock were excavated from it and piled up as two long, low heaps along the sides of the court. The front part of the court (where some form of entrance chapel would have been built) is unfortunately lost, but the rear part of the tomb, with its broad façade comprising a double row of rock-cut pillars and three chapels (one for the king himself and two probably for his wives), is still relatively well preserved. Since the surfaces of the walls have entirely flaked off, it is not known whether they were originally painted. Nevertheless, the Saff Dawaba appears to have been an impressive piece of architecture that reveals some of the fundamentals of the newly constituted kingship. Above all, there is not the slightest attempt to emulate Old Kingdom royal funerary architecture. Rather, the Theban kings created an explicitly Theban type of royal tomb from the stock of local tradition. Furthermore, unlike many rulers of the Old Kingdom, they did not strive for exclusivity of location. The royal tombs continued to be situated in the main cemetery of Thebes, directly opposite the town and its temples across the river. Here, the burial place of the king was surrounded not just by the tombs of a narrow circle of courtiers but by the cemetery of the local population. In addition, smaller tomb chapels along the sides of the court of the royal tomb provided space for the burials of some of his followers. The message conveyed by this architecture, therefore, was focused not only on the exalted position of the king, but also on the fact that these rulers were rooted in the Theban setting and in local society.

The immediate successors of Intef I (Wahankh Intef II and Nakht-Nebtepnefer Intef III) continued to build for themselves very similar *saff*-tombs in the necropolis of el-Tarif, parallel to the Saff Dawaba. When Mentuhotep II moved to the new site of Deir el-Bahri, it was perhaps only because the suitable building ground for monumental architecture at el-Tarif had been used up by his time.

King Wahankh Intef II (2112–2063 BC)

While Mentuhotep I and Intef I, the first two kings of the 11th Dynasty, reigned for only fifteen years, the fifty-year reign of Intef I's brother and successor, Wahankh Intef II, stands out as the most decisive phase in the development of the new monarchy. A large quantity of archaeological, epigraphic, and artistic evidence has survived from his reign, thus facilitating crucial insights into the nature of Theban kingship.

Intef II claimed the traditional title of dual kingship (*nesu-bit*) as well as the title 'son of Ra', which referred to the dogma of divine descent. He did not, however, assume the complete royal protocol with its five 'Great Names', the so-called royal fivefold titulary (see Chapter 1 for a discussion of the five royal names). In fact, he added only the 'Horus name' Wahankh ('enduring of life') to his 'birth name', Intef, and had no 'throne name' (which would traditionally have incorporated the name of the sun-god Ra). Unfortunately, only a few representations of the king have been preserved, so it remains impossible to decide whether he used the whole array of royal crowns and other insignia, although the present balance of evidence suggests that this is unlikely. The early Theban kings were evidently well aware of the limited character of their rule.

True to his social origins among the provincial magnates, Intef II created a biographical stele that stood in the entrance chapel to his *saff*-tomb in el-Tarif. This monument, which bears a depiction of the king accompanied by his favourite dogs, sums up in retrospect the accomplishments of his reign; and the statements made in the text are amply confirmed by the inscriptions of his followers.

As mentioned above, there is good reason to believe that the last non-royal Theban nomarch already held sway over a large part of southern Upper Egypt. Intef II, however, launched the decisive northward push. He captured the nome of Abydos, which, since the days of the Old Kingdom, had been the most important administrative centre in Upper Egypt, and he carried his attack even further into the territory of the 10th nome of Upper Egypt. This constituted a policy of open hostility against the Herakleopolitan kings, and for several decades war was to be waged intermittently in the stretch of land between Abydos and Asyut.

The King's Men

We know some of the men who served under Intef II. The Theban military officer Djary, for example, who fought the Herakleopolitan army in the Abydene nome and who pushed northwards into the 10th nome; Hetepy from Elkab, who managed the administration of the three southernmost nomes for the king; and Intef's treasurer Tjetjy, whose magnificent stele is now in the collection of the British Museum. Although the biographical inscriptions of these men were primarily intended to praise their owners' achievements, there cannot be the slightest doubt concerning the man to whom ultimate authority was due:

So says Hetepy: I was one beloved of my lord and praised by the lord of this land; and his majesty truly made this servant [i.e. Hetepy] happy. In fact, his majesty said: 'There is no one who [...] of (my) good command, but Hetepy!', and this servant did it exceedingly well, and his majesty praised this servant on account of it. And his nobles said: 'May this face praise thee!'.

Right: slab-stele of Djary (a military commander in Intef II's service) from his *saff*-tomb in the necropolis of el-Tarif. It is an excellent example of the bold—even bizarre—style of provincial art at this date. This is evident not only in the representation of Djary and his wife seated on a bench to receive funerary offerings, but also in the peculiar shapes and unusual arangements of many of the hieroglyphs, betraying the considerable distance that separates this piece from Old Kingdom artistic conventions.

It is no doubt extremely significant that there were no longer 'nomarchs' in the territory controlled by the Theban rulers, and none of the officials who carried out important missions for these kings was given the chance to establish himself as a local ruler mediating between the interests of his dominion and the king's demands. The newly founded state was organized not as a loosely knit network of semi-independent magnates, as the Old Kingdom had become towards its end, but as a powerful system relying on strong bonds of personal loyalty and on tight control.

Monuments and Art

Apart from his military feats, Intef II emphasizes in his biographical inscription that he had built many temples to the gods, and, in fact, the earliest surviving fragment of royal construction at Karnak temple is a column of Wahankh Intef II. At Elephantine, excavations in the temple of the goddess Satet have revealed an unbroken series of building stages reaching back to the Early Dynastic Period. While the rulers of the Old Kingdom dedicated only a few votive offerings to Satet on Elephantine, Intef II was the first king to erect chapels for both Satet and Khnum, and to commemorate his activity in inscriptions on their door frames. Each of his successors during the 11th Dynasty followed this example.

The sequence of events that has been revealed so clearly in the excavations at Elephantine was also true for many other temple sites. In fact, apart from a few

Facing, above: this rectangular 11th Dynasty slab-stele was probably originally erected in the tomb of Wahankh Intef II at western Thebes. The scene shows the king offering beer and milk to Ra and Hathor, and the accompanying text contains a long hymn that the king addresses to both deities. The relief work on this stele represents a superb example of the emerging 'court' style of the early 11th Dynasty.

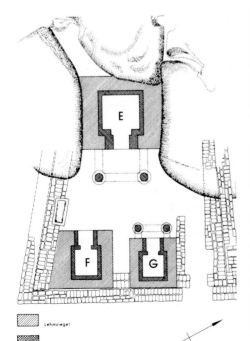

Lehmziegel

Stein

The 11th Dynasty rulers were the first to provide the temple of Satet at Elephantine with buildings adorned with inscribed stone architectural elements. The layout of the sanctuary in the time of Nakhtnebtepnefer Intef III shows an arrangement of three chapels. The most important one, dedicated to the goddess Satet, was inserted into a niche between huge granite boulders, where a shrine had been dedicated to her since the beginning of the pharaonic period. A second chapel, located in the court (marked F), served for the cult of Khnum, while the third shrine (G) was probably intended to house a statue of the king. The photograph above illustrates the right-hand half of an inscribed architrave of a similar chapel from the time of Wahankh Intef II.

specific exceptions, royal building activity in the provincial temples of Upper Egypt is attested only from the 11th Dynasty onwards. Intef II, therefore, may be said to have inaugurated a new policy of royal presence and activity in the sanctuaries throughout the country—a policy that was to be continued on an even larger scale by Senusret I and many later kings.

The private and royal monuments from the time of Intef II also include splendid examples of Theban 11th Dynasty art. Some of the lesser monuments, such as the stelae of Djary, still exhibit the bold artistic style of the First Intermediate Period in Upper Egypt, but at the same time the royal workshops were beginning to produce beautifully balanced works characterized by thick, rounded modelling, and often deriving a special aesthetic effect from the contrast between large, plain surfaces and areas filled with finely carved detail such as elaborately pleated kilts or intricately patterned hairstyles. In these works, there is a clearly visible desire for the creation of a fitting medium to convey the aspirations of the new Dynasty.

By concentrating on the developments in southern Upper Egypt, it is possible to trace the emergence of a new political structure that was to lead, in unbroken sequence, to the formation of the state of the Middle Kingdom. This process, which was to have an enormous effect on Egypt's future, should probably be regarded as the most important phenomenon in the history of the First Intermediate Period. We should not forget, however, that the Theban kingdom occupied only a small, remote, and relatively unimportant part of Egypt as a whole. The periods of war and conflict that make for such startling reading in biographical narrative were therefore no doubt only localized and short-lived episodes. At most places, for most of the time and for most of the people, the First Intermediate Period probably would have been a rather less thrilling experience.

Most of the country, during the First Intermediate Period, was in the hands of the Herakleopolitan successors to the ancient Memphite monarchy. To reach a balanced assessment of the period it is, therefore, crucial to concentrate on the situation in the Herakleopolitan realm just as much as that of the south.

The Herakleopolitan Kingdom

We know very little about the eighteen or nineteen kings who made up Manetho's Herakleopolitan Dynasty, occupying the throne of Egypt for a period of perhaps 185 years. Even their names remain largely unknown, and, with only one or two exceptions, it is impossible to assign the few named kings to their correct places within the dynastic sequence. In addition, none of the lengths of their reigns is known. According to Manetho, the Herakleopolitan Dynasty was founded by a king called Khety, and this piece of information is confirmed by contemporary epigraphic evidence that refers to the northern kingdom as the 'house of Khety'. We remain totally ignorant, however, either of the social origins of Khety or the circumstances of his rise to the throne.

Contemporary sources unequivocally corroborate Manetho's assertion of a connection between this dynasty and the town of Herakleopolis Magna. Most probably the kings actually resided at Herakleopolis, although the fact that Merykara (*c.*2025 BC), the final or penultimate Herakleopolitan ruler, was buried in a tomb in the ancient royal necropolis of Saqqara is a clear indication that the Herakleopolitan kings felt themselves to be within the tradition of the Memphite kingship. The fact that the throne name of Neferkara Pepy II—the last great ruler of the Old Kingdom—was assumed by at least one of the Herakleopolitan kings (like several of the rulers of the 8th Dynasty) obviously points in the same direction.

None of the Herakleopolitan kings left any monuments, or at least none has yet been found, although this may partly be due to the fact that the archaeological exploration of the site of Herakleopolis Magna itself (modern Ihnasya el-Medina) has only been under way since 1966. The fact that none of the Herakleopolitan pyramids has been hitherto securely identified in the necropolis of Saqqara may be regarded as evidence that these were rather inconspicuous buildings, perhaps similar to the small pyramid of the 8th Dynasty King Qakara Iby (see p. 117). Clearly the Herakleopolitans did not succeed in establishing a powerful centralized system along the lines of the state of the Old Kingdom, even in the heartlands of their own dominion.

Most of the contemporary references to the Herakleopolitan Dynasty derive from the monuments of private individuals, mainly comprising biographical inscriptions, from southern Middle Egypt and Upper Egypt, and they tend to centre on the Herakleopolitan–Theban war, an issue to which we will return later. The Herakleopolitan era also formed the historical setting for two of the most important literary and philosophical texts to have survived from ancient Egypt, the *Teachings for King Merykara* and the *Tale of the Eloquent Peasant.* Nowadays, there is widespread consensus that these 'wisdom texts' were actually composed during the Middle Kingdom, although the precise circumstances of their origins and the vicissitudes of their textual transmission remain the subject of controversy. The utmost caution is therefore advisable in any attempt to use them as historical sources. The *Teachings for King Merykara,* for instance, incorporate a background narrative in which the addressee's royal father is engaged in warding off Asiatic infiltration into the eastern Delta. Viewing the overall situation, such a scenario does not sound unlikely, but there is not yet any independent evidence that Asiatic immigration was a problem during the First Intermediate Period (although it is certainly attested for the later Middle Kingdom).

The Herakleopolitan Era in Social and Cultural History

Considering the lack of data concerning the Dynastic history of the Herakleopolitan rulers, it seems all the more important to investigate whether the Herakleopolitan kingdom can be regarded as a distinctive social and cultural entity. Turning to the archaeological evidence, we should focus attention on the core areas of the Herakleopolitan kingdom: the Memphite and Faiyum regions. From an archaeological point of view, southern Middle Egypt was effectively an Upper Egyptian region.

In the north, we face a twofold problem. The available sources of evidence do not form a rich and coherent historical framework like the data from Upper Egypt; it is, therefore, exceedingly difficult to establish a sound archaeological sequence. Furthermore, there are no key groups of material that can be firmly dated in dynastic terms. It, therefore, often remains doubtful as to which monuments are to be assigned to the Herakleopolitan period proper, and which, in fact, derive only from the time after the reunification of the country and the early Middle Kingdom.

In many respects, the development of the archaeological material in the north follows the same course as in Upper Egypt. For instance, wooden models of servants and workshops, cartonnage masks, and extensive family tombs all appear in both areas, and burial customs are in general largely the same. For some classes of artefacts, such as stone vessels and button seal amulets, the north and the south evidently drew on the same models. Judging from the archaeological material, the communities making up Herakleopolitan society seem to have undergone similar patterns of social and cultural development to the rest of the country.

Important differences, however, must not be overlooked. The development of the shapes of pottery vessels, for example, follows an entirely different course in the north. Here, the age-old ovoid pattern was not abandoned as it was in the south. Rather, a series of very special types of slender ovoid jars, often with pointed bases and quite peculiar cylindrical or funnel-shaped necks, emerged. The morphological patterns developed in the north during the First Intermediate Period evidently adhered much more closely to Old Kingdom tradition.

Even in the Herakleopolitan kingdom, however, the élite culture in the style of the Old Kingdom aristocracy did not survive. The social profile of the occupants of the ancient court cemeteries in the Memphite region therefore changed fundamentally. To earlier Egyptologists, who used to rely for their standards of judgement entirely on comparison with Old Kingdom court culture, this seemed to indicate dramatic events. Set against a broader background, however, it is clear that we are simply witnessing the change from very extraordinary conditions to a phase of comparative normality, when the Memphite necropoleis became similar to the cemeteries of provincial towns. Certainly, when Memphis lost its dominant status at the end of the Old Kingdom, this must undoubtedly have entailed severe changes in the living conditions of its inhabitants. But the archaeological record from the Memphite cemeteries cannot be construed as evidence for a social revolution or a civil war after the demise of the Old Kingdom.

At several important sites—Saqqara, Heliopolis, and Herakleopolis

Decorated limestone slab that formed the right-hand panel of a small offering niche in the tomb of a priestess of Hathor named Zat-ini-Teti at Saqqara. In the upper register of the representation, the owner of the tomb is shown seated in front of a table of offerings, a conventional scene that can be traced back to the 1st Dynasty. The offering list above specifies the individual items that were presented to her in the course of the ritual. The scenes below (three men throwing down a bull that is to be slaughtered, and a file of offering bearers) also derive from the standard corpus of Old Kingdom motifs.

Magna—small *mastaba*-tombs incorporating decorated offering chapels and false-door stelae are attested, thus allowing the style of Herakleopolitan art to be assessed. Old Kingdom tradition looms large. Ritual scenes and scenes of daily life, the arrangement of the decoration, and the style of carving closely follow Old Kingdom patterns—but everything is in miniature. Here, in the Memphite region and its surroundings, where the monuments of Egypt's glorious past were available for ready inspection and where its workshop traditions had been entrenched for centuries, the legacy of the Old Kingdom was not to be forgotten.

The full range of situations in which these traditions were exercised during the First Intermediate Period probably escapes us because of the state of archaeological research at the end of the twentieth century. Immediately after the reunification of the country, however, the 11th Dynasty King Nebhepetra Mentuhotep II was able to draw on the expertise of Memphite artists and stonemasons for the construction and the embellishment of his funerary temple at Deir el-Bahri. It is in his reign that we witness the sudden reappearance of a level of expertise that had not been attested since the pyramids of the Old Kingdom.

The Internal Organization of the Herakleopolitan Kingdom

During the early Herakleopolitan Period, southern Upper Egypt slipped out of royal control, but what happened to those parts of the country that remained under Herakleopolitan rule until its end? The relevant sources include the prosopographical records and biographical inscriptions from southern Middle Egypt. Among these, pride of place goes to the tombs of the overseers of priests at Asyut. During the latter part of the Herakleopolitan period, Asyut emerged as the most important military stronghold in Upper Egypt, remaining faithful to the Herakleopolitan kings in their struggle against the Theban rebels. The biographical inscriptions of three successive holders of office provide crucial information both on the course of political events and on current views on the ideology of rule.

Additional information can be derived from a group of graffiti that were inscribed on the walls of the travertine quarry at Hatnub by emissaries of a nomarch Neheri of the nome of el-Ashmunein, whose rock tomb is known at el-Bersha. A date for these texts immediately after the end of the Herakleopolitan Period seems most likely (although some would contest this). Certainly, however, their intellectual outlook is firmly rooted in Herakleopolitan tradition.

The topics addressed in these texts from Asyut and Hatnub are similar, in many respects, to those encountered in the texts from further south. Again, the local rulers' claims to have cared for their towns in critical situations feature prominently. The biographical inscription of the earliest overseer of priests at Asyut even provides a detailed description of the measures he took to improve the irrigation system in order to ensure sufficient harvests in bad years. Furthermore, the military prowess of the nomarchs is emphasized. Both their successes in struggles with a foreign enemy (the Theban ruler) and the establishment of public security within their own nomes are stressed. Lastly, the local magnates' care for the temples of their towns is not forgotten: both construction work in the temples and the making of provisions for the needs of the associated cults are mentioned.

In stark contrast to the text of Ankhtifi, however, the maintenance of close connections with the king plays an important part in the texts of the Asyut magnates. They themselves claim descent from venerable aristocratic stock, and close personal ties seem to have linked them with the Herakleopolitan house of rulers. One of them, for example, mentions that, in his childhood, he received swimming lessons together with the royal children. In addition, the intervention of the Herakleopolitan army in Upper Egypt is mentioned. Herakleopolitan rule, therefore, was something very real to the local rulers of southern Middle Egypt.

Our sources for the internal structure of the Herakleopolitan kingdom remain extremely sketchy. Nevertheless, the available material seems to suggest that the Herakleopolitan monarchs may have relied on a class of provincial aristocrats who stayed loyal to the Crown, particularly in those cases where there were strong personal bonds (perhaps through kinship, marriage, or friendship). These aristocrats, however, would, at the same time, have regarded their own towns as crucially important to them, perhaps even making them the principal focuses of their loyalty. In this respect, the Herakleopolitan kingdom again seems to have inherited one of the characteristics of the Old Kingdom: it may also, therefore, have shared one of its structural weaknesses.

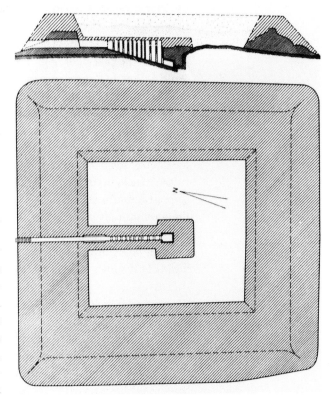

Plan and section of the so-called Kom Dara, the tomb of a local dynast who ruled in Middle Egypt during the ealier half of the First Intermediate Period. The layout of the building was derived from a type of square *mastaba*-tomb attested at the site during the late Old Kingdom, but its monumental dimensions greatly surpass the normal dimensions for the tombs of provincial administrators.

Kom Dara

In this context, an important, though rather enigmatic monument may be significant. In the cemetery of Dara, some 27 km. downstream from Asyut in Middle Egypt, a truly gigantic mud-brick *mastaba*-tomb, known as Kom Dara, occupies a commanding position. This building has not yet been properly investigated. In its present condition, an area of 138 × 144 m. (that is, 19,872 sq. m.) is delimited by massive outer walls that originally rose to a height of about 20 m. The remains of the mortuary chapel that must surely once have formed part of the complex have not yet been found. The interior, however, was reached by a sloping corridor entering the building in the middle of its north side, and leading down to a single subterranean burial chamber constructed from large limestone slabs.

The enormous size of this tomb, along with its square layout and the location of its burial chamber, are immediately reminiscent of a pyramid. Closer analysis of its construction, however, reveals beyond any doubt that the building was never planned as a pyramid. In fact, access to the burial chamber from the north is a fairly common feature in private tomb architecture of the late Old Kingdom, while the square layout of the superstructure is paralleled by lesser tombs in Dara cemetery itself. Kom Dara, therefore, may be understood as a monumental tomb that derived from a local prototype, very much in the way that the royal *saff*-tombs at Thebes developed from the simpler types of *saff*-tombs built for the funerary cults of the ordinary people.

On the basis of pottery, Kom Dara can be dated to the earlier half of the First Intermediate Period. Its owner remains unknown to us, and there is not yet any definite evidence to support the frequently repeated identification with an otherwise unattested King Khuy, whose name appears on a relief fragment found reused in another building at the site. The tomb itself, however, attests unequivocally to its owner's aspirations to a political role that far surpassed that of a mere nomarch, regardless of whether he actually dared to assume the titles of royalty.

There are no historical records that can tell us what was actually happening at this site, but the whole context makes it plain that the owner of the Kom Dara tomb did not in fact succeed in establishing an independent centre of power, as the Thebans did at a slightly later date. It is tempting, however, to speculate a little further. In the wide, fertile plains of Middle Egypt, every ambitious local dynast was bound to find himself immediately surrounded by a score of powerful competitors. The geographical situation itself, therefore, may have helped to stabilize the balance of power between a number of Middle Egyptian local rulers, which, in turn, could have been material in maintaining royal overlordship. In addition, it does not seem too far-fetched to assume that here, in one of the agriculturally most productive areas of the country, the Crown saw important interests at stake and, accordingly, felt rather less inclined to tolerate the political adventures of provincial rulers than in the remote stretches of the 'head of the south' (that is, the Theban region).

The Final War

Matters probably reached a head when Wahankh Intef II attacked the Thinite nome and pushed northwards, finding his advance eventually checked by the Asyut nomarchs. A record of at least one counter-attack by the Herakleopolitans has survived in the form of a very fragmentary inscription in the tomb of Ity-yeb (the second in a sequence of overseers of priests at Asyut), who reports successful military operations against the 'southern nomes'. In addition, the narrative recounted in the *Teachings for Merykara* claims that King Merykara's father had recaptured Abydos. Whether these facts are to be connected with the 'rebellion of Thinis', recorded on a stele from Mentuhotep II's fourteenth regnal year, remains a matter of speculation.

It is clear, however, that this Herakleopolitan military success had no lasting effect on the outcome, since the tomb of Ity-yeb's son, Khety II, from the time of King Merykara, contains a report concerning further conflict with the Theban aggressors. No record has survived of the sequence of events in this final phase of the war, but there can hardly be any doubt that Asyut was taken by force. In any event, the ruling family of Asyut did not survive the Theban victory.

Information on Mentuhotep II's advances further northwards is lacking, but it seems unlikely that he had to fight every step of the way. Instead, it is probable that the network of Herakleopolitan rule over Middle Egypt collapsed after Asyut had been defeated, and local rulers might then have been eager to side with the winning party before it was too late, thus hoping to save themselves and their towns from 'the terror which was spread by the [Theban] king's house'.

We do not know the fate of the last Herakleopolitan king nor the details of the capture of the town of Herakleopolis, but recent excavations in the cemetery of Ihnasya el-Medina show that its funerary monuments were literally hacked to pieces at some point in the early Middle Kingdom. It seems tempting to construe this archaeological observation as evidence for the eventual sacking and pillaging of Egypt's northern capital.

The First Intermediate Period in Retrospect

Modern Egyptologists still largely present a negative image of the First Intermediate Period. It is characterized as a period of chaos, decline, misery, and social and political dissolution: a 'dark age' separating two epochs of glory and power. This picture, however, is based only partly on an evaluation of sources contemporary with the period. It largely reproduces—sometimes with surprising naivety—the literary theme developed in a group of Middle Kingdom literary texts. The so-called *Admonitions of an Egyptian Sage* and the *Prophecy of Neferti* form the core of this genre, but several other 'pessimistic' texts, such as the *Complaints of Khakheperraseneb* and the *Dialogue between a Man Tired of Life and his 'ba'*, might also be added to this list. In this class of texts, a state of disorder is lamented and contrasted with the way in which things ought to be. Social order is turned upside down; the rich are poor, and the poor are rich; political unrest and insecurity prevails throughout the country; the administrative documents are torn to pieces; there are numerous different rulers in power at the same time; the country is invaded by foreigners; the moral basis of social life is destroyed; people neglect and hate each other; and the sacred scriptures are profaned. This state of general disturbance is not confined to the social world: it attains truly cosmic dimensions in that the river is sometimes said to be no longer flowing as it ought to do, and even the sun is found not to have retained its former brightness.

It should be noted that these texts do not actually claim to be set in the First Intermediate Period; nor do they mention any historical particulars. In the *Prophecy of Neferti*, the advent of Amenemhat I (1985–1956 BC) is foretold as bringing relief from a state of chaos which must be situated, chronologically, in the late 11th Dynasty and *not* in the First Intermediate Period. Careful scrutiny is, therefore, required if we are to determine whether these texts bear any relation to the history of the First Intermediate Period, and, even if they do, we need to investigate precisely *how* they relate to the actual historical events.

Texts deriving from the First Intermediate Period itself are entirely lacking in that very note of despair that is the hallmark of Middle Kingdom 'pessimistic' literature. They do talk about crisis, but crisis brilliantly overcome: vigour, self-confidence, and pride in one's own achievement characterize the mood of the time. Certainly there are a number of striking thematic similarities between First Intermediate Period biographies and the Middle Kingdom pessimistic texts (such as Nile failure, famine, social unrest, war, and a crisis affecting the foundations of the state), but these similarities prove, in the first place, *literary* connections between the two.

Another aspect of the textual evidence seems to be even more important. In First Intermediate Period inscriptions, tales of crisis served to legitimize the power of local rulers. In the same way, the greatly elaborated picture of a period of utter chaos in the later pessimistic literature provides the black background against which the tight politics of law and order implemented by Middle Kingdom kings can be justified and even made to appear beneficent. The foundations of the ruling ideology of Middle Kingdom monarchy, therefore, rest firmly on what we know of First Intermediate Period political thought.

These comparisons between Middle Kingdom 'pessimistic' literature and First Intermediate Period contemporary texts reveal just how deeply the impact of the First Intermediate Period affected the Middle Kingdom Egyptians' collective consciousness and their views on social and political relations. On the other hand, it would be extremely misguided to attempt to use Middle Kingdom literary texts as authentic sources for First Intermediate Period history. The view of the First Intermediate Period presented in this chapter has been entirely based on contemporary sources; this attempt to evaluate the surviving documentation in all its aspects makes it much more difficult to subscribe to the traditional negative view of the period. In contrast, one can only be struck by the dynamism and creativity of the period.

When Senusret I donated a statue of the 'count' Intef, the ancestor of the 11th Dynasty, to Karnak temple, he was acknowledging the origins of Middle Kingdom kingship in the struggles that local rulers fought for power and ascendancy during the First Intermediate Period. Apart from its political importance, the impact that the First Intermediate Period had on Egypt's cultural history cannot be denied. A whole range of new morphological types was developed in nearly every sphere of material culture, including such singularly successful new inventions as the scarab-shaped seal.

Above all, however, popular culture was given the opportunity to flourish at a time when the overpowering influence of court culture had faded, and when there was a great weakening of central government, which had previously (in the Old Kingdom) imposed heavy demands on provincial communities. In the First Intermediate Period the local populations throughout the country enjoyed conspicuous, if modest, wealth. They also acquired various new means of cultural expression and communication, and were able to arrange their lives within the small-scale horizon of their immediate concerns.

7 THE MIDDLE KINGDOM RENAISSANCE

(*c.*2055–1650 BC)

GAE CALLENDER

Unlike the First and Second Intermediate periods, the Middle Kingdom (2055–1650 BC) formed a political unity, the core of which comprised two political phases: the 11th Dynasty ruling from the Upper Egyptian city of Thebes, and the 12th Dynasty centred in the region of Lisht in the Faiyum. Earlier historians considered that the 11th and 12th Dynasties marked the full extent of the Middle Kingdom, but more recent scholarship shows clearly that at least the first half of the so-called 13th Dynasty (which apparently bears no resemblance to a proper political dynasty) belongs unequivocally to the Middle Kingdom. There was no shift of the location of the capital or royal residence, little diminution in the activities of the government, and no decline in the arts of the time—indeed, some of the finest works of Middle Kingdom art and literature date from the 13th Dynasty. There was, however, a decline in large-scale monumental building, a significant indication that the 13th Dynasty was neither as strong nor as inspired by the grandiose ideas that marked the reigns of the later 12th Dynasty rulers. Doubtless, this phenomenon was due to the brevity of reigns for the majority of 13th Dynasty kings, although the reasons for such changes in the political picture are as yet unknown.

The simplest way to gain some sense of the general flavour of Middle Kingdom history is to study the succession of kings and their achievements, since they set the tone for the political and cultural directions of the period. However, in pursuing this course, we are forced to confront one of the biggest problems in our understanding of Middle Kingdom history: the issue of the 'co-regencies' of the 12th Dynasty kings. Simply put, the question is: did some of these rulers share the throne with their successors? Crucial elements in the debate are so-called double-dated stelae, texts incorporating the names of two successive kings, together with different dates for each of these rulers. These stelae have left scholars divided on the issue of whether the records represent a sharing of power by two pharaohs or merely the years during which the owners of the stelae held office under each of the two kings.

The standard chronology for the 12th Dynasty has been remodelled over the years in the light of intensive studies of dated monumental records. Some of this new work has yielded much shorter reigns than those suggested by the fragmentary Turin Canon and the epitomes of Manetho. The most controversial reigns are those of Senusret II and III, and there are wide discrepancies between the proposed chronologies of different scholars. Discoveries of certain 'hieratic control marks' carved on the masonry of the monuments of Senusret III have added further confusion to these chronologies, so that the dating problems of the 12th Dynasty are still in a state of flux. Josef Wegner, for instance, has provided very strong evidence for a reign of thirty-nine years for Senusret III that—together with the discovery at Lisht of references to a 'year 30' of Senusret III and evidence for his celebration of a *sed*-festival (royal jubilee)—would argue for a much longer reign by this king than most modern chronologies suggest. There are also grounds for suspecting that the reign of Senusret II is more likely to have lasted for nineteen years (as suggested by the papyri discovered at the town of Lahun) rather than the shorter length of the revised chronologies, but there is some difficulty in accommodating these expanded reigns within the absolute dates proposed by some scholars. The evidence for longer 12th Dynasty reigns would fit in well with the co-regency theory, which is based on the double-dated monuments, but convincing arguments have also been put forward by a number of scholars seeking to refute individual co-regencies such as those of Amenemhat I–Senusret I, Senusret I–Amenemhat II, and Senusret III–Amenemhat III.

Since there are no true 'absolute dates' yet established in Egyptian history (apart from the radiocarbon-based chronologies) until the late New Kingdom at the earliest, and since argument still persists regarding the high, middle, and low dating schemes, there is room for revision in the chronologies for all pharaonic periods. It is possible that new archaeological material emerging from Tell el-Dabʿa (see Chapter 8) will help to solve some of the problems in Middle Kingdom chronology, but in the meantime the account given in this chapter leaves co-regencies out of the equation, pending further proof.

The 11th Dynasty

The first 11th Dynasty ruler to gain control of the whole of Egypt was Nebhepetra Mentuhotep II (2055–2004 BC), who probably succeeded Nakhtnebtepnefer Intef III (2063–2055 BC) on the Theban throne. Mentuhotep's tremendous achievement in reuniting Egypt was recognized by the ancient Egyptians themselves, and as late as the 20th Dynasty there were numerous private tombs containing inscriptions celebrating his role as founder of the Middle Kingdom. The increase in historical records and buildings, the evident prosperity of the land during the latter years of his reign, and the resurgence and development of all forms of art are particular indicators of his success in restoring peace. It is ironic to reflect that, after such a promising start, the 11th Dynasty was to collapse only nineteen years after his death.

Nebhepetra Mentuhotep II

Among the many rock carvings of various dates on the cliffs at Wadi Shatt el-Rigal, 8 km. north of Gebel es-Silsila, there is a relief incorporating a colossal figure of the 11th Dynasty ruler Nebhepetra Mentuhotep II dwarfing three other figures: his mother, his likely predecessor Intef III, and Khety, the chancellor who served both kings. This has long been taken as proof that Mentuhotep II was the son of Intef III. Further such proof seems to be provided by a relief on a masonry block from the site of Tod that portrays Mentuhotep II towering over a line of three kings named Intef, lined up behind him, thus again suggesting family connections with the Intefs as well as a lengthy royal ancestry. This insistence on 'lineage', however, seems to beg the question of Mentuhotep's actual origins, and it would not be surprising to discover either that Mentuhotep had not been a royal son or that these monuments were a deliberate attempt to counterbalance claims made by the Herakleopolitan rulers as members of the 'House of Khety' (see Chapter 6).

Mentuhotep II appears to have reigned quietly over his Theban kingdom for

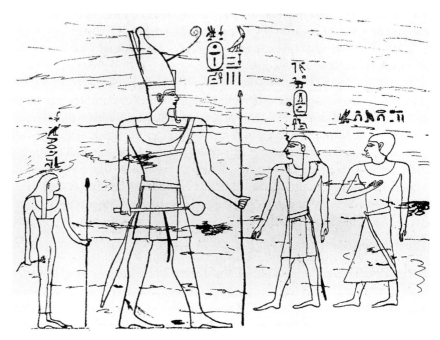

In the stele of Nakhtneb-tepnefer Intef III and Nebhepetra Mentuhotep II at Wadi Shatt el-Rigal, c.2055 BC, Mentuhotep is shown as if twice the height of the other figures. His mother is depicted behind him, while Intef III and the chancellor Khety are shown facing him. The reduced size of Intef might indicate that Mentuhotep, as Intef's successor, was greater than his predecessor had been. The figure of Khety also needs mentioning, for his figure is larger than that of King Intef and Queen Iah—a most unusual circumstance.

fourteen years before the last phase in the civil war between Herakleopolis and Thebes erupted. We know virtually nothing of this conflict, but a graphic image of its savagery may well have survived in the form of the so-called Tomb of the Warriors at Deir el-Bahri, not far from Mentuhotep II's mortuary complex. The unmummified linen wrapped bodies of sixty soldiers, clearly killed in battle and subsequently placed together in a rock-cut common tomb, were preserved by dehydration. Despite the absence of any embalming, these corpses are the best preserved of all Middle Kingdom bodies. Because they were buried as a group and within sight of the royal cemetery, it has been surmised that they died in some particularly heroic conflict, perhaps connected with the war against Herakleopolis.

The Herakleopolitan ruler Merykara died before Mentuhotep reached Herakleopolis, and with his death Herakleopolitan resistance must have collapsed, for Merykara's successor governed the northern kingdom for only a few months. Mentuhotep's victory over the last Herakleopolitan ruler provided him with the opportunity to reunite Egypt, but we have only indirect knowledge about how long this took and how severe such struggles were. This process may well have taken many years, for there are scattered references to other fighting throughout this stage of Mentuhotep's reign. One of the clues to the insecurity felt at this time is the inclusion of weapons among the grave goods of ordinary men; another is the depiction of administrators carrying weapons instead of official regalia on funerary stelae. However, as peace and material prosperity advanced within the country, such items seem to have diminished in frequency.

Part of Mentuhotep's reconquest included forays into Nubia, which had returned to native rule during the last stages of the Old Kingdom. There was at least one line of native rulers controlling parts of Nubia at the time when Mentuhotep II's armies descended upon them. An inscription on a masonry block from Deir el-Ballas, thought to belong to his reign, mentions campaigns in Wawat (Lower Nubia), and we also know that a garrison was established by Mentuhotep in the fortress at Elephantine, from which troops could more rapidly be deployed southwards.

In addition to the emphasis on his lineage, part of Mentuhotep's strategy to enhance his reputation with his contemporaries and successors was a programme of self-deification. He is described as 'the son of Hathor' on two fragments from Gebelein, while at Dendera and Aswan he usurped the headgear of Amun and Min, and elsewhere wears the red crown surmounted by two feathers. At Konosso, near Philae, he took on the guise of ithyphallic Min. Both this iconography and his second Horus name, Netjeryhedjet ('the divine one of the white crown'), emphasize his self-deification. Evidence from his Deir el-Bahri temple indicates that he intended to be worshipped as a god in his House of

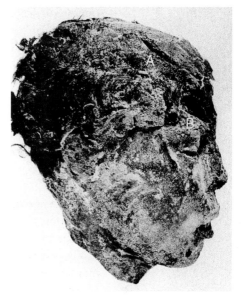

This head of a Theban soldier is one of the most striking images of the war between the rulers of Thebes and Herakleopolis in the early 11th Dynasty. It comes from the so-called Tomb of the Warriors at Deir el-Bahri, close to the mortuary complex of Nebhepetra Mentuhotep II. The tomb contained sixty unmummified bodies of soldiers evidently killed in battle.

Millions of Years, thus pre-dating by hundreds of years ideas that became a central religious preoccupation of the New Kingdom. It is evident that he was reasserting the cult of the ruler.

Mentuhotep's self-promotion was accompanied by a change of name as well as this process of self-deification. His Horus name was altered several times during his reign, each change evidently marking a political watershed. Sematawy ('the one who unites the two lands') was the last alteration, the earliest dated occurrence for this being year 39. However, prior to year 39 the king had celebrated his *sed*-festival, and perhaps this was the occasion when he took that name.

The government of the kingdom

Mentuhotep ruled from Thebes, which, until then, had not been a particularly prominent town in Upper Egypt. It was a good location from which to exercise control over the remaining nomarchs (regional governors), and most of Mentuhotep's officials were local men. The scope of their duties was wide: the vizier, Khety, conducted campaigns in Nubia for the king, while the chancellor, Meru, controlled the Eastern Desert and the oases. The latter office was much more significant than it had been in the Old Kingdom. In addition to the existing post of 'governor of Upper Egypt', an equally powerful new post, 'governor of Lower Egypt', was created. This strengthening of the central government increased the king's control over his officials while simultaneously curtailing the power of the nomarchs, who had enjoyed complete independence in the First Intermediate Period.

The numbers of nomarchs were probably reduced by Mentuhotep—the governors of Asyut, for instance, certainly fell from power because of their support for the Herakleopolitan cause. The nomarchs of Beni Hasan and Hermopolis, however, retained control as before, perhaps as their reward for assisting the armies of the Theban nomarchs. The governors of Nag el-Deir, Akhmim, and Deir el-Gebrawi also remained in office. The nomarchs' conduct, however, was monitored by officials from the royal court, who moved around the land at regular intervals.

Another indication of a return to a strong and united Egyptian government is found in the journeys being taken beyond Egyptian borders. One of the famous expedition leaders of this time was Khety (the official depicted on the Shatt el-Rigal relief described above), who patrolled the Sinai area and also carried out assignments in Aswan. Henenu, the 'overseer of horn, hoof, feather, and scale', was the king's steward; amid his numerous jobs, he travelled as far as Lebanon for cedar for his master. Such journeys suggest that Egypt was beginning to restore its influence in the outside world.

The building projects of Mentuhotep II

In addition to the numerous military campaigns launched by Mentuhotep in his fifty-one-year reign, he was also responsible for numerous building projects, although most of these have been destroyed. New temples and chapels were erected, the majority of these being located in Upper Egypt at Dendera, Gebelein, Abydos, Tod, Armant, Elkab, Karnak, and Aswan. A combined Dutch and Russian team has discovered a Middle Kingdom temple near Qantir, in the eastern Delta. Its architecture reflects that of Mentuhotep's mortuary complex at Deir el-Bahri, but firm dates have not been published.

Throughout the Middle Kingdom, the royal cemeteries were continually evolving, not only architecturally, but structurally and spatially. This constant change seems to reflect the search for a spiritual solution to the question of what constituted the most effective type of tomb, and this is very evident in Mentuhotep's mortuary monument, at Deir el-Bahri in western Thebes. This was by far the most impressive of his surviving buildings, although little remains of it today. The temple design was unique, for neither of his 11th Dynasty successors (Sankhkara Mentuhotep III and Nebtawyra Mentuhotep IV) completed their tombs, while the 12th Dynasty kings chose monuments inspired by Old Kingdom models. The *saff*-tomb (see Chapter 6) had been the tomb design used by previous Theban rulers in the el-Tarif region of western Thebes, but Mentuhotep's monument altered this tradition. Even though some of its architects seem to have been previously involved in the construction of *saff*-tombs, his complex reveals a vision previously absent from both the Theban and Herakleopolitan models; therefore it is rightly recognized as the most important building of the phase between the end of the Old Kingdom and the beginning of the 12th Dynasty.

This inspiring symbol of the reunification of Egypt epitomized a new beginning. It was, for example, the first royal structure overtly to stress Osirian beliefs—a reflection of the religious 'levelling' between the funerary cults of kings and commoners that had taken place in the First Intermediate Period. Significant innovations in this temple were the use of terraces, and the verandah-like walkways (or ambulatories) that were added onto the central edifice. The design incorporated groves of sycamore and tamarisk trees, which were planted in front of the temple, each in a pit cut 10 m. down into the rock and filled with soil. A long, unroofed causeway ran up from this tree-lined court to the upper terrace, upon which the central edifice was built. This main construction may have taken the form of a square *mastaba*-tomb (perhaps surmounted by a hill); behind it lay a hypostyle hall and the intimate cult centre.

The tombs of the king's wives, Queens Neferu and Tem, were included in the complex, the latter being buried in a dromos tomb at the rear of his temple, the former in a separate rock-cut tomb on the northern temenos wall in the forecourt. Several chapels and tombs for six other women, four of whom are named as 'royal wife', were found behind the central edifice, within the western walkway. Their original burials belong to the earliest phase of Mentuhotep's temple. When excavated, several of these tombs still contained their original burials, as well as the earliest evidence for the use of models depicting both the coffins and the bodies of the deceased—the precursors of the *shabti* figures that became more popular at a later date. These women buried in the western walkway seem to have been of lower status than Neferu and Tem, and all of them were young: the eldest, Ashaiyet, was 22, and the youngest, Mayt (whose badly destroyed chapel contains no indications of the title of 'wife'), was only a 5-year-old child. The significance of these less-important wives is uncertain; they may have been the daughters of nobles whom the king wished to keep in check, but most of them are named as priestesses of Hathor; therefore it has also been suggested that their tombs may have formed part of a Hathoric cult for the king within his mortuary monument. Another enigma is that the burials appear to be contemporaneous. Did these young girls die together in some disaster?

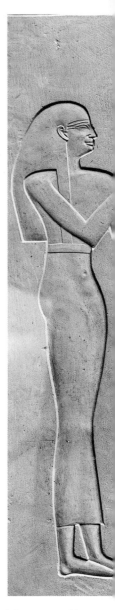

The six women's chapel tombs evidently belong to the same period in the development of the Deir el-Bahri monument as the tomb known as the Bab el-Hosan, which lies beneath the temple forecourt. This royal tomb is thought by Dieter Arnold to have been an earlier and incomplete burial for the king. It was in this structure that a black-skinned statue in festival robes was found. The unusual skin colour is another of the many references to Osiris, symbolizing the fertility and regenerative powers of Mentuhotep II.

Although the temple was decorated throughout, not enough of its art has survived to be able confidently to reconstruct the overall system of design and decoration, although there are some distinct themes. The king's supernatural and Osirian aspects are emphasized, but there are also scenes from court life. The regional nature of the artwork is evident in many of the surviving fragments of painted decoration, and such characteristic touches as thick lips, large eyes, and exaggeratedly thin and awkward bodies are all apparent. However, there is also some masterly carving (especially that from the chapels of the young wives), which is more typical of the Memphite school. This mixture of techniques reflects the political situation indicated by some of the craftsmen's biographies, which also show that they came from various regions of Egypt, bringing with them their local traditions. In time, the Memphite style prevailed, but it was several generations before it replaced the regional artistic genres throughout Egypt.

Although we cannot point to any monuments of Mentuhotep II in the Temple of Amun at Karnak, there is a reference to the god in Mentuhotep's temple, and the location of the latter in the curve of the cliffs at Deir el-Bahri is itself significant, being directly aligned with Karnak on the opposite bank. This position may have been intended to allow the king's funerary cult to benefit from

the annual visit of the god Amun to Deir el-Bahri in a rite known as the Beautiful Festival of the Valley. Certainly, the cult of Amun began to grow at Thebes from this time onwards.

Mentuhotep III and IV

Queen Tem was the mother of Sankhkara Mentuhotep III (*c.*2004–1992 BC), who was an energetic builder. In 1997 a Hungarian team led by Györö Vörös not only discovered a hitherto unknown Coptic sanctuary below the peak of Thoth Hill, on the west bank at Thebes, but also found an early Middle Kingdom tomb that surely belonged to Mentuhotep III. Its architecture may have been the inspiration for the *bab*-tombs of the early 18th Dynasty.

In this detail from the 11th Dynasty stone sarcophagus of Ashaiyet, one of the wives of Mentuhotep II, *c.*2055–2004 BC, the queen is being offered a duck, while behind her a girl fans her mistress. The transitional stage, combining artistic styles of the Memphite artists with the more attenuated forms of the regional artists is apparent here.

The reign of Mentuhotep III was characterized by a certain amount of architectural innovation, including a triple sanctuary at the site of Medinet Habu, which foreshadowed the 18th Dynasty temples to 'family' triads. In addition, the remains of the brick temple that he constructed on the 'hill of Thoth', the highest peak overlooking the Valley of the Kings, not only contained another triple shrine but also incorporated the earliest surviving examples of temple pylons. Not far from the temple lie the remains of another building of Mentuhotep III.

The art preserved from his brief reign is no less innovative, with the relief sculpture arguably reaching its peak for the Middle Kingdom at this point. The carving of the stone is extremely fine, the raised relief conveying tremendous spatial depth with a differentiation of no more than a few millimetres of thickness within the stone. The subtlety of the portraiture and details within clothing on his reliefs from Tod are far superior to the sculptures of Mentuhotep II.

Mentuhotep III was also the first Middle Kingdom ruler to send an expedition to the East African land of Punt to obtain incense, although such expeditions to the Red Sea and Punt became more frequent in the 12th Dynasty. Mentuhotep's expedition, led by an official called Henenu, was sent via the Wadi Hammamat, thus apparently necessitating the construction of ships on the shores of the Red Sea using timbers that had been transported across with them. He also attempted to protect the north-eastern border through the construction of fortifications in the eastern Delta.

When Mentuhotep III died, in about 1992 BC, there seem to have been 'seven empty years', corresponding to the reign of Nebtawyra Mentuhotep IV (who perhaps usurped the throne, since he is missing from the king-lists). His mother was a commoner with no royal titles other than 'king's mother', so he may not even have been a member of the royal family.

Little is known of Mentuhotep IV's reign, except for his quarrying expeditions. Inscriptions from the Hatnub travertine quarry suggest that some of the nomarchs in Middle Egypt might have been troublesome at about this time. The most important event attested from his reign was the sending of a quarrying expedition into the Wadi Hammamat. Amenemhat, the vizier who led the expedition, ordered the cutting of an inscription at the quarry to record two remarkable omens that the party were said to have witnessed. The first was a gazelle who gave birth to her calf on the stone that had been chosen for the lid of the king's sarcophagus, and the second was a ferocious rainstorm that, when it died down, disclosed a well, 10 cubits square, full of water to the brim. In such barren terrain, this would certainly have been a spectacular, even miraculous, discovery. It seems almost certain that the man who became the first king of the 12th Dynasty was this same Amenemhat. Like most of the 11th Dynasty high officials, he would have held various powerful posts; it may have been either the weakness of the king or the lack of a viable male heir that caused the throne to pass to the vizier.

The 12th Dynasty

The much greater sophistication of the 12th Dynasty, compared with the 11th, is perhaps the factor that has persuaded so many scholars that the Middle Kingdom only properly begins with the 12th Dynasty.

Amenemhat I

Sehetepibra Amenemhat I (Manetho's 'Ammenemes', *c.*1985–1956 BC) was the son of a man called Senusret and a woman called Nefret, who came from outside the royal family, and the names Amenemhat, Senusret, and Nefret were later to become popular with the 12th Dynasty kings and their wives. If Amenemhat the vizier really was the same person as Amenemhat I, then his reporting of the two miracles would appear to signal that he was the one for whom miracles were performed. His contemporaries must have understood that this man had been favoured by the gods.

The Prophecy of Neferty, a text which may have been composed at about the time of the beginning of the reign of Amenemhat I, starts with a list of problems in the land, then 'predicts' the emergence of a strong king:

> Then a king will come from the South,
> Ameny, the justified, by name,
> Son of a woman of Ta-Seti, child of Upper Egypt.
> He will take the white crown,
> He will wear the red crown;
> He will join the Two Mighty Ones [the two crowns]
>
> . . . .
>
> Asiatics will fall to his sword,
> Libyans will fall to his flame,
> Rebels to his wrath, traitors to his might,
> As the serpent on his brow subdues the rebels for him.
> One will build the Walls-of-the-Ruler,
> To bar Asiatics from entering Egypt . . .

Since this early 12th Dynasty 'prophecy' (the date of which is very questionable) clearly refers to King Amenemhat, we once again have a statement of divine intervention, calling attention to the king's supernatural status. There are a number of other texts that refer to the chaos before the arrival of new kings; however, the references to the Asiatics in *The Prophecy of Neferty* are new, as is the reference to the Walls-of-the-Ruler, a structure built by Amenemhat across the eastern approach to Egypt. It was during his reign that the first definitely attested Middle Kingdom military campaigns against the Near East were undertaken.

One of Amenemhat's most significant moves was to transfer Egypt's capital from Thebes to the new town of Amenemhat-itj-tawy ('Amenemhat the seizer of the two lands'), sometimes known simply as Itjtawy, a still-undiscovered site in the Faiyum region, probably near the Lisht necropolis. The name of the city implies a rather violent beginning to the reign, but the precise date of the transfer to Itjtawy is not known. Most scholars argue that it occurred at the beginning of Amenemhat's reign, although Dorothea Arnold advocates a date much later in his reign (around the twentieth year). While a case can be made for Amenemhat spending some years at Thebes, the fact that the building preparations on the platform near Deir el-Bahri identified as a possible tomb for Amenemhat I probably only took about three to five years suggests that the move may not have been as late as the twentieth year of his reign. The negligible number of Theban monuments constructed by Amenemhat I, and the suspicious absence of official burials after the time of Meketra (a high official buried in the vicinity of the above-mentioned platform), may suggest that the move took place in the earlier years of his reign. On the other hand, inscriptions on the foundation blocks of Amenemhat's mortuary temple at Lisht show firstly that Amenemhat I had already celebrated his royal jubilee, and, secondly, that year 1 of an unnamed king (thought to be Amenemhat's successor Senusret I) had already elapsed, thus suggesting an extremely late date for the Lisht pyramid complex. For these reasons, the date of the move to the Faiyum is still a source of considerable debate.

The site of Itjtawy may have been chosen because it was closer to the source of Asiatic incursions than Thebes had been, but it was also politically wise for Amenemhat to found a new capital, thus signalling a new beginning. It also meant that the officials who served him at Itjtawy would have been entirely dependent on the king rather than having their own power bases. This new beginning was celebrated in the king's second choice of Horus name, Wehemmesu ('the renaissance', or, more literally, 'the repeating of births', perhaps an allusion to the first of the 'miracles'). This was no empty phrase: the 12th Dynasty looked back to the Old Kingdom for its models (for example, the pyramidal form of the king's tomb and the use of Old Kingdom styles of artistic decoration) and also promoted the cult of the ruler. There was a steady but inexorable return to a more centralized government, together with an increase in the bureaucracy. There was also an exponential growth in the mineral wealth of the king, emphasized by the jewellery caches found in several 12th Dynasty royal burials. These changes resulted in rising living standards for middle-class Egyptians, whose level of wealth was proportional to their official posts.

Amenemhat's earliest use of the feudal armies was against Asiatics in the Delta; the scale of these operations is unknown. He then strengthened the region with the construction of the so-called Walls-of-the-Ruler, which play a dramatic role in the *Story of Sinuhe* and are also mentioned in the *Prophecy of Neferty*. No fortress of this date has yet been discovered at the north-eastern frontier of Egypt, but the remains of a large canal may date from this period. Other fortresses are known to have been constructed elsewhere in Amenemhat's reign, including one named Rawaty at Mendes, and the outposts of Semna and Quban in Nubia, the purpose of which was mainly to protect and service the gold mines in Wadi Allaqi.

Although the king and his conscript army pushed southwards as far as Elephantine quite early in his reign, they do not appear to have been active any further south before year 29. By this time, the policy towards Nubia had been transformed from the loose network of sporadic trading and quarrying ventures that characterized the the Old Kingdom to a new strategy of conquest and colonization, principally with the aim of obtaining raw materials, especially gold. An inscription at the lower Nubian site of Korosko, midway between the first and second Nile cataracts, states that the people of Wawat (Lower Nubia) were defeated in the twenty-ninth year of Amenemhat's reign. Only one military foray against the Libyans is recorded; this is said to have taken place in year 30, with the army under the command of the king's son Senusret. By the time the Libyan campaign had ended, Amenemhat was dead.

Senusret I

According to Fragment 34 of Manetho's history, a conspiracy took place at the end of Amenemhat's reign. *The Teaching of Amenemhat I* also hints at a dispute over the succession, and it was while Senusret was campaigning in Libya that he was told of his father's death. Amenemhat was almost surely murdered, and a text from Senusret I's times presents the account supposedly spoken by his father from beyond the grave:

It was after supper, when night had fallen, and I had spent an hour of happiness. I was asleep upon my bed, having become weary, and my heart had begun to follow sleep. When weapons of my counsel were wielded, I had become like a snake of the necropolis. As I came to, I awoke to fighting, and I found that it was an attack of the bodyguard. If I had quickly taken weapons in my hand, I would have made the wretches retreat with a charge! But there is none mighty in the night, none who can fight alone; no success will come without a helper. Look, my injury happened while I was without you, when the entourage had not yet heard that I would hand over to you when I had not yet sat with you, that I might make counsels for you; for I did not plan it, I did not foresee it, and my heart had not taken thought of the negligence of servants.

The manuscript from which this brief extract derives is thought to be an early 12th Dynasty composition, possibly created on behalf of Senusret I to support his claim to the throne. The piece would very well serve as a 'justification' for any punitive measures Senusret might have taken after he gained the throne.

The king-lists give Kheperkara Senusret I (*c.*1956–1911 BC) a reign of forty-five years, and this situation is backed up by a text at Amada, in Nubia giving a date of year 44 for him. It has been accepted for some time that Senusret I's reign consisted of thirty-five years of sole reign and ten years of a co-regency shared with his father, but this assumption was questioned by Claude Obsomer in 1995. If his claim is correct, then we can at last make sense of the ending of *The Teaching of Amenemhat I*, in which the king requests that Senusret succeed him. This poetic request is only explicable if there had been no co-regency to ensure the smooth transmission of the throne.

Senusret sent one expedition to Nubia, in the tenth year of his reign. Eight years later, he dispatched another army as far south as the second cataract. His general, Mentuhotep, went even further south, but it was the site of Buhen that became Egypt's new southern border. Here Senusret set up a victory stele, and constructed a fort, thus transforming Lower Nubia into a province of Egypt. While Kush (Upper Nubia) was mainly exploited for its gold, the Egyptians were also procuring amethyst, turquoise, copper, and gneiss for jewellery and sculpture. In the north, trading caravans passed between Egypt and Syria, exchanging cedar and ivory for Egyptian goods. These more prolific expeditions into Nubia and Asia show the extent to which foreign policy had changed between the 11th and the 12th Dynasties.

The king's numerous monuments were distributed from lower Nubia in the south to Heliopolis and Tanis in the north, and it was in order to obtain the raw materials for building, decorating, and equipping these constructions that officials were sent to exploit the stone quarries of Wadi Hammamat, Sinai, Hatnub, and Wadi el-Hudi. Just one of these expeditions extracted sufficient rock to make sixty sphinxes and 150 statues. The Egyptian Museum in Cairo includes a large collection of statues of Senusret retrieved from his mortuary temple, but many of his other monuments and statues were remodelled, copied, and replaced by later kings, so that few of the originals have survived. At Thebes, he is considered to have founded the temple of *Ipet sut* (Karnak) and erected an Egyptian alabaster bark shrine celebrating his *sed*-festival in the thirty-first year of his reign. The relief work of his time was particularly fine, judging from such surviving fragments as a damaged relief figure of the king from Koptos (now in the Petrie Museum, University College London), but his statues lack vivacity

The 'bark shrine' (or 'white chapel') of Senusret I (*c.*1956–1911 BC), which has been reconstructed in the 'open air museum' at Karnak. This kiosk, carved from Egyptian alabaster and embellished with superb raised reliefs, is one of the finest buildings in the Temple of Amun at Karnak.

and movement, and the portraits are impersonal. Nevertheless, the effect of this flurry of artwork had important results: because of Senusret's long reign, the 'royal style' reached the regions with sufficient force to cast its shadow throughout Egypt, and regional styles steadily retreated before it.

Senusret was the first to introduce a construction programme whereby monuments were set up in each of the main cult sites throughout the land. This move, which was an extension of the policy of later Old Kingdom pharaohs, had the effect of undermining the power bases of local temples and priests. Today there are only a few surviving remnants of the major sculptures and thematic works from these regions, thus reducing our impression of the impact of Senusret's programme. Among his more important measures, Senusret remodelled the temple of Khenti-amentiu-Osiris at Abydos. Following this royal impetus, the king's officials also erected numerous memorial stelae and small shrines (or 'cenotaphs') at Abydos, thus inaugurating a practice that was to become standard for devout men of means in both Middle and New Kingdoms. Because of the attention Senusret paid to the cult of Osiris, there was a great flowering of Osirian beliefs and practices in Egypt, as well as a more significant levelling between the king's belief in the afterlife and the beliefs of his subjects. John Wilson has described this as the 'democratization of the afterlife'.

The 'Hekanakhte papers'

By a stroke of good fortune, a collection of Middle Kingdom letters provide us with many details of agricultural life at about this time. The letters were written by an old farmer named Hekanakhte to his family, while he was absent on business for a considerable period of time. Although this material was, until recently, thought to date to the reign of Mentuhotep III, the fact that the papyri were found in association with pottery of the early 12th Dynasty suggests that they were actually written in the early years of Senusret I.

Hekanakhte's personality emerges from these letters, which are full of sharp commands to his several sons to do his bidding, to stop whingeing about the slender rations he has allowed them, and to be kind to his new wife. The letters provide a most intimate view of family dynamics in the 12th Dynasty, as well as indicating some of the ways in which richer farmers juggled their commitments and crops. They suggest that there was famine in Egypt in Hekanakhte's later years, a phenomenon also implied by the inscriptions in the roughly contemporary tomb of the nomarch Amenemhat at Beni Hasan (tomb BH 2).

The Hekanakhte papers include a rare letter from a woman to her mother—a find that raises the question of the extent to which ancient Egyptian women were able to read and write. Unfortunately, however, this does not constitute definite proof, given that the woman in question may have dictated the letter to a male scribe (as indeed many illiterate male correspondents would have done) and the style of the handwriting can provide no clues. References elsewhere to two Middle Kingdom female scribes suggest that a few women may nevertheless have been literate at this date.

Royal annals and the reign of Amenemhat II

Further information for the historical events of the 12th Dynasty comes from a set of official records (known as *genut* or 'day-books') that have been partly preserved in the temple at Tod. The king's building dedications also contain elements of these annals; P. Berlin 3029, for instance, describes the process by which the king founded a new building. These are some of the most useful surviving texts in terms of understanding the day-to-day world of the Egyptian palace. In addition, in 1974, the Egyptian Antiquities Organization discovered one of the most important *genut* inscriptions at Mit Rahina (ancient Memphis). Although the inscription mentions Senusret I, it clearly belongs to the reign of his son, Nubkaura Amenemhat II (*c*.1911–1877 BC). These annals contain very detailed descriptions of donations made to various temples, lists of statues and buildings, reports of both military and trading expeditions, and royal activities such as hunting. It is undoubtedly the most important text of Amenemhat II, but it also refers to other 12th Dynasty kings; more significantly, it reveals that the superficial 'peace' that was said to exist between Asia and Egypt at this time was only selective, with a number of treaties existing between Egypt and various individual Levantine cities. Herodotus' references to Asiatic wars and to the attitude of contempt held by 'Sesostris' towards the Asiatics (*Histories* 2. 106) are thus perhaps closer to historical reality than modern readers have tended to believe.

Wall paintings in the tomb of the nomarch Khnumhotep at Beni Hasan (BH 3) depict the visit of a Bedouin chieftain named Abisha, while numerous Egyptian statuettes and scarabs have been found at Near Eastern sites, reaffirming such Asiatic links. There had long been steady commerce with the Syrian port of Byblos, where the native rulers wrote short inscriptions in hieroglyphs, held the Egyptian titles of count and hereditary prince, referred to Egyptian gods, and acquired Egyptian royal and private statuary. In addition, the above-mentioned Mit Rahina annals of Amenemhat II identify the north Syrian city of Tunip as an Egyptian trading partner. Other Asiatic contacts appear to have been more warlike. The annals refer to a small group of Egyptians entering Bedouin territory (probably a region of Sinai) in order to 'hack up the land', and two more operations were directed against unknown walled towns. The victims are described as *Aamu* (Asiatics), and 1,554 of them are said to have been captured as prisoners. These large numbers of foreign captives may well explain the extensive lists of Asiatic slaves working in houses in Thebes in later times. There were also campaigns in the south at this time; thus the 'biography' in the tomb of Amenemhat at Beni Hasan mentions that he went on an expedition to Kush (Upper Nubia) and that the East African kingdom of Punt was visited by the king's official, Khentykhetaywer, in the twenty-eighth year of Amenemhat II.

Unlike so many of the 12th Dynasty rulers, Amenemhat II does not appear to have had a prolific building record, although this impression may be partly a result of later plundering. His pyramid complex, the so-called White Pyramid at Dahshur (poorly preserved and not yet thoroughly examined), was unique in being set on a platform. His daughters were buried in the forecourt and a queen called Keminebu was also buried within the complex. It was long thought that Keminebu was Amenemhat's wife, but it is now recognized, on the basis of her name and the style of her inscriptions, that she was actually a 13th Dynasty queen.

Senusret II and the inauguration of the Faiyum irrigation system

The reign of Amenemhat II's successor, Khakheperra Senusret II (1877–1870 BC), was a time of peace and prosperity, when trade with the Near East was particularly prolific. There are no records of military campaigns during his reign; instead, his greatest achievement appears to have been the inauguration of the Faiyum irrigation scheme. A dyke was built and canals were dug to connect the Faiyum with the waterway that is now known as the Bahr Yusef. These canals siphoned off some of the waters that normally would have flowed into Lake Moeris, resulting in a gradual evaporation of waters around the edges of the lake, the canals extended the amount of new land; the reclaimed land was then farmed. This was a far-sighted scheme, and would have been unique for its time, if it were not for the fact that land was reclaimed with a similar system of dams and drainage canals in the Copaic Basin of Boeotia, in central Greece, in the Middle Helladic Period (c.1900–1600 BC).

We do not in fact know how many of these irrigation works are to be ascribed specifically to the reign of Senusret II, but his connection with the overall revival of the Faiyum is probably indicated by the fact that he erected religious monuments at the edge of the region. The unique statue shrine of Qasr es-Sagha in the desert at the north-eastern corner of the Faiyum might date to around his reign by associated pottery. Like other buildings of his reign, however, this one was left undecorated and incomplete, thus contributing to the impression that he enjoyed only a short reign. The use of various sites in the Faiyum for royal pyramid complexes from this time onwards perhaps indicates the

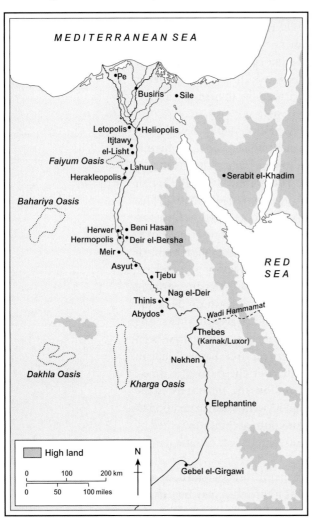

Map of Egypt showing the principal sites of the First Intermediate Period and Middle Kingdom.

MEDITERRANEAN SEA

Pe
Busiris • Sile
Letopolis • Heliopolis
Itjtawy
el-Lisht
Faiyum Oasis
Lahun
Herakleopolis
Serabit el-Khadim
Bahariya Oasis
Herwer • Beni Hasan
Hermopolis • Deir el-Bersha
Meir
Asyut • Tjebu
RED SEA
Nag el-Deir
Thinis
Abydos • Wadi Hammamat
Thebes (Karnak/Luxor)
Nekhen
Dakhla Oasis
Kharga Oasis
Elephantine
High land N
0   100   200 km
0   50   100 miles
Gebel el-Girgawi

importance of the irrigation scheme, since it is usually assumed that the royal palaces of each ruler would have been built close to their funerary monuments.

A small group of statues of Senusret II are known, at least two of which were usurped by Rameses II (1279–1213 BC). The wide, muscular shoulders are reminiscent of the statues of Senusret I, although the influence of Old Kingdom royal statuary is also apparent. The facial appearance of Senusret II is more vigorous and plastic, with none of the blandness that typified the statuary of his 12th Dynasty predecessors: his broad cheekbones are very distinctive, and probably indicative of actual portraiture, foreshadowing the startling studies of Senusret III (1870–1831 BC). The customary imitation of a royal trend by the wealthy members of society subsequently occurred, including many vivid examples of individuality among the private statuary of the late 12th Dynasty. The reign of Senusret II perhaps deserves to be regarded as one of the major phases of human portraiture in the history of Egyptian art.

Even better known than the king's statuary are a pair of highly polished black granite statues of Queen(?) Nefret now in the Egyptian Museum, Cairo. Larger than life, they depict a royal woman whose position at court is still uncertain. Although Nefret did not hold the title of 'royal wife', she possessed other titles held by queens. Was she perhaps the first wife of Senusret II, who may have died prior to her husband's fairly late accession, or was she his sister? As with many Egyptian queens, the records concerning Nefret are ambiguous and incomplete. Yet one more royal woman has emerged recently. In 1995 the remains of his chief wife, Khnumetneferhedjetweret, were discovered in the pyramid of her son (Senusret III) at Dahshur, together with a few items of jewellery.

Senusret II built his funerary complex at Lahun, the pyramid being a massive mud-brick structure with a rocky core; large limestone cross walls provided support for the brick sectors, which were then cased in limestone. Trees were planted at the southern end of the complex, and the entrance to the pyramid was also on the south. The layout of corridors and rooms within the pyramid is unique, and may reflect beliefs concerned with Osiris and the afterlife. It is suspected that another tomb, very well made and situated on the northern side of the complex (Tomb 621), could be a cenotaph like those in Old Kingdom royal complexes. The female members of the king's family may be represented by eight solid *mastaba*-tombs and a satellite pyramid; all of them were aligned with the northern side of the king's tomb, but they were apparently symbolic structures rather than actual burial places. In a shaft tomb at the southern end of the king's pyramid enclosure, the jewellery and other possessions of Princess Sathathoriunet were found by Petrie and Brunton in 1914; the workmanship of these pieces is among the best in the entire repertoire of Egyptian jewellery.

Nubian conquest under Senusret III

Although the Turin Canon gives Khakaura Senusret III (c.1870–1831 BC) a reign of over thirty years, the latest regnal year recorded by dated sources is 19. On the other hand, discoveries during the 1990s may support the longer date (see chronological discussion at the beginning of the chapter). There is no real evidence for a co-regency with Senusret II, but if one could be proven it would help resolve some difficulties caused by the unusually long reign.

Senusret is perhaps the most 'visible' monarch of the Middle Kingdom: his exploits gathered renown over time and substantially contributed to the character of 'Sesostris' (a kind of composite heroic Middle Kingdom ruler) described by Manetho and Herodotus. The king campaigned in Nubia in regnal years 6, 8, 10, and 16, and these wars appear to have been very brutal: Nubian men were killed, their women and children enslaved, their fields burnt, and their wells poisoned. Soon after this, the Egyptians were again mining and trading with the inhabitants, but conditions had changed. In the eighth and sixteenth regnal years, stelae were set up in the fortresses of Semna and Uronarti, at what appears to have been the southern border, with their inscriptions reminding everyone of Senusret's conquest and punishments. This frontier region was sealed off by reinforcing the huge fortresses, and guards were placed on round-the-clock duty, waiting for any movement. The year 8 stele at Semna states that no Nubians are allowed to take their herds or boats to the north of the specified border.

Seated diorite statue of the young Senusret III, from the temple at Medamud.

These forts emphasize the unsettled nature of the Egyptian control of Nubia. The so-called Semna dispatches—a set of military letters and accounts sent from Semna to Thebes in the 13th Dynasty—reveal just how rigorously the Egyptians policed the native people. They also show how closely these forts kept in contact with each other. Although the major forts were of comparable size, they fulfilled several different functions. Some, such as Mirgissa, were more involved with trade than others (bread and beer were exchanged for the native goods), while some (such as Askut) appear to have been used as supply depots for campaigns into Upper Nubia. Reports were sent backwards and forwards from the forts to the vizier, and in this way the king kept in touch with the limits of his domain. Senusret's final Nubian campaign, in year 19, was of lengthy duration and it was ultimately not particularly successful: the king had to retreat when the water level in the river dropped alarmingly, making journeys dangerous.

He undertook at least one campaign into Palestine, apparently similar to the expedition sent by Amenemhat II against the *Aamu* (Asiatics). There appear to have been large numbers of Asiatics in Egypt by this date; some of them were prisoners taken earlier, but the biblical account of Joseph's brothers selling him as a slave to an Egyptian master (Gen. 37: 28–36) may suggest another way in which some of these immigrants arrived. Egyptian intolerance toward the 'easterners' was already apparent in the reign of Senusret I, who described himself as 'the throat-slitter of Asia', and this general perception is reinforced by the so-called execration texts. These were lists of enemies inscribed on pottery objects and figurines, many of which name individual Asiatics and the people of Asia in general. The intention of the texts seems to have been to ensure the magical destruction of Egypt's enemies by burying or smashing the pots or figurines in question.

Senusret also took a different direction in his political reforms. Although he has often been credited with the dismantling of the system of nomarchs, there is no real evidence to support this assertion (see section on political change below). Nevertheless, his attempts to pull Egypt back into a more centralized form of government resulted in significant political and social readjustment (especially for the middle classes), and his reign is quite rightly regarded as a crucial watershed in Middle Kingdom history.

The tomb of Senusret III, a 60-metre-high mud-brick pyramid, cased with limestone blocks, was located at Dahshur, like that of Amenemhat II. *Mastaba*-tombs were built for his immediate family within the temenos wall, but their real burials lay below ground in galleries, one level for queens, the other for princesses. Dieter Arnold has shown that this complex takes some of its ideas from the 3rd Dynasty step-pyramid complex of Djoser at Saqqara. The burial chamber has a vaulted ceiling and is built of granite plastered over with white gypsum. Neither the king's chamber nor the sarcophagus appears to have been used. However, at the southern end of Abydos a second funerary complex was constructed for Senusret, consisting of a subterranean tomb and a mortuary temple, where a cult for the king lasted for over two centuries. Some scholars suspect that the Abydos complex may have been his actual burial place, but no remains were found there either.

One of the six granite statues of Senusret III found in the front court of Mentuhotep II at Deir el-Bahri. These must be classed among the most individual of royal portraits ever made, and are likely to be representative of the king's actual features. The mouth is characteristically downturned, the eyelids heavy, and these marks make it easy to identify the numerous statues of this king.

Amenemhat III: the cultural climax of the Middle Kingdom

Senusret's only known son was Nimaatra Amenemhat III (*c.*1831–1786 BC). It was arguably around the time of his long and peaceful reign that the Middle Kingdom reached its cultural peak. Consolidation of what had gone before

This small damaged head from a statue of Amenemhat III, carved in a dark green, shelly limestone, is a masterly portrait of the last of the major rulers of the Middle Kingdom.

appears to have been the hallmark of Amenemhat's style of government. He strengthened the Semna border and enlarged some of the fortresses. Other building works included numerous shrines and temples, and a huge structure at Biahmu (in the north-western Faiyum), featuring two colossal quartzite seated statues of the king facing onto the lake, which was later described by Herodotus (2. 149). He also constructed a large temple to Sobek at another Faiyum site, Kiman Faras (Crocodilopolis), and expanded the Ptah temple at Memphis. The surviving statues of Amenemhat III are striking, distinguished both by their originality and their workmanship, as in the case of a small head of the king now in the collection of the Fitzwilliam Museum, Cambridge, which is one of the most elegant and subtle of his many portraits. His so-called Hyksos sphinxes and parts of shrines were found reused in the Third Intermediate Period temples at Tanis, as were the twin black granite statues of the king in the guise of the Nile god, bringing offerings of fish, lotus flowers, and geese—a design later imitated by such New Kingdom rulers as Amenhotep III (1390–1352 BC).

Numerous inscriptions record Amenemhat III's mining activities. In the Sinai region alone, where the king's officials worked the turquoise and copper mines on a quasi-permanent basis, fifty-nine graffiti have been identified. The quarries at Wadi Hammamat, Tura, Aswan, and various Nubian sites were also worked. All this building and industrial activity symbolizes the prosperity that

Egypt enjoyed during the reign, but it may also have exhausted the economy and, combined with a series of low Nile floods, late in his reign, resulted in political and economic decline. Ironically, the large intake of Asiatics, which seems to have occurred partly in order to subsidize the extensive building work, may have encouraged the so-called Hyksos to settle in the Delta, thus leading eventually to the eventual collapse of native Egyptian rule.

Before the construction of the modern dams at Aswan and the creation of Lake Nasser, the annual Nile inundation was critical for Egypt's food supply. Amenemhat's records of inundation levels at Kumma and Semna in Nubia are numerous, revealing extremely high levels for the Nile during part of his reign, the highest being in year 30, when it reached 5.1 m. But these levels subsequently tapered away sharply, so that in year 40 the level was only 0.5 m. Such fluctuations must have had a destabilizing effect on the economy. Since the Faiyum is the only oasis in Egypt dependent upon the Nile, the Faiyum irrigation scheme would have needed to draw on some of the annual flood water, thus perhaps explaining the king's apparent intense interest in the flood levels. Alternatively, the high Niles may have been closely watched in order to allow possible flood damage in the north to be averted. Amenemhat III certainly maintained the Faiyum scheme, and later peoples worshipped him as Lamares, the god of the Faiyum, but, as with Senusret II, it is not clear just how much hydraulic work was undertaken in his particular reign. His deification may have taken place as early as the reign of his successor, Queen Sobekneferu, for she had the most to gain from elevating the man who was probably her own father.

Amenemhat built his first pyramid at Dahshur, but, as in the case of the 4th Dynasty Bent Pyramid of Sneferu, cracks appear to have developed in the structure during building. The finished pyramid had a mud-brick core and was originally encased in limestone (now robbed); its stone pyramidion is in the Egyptian Museum, Cairo. The remains of Queen Aat and another royal woman were found in two recently discovered corridors inside the south-western section of the pyramid. Their crypts were provided with separate entrances outside the pyramid, a feature that would have enabled access after the main entrance to the pyramid had been sealed. Queen Aat's sarcophagus is identical to that of the king.

The two queens' burial chambers at Dahshur each included a separate '*ka* chamber' where the canopic chests were placed. This was a type of funerary room that had once been the privilege of kings, thus presumably representing a rather specialized aspect of the so-called democratization of the afterlife (see section on religion below); it is likely that these chambers expressed new beliefs concerning the afterlife of royal women. Their corridors were linked with the king's, and they would have shared the tomb with him if it had not been for the structural faults that developed.

Amenemhat's final resting place, however, was at Hawara in the south-eastern Faiyum. His most famous monument was the mortuary temple attached to this pyramid, which may have been reminiscent of Djoser's *sed*-festival court, attached to his pyramid at Saqqara. The Hawara temple became known as the Labyrinth because of its maze of rooms and corridors. Although described by six classical writers, including Herodotus (2. 148–9), Strabo (17. I. 3, 37, 42) and Pliny (*Natural History* 36. 13), no details of its plan were coherent even when Petrie made his survey in 1888; therefore efforts at reconstructing its original appearance have been unsuccessful. Amenemhat's burial chamber at Hawara was originally intended to be shared with Princess Neferuptah, who was probably his sister, but she was later transferred to a small, separate pyramid (now almost totally destroyed by stone-robbers and water damage) a few kilometres away. The prominence of Neferuptah both during his reign and after her death, together with the mortuary privileges provided for her and for the two queens at Dahshur, suggests the increased status of royal women in the late 12th Dynasty.

Amenemhat IV and Sobekneferu

Given the long reign of Amenemhat III, there is a possibility that Maakherura Amenemhat IV (1786–1777 BC) might have been his grandson, but it is also possible that this last male ruler of the 12th Dynasty was an aged son whose life was nearing its end when he came to the throne, for he ruled for only nine years. He is likely to have been married to Queen Sobekkara Sobekneferu (1777–1773 BC), whom Manetho says was his sister. Few of his monuments have been preserved and little is known of events during his reign, which may have been primarily occupied in completing several temples begun by his predecessor, such as the limestone sanctuary of the harvest goddess, Renenutet, at Medinet Maadi in the south-western Faiyum. There were also continued expeditions to the turquoise mines in Sinai and further trade with the Levant.

There are only a handful of records relating to the last ruler of the 12th Dynasty, Queen Sobekneferu, but some of them offer very interesting clues relating to her reign. She is listed in the Turin Canon; there is a Nile graffito at the Nubian fortress of Kumma giving the height of inundation at 1.83 m. in the third year of her reign; and there is a fine cylinder seal bearing her name and titulary, which is now in

In this red quartzite headless statue of Sobekneferu, of unknown provenance, the queen wears an unusual costume: on top of a female shift, there is a masculine kilt with the usual kilt knot. The costume thus combines major elements of male and female dress, and it shows how the queen's sculptors tried to accommodate female iconography within the pharaonic form, perhaps later providing inspiration for the 18th Dynasty female ruler Hatshepsut.

the British Museum. Usually, the queen uses feminine titles, but several masculine ones were also used. Three headless statues of the queen were found in the Faiyum, and a few other items contain her name. She contributed to Amenemhat III's 'Labyrinth', and also built at Herakleopolis Magna.

There is an interesting, but damaged statue of the queen of unknown origin; the costume on this figure is unique in its combination of elements from male and female dress, echoing her occasional use of male titles in her records. This ambiguity might have been a deliberate attempt to mollify the critics of a female ruler. An intriguing statuette of Sobekneferu in the Metropolitan Museum, New York shows the queen wearing a *sed*-festival cloak and a most unusual crown, which may have resulted from the attempt to combine unfamiliar iconographic elements of male and female rulers. The queen's reign lasted for less than four years, and her tomb—like Amenemhat IV's—has not yet been identified.

The 13th Dynasty

The rulers of the 13th Dynasty continued to use Itjtawy as their capital, and carried on the policies of the 12th Dynasty rulers; but the new dynasty was made up of different lineages, and the question of how the king might have been chosen is unresolved. Stephen Quirke has suggested a 'circulating succession' among leading families, which would help to account for the great brevity of most of the reigns. Nevertheless, the bureaucracy continued to function in the same way as it had done throughout the 12th Dynasty. The Egyptians still controlled the area around the second Nile cataract, Nile floods were measured, trade still flourished, and royal monuments continued to be built (although these were far less impressive than those of the great 12th Dynasty kings). The visual arts, on the other hand, show no alterations in finesse or style from the best of the 12th Dynasty pieces. This continuity—broken at times—lasted until the reign of Neferhotep I.

Although many 13th Dynasty names have been recorded in the Turin Canon, we know little about the individual rulers. Wegaf Khutawyra was the first, followed by Khutawy-Sekhemra Sobekhotep II. After the reign of the third king, Sankhtawy-Sekhemra Iykhernefert-Neferhotep, Nile records were not kept for some time, and it is possible that this might have been a period of political unrest: it is perhaps significant that there are also few records during this time at the Sinai turquoise mines. Nevertheless, trading contacts continued, and the ruler of Byblos still described himself as the 'servant of Egypt'. Sealings from the Nubian forts show that affairs to the south ran as before. It is to this period that King Awibra Hor belongs; his burial—a mere shaft tomb—was discovered by Jacques de Morgan in the mortuary complex of Amenemhat III at Dahshur. In spite of the cultural continuity remarked above, nothing so clearly expresses the reduced circumstances of the rulers at this time as the impoverished nature of the tomb of Awibra Hor.

After this brief, unsettled period, a series of less ephemeral kings emerged, including Sekhemra-Khutawy Sobekhotep II, to whose reign is dated a most interesting papyrus revealing details of Theban court life for a period of twelve days. Stephen Quirke's analysis of this document (Papyrus Bulaq 18) has revealed a great deal about the hierarchical structure of the 13th Dynasty palace and its *modus operandi*. Some four reigns later, in about 1744 BC, Sekhemra-Sewadjtawy Sobekhotep III became king, and for a time it seemed that there would be a revival in the fortunes of Egyptian rulers. A relief carved in the cliff above Nag Hammadi, in Middle Egypt, provides very specific information about members of the king's family. His highest regnal date was year 5, although the Turin Canon gives him only three years and two months; despite this brevity, he left dated inscriptions on monuments from the Delta site of Bubastis down to Elephantine in the south.

Sobekhotep III's successor, Khasekhemra Neferhotep I (*c*.1740–1729 BC), was also evidently of non-royal stock, but he too left many monumental records, suggesting that his reign was a vigorous one. He was acknowledged as overlord by Inten, the ruler of Byblos, and his inscriptions have been found as far south as the island of Konosso, just south of the first cataract in Nubia. Despite these tokens of strength, however, he was not in control of the entire Egyptian kingdom, judging from the evidence of local rulers governing independently at Xois and Avaris in the Delta.

The throne passed to the two brothers of Neferhotep I, Sahathor and Sobekhotep IV, followed by the brief reign of the son of Sobekhotep IV. This mini-dynasty ended with Sobekhotep V in about 1723 BC. Nevertheless, enough evidence has survived of the reign of Sobekhotep IV to suggest that he had all the hallmarks of a strong king, and continued to hold some control over Nubia, where two of the king's statues were found south of the third cataract (other statues of this king survived reused at Tanis). It was, however, during the reign of Sobekhotep IV that the first signs of revolt emerged in Nubia, which was eventually to slip out of Egyptian control, to be ruled instead by a line of Nubian kings based at Kerma (see Chapter 8). By that time, Middle Kingdom Egypt had broken up into those spheres of interest that formed the basis for government in the Second Intermediate Period.

Processes of Political Change in the Middle Kingdom

Government in the Middle Kingdom was loosely based on the structure created under the Old Kingdom, but there were significant variations. The bureaucracy and the Crown were supported by taxation, although little direct information concerning the latter has survived from Middle Kingdom sources. The fiscal system was essentially based on assessment of yields from lands and waterways, and paid in kind. Temples and other pious foundations were often tax exempt in part, if not in full (see below). In addition, there was a system of enforced labour, whereby men and women of the middle and lower classes were enlisted

Many Middle Kingdom tombs contained funerary models depicting scenes from daily life. This model, from the tomb of Meketra at Thebes, portrays the cattle census, a regular event whereby the necessary amount of royal tax on live-stock would have been cal-culated.

to undertake specific physical tasks, including military service. This corvée sys-tem was organized through town officials, but there was central control under the office of the 'organization of labour'. Although it was possible to escape the burden of the work legitimately by paying another person to do it, those who avoided the corvée altogether were punished very severely, and their families, or anyone aiding their evasion, were also punished. Records from the fortress at Askut in Lower Nubia show that this was one place to which evaders of the corvée could be sent; no doubt other defaulters were sent to the quarry regions.

The corvée practice continued into the 17th Dynasty, and only the people of Nubia appear to have been exempt from both taxation and corvée impositions. For its part, the government kept the peace at home and patrolled the borders north of the second cataract and west of the Walls-of-the-Ruler. By means of raids into Palestine, and campaigns in Nubia, the Middle Kingdom rulers were able to extend Egypt's influence and prosperity. Trade was the king's monopoly, supervised by state officials, and in Nubia the rewards were extremely substantial.

Many of the titles held by Middle Kingdom officials were the same as those used in the Old Kingdom, but there were also a number of additional posts. One of the noticeable characteristics of the Middle Kingdom was a refining of official titles into more specific offices and duties, which must have been part of a general growth in the bureaucracy, although the range of activities within each office would have become more restricted. An exception to this narrowing of duties was that of 'royal sealbearer', who was given wide supervisory duties, especially under Mentuhotep II. The vizier, whose responsibilities are enumerated in a New Kingdom funerary text from the tomb of Rekhmira (*The Duties of the Vizier*), was still the chief minister under the king, albeit less prominently in the records after the 11th Dynasty. The practice of having two viziers is uncertain for the Middle Kingdom, although under Senusret I there do seem to have been two (Antefoker and Mentuhotep) who were serving at the same time.

The scant source material of the later Middle Kingdom suggests that there were other political changes between the Old and Middle Kingdoms: central government in the Middle Kingdom was much more pervasive in the regional areas (whereas there is little evidence for this in the Old Kingdom). There was also more control over individuals and the obligation that each was deemed to owe the government. This more intense intrusion into private life may be partially attributed to the Middle Kingdom custom of delegating so much local control to the mayors of the towns, but there was a marked change, too, in bringing the provinces into line with the styles and practices of the capital. Artwork is the most visible indicator of this phenomenon.

It was, however, the office of nomarch that experienced the widest fluctuation of all during the Middle Kingdom. Thanks to their distance from Memphis, the earlier nomarchs had always enjoyed a certain amount of independence in the Old Kingdom. This independence was strengthened by the collapse of the Memphite government, and a major goal of the Middle Kingdom rulers was to minimize it. Different kings chose different strategies to effect their policy.

Under Mentuhotep II the nomarchs were retained in many of the areas for which we have records (although much of this kind of evidence has not survived), but it appears that those nomarchs considered unhelpful to the Thebans would have automatically lost their positions. Throughout the 11th Dynasty the nomarchs played their traditional roles, but they were now supervised by the king's officials. Many of those who retained power still had delusions of grandeur: Count Nehry of the Hermopolite nome, for instance, dated his inscriptions to his own 'reign' during the time of Mentuhotep IV, and his statements at the Hatnub quarry strongly suggest challenges to the king.

The basic plan adopted by Amenemhat I was to make the individual town the focus of administration. Each town was controlled by a mayor, and only the chief official in the most important towns inherited the position of nomarch. With this concentration on the city as the basic unit of government, the political impact of the larger region of the nome now declined. Amenemhat I's nomarchs held the titles of 'great overlord, mayor, and overseer of priests', and were mainly located in the central and border regions of Egypt. The key factor in royal control over these men seems to have been the fact that, in the first two 12th Dynasty reigns at least, they were all personally appointed by the king (although by the time of Amenemhat II the office had once more become hereditary).

Such nomarchs made the most of their positions, some of them adapting titles for their own staff that imitated those at the royal court: one can find here and there a 'treasurer', a 'chancellor', and even an army captain in household retinues. Despite these pretensions, the great overlords were not allowed to forget their benefactor, the king, who had organized them in quasi-feudal fashion: they owed him direct allegiance and, in return for royal favours, they were obliged to protect the borders of Egypt, to undertake expeditions for the king, and probably to act as deputies for official receptions of foreigners, such as the arrival of the Bedouin traders in the Oryx nome, depicted in the tomb of Khnumhotep at Beni Hasan (BH 3), in the reign of Amenemhat II.

The main title of the nomarch, 'great overlord', disappeared about the time of Senusret III, and the conventional view is that this happened as a result of *force majeure* by the king. The real reason, however, is likely to have been somewhat different: by the time of Senusret III, only the nomarchs of el-Bersha and Elephantine are still definitely recorded as holders of the office of 'great overlord' (other areas were controlled by mayors, but records of many towns are missing, so we cannot be entirely certain). Detlef Franke has demonstrated that the practice under Senusret II was for the king to educate the sons of nomarchs in the capital, and then to give them appointments either at the capital or in other areas. With the family scions dissipated in this way, the office of nomarch would eventually have been eclipsed by that of the town mayors, who would inevitably not have enjoyed the same material wealth and power as the provincial governors. This would explain why the era of richly decorated provincial tombs came to an end. Senusret III is thus unlikely to have been the instrument of the nomarchs' demise, for the record shows that, although the office eventually expired under Senusret III, it had been in decline since at least the time of Amenemhat II.

Nevertheless, Senusret III did install other officials (based at the royal court) as governors of very large sections of the country, and in this way made a sharp break with practices of the past. Two bureaus (*waret*) were created, one each for the northern and southern areas of Egypt, operated by a hierarchy of officials. Other departments, such as the 'treasury', the 'bureau of the people's giving', and the 'organization of labour', were also inaugurated. The military sector was organized under a chief general, and there was a new 'bureau of the vizier'. In addition to these state departments, there was a separate administration for the palace. As a result of this new hierarchy, there were also fresh titles, and a corresponding increase in the size of the middle-class bureaucracy, which was reflected in greater numbers of funerary stelae for this period, a visible marker of the greater affluence of the middle class.

Outside the governmental boundaries were the estates of the temple and its dependencies. As the contracts for the mayor Djefahapy of Asyut reveal, this was an equally bureaucratic world. Djefahapy's ten contracts—which have survived because they were inscribed on an inner wall of his tomb—were drawn up to ensure that his mortuary cult would be maintained after his death. Apart from the legal implications, the contracts also reveal some of the other conditions applying to the temple, such as the fact that each person in the district was required to give the temple a *hekat* (nearly 5 litres) of grain from every field on his property on the occasion of the first harvest each year. The contracts are very specific, indicating that the temples were self-supporting, and that they too had to pay taxes to the Crown, unless they received an exemption decree from the king. Senusret I's policy of building provincial temples throughout the land effectively reduced the local temples' power bases.

The Royal Court

Very few explicit statements concerning the role of the pharaoh have survived from the Old Kingdom, but there are some Middle Kingdom texts that shed light on the nature of kingship, such as *The Teachings for Merykara*, *The Teaching of Amenemhat I*, and the *Hymns to Senusret III*. Some private records, too, can provide insights, as in the case of a long poem on the stele of Sehetepibra from Abydos (Egyptian Museum, Cairo), which describes the importance of the king to his people.

The concluding episodes of *The Tale of Sinuhe* (describing the return of an Egyptian courtier from exile) supply details of 12th Dynasty court life, but it is the 13th Dynasty Papyrus Bulaq 18 that provides the most revealing evidence concerning the social hierarchy of the royal family and the quantities of daily rations given out, thus indicating the relative importance of these and other palace dependants. This papyrus also indicates the fluidity of the movements of different people, with their sojourns away from the palace proper. With regard to the palace complex itself, the papyrus indicates that there were three inner divisions within its precincts. In descending order of importance, these were: the *kap*, or nursery, which was the domain of the royal family, their personal servants and select children being educated at the king's expense; the *wahy*, or audience area of the columned hall, a place where banquets were held; and the *khenty*, or outer palace, where the business of the court was conducted. These three groups of buildings were set within a less august area known as the *shena*, where provisions were handed out to the palace dependants. The vizier and senior officials occupied the *khenty*, while serving staff were restricted to the *shena*. The interior overseer of the *kap* appears to have been the only official who could operate in both the inner and outer parts of the palace. Without the information in Papyrus Bulaq 18, our knowledge of Middle Kingdom palace organization would barely extend further than the architectural plans of a 12th Dynasty palace at Tell Basta and an early 13th Dynasty palace at Tell el-Dabʿa in the Delta.

Urban life: The Pyramid Town at Lahun

The lives of ordinary people are accessible to us via the town of Hetep-Senusret beside the pyramid complex of Senusret II at the site of Lahun. Mistakenly named 'Kahun' by Flinders Petrie, who excavated there in 1888–9, it was closely associated with the funerary cult of Senusret II. Laid out in a single architectural plan like the much smaller New Kingdom walled villages at Amarna and Deir el-Medina (see Chapters 9 and 10), Hetep-Senusret was founded to accommodate the king's workers and their families. It is likely, however, that it included among its inhabitants many who were not connected with the funerary cult. It has been estimated, on the basis of the capacities of grain silos throughout the town, that a population as high as 5,000 could have been supported. The modern site, however, is barely distinguishable from the surrounding desert, since the mud brick has been almost entirely removed, leaving only the foundations and lower courses of the buildings.

The material from Lahun is particularly precious because it derives from the living world rather than the necropolis (although Middle Kingdom settlements have been excavated more recently at Abydos, Memphis, and Elephantine, allowing the Lahun material to begin to be viewed in a much broader geographical and social context). Unfortunately, much of the material left behind at Lahun, when it was first abandoned in the 13th Dynasty, was thrown into huge rubbish pits by the post-Middle Kingdom occupants of the site. Thus a great deal of the precious context of the material was destroyed long before the site was excavated. Nevertheless, some houses were left comparatively undisturbed, and these have the potential to provide glimpses into the lives of the kinds of individuals who tend not to feature in the surviving textual and funerary material. Thanks to Percy Newberry's collection of seed types during Petrie's expedition, it has even proved possible to recreate the vegetation of the area (despite a certain amount of contamination by Graeco-Roman botanical material). There were flowers such as poppies, lupins, mignonette, jasmine, heliotrope, and irises (as well as weeds), and vegetables, including peas, beans, radishes, and cucumbers.

The material from Lahun also includes such intriguing finds as a 'firestick' for lighting fires (probably the only surviving Egyptian example), the earliest known mud-brick mould (identical to those used by Egyptians today), a set of doctor's instruments, and many other tools used by farmers and professional craftworkers. There was also a rich variety of pottery, and a large number of papyri (some still unpublished), the contents of which shed light on many areas of religion and daily life. Among the most interesting of the texts from Lahun is the so-called Gynaecological Papyrus, which, as its name suggests, comprises the oldest surviving collection of remedies for women's ailments.

Foreign Trade

Commercial contacts between Middle Kingdom Egypt and the Aegean are indicated by a few sherds of Minoan pottery in the 12th Dynasty phase of the Lahun settlement, as well as a pyxis lid and fragments of local Egyptian pottery that were clearly imitating Minoan types. Because these sherds were found in refuse deposits, however, it is difficult to be sure of their dates or their original stratigraphic contexts. Curiously, they appear to have been common vessels used by the workmen (rather than luxury imports), perhaps even indicating the presence of foreign workers from Crete among the town's population. In the 12th Dynasty, there are also a few deposits of sherds from Minoan 'Kamares vessels' at such sites as Lahun, el-Haraga, and Abydos, and in a 12th Dynasty grave as far south as Elephantine. Numerous items from this time also reveal the presence of a Mediterranean network of artistic and iconographic exchange: Egyptian motifs can be found on items as far-flung as the dedicatory clay scarab beetles offered in the peak sanctuaries in parts of Crete. Egyptian stone vases also made their way to Crete, where their styles were imitated by Minoan craftsmen. Although such local imitations of Egyptian styles and iconography are often from undated contexts, they are nevertheless important in that they suggest frequent contact leading to exchange of *ideas* as well as materials and products.

At Lahun and Lisht, there is also early evidence for the distinctive Tell el-Yahudiya ware (see Chapter 8), comprising jugs that perhaps once contained Near Eastern oil. The Egyptian kings actively promoted imports of timber, oil, wine, silver, and perhaps ivory from Syria–Palestine. Both Cypriot and Minoan pottery are also attested from other occasional finds in Egypt. Egyptian goods, such as scarabs, statues, vases, jewellery, and even several sphinxes have been found in sites as far apart as Byblos, Ras Shamra, and Crete. Via Syria, further contacts were made with Cyprus and Babylon, but very little of this material comes from properly dated contexts.

Increasing contact with the Near East is suggested by the fact that Asiatic weights actually outnumber Egyptian ones at Lahun. In addition, one of the richest finds of the Middle Kingdom is a collection of Asiatic (or perhaps Minoan) gold and silver material discovered in four bronze caskets underneath the temple of Montu at Tod. Conversely, Pierre Montet discovered a hoard of 1,000 Egyptian items buried in a jar at the Syrian city of Byblos, including jewellery bearing a strong likeness to the 'treasure' from the tombs of 12th Dynasty princesses in the Lahun necropolis. Neferhotep and other Egyptian rulers were acknowledged as overlords by the local rulers of Byblos, who not only copied

Egyptian insignia and titles but also imitated Egyptian hieroglyphic inscriptions.

There were also strong contacts with the areas to the south of Egypt. Apart from their activities in Nubia, many of the Middle Kingdom rulers, particularly Mentuhotep III and Senusret I, maintained trading links with the African region of Punt (probably located somewhere in the vicinity of modern Eritrea). The 12th Dynasty port of Sa'waw has been discovered at the eastern end of the Wadi Gawasis, on the Red Sea coast (a short distance to the north of modern Quseir), and several inscribed stelae, found both along the wadi and at the port itself, provide records of 12th Dynasty journeys to Punt.

Religion and Funerary Practices

The most important developments in Middle Kingdom religion concerned the cult of Osiris, who had by then become the Great God of all necropolises. One of the reasons for the cult's growth was the patronage lavished on it by the Middle Kingdom rulers, especially at Abydos in the 12th Dynasty. This climaxed in the reign of Senusret III, whose 'cenotaph' at Abydos was the first royal monument to be erected there in the Middle Kingdom. A decree from the time of the 13th Dynasty ruler Wegaf (usurped by Neferhotep I) forbids tombs to be built on the processional way at Abydos. Sobekhotep III also erected stelae for several members of his family there, and Neferhotep I went to Abydos to take part in the mysteries of Osiris in the second year of his reign, erecting a stele to commemorate this event. Given the potency of Osiris and Abydos in terms of legitimizing royal power, the 13th Dynasty rulers' interest in Abydos may have been due to their mainly non-royal background, but the same cannot be said for the 12th Dynasty rulers. The growing influence of Osiris must have derived to some

This 12th Dynasty wand from Thebes is made from a hippopotamus tusk; its carved decoration includes depictions of the god Bes and other magical figures.

extent from active promotion of the site of Abydos and the so-called mysteries of Osiris. Some details of this set of rites are mentioned on a 12th-Dynasty stele (now in the Berlin Museum) that was set up at Abydos by Ikhernofret, the organizer of the annual festival during the reign of Senusret III.

The growth of the Osirian cult was accompanied by a cultural phenomenon sometimes described as the 'democratization of the afterlife': the extension of once-royal funerary privileges to ordinary people. Large numbers of stelae at Abydos in particular show that it was becoming increasingly common for private individuals to take part in the rites of Osiris, thus receiving blessings that had once been restricted to kings. As a result of this development, the funerary beliefs and rites of the entire population began to change. One of the earliest such changes was the practice of decorating non-royal coffins with the Coffin Texts, a combination of extracts from the royal Pyramid Texts with new funerary compositions, which emerged during the First Intermediate Period (see Chapter 6). In the mid-12th Dynasty, however, the use of these texts suddenly ceased, primarily as a result of further funerary changes, such as the introduction of the mummiform coffin, which, because of its more irregular shape, was less suited to long inscriptions of religious text.

Another religious development of the Middle Kingdom was the idea that all people (not just the king) had a *ba*, or spiritual force. The most evocative evi-

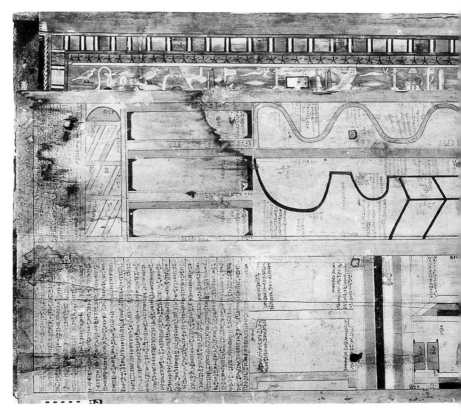

In the early- to mid-12th Dynasty, the floors of coffins began to be decorated with maps showing the routes to the underworld. Here, the interior of the 12th Dynasty wooden outer coffin of Gua from Deir el-Bersha (length of coffin 2.6 metres) is decorated with extracts from the so-called *Book of Two Ways*.

dence for this is the literary text, the *Dialogue between a Man Tired of Life and his 'Ba'*, which must be the world's earliest debate on the issue of suicide—a powerful philosophical treatise. There was also a noticeable emphasis on 'personal piety' (that is, direct personal access to deities rather than via the king or priests, a religious concept that further increased in popularity during the New Kingdom). Stelae from the Middle Kingdom stress the piety of their deceased owners, and out of this grew the concept of the 'negative confession' (ritual lists of misdemeanours that the deceased claimed not to have committed). Stelae themselves became popular memorials, especially those decorated with *wedjat*-eyes, the paramount symbol of protection, but other insignia (the *shen*-ring and the winged sun-disc, for instance)—like those found on royal stelae—also appeared during this period.

Royal mortuary complexes of the 11th and 12th Dynasties underwent considerable changes in design as the kings sought for the most appropriate architectural form to reflect their religious beliefs. Engineers and architects reached great heights of mastery, and the masons exceeded the considerable skills of their Old Kingdom counterparts. These skills were put to use not only in the service of the royal complexes, but also in the creation of larger and more skilfully constructed temples. In this period we find the complex internal engineering of the royal pyramids and structural experimentation in architecture,

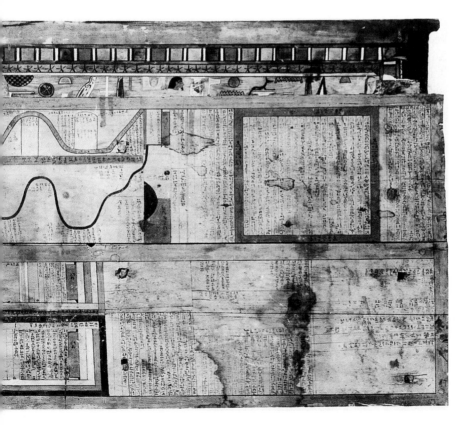

such as the terraced ambulatories of Mentuhotep II at Deir el-Bahri, the pylons and triple shrine of Mentuhotep III on the 'hill of Thoth' at Thebes, and the galleries of Senusret II in his pyramid at Lahun. Relief carving, previously found only in Old Kingdom mortuary complexes, now decorated the walls of Middle Kingdom temples for the gods, as well as kings. It was in this period, too, that the vast temple complex at Karnak was inaugurated and the once commanding temples and irrigation schemes of the Faiyum were built.

Experimentation is also to be found in the regional tombs of the nomarchs from the 11th Dynasty onwards: they indicate the world-view of these officials, with their interests in hunting, fishing, and wrestling matches, and their fascination with the exotic world of the Asiatics. The large, lavishly decorated rock-cut tombs usually featured pillared façades, and the tombs themselves were elevated above the burials of the members of their 'courts', scattered across the slopes below. The nomarchs' coffins—especially those from Deir el-Bersha—carry the finest artwork of all those that have survived. In a number of instances they are decorated with the earliest copies of the *Book of Two Ways*, which was a set of instructions for safely reaching the afterlife. As the nomarch's office diminished in importance, however, the character of the provincial necropolis changed: the size and number of the smaller tombs increased and there was less overt 'ranking' among the positions of graves. In the capital, on the other hand, things were rather different: the officials' tombs were located in the royal necropolises rather than their local family cemeteries, the *mastaba*-tombs became the preferred style of private tomb, and the provision of a memorial at Abydos became imperative for all.

By the Middle Kingdom, mummification had become much more widespread, but it was not effective. Although evisceration was more common, bodies were badly mummified and the residual flesh has seldom survived, despite the fact that their exterior wrappings were often lavish. The mummies were given cartonnage masks, which were often beautifully painted, and the bodies were placed on their sides in rectangular coffins oriented with regard both to the main compass points and to the texts written on their tomb walls.

A further significant change in funerary practices was the introduction of the *shabti*, a word that is sometimes also spelled *ushabti* or *shawabti*, and that may mean 'stick', 'answerer', or perhaps both. *Shabti*s were statuettes made from a variety of materials (wax, clay, pottery, faience, wood, or stone) which were meant to act as magical substitutes when work had to be done by the tomb-owner for Osiris. The earliest examples, dating to the time of Mentuhotep II, often took the form of small naked figures with no funerary formulas written on them, while others were mummiform in shape. These figurines were evidently three-dimensional reminders of Coffin Text spell 472, which appeared inside a few Middle Kingdom coffins. By the late 12th Dynasty, however, the text had begun to be written on the *shabti* itself. It is thought that the role of the *shabti* might be linked either with the corvée system by which each individual was obliged to work for the king, or with the work that ordinary people had to carry out in the maintenance of their local waterways. Like human workers, the later *shabti*s carried hoes and seed bags with which to undertake their tasks.

The Cultural Achievements of the Middle Kingdom

The Middle Kingdom was a time when art, architecture, and religion reached new heights but, above all, it was an age of confidence in writing, no doubt encouraged by the growth of the 'middle class' and the scribal sector of society, which was in turn due in no small measure to the expansion of the bureaucracy under Senusret III. Many different literary forms flourished, and the ancient Egyptians themselves appear to have regarded it as the 'classical' era of litera-ture. Such narratives as the *Story of Sinuhe* (the popularity of which is indicated by the many copies that have survived), *The Shipwrecked Sailor*, and the fantas-tical episodes in Papyrus Westcar were all composed in the Middle Kingdom, while religious and philosophical works (such as the *Hymn to Hapy*, the *Satire of the Trades*, and the *Dialogue between a Man Tired of Life and his 'Ba'*) were also very popular. Furthermore, a wide variety of official documents have sur-vived, including reports, letters, and accounts, which not only help to round out the overall picture of the period but also indicate that literacy was more widespread than it had been during the Old Kingdom.

Under the direction of the Middle Kingdom rulers, Egypt had its eyes opened to the wider world of Nubia, Asia, and the Aegean, benefiting from the ex-change of materials, products, and ideas. The Middle Kingdom was an age of tremendous invention, great vision, and colossal projects, yet there was also careful and elegant attention to detail in the creation of the smallest items of everyday use and decoration. This more human scale is present in the pervad-ing sense that individual human beings had become more significant in cosmic terms, whether in their obligations to the state (through taxation and the corvée work), their provisions for burial, or their increased presence within the litera-ture of the times. Neither Sinuhe nor the 'shipwrecked sailor' could ever have been central characters in any Old Kingdom tale, but these individuals sit com-fortably in the literature of the Middle Kingdom, which was an age of greater humanity.

8 THE SECOND INTERMEDIATE PERIOD

(c.1650–1550 BC)

JANINE BOURRIAU

The Second Intermediate Period is defined by the division of Egypt—the fragmentation of the Two Lands. 'Why do I contemplate my strength while there is one Great Man in Avaris and another in Kush, sitting united with an Asiatic and a Nubian while each man possesses his slice of Egypt.' This was the complaint of the Theban King Kamose (1555–1550 BC) at the end of the 17th Dynasty.

The beginning of the Second Intermediate Period is marked by the abandonment of the Residence at Lisht, 32 km. south of Memphis, and the establishment of the royal court and seat of government at Thebes, the Southern City. The end of the period came with the conquest of the capital of the Hyksos kings at Avaris in the eastern Delta by Ahmose, King of Thebes. The reunification of Egypt which Ahmose achieved was not to be broken again for over 400 years. The time between these two events was approximately 150 years. The final pharaoh at Lisht was probably Merneferra Ay (c.1695–1685 BC) because he is the last ruler of the 13th Dynasty (following the sequence given in the Turin Canon king-list) who has inscribed monuments in both Upper and Lower Egypt. The conquest of Avaris can be dated much more closely, between years 18 and 22 of Ahmose, 1532–1528 BC on the chronology used here.

In the course of a mere six generations (each calculated as twenty-five years), profound cultural and political changes took place, but the disunity of Egypt meant that they happened in different ways and at different rates in the various regions. Rather than presenting the history of the period as a single narrative, therefore, it seems better to describe it from the vantage point of each of the principal regions of Egypt, from north to south. The regions can only be

Facing: round-topped limestone stele of the late 13th Dynasty ruler Wepwawet-emsaf from Abydos, showing the king in the presence of the god Wepwawet-Ra, Lord of Abydos. The name of this king is not otherwise attested, apart from a possible mention among the hieratic graffiti on the walls of the rock tomb of Amenemhat at Beni Hasan.

defined by our sources and, given the gaps in the evidence, it is likely that the country was even more fragmented than we currently think. It is only after the beginning of the war between the Hyksos and Theban kings, eventually involving the whole of Egypt, that a single historical narrative seems appropriate.

The written sources present peculiar problems, due to abundance rather than scarcity, but the difficulty of integrating what they tell us with the archaeological evidence remains profound. They may be divided into six categories: the king-lists, of which the most detailed is the hieratic papyrus known as the Turin Canon (compiled from pre-existing lists at Memphis during the reign of Rameses II); Manetho's *Aegyptiaca*, a history written in the third century BC but surviving only in fragments excerpted by later chroniclers; contemporary and non-contemporary royal inscriptions written as 'propaganda', but for that reason, creating a vivid and dramatic *mise-en-scène*; contemporary private inscriptions, particularly 'funerary biographies'; the records of administration, both public and private; and, finally, literary and scientific texts such as Papyrus Sallier I and the Rhind Mathematical Papyrus. Such texts are always valuable, but ambiguities can be introduced because the most significant ones, the royal inscriptions, have often been removed from their original contexts. Most of the Theban royal stelae were found broken and reused in later buildings, while at Avaris none of the inscribed stone elements in the monumental mud-brick buildings of the Hyksos kings has been found in the stratum to which it originally belonged.

Archaeological sources have their own pitfalls, the most fundamental being gaps in the record either through poor survival or patchy excavation. No sites of the period have been excavated in the central or western Nile Delta, or in Middle Egypt between Maiyana and Deir Rifa. The mud-brick fortresses of the second-cataract region in Lower Nubia tell the history of relations between Egypt and Kush, but, after only partial excavation in the 1960s UNESCO campaign, they were lost in the waters of Lake Nasser. What remains is a large but sporadic patchwork of information. The adoption of a regional approach to the evidence serves to emphasize a recurring theme in Egypt's history: the rivalry between Upper and Lower Egypt, which was at its most extreme in the battle between Thebes and Avaris at the end of the period.

The Territory of Avaris

The question that lies at the heart of the Second Intermediate Period is the nature of the Hyksos. Most histories depend upon written sources, and, with few exceptions (the Rhind Papyrus is one), these emanate from the Egyptian side. There is no Hyksos counterpart to the Kamose texts. What we have instead is evidence from the systematic excavation of their capital, Avaris (Tell el-Dab'a). We now know what their palaces, temples, houses, and graves looked like, and we can observe how their culture evolved through time, but the Hyksos were not a single or simple phenomenon.

Aamu was the contemporary term used to distinguish the people of Avaris from Egyptians. It was used long before the Second Intermediate Period and was still in use long after (Rameses II, for instance, uses it of his opponents at Kadesh) in order to denote, in a general sense, the inhabitants of Syria–Palestine. Egyptologists conventionally translate *aamu* as 'Asiatics' (that is, inhabitants of Western Asia). The term 'Hyksos', on the other hand, derives, via Greek, from the Egyptian epithet *hekau khasut*, 'rulers of foreign (lit. mountainous) countries' and was applied only to the rulers of the Asiatics. In itself it held no pejorative meaning except to denote a lower status than that of the Egyptian king, and was used both by the Egyptians and by the Hyksos kings of themselves.

When their etymology can be established, all private and royal personal names of Asiatics in Egypt at this time derive from West Semitic languages. Earlier suggestions that some were Hurrian or even Hittite have not been confirmed. References to Asiatics are numerous in the Middle Kingdom: they worked in a variety of occupations, sometimes adopting Egyptian names while retaining the designation 'Asiatic' (*aamu*). These immigrants were thought to be economic migrants, but an inscription of the 12th Dynasty ruler Amenemhat II records, in unmistakable language, a campaign by sea to the Lebanese coast that resulted in a list of booty including 1,554 Asiatics. Such campaigns fit the archaeological evidence from Tell el-Habua, which shows that the eastern border of Egypt was as heavily fortified as the southern one. Tell el-Habua is a large

Plan of the historical landscape of Tell el-Dab'a (site of the Hyksos capital, Avaris). Excavated areas shown black.

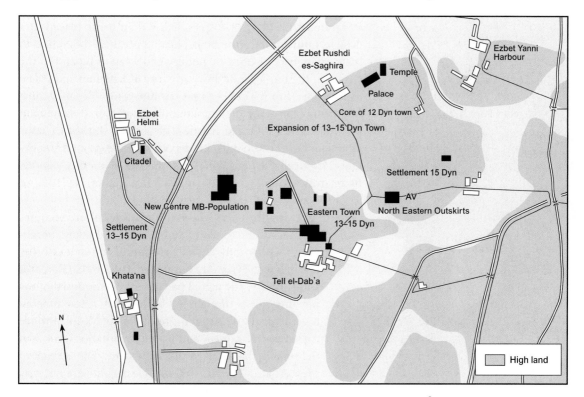

site situated to the east of Tell el-Dabʿa, dating from the Middle Kingdom onwards. Mohammed Maksoud, the excavator, has found traces of a major installation, probably a fort, judging from the thickness of the walls, underneath settlement strata of the Second Intermediate Period. By analogy with the Nubian second-cataract forts, patrols would doubtless have gone out to the surrounding desert recording in dispatches sent to the capital the movement of all people wishing to 'cross down into Egypt'.

There is evidence from Tell el-Dabʿa that a community of Asiatics, albeit very Egyptianized, existed there as early as the early 13th Dynasty. So far, however, this is the only convincing archaeological evidence for a population of Asiatics within Egypt (but living differently from the Egyptians) during the Middle Kingdom. There are also references in contemporary texts to 'camps of Asiatic workmen'.

It is likely that the oldest settlement at Tell el-Dabʿa, which dates to the First Intermediate Period, was deliberately built as a component in a defensive system constructed to protect the eastern boundary. During the late 12th and early 13th Dynasties the site expanded enormously, including the emergence of a settlement populated by Asiatics. The non-Egyptian character of the community is evident from the layout of the houses (apparently following a Syrian model) and from the fact that tombs were integrated with the living areas rather than being placed in a cemetery outside the settlement. Not only are there differences in material culture, defined by pottery and weapon types, but the nature of the burials indicates a mixture of Egyptian and Palestinian traits. From a robber's pit cut into a tomb chapel come fragments of an over-life-size limestone statue of a seated man holding a throwstick; the artistic style and the clothes are non-Egyptian, but the size indicates a person of the greatest importance. Ironically, the best parallel to this statue is a tiny wooden figure from a Middle Kingdom tomb at Beni Hasan, depicting an Asiatic woman and her baby.

In the next stratum (d/1), Middle Bronze Age culture becomes more pronounced, and tombs include burials of donkeys, sometimes in pairs. Other finds include an impression of a cylinder seal in North Syrian style, fragments of Minoan Kamares ware pottery, and a gold pectoral of two opposed hunting dogs, also thought to be Minoan. Such objects, together with the 'ordinary' testament of Middle Bronze Age imported pottery and Egyptian imitations, confirm the mixed character of the settlement. The origins of these Asiatics—if they had a single origin—are not easy

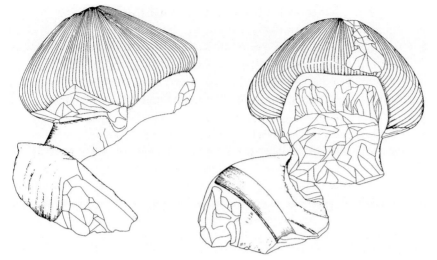

Far left: wooden statuette of an Asiatic woman from a 12th Dynasty burial at Beni Hasan, which is the nearest parallel to the colossal statue at Tell el-Dabʿa. *Left*: fragment of a colossal statue of an Asiatic from a robber's pit in a tomb chapel at Tell el-Dabʿa.

to determine. The Asiatic culture was certainly heavily adulterated by the underlying Egyptian one, the bulk of the pottery was Egyptian (although dropping from 80 per cent to 60 per cent by stratum d/1) and the administration, judging by the titles of officials on scarabs, was carried out on the Egyptian model. Parallels for the foreign traits have been found at southern Palestinian sites such as Tell el-Ajjul, at the Syrian site of Ebla, and at Byblos (in modern Lebanon). In a study of the non-Egyptian pottery from Tell el-Dabʿa, Patrick McGovern has postulated that most of it originated from the cities of Southern Palestine. Since the wealth of the late Middle Kingdom town at Tell el-Dabʿa centred around the seagoing trade along the Levantine coast, the caravan route across northern Sinai to Palestine (and perhaps also expeditions to the turquoise mines), the idiosyncratic culture of its inhabitants should not surprise us.

The culture of the people of Tell el-Dabʿa is not static but rapidly develops new traits and discards old ones. This makes the characterization of each stratum in terms of its architecture, burial customs, pottery, metal and other artefacts relatively clear, but leaves unanswered the question of why and how this cultural mixing and rapid development took place. One hypothesis is that the basic population of Egyptians received from time to time a new influx of settlers, first from the region of Lebanon and Syria, and subsequently from Palestine and Cyprus. The élite among them married local women—a suggestion supported by preliminary study of the human remains, although bone preservation is poor.

Diagram showing the interrelationships of regional chronologies in the eastern Mediterranean in the Middle Bronze Age.

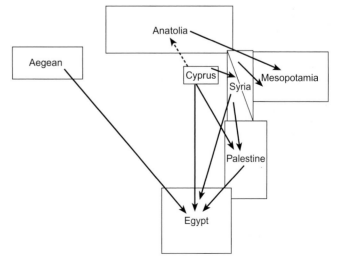

Tell el-Dabʿa has provided hundreds of artefacts that can be recognized as belonging to the well-known period of the Middle Bronze Age II A–C of Syria–Palestine. This material is found in nine strata (H–D/2), the upper and lower ends of which have been linked by the Austrian excavator Manfred Bietak to the reigns of two Egyptian kings, respectively Amenemhat IV (1786–1777 BC) and Ahmose (1550–1525 BC). He divides the resulting period by nine, allotting roughly thirty years to each stratum and thus obtaining a framework of absolute dates for his relative sequence. However, when these dates have been imported to sites in Syria–Palestine where objects similar to those from Tell el-Dabʿa have been found, there have sometimes been clashes with the existing chronology. The resulting fierce debates, when resolved, will eventually demand radical revisions not only in the dating of strata at Tell el-Dabʿa but in the methods used for dating the Middle Bronze Age over the whole east Mediterranean region.

The initial expansion of Tell el-Dabʿa was checked temporarily by an epidemic. In several parts of the site, Bietak has found large communal graves in which many bodies were placed, without any discernible ceremony. Thereafter, from stratum F onwards, the patterns of both settlements and cemeteries suggest a less egalitarian society than before. Large houses with smaller ones fitted in around them, more elaborate buildings in the centre than on the edge of the settlement, servants buried in front of the tombs of their masters: all suggest the social dominance of a wealthy élite group.

At this point in the city's history, its identification with the textually attested Hyksos capital of Avaris becomes clear. Two limestone door jambs were found naming the 'good god, lord of the two lands, son of Ra of his body, Nehesy'. Inscribed fragments from Tell el-Habua, Tanis, and Tell el-Muqdam provide further titles and epithets of this man, 'beloved of Seth, lord of Avaris, eldest king's son'. The last epithet is a title that implies high military rank but does not mean that the holder was literally 'son of the king'. The reference to the god Seth shows that his cult was already established, and that he was the local god of Avaris, just as Amun was the patron deity of Thebes. Seth's cult may have evolved from a blending of a pre-existing cult at Heliopolis with a cult of the North Syrian weather-god Baal Zephon, which was introduced by the Asiatics.

Nehesy is listed in the Turin Canon in the group generally identified as the 14th Dynasty, the capital of which—according to Manetho—was Xois in the western Delta. Nehesy was a high official who for a short time (no regnal years are known) assumed a royal status at Avaris. Probably Nehesy was an Egyptian, or perhaps a Nubian (the literal meaning of Nehesy); nothing in his inscriptions suggests otherwise. The king whom he originally served was probably still reigning from the city of Itjtawy, near Lisht, which was not abandoned until after 1685 BC, although Sobekhotep IV (c.1725 BC) was the last really powerful king of the 13th Dynasty. After Sobekhotep's reign, it is likely that the unity of Egypt began to break up, and an obvious candidate for elevation into an independent kingdom was the region around the rich and powerful city of Avaris.

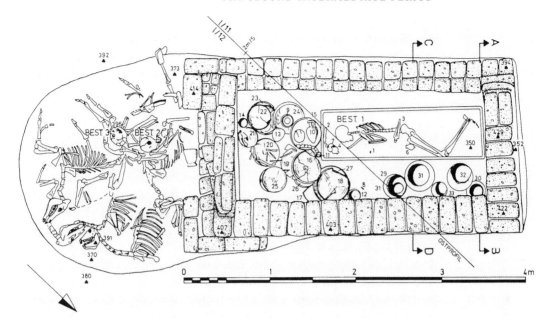

How far did the authority of King Nehesy extend? If we judge from the sites where his name occurs, his territory appears to have encompassed the eastern Delta from Tell el-Muqdam to Tell el-Habua, but the universal practice of usurpation and quarrying of earlier monuments complicates the picture. Given that the only examples that were certainly found at the sites where they once stood are those from Tell el-Habua and Tell el-Dabʿa, his kingdom may actually have been much smaller.

One of the Second Intermediate Period burials at Tell el-Dabʿa seems to confirm that the structure of Egyptian bureaucracy still existed at Avaris. The tomb owner is identified by a scarab on his finger as the Deputy Treasurer, Aamu ('the Asiatic'). His burial was an extremely wealthy one, but it was characterized by several non-Egyptian traits: the body lay in a contracted position (not extended, as is normal for Egyptian burials), the weapons and pottery were of Syro-Palestinian type, and in front of the tomb five or six donkeys had been buried. Such a high official would normally be interred close to his king, having expected to spend his life close to the royal residence, the seat of government, which, for him, was Avaris.

If the Danish Egyptologist K. S. B. Ryholt's reconstruction of the Turin Canon is accepted, in the columns allotted to the group of kings which include

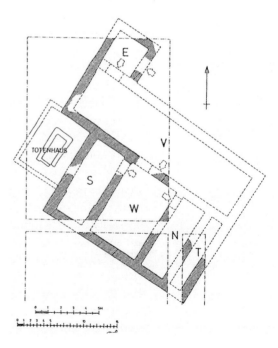

Above: grave of the Deputy Treasurer Aamu, from Tell el-Dabʿa. *Below*: typical house from strata F-E/3 at Tell el-Dabʿa—note the mortuary complex attached to the house.

Nehesy, there are 32 names, 17 lost names and two gaps, one covering the five predecessors of Nehesy and one of unknown length indicated by the scribe as present in the earlier manuscript from which the Turin Canon was copied.

For all except five of the named kings, the length of the reign is either missing or given as less than one year. Apart from Nehesy, only three of them appear elsewhere: Kings Nebsenra and Sekheperenra on a jar and a scarab respectively, and King Merdjedefra, who is shown on a contemporary stele, accompanied by 'the seal-bearer of the King, the treasurer, Renisoneb'. The findspot is unknown, but the eastern Delta, and more precisely Saft el-Hinna, about 30 km. north of Tell el-Yahudiya, has been suggested. The king is shown offering to Soped, Lord of the East, a god whose sphere was the desert routes to the Red Sea and the turquoise mines of Sinai. His cult centre in the 22nd Dynasty was Saft el-Hinna. The stela of Merdjedefra has significance beyond confirming the existence of a minor king, because it confirms that the names of the 14th Dynasty kings are not fictitious, although they are unlikely to represent a single line of kings ruling one after the other from the same place.

The inscription of Nehesy is the first contemporary evidence of the fragmentation of the Egyptian kingdom. According to Bietak, Nehesy fits into the relative chronology of Tell el-Dab'a at stratum F (or b/3), corresponding to the late 13th Dynasty. Thereafter, no single ruler was able to control the whole of Egypt, until the conquest of Avaris. Over 105 royal names are preserved from the period, and most of these occur in the Turin Canon. The implication of this is that records were kept at Memphis of the names of all these kings, however short their reigns, and however localized their rule. Ryholt's painstaking reconstruction of the damaged papyrus uses fibre matches as well as textual analysis and as a result we have a much more coherent record. The royal names now fall into four groups which correspond to Dynasties 14–17 of Manetho. Dynasties 14 and 15 were based in the eastern Delta with their capital at Avaris (although the 15th Dynasty also controlled part of Egypt south of Memphis, see below) and Dynasties 16 and 17 were centred at Thebes in Upper Egypt. The fragmentary nature of the papyrus allows for more than one interpretation even if Ryholt's physical reconstruction of the papyrus is accepted. One of his most debatable and far-reaching ideas is to assign the earlier group of Theban kings to Manetho's Dynasty 16. Africanus, the most accurate of the excerpters, described Dynasty 16 as 'Shepherd (Hyksos) Kings', while Eusebius records them as Theban. Ryholt's interpretation is followed here.

There are a few kings whose names occur on monuments but who cannot be identified in the Turin Canon (perhaps having been listed on a portion that is now missing). One such ruler is Sekerher, who bore a full Egyptian titulary (three out of his five names are preserved), but described himself as a *heka khasut* ('ruler of foreign countries'); his inscription is preserved on a door jamb found reused in an early 18th Dynasty building at Tell el-Dab'a. Bietak identifies him with Salitis, whose name is preserved in Josephus' version of Manetho's history as the conqueror of Memphis.

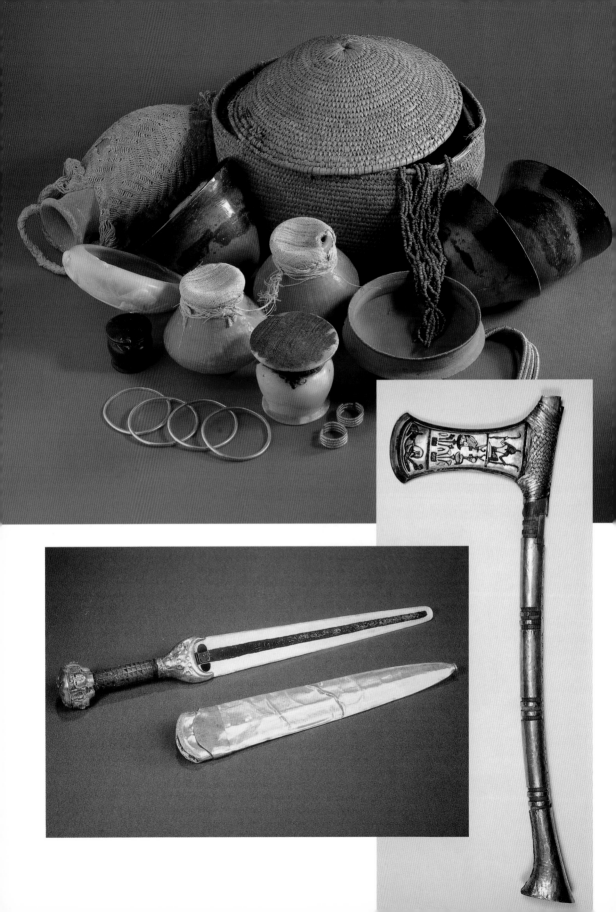

There is, however, also a large group of about 15 royal names that occur only on scarabs. These personal names are sometimes Egyptian, sometimes West Semitic, and are preceded by epithets such as 'the good god', 'the son of Ra', and 'the ruler of foreign countries'. The first two epithets were held by Egyptian kings for many hundreds of years, referring in the most general terms to the status of king. The term *nesu* ('king'), which is used in Egyptian sources such as the Turin Canon, is never employed to describe these rulers. Stylistically, the scarabs belong to a set of types that were made and used in both Egypt and Palestine. Their archaeological contexts show that they belong to the period following the 13th Dynasty, and their style links them with scarabs bearing the names of the kings of the 14th and 15th Dynasties. It is possible that we have here further examples of officials with a purely local authority abrogating to themselves royal epithets on their seals at a time and place where normally rigid protocols were no longer enforceable.

Without confirmation from other sources, it seems unsafe to use the distribution of scarabs as an indicator of the extent of the authority of such 'kings' or to use changes in scarab design and shape to place them into a chronological sequence. The finds from Tell el-Dabʿa do not, to date, help us to place any of them, except indirectly. It is likely, given the model of Middle Bronze Age IIB Palestine and a literal interpretation of the names adopted by Sekerher, that he was the overlord to whom minor kings paid tribute. If so, this would explain the use of the title 'ruler of foreign countries' both on the scarabs of otherwise unknown men and on the inscriptions of the rulers of Avaris.

Bietak associates the final Hyksos phase at Tell el-Dabʿa (strata b/1–a/2; E/2–D/2; VI–V) with Manetho's 15th Dynasty, and a fragment of the Turin Canon preserves '6 rulers of foreign countries ruling for 108 years'. Only the name of the last one, Khamudi, can be read. Sekerher, Apepi, and Yanassi, the son of Khyan, are recorded from Tell el-Dabʿa, and the first and last can be identified with Manetho's Salitis and Iannan. All evidence, written and archaeological, suggests that the authority of these rulers was very much greater than that of their predecessors. The father-to-son succession of two of them, and the exceptionally long reign of Apepi (at least forty years), shows that a real dynasty, in the sense of, for example, the Egyptian 12th Dynasty, was now ruling from Avaris.

At its largest extent, the city itself covered an area of almost 4 sq. km., which would have made it twice as large as it had been in the 13th Dynasty and three times larger than Hazor, the largest Middle Bronze Age II A–C site in Palestine. In the latest Hyksos stratum, D/2, a citadel was built on previously unsettled ground on the western edge of the city commanding the river, and a watchtower some 200 m. to the south-east guarding the land approach. Around these, an enormous enclosure wall was built, with walls 6.2 m. wide, later enlarged to 8.5 m., and buttressed at intervals. The fortifications were built over extensive gardens, which had originally been part of a large palace complex.

The zenith of the Hyksos period is the reign of Aauserra Apepi (*c.*1555 BC),

Facing, above: the intact burial of a late 17th Dynasty woman and her child at Thebes included six Kerma-ware beakers alongside the coffin.

Facing, below left: a ceremonial gold dagger was given by the early 18th Dynasty ruler Ahmose I to his mother Queen Ahhotep, and was included among the funerary equipment in her tomb at Thebes.

Facing, below right: the early 18th Dynasty tomb of Queen Ahhotep at Dra Abu el-Naga in Thebes included this axe, made from copper, gold, electrum, gemstones, and wood, which belonged to her son Ahmose I. This weapon suggests that early 18th Dynasty art was already being influenced by motifs and styles from the east Mediterranean.

The stratigraphy and
chronology of Tell el-Dabʿa.

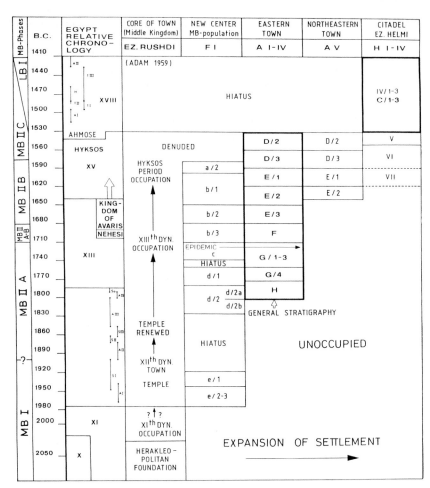

despite the fact that two Theban kings led campaigns against him. There are
signs of a conscious revival of Egyptian scribal traditions, indispensable for creating and controlling the complex bureaucracy needed to govern in the Egyptian mode. On the palette of a scribe called Atu, Auserra is described as 'a scribe
of Ra, taught by Thoth himself . . . with numerous [successful] deeds on the day
when he reads faithfully all the difficult [passages] of the writings, as flows the
Nile'. It was in the thirty-third year of his reign that the Rhind Mathematical
Papyrus was copied, a task that could have been undertaken only by a scribe
trained to the highest level of his craft and with access to a specialized archive of
mathematical texts such as could hardly have existed outside the Temple of
Ptah in Memphis. A stele from Memphis of post-New Kingdom date records
the genealogy of a line of priests going back to the 11th Dynasty. It also preserves
the names of reigning kings, and records Apepi and Sharek for the period
before Ahmose. Fragments of a shrine were found at Tell el-Dabʿa commemorating Apepi and his sister Tany and dedicated by two Asiatics whose scribes
adapted their West Semitic names to the Egyptian hieroglyphic script. A plate
inscribed in fine hieroglyphs for Apepi's daughter Herit was also found in the
tomb of the 18th Dynasty ruler Amenhotep I (1525–1504 BC).

194

As a cultural phenomenon, the Hyksos have been described as 'peculiarly Egyptian'. The mixture of Egyptian and Syro-Palestinian cultural traits—as expressed in objects from strata D/3 and D/2 (= reign of Apepi) at Tell el-Dab'a—can be recognized over a wide area of the Delta, from west to east: Tell Fauziya and Tell Geziret el-Faras, west of the Tanitic Nile branch and including Farasha, Tell el-Yahudiya, Tell el-Maskhuta, and Tell el-Habua to the east of it. These sites are all very much smaller than Tell el-Dab'a, and the principal period of occupation coincides in each case with the latest Hyksos strata, but two of them, Tell el-Maskhuta and Tell el-Yahudiya, had come to an end before the period represented by the last Hyksos stratum (D/2) at Tell el-Dab'a. Tell el-Maskhuta and its satellite sites are located in the Wadi Tumilat, which led to one of the main routes across northern Sinai to Palestine. It was a small settlement, perhaps only seasonally occupied. The wealth of Avaris derived from trade not only with Palestine and the Levant, but also, in its latest phase, especially with Cyprus. The Kamose stelae list the commodities imported by the Hyksos ('chariots and horses, ships, timber, gold, lapis lazuli, silver, turquoise, bronze, axes without number, oil, incense, fat, and honey'), but there is very little surviving evidence regarding the goods that the Hyksos kings were providing in exchange.

The ruler of Avaris claimed to be King of Upper and Lower Egypt, although from the stelae of Kamose we know that Hermopolis marked his theoretical southern boundary and Cusae, a little further south, the specific border point. This region includes both Memphis and Itjtawy, the capital of the 12th and 13th Dynasty kings. How was the authority of the king of Avaris exercised in this region and can we recognize the distinctive culture of the eastern Delta there?

Memphis: The Mansion of Ptah

Josephus claims to be quoting directly from Manetho in his description of the conquest and occupation of Egypt by the Hyksos:

> By main force they easily seized it without striking a blow; and having overpowered the rulers of the land, they then burned our cities ruthlessly, razed to the ground the temples of the gods . . . Finally, they appointed as king one of their number whose name was Salitis. He had his seat at Memphis, levying tribute from Upper and Lower Egypt, and always leaving garrisons behind in the most advantageous positions.

This picture of Hyksos rule is confirmed by the very fact that the Theban ruler Kamose rejected his status as vassal. The strict control of the border at Cusae, the imposition of taxes on all Nile traffic, and the existence of garrisons of Asiatics led by Egyptian commanders are all mentioned in the Kamose texts. The Hyksos kings seem to be following the model set up by the 12th Dynasty kings in their rule over Nubia, for which the bureaucratic and military institutions were probably still in place. The key role of Memphis is also clear from Kamose's account. Avaris was the Hyksos king's home city, the centre of his power, but Egypt, even the northern part of it, could not be ruled from the eastern Delta. Ruling Egypt meant controlling the Nile and every ruler of Egypt has done this from the apex of the Delta, the region of Memphis and modern Cairo.

Indisputable evidence of destruction and looting by the Hyksos is rare. Four colossal sphinxes of the 12th Dynasty ruler Amenemhat III and two statues of the 13th Dynasty ruler Smenkhera were found at Tanis, inscribed with the names of Aqenenra Apepi (another name of Aauserra Apepi). Their original dedication inscriptions to Ptah indicate that they were first set up at Memphis. It is usually assumed that they were looted by Apepi, taken to Avaris, and then removed in Ramessid times to Tanis, but all that we can be sure of is that Apepi claimed them by writing his name on them, and they may never have left Memphis at all until Ramessid times. Nevertheless, at least one royal monument of a 13th Dynasty king was violated: the pyramidion from the top of King Merneferra Ay's pyramid, which was probably built at Saqqara, was found at Faqus, close to Tell el-Dabʿa.

There is, to date, nothing to show that the Hyksos kings commissioned funerary monuments in the Memphite tradition in the Western Desert overlooking the city. However, we need to remember the wholesale demolition at Tell el-Dabʿa by the victorious Ahmose and the greed of later kings for building stone before we accept too readily an argument *ex silentio*. For example, two blocks, one of limestone and one of granite, carrying the names of Khyan (*c*.1600 BC) and Aauserra Apepi, have been found in the temple of Hathor at Gebelein. Since there is no unequivocal evidence that the Hyksos ever controlled this part of Egypt, let alone built monuments so far south, the blocks are more likely to originate from Memphis and to have been brought to Gebelein during the New Kingdom.

During the 1980s, as part of a survey of the vast ruin field of Memphis by the Egypt Exploration Society, a small area of the town was excavated, revealing strata of the Second Intermediate Period. The culture of this community, revealed by pottery, domestic architecture, mud sealings with scarab impressions, metalwork, and beads, is entirely Egyptian (especially when compared with that of Tell el-Dabʿa) and shows an unbroken cultural development from the 13th Dynasty. Similarities in Egyptian ceramics allow strata at Memphis to be related to those at Tell el-Dabʿa, and this reveals a major break at both sites after the last Hyksos stratum, Tell el-Dabʿa D/2. There follows at Memphis a sequence of sandy deposits in which no permanent structures were built and in which the ceramics contain increasing quantities of Upper Egyptian types dating to the very beginning of the 18th Dynasty. The subsequent phase shows buildings aligned quite differently and ceramics of pronounced early 18th Dynasty style. These sandy deposits are thought to coincide with the period of the Hyksos–Theban wars.

What is missing at Memphis is the presence of Middle Bronze Age traits such as those that are visible at Tell el-Dabʿa from the late 12th Dynasty onwards. Imports and Egyptian copies of Palestinian pottery are present at both sites, but at Memphis they represent less than 2 per cent and at Tell el-Dabʿa, 20–40 per cent, of the repertoire. There is no cultural break at Memphis from the earliest strata excavated, which are mid-13th Dynasty, until the end of the Second Intermediate Period. Can this pattern be observed at any of the other major centres of the region?

At Saqqara, the necropolis closest to Memphis, the focus for activity in the late Middle Kingdom was the mortuary temple of King Teti (2345–2323 BC). There are private tombs and evidence of the continuous celebration of the cult of the king until the first half of the 13th Dynasty. As far as the late 13th Dynasty and Second Intermediate Period are concerned, there is so far only one isolated intact burial comprising a man placed in a rectangular coffin. The man's name, Abdu, suggests that he was an Asiatic, and he was furnished with a dagger inscribed with the name of Nahman, a follower of King Apepi. Since the dagger is the only part of the find that has so far been published, it is not known whether the burial compares with those of similar date from Tell el-Dabʿa, but the rectangular coffin suggests that it does not. Nor do we know if the dagger is contemporary with the burial or an heirloom. Apart from this ambiguous find, there is clear evidence in the same area of an extensive cemetery of rich surface graves belonging to the reigns of the early 18th Dynasty rulers Ahmose and Amenhotep I.

At Dahshur, site of the mortuary complexes of two great kings of the 12th Dynasty, Senusret III and Amenemhat III, ritual activity must have continued at least into the early 13th Dynasty, because King Awibra Hor was buried there at that time. At some later date large mud-brick grain silos were built within the mortuary complex of Amenemhat III. When the silos had fallen into disrepair, they were used as convenient rubbish pits for the pottery discarded from a small nearby settlement. Similar pottery occurs at Memphis in strata below the sand deposits and at Tell el-Dabʿa in strata G/4 onwards. Its character is emphatically Middle Kingdom and Egyptian. It appears that buildings were erected on the sacred space at Dahshur some time after the early 13th Dynasty; these structures were associated with a settlement that continued to be occupied, although it is not yet clear how long this occupation lasted, except in relative terms. Thereafter there is no evidence of activity until Ramessid times. The 'silo' pottery at Dahshur is also present at Lahun, in the settlement which grew up close to the mortuary complex of Senusret II. Thereafter, at Lahun, there is a gap until pottery of the mid-18th Dynasty appears.

At Lisht, the necropolis closest to Itjtawy (the royal residence of the 12th and 13th Dynasty kings), the picture is more complex. A large private cemetery grew up around the pyramid of Amenemhat I, which eventually intruded into the royal funerary complex itself. Among these latest graves were a few fairly rich burials containing types of 'Tell el-Yahudiya' pottery vessels that occur both at Tell el-Yahudiya itself and at Tell el-Dabʿa in graves of strata D/3 and D/2 (that is, the strata dating to the end of the Hyksos period). These latest burials at Lisht are wholly Egyptian in character. A settlement of workers connected with the necropolis grew up during the 13th Dynasty in the same area, and some burial shafts were dug within house complexes both during and after their occupation. This un-Egyptian style of burial is paralleled at Tell el-Dab'a, but there is no further evidence to suggest that the inhabitants were not Egyptians. In the surface debris from the excavation of houses and graves were found two scarabs with the name of the 16th Dynasty ruler Swadjenra Nebererau I (*c*.1615–1595 BC). His dates, tentative though they are, fall within the range of those assigned by Bietak to D/3. There is no evidence of the 18th Dynasty at Lisht until the reign of Thutmose III.

Even this evidence both of the use of the necropolis at Lisht and of continuity of Middle Kingdom culture there until far into the Second Intermediate Period does not answer the question of when the king and his court moved from Itjtawy to Thebes. The last 13th Dynasty king known to have had monuments in the area is Merneferra Ay (*c*.1695–1685 BC). There is also the testimonial of an official called Horemkhauef, a chief inspector of priests who was sent to collect the temple statues of Horus of Nekhen (the local deity of Elkab) and of the goddess Isis. His funerary stele, found in the courtyard of his tomb at Elkab, describes a visit to Itjtawy in the course of this mission:

> Horus, avenger of his father, gave me a commission to the Residence, to fetch (thence) Horus of Nekhen together with his mother, Isis . . . He appointed me as commander of a ship and crew because he knew me to be a competent official of his temple, vigilant concerning his assignments. Then I fared downstream with good dispatch and I drew forth Horus of Nekhen in (my) hands together with his mother, this goddess, from the good office of Itjtawy in the presence of the king himself.

The divine images collected by Horemkhauef were presumably newly made or restored statuettes that had perhaps been used in a festival connected with the kingship. Significantly, therefore, the Residence appears at this time to have been the only place where craftsmen, scribes, and lector priests were able to make such images. This explains Horemkhauef's need to undertake a long journey and his pride in his success. Unfortunately for us, the king who sent him is never named. The making of such statues was one of the most significant acts of the Egyptian ruler, enabling him to validate his own divine status. References to the kings' creation of such images occur in all surviving royal annals going back to the beginning of the Old Kingdom. This tradition of sacred craftsmanship, of which the king was guardian, was evidently broken when the Residence was abandoned and ties with Memphis were cut.

One result of the loss of this artistic tradition was a break in what has been described as the 'hieroglyphic tradition'. The writing of the formulas used in funerary inscriptions changed because they were being produced under the influence of scribes trained in the cursive hieratic script (used in administrative documents), whereas previously the inscriptions had been created by the scribes who were specifically trained in the carving of hieroglyphic inscriptions on stone monuments. This change in the writing of the funerary formula can be used as a means of dating inscriptions to the period before or after the end of the Middle Kingdom. The writing on Horemkhauef's stele is of the post-Middle Kingdom type, which perhaps suggests that the political fragmentation may actually have taken place during his lifetime. A chronology has been deduced from genealogies of officials from Elkab recorded in inscriptions, and on this basis it is suggested that Horemkhauef's tomb was prepared between 1650 and 1630. If his visit to the Residence took place at the beginning of a twenty-year tenure of high office, it may date to between 1670 and 1650, at least fifteen years after the end of the reign of Merneferra Ay in 1685.

Three small cemeteries at the mouth of the Faiyum Oasis (Maiyana, Abusir el-Melek, and Gurob) date to the period of the wars between the Hyksos and the Thebans, which is otherwise represented only at Memphis. These Faiyum burials are Egyptian in character, with the bodies laid extended in rectangular coffins. At Gurob, two burials contain Kerma-ware pottery, indicating that they may belong to Kerma Nubians serving in the Theban army (see below). One intact burial at Abusir contained a scarab of the Hyksos ruler Khyan, which provides a *terminus post quem* for the burial.

The pottery at Maiyana (a small cemetery of men, women, and children, situated close to Sedment el-Gebel) includes cylindrical combed Tell el-Yahudiya juglets, like those in stratum D/2 at Tell el-Dab'a, as well as imported Cypriote base-ring I juglets, like those in the earliest 18th Dynasty strata both at Tell el-Dab'a and at Memphis. There are no weapons, apart from a throwstick, but the use of sheepskins and the decoration of the dead with feathers and flowers is not typically Egyptian. This small cemetery seems to record the short-lived existence of a foreign community, but one that was distinct from that flourishing at Avaris.

A small group of graves in the large New Kingdom cemeteries at el-Haraga and el-Riqqa provide parallels to the Maiyana–Gurob–Abusir el-Melek–Memphis pottery corpus and confirm that there is a short-lived but distinct archaeological phase marking the transition between the final phase of the Second Intermediate Period and the beginning of the 18th Dynasty in this region. Roughly 130 years before this period of transition, the king moved his Residence from Itjtawy to Thebes. Even before this defining event took place, the sacred spaces at the mortuary complexes of the 12th Dynasty kings began to be encroached upon, as the cults of the royal ancestors ceased to be celebrated. At Lisht, however, the cemetery (and possibly its settlement) continued in use until the end of the Second Intermediate Period. If the life of the necropolis paralleled that of the Residence, then it too continued in some form.

Cusae: The Boundary between the Egyptian and the Asiatic Nile

The Theban ruler Kamose was advised by his councillors: 'The middle country is with us as far as Cusae', and the texts from Kamose's reign remain our best written source for the history of Middle Egypt in the Second Intermediate

Map of the Nile Valley and
Palestine in the Second
Intermediate Period.

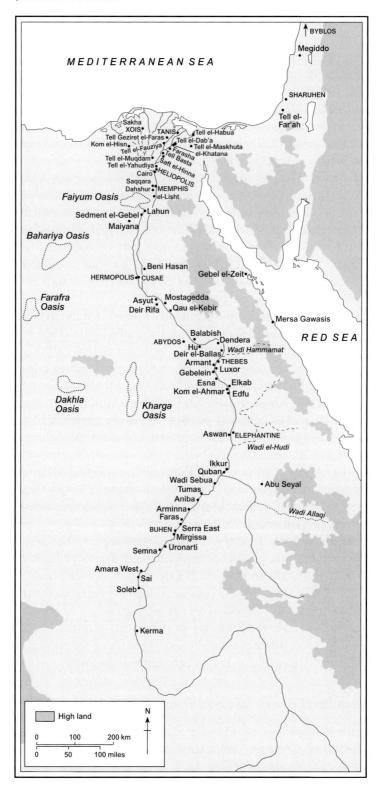

Period. An inscription of Queen Hatshepsut (1473–1458 BC) in the Speos Artemidos, 100 km. north of Cusae (el-Qusiya), records intensive restoration and reconsecration of temples in the area: 'I have raised up what was dismembered from the first time when the Asiatics were in Avaris of the North Land (with) roving hordes in the midst of them overthrowing what had been made ... The temple of the Lady of Cusae ... was fallen into dissolution, the earth had swallowed up its noble sanctuary, and children danced upon its roof.' This piece of royal propaganda was designed to show Hatshepsut in the traditional kingly role of restorer of order after chaos. Her scribe was writing more than eighty years after the Hyksos–Theban wars and it is as likely that the 'roving hordes' were the armies of Thebes as it is those of Avaris. It is interesting that, so long after the event, the rulers of Egypt were still boasting of the expulsion of the Hyksos.

Cusae lies about 40 km. south of Hermopolis (el-Ashmunein), which was the centre of the administration of the area during the Middle Kingdom. When Horemkhauef visited the Residence at Lisht, possibly between 1670 and 1650 BC, the river was still open, but shortly thereafter Cusae marked the boundary at which any traveller from the south had to pay tax to the ruler of Avaris if he wished to proceed.

Judging from Kamose's account of his arrest of a messenger with a letter from King Apepi to the king of Kush, the Hyksos appear to have controlled the route from 'Sako' (probably modern el-Qes) via the Western Desert oases to the Nubian site of Tumas, midway between the first and second Nile cataracts. This route gave the king of Avaris access to allies—the fierce kings of Kush—and to gold. At least three of the cataract forts (Buhen, Mirgissa, and Uronarti) were still functioning, although there is some debate as to whether they were subject to the rule of Egypt or of Kush; nevertheless the organization still existed to control the oasis route (from the southern end) and to send expeditions to the gold mines. Despite the boundary at Cusae, regular contact and exchange of goods continued between Lower Egypt and Nubia, via the oasis route. This is clear from finds of pottery and mud sealings both at the cataract forts and at the Kushite capital, Kerma. Moreover, at Buhen at least, that contact seems to have continued without a break from the 13th Dynasty until the beginning of the Hyksos 15th Dynasty (see below).

We can enlarge our picture of Middle Egypt by looking at a group of cemeteries excavated about 50 km. south of Cusae, at Deir Rifa, Mostagedda, and Qau. Cemetery S at Deir Rifa contains the burials of a group of Nubians known as 'pan-grave' people (because of their distinctive shallow oval graves), who were semi-nomadic cattle-breeders living on the edge of the desert. Their cemeteries and settlements appear in Egypt during the 13th Dynasty, and they have been identified with the Medjay of the Kamose texts, who were sent to scout the land in advance of Kamose's fleet. Their distinctive handmade pottery is ubiquitous in Middle Kingdom settlements and is found as far north as Memphis. At Deir Rifa, their graves contained Tell el-Yahudiya ware of types comparable with those from level E/1 at Tell el-Dabʿa, which are datable to the middle of the 15th Dynasty. The associated Egyptian pottery belongs to the Middle Kingdom style of the Memphis region and suggests that the cemetery goes back to the beginning of the 13th Dynasty.

Mostagedda, almost opposite Deir Rifa on the right bank of the Nile, also contained the burials of pan-grave people, and these can be placed into a chronological sequence according to the degree to which they follow Egyptian or Nubian burial customs (whereas the Deir Rifa cemetery is too poorly published to allow this to be done). Two phases before the beginning of the 18th Dynasty are present at Mostagedda and both contain Egyptian pottery remark-

An example of a Tell el-Yahudiya ware juglet of a type which first occurs in level E/1-b/1 at Tell el-Dabʿa during the 15th Dynasty.

ably different from that at Deir Rifa. These two phases, as well as earlier ones, have also been found in the large Egyptian cemetery at Qau, 15 km. to the south of Mostagedda and Deir Rifa. The pottery is characterized by elaborate incised decoration, the use of sandy marl clays, high-shouldered narrow-necked storage jars, and carinated jars. This ceramic corpus very clearly belongs to an Upper Egyptian tradition and provides the prototypes for vessels that appear at Memphis and Tell el-Dabʻa in fully developed form in the early 18th Dynasty strata.

The cemeteries of Deir Rifa and Mostagedda, on opposite sides of the river, belonged to the same Nubian cultural group, but the differences in funerary equipment show that Deir Rifa was in contact with the Memphis region, while Mostagedda was linked with Upper Egypt. The Nubian artefacts in both are similar enough to suggest that the difference between them is not one of time, but of wealth, status (Mostagedda being generally richer), and, above all, regional associations. Their location suggests that the region of Cusae did indeed, as the texts state, mark the border between Upper and Lower Egypt, and that the boundary existed at least by the beginning of the 13th Dynasty. It is possible to speculate that we have here the burial grounds of two groups of Medjay mercenaries patrolling the border region: perhaps one group based at Deir Rifa guarded the west bank for the Hyksos while the other looked after the east bank for the Theban kings.

Thebes, the Southern City: The Emergence of the 16th and 17th Dynasties

On the basis of Ryholt's reconstruction of the Turin Canon, we can now identify 15 names of kings (Dynasty 16 of Manetho) as the predecessors of the kings of the 17th Dynasty. Five of them occur in contemporary sources and these indicate that the centre of their power was in Upper Egypt. We cannot be certain that they all ruled from Thebes, and some may have been local rulers in important towns such as Abydos, Elkab, and Edfu. King Wepwawetemsaf, not listed in the Turin Canon, who left his modest stele at Abydos, may have been one of these local kings; the stele shows him offering to Wepwawet, the local deity after whom he was named. The style of its writing, design, and royal regalia place it in a line of development between the 13th and 17th Dynasty royal stelae.

King Iykhernefert Neferhotep, who definitely ruled from Thebes, left behind a much more impressive stele, on which he describes himself as a victorious king, beloved of his army, one who nourishes his town, who defeats rebels, who reconciles rebellious foreign lands. Neferhotep is shown protected by the gods Amun and Montu and by a goddess personifying the city of Thebes itself. She appears armed with a scimitar, bow, and arrows. The language of the formal eulogy is familiar from earlier hymns composed for kings but also for nomarchs, great warlords who, in the First Intermediate Period, ruled like local kings. The stele was set up, like those of Kamose, to celebrate a precise event, which may have been the raising of a blockade of Thebes. We do not know if

Neferhotep fought the Hyksos, their Egyptian vassals, or rival local rulers, but the Canadian Egyptologist Donald Redford has noted a destruction layer after the 13th Dynasty level in part of the town underlying East Karnak. Neferhotep's name is known also from contemporary monuments at Elkab and Gebelein. In such uncertain times, the king's role as army commander becomes more and more prominent and so enshrined in the royal litanies. The ideology as well as some of the phraseology survives into the 18th Dynasty.

Kings may fail but the officials who served them had their own monuments, and from the genealogies recorded there a relative chronology has been built up. Son often followed father into royal service, and kings took wives from the great official families, so that a network of interdependence gradually bound the king to the home towns of his officials, at Elkab and Edfu as well as at Thebes. Genealogical evidence suggests that only three generations separated the abandonment of Itjtawy from the reign of King Nebererau I, sixth king of the 16th Dynasty, and that the transition from the 13th to the 16th Dynasty group of kings went officially unremarked by the officials who served them.

We know a great deal more about the nine kings assigned (after Ryholt) to the 17th Dynasty, but so far only two are known to have been related to each other: the brothers Nubkheperra Intef VII and Sekhemra Intef VI. It is possible but not certain that their father was Sobekemsaf I. Their names do not occur in the Turin Canon, the relevant section having been cut away in antiquity, but they occur on other king-lists from Thebes; royal stelae have survived from reuse in later building, and excavations have produced rich objects from their burials. The bodies of Seqenenra Taa (*c.*1560 BC) and his wife Ahhotep, and possibly his mother Queen Tetisheri, were found in the Deir el-Bahri cache of royal mummies, and most curious of all, we have a tomb-robbers' description of the burial of King Sobekemsaf II and his wife, still intact over 600 years later in the 20th Dynasty. Kings' names also occur in private tombs, and on objects. These Theban kings are thought to have ruled at the same time as the Hyksos 15th Dynasty, but there is no fixed point for dating the beginning of the 17th Dynasty, only the end being marked by the death of Kamose at an unknown point in or after his third regnal year. The fortunes of the kings seem to have fluctuated: Nubkheperra Intef is mentioned on over twenty contemporary monuments, whereas Intef VI is known only from his coffin, now in the Louvre.

The continuing military ethos of the time is illustrated by the popularity of military titles such as 'commander of the crew of the ruler' and 'commander of the town regiment'. They show a defensive grouping of military resources around the king and confirm the importance of local militias based on towns. Instability remained characteristic of Upper Egypt for the rest of the Second Intermediate Period.

Rahotep, first king of the 17th Dynasty, boasts of restorations in temples at Abydos and Koptos, while an inscription of Sobekemsaf II shows that he sent a quarrying expedition of 130 men to the Wadi Hammamat. These quarries, however, were well within Theban territory, and the numbers of quarry-workers involved do not compare with the thousands of men sent to the wadi in the 12th Dynasty. Nevertheless, confidence was growing and both the territory and the activities of the king were expanding. Sobekemsaf's expedition has a distinctly *ad hoc* air: only one man holds the appropriate title of 'overseer of works', while the rest have honorific titles or offices connected with provisioning. The scribe does not observe the strict hierarchy of status in his listing, and uses a mixture of hieroglyphic and hieratic signs. It appears that traditional skills and protocols were having to be relearnt after a decisive breakdown. At the Gebel Zeit galena mines, overlooking the Red Sea, two modest stelae were found recording expeditions in the reigns of Nubkheperra Intef VII and Swaserenra Bebiankh of Dynasty 16, the latter previously hardly known beyond his listing in the Turin Canon. Large numbers of pan-grave sherds were also found there, suggesting another purpose for which the Theban kings may have used Nubian mercenaries.

Thebes was cut off from contact with Lower Egypt and denied access to the centres of scribal learning at Memphis. Such centres, with their archives, were not destroyed and may even have flourished under the Hyksos, but the Thebans would have been unable to consult them, thus perhaps necessitating the creation of a new compilation of texts needed for the all-important funerary rituals. One of the first collections of spells that we know as the *Book of the Dead* dates to the 16th Dynasty and comes from a coffin of Queen Mentuhotep, wife of King Djehuty. The funerary culture of Thebes also evolved in other ways, in response to an impoverishment of resources. Large rectangular coffins made of cedarwood were replaced with roughly shaped anthropoid coffins of sycamore painted in a feather pattern, but in so crude and idiosyncratic a style that no one is exactly like any other. This feature betrays a lack of training in the erstwhile rigid conventions of funerary art, which were perhaps also less in demand. However, a few coffins demonstrate that in some Theban workshops the tradition of Middle Kingdom coffin making survived well into the 18th Dynasty.

The location of five of the royal tombs of the 17th Dynasty, those of Nubkheperra Intef VII, Sekhemra Intef, Sobekemsaf II, Seqenenra Taa, and Kamose, is described in the Abbott Papyrus, which contains the record of a judicial enquiry into tomb robbery by the mayor of Thebes in the 20th Dynasty. In 1923 Herbert Winlock set out to relocate the tombs using the itinerary of the

Facing: coffin of King Nubkheperra Intef from Thebes.

inspectors given in the papyrus. He was also inspired by the fact that many objects from royal burials of the same date had appeared for sale from illicit excavations in the 1820s and 1859–60. The robbers of the 20th Dynasty described how they found the burial of Sobekemsaf II:

He was equipped with a sword and there was a . . . set of amulets and ornaments of gold at his throat; his crown and diadems of gold were on his head and the . . . mummy of the king was overlaid with gold throughout. His coffins were wrought with gold and silver within and without and inlaid with every splendid costly stone . . . we stole the furniture which we found with them, consisting of vases of gold, silver, and bronze.

These kings and their officials spent their increasing wealth at the end of the dynasty on the objects in their tombs rather than on the tomb structures themselves. Decorated tombs are rare; instead, earlier tombs were often taken over and reused. To understand where the wealth was coming from we need to look to the south, to Elephantine, to the forts guarding the second Nile cataract, and finally to Kerma, capital city of the King of Kush, over 800 km. south of Thebes.

Elephantine and the Cataract Forts

Elephantine, an island opposite the modern town of Aswan, is an interesting vantage point from which to study the Second Intermediate Period. As a provincial town, it provides a counterbalance to the Theban sources, and there is an unbroken series of private and royal dedications dating from the late 12th to the 16th Dynasty. The stratified town site and cemeteries of the same period are being excavated by the German Institute of Archaeology.

The fortunes of Elephantine are inextricably linked to those of Nubia. During most of the Middle Kingdom it did not mark the southern boundary at all; that was fixed by Senusret III at Semna, 400 km. to the south. However, during the nadir of the power of the Theban kings, it is possible that Elephantine was ruled independently and even that Nubians raided the city from time to time. Booty from a raid against Elephantine or the forts is the favoured explanation for the fact that a royal tomb at Kerma in the late Second Intermediate Period contained statues of a nomarch of Asyut and his wife who lived in the reign of Senusret I (1956–1911 BC).

The value of Lower Nubia lay in its quarries, principally of diorite, granite, and amethyst; its access to gold and copper mines; and its strategic location in terms of the control of the desert and river routes. A 6th Dynasty local official of Elephantine, Heqaib, was deified after his death, and a series of votive stelae and statues has been found in his shrine. The 13th–16th Dynasties are particularly well represented and, as at Memphis, the continuity is broken only with the advent of the 18th Dynasty. The genealogies recorded in the inscriptions show that the same families served both the late 13th Dynasty kings and those of the 16th Dynasty. The status of the mayor of Elephantine evidently changed from one of great local significance to a military one within the retinue of the King of

Thebes. One such man was Neferhotep, who was responsible to the king for the whole region from Thebes to Elephantine. After his time (the 16th Dynasty, judging from the orthography of his stele), dedications in the Heqaib shrine cease and it may be no coincidence that this is the period when the Prince of Kush was at his most powerful and even the cataract forts were falling under his control.

The fortunes of one of the forts, Buhen, may be pieced together from evidence not yet fully published. After the late 12th Dynasty, soldiers were buried with their families in Cemetery K at Buhen; these burials are characterized by pottery from the Memphite region, confirmation that the fort's supplies were still coming from the workshops of the Residence. Cemetery K shows continuous occupation until well into the Second Intermediate Period, and there are at least two groups of intact, multiple burials that contain Tell el-Yahudiya ware juglets, including one type that does not appear at Tell el-Dab'a until stratum E/1 (probably the early 15th Dynasty). One of the bodies has a large gold nugget around its neck, suggesting that settlers remained at Buhen primarily because of its proximity to the gold-mining region. By this time the boundary between Upper and Lower Egypt was in place, so that supplies from Lower Egypt could have reached Buhen only via the oasis route, which we know was in use during the reign of Apepi. Who, one wonders, was organizing this trade at the northern end? We may speculate that officials were still working at Itjtawy under the Hyksos king and we know that the Lisht cemetery was still in use. Avaris itself was the centre for the manufacture and distribution of Tell el-Yahudiya juglets, the contents of which have not yet been identified but were clearly much prized.

The fortress settlers must have felt themselves increasingly isolated and vulnerable, despite their links with Lower Egypt, and so had to accommodate themselves to the local military power, which was neither the Hyksos nor the Kings of Thebes, but the King of Kush. A family covering five generations left inscriptions at Buhen and these show that the last two generations served the King of Kush and even carried out local campaigns on his behalf; this period is marked archaeologically by the presence of pottery imported from Upper Egypt, from the Theban area, instead of pottery from Lower Egypt. The river was open between Thebes and the forts, but only, as the Kamose texts imply, if taxes were paid to the master of the southern Nile, the King of Kush. Buhen was eventually sacked (there are traces of a great fire) but more probably by the army of Kamose than by the Nubians. Other forts, Mirgissa and Askut, show a similar history of continued occupation by Egyptians, but alongside Nubians until the end of the Second Intermediate Period. Eventually control of the cataract region by the King of Kerma became intolerable to the Theban rulers, making it essential that they should retake the forts before they could proceed in safety against the Hyksos. In the third year of Kamose's reign, we have the earliest evidence that the region was again under Theban control. The building of a wall is recorded at Buhen, probably a renewal of the fortifications after the successful campaign mentioned in the letter from the Hyksos ruler Apepi to the King of Kush.

The Kingdom of Kush

The King of Kush is the name given in Egyptian sources to the king whose capital lay at Kerma. Archaeologists use Kerma as an adjective to describe the culture of the Kushites and to distinguish it from other contemporary Nubian cultures, such as C group and pan grave. Kerma is situated south of the third cataract, at the termination of the western oasis routes, and is being excavated by Charles Bonnet of the University of Geneva.

The Kerma people kept no written records, but we know that their culture, found throughout Nubia, goes back to the early Old Kingdom. The king was at his most powerful during the Classic Kerma phase, which corresponds roughly to the Second Intermediate Period. Kamose may have succeeded in retaking Buhen, but only much later in the 18th Dynasty, after at least three more long campaigns, was Kerma itself conquered. The destruction that followed was so thorough that it is difficult now to reconstruct the city as it stood during the reigns of the last independent rulers. We do know that the great tumulus tombs in which the kings were buried contained slaughtered servants and great stocks of provisions, many imported from Upper Egypt, which may have been the taxes paid by those wishing to pass south beyond Elephantine. Until at least the middle of the 13th Dynasty the king was trading with both Upper and Lower Egypt, a trade probably administered through the cataract forts.

The Kerma Nubians were cattle-breeders and warriors, particularly famous

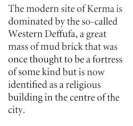

The modern site of Kerma is dominated by the so-called Western Deffufa, a great mass of mud brick that was once thought to be a fortress of some kind but is now identified as a religious building in the centre of the city.

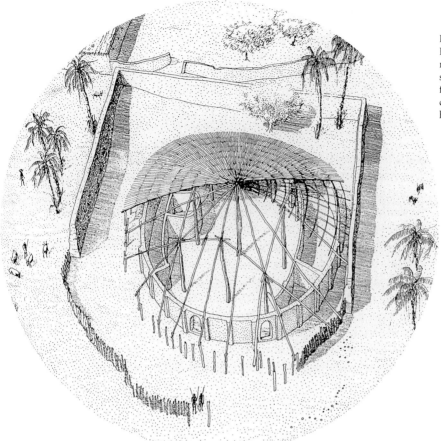

Reconstruction of the Great Hut at Kerma. This huge round hut set within a stockade seems to have functioned as a kind of ceremonial building at the heart of the city of Kerma.

as bowmen. The bows and arrows in their graves and the massive fortifications at Buhen designed to defend against archers, confirm this reputation. At the centre of the city was an enormous round hut set within a stockade which functioned in royal ceremonies. There were also large sacred sites and administrative buildings. An extensive building and rebuilding programme during the Classic Kerma phase testifies to the immense resources in materials and manpower at the king's disposal.

The presence of Kerma Nubians in the armies of Kamose and Ahmose is beyond dispute, but it is unclear whether they were there voluntarily or forcibly recruited during Kamose's campaign. It seems likely that the Kerma Nubians were a federation of tribes, not all of whom necessarily accepted the authority of the King of Kerma, and, with it, the policy of enmity towards the Theban kings. In any case, whatever the king's policy, trade flourished between Kerma and Thebes during the late Second Intermediate Period. People travelled as well as goods: Egyptian craftsmen to Kerma, perhaps, and certainly Kerma Nubians to Egypt. The burials of a handful of individuals have been found scattered between Thebes and Abydos. One rich burial, found intact at Thebes, is of the time of Kamose and belonged to a woman and her young child. It is entirely Egyptian in style and the woman wears a royal gift, 'the gold of honour', a necklace of many tiny gold ring beads. Beside her coffin was a carrying pole from which hung nets containing six pottery beakers, made in a style so diagnostic of the Kerma culture that it is called 'Kerma ware'. Gold drew the Thebans and the Kerma Nubians together, first as allies but finally and inevitably as enemies.

Avaris and Thebes at War

The scene was set for war. The Theban kings had mastered their own region; Kamose had retaken Buhen, so the route to the gold mines lay open to him; the Kerma Nubians had been driven south; and a battle fleet had been made ready. As Kamose phrases it, 'I will close with him that I may slit open his belly; for my desire is to rescue Egypt and to drive out the Asiatics.'

Most of our written sources for the war come from the Theban side and predictably they show the Thebans as both the stronger and the more belligerent of the protagonists. The war must have lasted for at least thirty years, since we know that Seqenenra Taa, the father of Ahmose, fought the Hyksos but that Avaris was not taken until between regnal years 18 and 22 of Ahmose. After the sack of the city, whether immediately or not, Ahmose took his army to Palestine in a campaign culminating in a three-year siege of Sharuhen, near Gaza. It is usually assumed that Sharuhen was the Hyksos king's last stronghold, but the sources are silent on this point. The war was not continuously fought: campaigns were short and armies, by modern standards, small. Ahmose, son of Ibana, an important military official who was buried in a rock tomb at Elkab, describes slaying two men and capturing another in battles around Avaris that were important enough for him to receive rewards of gold from the king.

The first known engagement occurred during the reign of Seqenenra Taa (now thought to be the same king as Senakhtenra Taa). A papyrus written in the reign of the 19th Dynasty ruler Merenptah (1213–1203 BC), about 350 years later, preserves fragments of a story of a quarrel between Seqenenra and Apepi. It begins with a complaint by Apepi that the roaring of the hippopotami at Thebes was keeping him from sleep. Seqenenra is described as the 'Prince of the Southern City' while Apepi is King (*nesu*), to whom the whole of Egypt pays tribute. The story breaks off as Seqenenra summons his councillors, but the narrative structure, so close to that of the Kamose texts, looks as if this is the prologue to a battle.

We have further evidence of military activity in Seqenenra's reign from Deir el-Ballas, the site of a settlement constructed on virgin ground at the desert edge, 40 km. north of Thebes. The interpretation of the remains, first excavated by George Reisner in 1900 and more recently examined by Peter Lacovara in 1980–6, is not straightforward, but the date of the site's first phase, the reigns of Seqenenra Taa, Kamose, and Ahmose, is not in doubt. During the reign of Seqenenra himself, a palace with an enormous enclosure wall was built. Like all the surviving buildings at Ballas, it was made of mud brick, with limestone door frames and columns. It consisted of a series of courts and a long entrance corridor around an elevated central area where, we presume, the private royal apartments stood. The walls were painted in a rough style, with scenes depicting men and weapons, and decorated with faience tiles. In an enclosure to the west were large animal pens. Beyond the enclosure wall were widely scattered groups of large private houses; an artificially laid-out group of smaller houses for workmen; an open area for food preparation; and a textile workshop. At the southernmost extremity, on a hill dominating the river and surrounding desert, was a platform supporting a building, now destroyed, reached by a monumental stairway. It seems most likely that this was a military observation post.

Among the pottery from Ballas was a large quantity of Kerma ware, especially types used for cooking and food storage. There can be no doubt that Kerma Nubians were living there alongside Egyptians in considerable numbers. It seems hard to avoid the conclusion that the purpose of this settlement, deliberately built in a remote place, was military, perhaps intended for the mustering of an army containing a large contingent of Kerma Nubians.

The examination of the mummy of Seqenenra shows that he died by violence. His forehead bears a horizontal axe cut; his cheek bone is shattered and the back of his neck carries the mark of a dagger thrust. It has been argued that the shape of the forehead wound is consistent only with the use of an axe of Middle Bronze Age type, similar to those found at Tell el-Dab'a. Egyptian axes, such as those depicted on the walls of the palace at Ballas, are of a different form. This is the most telling evidence so far that a major battle against the Hyksos took place in Seqenenra's reign—one in which the king himself was brutally slaughtered. The angle of the dagger thrust suggests that the king was already prone when it was inflicted.

Kamose succeeded Seqenenra Taa. It is often stated that he was the king's son, elder brother of Ahmose, but we do not know who his parents were and his coffin carried no uraeus, emblem of royalty. Only the third year of Kamose's reign is attested, on the stelae from Karnak and the inscription from Buhen. Both expeditions, to Buhen and to Avaris, took place in or before the third regnal year, the former preceding the latter. Kamose was a warrior, 'Kamose the Brave' being one of his most frequent epithets, but he probably died shortly after year 3. However, his funerary cult, associated with that of Seqenenra Taa, survived till Ramessid times and at least one of his Karnak stelae was still standing over 200 years after his death.

We can use the texts of the two 'Kamose stelae' and the near-contemporary copy found on a writing tablet in a Theban tomb to reconstruct his expedition to Avaris. Setting aside the hyperbole, this campaign was far from definitive, perhaps no more than a raid, given that the final destruction of Avaris did not take place until over twenty years later and that Kamose's opponent was Aauserra Apepi, the most powerful and long-lived of the Hyksos kings.

Kamose first moved north from Thebes with his army and battle fleet, sending Nubian scouts ahead to reconnoitre the position of enemy garrisons. The sack of Nefrusi, north of Cusae, is graphically described: 'as lions are with their prey, so were my army with their servants, their cattle, their milk, fat, and honey, in dividing up their possessions with joyous hearts.' As he continued north, he intercepted at Sako (el-Qes) a messenger sent from Apepi to the King of Kush, and this led him to send soldiers to Bahariya Oasis to cut communications and to 'prevent there being any enemies in my rear'. There follows a gap in the account until Kamose reaches Avaris, where he deploys his fleet on the waterways around the city to form a blockade while patrolling the banks to prevent counter-attacks. He describes the palace women peering out at the Egyptians from the citadel like 'young lizards from within their holes'. Then follows the traditional boastful speech to Apepi: 'Behold, I am drinking of the wine of your vineyards. . . . I am hacking up your place of residence, cutting down your trees', and a list of the plunder he was carrying away. Despite the bombast, it is clear that Avaris was not attacked and Apepi refused to engage him. The Kamose texts end with the king's happy return: 'every face was bright, the land was in affluence, the river bank was excited and Thebes was in festival.'

It is difficult from our vantage point to judge how much damage was inflicted on the Hyksos by Kamose's campaign. All his achievements, however, had to be repeated by his successor, and the admiral, Ahmose, son of Ibana, makes no mention of Kamose, although his father and he served successively in the battle fleets of Seqenenra Taa and Ahmose. There was no immediate follow-up by the Thebans and it was at least eleven years before an army under Ahmose began to fight its way north again. The reason for the lull was that both Kamose and his opponent Aauserra Apepi had died. They were succeeded by Ahmose and Khamudi respectively. Ahmose was a young boy at his succession, and the kingdom was held together by the queen mother, Ahhotep. Unique epithets are given to her: 'one who cares for Egypt; she has looked after her soldiers . . . she has brought back her fugitives, and collected her deserters; she has pacified Upper Egypt, and expelled her rebels.'

The final phase of the war was in the eleventh regnal year of an unknown king, sometimes identified as Ahmose, sometimes as Khamudi. The evidence consists of fragmentary notes on the verso of the Rhind Mathematical Papyrus. The recto was copied in year 33 of Aauserra Apepi, thus in a region where events were dated by the regnal years of Hyksos kings; the specialist subject matter and high quality of the papyrus suggest Memphis as the place of origin. On the verso are some notes: 'Regnal year 11, second month of *shemu*—Heliopolis was entered; first month of *akhet*, day 23—this southern prince broke into Tjaru. Day 25—it was heard tell that Tjaru had been entered.' Tjaru is probably to be identified as the fortress site of Tell el-Habua, and—in this author's view—the 'southern prince' is to be identified with Ahmose, while year 11 belongs to Khamudi, whose name, without regnal years, is given in the Turin Canon.

The strategy of Ahmose seems to have been to bypass Memphis to take Heliopolis and then, three months later, in mid-October (after the water level of the inundation had begun to fall, and men in chariots could move again in

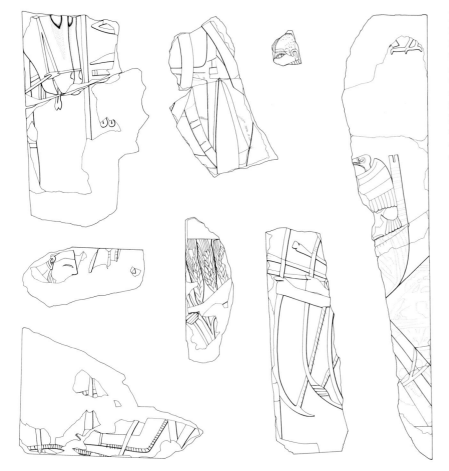

Many fragments of painted relief have been excavated from a temple at Abydos of the early 18th Dynasty ruler, Ahmose I. They include battle scenes evidently referring to wars against the Hyksos. Shown here: fragments of horses, chariots, fallen and captive enemies, archers, a raid on a corn field, and the royal battle ship.

the valley), to attack Tell el-Habua, which had the effect of cutting off the Hyksos from a retreat across northern Sinai to Palestine. The assault on Avaris followed.

We have three contemporary sources for the campaign: the biography of Ahmose, son of Ibana; the physical evidence from Tell el-Dabʿa; and fragments of narrative relief from Ahmose's temple at Abydos. Ahmose, son of Ibana, naturally focuses on his own role, so his perspective is a narrow one, but it is totally free of the grandiloquent posturing of the Kamose texts. Ahmose's Abydos reliefs (discovered in 1993) are discussed and illustrated here in advance of full publication, by courtesy of their excavator, Stephen Harvey. They give us fascinating glimpses of the protagonists: the horses and chariots of the Egyptians; the royal battle fleet; soldiers hacking at crops; a Hyksos captive, shown with shaved head, stubble beard, and rope around his neck; a Hyksos warrior with his arm upraised, and wearing a long-sleeved fringed garment; and the chaos of falling and struggling bodies. The relief may include episodes from the king's later campaigns in Syria and Palestine but the central narrative involves a battle fleet and this can only refer to the siege of Avaris.

Ahmose, son of Ibana, describes a series of engagements at Avaris, and, since we do not know how long the campaign lasted from siege to sack, his account may contain events spread over several years. The straightforward narrative style does suggest strongly that events are being reported in chronological order. Assuming this, we can reconstruct the campaign as follows: Ahmose, son of Ibana, is a member of the troop of soldiers on the ship 'Northern' (perhaps the king's ship), leading the battle fleet. They arrive at Avaris and, after a battle, the king begins the siege. While this continued, the army fought to pacify the surrounding area. Ahmose, son of Ibana, was appointed to a new ship, appropriately named 'Rising in Memphis', and fought on the water of Avaris, killing an enemy. He fought two more engagements, one 'again in this place'—presumably Avaris—and another south of the city. Only after these skirmishes does he laconically report: 'Avaris was despoiled and I brought spoil from there: one man, three women . . . his majesty gave them to me as slaves.'

Because Josephus considered the Hyksos to have been the founders of Jerusalem, his version of Manetho includes a detailed account of events after they were driven out of Egypt by Ahmose. Of the siege of Avaris he says: 'They [the Hyksos] enclosed [Avaris] with a high strong wall in order to safeguard all their possessions and spoils. The Egyptian king attempted by siege to force them to surrender, blockading the fortress with an army of 480,000 men. Finally, giving up the siege in despair, he concluded a treaty by which they should all depart from Egypt.'

Evidence from Avaris itself tends to confirm this picture of mass exodus rather than slaughter after Ahmose's victory. A clear cultural break is visible between the latest Hyksos stratum and that of the earliest 18th Dynasty all over the site, largely because of the appearance of a new ceramic repertoire. The same phenomenon appears also at Memphis (see above). After the break there is no evidence of any continued occupation by people with a mixed Egyptian/Middle Bronze Age culture and in some parts of the site occupation ceased altogether. On the other hand, the cult of Seth, retaining the attributes of a Syrian storm-god, continued and even expanded during the New Kingdom. The latest Hyksos stratum, as we have seen, saw the greatest expansion of the city and the building of immense defensive fortifications. These may have been carried out early in the reign of Khamudi, but they were not enough. Some explanation for defeat may be found in a clue that suggests that the ideal of a warrior élite among the Hyksos did not correspond to reality by the time of the Thebans' final assault. Battle axes and daggers from stratum D/3 were of unalloyed copper, whereas weapons from earlier strata were made of tin bronze, which produced a weapon with a far superior cutting edge. It has been suggested that an interruption in the supply of tin can be ruled out and the explanation lies rather in a change in the function of weapons from practical use to one of status and display. In contrast, weapons of the same period from Upper Egypt were made of tin bronze and this would have given the Thebans a clear advantage in hand-to-hand fighting.

It is generally thought that the Hyksos introduced the horse and chariot into Egypt, since there is no firm evidence of either during the Middle Kingdom yet they are present from the beginning of the 18th Dynasty. There is no evidence so far from Tell el-Dab'a of chariots, and the evidence for the presence of the bones of horses is equivocal. At Tell el-Habua, however, a complete skeleton, found in a late Second Intermediate Period context, has been positively identified as a horse. The Kamose texts mention the enemy's horses and the chariot teams of Avaris as part of Kamose's loot and this may account for their introduction into Upper Egypt. Both horses, and horses hitched to chariots, appear on the Ahmose reliefs at Abydos; moreover the chariots are not simple prototypes but exactly comparable with those shown in the mortuary temple of Tuthmose II.

Despite the defeat of the Hyksos, the boast of Queen Hatshepsut, 'I have banished the abomination of the gods, and the earth has removed their footprints', has been disproved by the painstaking work of Bietak and his team at Tell el-Dab'a.

The Reunification of the Two Lands under Ahmose

The sack of Avaris was only the first step in a series of campaigns needed to secure the unity of Egypt. The sequence of events is not universally agreed, but following the account of Ahmose, son of Ibana, after the Avaris campaign came a campaign to southern Palestine during which Sharuhen was taken. We do not know whether the intention was to destroy the remnants of the Hyksos or to exploit the vacuum they left to push on into Palestine and even as far as Lebanon. There are later references to the importation of cedars of Lebanon and the bullocks of 'Fenekhu'—a term thought to refer to Phoenicia. Ahmose, son of Ibana, continues, 'Now when his majesty had slain the nomads of Asia, he sailed south to Khent-hen-nefer (below the second cataract) to destroy the Nubian bowmen.' We have confirmation that King Ahmose restored (if that were necessary) Egyptian control of Buhen, because a door jamb shows him and his mother offering to Min and Horus (of Buhen) and names a commander of Buhen called Turo.

Fragment of a Minoan fresco from the earliest 18th Dynasty stratum at Tell el-Dab'a, showing a bull-leaper.

After Ahmose returned from Nubia, he had to deal with two uprisings. The first was a minor mutiny in which a non-Egyptian (possibly a Nubian) called Aata brought a small force into Upper Egypt from the north. This may have been no more than a raid for booty, since Aata did not seek to engage the king's army. He was found and defeated and he and his men were captured alive, two young warriors being given as a reward to Ahmose, son of Ibana. Assuming that Aata was a

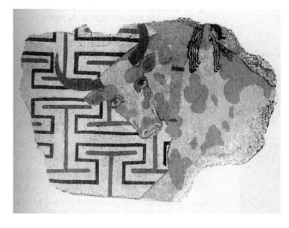

Nubian, and given that Kerma Nubians served in the army at Avaris and Memphis and disposed of enough wealth to have substantial burials, it is plausible that a group of such Nubians might have attempted to exploit the king's absence in Nubia to go on a plundering raid into Upper Egypt.

The second uprising was of a different character. It was led by an Egyptian, Teti-an, who 'gathered the malcontents to himself; his majesty slew him; his troop were wiped out'. The seriousness of this rebellion is shown by the severity of its punishment. We can only speculate that the malcontents were those who had, up till then, served Ahmose's rival, the king of Avaris. The last five years of Ahmose's reign were devoted to a massive building programme at the great cult centres (Memphis, Karnak, Heliopolis, and, above all, Abydos), and at the northern and southern boundaries of Egypt, Avaris, and Buhen.

The earliest 18th Dynasty stratum at Tell el-Dabʿa has produced discoveries, extraordinary even in the context of this unique site. In the immediate aftermath of the sack, the fortifications and palace of the last Hyksos king were systematically destroyed. Ahmose replaced them with similar fortifications and palatial buildings that were equally short lived and can now be reconstructed only from their foundations and from fragments of wall paintings found in dumps created as the buildings were levelled. The wall paintings are, in style, technique, and motif, Minoan, but there is as yet no consensus among Aegean scholars as to whether they were painted by Minoan artists or by Egyptians imitating them. Hundreds of fragments have been found, but in very poor condition, and it will take years of conservation and study before they can be fully assessed. Nevertheless, their presence in contexts over 100 years earlier than the first representations of Cretans in Theban tombs, and earlier than the surviving frescos at Knossos, whose subject matter they share, has revolutionized ideas of the relations between Egypt and Crete.

One of the buildings they came from was a royal palace and the only comparable building of the time is the North Palace at Deir el-Ballas. The few surviving wall paintings from there are utterly different, painted in a simple style similar to that of contemporary tomb paintings. The Tell el-Dabʿa frescos seem to owe little to the traditions of Egyptian wall decoration, which go back to the beginning of the Old Kingdom. By analogy with the Knossos frescos, they seem to have been executed to serve a ritual purpose, and are full of symbolic references to the Cretan ruler cult. Bull-leapers and acrobats, associated with motifs of the bull's head and maze pattern (labyrinth), belong totally to the Aegean world. The varying scales of the frescos, their subject matter, and background colour, all indicate that the decorative scheme was extremely complex and spread over not one but a series of buildings. Other frescos, less complex and more clearly imitations of the Minoan style, have been found at Tell Kabri in Palestine. One of their most puzzling features at Tell el-Dabʿa is that they appear in a vacuum. There is a small amount of Cretan Kamares ware pottery but it occurs in early 13th Dynasty strata and there is no continuity in buildings or artefacts between it and the strata of the frescos. Strangest of all, there are no

Cretan artefacts associated with the frescos themselves or in the strata from which they originally came.

The discovery of the frescos has revived old ideas, dismissed until now, that Ahmose was an ally of the Cretan kings and may have taken a Cretan princess as a wife. Evidence cited has been a Minoan style griffin on an axe of Ahmose, and the fact that Ahhotep, the king's mother, had a title 'mistress of the Hau-nebut' that was originally thought to refer to the islands of Greece, although it has recently been argued that this interpretation is implausible. Nevertheless, the frescos prove that Minoans were present at Tell el-Dabʿa, whether as artists themselves or as supervisors guiding Egyptian artists.

The questions posed by the frescos inevitably lead to another problem, the date of the eruption of the Thera volcano, since the best preserved frescos found so far are those from the Cycladic island of Thera sealed beneath layers of lava. The eruption is a key event for relating the chronological sequences of the Aegean and eastern Mediterranean to each other and to an absolute chronol-ogy. Much effort has been expended in attempts to identify the event in Egypt-ian sources so that it can be dated by regnal years. The Rhind Papyrus's references to storms, and a stele of Ahmose describing a destructive upheaval, have been produced in the argument, but the most telling evidence so far comes from Tell el-Dabʿa. Pumice, identified by analysis as deriving from the Thera volcano, has been found in settlement strata datable to the period from the reign of Amenhotep I until the beginning of that of Tuthmose III. However, the pumice occurs in a workshop where it was being used as raw material, and the context provides only a *terminus ante quem*, since the pumice could have been collected, from the seashore, for example, at an earlier date, and, in any case, could have lain there for some considerable time. Not all of the pumice derived from Thera: the source of at least one of the samples has been identified as an eruption in Turkey that took place over 100,000 years ago. It is remarkable that no pumice has been found so far in earlier strata at Tell el-Dabʿa and no ash (that is, 'fall-out' from the eruption) has been found at all. Using a combination of evidence, including data from records of ice cores and tree rings, where exceptional atmospheric conditions can sometimes be linked to historical events, it has been suggested that the Thera eruption occurred in 1628 BC. The evidence from Tell el-Dabʿa could be interpreted as support for the traditional date, *c*.1530 BC (within the reign of Ahmose), but much more work needs to be done to clarify the interpretation of the scientific data, and the question must be left open for the present.

Little of Ahmose's reign was left after his reconquest of Egypt. Many building projects were left unfinished, but the benefits of unification were clear to see. The fine objects from royal burials and lists of donations to the gods of Thebes testify to growing wealth and artistic skill. The fragments of relief from Abydos left to us after the depredations of Ramessid masons show that a style that we can easily recognize as 18th Dynasty had already evolved by the end of his reign.

9 THE EIGHTEENTH DYNASTY BEFORE THE AMARNA PERIOD

(c.1550–1352 BC)

BETSY M. BRYAN

Archaeological discoveries in the 1980s and 1990s, combined with the re-examination of older inscriptional evidence, suggest that the reunification of Egypt took place only in the last decade of the twenty-five-year reign of Ahmose (1550–1525 BC), first king of the 18th Dynasty. Thus the dynasty may be said to have begun officially around 1530 BC, but it was already well under way during Ahmose's reign. Indeed, the nature of the Egyptian state at the beginning of the dynasty was surely mainly a continuation of forms and traditions that had never been entirely disrupted by the internal squabbles of the Second Intermediate Period. It must have been in part the commanding faith in those traditions that enabled Ahmose's predecessors in the 17th Dynasty to consolidate a power base among other powerful Upper Egyptian families. As Ahmose and his successors later moved to assure their family's dynastic line, they created or modified aspects of the kingship that, together with external pressures from the north-east and south, profoundly affected the rest of the 18th Dynasty.

Ahmose and the Beginning of the New Kingdom

The inscriptions in the tomb of Ahmose, son of Ibana, at Elkab describe the defeat of the Hyksos by his namesake King Ahmose, as well as the latter's siege of the stronghold of Sharuhen in southern Palestine, and his campaigns in Kush, the capital of which was the city of Kerma near the third Nile cataract. The completion of this Nubian campaign was left to Amenhotep I (1525–1504

BC), and a series of monuments on the island of Sai commemorated the victories of both rulers; it is possible that all of these were erected by Amenhotep I, but the fact that Ahmose was active in the region is not disputed.

Early 18th Dynasty levels at Avaris (Tell el-Dabʿa) record the name of Ahmose, and the several kings who succeeded him. During this time, several monumental buildings decorated with Minoan frescos were in use at the site (see Chapter 8). Certainly this fact suggests that there was increased contact with the Aegean, even if only through itinerant artists commissioned to undertake or oversee the work. Since weapons found in the small coffin of Queen Ahhotep I (mother of Ahmose), in her tomb in western Thebes, illustrate Aegean or east Mediterranean motifs and craft techniques applied to Egyptian objects, the exotic foreign elements prized in the Delta appear to have been valued in Thebes as well, at least in an adapted form. Actual Aegean objects contemporary with the early 18th Dynasty are far more difficult to document in Egypt, although Egyptian small-trade items occur in fair numbers in Crete, and to a lesser degree on the Greek mainland. However, it remains unclear (if not doubtful) whether there was direct diplomatic exchange between Egypt and Crete in the early 18th Dynasty. Ahmose and his immediate successors may instead have continued to participate in an east Mediterranean exchange system, just as the Hyksos had. Whatever the case, the creativity in forging an Aegeanizing style, as seen on the objects of Ahmose's time, as well as the Minoan-style paintings at Tell el-Dabʿa, did not survive the early part of the 18th Dynasty. Ultimately, as was frequently the case in periods of strong kingship, traditional Egyptian iconography dominated. The few elements that persisted (the 'flying-gallop' motif, for example) were quickly adapted to more familiar iconographic contexts.

Two identical stelae were set up by the late 17th Dynasty ruler Kamose in the Temple of Amun at Karnak, commemorating his campaign against the Hyksos. The text on neither stele is complete but together they preserve virtually all of the original description.

Ahmose's most immediate construction project appears to have been within the capital of Avaris, which he had wrested from the Hyksos. Manfred Bietak's excavations have identified an early 18th Dynasty palace platform abutting a Hyksos fortification wall. Seals naming the rulers of the 18th Dynasty between Ahmose and Amenhotep II have been found in later strata, but Bietak considers that Ahmose was the builder of the original palace complex decorated with

Minoan frescos. He may have had other building projects in the Delta region, but Avaris was certainly planned to be a major centre—quite likely commercial—for the new government to utilize. It is clear from excavations during the 1980s and 1990s that Memphis was also redeveloped in the early 18th Dynasty: as the river moved eastwards, land was reclaimed and used for new settlement. Ceramic sequences and royal scarabs indicate that, already in the reign of Ahmose, Memphis was being resettled following a hiatus that may correspond to the wars between Thebes and Avaris, described in Chapter 8.

The temple monuments from the last years of Ahmose's reign constitute the foundations of a traditional pharaonic building programme, honouring gods whose temples had flourished in the Middle Kingdom—Ptah, Amun, Montu, and Osiris. Ahmose certainly venerated the traditional deities of Egypt's cult centres. Ahmose's affiliations with the moon-god Iah (represented in the 'Ah' element of his name) are best attested in the inscriptions on the jewellery of Ahhotep I and Kamose (1555–1550 BC), which describe Ahmose as 'son of the moon-god, Iah'. This god's major cult centre is unknown, despite the ubiquitous presence of the 'Ah' element in the royal family names. Perhaps, at the very time that he effected the reunification, Ahmose began to have his name written with the lunar crescent of Iah pointing its ends downward. All monuments showing this form of the name Ahmose must, therefore, date after years 17 or 18 of his reign. Being the first king in more than 100 years to be able to erect monuments for the gods of both southern and northern Egypt, Ahmose opened limestone quarries at Maasara with a view to building at Memphis, the old and venerated northern centre, and also at Thebes, the home of Amun and Montu. Although his constructions at Memphis have not been found, some from Thebes, and elsewhere, are still extant.

Ahmose undoubtedly made significant contributions to the cult of Amun at Karnak. If he had lived longer, he would perhaps have begun the rebuilding in stone of far more buildings there, but his surviving monuments nevertheless comprise a doorway and several stelae, as well as perhaps a boat shrine, probably located near the entrance ways to the temple. His desire to be recognized as Amun's pious dedicant would, therefore, have been apparent not only to those whose priestly offices or élite status gained them access to the god's home, but also to the lesser inhabitants of Thebes who were able to visit the front courtyards only at festival times.

Several limestone stelae recording major episodes connected with Karnak temple are known from Ahmose's reign—probably all from the last seven or so years of the reign. On two stelae discovered in the foundations of the Third Pylon at Karnak, the king presents himself as a propitiator and benefactor to the temple. On one of these, the so-called Tempest Stele, the king claims to have rebuilt the tombs and pyramids in the Theban region destroyed by a storm inflicted on Upper Egypt by the power of Amun, whose statue appears to have been left in extreme want. Ahmose describes the fact that the land was covered with water and that he had brought costly goods to support the restoration of the region. The other stele from the Third Pylon (known as the Donation Stele) records the purchase by King Ahmose of the 'second priesthood of Amun' on behalf of his wife, the god's wife of Amun, Ahmose-Nefertari. The cost of this office was paid to the temple by the king, thus making him its benefactor again, and also securing the tie between the god and the royal family.

A third stele of Ahmose, from the Eighth Pylon court at Karnak, dates to year 18 of his reign; it extols the universal power of the royal family, and details the cult equipment that Ahmose had fashioned and dedicated to Karnak temple: gold and silver libation vessels, gold and silver drinking cups for the god's statue, gold offering tables, necklaces and fillets for the divine statues, musical instruments, and a new wooden boat for the temple statue's processions. The objects donated by the king to Karnak are the most essential cult furniture, and their dedication may indicate that the temple was utterly without precious metal objects at this point. It is impossible to say whether this would have been due to the action of a great storm, as the king asserts in the Tempest Stele, but temple cult objects, along with royal burial objects, might also have been important financial resources for the Thebans during the arduous years of the 17th Dynasty.

It is important to note the great dearth of precious metal objects known from Upper Egypt in the Second Intermediate Period. Only with the funerary equipment of Ahmose's mother, Ahhotep, and the mummy of Kamose is there evidence again of extravagant gold royal funerary objects, such as were known in the Middle Kingdom. Despite the claims of tomb-robbers several hundred years after the Second Intermediate Period, that they had robbed the gold-laden body of King Sobekemsaf II of the 17th Dynasty, only comparatively modest coffins and funerary objects have been recovered for the period preceding Ahmose. Could the king's Karnak inscriptions have been an official explanation for the impoverishment of the Theban region and, more importantly, Ahmose's role in restoring the riches of the Karnak temple and its god? This is not to suggest either that there was no tempest in Ahmose's reign or that there was no purchase of the 'second priesthood' for Ahmose-Nefertari, but rather that these particular events might have been recounted on the stelae simply in order to suit historico-religious purposes.

Royal and Élite Tombs in the Late 17th and Early 18th Dynasties

Ahmose also built monuments at a number of other sites traditionally favoured by kings, including Abydos, the major site of Osiris's cult. These remains, currently being excavated and analysed by Stephen Harvey during the 1990s, are known to have included pyramid monuments as well as temples. Abydos had long been a site that honoured Osiris and the royal ancestors who had merged with Osiris at their deaths. Pyramids were used to mark the Theban tombs of the 17th Dynasty kings, and their brick remains may still have been visible in the Theban region of Dra Abu el-Naga as recently as the nineteenth century.

Although the body of Ahmose was found in the royal mummy cache at Deir el-Bahri (see below), the location of his tomb remains unknown.

Ahmose's mother, Ahhotep, was almost certainly buried in the Theban cemetery, as were kings and queens from earlier in the dynasty. Excavation in the region during the 1990s has focused on what may be one of these royal tombs, and, although no certain evidence yet exists, Daniel Polz's work at Dra Abu el-Naga has shown the continuity of this north Theban cemetery from the 17th to the early 18th Dynasty. He has also demonstrated the existence of élite tomb clusters (each comprising smaller graves scattered around a large tomb), in which single free-standing cult structures may have been shared by several adjacent graves. These clusters of graves are located on the desert floor beneath the Dra Abu el-Naga hills, just south of the entrance to the Valley of the Kings. The royal tombs, some of which were perhaps reused Middle Kingdom chapels, are cut into the hills themselves, overlooking the lesser graves.

So far, the archaeological evidence suggests that funerary wealth was indeed curtailed in the 17th Dynasty, and that decorated tombs were almost unknown in Thebes at this time. Still, the practice of clustering the graves of the élite and the slightly less wealthy beneath royal burial places, despite recalling the old practice of burying followers near the king, may also reflect some new organizational pattern (although without further study it is impossible to conclude more). It is interesting to point out in this regard, however, that in the Saqqara region a non-royal cemetery of the time of Ahmose and Amenhotep I consisted of surface graves, described as rich. Since the burial places of the highest officials of these two reigns (viziers, high priests, treasurers) are largely unknown, identifying the patterns of cemetery development could ultimately help to locate missing tombs. Such work has already been undertaken by Geoffrey Martin and Martin Raven in central Saqqara south of Unas' causeway, and by Alain Zivie in North Saqqara.

The bodies of some rulers and the coffins and funerary equipment of others were moved from their original locations in antiquity (and perhaps also in more recent times). Priests of the late New Kingdom and early Third Intermediate Period reburied some royal mummies in a tomb near Deir el-Bahri, where the mummies of Ahmose and Seqenenra Taa (*c.*1560 BC) were found, both placed in non-royal coffins of slightly later date. The large outer coffin of Ahmose's mother, Ahhotep, made probably at the time of her death (perhaps as late as the reign of Amenhotep I), was also found in the cache, although her inner coffin (presuming both belonged to a single queen named Ahhotep) was found earlier in what may have been her tomb. It contained objects naming both Ahmose and Kamose. The area of Dra Abu el-Naga continued for centuries to be associated with the royal family of Ahmose and with Ahhotep and Ahmose-Nefertari particularly, and later Ramessid tombs, chapels, and stelae in the region venerated their memory.

The cemetery area itself changed dramatically, however, after the early 18th Dynasty. Once royal tombs were no longer being constructed at Dra Abu el-

Naga, it retained its status as the most élite portion of the Theban necropolis only for another thirty years or so, up to the reign of Hatshepsut (1473–1458 BC). With the establishment of the Valley of the Kings as the royal burial ground, a few élite burials began to be placed in Sheikh Abd el-Qurna, the line of hills to the south of Deir el-Bahri. The clusters of valley shaft tombs, largely without chapel structures, followed the movement of the cemetery southward, and through the reign of Hatshepsut, and into that of Thutmose III (1479–1425 BC), shafts were dug into Deir el-Bahri and the Asasif to make family tombs of one or more chambers similar to those at Dra Abu el-Naga. With the sudden increase of wealth held by the élite in the later reign of Thutmose III, this practice seems to have largely disappeared. Tomb-builders were kept busy excavating and decorating rock-cut tombs at Sheikh Abd el-Qurna for the growing royal administration.

Amenhotep I and the Nature of the 18th Dynasty

Like his father, Amenhotep I may not yet have been an adult at his accession, particularly since another elder brother had been a designated heir only about five years earlier. There may have been a brief co-regency with Ahmose to ensure the peaceful transition and continuity of the recently established Dynasty, and his mother, Ahmose-Nefertari, certainly figured prominently in his reign. In a general way, Amenhotep I's reign was a continuation of his father's; buildings that may have been conceived by Ahmose were constructed, and military expeditions in the south, completing earlier campaigns, were carried out. Despite this apparent lack of personal *imprimatur*, Amenhotep I was successful as a ruler in his own right. This is perhaps best borne out by the fact that, soon after his death, both he and his mother were deified and worshipped at Thebes, especially at Deir el-Medina, the royal tomb-workers' village.

Deir el-Medina, situated in western Thebes to the south of the hill of Sheikh Abd el-Qurna, was built early in the 18th Dynasty to house the craftsmen who would build and decorate the royal tombs. Thutmose I is the earliest attested royal name from contemporary monuments, but Amenhotep I and his mother, Ahmose-Nefertari, were patron-deities of the village throughout the New Kingdom and quite likely from the founding of the settlement. Not only were there cult centres for the two in the town, but most houses of the Ramessid era contained in their front rooms a scene honouring the king and queen. The factors linking Amenhotep I and his mother with the necropolis region, with deified rulers, and with rejuvenation generally was visually transmitted by representations of the pair with black or blue skin—both colours of resurrection. The third month of *peret* was devoted to (and named after) Amenhotep I, and within Deir el-Medina several rituals that dramatized his death, burial, and return took place during that period. However, Amenhotep I was a major god of the region and as such had festivals throughout the year. It is probable that the king and his mother became important deified rulers because of their

Facing: a detail from the decoration of the quartzite chapel of Hatshepsut, *c.*1473–1458 BC, portrays a scene from the queen's *sed*-festival (royal jubilee).

connection to the beginning of the New Kingdom and their activity in building on the west bank of the river.

Amenhotep's military successes and consequent financial gains from Nubia began to improve the overall economy of Egypt, and his temple monuments made a significant impact as symbols of royal power. Military action against Nubians south of the second cataract took place around year 8, judging from inscriptions dating to years 8 and 9. Although it is not possible to ascertain with certainty, this may be the campaign described in the tombs of Ahmose, son of Ibana, and Ahmose Pennekhbet at Elkab. It is important to point out, however, that both of these men's autobiographies derive from tombs constructed long after the events retold in their narratives—as much as sixty or seventy years after.

According to Ahmose son of Ibana, he himself carried the king to Kush, where 'his Majesty killed that Nubian bowman in the midst of his army' and then pursued the people and cattle (presumably inland). Ahmose was later rewarded with gold after bringing the king back to the Nile Valley in two days, from an area designated as the Upper Well. An extremely eroded stele left at Aniba and bearing a date in year 8 records that the Bowmen (*iuntyu*) and the Eastern Desert dwellers (*mentyu*) delivered gold and large quantities of products to the king. This stele may commemorate the fact that the successful expedition to Kush was followed up by an official visitation to a secure part of Lower Nubia by the royal family.

By the end of Amenhotep I's reign, the main characteristics of the 18th Dynasty had already been established: its clear devotion to the cult of Amun of Karnak, its successful military conquests in Nubia aimed at extending Egypt southwards for material rewards, its closed nuclear royal family (which avoided political or economic claims on the kingship), and a developing administrative organization presumably drawn from powerful families and collateral rela-

Agricultural scenes in the 18th Dynasty rock-tomb of the high official Pahery at Elkab (tomb EK3).

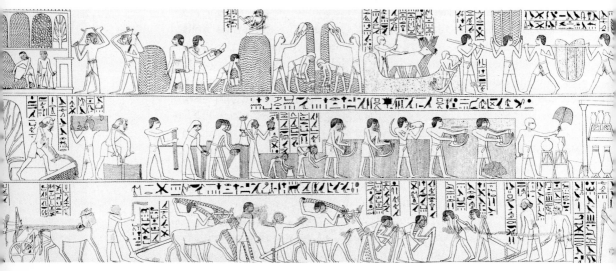

tions, primarily associated, at this point, with the regions of Elkab, Edfu, and Thebes. However, only a small number of the tombs of the high officials of the first two reigns have so far been located.

The Monuments of Amenhotep I

It has been pointed out that Amenhotep I enjoyed at least a dozen years of peaceful rule during which he was able to revive traditional activities associated with monument building: the opening of the Sinai turquoise mines (and consequent expansion of the Middle Kingdom Hathor temple at the Serabit el-Khadim mines), the quarrying of Egyptian alabaster at Bosra (in the name of Ahmose–Nefertari) and at Hatnub, and the opening of work at the sandstone quarries of Gebel el-Silsila, providing most of the stone necessary to rebuild Karnak temple.

Amenhotep I built at several of the sites where his father had been active: at Abydos, for example, he erected a chapel that commemorated Ahmose himself. Following successes in Upper Nubia, Amenhotep dedicated monuments on Sai Island, including a statue similar to that of his father and perhaps some type of building, judging from the survival of blocks inscribed in his name and that of his mother, Ahmose-Nefertari.

Amenhotep I's interest in Delta sites and at Memphis remains unverified, but Karnak figured prominently in his designs. A large limestone gateway at Karnak, now reconstructed, was decorated with jubilee festival decoration. According to its inscription, this was a 'great gate of 20 cubits' and a 'double façade of the temple'. It may once have been the main south entrance that was later replaced by the Seventh Pylon. To the east the king built a stone enclosure around the Middle Kingdom court, with chapels on the interior of the wall. These chapels contained scenes depicting the king, the god's wife, Ahmose-Nefertari, and other temple personnel performing the ritual for Amun, and dedications on behalf of the 11th Dynasty rulers. Thutmose III dismantled all these chapels and rebuilt them in sandstone some forty or fifty years later, but blocks and lintels with offering texts were found in several locations within Karnak. A jubilee peripteral chapel for Amenhotep I probably stood along the southern alleyway and was of a type similar to that of Senusret I (1956–1911 BC) from the 12th Dynasty. Indeed, the style of Amenhotep I's relief carving on the limestone monuments at Karnak so consciously emulated that of Senusret I's artisans that some blocks have been difficult to assign to the proper ruler.

Clearly Karnak's function as a site for venerating the kingship was central to Amenhotep I's construction plans. Whether that emulation included celebrating a royal jubilee prior to thirty years of reign (the ideal time a king waited before his first *sed*-festival), or whether he erected the monuments in anticipation of ruling three full decades, is unknown. Several of Amenhotep I's buildings, none the less, mention the jubilee, such that it is certain the king intended to claim the honour, just as did the great Middle Kingdom rulers.

Facing: the terraced style of the cult temple of the 18th Dynasty ruler Queen Hatshepsut (*c.*1473–1458 BC) at Deir el-Bahri was modelled on the appearance of the adjacent 11th Dynasty temple of Mentuhotep II.

Limestone jambs unearthed from the foundations of the Third Pylon at Karnak provide a list of religious festivals and their dates of celebration. Anthony Spalinger's study of these blocks has indicated that in his festal calendar, as in most things at Karnak, Amenhotep I was heavily influenced by 12th Dynasty calendars. Amenhotep I also had a bark shrine built for the god Amun erected (most likely) in the west front court of the temple.

Across the river from Karnak, Amenhotep I left funerary monuments in the bay of Deir el-Bahri and to the north and east along the edge of the cultivation. Built from mud brick, the Deir el-Bahri monument has been reconstructed with a pyramid, but only a few bricks naming Amenhotep I and Ahmose-Nefertari were found there *in situ*. No tomb has been certainly identified for either.

The building sites of Amenhotep I and his successors may relate to the question of where and how astronomical observations for calendrical purposes were carried out (see Chapter 1). Some discussions have argued that Elephantine may have housed an observatory for Sothic sightings, and recently a graffito from the Hierakonpolis region has suggested that some sightings took place in desert locations. Renewed interest in the cult sites between Aswan and Thebes during the 18th Dynasty does indicate a similar concern with the natural phenomena associated with these cults, such as the rise of the dog-star Sirius (Sopdet/Sothis), the beginning of the rise of the Nile, and attendant lunar cycles. The existence of a festival calendar recorded on papyrus for the reign of Amenhotep I (Papyrus Ebers verso), raises the possibility that the king wished to rework earlier calendars.

The Significance of the Royal Women of the Early 18th Dynasty

A number of princesses, some of whom were also royal wives, are known from the royal cache of mummies at Deir el-Bahri. They were offspring of rulers from the end of the 17th or the beginning of the 18th Dynasty, and their names are often known also from late New Kingdom private tomb chapels that venerated the royal family of the early 18th Dynasty. The titles held by these women, and the absence of husbands other than kings, show the limitations that were placed on females born of the king. The success of the dynastic line in the early 18th Dynasty was certainly attributable, in part, to a decision to limit access to the royal family. In economic terms, this would have meant that holdings gained in the wars were not divided with families whose sons married a princess. The kings were therefore free to enrich military followers as they wished, and thereby build new constituencies. Followers such as Ahmose, son of Ibana, and Ahmose Pennekhbet are two examples of these new members of the élite, but legal documents later in the New Kingdom inform us of other men whose fortunes derived from grants by Ahmose.

In political and religious terms, the closed royal family apparently reached back into the Middle Kingdom (and the Old Kingdom before it), when

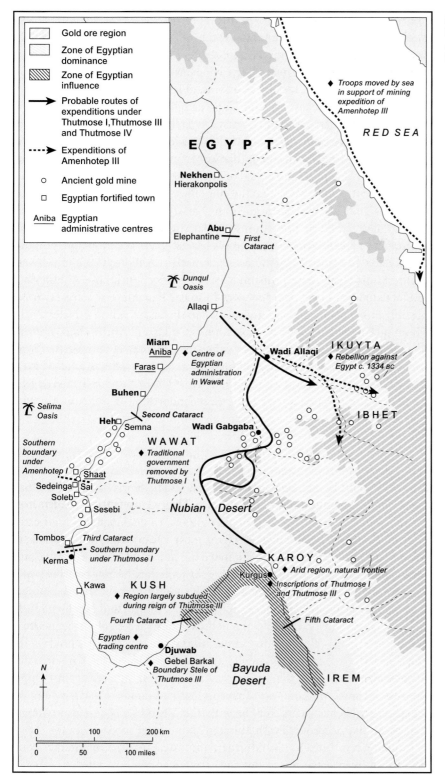

Map of Egypt and Nubia between the reigns of Ahmose and Amenhotep III (c.1550–1352 BC).

Gold ore region

Zone of Egyptian dominance

Zone of Egyptian influence

Probable routes of expeditions under Thutmose I, Thutmose III and Thutmose IV

Expeditions of Amenhotep III

○ Ancient gold mine

□ Egyptian fortified town

Aniba — Egyptian administrative centres

E G Y P T

RED SEA

◆ Troops moved by sea in support of mining expedition of Amenhotep III

Nekhen □
Hierakonpolis

Abu □
Elephantine — First Cataract

Dunqul Oasis

Allaqi □

Miam □
Aniba
◆ Centre of Egyptian administration in Wawat

Faras □

Wadi Allaqi ●
I K U Y T A
◆ Rebellion against Egypt c. 1334 BC

Buhen □

I B H E T

Selima Oasis

Heh □
Semna
Wadi Gabgaba ●

W A W A T
◆ Traditional government removed by Thutmose I

Second Cataract

Southern boundary under Amenhotep I
Shaat □
Sedeinga □ Sai
Soleb
□ Sesebi

Nubian Desert

Tombos □
Third Cataract
Southern boundary under Thutmose I
Kerma ●

Kawa □

K A R O Y ○
◆ Arid region, natural frontier

Kurgus ●
◆ Inscriptions of Thutmose I and Thutmose III

K U S H
◆ Region largely subdued during reign of Thutmose III

Fourth Cataract

Fifth Cataract

Egyptian ◆ trading centre
● **Djuwab**
Gebel Barkal
◆ Boundary Stele of Thutmose III

Bayuda Desert

I R E M

N

0   100   200 km
0   50   100 miles

227

princesses were frequently married to kings or associated throughout life with their reigning fathers. In order to assure the exclusivity of the line, however, the family of Seqenenra and Ahhotep apparently established the additional prohibition that royal daughters were to marry no one other than a king. This was not the case in the Old and Middle kingdoms, at least not always, since we know examples of high officials marrying kings' daughters, but, once the custom was established at the end of the 17th Dynasty, it persisted through the 18th Dynasty. Only with the reign of Rameses II do we again have definite evidence of princesses marrying anyone other than kings.

There were no enfeebling effects on the kinship line as a result of this practice, because it did not mean that the kings themselves were only able to marry princesses. Indeed, throughout the 18th Dynasty, kings were most commonly born to their fathers by non-royal secondary queens, such as Tetisheri. If our understanding of the documentation is correct, then Tetisheri bore both the mother and father of King Ahmose. His mother, Ahhotep, bore him by her brother (full or half), most probably Seqenenra, possibly Kamose. Ahhotep had several daughters as well, but Seqenenra also had daughters by at least two and possibly three other women. Ahmose married his sister, Ahmose-Nefertari, by whom he fathered at least two sons, Ahmose-ankh and Amenhotep. He may, however, have fathered children by other women as well. At least two princesses, Satkamose and (Ahmose-) Merytamun, had the titles of king's daughter, king's sister, great royal wife, and god's wife. The first was described on later stelae as a sister of Amenhotep I, while the second is often identified as Ahmose-Nefertari's daughter, who also married her brother, Amenhotep I, although no document actually states this explicitly.

Despite the restrictions on marriage for kings' daughters, several princesses who emerged as major queens (Ahhotep, Ahmose-Nefertari, Hatshepsut) were extremely active in the reigns of their husbands and heirs. Ahmose's mother, Queen Ahhotep, whose large outer coffin was found in the Deir el-Bahri royal cache, was, according to her titles on that coffin, a king's daughter, king's sister, great royal wife, and king's mother. On Ahmose's year 18 stele from Karnak, he honoured Ahhotep with titles that implied her *de facto* governance of the land. Although we are ignorant of Ahmose's age at accession, he may have been only a boy for some period of his reign. It is highly significant that the queen mother was honoured later by her son for pacifying Upper Egypt and expelling rebels. Ahhotep apparently carried on the fight without successful challenge from within the region—although the implication is that the family's hold on the kingship was tested during this period. Claude Vandersleyen has suggested that the battles that Ahmose fought against Aata and Teti-an were against Upper Egyptian enemies, the latter perhaps representing a family line with whom the 17th Dynasty Theban rulers Nubkheperra Intef VI and Kamose had also fought (and this would accord well with Ahhotep's honouring Sobekemsaf, the widow of Nubkheperra Intef VI, at Edfu). In any case, Ahhotep apparently commanded the respect of local troops and grandees to preserve a fledgling dynastic line, and she continued to function as king's mother well into the reign of Amenhotep I.

Perhaps not long after year 18 of Ahmose's reign, Ahhotep ceded pride of place to Princess Ahmose-Nefertari, who may have been her daughter. Ahmose's Donation Stele at Karnak (mentioned above) is the first known monument on which Ahmose-Nefertari figures; she is described on this stele as king's daughter, king's sister, king's great wife, god's wife of Amun, and, like Ahhotep, mistress of Upper and Lower Egypt. Ahmose and Ahmose-Nefertari are depicted with their son, Prince Ahmose-ankh. Only a few years after this inscription was made, in year 22, Ahmose-Nefertari claimed the title of king's mother, although it is not known whether the designation referred to Ahmose-ankh or Amenhotep. In any case, the queen survived her husband Ahmose and even her son Amenhotep I, and still held the position of god's wife of Amun in the reign of Thutmose I (1504–1492 BC).

Ahmose-Nefertari used the god's wife title more frequently even than that of great royal wife. She also operated independently of both her husband and her son in monument building and cult roles. When she died, a stele of a non-royal contemporary recorded simply that 'the god's wife . . . had flown to heaven'. The emphasis on her role as priestess was perhaps due to the independent economic and religious power ceded to the office of god's wife by Ahmose. The Donation Stele records Ahmose's creation of a trust relating to the 'second priesthood of Amun', whose benefices were then granted to the god's wife in perpetuity, to be passed on, without interference, to whom she wished. The institution of the divine adoratrice, an office separate from the god's wife but also held by Ahmose-Nefertari, was also mentioned on the Donation Stele. The economic holdings of the priestess institution apparently continued to grow, such that some 100 years after Ahmose's death, and following reorganization of the descent of the offices, the produce of the 'house of the adoratrice' were a significant focus of account papyri.

Ahmose-Nefertari functioned as great royal wife and particularly god's wife of Amun throughout her son's reign. No certain wife is known for Amenhotep I of his own generation, although it is often presumed that the 'king's daughter, god's wife, great royal wife, united to the white crown, lady of the two lands' (Ahmose-)Merytamun, whose coffin was found in a tomb at Deir el-Bahri, was his sister and consort. It should be noted, however, that the only connection between the two is the fact that her coffin (like those of Ahhotep and Ahmose-Nefertari) dates stylistically to Amenhotep I's reign. There are no monuments of this date that refer to (Ahmose-)Merytamun, apart from a possible reference to her on a monument in Nubia. On his year 8 stele, the figure of Amenhotep I was followed by king's mother Ahmose-Nefertari and a second god's wife, king's daughter, sister, and king's wife (not 'great') whose name was later restored as Ahmose-Nefertari, before Horus of Miam (Aniba). This may instead have been Merytamun, who had been elevated to queen, but then predeceased Ahmose-Nefertari. Monuments that represent the presence of female royal family members at border regions are attested several times in the 18th Dynasty, perhaps following an older tradition. There are representations of this type at Sinai, the Aswan rock outcrops, and Nubia from the first to the fourth cataracts, in the Middle and New kingdoms. Perhaps they are meant to link the queens and princesses to Hathor, goddess of foreign lands, whose role as daughter of the sun-god was to be protective of her father.

Another female family member in the early 18th Dynasty was Amenhotep I's daughter, king's sister, and god's wife, Satamun, who is known both from her coffin in the royal mummy cache and from two statues at central and southern Karnak. Attested from the reign of Ahmose onwards, she never became queen, but appears to have been honoured by Amenhotep I, along with Ahmose-Nefertari, for her priestly role as Amun's wife. Even in the Ramessid Period, Satamun and Merytamun were both venerated as members of the family of Ahmose-Nefertari and were included in scenes depicting the deified royal family. Precise chronology of the early 18th Dynasty and specific genealogy of the family appears to have been as obscure to the late New Kingdom Thebans as it is to us today, so we cannot rely on these votive references to provide secure parentage.

It is interesting to note that, notwithstanding the kings' apparent ability to marry as many women as they wished, no offspring of Amenhotep I have been identified with certainty, despite his twenty-year reign. A king's son Ramose known from a statue now in Liverpool may have been from the Ahmosid family, but his specific parentage is not given. None the less, perhaps owing to the stability provided by Amenhotep's rule, the succession passed without event to Thutmose I, who is not known to have been a member of the Ahmosid family.

Thutmose I and his Family

The first succession of the 18th Dynasty that did not descend from father to son did not result in a lengthy reign. In 1987 Luc Gabolde published a study of the chronology of the reigns of Thutmose I and II, estimating eleven years for the former and three for the latter. The short duration of Thutmose I's rule was in inverse proportion to its impact on the character of later 18th Dynasty kingship. Thutmose's interest in the military and economic exploitation of Nubia may have built upon the efforts of Amenhotep I, but his expedition to Syria opened new horizons that led later to Egypt's important role in the trade and diplomacy of the Late Bronze Age Near East. The effect of Thutmose's efforts on cultural material generally is most visible today in Thebes and Nubia, but the importance of Memphis, and regions further north, is also evident.

Thutmose I's father is unknown, but his mother was named Seniseneb, a rather common name of the Second Intermediate Period and early 18th Dynasty. The families of both Ineni and Hapuseneb (high priest of Amun under Hatshepsut) contained female members with this name. Seniseneb appeared behind Thutmose I and in front of Ahmose-Nefertari on the Wadi Halfa copy of the coronation stele of Thutmose's first regnal year. Seniseneb's parentage is equally unknown, but she had no title during her son's reign other than 'king's mother'. Thutmose's principal wife was Ahmose, who had the titles 'king's sister, great royal wife'. Claude Vandersleyen has assumed that she was Thutmose's own sister, primarily because she lacked the title 'king's daughter'. The king would then have been attempting to recreate the situation of the two preceding reigns, with brother and sister rulers. Her name may suggest, however, that Ahmose was a member of Amenhotep I's family, perhaps by Prince Ahmose-ankh, and that it was her important connection to the Ahmosid family that facilitated Thutmose's accession to the throne. At present Ahmose's origins and the succession of Thutmose cannot be better explicated.

It was by Ahmose that Thutmose I fathered the future Queen Hatshepsut and probably also a princess called Nefrubity, to judge from the latter's appearance with them in scenes from the temple of Hatshepsut at Deir el-Bahri. The 'god's wife of Amun', Ahmose-Nefertari, died in the reign of Thutmose I and was replaced by Hatshepsut. By a non-royal wife, Mutnefret, the king fathered the future King Thutmose II (1492–1479 BC); the female parentage of his two other sons, Amenmose and Wadjmose, is uncertain, but the latter was honoured along with Thutmose I on a statue of Mutnefret dedicated by Thutmose II in the chapel on the south side of the Ramesseum. Indeed, it has been suggested that this chapel was a family funerary temple; it would have been, therefore, more specifically a family temple for Thutmose I's heirs by Mutnefret.

The Monuments of Thutmose I

Thutmose I and his viceroy Turi left monuments and inscriptions at a number of sites in Upper and Lower Nubia. Several brick installations may date from his reign in the region of Kenisa (at the fourth cataract) and at Napata. Blocks from buildings (or fragments of blocks) have survived at Sai Island, held at least since Ahmose's reign, and traces remain at Semna, Buhen, Aniba, Quban, and Qasr Ibrim. The probability is that, apart from stelae, the monuments were small in scale, comprising stone elements within brick structures. Thutmose III and Hatshepsut may well have reconstructed brick buildings of this type in sandstone, particularly at Semna and Buhen. Within the traditional borders of Egypt, Thutmose I left indications of building at Elephantine, Edfu (probably), Armant, Thebes, Ombos (near the late 17th to early 18th Dynasty palace centre at Deir el-Ballas), Abydos, el-Hiba, Memphis, and Giza. Votive objects dedicated in his name have been found in Sinai at the temple of Serabit el-Khadim.

The materials from Thebes, Abydos, and Giza are of particular interest. Giza became a major pilgrimage site during the New Kingdom, as the location of the tombs of Khufu and Khafra, and as the cult place for the god identified with the Great Sphinx, Horemakhet ('Horus in the horizon'). It is no coincidence that the monuments at Giza, like those at Abydos and Karnak, emphasized the ven-

Facing: map of Egypt and the Levant, showing the limits of incursions into the Near East between the reigns of Ahmose and Amenhotep III (*c*.1550–1352 BC).

eration of rulers. Like Ahmose and Amenhotep I before him, as well as the next four monarchs, Thutmose I chose to embellish cult places that promoted the connections between king and god and between king and king. However, he seems to have associated himself with distant royal precursors rather than immediate ones.

At Abydos, Thutmose I left a stele recording his contributions to the temple of Osiris. Instead of honouring his royal predecessors directly, he donated cult objects and statues. According to the stele, priests then proclaimed him as the offspring of Osiris, whose intended role was to restore the divine sanctuaries with the vast wealth given to him by the earth deities Geb and Tatjenen. Thutmose I did not choose to honour the two previous kings, perhaps because their monuments stressed the Ahmosid family line of which he was not a part; instead he wished to claim his kingship from the great gods themselves. As a royal ideology, divine descent was common to the 18th Dynasty kings, but it may well have received its first emphasis in the reign of Thutmose I. It was subsequently consistently exploited in royal inscriptions from Hatshepsut (1473–1458 BC) to Amenhotep III (1390–1352 BC).

At Karnak, Thutmose I left an indelible mark. He enlarged and completed an ambulatory worked on by Amenhotep I around the Middle Kingdom court, and he extended its walls westwards to join two new pylon gates (the Fourth and Fifth) which he built as the entrance to the temple. He then finished the court space between the two gateways. He also completed the decoration of Amenhotep I's alabaster chapel, which appears to be his only claim to direct connection with his predecessor. In northern Karnak, he replaced a monument of Ahmose with his 'treasury', but appears to have preserved a block from the earlier structure and built it into his own.

The Policy of Thutmose I in Nubia and Syria-Palestine

Thutmose I's campaign to Nubia was very likely the true death knell to Kush and its capital at Kerma. The tombs of three of his officials—Turi (king's viceroy of the south), Ahmose son of Ibana, and Ahmose Pennekhbet—all contained descriptions of this campaign, which probably took place during the second and third years of his reign. The longest description of the major battle, however, was inscribed on the rock outcrop of Tombos, at the third cataract, a stone's throw from the entrance to Kerma. The king's inscription described the campaign's successes in the third and fourth cataract regions, in vividly violent terms: 'The Nubian bowmen fall by the sword and are thrown aside on their lands; their stench floods their valleys . . . The pieces cut from them are too much for the birds carrying off the prey to another place.'

Thutmose's armies (like those of Amenhotep I before him) then struck out eastwards away from the Nile Valley and into the desert behind Kerma, eventually reaching the fourth cataract area around Kurgus and Kenisa. Since the river makes a great bend between the third and fourth cataracts, a west–east overland

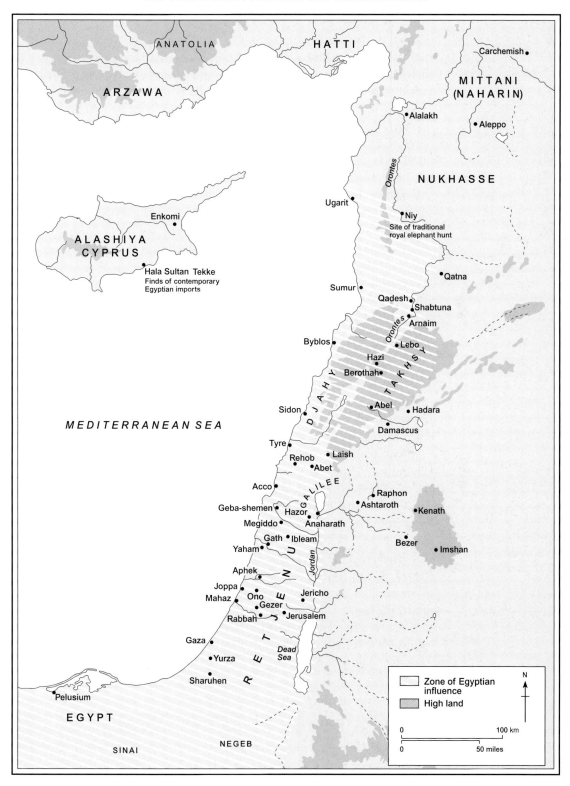

ANATOLIA

HATTI

ARZAWA

Carchemish

MITTANI
(NAHARIN)

Alalakh

Aleppo

Orontes

NUKHASSE

Ugarit

Niy
Site of traditional
royal elephant hunt

Enkomi

ALASHIYA
CYPRUS

Qatna

Hala Sultan Tekke
Finds of contemporary
Egyptian imports

Sumur

Qadesh
Shabtuna

Arnaim

Byblos

Lebo

Orontes

Hazi

Berothah

T A K H S Y

D J A H Y

Abel

Hadara

MEDITERRANEAN SEA

Sidon

Damascus

Tyre

Rehob
Abet

Laish

Acco

G A L I L E E

Raphon
Ashtaroth

Kenath

Geba-shemen
Hazor

Megiddo
Anaharath

Gath
Ibleam

Bezer

Imshan

Yaham

C A N A A N

Jordan

Aphek

Joppa
Mahaz
Ono
Gezer
Rabbah

Jericho

Jerusalem

R E T E N U

Gaza

Dead
Sea

Yurza

Sharuhen

Pelusium

EGYPT

SINAI

NEGEB

Zone of Egyptian
influence

High land

N

0   100 km

0   50 miles

route connected the two cataracts. Thutmose I then left an inscription at Kenisa. According to Ahmose son of Ibana, on his consequent return from Kerma to Thebes, 'his Majesty sailed northward, all countries in his grasp, with that defeated Nubian bowman [probably the ruler of Kush] being hanged head down at the [front] of the [boat] of his Majesty, and landed at Karnak.'

Following this success, Thutmose I led his army to Syria for a first campaign in that region. No doubt well aware of the Mitanni overlords in the vicinity, the king steered clear of direct confrontation with them, and, following several local successes, departed southwards to Niy, where he may have hunted elephants. The descriptions of this expedition derive only from the tombs of Ahmose Pennekhbet and Ahmose, son of Ibana, both built and decorated in the reign of Thutmose III (and later). They characterize Syria as the Mitanni aggressor with accompanying epithets otherwise unknown until late in the fourth decade of Thutmose III's reign. No document contemporary with the reign of Thutmose I mentions this campaign.

Egyptian engagement with Mitanni was extremely limited in the early 18th Dynasty. Skirmishes with Mitanni vassals first occurred during Thutmose I's reign, but the conquest of north eastern regions did not occur until at least thirty-six years later, when Thutmose III began his Syrian expedition. Perhaps Thutmose I, on his brief expedition to Syria, encountered enemies and military technology beyond the capability of Egypt's armies, which almost certainly had fewer chariots than the Mitanni at the time. Newly found relief fragments of the time of Ahmose at Abydos, however, show that chariots were already being depicted at the very beginning of the 18th Dynasty. Had Thutmose I made substantial territorial or material gains, it is difficult to believe that Mitanni would not have been mentioned more frequently on the preserved monuments of Thutmose I, Thutmose II, or Hatshepsut. It is instead far more likely that Thutmose I simply found the Mitanni vassals to be superior military powers and that he departed after leaving an inscription and perhaps conducting an elephant hunt in the region of Niy, which lay to the south of the Mitanni-dominated cities.

A brief reference to Thutmose I's Syro-Palestinian expedition has been preserved in a fragmentary inscription at Deir el-Bahri, associated with the description of Hatshepsut's Punt expedition. This text, which essentially celebrates the fame of Thutmose I, mentioning elephants and horses, as well as the region of Niy, suggests that, in the time of Hatshepsut, Thutmose I was vaunted primarily for bringing back the exotica of the land of Niy, rather than for having conquered Mitanni.

The Tomb of Thutmose I and Royal 'Ancestor Worship'

Thutmose I's original burial location remains a subject of debate. His name occurs on sarcophagi from two tombs in the Valley of the Kings (KV 20 and

KV 38), but there is no agreement on which of the locations is earlier or whether either was originally excavated for Thutmose. The body of the king may be among those from the royal cache, but this too is uncertain. Two coffins of Thutmose I, usurped for Pinudjem I (one of the chief-priests of Anum at Thebes in the 21st Dynasty), contained an unidentified mummy, which may possibly be the body of the king himself. One of his high officials, Ineni, describes his overseeing of the work on Thutmose's tomb: 'I oversaw the excavation of the cliff tomb of his Majesty, in privacy; none saw, none heard.' His vague description of the tomb as a *heret*, usually taken to mean 'cliff' tomb, may indicate a location in the Valley of the Kings, but the question remains unsettled.

There is no known funerary temple for Thutmose I; bricks bearing his name—and some bearing both his and Hatshepsut's—are attested from several locations near Deir el-Bahri's 'valley temple'. A chapel honouring Thutmose I was included by Hatshepsut in her temple, but this does not necessarily mean that he had no funerary cult before her reign. Rather, she venerated her ancestral line within her funerary temple, because such temples were both 'family' shrines and temples honouring the union between the god Amun and the king. This 'ancestor worship' was already evident in the monuments of Ahmose and Amenhotep I at Abydos, while non-royal tomb chapels of contemporary and mid-18th Dynasty date frequently included niches or scenes venerating living and deceased family members.

The Brief Reign of Thutmose II

The highest preserved year date for the reign of Thutmose II is his first, and scholarship in the 1980s and 1990s suggests that his reign lasted for no more than three years. Hatshepsut, the half-sister of Thutmose, served as his 'great royal wife' and was also 'god's wife of Amun'. Like Ahmose-Nefertari, from whom she inherited her religious role, Hatshepsut was frequently featured in the reliefs decorating the Theban monuments of her husband, most commonly in the guise of 'god's wife'. Thutmose II's brief tenure has left few records of external activities, but the Egyptian army continued to quell uprisings in Nubia and brought about the final demise of the kingdom of Kush at Kerma.

The nearly ephemeral nature of Thutmose II's rule is underlined by the paucity of his monuments generally, and their absence in the north of Egypt. Thutmose II left no identifiable tomb (not unusual in the early 18th Dynasty) or any completed funerary temple. There are indications that the temple of Hatshepsut at Deir el-Bahri was originally begun in the reign of Thutmose II, perhaps even then under the queen's direction. However, it may have been intended as his (and her) funerary cult location. A small temple near Medinet Habu was erected for him by Thutmose III, perhaps carrying out a plan already contemplated by Thutmose II.

Thutmose II's only major monuments are from Karnak: a pylon-shaped limestone gateway was erected at the front of the Fourth Pylon's forecourt. Both the gate and another limestone structure of unknown type were later dismantled and the blocks placed in the Third Pylon foundations. The gateway has been reconstructed in the Karnak 'Open Air Museum'. The structure with raised relief scenes contained a preponderance of scenes of the king, some showing him with Hatshepsut, and some depicting Hatshepsut alone. This building was completed in the first years of Thutmose III (during the Hatshepsut regency); following her accession, the queen's agents actually replaced the small boy-king's name in a few places with her own cartouches. On one face of a four-sided pillar fragment Thutmose II is shown receiving crowns, while two other sides bear reliefs of Nefrura (his daughter) and Hatshepsut receiving life from the god. This monument may have been created after Thutmose II had died, but it is undeniable that Hatshepsut was already an important influence on the monarchy before her brother's death.

Other constructions in the name of Thutmose II are known from Napata, where Thutmose I may already have left building remains. At Semna and Kumma, as well as at Elephantine, there are surviving blocks from buildings of Thutmose II. In addition, recent exavations at Elephantine have revealed a statue that was dedicated by another ruler (presumably Hatshepsut) in the name of her 'brother'; Vandersleyen notes that there is also an identical uninscribed royal torso in the Elephantine Museum.

The only known military expedition of Thutmose II's reign is recorded on a rock-cut stele at Sehel, south of Aswan. It is dated to the first year of his reign and describes a local uprising in Kush that was punished with the death of all involved, except for one son of the ruler of Kush, who was brought back as a hostage, evidently resulting in the restoration of peace. Clearly this was a minor rebellion, but the family of the local Kerma king was still active, so the action was brutal and swift. This effectively ended Egypt's major problems with Kush. Inhabitants of the region were pursued through the desert from near an Egyptian fortress on the river.

Ahmose Pennekhbet notes in his funerary inscriptions that numerous Shasu were brought away as prisoners for Thutmose II during an otherwise unattested campaign. Since the ethnic term Shasu could refer to peoples of either Palestine or Nubia, this brief entry probably referred to the year 1 Nubian expedition. It is important to note again, however, that these autobiographies were carved on the wall several decades after the events they describe. The effects of creating a single narrative may have made any single entry somewhat less than complete.

Thutmose II's mother, Mutnefret, was alive in his reign, to judge from the statue dedicated for her in the Wadjmose chapel at Thebes mentioned above. Although the king's age at accession (and death) is unknown, it is quite possible that he was younger than his sister and wife Hatshepsut. She was the offspring of Thutmose I and Ahmose, the queen officially recognized in the previous reign. A stele of Thutmose II's reign shows the king followed by Ahmose and Hatshepsut. Apparently the latter was already 'god's wife of Amun' in the reign of Thutmose I, following Ahmose-Nefertari's death. Thutmose II was not so young that he could not father a child, however, since Nefrura is portrayed at Karnak with him and Hatshepsut.

The Regency of Hatshepsut

The fifty-four-year reign of Thutmose III began in his early childhood with Hatshepsut, his aunt and stepmother, acting as regent. According to Ineni, whose funerary 'autobiography' ended just before Hatshepsut became ruler: 'his [Thutmose II's] son was set in his place as king of the Two Lands upon the throne of him who engendered him. His sister, the god's wife Hatshepsut, executed the affairs of the Two Lands according to her counsels. Egypt worked for her, head bowed, the excellent seed of the god, who came forth from him . . . '. Ahmose Pennekhbet's inscription similarly refers to Hatshepsut's regency in unabashed terms, not only describing her as god's wife but also calling her Maatkara, which was her chosen throne name (prenomen).

It has been argued that Hatshepsut saw herself as Thutmose I's heir even before her father died, thus implying that the dating of Thutmose III's rule may have applied to her own reign as much as to the child king's. It is also possible that she capitalized on the role of 'god's wife of Amun', its economic holdings, and its connection to the family of Ahmose-Nefertari (possibly Hatshepsut's own genealogical link, through her mother, Ahmose) in order to support her regency in a manner similar to her female predecessors, Ahhotep and Ahmose-Nefertari. She also appears to have been preparing Nefrura for the same type of role.

However, once Hatshepsut had given herself a throne name and begun to transform herself publicly into a king, she can have had only one certain earlier model to follow: Sobekkara

Sobekneferu (1777–1773 BC), the woman who ruled at the end of the 12th Dynasty (see Chapter 7). Hatshepsut did not attempt to legitimize her reign by claiming to have ruled with or for her husband Thutmose II. Instead she emphasized her blood line, and in the period before she had taken a throne name the royal steward Senenmut left an inscription at Aswan (commemorating the quarrying of her first obelisks), naming her as: 'king's daughter, king's sister, god's wife, great royal wife Hatshepsut'. At Deir el-Bahri, scenes and texts of Hatshepsut claim that Thutmose I had proclaimed her as heir before his death, and that Ahmose had been chosen by Amun to bear the new divine ruler. Hatshepsut had the same pure genealogy as Ahmose-Nefertari, Ahhotep, and Sobekneferu. The latter was never a queen: she was a king's daughter, whose embodiment of the pure family line was apparently sufficient to maintain her rule as pharaoh. Hatshepsut must have felt she embodied the same aspects, and for nearly twenty years she was correct.

Her only known offspring (by Thutmose II) was Nefrura, who was frequently described as 'king's daughter' and 'god's wife', and also, more than once, 'mistress of the two lands' and 'lady of Upper and Lower Egypt'. The debate continues as to whether she was wife to Thutmose III during the co-regency period, but she did appear as 'god's wife' with him as late as the twenty-second or twenty-third year of his reign. At some time Thutmose III replaced her name with that of Sitiah, whom he married after his sole rule began. If Nefrura was ever 'king's great wife' to Thutmose III, the king must have ended the formal relationship soon after Hatshepsut's disappearance in the twentieth or twenty-first year of his reign. Children born to Nefrura are not explicitly identified, although the prince Amenemhat has been suggested as her son on purely circumstantial grounds.

Hatshepsut's Ambitious Building Projects

As ruler, Hatshepsut inaugurated building projects that far outstripped those of her predecessors. The list of sites touched by Thutmose I and II was expanded in Upper Egypt, to include places that the Ahmosid rulers had favoured: Kom Ombo, Nekhen (Hierakonpolis), and Elkab in particular, but also Armant and Elephantine. Both Hatshepsut and Thutmose III left numerous remains in Nubia: at Qasr Ibrim, at Sai (a seated statue of the queen recalling those of Ahmose and Amenhotep I), Semna, Faras, Quban, and especially Buhen, where the queen built for Horus of Buhen a peripteral temple of a type common in the mid-18th Dynasty. The scenes on the walls of the temple originally included figures of both Hatshepsut and Thutmose III, but he later replaced her name with his own and that of his father and grandfather. The Buhen temple (now entirely moved to the Khartoum Museum) contains scenes of Hatshepsut's coronation and veneration of her father.

Memphis may have received attention from Hatshepsut as ruler. An alabaster jar fragment from the region of the Ptah temple has been identified, but, more significantly, the colossal Egyptian alabaster sphinx that sits within the south wall of the Ramessid temple precinct may have formed part of an earlier approach to the temple and was very likely accompanied by a second sphinx. The Hatnub quarries, probable source of stone for the sphinx, were located in Middle Egypt, not very far from another of her monuments, the rock-cut shrine at Beni Hasan that is now called the Speos Artemidos. Apart from the evidence of quarrying at Hatnub, there is no record of 18th Dynasty kings building in Middle Egypt before Hatshepsut, and her lengthy inscription at Speos Artemidos documented that she was the first to restore temples in the area since the destructive days of the wars with the Hyksos. During those wars, Middle Egypt was a strategic region, owing to the roads stretching through the Western Desert to oases, and thence south to Nubia.

Hatshepsut claimed in her inscription to have rebuilt temples at Hebenu (the capital of the Oryx nome), at Hermopolis, and at Cusae, and to have acted for the lioness-goddess Pakhet sacred to the region around the Speos itself. This work must have been carried out under the supervision of Djehuty, overseer of the treasury and also nomarch in Herwer in Middle Egypt, as well as overseer of priests of Thoth in Hermopolis. The inscriptions in his tomb at Dra Abu el-Naga mention the numerous works he supervised on behalf of Hatshepsut, and invoke a number of regional deities, including Hathor of Cusae. The gods of those cult centres (Horus, Thoth, and Hathor, respectively) therefore received—like the other deities of Nubia and Egypt—a new share of the economic resources of Egypt.

However, no site received more attention from Hatshepsut than Thebes. The temple of Karnak grew once more under her supervision, with the constructon work being directed by a number of officials, including Hapuseneb (her high priest of Amun), Djehuty (the overseer of the treasury, mentioned above), Puyemra (the second priest of Amun), and, of course, Senenmut (the royal steward, also mentioned above). With the country evidently at peace during most of the twenty years of her reign, Hatshepsut was able to exploit the wealth of Egypt's natural resources, as well as those of Nubia. Gold flowed in from the eastern deserts and the south; the precious stone quarries were in operation, Gebel el-Silsila began to be worked in earnest for sandstone, cedar was imported from the Levant, and ebony came from Africa (by way of Punt, perhaps). In the inscriptions of the queen and her officials, the monuments and the materials used to make them were specifically detailed at some length. Clearly Hatshepsut was pleased with the amount and variety of luxury goods that she could acquire and donate in Amun's honour; so much so that she had a scene carved at Deir el-Bahri to show the quantity of exotic goods brought from Punt. Likewise, Djehuty detailed the bounties from Punt that Hatshepsut donated to Amun, and he also described the electrum from the mines in the Eastern Desert, with which he was entrusted to embellish Karnak. Djehuty, Hapuseneb, and Puyemra all described participating in the making of the ebony shrine donated at Mut's temple of Isheru at Karnak. Work in that temple was conducted for Hatshepsut by Senenmut, whose name occurs on a gate excavated there, but Hapuseneb also left a statue in the precinct.

At Karnak Hatshepsut left, most significantly in terms of her personal *imprimatur*, the Eighth Pylon, a new southern gateway to the temple precinct. Lying along the north–south processional way that connected Karnak central to the Mut precinct, the new sandstone pylon was the first stone-built one on that route. Ironically, evidence of Hatshepsut's building effort is today invisible, since the face of the pylon was erased and redecorated in the first years of Amenhotep II (1427–1400 BC), son of Thutmose III. Nevertheless, Hatshepsut's desire to create a new main entrance was part of a grander plan, designed to ensure that her involvement with the temple would not be forgotten easily. By connecting Karnak to Mut's temple, the queen was perhaps deliberately shifting attention away from Thutmose II's gateway before the Fourth Pylon. She likewise built a temple in the north–south alley dedicated to Amun-Ra-Kamutef, a creator form of the god. Taken together, her constructions at Luxor temple, to the south, which housed the yearly royal renewal festival, the Mut temple, where Amun's consort resided, and the Kamutef shrine formed a set of buildings in which Hatshepsut could describe and celebrate her birth from Amun, gain the favour of the deities for her rule, and expand the claim to divinity for the kingship itself.

Elsewhere in Karnak central Hatshepsut had a palace built for her ritual activities, and she constructed a series of rooms around the central bark shrine where she had depicted her purification and acceptance by the gods. Precisely where she had her great quartzite bark shrine set up remains an issue of debate, but it is now being reconstructed in the Open Air Museum at Karnak. This shrine bears depictions of the processions associated with the Opet Festival (in which Amun of Karnak visited Luxor temple) and the Beautiful Feast of the Valley. During the latter festival, Amun left Karnak to travel westwards to Deir el-Bahri and the temples of other rulers. This festival became the most prized one on the Theban west bank during the New Kingdom.

Hatshepsut had a tomb excavated in the Valley of the Kings for herself as ruler. Tomb KV 20 appears to be the earliest tomb in the valley, and Hatshepsut had it enlarged to accommodate both her own sarcophagus and a second that had been initially carved for herself but then recarved for her father Thutmose I. Both Hatsheput and Thutmose I may have initially been laid to rest there, but Thutmose III later removed Thutmose I's body to KV 38, which he had built for a similar purpose. The confusion of multiple tombs and sarcophagi for Hatshepsut is not entirely at an end, but research by Luc Gabolde and others has contributed to a better understanding of early work in the Valley of the Kings. The queen also built a temple to Amun at Medinet Habu at the southern end of Thebes. Completed by Thutmose III, this chapel housed an important cult of the god on the west, becoming part of the regular festival processional cycle which included Deir el-Bahri and Karnak, and later also involved Osiris.

The Temple at Deir el-Bahri: A Statement of Hatshepsut's Reign

The temple at Deir el-Bahri remains Hatshepsut's most enduring monument. Built of limestone and designed in a series of terraces set against the cliff wall in a bay formed naturally by river and wind action, the temple called 'Holy of Holies' (*djeser djeseru*) was Hatshepsut's most complete statement in material form about her reign. The design of the temple followed a form known since the First Intermediate Period, and particularly inspired by the 11th Dynasty temple of Mentuhotep II (2055–2004 BC) just to the south. Terrace temples, however, had continued to be built in the Second Intermediate Period and, more recently, in the early 18th Dynasty (most particularly by Ahmose at Abydos). Hatshepsut borrowed forms developed by many of her royal ancestors; for example, colossal Osirid statues set in front of square pillars on her colonnades resemble closely statues of Senusret I. Hatshepsut's inspiration may instead have been her father, Thutmose I, however, since his Osirid colossi at Karnak, although of sandstone, were similar to those at Deir el-Bahri.

By the time of its completion, the temple contained scenes and inscriptions that carefully characterize a number of aspects of the life and rule of Hatshepsut. The most accessible areas, the lower and middle colonnades, showed, for example, a Nubian campaign, the transport of obelisks for Karnak temple, an expedition to Punt to bring back incense trees and African trade products, and the divine birth of the ruler. Officials associated with the work were mentioned by name, including the treasurer Nehesy, and Senenmut. The funerary inscriptions of Djehuty and Senenmut suggest that they were active in the building and embellishment of the 'Holy of Holies' temple at Deir el-Bahri.

On the south end of the middle terrace, a chapel was constructed for Hathor, goddess of the western cemetery, and it was fronted by a pillared court, whose capitals were fashioned as emblems of the cow-faced deity. Scenes of the king feeding the sacred cow flank the entrance to the chapel itself. On the upper terrace there was a central door into a peristyle court behind which was the main temple sanctuary. Scenes of the Beautiful Feast of the Valley procession decorated the north side of the court, while the Opet Festival appeared on the south. Another enclosed court to the north contained niche shrines to the gods, including Amun, and a large Egyptian alabaster open-air altar for the sun-god Ra-Horakhty. This sun-temple feature was a significant addition to the complex, recalling an old form seen as early as the 3rd Dynasty Step Pyramid at Saqqara. Its meaning for the royal cult was further underscored in rooms on the south of the central court, where the ruler's desire to accompany the sun-god on his daily route through the heavens and the netherworld was expressed in scenes and texts. Hymns describing the deities who governed each hour of the day and night gave Hatshepsut power over time itself so that she could merge with the sun for eternity. On this terrace, too, were chapels for Hatshepsut herself and for her father, Thutmose I. An inscription accompanied a scene of the king declaring his daughter's future reign.

A set of phrases designed to communicate with the few who could read and who would actually see these private areas of the temple allude obliquely to the unusual nature of Hatshepsut's rule. Her high officials are twice warned: 'he who shall do her homage shall live, he who shall speak evil in blasphemy of her Majesty shall die.' It is likely that this was the official court position of the time and that the inscription merely monumentalized a statement well known to élite circles of the time. Hatshepsut was very generous to those who supported her, judging from the sudden increase in large decorated private tombs at Thebes and Saqqara, as well as the increasing number of private statues dedicated in temples such as Karnak. The ruler appears to have forged a symbiotic relationship with her nobles, so that she became as important to them as they were to her. During this period, for the first time in Theban private tombs, the enthroned ruler appears arrayed like the sun-god himself, acting as an eternal intermediary for the tomb-owner. The Theban tombs of the royal steward Amenhotep (TT 73) and the royal butler Djehuty (TT 110) show Hatshepsut in this manner, and several tombs dating to the sole rule of Thutmose III continued the practice. Such loyalist representations recall the inscribed stelae of the Middle Kingdom élite that described how the 12th Dynasty kings acted for the good of Egypt.

Foreign Relations in the Reign of Hatshepsut

Hatshepsut's co-regency with Thutmose III was not a period of protracted warfare. There were several Nubian military expeditions that appear to have dealt with local uprisings, but nothing indicates that overall administration of the south by the 'viceroy and overseer of southern countries' was interrupted. The viceroy Seni gave way to Amennakht during Hatshepsut's reign, and the latter ceded to Nehy under Thutmose III's sole rule. At least one other viceroy was in service at the end of Hatshepsut's tenure, but his name is uncertain. Each of these men not only governed Nubia but also supervised construction projects. They oversaw the delivery of Nubian products as 'tribute' to the ruler, but no doubt saw little direct military action.

Hatshepsut's trade mission to Punt was promoted in Egypt as a major diplomatic *coup*. The African products that were brought back, along with gold and incense (including the incense trees themselves), stimulated interest in exotic luxury goods. Soon the Nubian tribute-bearers were pictured in private tomb paintings bringing the same items: ivory tusks, panther skins, live elephants, and, of course, gold. It is not entirely clear how the mission to Punt opened more extensive trade to areas of Africa south of Egypt's control, but it was only after this time that consistent reports of Nubian tribute from the conquered regions were recorded, including lists of the exotic materials obtained.

The possibility exists that Egypt's connection to the Aegean, as attested by the Minoan paintings at Tell el-Dab'a (Avaris), underwent a change during Hatshepsut's reign. Although Avaris continued to be occupied until the reign of Amenhotep II, there is no certain indication that Egypt was in contact with Crete following the first part of the 18th Dynasty. Trade may have been maintained through Cyprus and the Levant, however, since imported pottery occurs in some quantities. In the reign of Hatshepsut, when delegations of Keftiu (Minoans, judging from the Egyptian representations) appear alongside other foreign emissaries in mural paintings from Theban private tomb chapels, Egypt may have forged its own trade connection with Minoan Crete or Mycenaean Greece. The consistency of the contact, however, is dubious. Similar paintings in the reigns following Hatshepsut show less familiarity with the dress and trade objects from Crete, and scholars have concluded that the trade contact may have been through Syria–Palestine rather than directly.

Thutmose III's Sole Rule

The kingship reverted to Thutmose III alone sometime in the twentieth or twenty-first year of Hatshepsut's reign. He then wasted little time in establishing a reputation both for himself and for Egypt that was to be remembered a millennium later, if somewhat imperfectly. Thutmose III must have carefully assessed his situation as a now mature but unproven ruler and, no doubt with counsel from associates and fellow military colleagues, identified the potential for glory and wealth lying to the north-east. The rewards of conquering Nubia could not belong to Thutmose III, and Hatshepsut had reaped what there was from establishing contact with Punt. The new locale for quick gains was the Levant, where Egypt might gain control of the trade routes that had until then been dominated by Syrian, Cypriot, Palestinian, and Aegean rulers and traders. At the end of some seventeen years of military campaigns, Thutmose III had successfully established Egyptian dominance over Palestine and had made strong inroads into southern Syria. His own reputation was assured, and the proceeds were extravagantly expended on behalf of the temples of Amun and other gods, as well as on those men who followed the king on his quests.

The king did not dishonour the name and monuments of Hatshepsut until the last years of his reign, but instead attempted to fill the landscape of the Nile Valley with reminders of his own reign. It is interesting to note that the artistic style and portraiture of Thutmose III are extremely difficult to differentiate from those of Hatshepsut in her later monuments. Only in his body type did Thutmose choose to be shown somewhat differently, for his images routinely show him with broader shoulders and a heavier upper torso than Hatshepsut in both relief and statuary, and this more virile body type was the one used later by Amenhotep II. The face of Thutmose III continued the 'Thutmoside' profile seen already with Thutmose I, comprising a long nose with slight hump and downturned end, broad at the base. The mouth was wide, with a protruding upper lip due to the overbite that ran in the family.

Thutmose III used his thirty-two years of sole rule to make his name prominent throughout Egypt and Nubia. He was active at Gebel Barkal at the farthest southern point in Nubia, at Sai, Pnubs at the third cataract, Semna, Kumma, Uronarti, Buhen, Quban, Amada, Faras, and Ellesiya, as well as several other locations where blocks are known in his name. His monuments further north are well attested at Elephantine, where he built a temple to the goddess Satet of the first-cataract region, at Kom Ombo, Edfu, Elkab, Tod, Armant, Thebes, Akhmim, Hermopolis, and Heliopolis. A statue of the overseer of works Minmose, active in the later reign of Thutmose III, listed cult sites at which he worked. He named, in addition to the places mentioned already, Medamud, Asyut, Atfih, and a number of localities in the Delta, including Buto, Busiris, and Chemmis. Although no buildings of Thutmose III have yet been identified in the Delta, Minmose's inscription suggests that he and earlier 18th Dynasty kings may well have been active there.

Karnak continued to be a favoured site. Thutmose III somewhat ruthlessly restructured the central areas of the temple, removing Amenhotep I's cult chapels of limestone and replacing them in sandstone. Soon after beginning his period of sole rule, he inaugurated the construction of his major building in Karnak: '[Thutmose III is] Effective of Monuments' (*akh menu*). The overall theme of the relief scenes in the building concerns the renewal of Thutmose III's kingship, primarily through the *sed*-festival, which he first celebrated in the thirtieth year of his reign. The veneration of kingship generally fitted well with this purpose for the building and connected it with the chapels around the central court. Later in his reign, Thutmose III had the entire central area redecorated with scenes and particularly inscriptions detailing his campaigns in Asia. These *Annals*, inscribed in the forty-second year of his reign, have become the primary historical record of the king's conquests, containing, as they do, specific episodes of the warfare and lists of booty taken. The enrichment of the Amun temple was enormous as described in the *Annals*: the buildings alone were numerous. The Sixth and Seventh Pylons were added by the king, the latter covered with scenes and inscriptions naming the places over which he claimed mastery. A temple to the god Ptah was built on the north side of the precinct, and a granite bark shrine was made for the centre of the temple, as well as an Egyptian alabaster one later joined to a shrine of Thutmose IV (1400–1390 BC) and set near the Fourth Pylon. Transformations to the works of Hatshepsut also took place in the reign of Thutmose III and were completed by his son Amenhotep II, but even without these the activity was unceasing. The king's high priests of Amun included the energetic Menkheperraseneb, owner of Theban tomb 86, his nephew of the same name (TT 112), and Amenemhat (TT 97). Amenemhat was probably Thutmose III's last high priest of Amun and largely in service under Amenhotep II, after Menkheperraseneb handed over the office to his nephew for a brief period.

The high priests were responsible not only for Karnak, but for works on Amun's behalf on the west bank as well. Thutmose III was extremely active at Medinet Habu, where he completed the small temple to Amun and also built a memorial temple for his father just to the north. Late in his reign, he converted an elevated shrine at Deir el-Bahri into his own chapel called 'Sacred Horizon' (*djeser akhet*). The tomb of Thutmose III in the Valley of the Kings (KV 34) was hewn high in a cliff, descending deep into the rock face. The walls of the burial chamber are covered with black- and red-painted hieratic renditions of the netherworld texts: the *Litany of Ra*, which calls upon the names of the sun-god to aid the king in his afterlife journeys, and the *Book of what is in the Netherworld* (*Amduat*), which provided the king with a map of the underworld and spells to help him achieve eternal justification.

Thutmose III in the Levant

Almost immediately after his sole rule began, Thutmose III began an expedition to the Levant, where he sought to wrest control of a number of city states and towns who recognized a Mitannian overlord from north-east Syria. Having apparently taken as an excuse the need to deal with local squabbles in Sharuhen and its vicinity, the king went to Gaza from the Egyptian border fortress at Tjaru. Gaza had been under Egyptian rule at least since Ahmose's time, and we presume that Sharuhen's loyalty had been expected since the same reign. The *Annals* record that in this first campaign of his twenty-third regnal year Thutmose III left Gaza and planned his attack on Megiddo from the city of Yehem, a major city-state then occupied by the ruler of Kadesh. It was also protected by a group of chiefs representing regions of the Levant as far as Nahrin (Mitanni and Mitanni-dominated Syria). Thutmose's inscription indicated that these chiefs should have been loyal to Egypt, and this must be seen as the true threat. Access to Lebanese cedar, copper and tin sources, and other prized products may have been jeopardized by Mitanni overlordship in northern Palestine and the coastal strip.

Once in the field, Thutmose III discovered the actual rewards of war. The spoils were evidently so great that he continued to campaign intermittently, until the forty-second year of his reign, in the regions of northern Palestine, the Lebanon, and parts of Syria. The spoils taken from the battle of Megiddo, together with the peace offerings that ended the seven-month siege of the town, were considerable and included 894 chariots, including two covered with gold, 200 suits of armour and two of bronze belonging to the chiefs of Megiddo and Kadesh, as well as over 2,000 horses, and 25,000 animals. Following the siege of Megiddo, Thutmose III replaced the defeated local chiefs and continued northward in the direction of the Litani River. The luxury objects taken from the several towns he defeated were meticulously described in the *Annals*, and the different classes of captives taken were also enumerated. The campaigns of years 24–32 detailed the king's focus on the Levantine littoral, with its forests and harbours, as well as areas of west Syria. The Egyptian proceeds included a range of materials from precious metals (gold, silver, copper, and lead) to wood, oils, and even foodstuffs and cereal harvests. The king sent the children of the city rulers back to Egypt to be Egyptianized. According to the *Annals* for year 30, 'whoever died from among these chiefs, his Majesty caused that his son stand in his place'.

If we are correct in assuming that the toponym Nahrin does not feature in Egyptian inscriptions before Thutmose III's eighth campaign (in year 33 of his reign) simply because they were regarded as too powerful to be mentioned on Egyptian royal monuments, then the king's conquest of the Syrian vassals was a truly significant achievement. The hitherto poorly attested state of Nahrin suddenly appears in the later years of Thutmose III's reign in every type of hiero-glyphic inscription: in addition to the *Annals* of Thutmose III, the king's apparent crossing of the Euphrates appears in the Gebel Barkal Stele erected at the fourth cataract in Nubia, on a Karnak obelisk, on the Poetical Stele from Karnak, and on the Armant Stele. References to Nahrin also occur among the numerous toponym lists from the reign. The amount of booty taken during the Syrian campaigns was impressive, both for the ruler and for his soldiers. With the exception of the aftermath of the eighth campaign, in year 33, throughout the *Annals* revenue from Nahrin was listed as booty, either the plunder of the army or what the king captured. Apparently Nahrin did not at this time offer yearly deliveries (*inu*), as the *Annals* clearly indicate by contrasting its one-time

On the Seventh Pylon of the Temple of Amun at Karnak, Thutmose III is shown smiting foreigners in the classic royal pose.

246

delivery after the year-33 campaign with that of other areas designated as 'from this year'. This might be interpreted to mean that the defeated Mitanni vassals alone were the source of Egypt's revenues, not the Mitanni king in his capital, Washshukanni. Although the listed objects and people taken from Nahrin are sizeable, the yearly deliveries from Retenu and Djahy included far more items of precious materials. Clearly Thutmose III was still at war with the Mitanni.

The participation in the conquest of Syria, including Nahrin, by a newly formed Egyptian military élite is commemorated in at least eleven Theban tombs from the reign of Thutmose III and early in that of Amenhotep II, in addition to numerous private statue and stele inscriptions (tombs TT 42, 74, 84, 85, 86, 88, 92, 100, 131, 155, and 200). In these tomb chapels, the emphasis was upon the captives of military expeditions and upon the wars or soldiers themselves, as much as it was upon luxury items acquired from foreign deliveries. The military aspect of Egyptian–Mitanni encounters was to be short lived, however. Instead, the prestige of things Syrian began to soar. Tombs decorated after the first decade of Amenhotep II's rule celebrated the revenues as foreign impost, particularly of an exotic nature, the elements of conquest being formalized within celebratory processions. For example, in the tomb of Kenamun (TT 93), decorated late in the reign of Amenhotep II, there is no text describing the Syrian wars, no accounting of booty as in Suemniwet's chapel (TT 92), or presentation of the foreign chiefs' children, as in Amenemheb's (TT 85). Instead, one wall shows the New Year's presents for the king. Among them are numerous weapons and coats of armour, as well as two chariots. The label for the chariot in the higher register boasts of the wood being brought from the foreign country of Nahrin, while a chariot below it is designated for use in warfare against the southerners and the northerners. A pile of Syrian-style helmets is beneath the upper chariot, while a heap of ivory is beneath the lower one— clearly an allusion to former warfare in the two regions (Asia and Nubia respectively).

Also among the New Year's gifts in Kenamun's tomb is a group of glass vessels imitating marble. This type of glass was particularly characteristic of northeast Syria and northern Iraq. Indeed, the large-scale introduction of core-formed glass into Egypt may well have been a direct result of the Mitanni wars. Quite possibly first developed in Mitanni centres, such as Tell Brak and Tell Rimah, glass vessels quickly became among the prized objects copied (and frankly improved upon) in Egypt. Silver and gold vessels (often described in the booty lists as 'flat bottomed') associated with the Mediterranean littoral (referred to as the 'workmanship of Djahy') also came as revenue from Nahrin (in year 33), and, as with glass, Egyptian-style copies of these Syrian vessels rapidly became fashionable. The famous flat-bottomed silver vessel inscribed for the soldier Djehuty under Thutmose III is just such a bowl; a gold bowl of Djehuty, also at the Louvre, may be a modern copy of the silver one, and there are numerous representations of them from temple and tomb walls in Thebes.

Along with Syrian-style luxury items came the gods of the region, and it is in the reign of Amenhotep II that the cults of the Asiatic deities Reshef and Astarte were heavily promoted in Egypt. It is significant that the fashion for Mitanni-style items far outlasted the fashion for military decoration. A special type of gold lion award that was issued to soldiers in the Syrian campaigns is not found after the early reign of Amenhotep II, but Syrian-style metal and glass vessels continued to be status symbols throughout the 18th Dynasty and were copied in a variety of forms within Egypt. Likewise, the scenes of presentation of Mitanni war captives and booty gave way after the early reign of Amenhotep II to the preferred scene of foreign representatives offering their prized luxury objects in obeisance to the pharaoh.

In the iconographical transformation of Mitanni from arch-enemy to a compliant source for prestige luxury goods, we can track Egypt's path towards an alliance with Nahrin. It is not certain that the three wives of Thutmose III buried in the Wadi Qubbanet el-Qirud (in western Thebes) were Syrian, but their names were certainly Asiatic and their wealth in gold was profound. This perhaps reflects the changing Egyptian view towards the east—the same king who campaigned to conquer Retenu and Nahrin for twenty years then married women from the region and showered them with riches. Despite the battles of Amenhotep II yet to be fought in Syria, Egypt's interest in peace was imminent at the close of Thutmose III's reign.

Thutmose III's wives included one woman called Sitiah, daughter of a royal nurse. She had the titles of 'great royal wife' and—in one surviving text—'god's wife'. If she in fact replaced Nefrura in the priestess's position, it was only until Thutmose III's daughter Merytamun was old enough to take up the role. Sitiah is not definitely known to have had any children, while the mother of Amenhotep II, Merytra, appears to have produced several children. Merytra (daughter of Huy, a divine adoratrice of Amun and Atum, and chief of choristers for Ra) apparently gave birth to Amenhotep, Princess Mery(t)amun, prince Menkheperra, Princesses Isis and another Mery(t)amun, and a small Princess Nebetiunet. Merytra as queen appeared in the temple of Medinet Habu and in the tomb of Thutmose III. A third wife, Nebetta, and a Princess Nefertiry are depicted in the royal tomb.

Amenhotep II

It is not known whether any members of Hatshepsut's branch of the family (descended from Queen Ahmose) were still alive at the end of Thutmose III's reign. The ageing king, however, did take his son Amenhotep as co-regent in the fifty-first year of his reign, and then shared the monarchy with him for a little more than two years. The so-called dishonouring of Hatshepsut, which had begun around year 46 or 47, may have paved the way for the joint rule, for Amenhotep II himself completed the desecration of the female king's monuments. In order to eliminate the claims of Hatshepsut, and her family line, her monuments were systematically adjusted: some were obscured by new work; some were mutilated to remove any evidence of her name; and many were altered such that the names of Thutmose III or Thutmose II replaced those of Hatshepsut. Since Thutmose sought to destroy the memory of the queen twenty-five years after her disappearance, it is unlikely that this was carried out as pure vengeance against his stepmother, particularly since the king had retained a number of Hatshepsut's officials, who completed their career and built tombs with the name of Thutmose III prominently inscribed in them. Perhaps the death of men who served both rulers, such as Puyemra, second priest of Amun, and Intef, the mayor of Thinis (the region of Abydos) and governor of the oases, also vitiated objections to the execration of Hatshepsut.

Amenhotep II's reign was a pivotal one in the early New Kingdom, although today it is often dwarfed by the shadow of his two predecessors and his successors in the late 18th Dynasty. During a reign of nearly thirty years (with a highest known regnal year of twenty-six) the king had military successes in the Levant, brought peace to Egypt together with its economic rewards, and faithfully expanded the monuments to the gods. In his own time Amenhotep II commanded recognition most particularly for his athleticism, and his monuments often allude to this capability. As a young man, the king lived in the Memphite region and trained horses in his father's stables (if we are to believe the inscription he left on a stele at the Sphinx temple at Giza). His greatest athletic achievement was accomplished when he shot arrows through copper targets while driving a chariot with the reins tied around his waist. The fame of this deed was monumentalized not only in the stele inscription from Giza but in

A fragment of painted decoration from the 18th Dynasty tomb of Nebamun at Thebes shows a scribe assessing a field of grain for taxation.

carved relief scenes in Thebes. It was also miniaturized on scarabs that have been found in the Levant. Sara Morris, a classical art historian, suggests that Amenhotep II's target shooting success formed the basis hundreds of years later for the episode in the *Iliad* when Achilles is said to have shot arrows through a series of targets set up in a trench.

The majority of Amenhotep II's reign was peaceful, providing a lengthy period of stability. Several administrative papyri from his reign document flourishing agricultural and industrial organizations in several areas of Egypt. A well-developed bureaucracy was at work, and Amenhotep II appears to have made good use of the services of administrators. He encouraged men who had served his father to stay on, and he installed close friends of his own in key roles. Several Middle Kingdom literary compositions were recopied at this time, suggesting a growing interest in cultural refinement rather than military valour. Although royal art remained as idealized and highly formal as it had been in the reign of Thutmose III, painting style in non-royal contexts began to betray an artistic individualism that was later to be accentuated.

Amenhotep II's Building Programme

Amenhotep II left buildings or additions to standing monuments at nearly all the major sites where his father had worked. In the first three years of his reign, constructions in the names of the two kings were erected, most notably at Amada in Lower Nubia, where a temple celebrating both equally was built to honour Amun and Ra-Horakhty, and at Karnak, where both kings participated in eliminating the vestiges of Hatshepsut's monuments by masking them with their own. In the court between the Fourth and Fifth pylons the columns added and the masonry placed around the queen's obelisks carried sometimes the name of one ruler and sometimes the name of the other. It remains impossible to say whether the alterations were effected simultaneously (during a co-regency) or consecutively.

He left monuments at Pnubs on Argo Island, at Sai, Uronarti, Kumma, Buhen, Qasr Ibrim, Amada, Sehel, Elephantine, Gebel Tingar (a chapel near the quartzite quarry on the west bank at Aswan), Gebel el-Silsila, Elkab, Tod (a bark chapel of the co-regency), Armant, Karnak, Thebes (including his tomb, KV35 in the Valley of the Kings and a now-destroyed funerary temple), Medamud, Dendera, Giza, and Heliopolis. A temple construction of limestone was the object of the reopening of the Tura quarries in year 4 of the reign, but the location of that temple is uncertain; it was not the king's funerary temple at Thebes, since that structure was built of sandstone and brick.

The sites where Amenhotep II's construction efforts left the deepest impressions were Giza and Karnak, despite the fact that the king's work at Giza was not particularly ambitious. None the less, he built a temple to the god Horemakhet, the sun-god identified with the Great Sphinx. It has been noted that, since the time of Thutmose I's reign, the area around the Sphinx was frequented by princes and pilgrims who visited the great pyramid complexes of Khufu and Khafra. The Sphinx and its amphitheatre became the site of a cult of royal ancestors, including Amenhotep II himself and his son, Thutmose IV, who set up the Sphinx Stele between the paws of the great lion statue. The cult of Horemakhet and the royal veneration continued into Roman times, such that pilgrims left votive offerings in the enclosure wall of the amphitheatre or in the chapels if possible. Amenhotep II's dedication of a small temple to Horemakhet (also described as Hauron on the king's foundation deposit from the site) was thus an important development in the history of the Sphinx as a focus of worship. His own sons left stelae in his temple, some bearing depictions that indicate that a statue of Amenhotep II once stood against the breast of the Sphinx. Mark Lehner has reconstructed the appearance of the Sphinx with this 18th Dynasty statue in place.

When Amenhotep II had finished his programme of erasures on the monuments of Hatshepsut at Karnak, he was able to concentrate on preparations for the royal jubilee at this temple. Just as Thutmose III had constructed the festival temple known as 'Effective of Monuments' in the precinct of Amun at Karnak, so Amenhotep II created a building for his *sed*-festival. His pavilion, as reconstructed by Charles Van Siclen, was a court of relief-carved square pillars with decorated walls on the sides. Dated to the later part of his reign both by its artistic style and its inscriptions, it fronted the temple's south entrance at the Eighth Pylon, effectively creating a new main gateway to the complex, just as Hatshepsut had done before him. In front of this *sed*-festival court were the estates of Amun, or gardens that produced vegetables and other sweet plants. The pillars carried the unusual dedication of 'a first occasion of repeating [or "and repetition of"] the *sed* festival' which may imply that he had already celebrated a jubilee before building this court. These formulas are, however, difficult to interpret and may simply be wishes expressed for the king's coming jubilees. Following an old tradition, Amenhotep II's relief decoration in the festival pavilion contained elaborate royal regalia for the king, that particularly emphasized solar connections—for example, multiple sun discs on top of crowns, and tiny falcons set above the sun discs, creating identity with the falcon-headed Ra-Horakhty.

The small temple of Thutmose III at Deir el-Bahri had used similarly extravagant solar symbolism and was also a monument dating to the period after the king's jubilee preparations had been made. Amenhotep II's festival building included scenes of his mother, Merytra, who served as his queen and, more importantly, 'god's wife of Amun'. The building was dismantled at the end of the 18th Dynasty, to accommodate alterations of the quadrant by Horemheb (1323–1295 BC), and it was later rebuilt in a different architectural form by Sety I (1294–1279 BC) at the beginning of the 19th Dynasty.

Amenhotep II also built a temple to Amun in northern Karnak, a precinct later dedicated to Montu of Thebes. However, the blocks of this building now form part of the foundations of a temple constructed under Amenhotep III and later adapted in the Ptolemaic Period. Its original function remains unknown. Other gateways and blocks from North Karnak, however, indicate that the king was interested in developing this sector, perhaps because of its position in terms of extending the north–south axis of the central part of Karnak. Stone door elements from a palace of the king were found north of the temple proper, perhaps indicating the location of a ceremonial residence for Amenhotep II. The king's interest in Montu's temple at Medamud some 8 km. to the north is perhaps also notable, since later there was certainly a processional way between northern Karnak and Medamud.

Amenhotep II in the Levant

Amenhotep II carried out two campaigns in Syria, the first probably in year 7, the latter in year 9. These are described on stelae left at Amada, Memphis, and Karnak. The first campaign concentrated on the defeat of unaligned chiefs and rebellions among recently acquired vassals. Among the latter, the region of Takhsy, mentioned in the Theban tomb of Amenemheb (TT 85), was a primary, and successful, target. The seven defeated chiefs of that region were taken back to Thebes, head-down on the royal barge, where six were hung upon the temple wall. One was carried all the way to Napata, in the Sudan, where his body was hung, no doubt as an example to the local population. According to the stelae, the plunder claimed from Amenhotep's first campaign comprised a staggering 6,800 *deben* of gold and 500,000 *deben* of copper (1,643 and 120,833 pounds respectively), along with 550 *mariannu* captives, 210 horses, and 300 chariots. The second campaign in year 9 was largely carried out in Palestine.

Apart from the standard toponyms in 'name rings', none of the monumental texts of Amenhotep II contains a hostile reference to Mitanni or Nahrin (despite the fact that the inscriptions narrated his Syrian campaigns)—and this is probably intentional. Instead of Thutmose III's designation, 'that foe of Nahrin', Amenhotep II several times uses the archaic Egyptian generic term *set-jetyu* ('Asiatics'). The language of the stelae, composed after the conflicts had ended, in year 9 or later, reflects the fact that peace with Mitanni was at hand. Indeed, the Memphis stele contains an addition at the end, reporting that the chiefs of Nahrin, Hatti, and Sangar (Babylon) arrived before the king bearing gifts and requesting offering gifts (*hetepu*) in exchange, as well as asking for the breath of life. This was certainly the first official announcement of the creation of a Mitanni peace, although good relations with Babylon and others already existed in the reign of Thutmose III.

The importance of Amenhotep II's new alliance with Nahrin was underlined by its exposition in a column inscription from the Thutmosid *wadjyt*, or columned hall, between the Fourth and Fifth Pylons at Karnak. This location was significant, because the hall was venerated as the place where Thutmose III received a divine oracle proclaiming his future kingship. In addition, the association of the hall with the Thutmosid line going back to Thutmose I, the first king to venture to Syria, made it a logical place to boast of the Mitanni relationship. The inscription singles out Syria, stating: 'The chiefs (*weru*) of Mitanni (*My-tn*) come to him, their deliveries upon their backs, to request offering gifts (*hetepu*) from his majesty in quest of the breath of life.' By the close of Amenhotep II's reign the portrayal of Mitanni, so recently the vile enemy of the king, was brought into line with that of Egypt's other close allies. In monuments within the Nile Valley, these brother kings of Babylon, Hatti, and Nahrin were always portrayed as suppliants who requested life from the Egyptian king. The hard-won peace with Syria is betrayed, however, by Amenhotep II's enthusiasm for it. Clearly Amenhotep II considered this alliance to be a boon at home as well as abroad.

Royal Wives in the Mid-18th Dynasty

A number of princes can be documented for the reign of Amenhotep II: Amenhotep, Thutmose, Khaemwaset(?), Amenemopet, Ahmose, Webensenu, and Nedjem, as well as the unnamed Princes A and B known from stelae left at Giza. Perhaps another, named Aakheperura, was born late in Amenhotep's reign, or in Thutmose IV's. In striking contrast to earlier reigns, princesses are difficult to document. The plurality of young royal males is in contrast to the earlier part of the dynasty when adult princes appeared to be scarce, perhaps because they died on military campaigns, or from childhood illnesses. The scarcity of princes, perhaps due in part to the dynastic preference for princess sisters as queens, may have inspired rulers to take minor queens in addition to their great royal wives. These 'royal wives', such as Nebetta and the three Levantine queens of Thutmose III, all mentioned above, were probably distinct from court females of unknown rank with whom the kings had sexual liaisons. The latter women, such as Mutnofret, Isis, Tiaa, and Mutemwiya, produced sons who became king and promoted their mothers as queens. It is not known, however, which women (apart from Tiaa, mother of Thutmose IV) were the mothers of Amenhotep II's numerous offspring.

It was not only his able procreative powers that separated Amenhotep II from his predecessors. Unlike those before him, this king had no publicly acknowledged wife other than his mother, Merytra, who served as 'great royal wife' for much of Amenhotep's reign. The absence of wives might be considered a conscious rejection of the dynastic role played by princesses as queens and 'god's wives of Amun' from the establishment of the dynasty through to the reign of Hatshepsut. Perhaps Thutmose III and Amenhotep II now realized that queens like Hatshepsut, who represented the dynastic family, could be dangerous if they were too wealthy and powerful. In addition the queen-turned-king's usurpation of the throne may have given Thutmose III and Amenhotep II a particular incentive to produce sons. This conclusion further motivated kings to choose as great royal wives women from outside the main royal line, as did Thutmose III in choosing Sitiah and Merytra.

The Legitimization of Thutmose IV

The succession of Thutmose IV appears to have had no recognition at all by Amenhotep II, either by co-regency or announced intent. On a statue dedicated in the reign of Amenhotep II by Prince Thutmose (later Thutmose IV) in the Temple of Mut at Karnak, the tutor accompanying the prince, named Hekareshu, was designated simply as nurse of the royal children; however, after Thutmose's accession, Hekareshu was retrospectively termed 'god's father' and 'nurse of the king's eldest son'. Although Merytra may have appeared on Thutmose III's late monuments, Thutmose IV's mother, Tiaa, cannot be certainly attested on a monument of Amenhotep II's other than as a later addition by Thutmose himself. There is no evidence before her son's reign that Tiaa's position influenced the succession.

Royal nurses (male and female), together with tutors from the ranks of retired courtiers, nurtured and educated royal children during the 18th Dynasty. The burgeoning documentation for princes at this time is thus probably no accident at all. Competition among the swelling ranks of capable young princes, particularly with the cessation of regular military campaigns in Asia after the first decade of Amenhotep II's reign, is not difficult to imagine. And competition can erupt unexpectedly into struggle among ambitious youths. The story of Thutmose IV's elevation to the kingship related by the Giza Sphinx Stele inscription has been interpreted in the past to suggest that he was not the legitimate heir, but it need tell us no more than that royal ideology often drew upon divine legitimization in the New Kingdom. The sheer romance of the 'Sphinx Stele' is perhaps a good enough reason to quote part of it here:

Now the statue of the very great Khepri [the Great Sphinx] rested in this place, great of fame, sacred of respect, the shade of Ra resting on him. Memphis and every city on its two sides came to him, their arms in adoration to his face, bearing great offerings for his *ka*. One of these days it happened that prince Thutmose came travelling at the time of midday. He rested in the shadow of this great god. [Sleep and] dream [took possession of him] at the moment the sun was at zenith. Then he found the majesty of this noble god speaking from his own mouth like a father speaks to his son, and saying: 'Look at me, observe me, my son Thutmose. I am your father Horemakhet-Khepri-Ra-Atum. I shall give to you the kingship [upon the land before the living]. . . . [Behold, my condition is like one in illness], all [my limbs being ruined]. The sand of the desert, upon which I used to be, (now) confronts me; and it is in order to cause that you do what is in my heart that I have waited.'

The request addressed to Thutmose to excavate the Sphinx from the sand was answered, and the king's retaining wall around the amphitheatre, as well as a set of stelae set up around the arena, document his work in the region. Possibly his construction efforts were intended to distract attention from problems with the succession. The suggestion of a struggle for the throne can be seen in several monuments dedicated by Thutmose's brothers at their father Amenhotep II's Giza Sphinx temple. They were found broken and mutilated, and their defacement suggests some sort of *damnatio memoriae*, but there is presently no way to demonstrate what provoked it. Prince Webensenu is the most likely son of Amenhotep to have been the owner of defaced Giza stelae A and B. Webensenu's canopic jars and *shabtis* were found in Amenhotep II's tomb (KV 35 in the Valley of the Kings), but it is difficult to know when they were placed there. We may suppose that this prince was of some importance, but more than this is not possible. The defaced Giza stelae should thus not be ignored as evidence of a struggle, but we cannot confirm or deny that Thutmose IV was the usurper.

The Monuments of Thutmose IV

Thutmose IV's reign of at least eight years was brief but active. It is a common-place observation that Egyptian rulers built numbers of monuments in direct proportion to the amount of peace and affluence they enjoyed. As king, Thutmose IV had the wealth and peace, but time apparently was cut short. He began construction at most of Egypt's major temple sites and at four sites in Nubia. The original sizes of the monuments and of their remains vary greatly, but in general he added to pre-existing temples. The distribution of Thutmose IV's monuments, within the context of the mid-18th Dynasty, is unremarkable. He honoured the established cult centres and was hardly an iconoclast. On the other hand, at several locations he left certain harbingers of things to come. Indeed we may suggest that he deliberately followed in the footsteps of his grandfather and father, building additions to their temples, and in similar fashion suggested new sites and monuments to his son.

Monuments of the reign have been found at the following places: in the Delta at Alexandria, Seriakus, and Heliopolis (?); in the Memphite region at Giza, Abusir, Saqqara, and the city of Memphis itself; in the Faiyum at Crocodilopolis; in Middle Egypt at Hermopolis and Amarna; and in Upper Egypt at Abydos (where he left a chapel of brick with limestone revetments), Dendera, Medamud, Karnak, Luxor, western Thebes (where he built a mortuary temple and a tomb, KV43, in the Valley of the Kings), Armant, Tod, Elkab, Edfu, Elephantine, and Konosso. In Nubia he left blocks at Faras (?) and Buhen. He decorated the peristyle court at Amada, began a building at Tabo (later completed by Amenhotep III), and left a foundation deposit at Gebel Barkal. In addition, some decoration was carried out in the Hathor temple at the Serabit el-Khadim turquoise mines in Sinai.

The king's interest in the sun-gods may be documented throughout his building campaigns and in his inscriptions as well. At Giza, he devoted himself not to a display of equestrianism and archery, but to the god Horemakhet and the Heliopolitan cult. He made no reference to Amun-Ra on the Sphinx Stele, allowing the northern deity (Horemakhet-Khepri-Ra-Atum) to dominate both as sun-god and as royal legitimator. Given that Amun, even on Amenhotep II's Sphinx Stele, was the primeval creator and the god who determined the kingship, Thutmose's omission of Amun from his stele must surely have been deliberate, perhaps reflecting both the increasing importance of the Heliopolitan gods and the political influence of the north itself as the administrative centre of Egypt.

At Karnak, the king shifted the main axis back to east–west, thus reducing the importance of Amenhotep II's north–south entranceway. Placing a porch and door before the Fourth Pylon, Thutmose IV probably first left the original court untouched and changed only the monumental doorway itself. He erected a porch for the Fourth Pylon doorway with columns made of wood (ebony and *meru* according to an inscription), probably gilded with electrum. This porch would have been a protected space used during court rituals, and two contemporary representations of it have been preserved.

This presentation scene from the Theban tomb of Sobekhotep (TT 63), shows foreigners bringing gifts for Thutmose IV (*c.*1400–1390 BC) and requesting peace.

A few years later he created a new appearance for the Fourth Pylon limestone court erected by Thutmose II. Over the earlier limestone walls, Thutmose IV built a sandstone peristyle court elaborately decorated with reliefs showing treasures donated by the king to the god Amun. This was to have commemorated the celebration of a first jubilee planned without waiting for thirty years to elapse, as was certainly the case with Amenhotep II too. The style of Thutmose's sculpture from Karnak changed in the last years of rule, becoming more elaborate and expressive.

The king also erected a single obelisk at the eastern end of the precinct at Karnak. It had been produced for Thutmose III but lay in the stone workshop for thirty-five years until Thutmose IV ordered it to be set up. It became a focus of the solar cult place designed by Thutmose III, and it was placed directly on the temple axis.

Thutmose IV in Syria-Palestine and Nubia

With regard to foreign policy in the east, Thutmose IV's contacts with Mitanni are best considered in the context of the pre-existing peace with that power. This situation would have restricted military activity to campaigns against either upstart Egyptian vassals or Mitanni kinglets asserting pressure on the Egyptian city states. Thutmose IV took a daughter of the Mitanni ruler Artatama as wife, in order to seal a diplomatic relationship with the king.

The best-known inscription noting military activity for Thutmose IV is the laconic dedication text on a statue at Karnak that consists of a single line: 'from the plunder of his Majesty from [. . .]na, defeated, from his first campaign of victory'. The toponym referred to on his Karnak dedication (and a statue base from Luxor temple) is likely to have been in Syria, given the several references in the Amarna Letters to the king in that region. The two most likely cities to restore on the Karnak dedication would have been Sidon (*Zi-du-na*), where Thutmose IV was known to have travelled and where Egypt clearly lacked support in the Amarna period; or Qatna, near Tunip in Nukhashshe (an amorphous area to the east of the Orontes). Whether the toponym was Qatna or Sidon or some other city, the northern Levant remains the likely area for the main campaign. This is all the more evident since the Mitannian king Artatama would have been impressed by a show of strength at his doorstep, particularly if negotiations for a diplomatic renewal were in progress.

A scene in the tomb of the standard-bearer Nebamun (TT 90) records the man's promotion in year 6 and shows the Chiefs of Nahrin before the king in his kiosk. Captives also appear in this scene and are rare enough after the reign of Amenhotep II that they should be taken seriously. However, as captives taken in a campaign against both Mitanni vassals and rebellious Egyptian city states, these foreigners make the statement of Egypt's obvious superiority over Mitanni. Such an assertion of dominance would have been appropriate at the moment of Egypt's treaty renewal with Washshukanni. It may be that, rather than help us to document a war against the Mitanni ruler, this scene informs us of the date for Thutmose IV's diplomatic marriage with the Syrian princess.

In the southern regions of Palestine, Thutmose can only be said to have taken punitive action against Gezer; actual warfare cannot be proven, but some of the population of this town were transported to Thebes. It is presently impossible to prove that the Levantine holdings of Egypt at the end of Thutmose's reign were not similar to those of Amenhotep II. And it is similarly impossible to demonstrate that Artatama I could have been dealing from a position of strength when he decided to form a brotherhood with Thutmose IV. Thutmose never fought the Mitanni ruler directly, but his power in the far northern provinces was intact. Thus Artatama may have been renewing a diplomatic relationship established under Amenhotep II, or he may have been reaching an accord to achieve stability for the region as a whole (particularly as the threat of a united Assyria and Babylon may already have been looming). The Egyptians were hardly disgraced in this peace—they appear to have given up nothing.

Turning to the areas south of Egypt, there is no clear attestation of Thutmose IV's military activity in Nubia proper. The Konosso Stele, carved on the rock south of Aswan, details a journey by Thutmose IV over the gold-mine routes east of Edfu; it is very likely that the Nubians were interfering with gold transports, attacking from hiding places in the high desert where the mines themselves were located. Since the expedition terminated at Konosso, it is possible that the king used the Wadi el-Hudi to return, having taken an elliptical route eastwards through the Wadi Mia, then south, then westwards back to the Nile Valley. There is, however, little in the text to imply any major warfare against these Nubians. Rather, this was a desert police action that merited attention because of a threat to transportation through the desert.

Kingship and Royal Women in the Reign of Thutmose IV

Thutmose IV may have begun a course that Amenhotep III completed, particularly in deliberately identifying himself with the sun-god. At Giza, on one stele he was shown wearing the gold *shebiu*-collar and armlets strongly associated with the solar deity's favour. These jewels are often shown on representations of the king in funerary contexts, but on this stele (as well as on an ivory armlet from Amarna, and on the king's chariot) Thutmose IV is shown wearing them as a living ruler. Thutmose IV left a statue of himself as falcon king at Karnak (now in the Cairo Museum), and on a relief from his sandstone court at Karnak a statue of the king as falcon was pictured among other royal statuary. In these images the divine and solar aspects of the kingship are supreme.

The trend of elevating the royal associations with Egypt's major gods (as seen in Thutmose III's veneration of his own and earlier kingships in his jubilee temple within the precinct of Amun) became even more prominent during Thutmose IV's reign. While never abandoning the notion that the dynastic line was best strengthened by marriage of the king to a king's daughter (for both politi-

The Theban tomb of Sobekhotep includes a depiction of the delivery of African 'tribute' to Thutmose IV. The Nubians are carrying gold rings, ebony logs, incense, and other luxury goods.

cal and economic reasons), Thutmose IV, like Amenhotep II, increasingly emphasized divine associations of royal females. He placed his mother in the role of 'god's wife of Amun', as if she were the goddess Mut herself. This was her primary role, although Tiaa also held the titles of 'king's mother' and 'great royal wife' during most of Thutmose IV's reign. Monuments with her name are known from Giza, the Faiyum, Luxor, Karnak, and the Valley of the Kings. This intentional association with the mother-goddess Mut was supplemented by iconographic and inscriptional connections between Tiaa and the goddesses Isis and Hathor. The king appears to have apportioned the ceremonial roles of priestess and queen among Tiaa and two other great royal wives. Tiaa appears in the Karnak jubilee court of her son, where she holds a mace while witnessing the monument's foundation ceremony. In Amenhotep II's jubilee pavilion

Merytra (name later changed to Tiaa) was shown likewise holding a mace and a sistrum in her other hand. The imagery here probably signifies these queens' status as 'god's wives of Amun'. The mace became a standard iconographic element of the 'god's wives' later on.

A non-royal wife Nefertiry, attested in Giza and the Luxor temple, was 'great royal wife' alongside Tiaa during the earlier years of rule, and Thutmose capitalized on this mother–son–wife triad (as did Amenhotep III later) to portray roles—for example, at Luxor temple—where he, as both god and king, accompanied his mother and wife goddesses enacting the roles of mother, wife, and sister-goddesses. Later, after Nefertiry had apparently either died or been set aside, he followed the trend of his family and married a sister, whose name may be read as Iaret. It is possible that he may have had to wait for Iaret to reach a marriageable age. Amenhotep III's mother, Mutemwiya, was never acknowledged by Thutmose IV, either as major or minor queen, but a statue of Amenhotep's court counsellor, the treasurer Sobekhotep (buried in TT 63), shows the Prince Amenhotep in a favoured position before his father's death. The tomb of Amenhotep's royal nurse, Hekarnehhe (TT 64) also shows the young heir, but, since the tomb was completed in Thutmose IV's reign, Mutemwiya does not appear. Several other princes are mentioned in texts in Hekarnehhe's tomb, as well as in a rock graffito at Konosso, but it is not clear whether these are sons of Amenhotep II or Thutmose IV.

Amenhotep III

The thirty-eight-year reign of Amenhotep III was primarily a period of peace and affluence. The construction of royal monuments during the reign was on a scale with few parallels, and the retinue of the king left tombs, statues, and shrines that rivalled those of many former rulers. Sadly, as in most periods, it is impossible to compare the fortunes of the rich with those of the poor. Whether the peasant's life was economically improved due to the overall wealth in Egypt is unknown. The official documentation might suggest that the population as a whole enjoyed prosperity at some point, since Amenhotep III and his granary official Khaemhet boasted of the 'bumper' crop of grain harvested in the king's crucial jubilee year 30. The king was remembered even 1,000 years later as a fertility god, associated with agricultural bounty. Still, this type of evidence is hardly unbiased, so we must admit our ignorance.

It is probable that Amenhotep III was a child at his accession. A statue of the treasurer Sobekhotep holding a prince Amenhotep-mer-khepesh probably shows the king shortly before his father's death, and a wall painting in the tomb of the royal nurse Hekarnehhe (TT 64) describes the tomb-owner as the royal nurse of Prince Amenhotep, portraying the prince as a youth rather than a small naked child. The age of the king at accession could have been anywhere between 2 and 12, with a later age perhaps to be preferred given that Amenhotep's mother, Mutemwiya, was barely more visible than Tiaa and Merytra, the preceding two kings' mothers. A regency by Mutemwiya appears unlikely, and, if the king was indeed a small child at accession, his rule was conducted for him quite unobtrusively. An alternative possibility might be that members of Queen Tiye's family assisted the king in his early rule. A scarab dated in year 2 of Amenhotep's reign established the early date of his marriage to Tiye, and the identification on another scarab of the queen's parents, Yuya and Tuya, underscores their prominence. There is, at present, no documentary evidence that Tiye's family acted as a power behind the throne. This presumption has become so strong, however, that other non-royal 'king-makers', such as Ay (whose name in Egyptian resembles that of Yuya), have been thought to be from the same Akhmim family. The discovery of colossal statuary of the late 18th Dynasty at Akhmim, along with some of Amenhotep III, appears to give support to this idea, in so far as that geographic region benefited during the reigns of Amenhotep III and Tutankhamun/Ay.

The Divinity of Amenhotep III

Recent discussions of the reign of Amenhotep III have suggested that he was deified during his lifetime, not only in Nubia, where he built a cult temple for himself, but also in Egypt proper. Raymond Johnson has argued that Amenhotep III's insistent identification with the sun-god in his monumental iconography and inscriptions should be understood as his deification, and he further contends that Amenhotep IV/Akhenaten (1352–1336 BC) transformed his deified father into the disembodied solar disc Aten, thereby worshipping the living Amenhotep III as the sole god of the world. The view that Amenhotep IV worshipped his father as the Aten (albeit after his death) was earlier espoused by Donald Redford. It must be observed that, at the same time, such a transmogrification would have deprived the father of both his physical existence and his name, and it would also have forced Amenhotep III to participate in the ruination of the god celebrated in his own name, Amun. Although the interpretation of Amenhotep III as his son's god carries within it the unmistakable influence of modern Freudian psychology, Egyptian notions of the king's relationship to the gods might support the basis of this idea.

While there is at present no text or iconography within Egypt proper that identifies Amenhotep III as a cult deity during his lifetime, all kings (whom Jaromir Malek describes in Chapter 5 as *netjeru neferu*, 'junior gods') were considered to be major gods at their decease and were frequently invoked as intercessors by their successors and by private persons as well. Moreover, it is arguable that Amenhotep III intended to be identified with the sun-god from the time of his first jubilee in years 30–31, since scenes representing that festival show him taking the specific role of Ra riding in his solar boat. The degree to which Amenhotep III was associated with the sun-god on monuments might well have encouraged the view that, having merged with the sun, as the king was expected to do after death, he was present in Akhenaten's deity, the solar disc

The 'Colossi of Memnon' are two colossal seated statues of Amenhotep III that originally stood at the entrance to the king's mortuary temple on the west bank at Thebes. Most of the temple, however, was dismantled at least as early as the 19th Dynasty, so that the masonry could be reused in the mortuary temples of some of his Ramessid successors (particularly that of Merenptah).

Aten. To claim that this was Akhenaten's intention remains a psychologically informed speculation.

It is also noteworthy that Amenhotep III named his own palace complex 'the gleaming Aten' and used stamp seals for commodities that may be read 'Nebmaatra [his prenomen] is the gleaming Aten'. Of course, sealings are economic documents and could as such refer to the palace complex itself; they might, therefore, have been intended to be read as 'the gleaming Aten of Nebmaatra'. What is certain is that the association of the Aten with Amenhotep III was well established in his own documentation prior to the reign of Amenhotep IV/ Akhenaten.

It is impossible at this point to prove or disprove Johnson's argument. There are no stelae or statues that were, with certainty, dedicated to Amenhotep III as a major deity within Egypt in his lifetime—much less as the Aten. The deification of Rameses II, some 100 years later, was accompanied by significant numbers of monuments, both royal and private, that identified the god Rameses in a number of cult locations within Egypt proper. These monuments date

262

from the reign of Rameses himself and do not refer to the king as 'beloved of X-deity' (as the numerous monuments of Amenhotep III do). They name Rameses himself as the god and show him being offered to, usually as a statue. Nothing of this type exists for Amenhotep III in Egypt, and the examples that most closely parallel monuments offered to gods cannot be safely assigned to the king's lifetime. One stele from Amarna shows Amenhotep and Tiye receiving food offerings under the bathing rays of the Aten. While this might be seen to contradict Johnson's thesis that Amenhotep III *was* the Aten, it is perhaps significant that it derives from the late years of Akhenaten's reign. It therefore raises the question as to whether the king and queen were still alive, or whether the stele, from a private house owner's shrine, venerated the deceased royal couple to invite their intercession. Such votive stelae offered to deceased kings were common in houses at Deir el-Medina both earlier and later than the Amarna Period.

A major obstacle is our inability to ascertain whether Amenhotep III and his son Amenhotep IV/Akhenaten ruled as co-regents for an appreciable length of time. Were this proposition (supported by Johnson's thesis) to be demonstrated, then objects venerating Amenhotep III and made in Akhenaten's reign could be seen as worship of him as a living deity, but not necessarily as the Aten. Co-regency was rare enough in ancient Egypt that scholars remain uncertain as to whether it had consistent hallmarks (see Chapters 1, 7, and 10). After years of debate, we are no closer to a resolution of the debate about co-regency or about the deification of Amenhotep III as the Aten. It might not be unfair to suggest, however, that Amenhotep III would have been pleased that, 3,350 years after his death, it is difficult to ascertain whether he ruled as a living god or merely strived to give that impression.

The Building Programme of Amenhotep III

It may be fair to describe the numerous constructions of Thutmose III as a building programme, in that he developed and expanded cults at a number of sites, including Amada (for Amun and Ra-Horakhty), Karnak (the East Temple for the sun-god and his own festival building), and Hermopolis. More importantly, however, at Karnak his impact was thematic and left the dramatic impression of the warrior pharaoh whose victories simultaneously honoured the king himself and the god Amun. The geographic regions that he conquered appear there in eternal captivity to the god, and the king proudly claimed Amun's favour when he built his festival temple known as 'Effective of Monuments', a cult place that overshadowed those of his royal predecessors at Karnak. Thutmose III's divinity as he designed it for eternity described him as the 'best among equals', referring to the earlier kings of Egypt. This divinity gained him entrance to the council of supreme deities such that he shared the solar boat with Ra and was introduced before Amun.

Amenhotep III's building programme gave him space to design an eternal divinity for himself that reached beyond Thutmose III's vision. He consistently identified himself with the national deities, not his deceased royal predecessors, and he represented himself as the substitute for major gods in a few instances. In addition, his buildings document an unparalleled emphasis on solar theology, such that the cults of Nekhbet, Amun, Thoth, and Horus-khenty-khety, for example, were heavily solarized during Amenhotep III's reign. Trends apparent in 18th Dynasty funerary literature reveal that the sun's cyclicity and its potential for fertility or famine were manifest in the world and in the ruler, but monuments and objects made in Amenhotep III's time may have disseminated these notions more widely. It is impossible to ascertain whether the intellectuals of the age influenced the royal iconography or were requested to formulate it.

Amenhotep built temples or shrines in Nubia at Quban, Wadi es-Sebua, Sedeinga, Soleb, and Tabo Island. There are building elements or stelae in his name at Amada, Aniba, Buhen, Mirgissa, and Gebel Barkal (perhaps reused in the latter). There are statues or scarabs in his name at a variety of sites, including Gebel Barkal and Kawa, and most of the statues originated at other sites, particularly at Soleb. In Egypt proper the king built a shrine at Elephantine (now destroyed) and completed a chapel at Elkab, probably partially erected by his father. Some 20 km. south of Thebes Amenhotep III built a temple at Sumenu, site of a cult to the crocodile Sobek. Although the temple itself remains elusive, numerous objects from it and the cemetery associated with its town, have come to light since the 1960s.

It is in Thebes that Amenhotep's penchant for the colossal is most visible today. The Colossi of Memnon were the towering quartzite images of Amenhotep that protected the king's first pylon at his funerary temple (the single largest royal temple known from ancient Egypt). More fragments of colossal sculpture have been found within his mortuary temple than in any other known sacred precinct. Buildings on the east bank of the Nile at Thebes included a series of constructions at Karnak, as well as Luxor temple, which was entirely rebuilt.

Amenhotep's tomb, KV 22, was excavated in a western valley wadi, away from earlier royal tomb locations. Excavations during the 1990s by a Japanese team have carefully mapped this remarkably large and beautifully finished tomb. The body of Amenhotep III himself (or a mummy so labelled) was found in the tomb of Amenhotep II (KV 35).

On the west bank of Thebes, south of the king's enormous funerary temple, was located his enormous palace of 'the gleaming Aten', now termed Malkata after the Arabic designation for the Queen's Valley nearby. Still further south, at Kom el-Samak, the king built a jubilee pavilion of painted mud brick. A Japanese expedition excavated and carefully recorded this building, which is now destroyed. Next to the Malkata complex is the great harbour that Amenhotep created for use during his constructions and habitation at the palace. In the early 1970s the Birket Habu harbour was the subject of an investigation by

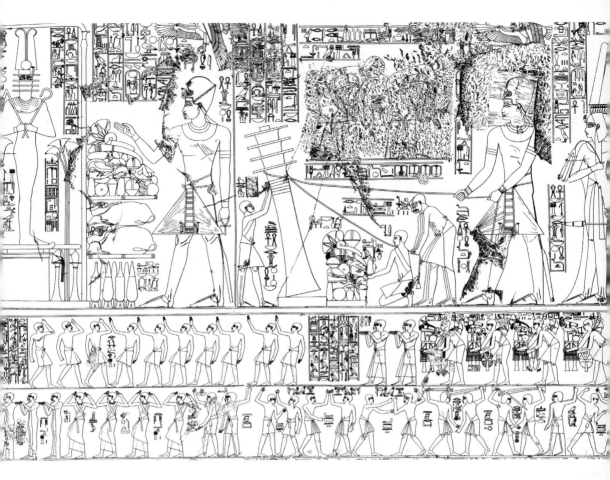

David O'Connor and Barry Kemp, who also studied the Malkata palace. A Japanese expedition worked at the palace in the 1980s.

A painted scene in the tomb of Kheruef (TT 192) shows the 18th Dynasty ruler Amenhotep III and his wife Tiye celebrating the king's third *sed*-festival.

Amenhotep was particularly active in Middle Egypt, although little remains of his temple works at Hebenu and Hermopolis. To the north, blocks of brown quartzite with relief decoration remain from the king's great temple in Memphis, 'Nebmaatra United with Ptah'. Colossal quartzite statues of Ptah, reworked by Rameses II, now stand in the foyer of the Egyptian Museum, Cairo, but probably derived from the Memphite temple of Amenhotep III. In the 1990s the Egypt Exploration Society with W. Raymond Johnson have investigated limestone blocks of a small temple of Amenhotep reused by Rameses II. The king's interest in Memphis is further attested by his association with the first known Apis-bull burial in the Serapeum through the agency of his son Thutmose, the high priest of Ptah. Building elements at Bubastis, Athribis, Letopolis, and Heliopolis attest to the king's interest in the eastern Delta. At Athribis a temple was constructed under the supervision of the king's confidant Amenhotep, son of Hapu.

The work of Amenhotep III at Karnak, Luxor, and his funerary temple reveals his interest in stressing the royal identification with the sun-god. After completing the monuments of his father, Thutmose IV, he changed the face of the Karnak temple. At some undetermined point in his reign, Amenhotep III's workers dismantled the peristyle court in front of the Fourth Pylon and the shrines associated with it, using them as fill for a new pylon, the Third, on the east–west axis. This created a new entrance way to the temple, and two rows of columns with open papyrus capitals were erected down the centre of the newly formed forecourt. He also began the construction of the Tenth Pylon at the south end of Karnak, changing its orientation slightly from that of the Seventh and Eighth in order that it led to a new entrance for the precinct of the goddess Mut, for whom he may also have built or begun a temple. Balancing the south-temple complex was a new building to the north of central Karnak, which was a shrine to the goddess Maat, the daughter of the sun-god. Both Mut and Maat could represent the solar eye of Ra, his agent in the world. David O'Connor has noted that the north–south opposition corresponds to heavenly and terrestrial settings, a fact that accords well with the divine roles of Maat and Mut respectively. The rituals and offerings that Amenhotep III provided may have been designed to demonstrate architecturally and inscriptionally his ability, like the sun-god, to create stability in the cosmos. Deeply carved reliefs from a granary within Karnak show the king in elaborate regalia, crowned with multiple solar discs, and bejewelled on his kilt apron and body with solar imagery. In addition, the king's face is childlike, and his body type is thicker and shorter waisted than on most of the temple reliefs. This is a rejuvenated Amenhotep III, who also exhibits the jubilee iconography with elaborated divine, and particularly solar, elements.

The construction of Luxor temple by Amenhotep III may have been carried out in several stages. He replaced an earlier Thutmosid building with a sandstone temple that celebrated the renewal of the divine kingship during the Opet feast, added into it a birth room wherein he was born of the union of Amun-Ra

One of the relief blocks from a granary at Karnak showing Amenhotep III wearing an elaborate solar headress and making an incense offering.

and his real mother, Mutemwiya, and completed the temple with a new cult place for Amun of *Ipet resy*, or Luxor.

The royal penchant for ritual drama was further monumentalized in Amenhotep III's funerary temple. The temple contained large numbers of life-sized and colossal statuary in the form of both well-known and obscure deities, frequently with human bodies topped by animal heads. These statues represented both the gods of the jubilee and a three-dimensional astronomical calendar to guarantee a propitious festival year. A litany to satisfy Sekhmet, the solar eye of Ra, began the rituals in Thebes, and it was followed in the king's temple in the Sudan, at Soleb, with the ritual propitiation of the deified Nebmaatra, the lunar eye of Ra. After this sequence, the jubilee began in earnest.

Queen Tiye

Tiye was the most influential woman of the king's reign, and she survived her husband by at least a few years. She was so important to him that she not only appears with him on temple walls at Soleb and west Thebes, accompanying him at the jubilee festivities, but she was deified in her own temple at Sedeinga in Upper Nubia and became part of the royal solar programme. As the solar eye of Ra in the Sudan, she would have joined the deity Nebmaatra to return to Egypt and restore order ('Maat') to the world. The role she did not play was that of 'god's wife of Amun', and it is this fact that accounts for her scarcity on the monuments from Karnak and Luxor. She is known only from a small shrine at Karnak later usurped for Tutankhamun—not at all at Luxor.

After her husband's death, the king of Mitanni, Tushratta, wrote to Tiye asking her to remind her son Amenhotep IV/Akhenaten of the close relationship between him and Amenhotep III. Perhaps upon her own death she was first entombed at Amarna, then moved to either (or both) KV 22 or 55. Tiye gave birth to Satamun, Henuttaneb, Nebetiah, and Isis, all of whom appear on statues and smaller objects associated with the royal couple. Satamun was the most elevated of Tiye's daughters, and chairs made for her were found in the tomb of Yuya and Tuya (KV 46). She bore the title of 'great royal wife' simultaneously with Tiye, while the other daughters were called 'king's wife' or 'king's consort'. The economic and, particularly under Amenhotep III, religious significance of the king's marriage to his own daughters has been discussed a number of times already in this chapter and dates back to the beginning of the dynasty. In pairing his wife and daughter(s) with himself on monuments, Amenhotep encouraged the image of the sun-god accompanied by the mother goddess (Nekhbet, Nut, Isis) and the daughters of Ra (Hathor, Maat, Tefnut). More practically, the king enlarged his own holdings, not by giving his daughters to non-royal men to marry, but by himself marrying into wealth. He asked for and received a Babylonian princess as wife, and he married two Mitannian princesses (one of the latter, Taduhepa, having reached Egypt only just in time to become a widow and then marry Amenhotep IV).

Male offspring of Amenhotep III and Tiye certainly included Amenhotep IV. The mother of a king's son and *sem*-priest Thutmose, who may have been older than Amenhotep, is unknown. Whether the king had offspring by his foreign wives is unknown, but there are a number of court women, princes, and princesses known by name from funerary objects unearthed near Malkata. Some of these may have been royal family members, others minor wives.

The body of a royal woman was found in the cache of mummies in the tomb of Amenhotep II (KV 35). She has been identified as Queen Tiye on the basis of hair samples matched to strands of the queen's hair carefully boxed in Tutankhamun's tomb. The certainty of this identification is in question, and confusion persists, given that objects in the name of Tiye were found both in KV 22 and in the enigmatic KV 55. The Japanese expedition at KV 22 has found elements of a coffin that could belong to a queen, but whether that would be Tiye or Satamun, the daughter whom Amenhotep III took as 'great royal wife' during his reign, is unknown.

International Relations in the Reign of Amenhotep III

A Nubian campaign took place in year 5 of Amenhotep III's reign and was commemorated on the Island of Sai, as well as at Konosso and along the road south of Aswan. The viceroy of Kush may have supervised the military action, but whether this was Merymose or the earlier office-holder Amenhotep is unknown. Merymose left his own inscription at Semna, describing an action against Ibhet (probably Lower Nubia). The year 5 campaign was in Kush, perhaps even to the south of the fifth cataract. The building of the fortress of Khaemmaat at Soleb, where the king also constructed a temple, may have been intended to prevent further disruptions from Upper Nubia. The earlier Upper Nubian capital at Kerma was almost directly across the river from Soleb, so the site may have been chosen to underscore Kushite subjection to Egypt.

International relations with the rest of the ancient world were conducted through diplomatic missions. The amount of Egyptian material on the Greek mainland increased dramatically in the reign of Amenhotep III, and the names of Aegean cities, including Mycenae, Phaistos, and Knossos, appear for the first time in hieroglyphic writing on statue bases from the king's funerary temple. Letters between Amenhotep III and several of his peers in Babylon, Mitanni, and Arzawa are preserved in cuneiform writing on clay tablets. These letters, many found in the archive of Akhenaten's capital of Amarna, demonstrate the powerful position enjoyed by Amenhotep III as he negotiated to marry the daughters of other rulers. A strong connection between Amenhotep III and the Mitanni king Tushratta is apparent in the letters, while the Babylonian king Burnaburiash, who came to power late in Amenhotep's rule, appears more suspicious of Egyptian strength. The mid-14th century BC certainly represents one of the high points of Egypt's influence in the ancient world, and it was the culmination of activities by nearly all the rulers of the 18th Dynasty.

Administration in the 18th Dynasty

The overall administrative structures in use during the 18th Dynasty are characterized both by clear trends and by some inconclusive situations. Too few of
the officials of Ahmose and Amenhotep I have been securely identified to indicate the families and regions represented in the early 18th Dynasty royal retinue.
By the middle of the dynasty, however, the kings' closest associates were buried
either in Thebes or at Saqqara, with more of our documentation deriving from
the southern city. From the reign of Hatshepsut onwards, the élite officials for
whom we may expect to find a decorated tomb chapel and burial shaft at
Thebes or Saqqara included the vizier, the treasurer (literally the overseer of the
seal), overseers of gold and silver houses, royal stewards, overseers of the granary (of Egypt or Amun), the king's son and overseer of southern countries,
royal heralds or butlers (often involved in diplomacy), royal nurses (male and
female), regional mayors (sometimes buried in their home districts), the high
priest of Amun (Thebes), the high priest of Ptah (Saqqara), the second, third,
and fourth priests of Amun, and overseers of the army, as well as various levels
of royal scribes.

The 18th Dynasty pharaohs' need to garner support from powerful élite families has been mentioned with respect to scenes of the enthroned ruler in private
tombs of the reign of Hatshepsut and Thutmose III, and powerful families held
the positions of vizier and high priest of Amun during the reigns of Hatshepsut
and Thutmose III. Important members of Thutmose III's retinue, including
the vizier User (TT 61 and TT 131), his steward and counter of grain for Amun,
Amenemhat (TT 82), and the overseer of the granary of Amun, Minnakht
(TT 87), had burial chambers with similar versions of the *Litany of Ra* and the
Amduat. Erik Hornung's recent study of User's texts has underscored the royal
prerogatives assumed by élite individuals in the time of Hatshepsut and Thutmose III. One of the two tombs of Senenmut (TT 71 and TT 373) was designed
to emulate a royal burial, including an astronomical ceiling such as those later
used in the Valley of the Kings. Privileged access to the king arose in other ways
as well (for example, through burials granted in the Valley of the Kings). This
was true for the reigns of Thutmose III and Amenhotep II.

In contrast to the élite families well known in the time of his aunt and father,
many of Amenhotep II's close associates had earlier served in the military both
under Thutmose III and under Amenhotep himself. Such close relations as
army service can foster were perhaps made all the stronger by their origins in
youth, when the king and his court associates learned to hunt and drive chariots. Usersatet, the 'viceroy of southern countries', may well have been one of
these childhood friends who then served as a royal herald abroad under Thutmose III. The inscription on a stele which he left at the fortress of Semna in the
second-cataract region contains within it the text of a remarkable letter sent by
Amenhotep II to his old friend posted abroad: 'You sit . . . a chariot-soldier who
fights for his Majesty . . . the [possessor of a wo]man from Babylon, and a ser-

vant from Byblos, of a young maiden from Alalakh, and an old lady from Arapkha.' Another man who had served Thutmose III, Amenemheb (TT 85), must have died rather early in Amenhotep II's reign. In an inscription from his tomb, Amenemheb described the appointment of Amenhotep as king and then related how the king spoke to him: 'I knew your character when I was (still) in the nest, when you were in the retinue of my father. May you watch over the élite troops of the king.'

A courtier who perhaps best typifies the whole of Amenhotep II's rule was a friend from the military campaigns and childhood play. The great steward Kenamun fought together with Amenhotep in Retenu. When recognized for his service, Kenamun was appointed as steward of Peru-nefer, the seat of a large naval dockyard and ship-building centre. A royal residence was also active there in the mid-18th Dynasty. Later in his life Kenamun's sinecure included the profitable stewardship of the king's own household. Kenamun appears to have been active for almost the whole of Amenhotep II's reign. His tomb (TT 93) shows elegant stylistic elements known only from tombs painted late in this three-decade period, but there is no hint that Kenamun survived into Thutmose IV's rule. The decidedly non-military character of Kenamun's chosen tomb-painting themes, coupled with images of the prosperous élite lifestyle, are in harmony with the tone set by tomb paintings contemporary with both Thutmose IV and Amenhotep III.

Two other men were greatly advanced in the time of Amenhotep II, probably because of early court acquaintance. The vizier Amenemopet and his brother the mayor of Thebes, Sennefer, became extremely affluent owing to the king's attentions. These two men were so influential in the Theban region that they were both afforded burial in the Valley of the Kings, and Sennefer's wife Sentnay, a royal nurse, was interred there as well. Both men also had large tomb chapels at Sheikh Abd-el-Qurna on the Theban west bank (TT 29 in the case of Amenemopet); indeed Sennefer had two tombs (TT 96 upper and lower) in order to accommodate several different female contemporaries, probably including both wives and sisters. The elder daughter of Sennefer, Muttuy, shown on statuary and in the lower part of tomb TT 96, appears to have married a man called Kenamun who succeeded Sennefer as mayor of Thebes. This couple, Muttuy and Kenamun, were contemporaries of Amenhotep III and were interred in tomb TT 162.

Thutmose IV's approach to the administration was to allow the military offices to shrink, replacing them with bureaucrats, often selected from long-established élite families. However, every king had his favourites, and Thutmose IV's was the steward Tjenuna (TT 76). Tjenuna's fragmentary tomb biography suggests he had a personal relationship with Thutmose IV that resembled that of a son to a father: he called himself 'true foster child of the king, beloved of him'. Although there is not sufficient documentation to support the notion that Tjenuna was as powerful as either Senenmut or Kenamun, Thutmose IV may well have trusted his chief steward (who was also steward for

Amun) as much as any other single individual. An official called Horemheb must also have been a powerful and close ally, to judge both from the size of his burial (TT 78) and from the fact that it contained a depiction linking him with one of Thutmose IV's daughters, Amenemopet.

The civil officials often represented traditional families of influence. Hepu was vizier in the south during Thutmose IV's reign, and a Ptahhotep administered the north. That the two viziers existed simultaneously is confirmed by the Munich papyrus dated to Thutmose's reign in which both men called 'vizier' appear as judges. Hepu's tomb (TT 66) is situated in the prestigious cemetery of Sheikh Abd el-Qurna, a placement that conforms to that of viziers under Thutmose III and Amenhotep II. Although it is the most deeply placed tomb of the reign, it is rather small and comparatively unimpressive when viewed beside others of the period (for example, TT 76 and TT 63).

Clearly the royal administration prospered during Thutmose IV's rule, court and bureaucratic connections supplanting military ones almost entirely. The rank of 'general' or 'military officer' is practically unknown in the period, while that of 'royal scribe' abounds, such that even the viceroy of Nubia Amenhotep came from a 'paper-pusher's' background. The office of 'scribe of recruits' was never so well attested, but the fact that the holders were often clearly court associates suggests the position required not the hardened military man but the loyal civil official. With the exception of the Konosso 'police action' (see above, in the section headed 'Thutmose IV in Syria–Palestine and Nubia'), even the employment to which the levied 'recruits' were put in this period and later remains a mystery. It would not surprise us to find that they were as common in quarry expeditions and building enterprises as in military manœuvres.

The court of Amenhotep III is unusual in being known to us nearly as much from monuments outside Thebes as from those within it. The king's treasurers, Sobekmose and his son Sobekhotep (Panehsy), do not have Theban tombs, but the former was buried in Rizeikat. Tombs of the reign, including one of a vizier, Aper-el, have been discovered at North Saqqara by Alain Zivie, and numerous stelae found in the 19th century at that same site name people from the reign. The king's best-known associates, however, did reside in or leave tombs in Thebes. His viziers Ramose (TT 55) and Amenhotep both built extravagant chapels of carved limestone in Thebes, but the latter's is destroyed. This family, though associated heavily by titles with the Memphite region, may, as William Murnane notes, have in fact been Theban. The chief of the king's granary, Khaemhet, likewise left a relief carved tomb at Thebes (TT 47), as did Queen Tiye's steward, Kheruef (TT 192). The most beloved courtier of all was Amenhotep, son of Hapu, to whom the king granted the privilege of his own funerary temple, overlooking the funerary temple of Amenhotep III himself. Amenhotep, son of Hapu, a military scribe from a Delta family, oversaw the completion of many of Amenhotep III's most challenging monuments; the king's recognition of his service led to his eventual deification in the first millennium BC.

10 THE AMARNA PERIOD AND THE LATER NEW KINGDOM

(c.1352–1069 BC)

JACOBUS VAN DIJK

When Amenhotep III died, he left behind a country that was wealthier and more powerful than it had ever been before. The treaty with Mitanni concluded by his father had brought peace and stability, which resulted in a culture of extraordinary luxury. A large percentage of the income generated by Egypt's own resources and by foreign trade went into building projects of an unprecedented scale; inscriptions enumerate the enormous quantities of gold, silver, bronze, and precious stones used in the construction and decoration of the temples. Egypt's wealth was symbolized by the sheer size of the monuments—everything had to be bigger than before, from temples and palaces to scarabs, from the colossal statues of the king to the *shabti* figures of his élite.

Peace had also changed the Egyptians' attitude towards their foreign neighbours, who were no longer primarily seen as the hostile forces of chaos surrounding Egypt, the ordered world created at the beginning of time. Amenhotep's court had become a diplomatic centre of international importance, and friendly contact with Egypt's neighbours had led to an atmosphere of openness towards foreign cultures. During the earlier part of the dynasty, immigrants had introduced their native gods into Egypt and some of these deities had become associated with the Egyptian king, especially in his warlike aspect, but now foreign peoples were themselves seen as part of god's creation, protected and sustained by the benevolent rule of the sun-god Ra and his earthly representative, the pharaoh.

New Kingdom Religion

The sun-god and the king lay at the heart of Egyptian theological thinking and cultic practice as they had developed over the previous centuries. The daily course of the sun-god, who was also the primeval creator-god, guaranteed the continued existence of his creation. In the temple, the sun-god's daily journey through the heavens was symbolically enacted by means of rituals and hymns, the principal aim of which was to maintain the created order of the universe. The king played a crucial role in this daily ritual; he was the main officiant, the sun priest, who had an intimate knowledge of all aspects of the sun-god's daily course. Every sunrise was a repetition of the 'first occasion', the creation of the world in the beginning. Ra himself went through a daily cycle of death and rebirth; at sunset he entered the netherworld, where he was regenerated and from which he was reborn in the morning as Ra-Horakhty. Light could not exist without darkness; without death there could be no regeneration and no life. Together with the sun-god the dead were also reborn; they joined Ra on his daily journey and went through the same eternal cycle of death and rebirth. Osiris, the god of the dead and the underworld, with whom the deceased were traditionally identified, was increasingly seen as an aspect of Ra, and the same held true for all other gods, for, if the sun-god was the primeval creator, then all the other gods had emerged from him and were therefore aspects of him. In this sense a tendency towards a form of monotheism is inherent in the religion of New Kingdom Egypt.

Towards the end of the reign of Amenhotep III the cult of many gods as well as that of his own deified self were increasingly solarized, but at the same time the king appears to have tried to counterbalance this development by commissioning an enormous number of statues of a multitude of deities and by developing the cult of their earthly manifestations as sacred animals. However, in hymns from the very end of the reign, the sun-god is clearly set apart from the other gods—he is the supreme god who is alone, far away in the sky, whereas the other deities are part of his creation, alongside men and animals. Amenhotep III's successor was soon to find a radically different solution to the problem of unity and plurality.

Although the seat of government during most of the New Kingdom was the northern capital, Memphis, the 18th Dynasty kings had originated from Thebes, and this city remained the most important religious centre of the country. Its local god, Amun ('the hidden one'), had become associated with the sun-god Ra and as Amun-Ra King of the Gods was worshipped in every major temple in Egypt, including Memphis. The king was the bodily son of Amun born from the union of the god with the queen mother in a sacred marriage that was ritually re-enacted during the annual Opet Festival in Amun's temple at Luxor. During the great processions that formed part of this important festival, the king was publicly acclaimed as the earthly embodiment of Amun; thus the king and the god were intimately linked by a powerful amalgam of religious and political ties. All of this had made Amun-Ra the most important god of the country, whose temple received a substantial part of Egypt's wealth and whose priesthood had acquired considerable political and economic power. This, too, was soon to change under Amenhotep's successor.

Amenhotep IV and Karnak

There can be little doubt that Amenhotep IV was officially crowned by Amun of Thebes, for he is described as 'the one whom Amun has chosen (to appear in glory for millions of years)' on some scarabs from the beginning of his reign, but this token reference to Amun cannot conceal the fact that the new king was clearly determined right from his accession to go his own way. When exactly this accession took place is still the subject of controversy; clearly Amenhotep was not originally meant to succeed his father, for a crown prince Thutmose is known from earlier in Amenhotep III's reign. Amenhotep IV is mentioned as 'real king's son' on one of the many mud jar sealings found in his father's palace at Malkata, most of which are associated with the three *sed*-festivals (jubilees) celebrated by Amenhotep III during the last seven years of his reign. Opinions

Two scenes from the tomb of Ramose (TT 55) at Thebes, one showing Amenhotep IV seated under the royal baldachin and accompanied by the goddess Maat (who presents him with a sceptre symbolizing eternal rule), and the other showing the king (now identified by his later name of Akhenaten) standing with Queen Nefertiti on the palace balcony at the temple of Gempaaten in Karnak, dispensing gifts and honours to the official Ramose. The scene on the left is executed in the traditional style, while that on the right is in the new 'Amarna' style.

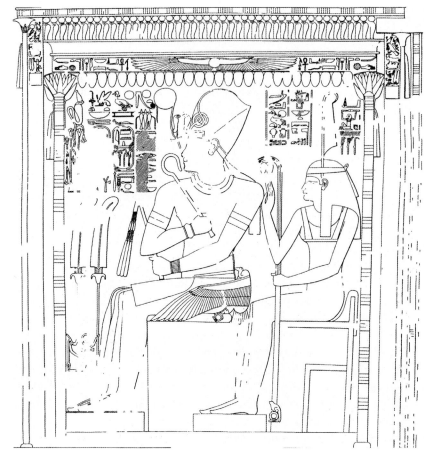

are divided over the issue of a possible co-regency between Amenhotep III and IV; some scholars have opted for such a period of joint rule lasting for some twelve years, others have at best admitted the possibility of a short overlap of one or two years, whereas the majority of scholars reject it entirely.

Amenhotep IV began his reign with a major building programme at Karnak, the very centre of the cult of Amun. The exact location of these temples is unknown, but some, perhaps all of them, were situated to the east of the Amun precinct and orientated towards the east—that is, to the place of sunrise. The temples that he started to build here and elsewhere were dedicated not to Amun, however, but to a new form of the sun-god whose official name was 'The living one, Ra-Horus of the horizon who rejoices in the horizon in his identity of light which is in the sun-disc', a long formula that was soon enclosed in two cartouches just like the names of a king, and that was often preceded in royal inscriptions by the words 'my father lives'. The name of the god could be shortened to 'the living sun-disc' or simply 'the sun-disc' (or, to use the Egyptian word, the Aten). The word itself was not new; it had previously been used to refer to the visible celestial body of the sun. During the reign of Amenhotep III this aspect of the sun-god had become increasingly important, especially in the later years of his reign. During the king's *sed*-festivals, his deified self had been

identified with the sun-disc and in several inscriptions, most clearly in one on the back pillar of a recently discovered statue, the king calls himself 'the dazzling Aten'. Originally this 'new' form of the sun-god was depicted in the traditional manner, as a man with a falcon's head surmounted by a sun-disc, but early in the reign of Amenhotep IV this iconography was abandoned in favour of a radically new way of depicting a god—as a disc with rays ending in hands that touch the king and his family, extending symbols of life and power towards them and receiving their offerings. Although the Aten clearly takes precedence over the other gods, he does not yet replace them entirely.

One of the Karnak temples is devoted to a *sed*-festival, a remarkable fact because kings did not normally celebrate their first jubilee until their thirtieth regnal year. Unfortunately there is no indication of the exact date of this festival of Amenhotep IV, but it must have taken place within the first five years of the reign, possibly around years 2 or 3; if so, it might well have come at the regular interval of three years after the last *sed*-festival of Amenhotep III, which had been celebrated not long before the latter's death. This would provide an additional argument against the assumption of a co-regency between Amenhotep III and IV. The Aten, who is present in every single episode of the jubilee rituals depicted on the walls of the new temple, is now evidently identical with the deceased solarized Amenhotep III, and the *sed*-festival celebrated by his son is as much a festival for the Aten as for the new king, even though the latter is of necessity the chief actor in the rituals. The Aten is the 'divine father' who rules Egypt as the celestial co-regent of his earthly incarnation, his son. That the Karnak jubilee was not considered to be Amenhotep IV's own official first *sed*-festival is proved by a later inscription in which a courtier at Amarna includes a wish to see the king 'in his first jubilee' in his funerary prayers, clearly indicating that such a festival had not yet taken place.

Another extraordinary feature of the Karnak buildings of Amenhotep IV is the unprecedented prominence of the king's wife, Nefertiti, in their decoration, and hence in the rituals that took place in them. One structure is devoted entirely to her alone, her royal husband being absent from the reliefs. Nefertiti is given a new name, Neferneferuaten, and she, often accompanied by her eldest daughter, Meritaten, performs many rituals that had until then been reserved for the king, including those of 'presenting Maat' (maintaining the order of the universe) and 'smiting the enemy' (subduing the powers of chaos). At this early stage of the reign it is not so much that she is acting as an official co-regent of her husband, but rather that the royal couple together now represent the mythical twins that in the traditional religion were called Shu and Tefnut, the first pair of divinities to issue from the androgynous creator-god Atum. The original triad consisting of Atum, the primeval father, his son Shu, and his daughter Tefnut is now replaced by a triad consisting of the Aten as the father and the living king and queen as his children. The unique iconography of both royals as displayed in statuary and reliefs reflects this new interpretation of their divine status.

Akhenaten and Amarna

Early in the fifth year of his reign, Amenhotep IV decided to sever all links with the traditional religious capital of Egypt and its god Amun, and to build an entirely new city on virgin soil that would be devoted solely to the cult of the Aten and his children. At the same time he changed his name to Akhenaten, meaning 'he who acts effectively on behalf of the Aten' or perhaps 'creative manifestation of the Aten'. The new city, nowadays known as Amarna, was called Akhetaten, 'Horizon of the Aten'—that is, the place where the Aten manifests himself and where he acts through his son, the king, who is 'the perfect child of the living Aten'. Whether there were political as well as religious motifs for this drastic decision remains unknown, although the king appears to hint at opposition to his religious reforms in the decree inscribed on a series of 'boundary stelae' defining the territory of Akhetaten. Opposition there must have been, especially among the dispossessed priestly establishment of the great temples of Amun at Thebes and probably elsewhere as well. Even before the move to Akhetaten some of the revenues of the established cults had been diverted to the cult of the Aten, and the situation must have deteriorated even further when the king abandoned the city of Amun for his new capital.

Before we examine this city, its inhabitants, and the new Atenist religion as it was practised there, we must briefly summarize the main political events of the reign of Akhenaten. We do not know when exactly he took up residence in Akhetaten, but presumably it was within a year or two of its foundation; the oaths sworn on that occasion by the king regarding the boundaries of the city's territory were renewed in regnal year 8. As soon as the decision to move had been made, all building activities at Thebes ceased, although the king's original name was removed from the inscriptions and replaced by the new one.

Once Akhenaten was firmly settled in his new residence, a further radicalization of his religious reforms took place. In year 9, the official name formula of the Aten was changed to 'the living one, Ra, ruler of the horizon who rejoices in the horizon in his identity of Ra the father who has returned as the sun-disc'. Clearly this new formula, while on the one hand removing the name of the god Horus, which smacked too much of traditional concepts, on the other hand puts even more emphasis on the father-son relationship between Aten and the King. Probably at the same time as this name change took place, the traditional gods were banned completely and a campaign was begun to remove their names and effigies (particularly those of Amun) from the monuments, a Herculean task that can only have been carried out with the support of the army. The traditional state temples were closed down and the cults of their gods came to a standstill. Perhaps most important of all, the religious festivals with their processions and public holidays were no longer celebrated either.

The role of the military during the Amarna Period has long been underestimated, partly because Akhenaten was thought to have been a pacifist. More recently, however, it has been recognized not only that the king's programme of

Facing: the 'year 3' hieratic graffito in the tomb of Pere⁽ᶜ⁾ (TT 139) at Thebes.

political and religious reform could never have succeeded without active military support, but also that Akhenaten sent his army abroad to quash a rebellion in Nubia in year 12. It has even been suggested that he may have been involved in a confrontation with the Hittites, who during Akhenaten's reign defeated the Hurrian empire of Mitanni, Egypt's ally, thus destroying the carefully maintained balance of power that had existed for several decades, although the diplomatic archive from Akhetaten (the 'Amarna letters') shows that Egyptian military activity in northern Syria usually took the form of limited police actions, the main goal of which was to prevent the volatile vassal states in the area from switching sides. It was also in year 12 that a great ceremony took place, during which the king received the tribute from 'all foreign countries gathered together as one', an event that may well be connected with the Nubian campaign of the same year.

Royal Women in the Amarna Period

At about the same time as these political events, an important change took place within the royal family. Nefertiti had so far produced six daughters, but no son, and, although she never lost her prime position as 'great royal wife', a second wife of Akhenaten had appeared on the scene at Akhetaten. It has often been speculated that she was a Mitannian princess, but her name Kiya is a perfectly normal Egyptian one and there is nothing to suggest that she was of foreign extraction. She was given the newly created title 'greatly beloved wife of the king', which sets her apart from other ladies in the royal harem, while at the same time distinguishing her clearly from Nefertiti. In or shortly before regnal year 12 she suddenly disappears from the monuments; her name was erased from the inscriptions and replaced by those of Akhenaten's daughters, most frequently that of Meritaten, and her representations were likewise altered. Since even the funerary equipment prepared for her, including a magnificent anthropoid coffin, was adapted for a different royal person, it is most likely that Kiya at some point fell from grace, perhaps because she had become too much of a rival to Nefertiti after she had borne Akhenaten not only a further daughter, but perhaps also a male heir. There is no hard evidence to support this theory, but a single inscription from about this time mentions 'the King's bodily son, his beloved, Tutankhaten' (the future king Tutankhamun (1336–1327 BC)), who was almost certainly a son of Akhenaten, but not of Nefertiti.

The latter's influence increased even further during the later part of the reign, when she became the official co-regent of her husband as Neferneferuaten with the throne name Ankh(et)kheperura; her role as queen consort was taken over by her eldest daughter, Meritaten. What prompted Akhenaten to appoint a co-regent, a step taken only in exceptional circumstances, is unknown. Perhaps opposition to his regime elsewhere in the country (that is, in Thebes) was threatening to get out of control, making it necessary to have someone who could act as king and perhaps even take up residence outside

Plan of the site of Amarna, showing the main city and the outlying temples, shrines, and settlements.

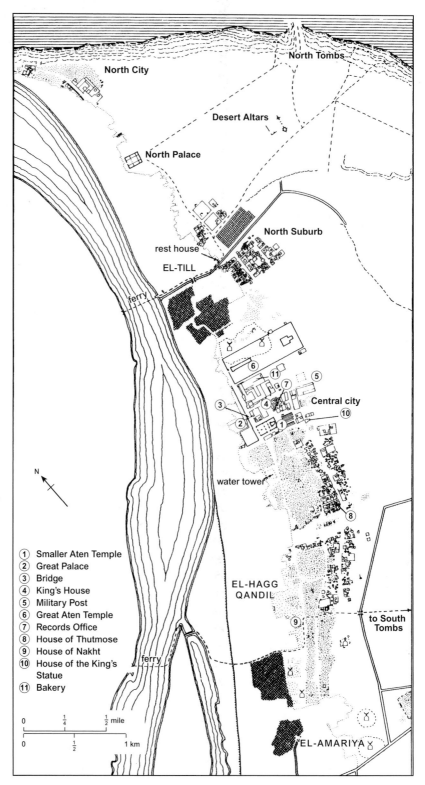

North City

North Tombs

Desert Altars

North Palace

North Suburb

rest house

EL-TILL

ferry

Central city

water tower

EL-HAGG QANDIL

to South Tombs

ferry

EL-AMARIYA

N

① Smaller Aten Temple
② Great Palace
③ Bridge
④ King's House
⑤ Military Post
⑥ Great Aten Temple
⑦ Records Office
⑧ House of Thutmose
⑨ House of Nakht
⑩ House of the King's Statue
⑪ Bakery

0   ¼   ½ mile

0   ½   1 km

Amarna; at any rate, a Theban graffito dated to her regnal year 3 reveals that Neferneferuaten owned a 'Mansion of Ankhkheperura in Thebes' that employed a scribe of divine offerings of Amun, a clear indication that an attempt at reconciliation with the old cults was undertaken. Most of this text consists of the scribe's prayer to Amun, with a poignant appeal to the god to come back and dispel the darkness that had descended upon his followers.

Whether or not Nefertiti survived Akhenaten, who died in his year 17, is uncertain. An ephemeral king Smenkhkara with virtually the same throne name as Nefertiti/Neferneferuaten appears in some inscriptions from the end of the Amarna Period; in one or two rare representations he is accompanied by his queen Meritaten. The identity of this Smenkhkara is uncertain. Many scholars continue to see him as Nefertiti's male successor, perhaps a younger brother or even another son of Akhenaten, but there is a strong possibility that 'he' was actually none other than Nefertiti herself who, like Hatshepsut before her, had assumed a male persona and ruled alone for a brief period after the death of Akhenaten, with Meritaten in the ceremonial role of 'great royal wife'. Akhenaten's successor probably did not survive him for very long, and, when he/she died, the very young Tutankhaten, the only remaining male member of the royal family, mounted the throne. Early in his reign he and his queen, his halfsister Ankhesenpaaten, abandoned Amarna and restored the traditional cults. With him, one of the most incisive periods in Egyptian history came to an end.

The Art and Architecture of the Amarna Period

The earliest representations of Amenhotep IV show him in a traditional style closely resembling the one used to portray both Thutmose IV and Amenhotep III, but not long after his accession Amenhotep IV had himself depicted with a thin, drawn-out face with pointed chin and thick lips, an elongated neck, almost feminine breasts, a round protruding belly, wide hips, fat thighs, and thin, spindly legs. At first the new style was still fairly restrained, but on most of the Theban monuments and during the early years at Amarna the king's features were depicted in such an exaggerated way as to make him look like a caricature; later in the reign a more balanced style developed. It was not only Akhenaten, Nefertiti, and their daughters who were depicted in this style, but all other human beings as well, albeit in a less exaggerated form. This is not surprising, since representations of private individuals had always followed the artistic model of the king of their time, and Akhenaten in particular put much emphasis on the fact that he was the 'mother who gives birth to everything' who had 'created his subjects with his *ka*'. He was the creator-god upon earth who fashioned mankind after his own image.

There can be little doubt that the extraordinary manner in which Akhenaten portrayed himself, his family (and, to a lesser extent, all other human beings) on his monuments somehow reflects the king's actual physical appearance, albeit in an exaggerated style that has been termed 'expressionist' or even 'surrealist'. Inscriptions tell us that it was the king himself who instructed his artists in the new style. Not only the human figure is affected by it, but also the way they interact. Scenes of the royal family display an intimacy such as had never before been shown in Egyptian art even among private individuals, let alone among royalty. They kiss and embrace under the beneficent rays of the Aten, whose love pervades all of his creation. Another characteristic feature of the Amarna style is its extraordinary sense of movement and speed, a general 'looseness' and freedom of expression that was to have a lasting influence on Egyptian art for centuries after the Amarna Period had come to an end.

In a different way, speed is also the determining factor of a new building technique. Again, the earliest structures of Amenhotep IV employed the traditional large sandstone blocks commonly used for temple walls, but these were soon replaced in both Thebes and Amarna by very much smaller blocks, the so-called *talatat*, typically measuring about 60 × 25 cm. and therefore small enough for a single man to lift and carry. This made it much easier to erect a large building in a relatively short space of time. The new method was abandoned again after the Amarna Period, perhaps because it had by then become apparent that the reliefs carved on walls constructed of such small blocks, needing as they did a great deal of plaster finishing to close the gaps between individual stones, did not withstand the test of time as well as traditionally built walls. Certainly Akhenaten's successors soon found out that it also took far less time and effort to demolish buildings constructed of *talatat*.

The 'looseness' of the Amarna art style is perhaps also matched by the city plan of Akhetaten, at least as far as the living quarters are concerned. Despite the fact that it was a newly planned city, it was not built on a rigid orthogonal grid like the Middle Kingdom town of Kahun, which had reflected the highly structured, bureaucratic society of its time. The layout of Amarna is far more like a cluster of small villages centred around loosely grouped houses both large and small, each with its own subsidiary buildings such as grain silos, animal pens, sheds, and workshops. The variety in size of these compounds matches the differences in wealth and status between their owners. Many of them have their own well, a unique feature of this city, which made its inhabitants independent of the Nile for their daily water supplies. In general Amarna looks more like a city that developed naturally over a period of time, rather than as a result of careful planning.

Needless to say, however, the temples and palaces are a different matter. Both were intimately linked with Akhenaten's religious ideas and for this reason they must have been designed and planned by the king himself in close cooperation with architects and artists who worked under his personal 'instruction', as inscriptions never tire of telling us. We cannot describe these buildings in detail here, but a few significant features must be mentioned. First of all, Akhenaten and his family lived some distance away from the main city in what is now known as the North Riverside Palace. A long spacious avenue, the 'royal road', ran via the North Palace (the queen's residence) in a straight line of about

3.5 km. to the Central City with its two palaces (one used among other things for ceremonial state occasions like the reception of foreign envoys, the other serving as the king's working palace with a 'window of appearances', through which he rewarded loyal officials), and two major Aten temples. Of these, the Great Temple to the Aten was the Amarna equivalent of the great temple enclosure of Amun-Ra at Thebes; it contained several separate buildings, including a structure with a *benben*-stone, the sacred sun symbol, the archetype of which stood in the temple of Ra at Heliopolis. This is one of the indications of the influence of Heliopolitan theology on Akhenaten's thinking, another being that the king had planned a cemetery for the sacred Mnevis bull of Ra-Atum of Heliopolis at Amarna. The other Aten temple was very much smaller and lay immediately to the south of the king's working palace. It appears to have been dedicated to the king as well as to the Aten and may have been the equivalent of the traditional so-called temples of a million years, and, like the temples of that name on the Theban west bank, may have served as a mortuary chapel for Akhenaten that was orientated towards the entrance of the wadi in which the royal tomb was located.

The most conspicuous difference between, on the one hand, the Aten temples both at Amarna and earlier on at Karnak, and, on the other hand, the traditional temples is that the former are open to the skies. A typical temple of the traditional type began with a pylon and an open peristyle court followed by a succession of further courts and rooms, which gradually became smaller and darker as the worshipper penetrated further into the building. In the innermost sanctuary the cult image of the god was kept in a shrine that for most of the time was in total darkness. Akhenaten's god was there for all to see, however, and no man-made cult image was, therefore, needed. The only statues to be found in Atenist temples are representations of Akhenaten and other members of the royal family. In the architecture of these temples a deliberate effort has been made to create as little shadow and darkness as possible; even the lintels above the doorways were open in the middle. These 'broken' lintels were an architectural innovation that continued to be used for certain temple doorways until Graeco-Roman times. The king worshipped his god in open courtyards studded with a large number of small altars on which offerings to the Aten were made. Why there are so many altars remains a mystery; perhaps the most likely explanation is that they are altars for the dead who are being fed in the temples as part of the daily cult.

Light was the most essential aspect of the Aten, who was a god of the light that emerged from the sun's disc and kept every living being alive in continuous creation. He was the creator-god who ruled the world as the celestial king. And, just as the Aten was king of the world, so Akhenaten was the god of his subjects. His daily 'procession', when he drove in his chariot along the royal road from the North Riverside Palace to the Central City, replaced the traditional divine processions during which the inhabitants of a town could come into contact with the deities whose statues were normally hidden from view in the temple.

Akhenaten was, as his name indicates, the 'creative manifestation of the Aten', through whom the Aten does his beneficial work. It was the king who 'made' mankind and especially his élite, whom he had chosen himself. In their inscriptions these officials denied their true background, even though some of them must surely have come from influential families; they all presented themselves as having been poor, wretched orphans, owing their whole existence to the king who had 'created them with his *ka*'. The king's work was likened to the annual inundation of the Nile, which sustained mankind and all other living beings. Personal piety was now identical with total loyalty towards Akhenaten personally. In their private houses the Amarna élite kept small shrines with altars and stelae representing the holy royal family, which replaced the old household shrines for local deities.

Tombs and Funerary Beliefs at Amarna

Even in the tombs of the élite at Akhetaten, the king totally dominated the wall decoration. Representations of Akhenaten and his wife and children (as well as depictions of the various temples of Akhetaten) were ubiquitous, and hymns and offering formulas were dedicated as often to the king as to the Aten. It is notable that these offering formulas were frequently—although not exclusively—addressed to the god by the king himself rather than by the tomb-owner. The only surviving copies of the famous *Great Hymn to the Aten*, the most comprehensive text on the main dogmas of the new religion (probably composed by Akhenaten himself), are found in these tombs. This hymn and all other texts at Amarna were written in a newly created official language that was much closer to everyday speech than the classical Egyptian that had so far been used for official and religious texts. The boundary between official and vernacular language did not disappear completely, but the use of the latter for literary compositions was greatly stimulated by this development and gave rise to a whole new literature in the centuries after the Amarna Period.

Osiris, the most important god of the dead, appears to have been proscribed from the very beginning of Akhenaten's reign. Even the doctrine that viewed Osiris as the nocturnal manifestation of the sun-god, well established in funerary religion long before Amarna, was rejected by Akhenaten. The Aten was a god of life-giving light; during the night he was absent, but it is unclear where he was thought to go. Darkness and death were completely ignored instead of being regarded as a positive, necessary state of regeneration. At night the dead were simply asleep like every other living being and like the Aten himself. They were not in the 'Beautiful West', the underworld, and their tombs were not even physically located in the west but in the east, where the sun rises. The 'resurrection' of the dead took place in the morning, when the Aten arose. The Aten himself represented 'the time in which one lives', as the *Great Hymn* expressed it. The mode of existence of the dead was, therefore, one of a continual presence with the Aten and the king in the temple, where they (or their *ba*-

souls) fed on the daily offerings. For this reason the Amarna private tombs were full of representations of the temples of the Aten and of the king driving along the royal road towards the temples and offering in them. The temples and palaces of Akhetaten were the new hereafter; the dead no longer lived in their tombs but on earth, among the living. The tombs, therefore, served only as their nightly resting places. Mummification persisted, because at night the *ba* returned to the body until sunrise. For this reason, funerary rites, including offerings and tomb equipment, appear to have continued as well, although most *shabti* figures no longer have the chapter from the *Book of the Dead* traditionally inscribed on them. It is difficult to be sure what the Amarna Period private coffins and sarcophagi looked like, since no examples have ever been found at Amarna. On Akhenaten's own large stone sarcophagus the four winged goddesses who traditionally stood at the corners were replaced by figures of Nefertiti, and some finds from other sites suggest that private sarcophagi may also have been decorated with depictions of members of the family of the deceased rather than funerary deities. There was also no 'judgement of the dead' before the throne of Osiris, which the deceased formerly had to pass through in order to gain the status of a *maaty* ('righteous one'); instead, the king's officials earned their life after death by following Akhenaten's teaching and by being totally loyal to him during their lifetime. Akhenaten was the god who granted life and a burial after old age in his favour; he embodied *maat* and it was

The tomb of the priest Panehsy at Amarna (EA6) includes a relief showing the king and queen, Akhenaten and Nefertiti, processing through the city of Akhetaten in a chariot.

285

Changes in funerary belief during the Amarna Period led to the deceased being portrayed wearing a festive pleated linen costume rather than being shown as a mummy, as on these sarcophagus fragments in the Strasbourg Museum.

through loyalty to him that his subjects could become *maatyu*. Without this there would be no life after death, and continued existence upon earth depended on the king, who therefore monopolized all aspects of the Amarna religion, including funerary beliefs.

Life outside Amarna during the Amarna Period

Most of our knowledge of Akhenaten's new religion derives from his early monuments at Thebes and from the city at Amarna itself. What happened in the rest of the country, especially after the king had moved to his new city , is very much less clear. Akhenaten would almost certainly have travelled outside Akhetaten; he even stipulates (on the 'boundary stelae') that, if he were to die elsewhere, his body should be brought back to Amarna and buried there. Apart from early building activities in Nubia, we know of Aten temples in Memphis and Heliopolis and there may have been others. Some Memphite blocks display the late form of the Aten name (after regnal year 9), and a stray block from Thebes also has this form; therefore, even after the radicalization of Akhenaten's reform, construction work outside Amarna obviously continued. What we do not know is the extent to which the traditional cults were really abolished; our picture is very much coloured by a later description of the situation in the

Restoration Decree of Tutankhamun, the tenor of which is quite obviously propagandistic.

In everyday practice, the new religion probably only replaced the official state cult and the religion of the élite; the majority of the people must have continued to worship their own traditional, often local gods. Even at Amarna itself there are a fair number of surviving votive objects, stelae, and wall paintings that depict or mention gods such as Bes and Taweret (both connected with childbirth); the harvest-goddess Renenutet; the protective deities Isis and Shed ('the saviour', a new form of Horus not found before Amarna); Thoth (the god of the scribes); Khnum, Satet, and Anuket (the triad of Elephantine); Ptah of Memphis; and even Amun of Thebes.

It is not always easy to decide whether tomb reliefs, stelae, and items of burial equipment that mention the Aten together with traditional gods such as Osiris, Thoth, or Ptah date from the beginning of the reign or later, or even from the time immediately after the Amarna Period. Nor do we know whether the deceased buried in a necropolis other than that of Akhetaten were supposed to partake of offerings in the Aten temple at Amarna or in their home town, or how the dead were thought to live on in places where there was no Aten temple at all. Much further research is needed here, particularly in the necropolis of Memphis, where many tombs of this period have yet to be discovered.

It is also unclear what happened to the civil administration during the Amarna Period. Clearly Akhetaten had replaced Thebes as the religious capital and the centre of the state cult, but did it also replace Memphis as the administrative capital? One of the two viziers resided at Amarna, but his northern colleague remained posted at Memphis. It is probable that this city in fact retained its position of administrative centre for the country throughout the Amarna Period. The situation during the Saite Period may well afford a parallel: the 26th Dynasty kings greatly favoured Sais, their home town (although they were originally of Libyan descent), which functioned as their capital, and much of the state revenues went to the temple of its goddess Neith. Yet Memphis remained the administrative centre of Egypt throughout the Saite Period, a situation that persisted until the successor of Alexander the Great removed the latter's mortal remains to Alexandria and made this city the centre of Ptolemaic and Roman Egypt.

The Aftermath of the Amarna Period

Although the Amarna episode lasted barely twenty years, its impact was enormous. It is perhaps the single most important event in Egypt's religious and cultural history and it left deep scars on the collective consciousness of its inhabitants. Superficially, the country returned to the traditional religion of the time before Akhenaten, but in reality nothing would ever be the same again. Some of the changes can be detected in the burial arrangements of the élite, always a good barometer of shifting religious attitudes. Most conspicuous are

Facing: the gold mask and trappings of the mummy of Tutankhamun. The King wears the *nemes* headcloth with vulture and cobra at his brow

the developments in tomb architecture. At Memphis in particular, free-standing tombs appear that in all essential aspects resemble temples. In Thebes rock tombs continue to be used, but their architecture and decoration are adapted to the same new concept, that of the tomb as the private mortuary temple for its owner, whose funerary cult is integrated with the cult of Osiris. This god, who had been banned by Akhenaten, was now universally seen as the nocturnal manifestation of Ra, and his role in funerary matters increased dramatically as compared to the days before the Amarna Period. In these tombs, the solar symbol *par excellence*, the pyramid, previously a royal prerogative, sat on the roof of the central chapel, usually with a capstone (pyramidion) showing scenes of worship before Ra and Osiris. In the central chapel itself the main stele, the focal point of the cult, often showed a symmetrically arranged double scene comprising both of these gods seated back to back. Statues that had previously been typically placed in temples began to appear in private tombs, including images of various deities and naophorous statues that show the deceased holding a shrine with an image of a god.

The reliefs and paintings on the walls of the tombs were no longer primarily concerned with scenes from the owner's career and professional occupation,

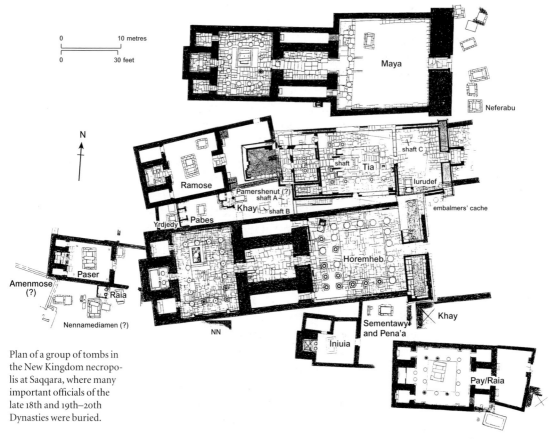

Plan of a group of tombs in the New Kingdom necropolis at Saqqara, where many important officials of the late 18th and 19th–20th Dynasties were buried.

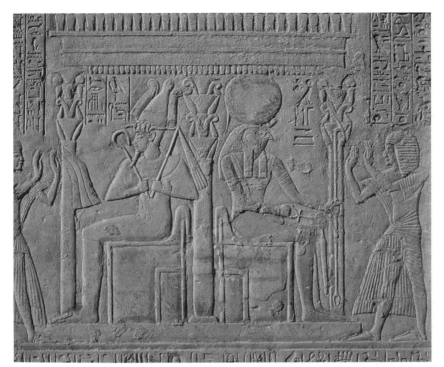

The central funerary stele from the late 18th Dynasty tomb of Pay at Saqqara shows the gods Ra and Osiris in the top register.

although such scenes do not disappear completely, but instead concentrate on showing him adoring Ra, Osiris, and a wide variety of other gods and goddesses, wearing a long pleated linen costume (often wrongly called the 'dress of daily life') and an elaborate wig. The same festive costume also appears on anthropoid sarcophagi and *shabtis*, which hitherto had shown the deceased exclusively as a mummy. Apart from one or two examples from very early in the reign of Tutankhamun, scenes in which the deceased is shown presenting offerings to the king disappear completely; his place is now occupied by Osiris enthroned. In general, religious scenes and texts, often taken from the *Book of the Dead*, dominated the post-Amarna tomb decoration. Illustrations and textual excerpts from various exclusively royal funerary compositions such as the *Litany of Ra* and the so-called *Books of the Underworld* began to appear on the walls of private tombs, first at Deir el-Medina, but soon elsewhere as well. All of these features may be explained as a reaction against Akhenaten's total monopolization of the funerary cult of his subjects and the role that the Aten temples had played in Amarna religion as the new 'hereafter'. The tomb-owners now had their own temples in which they themselves worshipped the gods, without the intervention of the king, whose role was thus minimalized.

The changes in funerary culture just outlined are symptomatic of the totally different relationship between the gods and their worshippers, and the role played by the king in this relationship. In another 200 years, the ultimate consequence of this new world-view would be shown by the realization of the so-called Theban theocracy, whereby Amun himself was thought to rule as king of

Facing, above: aerial view of the temple complex at Karnak.

Facing, below: watercolour by Henry Salt of a painted relief in the early 19th Dynasty tomb of Sety I.

Egypt, governing his subjects by means of direct intervention in the form of oracles. Before we can discuss this development, however, we must return to the political and dynastic history of Egypt following the end of the Amarna Period.

Tutankhamun

The young Tutankhaten, still a child, had ascended the throne at Amarna, but soon afterwards, perhaps as early as his first regnal year or shortly afterwards, he abandoned the city founded by his father. People continued to live in Akhetaten for some time, but the court moved back to Memphis, the traditional seat of government. The old cults were restored and Thebes once more

In the Amarna period, the name and depictions of the god Amun were removed from many monuments, but, as the top of this Karnak obelisk of Hatshepsut demonstrates, they were often restored in the late 18th Dynasty and Ramessid period.

became the religious centre of the country. The king's name was changed to Tutankhamun and the epithet 'ruler of southern Heliopolis', a deliberate reference to Karnak as the centre of the cult of the sun-god Amun-Ra, was added to it. The name of his great royal wife, his half-sister Ankhesenpaaten, was likewise altered to Ankhesenamun. Tutankhamun was by no means the first ruler in the history of the dynasty to have ascended the throne as a child. Both Thutmose III and Amenhotep III had been very young at their accessions, but in both cases a senior female member of the royal family (Hatshepsut and Mutemwiya, respectively) had acted as regent during their early years. No such option was available now; therefore the role of regent was played by a senior military official with no bloodlinks with the royal family, the commander-in-chief of the army, Horemheb. His titles as regent indicate that he gained the right to succeed Tutankhamun if he were to die without issue. Horemheb would in fact eventually become king himself, and in his Coronation Text (a unique inscription giving an account of his rise to power, carved on the back of a statue now in the Egyptian Museum, Turin), he seems to suggest that it was he who advised the king to abandon Amarna 'when chaos had broken out in the palace' (that is, after the deaths of Akhenaten and his ephemeral successor). Obviously the army had come to the conclusion that Akhenaten's experiment had ended in disaster and had withdrawn its support from the religious reforms they had initially helped to carry through, another tell-tale sign of the important role played by the military in this whole affair.

The most important document of Tutankhamun's reign is the so-called Restoration Stele, which presents an extremely negative description of the state in which Akhenaten's reforms had left the country. The temples of the gods had become ruins, their cults abolished. The gods had, therefore, abandoned Egypt; if one prayed to them, they no longer answered, and, when the army was sent to Syria to expand the boundaries of Egypt, it met with no success. The prominence of this last phrase probably indicates why the army no longer supported the Amarna policy. During Akhenaten's reign, Egypt's ally Mitanni had been defeated by the Hittites, who were now the major power in the north. This had prompted some of Egypt's vassals, notably Aziru of Amurru, to try to establish an independent buffer state between the two rival superpowers. Egypt was beginning to lose some of its northernmost territory, and the army, restricted to limited police actions in Syria, was obviously unable to do anything about it. With the accession of Tutankhamun, these restrictions were evidently lifted, since the reliefs in the inner courtyard of Horemheb's magnificent Memphite tomb (decorated around this time) include the claim that his name was 'renowned in the land of the Hittites', thus suggesting that, early in Tutankhamun's reign, Horemheb must have been engaged in military confrontations with the Hittites. These skirmishes, as well as later ones, seem to have failed to establish a new balance of power. On the other hand, simultaneous attempts to reassert Egyptian authority in Nubia, documented by these same reliefs, were probably more successful.

In Egypt itself, a major campaign to restore the traditional temples and to reorganize the administration of the country was set in motion. The enterprise was led by the chief of Tutankhamun's treasury, Maya, who was sent on a major mission to temples from the Delta to Elephantine, in order to levy taxes on their revenues, which had previously been diverted to the Aten temples. Some of the measures later described in Horemheb's Coronation Text and in his great Karnak Edict may actually have been carried out during the reign of Tutankhamun. Maya was also responsible for the gradual demolishing of the temples and palaces of Akhenaten, first at Thebes, but later at Amarna as well. Most of the Theban *talatat* found their way into the foundations and pylons of new construction works in Luxor and Karnak. As overseer of works in the Valley of the Kings, Maya must have organized the transfer of Akhenaten's mortal remains to a small undecorated tomb in the valley (assuming that the body found in KV 55 is indeed Akhenaten's, as seems likely); later he was responsible for the burials of Tutankhamun and his successor Ay (1327–1323 BC) and for the reorganization of the workmen's village at Deir el-Medina when work began on the tomb of Horemheb.

The Reigns of Ay and Horemheb

The events surrounding the death of Tutankhamun are still far from clear. The king died unexpectedly in his tenth regnal year, at a time when Egypt was engaged in a major confrontation with the Hittites that ended in an Egyptian defeat at Amqa, not far from Qadesh. News of this disaster reached Egypt at about the time of Tutankhamun's death. We do not know whether Horemheb himself was leading the Egyptian troops in this battle, but the fact that he does not appear to have been involved in the burial arrangements for Tutankhamun, despite his role as regent and heir presumptive, is highly suggestive. Instead, Ay, a senior court adviser who had been one of Akhenaten's most trusted officials and may have been a relative of Amenhotep III's wife, Queen Tiy, conducted the obsequies and shortly afterwards ascended the throne. Apparently he did so at first as a kind of interim king, for Tutankhamun's widow, Ankhesenamun, was trying to negotiate a peace with the Hittites by writing to the Hittite king Shupiluliuma to ask him for a son who could marry her and become king of Egypt, in order that Egypt and Hatti should become 'one country', an extraordinary step which may possibly have been instigated by Ay. This request met with much suspicion in the Hittite capital and, when Shupiluliuma was finally convinced of the Egyptian queen's honorable intentions and sent his son Zannanza to Egypt, the unfortunate prince was murdered *en route*, perhaps by forces loyal to Horemheb in Syria. The result was prolonged warfare with the Hittites.

King Ay, who must have been fairly aged when he mounted the throne, ruled for at least three full years. A fragmentary cuneiform letter appears to suggest that he tried to make amends with the Hittites, denying all responsibility for the death of the prince, but to no avail. He also made a conscious effort to prevent Horemheb from asserting his rights after his death, for he appointed an army commander called Nakhtmin (possibly a grandson of his) as his heir. Despite this, however, Horemheb succeeded in ascending the throne after Ay's demise and soon set out to deface the monuments of his predecessor and to destroy those of his rival Nakhtmin.

If Horemheb's path to the throne had been beset with difficulties, his actual reign (1323–1295 BC) appears to have been relatively uneventful. It should be borne in mind, however, that there are few inscriptions from the later part of his reign. Even its length is still uncertain; his highest attested date is year 13, but on the basis of Babylonian chronology and two posthumous texts many claim that he reigned for nearly twice as long as this. The unfinished state of his royal tomb in the Valley of the Kings (KV 57), however, even if it was not begun before his year 7, is difficult to reconcile with such a long reign. Trouble with the Hittites over territories in northern Syria continued, and around regnal year 10 the Egyptians appear to have made an unsuccessful attempt to reconquer Qadesh and Amurru, although it is typical of the reign that our sources for this confrontation are Hittite, and not Egyptian texts. It is even possible that Horemheb finally came to an agreement with his enemy, for a later Hittite text refers to a treaty that had been in force before it was broken during the reigns of Muwatalli and Sety I (1294–1279 BC).

At home, Horemheb embarked on a number of major building projects, including the Great Hypostyle Hall in Karnak. He may also have begun the systematic demolition of the city of Amarna, still inhabited at this time. Two stone fragments including a statue base bearing his cartouches were found there. The reorganization of the country was also taken in hand with great gusto. The Great Edict, which he published on a stele in the temple of Karnak, enumerates a large number of legal measures enacted in order to stamp out abuses such as the unlawful requisitioning of boats and slaves, the theft of cattle hides, the illegal taxation of private farmland and fraud in assessing lawful taxes, and the extortion of local mayors by officials organizing the king's annual visit to the Opet Festival during the journey from Memphis to Thebes and back. Other paragraphs deal with the regulation of the local courts of justice, the personnel of the royal harem and other state employees, and the protocol at court.

Perhaps the most salient feature of Horemheb's reign is the way that he legitimized it; after all, he was of non-royal blood and was, therefore, unable to claim a 'genealogical' link with the dynastic god Amun. It is often maintained that his queen, a songstress of Amun called Mutnedjmet, should be identified with a sister of Nefertiti of that name, but this is not very likely as she appears to have become his wife well before his accession, quite apart from the fact that the legitimizing force of such a royal marriage may well have been questionable, given the circumstances. In his Coronation Text Horemheb does not hide his non-royal background, but instead puts much emphasis on the fact that, as a young man, he was chosen by the god Horus of Hutnesu, presumably his home town, to be king of Egypt; he then goes on to describe how he was carefully prepared for his future task by being the king's (that is, Tutankhamun's) deputy and prince regent, a claim largely substantiated by the inscriptions in his preroyal tomb in the Memphite necropolis. It is Horus of Hutnesu who finally presents him to Amun during the Opet Festival procession, and who then proceeds to crown him as king. Horemheb thus owes his kingship to the will of his personal god and to divine election during a public appearance of Amun (that is, by means of an oracle). In this respect Horemheb's coronation resembles that of Hatshepsut (1473–1458 BC), who had also been elected by an oracle of Amun after having been regent. However, Hatshepsut was at least able to claim to be of royal blood herself and actually stressed that Amun had fathered her by the queen mother, a subject that Horemheb carefully avoids in his Coronation Text.

Rameses I

The principle of electing a non-royal heir was adopted by Horemheb and the early Ramessid rulers, the first of whom was appointed by Horemheb as prince regent during his lifetime with much the same titles as he himself had held under Tutankhamun. This man, Paramessu, acted as Horemheb's vizier as well as holding a number of military titles including that of commander of the fortress of Sile, an important stronghold on the landbridge connecting the Egyptian Delta with Syria–Palestine. The role assigned to Paramessu once more reveals Horemheb's preoccupation with the military situation in Egypt's northern territories. Paramessu's family came from Avaris, the former capital of the Hyksos, and the role of its local god Seth, who had retained strong connections with the Canaanite god Ba'al, appears to have been comparable with that of Horus of Hutnesu in Horemheb's career. In the light of this it is interesting to observe that Horemheb built a temple for Seth at Avaris. The Ramessid royal family considered the god Seth to be their royal ancestor, and a fragment of an obelisk (originally from Heliopolis), recently discovered on the seabed off the coast of Alexandria, shows Sety I as a sphinx with the head of the Seth-animal offering to Ra-Atum.

When Horemheb died, apparently childless, Paramessu succeeded him as Rameses I (1295–1294 BC). With him began a new dynasty, the 19th, although there is some evidence to suggest that the Ramessid pharaohs considered Horemheb as the true founder of the dynasty. Rameses I must have been old when he mounted the throne, since his son and probably also his grandson had already been born before his accession. During his short reign (barely one year), and maybe even before, his son Sety was appointed vizier and commander of Sile but also held a number of priestly titles linking him with various gods worshipped in the Delta, including that of high priest of Seth. In his Coronation Text Horemheb had mentioned that he had equipped the newly reopened temples with priests 'from the pick of the army', providing them with fields and cattle. From other documents we know that retired soldiers were often given a priestly office and some land in their native towns, so Sety may also not have been particularly young when his father mounted the throne.

Sety I and the 'Restoration'

Sety I must be credited with the bulk of the restoration of the traditional temples, continuing and surpassing the efforts of his predecessors. Everywhere inscriptions of pre-Amarna pharaohs were restored, and the names and representations of Amun hacked out by Akhenaten were recarved. He also soon embarked on an ambitious building programme of his own. Practically everywhere in the country, and particularly in the great religious centres of Thebes, Abydos, Memphis, and Heliopolis, new temples were erected or existing ones expanded. Among the latter was the temple of Seth at Avaris, a city that was soon to become the new Delta residence of the Ramessid rulers. At Karnak, Sety continued the construction of the Great Hypostyle Hall begun by Horemheb, which was connected with his own mortuary temple at Abd el-Qurna, directly opposite Karnak on the west bank of the Nile. Together with Hatshepsut's temple at Deir el-Bahri, which he restored, these buildings provided a splendid new setting for the important annual Beautiful Feast of the Valley, during which Amun of Karnak visited the gods of the west bank and people came to the tombs of their deceased relatives to eat, drink, and be merry in their company. At Abydos Sety I built a magnificent cenotaph temple for the god Osiris, following Middle Kingdom and early 18th Dynasty examples. The famous kinglist in this temple, a list of the royal ancestors participating in the offering cult for Osiris, provides the first evidence that the Amarna episode was now completely obliterated from official records. In the list Amenhotep III is directly followed by Horemheb, and other sources indicate that the regnal years of the kings from Akhenaten to Ay were added to those of Horemheb.

Sety's building programme was made possible because he reopened several old quarries and mines, including those in Sinai, and also because, like his predecessors, he raided Nubia for captives who could be employed as cheap labour. Security was another reason for these Nubian campaigns, for the finances for his building projects came from the exploitation of gold mines both there and in the Eastern Desert. The mines in the latter area in particular were worked on behalf of Sety's great Osiris temple at Abydos; in regnal year 9 the road leading to them was provided with a resting-place, a newly dug well, and a small temple. In Nubia there was a failed attempt to sink a new well to make the more profitable mines in some of the remoter areas accessible.

Further resources had previously come from the Egyptian territories in Palestine and Syria and it was now essential to reassert Egyptian authority over these areas. Sety began in his regnal year 1 with a relatively small-scale campaign against the Shasu in southern Palestine, soon followed by military expeditions further north. In a later war he moved into territory held at the time by the

The military campaigns of Sety I depicted in series of reliefs on the walls of the Temple of Karnak show the king riding his chariot into battle.

Hittites and managed to reconquer Qadesh, which in turn prompted Amurru to defect to the Egyptian side. The result was a war with the Hittites during which both vassal states were lost again, followed by a period of guarded peace. Sety I was also the first king to have to face incursions by Libyan tribes along the western border of the Delta. These tribes, who appear to have been motivated primarily by famine, were to continue to cause problems throughout the rest of the New Kingdom, but little is known about this first attempt to settle in Egypt, other than the fact that Sety's campaign against them probably took place before his confrontation with the Hittites.

The reliefs on the northern exterior wall of the Great Hypostyle Hall documenting the Libyan and Syrian campaigns are in a new, much more realistic style, which, despite a few precursors from the time of Thutmose IV and Amenhotep III, was clearly influenced by the realism of the Amarna style. More than the traditional scenes of slaying the enemy with their strong symbolic content, these battle reliefs create the feeling that we are looking at a real, historical event. An important role in these reliefs is played by a 'group-marshaller and fan-bearer' called Mehy (short for Amenemheb, Horemheb, or some similar name), who accompanies Sety in a number of scenes. It is unlikely that this man was ever more than a trusted military officer who perhaps conducted some of the campaigns instead of the king himself, but Sety's successor Rameses II (1279–1213 BC), eager to stress his own role on the battlefield during the reign of his father, had Mehy's names and figures erased and in some cases replaced by his own as crown prince.

Rameses II

Unfortunately it is not known how long Sety I occupied the throne. His highest attested regnal year is his eleventh, but he may have ruled for a few years more. Towards the end of his reign—we do not know exactly when—he appointed his son and heir Rameses as co-regent while the latter was still 'a child in his embrace'. The sources for this co-regency all date from Rameses' reign as sole king, however, and he may well have exaggerated its length and importance. It is nevertheless significant that Rameses received the kingship in this way. Although clearly a son of Sety I, he was almost certainly born during the reign of Horemheb, before his grandfather ascended the throne, and at a time when both Rameses I and Sety I were still simply high officials, a fact later emphasized rather than disguised by Rameses II himself in much the same way as Horemheb had done in his Coronation Text. Although his father was obviously king when Rameses II was crowned as co-regent, his election resembles that of Horemheb. Clearly the succession of the crown prince was not a foregone conclusion and had to be secured while his father was still alive. Only later, when Rameses II ruled alone, did he revert to the old 'myth of the birth of the divine king' that had legitimized the rulers of the 18th Dynasty.

Very early in his reign, probably still as co-regent of his father, he went on his first military campaign, a limited affair aimed at quelling a 'rebellion' in Nubia. Reliefs in a small rock temple at Beit el-Wali commemorating the event show the young king in the company of two of his children, the crown prince, Amunherwenemef, and Rameses' fourth son, Khaemwaset, who, although shown standing proudly in their chariots, must have been mere striplings at the time. Throughout the Ramessid Period the royal princes, who in the 18th Dynasty had only occasionally been depicted in the tombs of their non-royal nurses and teachers, would be prominent on the royal monuments of their father, perhaps in order to emphasize that the kingship of the new dynasty was now well and truly hereditary again. Almost without exception every Ramessid crown prince held the title, honorific or real, of 'commander-in-chief of the army', a combination first seen in the case of Horemheb, the founder of their dynasty.

In his fourth regnal year Rameses II mounted his first major campaign in Syria, as a result of which Amurru once again returned to the Egyptian fold. This was not to last long, however, for the Hittite King Muwatalli decided at once to reconquer Amurru and to try to prevent further losses of territory to the Egyptians, with the result that the following year Rameses again passed the border fortress at Sile, this time in order to wage war directly against his rival. The battle of Qadesh that followed is one of the most famous armed conflicts of antiquity, perhaps not so much because it was significantly different from earlier battles, but because Rameses, despite the fact that he was unable to achieve his goals, presented it at home as a huge victory described at large in lengthy compositions, which, in a propaganda campaign of unprecedented proportions, were carved on the walls of all the major temples.

In actual fact, Rameses had wrongly been led to believe that the Hittite king was in the far north at Tunip, too scared to confront the Egyptians, whereas in reality he was nearby on the other side of Qadesh. Rameses had, therefore, made a quick advance to Qadesh with only one of his four divisions and was then suddenly obliged to face the huge army that the Hittite king had mustered against him. Muwatalli first destroyed the advancing Egyptian second division, which was about to join the first, then turned around to crush Rameses and his troops. In his later descriptions of the battle Rameses tells us that this was his true moment of glory, for, when even his immediate attendants were ready to desert him, he called out to his father Amun to save him, then almost single-handedly managed to fight off the Hittite attackers. But Amun heard his prayers and rescued the king by causing an Egyptian support force from the coast of Amurru to arrive in the nick of time. These forces now attacked the Hittites in the rear and, together with Rameses' division, severely reduced the number of the enemy's chariots and sent the remainder fleeing, many of them ending up in the river Orontes. With the arrival of the third division at the close of the combat, followed by the fourth at sunset, the Egyptians were able to reassemble their forces and were now ready to face their enemy the next morning. But, despite the fact that the Egyptian chariotry now outnumbered their Hittite counterparts, Muwatalli's formidable army was able to hold its ground and the battle ended in stalemate. Rameses declined a Hittite peace offer, although a truce was agreed. The Egyptians then returned home with many prisoners of war and much booty, but without having achieved their goal. In subsequent years several other fairly successful confrontations in Syria–Palestine took place, but each time the vassal states conquered on these occasions quickly returned to the Hittite fold once the Egyptian armies had gone home, and Egypt never regained Qadesh and Amurru.

In year 16 of Rameses II's reign, Muwatalli's young son Urhi-Teshub, who had succeeded his father as Mursili III, was deposed by his uncle Hattusili III and, two years later, after some failed attempts to regain his throne with the help first of the Babylonians, then of the Assyrians, he finally fled to Egypt. Hattusili immediately demanded his extradition, which was refused, and so the Hittite king was ready to wage war against Egypt again. Meanwhile, however, the Assyrians had conquered Hanigalbat, a former vassal state that had recently defected to the Hittites, and were now threatening Carchemish and the Hittite empire itself. Faced with this menacing situation Hattusili had no choice but to open peace negotiations with Egypt, which finally led to a formal treaty in regnal year 21. Although the Egyptians had to accept the loss of Qadesh and Amurru, the peace brought a new stability on the northern front, and, with the borders open to the Euphrates, the Black Sea, and the eastern Aegean, international trade soon flourished as it had not done since the days of Amenhotep III. It also meant that Rameses II could now concentrate on the western border, which was under constant pressure from Libyan invaders, particularly on the fringes of the Delta, where Rameses built a whole series of fortifications. In year

34 the bond with the Hittites was further strengthened by a marriage between Rameses and a daughter of Hattusili, who was received with much pomp and circumstance and was given the Egyptian name Neferura-who-beholds-Horus (i.e. the King).

This Hittite princess was only one of seven women who gained the status of 'great royal wife' during Rameses' very long reign of sixty-seven years. When he had become his father's co-regent he had been presented with a harem full of beautiful women, but apart from these he had two principal wives, Nefertari and Isetnefret, both of whom bore him several sons and daughters. Nefertari was 'great royal wife' until her death in about year 25, when the title passed on to Isetnefret, who appears to have died not long before the arrival of the Hittite princess. Four daughters of Rameses also held the title, Henutmira, long believed to have been his sister rather than a daughter, Bintanat, Merytamun, and Nebettawy. These were the most exalted among the king's daughters, of whom there were at least forty in addition to some forty-five sons. Many of them appear in long processions on the walls of the great temples built by their father, who was to outlive several of his children. They were buried one after the other in a gigantic tomb in the Valley of the Kings (KV 5), which has recently been rediscovered. It resembles the underground galleries that Rameses started to build at Saqqara for the burial of the sacred Apis bulls of the god Ptah, which had until then been placed in separate tombs.

During his long years on the throne, Rameses II carried out a vast building programme. He began by adding a great peristyle courtyard and pylon to the temple of Amun in Luxor, built by Amenhotep III and completed by the last 18th Dynasty kings. The courtyard was planned at a curious angle to the rest of the temple, presumably in order to create a straight line across the river to the site of the king's mortuary temple, the Ramesseum, in much the same way as his father had done with the Great Hypostyle Hall at Karnak and his Abd el-Qurna temple on the west bank. Rameses also built a temple for Osiris at Abydos, smaller than his father's, but equally beautiful. During the rest of his reign he gradually filled the country with his temples and statues, many of which he usurped from earlier rulers; there is hardly a site in Egypt where his cartouches are not found on the monuments. Particularly impressive is the astonishing series of eight rock temples in Lower Nubia, including two at Abu Simbel, most of which must have been built with a work-force rounded up from among the local tribes, as is attested in the case of Wadi es-Sebua, built for the king by Setau, the viceroy of Nubia, after a *razzia* in year 44.

Among the hundreds of statues of deities and kings that Rameses usurped, those erected by Amenhotep III, the last king before the Amarna Period, were particularly favoured, as were those made by the kings of the 12th Dynasty, the great rulers of the classical period of Egyptian history that served as a model for the new Egypt now taking shape, after the radical break in the tradition consti-tuted by the Amarna Period. The same reflection on a great past is also evident from a renewed interest in the classical writers of the Old and Middle kingdoms, especially the 'teachings' or 'instructions' of old sages such as Ptahhotep and Kagemni, and descriptions of chaos such as those of Neferti and Ipuwer. It was perhaps because Ramessid scribes felt that these earlier works could not be equalled, let alone surpassed, that contemporary literature, such as love poetry and folk tales and mythical stories that sprang from an oral tradition, was written not in classical Egyptian, but in the modern language first introduced in inscriptions by Akhenaten.

Rameses II was also the king who expanded the city of Avaris and made it his great Delta residence called Piramesse ('house of Rameses'), the Ramses of biblical tradition. Its location has long been disputed, but it has now been established beyond reasonable doubt that it is to be identified with the extensive remains at Tell el-Dab'a and Qantir in the eastern Delta. The city was strategically situated near the road leading to the border fortress of Sile and the provinces in Palestine and Syria and also along the Pelusiac branch of the Nile, and it soon became the most important international trade centre and military base in the country. Asiatic influence had always been strong in the area, but now many foreign deities such as Ba'al, Reshep, Hauron, Anat, and Astarte, to mention only a few, were worshipped in Piramesse. Many foreigners lived in

The excavations of the Ramessid city of Piramesse (modern Qantir) during the 1980s and 1990s revealed military stables as well as armoury workshops where craftsmen were evidently using stone moulds to produce Hittite-style shields for the Egyptian army.

the city, some of whom eventually became high-ranking officials. One office that was more often than not held by foreigners was that of 'royal butler', a senior executive position outside the normal bureaucratic hierarchy, the holder of which was often entrusted with special royal commisions. As a result of the peace treaty with the Hittites, specialist craftsmen sent by Egypt's former enemy were employed in the armoury workshops of Piramesse to teach the Egyptians their latest weapons technology, including the manufacture of much sought-after Hittite shields. Indeed, by this date the Egyptian army itself counted among its ranks large numbers of foreigners who had come to Egypt as prisoners of war and had subsequently been incorporated into the country's combat forces.

Many of Rameses' high officials lived and worked in Piramesse, but most of them appear to have been buried elsewhere, particularly in the necropolis of Memphis. About thirty-five tombs of the Ramessid Period have so far been excavated there, some of them very large. These tombs still took the form of an Egyptian temple, but, compared to the tombs of the late 18th Dynasty, the workmanship had declined. The earlier tombs had walls built of solid mud-brick masonry with a limestone revetment set against the interior faces, but now the walls consisted entirely of a double row of limestone orthostats with the space in between filled with rubble, and the same technique was used for their pylons and pyramids. In addition, the quality of the limestone itself was often not very good, and, rather than carefully making the blocks fit against each other, a liberal amount of plaster was used to fill the gaps between the blocks. Nor do the reliefs carved on them compare favourably with those in the older tombs in the cemetery. This general decline in the quality of the work-manship can be observed throughout the country, even in the king's own tem-ples; of the two main relief-sculpting techniques, the superior, but more time-consuming and more expensive, raised relief all but disappeared after the first years of the reign, in favour of the common sunk relief. Generally speaking, Rameses' monuments impress more by their size and quantity than by their delicacy and perfection.

Rameses II was the first king since Amenhotep III to celebrate more than one sed-festival. The first took place in year 30 and then another thirteen followed, at first at more or less regular intervals of about three years, and then, towards the end of his long life, annually. Amenhotep III had become deified during his three jubilees, but in this respect Rameses had less patience than his great pre-decessor, for already by his eighth year we hear of a colossal statue being carved which was given the name 'Rameses-the-god'. Colossal statues of the king with similar names were set up in front of the pylons and by the doorways of all the great temples and these received a regular cult as well as being objects of public worship for the inhabitants of the towns in which they stood. Inside the tem-ples, Rameses-the-god had his own cult-image and processional bark along with the other deities to whom they were dedicated; in reliefs Rameses II is often shown offering to his own deified self.

Among the king's many sons who held high positions, the second son of Queen Isetnefret, Khaemwaset, must be singled out. He was high priest of Ptah in Memphis and acquired a reputation as a scholar and magician that would survive until Roman times. No other son of Rameses II left so many monuments and many of these were inscribed with learned, sometimes archaic, texts. Although, as we have seen, the reign of Rameses II saw a marked revival of classical traditions, Khaemwaset must clearly have had a special interest in Egypt's glorious past, for he also restored several pyramids of Old Kingdom pharaohs in the Memphite necropolis, and in some of his own monuments tried to copy the style of Old Kingdom tomb reliefs. As high priest of Ptah, one of his duties was to see to the burial of the sacred Apis bull and it is to Khaemwaset that the first galleries (rather than individual tombs) of the Serapeum are due. He also travelled the length and breadth of the country in order to announce his father's first five *sed*-festivals, which were traditionally proclaimed from Memphis. By year 52 of his father's reign, Khaemwaset was the eldest surviving son and therefore became crown prince, but at that stage he must have been in his sixties already, and he died a few years later, around year 55. He was almost certainly buried in the Memphite necropolis and not in the princely gallery tomb in the Valley of the Kings (KV 5), but whether he was really interred in the Serapeum, as many believe, is less certain.

After Khaemwaset's death Rameses II lived on for another twelve years until he finally died in the sixty-seventh year of his reign, the longest reigning monarch since Pepy I (2321–2287 BC) of the 6th Dynasty. During the last years of his reign he had become a living legend and he was clearly much admired (and envied) by his successors. His memory would live on in later traditions both under his own name and under that of Sesostris, in reality the name of several Middle Kingdom rulers whose monuments he had so avidly usurped. His twelve eldest sons had died before him, and it was Merenptah (1213–1203 BC), the fourth son of Isetnefret and crown prince since the death of Khaemwaset, who eventually succeeded him.

Rameses II's Successors

During the first years of his reign Merenptah, who must have been fairly advanced in years already, sent several military expeditions abroad, not only to Nubia, but also into Palestine, where he subdued the rebellious vassals of Ashkelon, Gezer, and Yenoam; the 'victory stele' that records these victories also contains the first reference in Egyptian sources to Israel, albeit not as a country or city, but as a tribe. The major event of Merenptah's reign occurred in his year 5, however, and the victory stele really deals with this: a campaign against the Libyans. They had been a problem even during his father's and grandfather's reigns, but the fortresses Rameses II had built along the western borders of the Delta were obviously unable to prevent the invasion of a massive coalition of Libyan and other tribes led by their king, Mereye.

The previous decades had seen a great migration in the Aegean and Ionian world that had probably been caused by widespread crop failure and famine. According to a long inscription at Karnak (between the Seventh Pylon and the central part of the temple), Merenptah had actually sent grain to the starving Hittites, still Egypt's ally in the East. Many important centres of Mycenaean Greece had been violently destroyed and the western fringes of the Hittite empire had begun to collapse. The marauding 'Sea Peoples', as they were soon to be called in Egypt, had also reached the coast of North Africa between Cyrenaica and Mersa Matruh, which in the Late Bronze Age was seasonally occupied by foreign seafarers sailing from Cyprus via Crete to the Egyptian Delta. In this area, the Sea Peoples joined the Libyan tribes and with a force of some 16,000 men marched on Egypt; since they brought their women and children with them, as well as cattle and other belongings, they were obviously planning to settle in Egypt. They had actually penetrated the western Delta and were moving southwards, threatening Memphis and Heliopolis, when Merenptah confronted them and, in a battle that lasted for six hours, managed to defeat them. The Libyans were destined to fail on this occasion because, as Merenptah says on his victory stele, their king, Mereye, had already been 'found guilty of his crimes' by the divine tribunal of Heliopolis, and the god Atum, who presided over the tribunal, had personally handed the sword of victory to his son Merenptah, making the battle nothing less than a 'holy war'. Thousands of enemies were killed, but great numbers were also captured and settled in military colonies, especially in the Delta, where their descendants would become an increasingly important political factor (see Chapter 12).

The rest of Merenptah's reign appears to have been peaceful, and the king used it to build at least two temples and a palace in Memphis. He must have realized that he did not have many years left, however, for his mortuary temple on the Theban West Bank is constructed almost exclusively from blocks removed from earlier structures, particularly the nearby temples of Amenhotep III. He died in his ninth year. After his death, trouble over the succession broke out, for, although the next king, Sety II (1200–1194 BC), was almost certainly the eldest son of Merenptah, a rival king, Amenmessu, ruled for a few years, at least in the south of the country. When exactly this happened is still the subject of much controversy; it has been suggested that Amenmessu deposed Sety II for some time between the latter's years 3 and 5, but others have the trouble set in at the beginning of the reign. Whatever the truth may be, Sety ruthlessly erased and usurped all of Amenmessu's cartouches and later texts refer to the rival ruler as 'the enemy'.

When Sety II died, after a reign of almost six full years, his only son, Saptah (1194–1188 BC), succeeded him. However, Saptah was not a son of Sety's principal queen, Tausret (1188–1186 BC); instead he had been born to him by a Syrian concubine called Sutailja. More importantly, he was only a young boy who suffered from an atrophied leg caused by poliomyelitis; his stepmother, Tausret, therefore remained 'great royal wife' and acted as regent. She was not the

303

only power behind the throne, however, for a powerful official called Bay, described as the 'chancellor of the entire land', who was himself a Syrian, appears to have been the true ruler of the country at this date. He is depicted several times with Saptah and Tausret and in some inscriptions he even claims that it was he who 'established the king on the throne of his father', an extraordinary phrase normally reserved for the gods. When Saptah died in his sixth regnal year Tausret reigned on as sole ruler for another two years, doubtless with the support of Bay. After Hatshepsut and Nefertiti she was the third queen of the New Kingdom to rule as pharaoh. With her death the 19th Dynasty came to an end.

Rameses III and the 20th Dynasty

How the next dynasty gained power remains unclear. The only indications of the political events at this date derive from a stele erected on the island of Elephantine by its first ruler, Sethnakht (1186–1184 BC), and an account written down in the Great Harris Papyrus from the beginning of the reign of Rameses IV (1153–1147 BC), some thirty years later. On the stele, Sethnakht relates how he expelled rebels who on their flight left behind the gold, silver, and copper they had stolen from Egypt and with which they had wanted to hire reinforcements among the Asiatics. The papyrus describes how a state of lawlessness and chaos had broken out in Egypt because of forces from 'outside'; after several years in which there was no one who ruled, a Syrian called Irsu (a made-up name meaning 'one who made himself'—that is, 'upstart') seized power, and his confederates plundered the country; they treated the gods like ordinary human beings and no longer sacrificed in the temples, a description that resembles the one given of the Amarna Period in the years of the Restoration. The gods then chose Sethnakht to be the next ruler, just as they had Horemheb at the end of the 18th Dynasty, and he re-established order.

From these texts we may perhaps conclude that, after the death of Tausret, Bay had tried to seize power and may even have succeeded for a brief time until he was expelled by Sethnakht. The date of the Elephantine stele is not Sethnakht's regnal year 1, as one might expect on a victory stele, but year 2, and this date is not given at the beginning of the text, as was customary on stelae, but towards the end. It has, therefore, been suggested that it represents the date of Sethnakht's victory and at the same time the true date of his accession, having counted in retrospect the time it took him to overcome his adversaries as his first year. Be that as it may, he did not enjoy his newly gained kingship for long, for he died soon afterwards and was succeeded by his son Rameses III (1184–1153 BC).

Although the new king inherited peace and stability from his father, he soon had his fair share of troubles as well. In year 5 he had to fight off further advances by Libyan tribes, who had used the period of internal struggle to penetrate into the western Delta as far as the central Nile branch. By this time the Egyptians appear to have accepted this peaceful immigration as inevitable, but, when a revolt against the pharaoh broke out because he interfered in the succession of their 'king', Rameses III quickly responded and brought them back under Egyptian control. A further Libyan campaign took place in year 11. Far more challenging, however, was the great battle against the Sea Peoples in year 8.

Since the days of Merenptah, when some of the Sea Peoples had first tried to enter Egypt from the west, their movements had turned the whole of the Middle East upside down. They had destroyed the Hittite capital Hattusas and swept away their whole empire; they had conquered Tarsus and many of them had settled in the plains of Cilicia and northern Syria, razing Alalakh and Ugarit to the ground. Cyprus had also been overwhelmed and its capital Enkomi ransacked. Clearly their ultimate goal was Egypt, however, and in year 8 of Rameses III they launched a combined land and sea attack on the Delta. But the Egyptians were well aware of the imminent danger and had moved a large defence force to Djahy (southern Palestine, perhaps the Egyptian garrisons in the Gaza strip) and fortified the mouths of the Nile branches in the Delta. When the assault finally came, Rameses' troups were well prepared for it and were able to beat the invaders back. Although the Sea Peoples had changed the east Mediterranean world for good, they never succeeded in conquering Egypt and their presence in Syria–Palestine does not at first seem to have affected Egypt's sway over its northern territories.

At home, Rameses III spent a lot of time and energy on his building projects, foremost of which was his large mortuary temple at Medinet Habu, begun shortly after his accession and finished by year 12; it still stands today as one of the best preserved temples of the New Kingdom (the decoration on its exterior walls including scenes from the battle with the Sea Peoples). It was closely modelled on the Ramesseum of his great predecessor Rameses II, whom Rameses III tried to emulate in many other ways; his own royal names were all but identical to those of Rameses II and he even named his sons after the latter's numerous offspring. The building of Medinet Habu and other projects, including the expansion of Piramesse, do not appear to have been hampered by the various threats to Egypt's borders. We also hear of a major expedition to Punt, perhaps the first since the famous venture to that remote land in the days of Hatshepsut, and another one to Atika, perhaps the copper mines of Timna.

All was not well in Egypt, however. The period of turmoil before Rameses' accession had led to corruption and various abuses, and he was forced to inspect and reorganize the various temples throughout the country. The Great Harris Papyrus enumerates the huge donations of land he made to the most important temples in Thebes, Memphis, and Heliopolis, and to a lesser extent to many smaller institutions as well. By the end of his reign a third of the cultivable land was owned by the temples and of this three-quarters belonged to Amun of Thebes. This development upset the balance between temple and state and between the king and the ever more powerful priesthood of Amun. An overall loss of control over the state finances and economic crisis were the result; grain prices soared and the monthly rations to the workmen at Deir el-Medina, which had to be paid by the state treasury, were soon in arrears, leading in year 29 to the first recorded organized strikes in history. Things were made worse by repeated raids by groups of Libyan nomads in the Theban area, which created a general sense of insecurity.

This gradual breakdown of the centralized state may well have been one of the reasons behind an attempt on the life of Rameses III, or, if it was not, the general unrest and insecurity may at least have given the conspirators the idea that they could count on general support if they succeeded. The plot originated in the king's harem, presumably in Piramesse, where one of the officials involved, the scribe of the harem, Pairy, had a house. He was just one of several harem officials implicated; the ringleaders were one of Rameses' wives, called Tiy, and some other women from the harem, as well as several royal butlers and a steward; all of them were 'stirring up the people and inciting enmity in order to make rebellion against their lord'. The ultimate goal was to put Tiy's son Pentaweret on the throne instead of the king's lawful heir. Apparently the plan was to murder the king during the annual Opet Festival in Thebes, but included in the preparations were also magical spells and wax figurines, which were smuggled into the harem. The plot must have failed, however, for the king's mummy shows no signs of a violent death, and his crown prince, Rameses IV, and not Pentaweret eventually succeeded him. When all of this happened we do not know, but the records of the court hearings and the sentences passed on 'the great criminals' (most of them were forced to commit suicide) were written down at the beginning of the reign of Rameses IV, who also compiled the Great Harris Papyrus, which contains his father's 'testament', suggesting that the assassination attempt took place towards the end of Rameses III's thirty-one-year reign.

Rameses IV

All of the remaining 20th Dynasty kings were called Rameses, a name they adopted at their accession, adding it to their birth-name. They were probably all related to Rameses III, although in some cases we do not know exactly how. During their reigns, Egypt lost control over its territories in Syria–Palestine and the importance of Nubia was rapidly declining as well. Apart from the temple of Khonsu in Karnak, no major temples were built even by those Ramessid rulers who reigned long enough to do so. Rameses IV was the fifth son of his father and had become crown prince around the latter's regnal year 22, after four older brothers had died. The sons of Rameses III were not buried in a gallery tomb in the Valley of the Kings like those of Rameses II, but in separate tombs in the Valley of the Queens. Judging by the name of his mother, Rameses III's Great Royal Consort Isis-Ta-Habadjilat, the new king must have had at least some foreign blood running through his veins. At the beginning of his reign he embarked on several building projects, especially his royal tomb and mortuary temple at Thebes, for which he doubled the workforce of Deir el-Medina to 120 men. Probably in connection with these projects he mounted several expeditions to the quarries of the Wadi Hammamat, where little activity had taken place since the days of Sety I, as well as to the turquoise and copper mines in Sinai and Timna. None of his building plans came to fruition, however, for he died after a reign of five (perhaps seven) years, before he could complete any of them, despite his prayers on a large stele in Abydos asking Osiris to grant him a reign twice as long as the sixty-seven years of Rameses II.

During Rameses IV's reign, further delays in the delivery of basic commodities at Deir el-Medina occurred; at the same time the influence of the high priest of Amun was growing. Ramesesnakht, holder of that high office, was soon accompanying the state officials when they went to pay the men their monthly rations, indicating that the temple of Amun, not the state, was now at least partly responsible for their wages. The highest state and temple offices were in fact in the hands of the members of two families. Thus Ramesesnakht's son Usermaatranakht was 'steward of the estate of Amun' and as such administered the land owned by the temple, but he also controlled the vast majority of the state-owned land in Middle Egypt. The holders of the offices of 'second and third priest' and of 'god's father of Amun' were all related to Ramesesnakht by marriage. This well illustrates the marked tendency of these high positions, including that of high priest itself, to become hereditary, and Ramesesnakht himself was to be succeeded by two of his sons. The office became more and more independent and the king had only nominal control over who was appointed high priest.

The Final Reigns of the 20th Dynasty

Rameses IV was succeeded by his son, who became Rameses V (1147–1143 BC) upon his accession. A major crime and corruption scandal among the priesthood at Elephantine, which had in fact evolved during the reign of his father, is the main event known from his reign, although he also continued the latter's mining activities in Timna and Sinai. After four years, Rameses V died of smallpox at a young age.

The next king, Rameses VI (1143–1136 BC), was a younger son of Rameses III. He usurped the royal tomb and mortuary temple begun by his nephew, whose burial had therefore to be delayed until an alternative tomb had been found for him in Rameses VI's year 2. It has, therefore, been concluded by some researchers that the succession was accompanied by civil unrest, especially as there are some entries in a necropolis journal that state that the workmen of Deir el-Medina, whose numbers were soon afterwards reduced to sixty again, stayed at home 'for fear of the enemy'. This does not seem very probable, however, although the mere fact that most officials remained in office from one reign to the next is hardly enough proof to the contrary, for the same had been the case at the end of the 18th and 19th Dynasties, when there had certainly been troubles. The 'enemy' mentioned in the journal is more likely to have been a group of Libyans, who continued to be a nuisance in the area. Rameses VI reigned for seven years; he is the last king whose name is attested in Sinai. During the seven-year reign of Rameses VII (1136–1129 BC), grain prices soared to their highest level, after which they gradually came down again. His successor Rameses VIII was probably yet another son of Rameses III, which might explain why his reign was so brief.

The exact family background of the last three Ramessid rulers is unknown. The eighteen years or so of the reign of Rameses IX (1126–1108 BC) were marked by increasing instability. In regnal years 8–15 we regularly hear of Libyan nomads disturbing the peace in Thebes, and there were also strikes again. It is, therefore, hardly surprising that this period witnessed the first wave of tomb-robberies, known from a whole series of papyri that record the trials of the thieves who had been apprehended. However, the tombs in the Valley of the Kings were not involved; in fact only one 17th Dynasty royal burial in Dra Abu el-Naga and a number of private tombs were robbed, and various thefts from temples were also investigated. At the beginning of the reign, Ramesesnakht (the high priest of Amun mentioned above) had died; he was succeeded as high priest firstly by his son Nesamun, and then by the latter's brother Amenhotep. In two reliefs at Karnak Amenhotep had himself depicted on the same scale as Rameses IX, a fair indication of the virtual equality that now appears to have existed between the king and the high priest of Amun. One of these scenes commemorates an event in year 10, when Rameses rewarded Amenhotep for his services to king and country with the traditional 'gold of honour'. The many gifts bestowed upon him on this occasion must certainly have been very impressive, but their quantities are nevertheless a revealing illustration of the state of the economy, or at least of the king's wealth. Among the gifts received by Amenhotep were 2 *hin* of a costly ointment; some 200 years earlier, during the reign of Horemheb, one of Maya's subordinates, a mere scribe of the treasury, had contributed 4 *hin* of the same ointment to the burial goods of his master.

Almost nothing is known about the reign of Rameses X, which seems to have lasted for nine years. Rameses XI (1099–1069 BC), on the other hand, ruled for thirty years, although certainly during the last ten years the geographical extent of his power was virtually reduced to Lower Egypt (that is, the Delta). During his reign, the crisis that had gripped the Theban area in the previous decades deepened even further: persistent trouble with Libyan gangs preventing the workmen on the west bank from going to work, famine (the 'year of the hyenas'), further tomb robberies and thefts from temples and palaces, and even civil war. At some point, in or before year 12, Panehsy, the viceroy of Nubia, appeared in Thebes with Nubian troops to restore law and order, perhaps at the request of Rameses XI himself. In order to feed his men in a city that was already suffering from economic malaise, he was given, or perhaps usurped, the office of 'overseer of the granaries'. This must have brought him into conflict with Amenhotep, the high priest of Amun, whose temple owned the bulk of the land

and its produce. The conflict quickly escalated and during a period of eight or nine months (sometime between years 17 and 19) Panehsy and his troops actually besieged the high priest at Medinet Habu. Amenhotep then appealed to Rameses XI for help and this resulted in a civil war. Panehsy marched north, reaching at least as far as Hardai in Middle Egypt, which he ransacked, but probably actually pushing much further north, until he was eventually driven back by the king's army, which was almost certainly led by a general called Piankh. Eventually Panehsy had to withdraw to Nubia, where trouble persisted for many years, and where he was eventually buried.

In Thebes, General Piankh took over the titles of Panehsy as well as styling himself vizier, and after the death of Amenhotep, who may or may not have survived Panehsy's assault, he also became high priest of Amun, uniting the three highest offices of the country in one person. With Piankh's military *coup* begins the period of the *wehem mesut*, the 'renaissance', a term that had also been used by kings at the beginning of the 12th and 19th Dynasties to indicate that the country had been 'reborn' after a period of chaos. In the Theban area documents were now dated in years of the 'renaissance' rather than regnal years of the king. Years 1 to 10 of the renaissance were identical with regnal years 19 to 28 of Rameses XI. After the death of Piankh, his son-in-law Herihor took over all his functions, and after the death of Rameses XI the former even assumed royal titles. In the north of the country Smendes (1069–1043 BC) mounted the throne, and with these two men the 21st Dynasty begins.

After Rameses III the Egyptians finally lost their provinces in Palestine and Syria, which after the invasion of the Sea Peoples and the disappearance of the Hittite empire had broken up into several small states. Problems in the north had been made worse by the gradual sanding-up of the harbour of Piramesse owing to the slow but inexorable eastward shift of the Pelusiac branch of the Nile. Nor did the kings of the 20th Dynasty any longer have the power and the resources to mount major expeditions to the gold mines in Nubia. Towards the end of the dynasty the treasury of the temple of Amun sent some small-scale expeditions to the Eastern Desert in search of gold and minerals, but the quantities with which they came back were small. During the years of the renaissance, Piankh and his successors, assisted by the descendants of the workmen of Deir el-Medina who were now living at Medinet Habu, began to tap a different source of gold and precious stones: the very same tombs in the Valley of the Kings that their fathers and grandfathers had carved and decorated, as well as many other tombs both royal and private in the Theban necropolis. Over the next century and later, the tombs were gradually despoiled of their gold and other valuables; eventually they would be emptied out completely, and even the mummies of the great pharaohs of the New Kingdom would be unwrapped and stripped of their precious amulets and other trappings and reburied together in an anonymous tomb in the Theban cliffs. By some strange irony only two royal mummies would escape this fate: that of Tutankhamun (in KV 62) and that of his father, Akhenaten, the 'enemy of Akhetaten' (in KV 55).

The Historical and Social Repercussions of the Amarna and Ramessid Periods

There can be no doubt that the great kings of the Ramessid Period were immensely powerful rulers. Even Rameses XI was obviously still able to mobilize an army that was strong enough to repel his opponent's troops all the way back to Nubia. And yet it is undeniable that royal prestige had gradually eroded in the course of the 19th and 20th Dynasties. As we have seen, political and economic developments, which had led to the breakdown of the central government and the concentration of ever more power in the hands of the high priests of Amun, greatly contributed to this erosion. On the other hand, these developments may themselves be seen as the result, or at least the symptoms, of a much more fundamental change. At the root of this change is yet again the Amarna Period.

Akhenaten had tried to remake society and had failed, even though he had initially enjoyed the support of the army. What was worse, however, is that in the eyes of all but a few of the Amarna élite he had actually wrecked society. We have already seen how burial customs after the Amarna Period reflect a totally different attitude towards the king, as a reaction against the way Akhenaten had tried to monopolize the funerary beliefs of his subjects. This monopoly was not limited to life in the hereafter, however, but also deeply affected life on earth.

A relief from the tomb of Iniuia at Saqqara shows the deceased and his wife Iuy, with their daughter and two sons (both employed by the Memphite temple of Aten). The scene shows Amarna influence on its artistic style.

Traditionally, access to the god's cult image in the temple was restricted to the king and the professional priesthood representing him; for the vast majority of the population the only means of getting in contact with the gods of their home town, without the intervention of the state or the official temple cult, was during regularly held processions, when the images of the gods were carried from one temple to another on the occasion of a religious festival. These festivals, which were quite frequent, were public holidays, and they played an enormously important part in people's religious and social lives. Most Egyptians had a strong emotional bond with their native town and its god, the 'city-god', to whom they showed a life-long loyalty. The city-god was also the god of the local necropolis, the 'lord of the burial' who granted 'a goodly burial after old age' to his loyal servants.

Akhenaten had not only banned all gods other than the Aten and abolished the daily rituals in their temples, but with them he had also put an end to the festivals with their processions, and in doing so he had undermined the social identity of his subjects. Instead, he had claimed all devotion and loyalty for himself and the prosperity of the country and the happiness of its inhabitants depended on him alone. He was the 'city-god' not just of Akhetaten, but of the whole country, and his daily chariot ride along the royal road at Amarna replaced the divine processions. The history of the 18th Dynasty before the Amarna Period had seen a clear development towards a more personal relationship between the various deities and their worshippers. This development came to a sudden halt when Akhenaten proclaimed a god who could only be worshipped by his son, the king, whereas all individual, personal devotion had to be diverted to the king himself. This total usurpation of personal piety had seriously compromised the credibility of the dogma of divine kingship.

In the period after Amarna, the balance between god and king underwent a dramatic change. The king lost for good the central position he had occupied in the lives of his subjects; instead, the god now acquired many traditional aspects of kingship. In the traditional representative theocracy, the gods embodied the cosmic order that they had created at the beginning of time, while the king, as their intermediary, represented the gods upon earth, maintained cosmic order by means of the temple ritual, and carried out their will by his government. Only very rarely did the gods reveal themselves directly, and, when they did, they did so to the king.

After the Amarna Period, the problem of the unity and plurality of the gods, which Akhenaten had tried to solve by denying the existence of all but one sole god, was solved in a different way: Amun-Ra became the universal, transcendent god, who existed far away, independent of his creation; the other gods and goddesses were aspects of him, they were his immanent manifestations. This situation is elegantly expressed in a collection of hymns to Amun (preserved in a papyrus now in Leiden), according to which Amun 'began manifesting himself when nothing existed, yet the world was not empty of him in the beginning'. This universal god was now the true king, and, although the pharaoh's traditional titles—which were rooted in mythology and express his divinity—did not change, he had in actual fact become more human than ever before in the history of Egypt. The fact that Ay, Horemheb, Rameses I, and even Sety I had all been commoners before they mounted the throne may have had something to do with the speed with which this change took place. The representative theocracy had become a direct theocracy: no longer was the king the god's divine representative upon earth who carried out his will; rather, the god revealed his will directly to every human being and intervened directly in the events of everyday life and in the course of history.

The new transcendent god had at the same time become a personal god whose will determined the fate of the country and of the individual. Texts express this by bridging the gap between the opposites of being far away and yet nearby: 'Far away he is as one who sees, near he is as one who hears.' Amun-Ra looked down upon his worshippers from afar, but at the same time he was near because he heard their prayers and revealed himself in their lives by the manifestation of his will, by his divine intervention.

Private votive stelae of the Ramessid period sometimes indicate that individuals expected to be rescued from difficulties by the direct intervention of deities. In this particular instance of 'personal piety' this priest of Amun(?) is recording the fact that the god Wepwawet has saved him from an attack by a crocodile (dispatched by the god in the bottom register, while the man himself is shown escaping).

This new form of religious experience, usually called 'personal piety', was wholly characteristic of the Ramessid Period, although its beginnings, suppressed by Akhenaten, went back to the mid-18th Dynasty. Penetential psalms, inscribed on votive stelae and ostraca by literate members of the ordinary population, were one form in which this piety was expressed. When an individual had commited a sin, divine intervention could mean divine retribution, particularly when this sin had gone undetected and unpunished by a human court of justice. These penetential hymns attributed illness (often blindness, although this word is probably used in a metaphorical sense) to the state of being guilty of a hidden sin, which once revealed in the text on a votive stele was no longer hidden, so that god would 'return' to his worshipper and make him 'see' again. It was not only the individuals who could sin, but also the country as a whole. In a text of this type inscribed on a Theban tomb wall (TT 139) at the end of the Amarna Period, Amun is begged to return, and in Tutankhamun's Restoration Stele the gods are also said to have abandoned Egypt.

Another type of votive stele demonstrates that God was also thought to be able to intervene positively in the life of his worshipper—for example, by saving him from a crocodile or making him survive the sting of a scorpion or the bite of a snake. Many gods received specially made stelae or other objects as a thanksgiving for saving their worshippers; there is even a special god Shed, whose name means 'saviour', and who, probably not by chance, appears for the first time at Amarna, possibly in spite of official repression. Some people even went one step further and put their whole lives in the hands of their personal patron god or goddess, even to the extent of assigning all their possessions to his or her temple.

Even the king might appeal to his god in his hour of need. When all seemed lost and Rameses II was about to be captured or even killed by his Hittite enemies at the Battle of Qadesh, he called out to his god Amun, and the arrival of the king's support force at the critical moment was interpreted as proof of the god's personal intervention. This shows clearly that the king no longer represented god on earth, but was subordinate to him; just like all other human beings, he was subject to the will of god, even though in traditional mythological terms he was still viewed as the divine pharaoh and on his monuments this aspect would continue to be emphasized. Clearly the divide between theological dogma and everyday reality had widened considerably.

Once it had been recognized that god's will was the governing factor in everything that happened, it became mandatory to know his will in advance. Oracles, which had originally been consulted only by the king, perhaps as early as the Old Kingdom (and which had during the 18th Dynasty been used to seek the god's approval of a king's accession or a major trade or military expedition), began to be used in the Ramessid Period to consult the god on all sorts of affairs in the lives of ordinary human beings. Priests would carry the portable bark with the god's image in procession out of the temple and a piece of papyrus or an ostracon bearing a written question would be laid before him; the god would then indicate his approval or disapproval by making the priests move slightly forwards or backwards or by some other motion of the bark. Appointments, disputes over property, accusations of crimes, and later even questions seeking the god's reassurance that one would safely live on in the hereafter, were thus subjected to the god's will.

All of these developments further minimalized the role of the king as god's representative on earth; the king was no longer a god, but god himself had become king. Once Amun had been recognized as the true king, the political power of the earthly rulers could be reduced to a minimum and transferred to Amun's priesthood. The mummies of their royal ancestors were no longer considered the erstwhile incarnations of god on earth, and so, with few scruples, their tombs could be robbed and their bodies unwrapped.

11 EGYPT AND THE OUTSIDE WORLD

IAN SHAW

From the earliest times, expeditions concerned with trade, quarrying, and warfare brought the Egyptians into repeated contact with foreigners. The regions with which Egypt gradually fostered commercial and political links can be grouped into three basic areas: Africa (primarily Nubia, Libya, and Punt), Asia (Syria–Palestine, Mesopotamia, Arabia, and Anatolia) and the northern and eastern Mediterranean (Cyprus, Crete, the Sea Peoples, and the Greeks).

The Egyptians' African neighbours to the south included, over the course of time, a number of different ethnic groups in Nubia (primarily the A Group, the C Group, the Kerma civilization, the pan-grave culture, the kingdom of Kush, the Ballana culture, and the Blemmyes), and Ethiopia (the pre-Axumite cultures and the Axum civilization), while to the north-east, beyond the Sinai peninsula, they encountered many towns and villages in the hills and coastal plain of the Levant (and, further to the north and east, a constantly changing mosaic of kingdoms and empires in Anatolia and Mesopotamia). To the west, in the Sahara, they came into contact with several different peoples whom we now group under the general term 'Libyans'. Little archaeological evidence has survived concerning the latter, although it is usually assumed on the basis of textual references that they were nomadic or at least dependent on forms of pastoralism for their subsistence, and it is only when they become part of Egyptian society in the late New Kingdom and the Third Intermediate Period that aspects of their culture can be glimpsed or hypothesized (see Chapter 12).

The Racial and Ethnic Identity of the Egyptians

There are a number of different ways in which we can define the ancient Egyptians themselves as a distinct racial and ethnic group, but the question of their roots and their sense of their own identity has provoked considerable debate. Linguistically, they belonged to the Afro-Asiatic (Hamito-Semitic) family, but this is simply another way of saying that, as their geographical position implies, their language had some similarities to contemporary languages both in parts of Africa and in the Near East.

Anthropological studies suggest that the predynastic population included a mixture of racial types (negroid, Mediterranean, and European), but it is the question of the skeletal evidence at the beginning of the pharaonic period that has proved to be most controversial over the years. Whereas the anthropological evidence from this date was once interpreted, by Bryan Emery and others, as the rapid conquest of Egypt by people from the east whose remains were racially distinct from the indigenous Egyptians, it is now argued by some scholars that there may have been a much slower period of demographic change, probably involving the gradual infiltration of a different physical type from Syria–Palestine, via the eastern Delta.

The iconography of the Egyptians' depictions of foreigners suggests that for much of their history they saw themselves as midway between the black Africans and the paler Asiatics. It is also clear, however, that neither Nubian nor Syro-Palestinian origins were regarded as particularly disadvantageous factors in terms of individuals' status or career prospects, particularly in the cosmopolitan climate of the New Kingdom, when Asiatic religious cults and technological developments were particularly widely accepted. Thus the demonstrably negroid features of the high official Maiherpri did not prevent him from attaining the special privilege of a burial in the Valley of the Kings at about the time of Thutmose III (1479–1425 BC). In the same way, a man called Aper-el, whose name indicates his Near Eastern roots, rose to the rank of vizier (the highest civil office below that of the king himself) in the late 18th Dynasty.

The Iconography of Warfare and Conquest: Textual and Visual Evidence

The term 'Nine Bows' was frequently used to refer to the enemies of Egypt, the specific identity of whom varied from one time to another, although they usually included Asiatics and Nubians. They were generally symbolized by depictions of rows of bows or bound captives, the number of which varies, and the motif often decorated such royal items as sandals, footstools, and daises, so that the pharaoh could symbolically tread on his enemies. The depiction of nine bound captives surmounted by a jackal, on the seal of the necropolis of the Valley of the Kings, was evidently intended to protect the tomb from the depredations of foreigners and other sources of evil.

Depictions of bound foreign captives frequently feature in Egyptian art. Various prestige items of the late Predynastic and Early Dynastic periods (such as the Narmer Palette) include scenes in which the king dispatches or humiliates bound foreigners. The scene of the smiting pharaoh is not only one of the most enduring aspects of pharaonic art (appearing on temple pylons as late as the

Roman Period) but also one of the first recognizable icons of kingship, the earliest known instance being a sketchy depiction painted on the wall of the late predynastic Tomb 100 at Hierakonpolis in the late fourth millennium BC.

The excavations of the 5th and 6th Dynasty pyramid complexes of Raneferef, Nyeuserra, Djedkara, Unas, Teti, Pepy I, and Pepy II at Saqqara and Abusir have yielded a large number of statues of foreign captives, which may perhaps have been placed in rows along the sides of the causeway leading from the val-

The 'Battlefield' (or 'Vultures') Palette, *c*.3200 BC, is one of the first Egyptian depictions of the slaughter of enemies on the battlefield, with birds of prey swooping down on the corpses, and in the centre a lion (perhaps symbolizing the king) savaging a foreigner. Compared with the elegant vignette of the king smiting his enemy on the Narmer Palette, this is a darker and more anarchic view of warfare.

Facing: this wooden statuette of an Asiatic captive, from the mortuary temple of Raneferef at Abusir, *c*.2448–2445 BC, is one of several sculptures representing captive foreigners that have been found in and around the funerary complexes of late Old Kingdom rulers. It is possible that these images of bound and humiliated foreigners may once have lined the causeways linking mortuary and valley temples in the Memphite royal cemeteries.

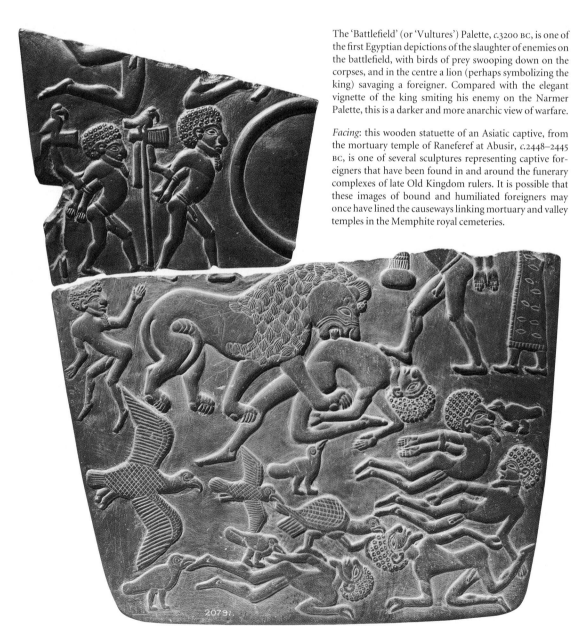

ley temple to the pyramid temple. At a slightly later date, representations of bound captives were used in cursing rituals, as in the case of five early 12th Dynasty alabaster captive figures (now in the Egyptian Museum, Cairo) inscribed with hieratic execration texts comprising lists of the names of Nubian princes accompanied by insults.

Throughout the pharaonic and Graeco-Roman periods the depiction of the bound captive was a popular theme in the decoration of temples and palaces. The inclusion of bound captives in the decoration of aspects of the fittings and furniture of royal palaces served to reinforce the pharaoh's total suppression of foreigners and probably also symbolized the elements of 'unrule' that the gods required the king to control. There are, therefore, a number of depictions in Graeco-Roman temples showing lines of gods capturing birds, wild animals, and foreigners in clapnets.

The *rekhyt*-bird (a type of lapwing or plover with a distinctive crested head) was often used as a symbol for foreign captives or subject peoples, probably because, with its wings pinioned behind its back, it roughly resembled the hieroglyph for a bound captive. The first depiction of this bird is attested in the upper register of relief decoration on the late predynastic Scorpion Macehead (*c*.3100 BC), comprising a row of lapwings hanging by their necks from ropes attached to the standards representing early Lower Egyptian provinces. In this context the *rekhyt* appears to be representing the conquered peoples of northern Egypt during the crucial

period when the country was transformed into a single unified state. In the 3rd Dynasty (2686–2613 BC), however, another row of lapwings were depicted in the familar pinioned form, alongside the Nine Bows, crushed under the feet of a stone statue of Djoser from his Step Pyramid at Saqqara. From that point onwards there was a continual ambiguity in the symbolic meaning of the birds (to modern eyes at least), since they could, in different contexts, be taken to refer either to the enemies of Egypt or to the loyal subjects of the pharaoh.

Facing: map of Egypt and the Ancient Near East, showing links and trade routes.

Where did the Outside World Begin?

The traditional physical borders of Egypt—the Western and Eastern deserts, Sinai, the Mediterranean coast, and the Nile cataracts south of Aswan—were sufficient to protect Egypt's independence for thousands of years. But perhaps the most intriguing issue in the geography of ancient Egypt—especially with regard to attitudes to Africa and Asia—is the question of the slowly changing Egyptian conception of where the outside world began. To what extent, for instance, were those areas outside the Nile Valley (but within the borders of modern Egypt), particularly the Eastern Desert and the Sinai peninsula, regarded as 'non-Egyptian' territory?

The Egyptians used two words to refer to a border: *djer* (an eternal and universal limit) and *tash* (an actual geographical frontier, which might be set by people or deities). The latter was, therefore, essentially movable, and all pharaohs were in theory entrusted with the responsibility of 'extending the borders' of Egypt, given that their royal names and titles implied a potentially infinite area of political domination. The furthest extent of the actual borders was evidently established in the reign of Thutmose III in the 18th Dynasty, when triumphal stelae were erected at the River Euphrates in Asia and at Kurgus (between the fourth and fifth cataracts) in Nubia.

In the Early Dynastic Period and the Old Kingdom, the border with Lower Nubia traditionally lay at Aswan, the modern name of which derives from the ancient Egyptian word *swenet* ('trade'), clearly indicating the commercial opportunities afforded by its location. The first cataract, just a short distance to the south, represented a substantial obstacle to Nile boats, therefore all trade goods had to be carried along the bank; this land route to the east of the Nile was protected by a huge mud-brick wall, almost 7.5 km. long, probably primarily a 12th Dynasty construction.

By the 12th Dynasty, however, the border with Nubia lay much further to the south, at the Semna gorge, the narrowest part of the Nile Valley. It was here, at this strategic location, that the 12th Dynasty pharaohs built a cluster of four mud-brick fortresses, Semna, Kumma, Semna South, and Uronarti. Several 'boundary stelae' erected by Senusret III in the fortresses of Semna and Uronarti spelled out the Egyptians' complete control over the region, including regulations concerning the ability of Nubians to trade along the Nile Valley (see p. 116).

From at least the beginning of the 12th Dynasty, the border with Palestine in the eastern Delta was also defended by a line of fortresses, known as the 'Walls of the Ruler' (*inebu heka*), and, at about the same time, a fortress seems to have been established in Wadi Natrun in order to protect the western Delta from the 'Libyans'. This policy was maintained throughout the Middle Kingdom, and a number of new fortresses were built in the New Kingdom, including the easterly sites of Tell Abu Safa, Tell el-Farama, Tell el-Heir, and Tell el-Maskhuta, and the westerly sites of el-Alamein and Zawiyet Umm el-Rakham.

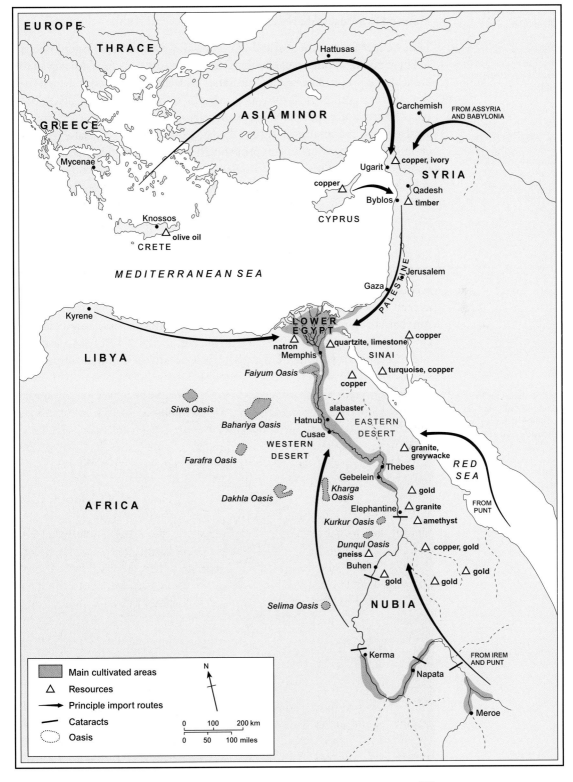

EUROPE

THRACE

Hattusas

ASIA MINOR

GREECE

Mycenae

Carchemish

FROM ASSYRIA
AND BABYLONIA

copper, ivory

SYRIA

copper

Ugarit

Qadesh

Byblos

timber

CYPRUS

Knossos

olive oil

CRETE

MEDITERRANEAN SEA

Jerusalem

Gaza

PALESTINE

Kyrene

LOWER
EGYPT

copper

LIBYA

natron

Memphis

quartzite, limestone

SINAI

Faiyum Oasis

turquoise, copper

copper

Siwa Oasis

Bahariya Oasis

alabaster

Hatnub

EASTERN
DESERT

Cusae

Farafra Oasis

WESTERN
DESERT

granite,
greywacke

Thebes

RED
SEA

Gebelein

AFRICA

Kharga
Oasis

gold

FROM
PUNT

Dakhla Oasis

Elephantine

granite

Kurkur Oasis

amethyst

Dunqul Oasis

copper, gold

gneiss

Buhen

gold

gold

gold

Selima Oasis

NUBIA

Kerma

FROM IREM
AND PUNT

Napata

Meroe

Main cultivated areas

N

Resources

Principle import routes

Cataracts

0   100   200 km

Oasis

0   50   100 miles

319

Material Evidence of Early Contacts with Asia and Nubia

The evidence for commercial and diplomatic links between the emerging state
of Egypt and its various neighbouring cultures and states often survives in the
form of exotic raw materials and products, as well as the vessels in which they
were carried. Although Egypt was clearly self-sufficient in a wide diversity of
rocks, plants, and animals, there were nevertheless many much-prized materials that were not obtainable within the Nile Valley itself. Turquoise could be
obtained only from Sinai; silver probably from Anatolia or the north Mediterranean, via the Levant; copper from Nubia, Sinai, and the Eastern Desert; and
gold from the Eastern Desert and Nubia; while such fine woods as cedar,
juniper, and ebony, as well as products such as incense and myrrh, had to be
imported from western Asia and tropical Africa.

One of the most well-travelled and sought-after materials was lapis lazuli, a
deep blue stone, streaked with glistening pyrite and calcite, which was known to
the Egyptians as *khesbed*. It was used for jewellery, amulets, and figurines from
at least as early as the Naqada II Period (*c.*3500–3200 BC), but the principal
ancient source seems to have been located at Badakhshan in north-eastern
Afghanistan (some 4,000 km. from Egypt), where four ancient quarries have so
far been identified: Sar-i-Sang, Chilmak, Shaga-Darra-i-Robat-i-Paskaran,
and Stromby. Badakhshan lay at the centre of a wide commercial network

The Palestinian pottery
in tomb U-j Abydos is an
indication of the degree to
which powerful Egyptians
were already gaining access
to Asiatic commodities as
early as 3200 BC.

through which lapis lazuli was exported over vast distances to the early civilizations of western Asia and north-east Africa, no doubt passing through the hands of many middle men *en route*.

Some of the most important archaeological data for the earliest Egyptian links with the outside world take the form of the pottery vessels in which many commodities (usually food, drink, or cosmetics) were transported to and from the Nile valley. The cache of about 400 Palestinian-style vessels that filled one chamber of Tomb U-j, in the Naqada III Cemetery U at Abydos (see Chapter 4), shows that this élite tomb-owner in *c*.3200 BC—perhaps an early ruler—was able to exert considerable commercial influence in order to obtain these grave goods (probably wine jars). Very few of these vessels have been identified with pottery from contemporary sites in Palestine; therefore they seem to have been types produced specifically for export. The same tomb also contained wavy-handled Egyptian vessels, the style of which was derived from Palestinian vessels, as well as a fragment of carved ivory handle, which appears to show rows of Asiatic captives and women carrying pottery vessels.

Pottery found at early urban sites in southern Palestine itself suggests that an Egyptian trade network may have been flourishing in this region as early as the first phase of the Early Bronze Age. It has been suggested that the expansion of the Naqada culture into the Delta region in the late Predynastic Period may well have resulted from the Upper Egyptian rulers' desire to gain direct commercial contact with Palestine, rather than obtaining goods via the middlemen of Maadi and other Lower Egyptian sites. By at least the 1st Dynasty, the newly unified Egyptian state had expanded beyond the Delta into southern Palestine, with a thriving trade route passing through several hundred encampments and way stations along the northern end of the Sinai peninsula (see Chapter 4). Several of the Early Dynastic royal tombs at Abydos contained fragments of Palestinian vessels, showing that the rulers of Egypt included imported Asiatic commodities among their funerary equipment.

At about the same time that Egyptians were first establishing commercial links with the inhabitants of Early Bronze Age Palestine, they were also making contact with the people of Lower Nubia (primarily in order to gain access to the exotic products of tropical Africa, as well as the mineral resources of Nubia itself). The archaeological traces of these people, whom George Reisner named the 'A Group', have survived throughout Lower Nubia, dating from about 3500 to 2800 BC. The grave goods often include stone vessels, amulets, and copper artefacts imported from Egypt, which not only help to date these graves but also demonstrate that the A Group was engaged in regular trade with the Egyptians of the Predynastic and Early Dynastic periods. Bruce Williams has made the controversial suggestion that the chiefdoms of the early A Group were actually reponsible for the rise of the Egyptian state, but this has been refuted by most scholars (see Chapter 4).

The wealth and quantity of imported items appear to increase in later A-Group graves, suggesting a steady growth in contact between the two cultures.

Facing, above: the palace of the mortuary temple of Rameses III at Medinet Habu, *c*.1180 BC, contained these faience tiles decorated with detailed figures of foreigners.

Facing, below: although the 18th Dynasty ruler Tutankhamun is better known for his intact tomb than his military prowess, tradition demanded that items such as this painted box should portray him in his war-chariot leading an attack against Syrians.

Sites such as Khor Daoud (comprising no settlement remains but hundreds of silos containing Naqada-culture pottery vessels that originally held beer, wine, oil, and perhaps cheese) were evidently trading posts at which exchange of goods took place between the late predynastic Egyptians, the A Group, and the nomads of the Eastern Desert. Judging from some of the rich tombs at the Sayala and Qustul cemeteries, which contain prestige goods imported from Egypt, the élite within the A Group were able to profit substantially from their role as middlemen in the African trade route. However, a rock carving at the Lower Nubian site of Gebel Sheikh Suleiman (now on display in the Khartoum Museum) appears to record a 1st Dynasty campaign as far south as the second cataract, suggesting that contacts with the A Group had by this date become somewhat more militaristic.

A process of severe impoverishment appears to have taken place in Lower Nubia during the 1st Dynasty, probably as a direct result of the depradations of early Egyptian economic exploitation of the region. It has been suggested that there might have been an enforced reversion to pastoralism (perhaps partly due to environmental changes) or that the local Nubian population might even have temporarily abandoned the region, perhaps moving south and eventually returning as the so-called C Group (once regarded as quite separate from the A Group, but now seen to have a number of cultural features in common).

The C-Group people were roughly synchronous with the period in Egyptian history from the mid-6th Dynasty to the early 18th Dynasty (c.2300–1500 BC). Their principal archaeological characteristics included hand-made black-topped pottery vessels bearing incised decoration filled with white pigment, as well as artefacts imported from Egypt. Their way of life seems to have been dominated by cattle-herding, while their social system was probably essentially tribal (until they began to be integrated into Egyptian society). In the early 12th Dynasty their territory in Lower Nubia was taken over by the Egyptians, perhaps partly in order to prevent them from developing contacts with the more sophisticated Kerma culture that had emerged in Upper Nubia (see Chapter 8).

The Kingdom of Punt

Egyptian contacts with Africa gradually extended even further than Lower and Upper Nubia, bringing them into contact with a region in East Africa that they describe as Punt. Trading missions were sent there from at least the 5th Dynasty (2494–2345 BC) onwards in order to obtain such products as gold, aromatic resins, African blackwood, ebony, ivory, slaves, and wild animals (for example, monkeys and cyncocephalous baboons). By the New Kingdom, such expeditions were being depicted in temples and tombs, showing the inhabitants of Punt as a people with a dark-reddish complexion and fine features; they were shown with long hair in the earlier paintings, but from the late 18th Dynasty onwards they had evidently adopted a more close-cropped style. The last

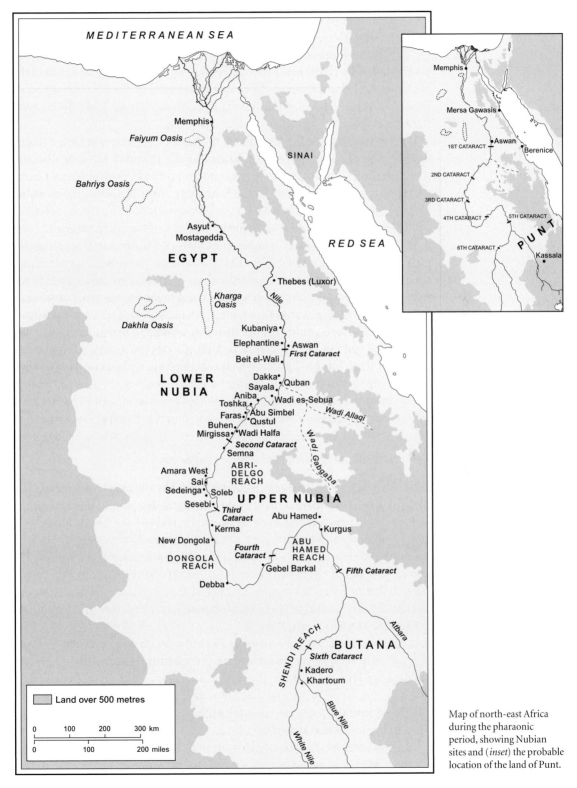

Map of north-east Africa during the pharaonic period, showing Nubian sites and (*inset*) the probable location of the land of Punt.

323

definite indications of expeditions to Punt date to the time of the 20th Dynasty ruler Rameses III.

There is still some debate regarding the precise location of Punt, which was once identified with the region of modern Somalia. A strong argument has now been made for its location in either southern Sudan or the Eritrean region of Ethiopia, where the indigenous plants and animals equate most closely with those depicted in the Egyptian reliefs and paintings.

It used to be assumed (primarily on the basis of the scenes at Deir el-Bahri depicting Hatshepsut's expedition to Punt in the mid-18th Dynasty) that the trading parties always travelled by sea from the ports of Quseir or Mersa Gawasis, but it now seems possible that at least some of the Egyptian traders sailed south along the Nile and then took an overland route to Punt, perhaps making contact with the Puntites in the vicinity of Kurgus, at the fifth cataract.

The Deir el-Bahri scenes include depictions of the unusual Puntite settlements, comprising conical reed-built huts set on poles above the ground, and entered via ladders. Among the surrounding vegetation are palms and myrrh trees, some of the latter already in the process of being hacked apart in order to extract the myrrh. The scenes also show myrrh trees being loaded onto the ships so that the Egyptians could produce their own aromatics from them (and it has been argued that this in itself may be an argument for the combined Nile–overland route from Punt to Egypt, given the fact that such plants might well have died during the more difficult voyage northwards along the Red Sea coast). These myrrh trees might even have been replanted in the temple at Deir el-Bahri itself, judging from the surviving traces of tree pits there.

'Imperialism' in the Middle and New Kingdoms

In the Middle and New kingdoms, Egypt gradually obtained a degree of economic control over the regions of Nubia and Syria–Palestine. Opinions differ, however, as to which of these territories can be said to have been politically or socially 'colonized', or whether the situation was much more erratic, perhaps characterized only by periodic raids designed to safeguard trade routes and provide supplies of war booty. Debate also centres on the question of the possible motivations for ancient imperialism: were the Egyptian inroads into Nubia and the Levant dictated by ideological imperatives, by economic necessity, or by some other socio-political factor?

In practice, the answers to these questions are by no means straightforward and, not surprisingly, vary according to the specific place and period. In the Middle Kingdom, for instance, the situation is in some respects clearer: as far as Nubia is concerned, we know that the 12th Dynasty pharaohs used military force to control the region as far south as the third cataract at least, building a chain of fortresses that would have given them a stranglehold over Nile commerce. The fortresses contained garrisons and extensive storerooms that would not only have ensured a continuous military presence in Lower Nubia, but would also have provided the potential to send campaigns further south, when necessary to oppose any perceived or actual threat.

The enormous amount of space devoted to granaries at such fortresses as Askut, together with the traces of buildings interpreted by Barry Kemp as royal 'campaign palaces' at Uronarti and Kor, all suggest the use of the Lower Nubian fortresses as a 12th Dynasty springboard into Africa rather than just a heavily defended border. The storage space in the fortresses was also no doubt utilized to store the materials and products imported by the Egyptians, while they were *en route* for Thebes or Itjtawy.

In Palestine, however, there is very little evidence for any permanent Egyptian presence during the Middle Kingdom. There were certainly contacts both with the Levant and the Aegean during the 12th and 13th Dynasties, but it remains unclear to what extent Egypt gained political or economic control over any parts of the eastern Mediterranean. A fragment of Amenemhat II's annals preserved at Memphis records at least two invasions of the Levant during his reign, and the stele of Khusobek (at Manchester Museum) records an expedition launched against the Palestinian city of Shechem in the reign of Senusret III. Apart from these references, however, the only other indications of military designs on the Levant are to be found in élite epithets and titles (which may well be primarily bombastic rather than historical), or in descriptions of produce obtained from western Asia (which tend not to specify whether the goods or livestock were obtained by force). A reasonable archaeological case, however, can be made for a fairly strong and continuous Middle Kingdom Egyptian *economic* presence in Palestine and Byblos (see below), probably periodically reinforced by military pressure. The increasingly high numbers of Asiatics known to have been living in Egypt during the Middle Kingdom (see Chapter 7) suggests that at least some were being brought in as prisoners of war.

Egyptian activities in the Levant during the New Kingdom are attested in some detail both by archaeological and textual sources. The latter consist not only of triumphal Egyptian 'victory stelae' and temple reliefs, presenting glowing accounts of the spoils obtained by the king on behalf of the gods, but also clay cuneiform tablets from a number of sites (for example, Taʿanach, Kamid el-Loz, and Hattusas), documenting the diplomatic, administrative, and economic links between the various states of the Near East. From an Egyptian point of view, the most important of these 'archives' is a set of 382 tablets found at Amarna in Middle Egypt, consisting mainly of correspondence between foreign leaders and the Egyptian king in the mid-14th century BC (the late 18th Dynasty). The 'Amarna Letters' thus provide insights first into the diplomatic relations between Egypt and the other great powers (for example, Mitanni and Babylon) and, second, into the labyrinthine politics of the small city states of Syria–Palestine, disputing and allying among themselves as they slipped back and forth between the spheres of influence of Mitanni, Egypt, and the Hittite kingdom.

The principal debate concerning Egyptian involvement in Syria–Palestine

This cuneiform tablet bearing a letter from King Ashuruballit I of Assyria to King Akhenaten of Egypt, *c.*1350 BC, is part of an extensive archive of letters from foreign rulers that was excavated at Amarna and is now spread among the collections of several museums.

during the New Kingdom centres on the question of the degree to which Egypt maintained a *permanent* military and/or civilian presence at the various towns and cities that they had conquered. Some scholars argue that there is sufficient archaeological and textual evidence to suggest that Egypt had effectively colonized some of the towns of Palestine at least (perhaps initially inheriting the control of this region when they pursued the defeated Hyksos into their homeland at the end of the Second Intermediate Period (see Chapters 8 and 9)). According to this theory—primarily based on the Amarna Letters and the presence of Egyptian artefacts at many Levantine sites—the whole area of Syria–Palestine was divided up into three zones (north–south: Amurru, Upe, and Canaan), each ruled by an Egyptian governor via a number of small garrisons scattered among the local settlements. Other scholars, however, argue that the material culture of Egyptian sites in the eastern Delta is so clearly distinct from that of the nearest towns in Palestine, just on the other side of Sinai, that it seems highly unlikely that there were ever many Egyptians actually living among the local populations (in contrast to the extensive architectural and artefactual evidence of Egyptians colonizing Nubia in the New Kingdom).

The motivation for the significant New Kingdom Egyptian presence in Lower Nubia may well have been primarily economic, but it has been pointed out by a number of scholars that the archaeological and textual evidence actually amount to a very complex web of information concerning Egyptian attitudes to Nubia. To begin with, there is the continuation, throughout the Middle and New kingdoms of the essentially xenophobic ideology described above, whereby stereotypical barbaric Nubians were portrayed in official art and literature as worthless representatives of chaos. This has to be contrasted, however, with two important factors: first, that many foreigners (including Nubians and Asiatics) were living happily alongside native Egyptians in many of the towns in Egypt proper, and, second, that there is good evidence of a deliberate New Kingdom policy of acculturation both in Nubia and the Levant, so that the local élite were encouraged to adopt Egyptian customs and nomenclature, and their children were sometimes forcibly removed to be 'educated' in Egypt, eventually returning to their home countries fully indoctrinated with the Egyptian way of life.

The overall image of Egyptian 'imperialism', therefore, is multifaceted, the economic and political pragmatism of the pharaohs often being cloaked in the hyperbole of royal rhetoric and piety. The debate concerning ideology versus economics is difficult to resolve because we rely primarily on a combination of royal religious and funerary texts for our reconstruction of Egyptian behaviour in the outside world, yet the real story probably lies in the more prosaic archival material that has so rarely survived.

Byblos

The town of Byblos (or Jubeil) was located on the coast of Canaan (about 40 km. north of modern Beirut). The principal settlement, known in the Akkadian language as Gubla, has a long history extending from the Neolithic to the Late Bronze Age, when the population appears to have moved to a nearby site now covered by a modern village. The importance of Byblos lay in its function as a port, and from around the time of Egypt's unification it was used by the Egyptians as a source of timber. The famous cedars of Lebanon, and other goods, passed through it, and Egyptian objects are found there from as early as the 2nd Dynasty (2890–2686 BC). The site included several religious buildings, such as the so-called Obelisk Temple, dedicated to Ba'alat Gebal, the 'Lady of Byblos' (a local form of Astarte, who was also identified with the Egyptian goddess Hathor), where one of the obelisks was inscribed with hieroglyphs.

Egyptian culture of the Middle Kingdom had an especially strong influence on the court of the Middle Bronze Age rulers of Byblos, and among the objects found in the royal tombs of this period are several bearing the names of the late 12th Dynasty rulers Amenemhat III and IV. Egyptian objects included ivory, ebony, and gold, while local imitations used other materials and were executed in a less accomplished style.

In the New Kingdom, the city features prominently in the Amarna Letters, since its ruler, Ribaddi, sought military assistance from the Egyptian pharaoh. On this occasion Byblos fell into enemy hands, but was later regained. A sarcophagus found with objects of Rameses II (1279–1213 BC) and showing Egyptian influence is important for its later (tenth century BC) inscription for Ahiram, a local ruler, which is in early alphabetic characters. Various Egyptian artefacts found at Byblos itself attesting to strong royal diplomatic contacts between the pharaohs and the rulers of Byblos include a vessel bearing the name of Rameses II from the tomb of the above-mentioned Ahiram, inscribed door jambs of Rameses II from a temple, and fragments of statues of Osorkon I and II (the Osorkon I statue bearing a Phoenician inscription and dating to the reign of Abibaal).

The archaeological evidence therefore suggests a peak of Egypto-Byblian contact in the 19th Dynasty, followed by decline in the 20th and 21st Dynasties (documented by the *Tale of Wenamun*, a quasi-historical description of a late 20th Dynasty expedition to Byblos), and finally a resurgence of links in the 22nd and 23rd Dynasties. After the Third Intermediate Period, the importance of

Byblos gradually appears to have declined in favour of the neighbouring ports of Tyre and Sidon.

The Sea Peoples

In the 13th and 12th centuries BC, a series of major crop failures in the northern and eastern Mediterranean appear to have triggered off large-scale migrations through Anatolia and the Levant. These agricultural problems evidently led the Egyptian 19th Dynasty ruler Merenptah to send grain to the famine-stricken Hittites (now in decline), and many Mycenaean urban centres appear to have

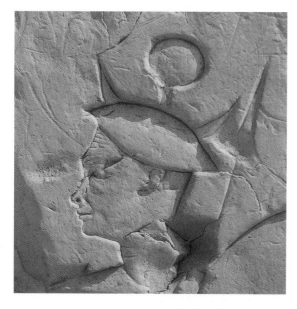

been destroyed at this date. Among the new migrants in the Mediterranean region at this date were a loose confederation of ethnic groups from the Aegean and Asia Minor, known to the Egyptians as Sea Peoples. Some of these groups, such as the Denen, Lukka, and Sherden, were already active by the reign of Akhenaten (1352–1336 BC), while members of the Lukka, Sherden, and Peleset are portrayed as mercenaries fighting for the army of Rameses II (1279–1213 BC) at the Battle of Qadesh.

Later in the Ramessid Period, the Sea Peoples are described and depicted on reliefs at Medinet Habu and Karnak as well as the Great Harris Papyrus, a list of temple endowments in the reign of Rameses III (1184–1153 BC). The latter sources indicate that the Sea Peoples were not simply engaged in random acts of plundering but were

By the Ramessid period, the Egyptian army had begun to incorporate many mercenaries from the eastern Mediterranean whose distinctive physical features and weapons were faithfully reproduced by the artists of the time, as in this detail of a Sherden soldier in the depiction of the Battle of Qadesh on the external walls of the temple of Rameses II at Abydos.

part of a significant movement of displaced peoples migrating into Syria–Palestine and Egypt. It is clear that they planned to settle in the areas that they attacked, since they are portrayed not merely as armies of warriors but also as whole families bringing their possessions with them in ox-drawn carts. Study of the 'tribal' names recorded by the Egyptians and Hittites has shown that various groups of the Sea Peoples can be linked either with particular homelands, or at least with the places in which they finally settled. Thus, the Ekwesh and Denen may possibly be correlated with the Achaean and Danaean Greeks of the *Iliad*, the Lukka may have derived from the Lycian region of Anatolia, the Sherden may have originated in Sardinia, and the Peleset are almost certainly to be identified with the biblical Philistines (who gave their name to Palestine).

The Sea People's first attack on the Egyptian Delta, in alliance with the Libyans, dates to the fifth year of the reign of Merenptah (1213–1203 BC). The individual groups of Sea Peoples (in addition to the Libyan Meshwesh) are named as the Ekwesh, Lukka, Shekelesh, Sherden, and Teresh. According to Merenptah's reliefs on one of the walls of the temple of Amun at Karnak and the text of a stele from his funerary temple (the so-called Israel Stele), he success-fully repelled them, killing 6,000 and routing the rest. Moshe Dothan's excava-tions at the Philistine city of Ashdod in 1962–9 uncovered a burnt layer dating to the thirteenth century BC, which may perhaps correspond either to the Lev-antine campaign of the pharaoh Merenptah or the arrival of the Peleset them-selves.

From an Egyptian point of view, the final confrontation with the Sea Peoples took place in the eighth year of Rameses III's reign, by which time they had probably captured the Syrian cities of Ugarit and Alalakh. They attacked Egypt by both land and sea, the latter confrontation being depicted in the celebrated sea-battle reliefs on the external walls of Rameses' mortuary temple at Medinet Habu. This victory protected Egypt from overt invasion from the north, but ultimately it was to be the more insidious infiltration of Libyan peoples from the west that was more successful as a means of gaining control of Egypt (see Chapter 12).

Conclusion

The history of Egypt's contact with the outside world is above all concerned with power and prestige. In the earliest commercial links between the Egyptians and their neighbours in Africa and the Near East, the principal motivation appears to have been to obtain rare or exotic materials and products that could serve to bolster the power base of the individuals or groups concerned. Trade, whether inter-regional or international, was an integral part of the formation and expansion of the early Near Eastern states.

By the time that the full national administrative apparatus was operating, in the Middle and New kingdoms, there were large sectors of royal bureaucracy and military power dedicated solely to the process of obtaining taxes and con-scripted labour from the provinces of Egypt. This efficient national economic system formed the ideal basis for the process of exacting tribute (*inu*) and spoils from the lands outside Egypt's borders. Both ideologically and economically, the acts of conquering and ruling were inseparable from the idea of absorbing new wealth into the estates of the king and the major religious cults.

It was not, however, simply a question of importing materials and com-modities into Egypt. There also appears to have been a steady influx of people, as well as linguistic and cultural influences, leading to the creation of a distinctly cosmopolitan and multicultural society from at least the New Kingdom onwards. The apparent tolerance of foreigners within Egyptian society was nevertheless accompanied by a tremendous continuity in terms of the core val-ues and beliefs of the indigenous population (so far as we can tell, given the bias of surviving data towards the élite end of society). Egyptian culture was appar-ently strong and flexible enough to survive long periods of Libyan, Kushite, Persian, and Ptolemaic domination without the essence of the Egyptians' iden-tity as a nation being affected.

12 THE THIRD INTERMEDIATE PERIOD

(1069–664 BC)

JOHN TAYLOR

This 400-year period, comprising the 21st to 25th Dynasties (1069–664 BC), may justly be regarded as marking a new phase in Egypt's history. The period is characterized by significant changes in Egypt's political organization, society, and culture. Centralized government was replaced by political fragmentation and the re-emergence of local centres of power; a substantial influx of non-Egyptians (Libyans and Nubians) permanently modified the profile of the population, while Egypt as a whole became more inward-looking, its contacts with the outside world (and its impact on the Levant in particular) greatly reduced in scale. These, and other, factors had important consequences for the functioning of the economy, for the structure of society, and for the religious attitudes and funerary practices of the inhabitants. It is true that the period was marked by tensions over control of territory and resources, leading on occasion to conflicts, but violence was not endemic; the period as a whole was stable and represents far more than a temporary lapse from traditional pharaonic rule (an unfortunate implication of the customary designation 'Intermediate'). Many of the events and trends of these years were permanent in their effect and played a crucial role in shaping the Egypt of the later first millennium BC.

A sound historical framework for these centuries has proved more difficult to establish than for any other major period of Egyptian history. No pharaonic king-lists include the 21st–25th Dynasties, and the Egyptologist is thus forced to rely more heavily than is strictly desirable on the often garbled excerpts from the history of Manetho (itself derived chiefly from Delta-based sources and thus offering, at best, an incomplete picture). Careful collation of the Manethonian lists with the scattered inscriptions of kings and local dignitaries of the period and cross-references to Near Eastern sources has yielded a chronology that is accepted in its main points by most scholars, but some areas remain subjects for debate (notably the relationships and spheres of influence of some of the provincial rulers who adopted royal status during the late ninth and eighth centuries BC). With the exception of sites such as Tanis, the survival of evidence from this period in the Delta is, as always, relatively poor, and, while Thebes has yielded a very large quantity of artefacts, private statuary and funerary equipment tend to predominate, whereas economic sources such as administrative papyri are very rare. Since it was in the north that many of the most significant developments were taking place at this time, a balanced picture of the country as a whole is difficult to achieve.

Historical Outline

The Third Intermediate Period was inaugurated by a major political upheaval and a weakening of the economy. The civil war fomented by Panehsy, the viceroy of Kush, shook the country, and his subsequent defeat and expulsion beyond the southern frontier amounted to only a partial victory for the government. Military action against Panehsy by General Piankh failed to re-establish Egyptian authority in Nubia, and control over the resources of the southlands—the gold mines and the lucrative trade in the products of sub-Saharan Africa—was lost. Hence, at the very outset of the period, Egypt suffered a serious reduction in revenue from its former dependencies; as the *Tale of Wenamun* (a narrative describing an expedition supposedly sent to Byblos by Herihor) hints, the new Egyptian rulers may also have lacked the prestige in the Levant that their predecessors had enjoyed.

Following the death of Rameses XI, *c.*1069 BC, the 20th Dynasty—and with it the Renaissance era—came to an end, but the foundations of a new power structure were already in place, and transition to a new regime occurred smoothly. Under the 21st Dynasty Egypt was—to outward appearances—politically united, but in reality control was divided between a line of kings in the north and a sequence of army commanders, who also held the post of high priest of Amun, at Thebes. Smendes (1069–1043 BC), an influential figure of unknown origin, founded the dynasty in the north, with his power base at the eastern Delta site of Tanis, a new city whose chief monuments were constructed largely of reused materials brought from Piramesse and other northern sites. Tentamun, probably Smendes' wife, is thought to have been a member of the Ramessid royal family. While this connection may have been a factor in the new ruler's rise to power, the growing influence of the cult of Amun and its officials was undoubtedly also significant. During this period, the government of Egypt was in effect a theocracy, supreme political authority being vested in the god Amun himself. In a hymn to Amun on a papyrus from Deir el-Bahri, which has been dubbed the '*credo* of the theocracy', the god's name is written in a

Plan of the remains of the
temples and tombs at the
eastern Delta site of Tanis.

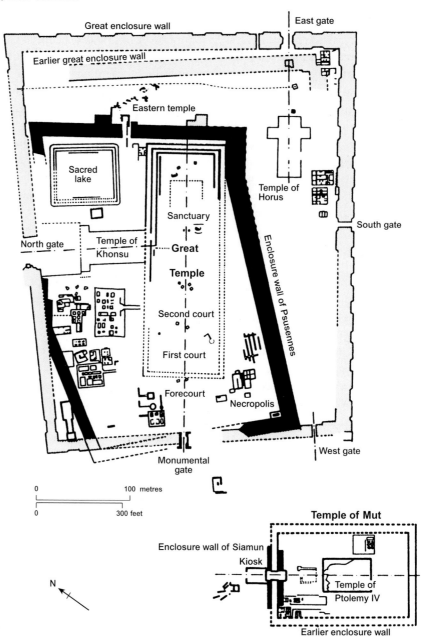

cartouche and he is addressed as the superior of all the gods, the fountainhead of creation, and the true king of Egypt. The pharaohs were now merely temporal rulers who were held to be Amun's appointees and to whom the god's decisions were communicated via oracles. The workings of the theocratic government are explicitly documented at Thebes, where oracular consultations were formalized by the institution of a regular Festival of the Divine Audience, held at Karnak. The same principles are implied for the north as well—

Smendes and Tentamun are described in *Wenamun* as 'the pillars which Amun has set up for the north of his land', while the city of Tanis was developed as a northern counterpart to Thebes, Amun's principal cult centre. Temples to the Theban triad were erected there and Tanis's role as a holy city was enhanced by the siting of the tombs of the 21st Dynasty kings within the temple precinct. To what extent Tanis was really a *political* power base at this time may be questioned, since excavations have so far revealed no dwellings, private monuments (other than a few reused blocks from courtiers' tombs), or donation stelae (that is, records of the bestowal of cultivable land on the gods of local temples) in the area. There is evidence, however, that Memphis functioned as a residence of the northern kings—a decree of Smendes is recorded as having been issued there—and the ancient city may once more have served as a major administrative base.

The activities of the northern rulers during the 21st Dynasty are poorly documented. Building works at Tanis and Memphis by Psusennes I (1039–991 BC) and Siamun (978–959 BC) are the most prominent remains within Egypt itself, and relations with the Levant seem to have been sporadic and unadventurous. The marriage of a royal princess (perhaps a daughter of Siamun) to Solomon of Israel is a striking testimony to the reduced prestige of Egypt's rulers on the world stage. At the height of the New Kingdom, pharaohs regularly took to wife the daughters of Near Eastern princes, but refused to permit their own daughters to be married off to foreign rulers.

The most prominent of the southern commanders at the inception of the Third Intermediate Period was the chief general Herihor. Through his assumption of the office of high priest of Amun—and even, on occasion, the titles and trappings of a pharaoh—supreme civil, military, and religious authority was combined in the hands of a single individual. However, it was to the family of Herihor's colleague General Piankh that long-term control of Upper Egypt subsequently passed. All of these men held the offices of chief general and high priest of Amun. Under the auspices of the theocracy they derived their executive powers from oracles of Amun, Mut, and Khons, by whom clerical appointments and major policy decisions of the rulers were sanctioned. Although the temporal authority of the Tanite kings was formally recognized throughout the whole of Egypt, and the Theban commanders made only limited pretensions to royal status, it was none the less they who were in effective control of Middle and Upper Egypt. A formal frontier between the two regions was fixed at Teudjoi (el-Hiba), south of the entrance to the Faiyum. Here, and at other sites along the Nile, the southern rulers erected a series of fortresses. Otherwise the principal activity documented in the south during the 21st Dynasty was the systematic dismantling of the New Kingdom royal burials in the Theban necropolis. The Valley of the Kings ceased to be the royal burial ground, the tomb-builders' community of Deir el-Medina was disbanded, the contents of the tombs were appropriated and the mummies secreted in caches.

After the reigns of Smendes and his successor Amenemnisu (1043–1039 BC), the throne in the north passed to Psusennes I, son of the Theban commander

Drawing by Lack

A relief in the temple of
Khons at Karnak showing
Herihor, the chief general
and high priest of Amun, as
a king being purified by the
gods Horus and Thoth.

Pinudjem I, and control of Upper Egypt to his brother Menkheperra. Thus for a time the same Theban line governed all Egypt, and amicable relations between the north and the south were maintained through the intermarriage of several members of the rulers' extensive families. Yet the division of the realm persisted—an indication that decentralization was tolerated by these rulers. About 984 BC a new family took control in the Delta, with the accession of Osorkon the Elder (984–978 BC), the son of the Chief of the Meshwesh Sheshonq, a ruler whose name and parentage proclaim his Libyan origins. The Theban commanders dropped all claims to royal status, and more openly made use of the names and date lines of the northern monarchs in documents. Nevertheless, the Theban high priest Psusennes ultimately became king in the north as Psusennes II (959–945 BC), last ruler of the 21st Dynasty.

By this time, Libyans constituted a substantial and influential presence in

Egypt. Although major incursions of Meshwesh and Libu had been repulsed by Merenptah and Rameses III, the settlement of immigrants, war captives, and garrison troops continued, particularly in the Delta and in the area between Memphis and Herakleopolis; it has been suggested that by the end of the New Kingdom the Egyptian army was almost entirely made up of Libyan mercenaries. The incipient decentralization of government during the 21st Dynasty facilitated the growth of provincial power-bases, and local dynasties of Libyan chieftains, descended from the settlers of the late New Kingdom, were able to increase their autonomy; the ruling families in both north and south during the 21st Dynasty included individuals who bore patently Libyan names—and since some form of acculturation was doubtless practised (see below), many more are probably disguised in the record under Egyptian names. It was, therefore, only the culmination of an established trend when, at the beginning of the 22nd Dynasty, the throne in Tanis passed to the Chief of the Meshwesh Sheshonq (King Sheshonq I (945–924 BC)). He belonged to a family settled at Bubastis, whose members had, through judicious marriages with the royal family and links with the high priests at Memphis, become highly influential in the Delta. The transfer of power from Psusennes II appears to have been accomplished with a minimum of opposition—it was undoubtedly eased by the fact that Sheshonq was the nephew of the earlier Tanite king Osorkon the Elder, while his own son, the future Osorkon I (924–889 BC), was married to Psusennes II's daughter Maatkara.

Sheshonq's reign (945–924 BC) stands out as a high point in the Third Intermediate Period. Rejecting the internal divisions of the 21st Dynasty in favour of New Kingdom models of pharaonic rule, Sheshonq sought to re-establish the political authority of the king. The theocracy continued to function but in a modified form—oracular consultations still occurred, but no longer feature as a regular instrument of policy. The new reign was marked by a change in the attitude of the throne towards the integrity of the country, the adoption of an expansionist foreign policy, and an ambitious royal building programme.

The attempt to exert direct royal control over the whole of Egypt involved curtailing the virtually independent status of Thebes. To achieve this, the post of high priest of Amun was handed to one of Sheshonq's sons, Prince Iuput, who was also army commander—a policy followed by subsequent pharaohs. Other members of the royal family and supporters of the dynasty were also appointed to important offices, and loyalty on the part of local power-holders was encouraged by marriages to daughters of the royal house.

After more than a century of passivity on the part of Egyptian rulers, Sheshonq I intervened aggressively in the politics of the Levant to reassert pharaonic prestige there. His Karnak inscriptions record a major military expedition c.925 BC against Israel and Judah and the principal towns of southern Palestine, including Gaza and Megiddo. The Old Testament records the same event, stating (1 Kgs. 14: 25–6) that, in the fifth year of Rehoboam, 'Shishak, king of Egypt' seized the treasures of Jerusalem, and adding (2 Chr. 12: 2–9) that he came with

1,200 chariots and an army that included Libyans and Nubians. These sources indicate that the campaign was launched in support of Jeroboam, an exile in Egypt who claimed the throne of Judah. However, if this was meant to be the first stage of a programme to re-establish Egyptian authority in Palestine, it remained only a flash in the pan. Sheshonq died soon after his return to Egypt and under his successors relations with the Levant appear to have reverted to purely commercial contacts—notably the reopening of relations with Byblos. Sheshonq I's building programme included plans for a great court in the temple of Amun at Karnak, but this remained unfinished at the king's death. The gateway, known as the 'Bubastite portal'—the only section completed—was inscribed with a record of Sheshonq's victories in Palestine, which is one of the most valuable historical sources for the entire period.

Efforts to consolidate the unity of the realm continued under Sheshonq's successors, but the growing power of provincial rulers led to the weakening of royal control and a consequent fragmentation of the country. The post of high priest of Amun and other key offices were once more permitted to become hereditary, and this facilitated the development of independent power bases. The appointment of close relatives of the kings to important posts in major cen-

The triumphal relief of the early 22nd Dynasty ruler Sheshonq I, c.945–924 BC, at Karnak (on the so-called Bubastite Portal) commemorates his campaigns against the cities of Palestine, which are also recorded in the Old Testament. After his reign, however, the Egyptian presence in the Levant seems to have diminished to such an extent that the only known consistent diplomatic contacts were with Byblos.

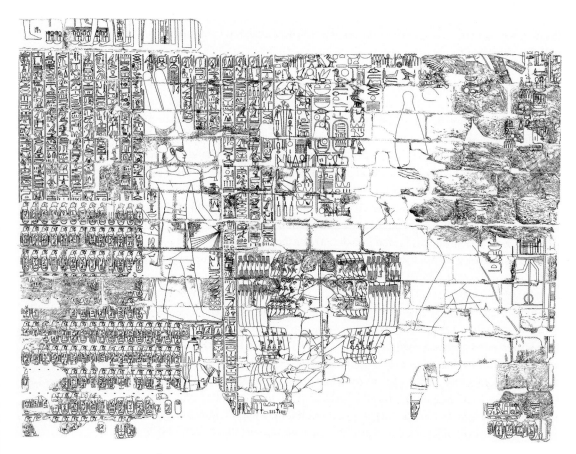

tres such as Memphis and Thebes failed to halt the growing independence of the provinces, and indeed probably accelerated the process. In an interesting inscription on a statue from Tanis, Osorkon II (874–850 BC) petitions Amun to confirm the appointment of his children to various high civil and religious offices, with the significant proviso that 'brother should not be jealous of brother'. From the mid-ninth to the mid-eighth century BC the process of decentralization continued and the power of the 22nd Dynasty diminished, as provinces ruled by royal princes and Libyan chiefs became increasingly autonomous. At Thebes, the high priest Harsiese declared himself king, and was buried at Medinet Habu in a falcon-headed sarcophagus in clear imitation of the funerary traditions of the Tanite rulers. Eventually, northern attempts to impose authority over Thebes led to violence. A long inscription of Prince Osorkon, son of Takelot II (850–825 BC), carved on the Bubastite portal at Karnak (the so-called *Chronicle of Prince Osorkon*), describes a series of conflicts that arose as he sought to implement his authority as high priest of Amun in Thebes against a rival group.

During the reign of Sheshonq III (825–773 BC) and in the years that followed, numerous local rulers—particularly in the Delta—became virtually autonomous and several declared themselves kings. The first of these was Pedubastis I (818–793 BC), who may have been related to the royal family of the 22nd Dynasty. The location of his power base is uncertain, but at Thebes it was his authority and that of his successors that was recognized, in preference to the rule of Tanis. While these local kings are assigned by some scholars to the 23rd Dynasty, it remains unclear which, if any, of them are to be equated with the '23rd Dynasty' as recorded by Manetho, which was perhaps composed of successors to the 22nd Dynasty at Tanis. By *c.*730 BC there were two kings in the Delta (at Bubastis and Leontopolis), one at Hermopolis, and one at Herakleopolis in Upper Egypt; besides those in the Delta, and virtually independent, were a 'Prince Regent', four Great Chiefs of the Ma, and a Prince of the West in Sais. This last, Tefnakht (king 727–720 BC), had taken over all the territories of the western Delta and Memphis, and was expanding into the northern reach of Upper Egypt.

This illuminating snapshot of the political geography of Egypt is to be found on a stele set up at Gebel Barkal near the fourth cataract by the Nubian ruler Piy (747–716 BC). During the second half of the eighth century BC, the rulers of Kush had emerged as strong contenders for power over Egypt. Following initial assertions of authority by Kashta, Piy (Kashta's son) launched a military expedition into Egypt—ostensibly to halt the expansionist policies of Tefnakht of Sais. Piy's troops appear to have taken Thebes without a struggle, perhaps owing to a previous agreement with the local representatives of the 23rd Dynasty, and the towns and cities of northern Upper Egypt rapidly capitulated or were besieged and captured. Memphis offered resistance and was taken by assault, after which the dynasts submitted to Piy, acknowledging him as their overlord.

After this show of strength, Piy returned to Nubia, leaving the political situation in Egypt virtually unchanged. During the following decade Tefnakht assumed the status of king; he and his successor Bakenrenef (Bocchoris) constitute the 24th Dynasty. Although based at Sais, Bakenrenef's authority was soon acknowledged throughout the Delta and as far south as Herakleopolis. But the Nubians, having once tasted power in Egypt, were not prepared to countenance its loss. In *c.*716 BC Piy's successor Shabaqo (716–702 BC) launched a new invasion. On this occasion Egypt was formally annexed to Kush and Shabaqo and his successors—Shabitqo, Taharqo, and Tanutamani—were recognized by later historians as the 25th Dynasty. According to Manetho, Bakenrenef was executed, but fully centralized government was not restored. Instead, the Kushite monarchs ruled as overlords and permitted the dynasts to remain in control of their fiefs. In order to be recognized as authentic Egyptian pharaohs, they displayed special respect for Egyptian religious and cultural traditions, and intentionally sought an ideological link with the great eras of Egypt's past—in particular with the Old Kingdom. To this end, Memphis was promoted to become the Kushites' preferred residence in Egypt, and nascent archaizing tendencies were boosted, leading to a revival of artistic, literary, and religious trends drawing inspiration from earlier ages. In the south, Thebes retained its pre-eminent status, but the power of the high priest of Amun was eclipsed. In its place the office of 'god's wife of Amun' grew in importance; this celibate priestess was usually a royal princess, and each 'god's wife' adopted her successor from among the junior members of the royal family, eliminating the possible emergence of a Theban-based subdynasty to threaten the king's political authority.

The Nubian rulers also pursued an aggressive policy with regard to the former Egyptian dependencies and commercial partners in Palestine. Intervention in the politics of this region during the early seventh century BC led, unfortunately, to direct confrontation with the might of Assyria, which was in the process of exerting its control over this area of the Levant. In consequence, much of the reign of Taharqo (690–664 BC) was occupied by increasingly desperate struggles to defend Egypt against Assyrian aggression. Finally, after the sack of Thebes by Ashurbanipal's forces (663 BC), the last Kushite monarch was permanently expelled from Egypt, and it was left to Psamtek of Sais (who had been installed by the Assyrians as a vassal ruler) to recover Egypt's independence.

The 21st to 24th Dynasties: the Libyan Period

The Libyans who settled in Egypt before and during the Third Intermediate Period were drawn predominantly from the Meshwesh (or Ma) and the Libu, the principal groups who had threatened Egypt's security during the New Kingdom. Their homeland appears to have been Cyrenaica, where they followed an economy based mainly on pastoral nomadism, although there is also some evidence for settlements. A low degree of infiltration by these people along Egypt's western fringe was probably endemic; its culmination in large-scale migrations under Merenptah and Rameses III seems to have been a consequence of displacement of populations in Cyrenaica, perhaps on account of local food shortages and the incursions of the Sea Peoples along the North African coast. Possibly an additional factor was the development of more concrete political cooperation and military organization among the Libyans of the later New Kingdom, which might have prompted a more constructive impetus towards settlement in Egypt. Under the successors of Rameses III a steady influx continued. The existence of different population groups among the Libyans and their semi-nomadic lifestyle doubtless meant that numerous groups, large and small, moved into Egypt independently. Some of these Libyans were captives or mercenaries who were settled in military communities as a policy of the 20th Dynasty kings, but there were probably many smaller groups that settled without coming under official control.

The Libyan element in Egyptian society
Numbers of these Libyans were settled in the area between Memphis and Herakleopolis, and in the oases of the Western Desert, but by far the largest concentration of them was in the western Delta. Settlement here was facilitated by the natural proximity of the area to the Libyans' homeland, and by the relatively unimportant status of this part of Egypt in the eyes of the pharaohs; thinly populated and of low agricultural productivity, it was mainly used for grazing cattle.

On account of the growing military and political efficiency of the Libyans towards the end of the New Kingdom, their chiefs were able to secure positions of local influence. There had already arisen in Egypt a class of ex-military men who had been rewarded for their services with land and who could rise to high office in the bureaucracy. The chiefs of Libyan mercenary groups were probably no less able to take advantage of this situation, and in this way a number of principalities developed, each based at an important town and each controlled by a Libyan chief—and this not only in the Delta but at strategic points along the Nile Valley, notably at Memphis and in the area around Herakleopolis. Unfortunately the sparsity of evidence for the 21st Dynasty conceals the precise stages by which these chieftains rose to power, but Libyans with high military rank are attested in the Herakleopolis area from the beginning of the Third Intermediate Period, and the appearance of a ruler named Osorkon on the throne at Tanis in the second half of the 21st Dynasty is the clearest indication that they had attained the first rank of Egyptian society.

The Libyans' consolidation of power was probably achieved in a variety of ways. The development of the theocratic form of government in the 21st Dynasty doubtless helped to render their rule palatable in the crucial transitional stage, by lending divine authority to their policies. Integration into Egyptian society could have been further enhanced by acculturation. Although increased contact with foreign lands and customs during the New Kingdom had made Egypt a cosmopolitan society with a mixed population, foreign settlers still underwent a process of Egyptianization, the main manifestations of which were the adoption of Egyptian names, dress, and burial customs. Evidence for acculturation of the Libyans can be adduced, though it is by no means conclusive. There is no trace of a characteristic material culture for the Libyans in Egypt, though, in view of the scanty archaeological documentation of both the Nile Delta and the Libyans' homeland of Cyrenaica, this picture may yet be transformed by further investigations. More significantly, the Libyans of the 21st–24th Dynasties do not figure as 'foreigners' in the Egyptian graphic or textual record. The distinctive ethnic features associated with Libyans in New Kingdom art (yellow skin, sidelocks, tattoos, feathered headgear, penis sheaths, and decorated robes) no longer appear, though this is not altogether surprising, since the Libyans were distinguished from the Egyptians in such depictions for ideological reasons rather than as a faithful reflection of their appearance. In the same way, the depiction of kings and officials of Libyan origin with traditional Egyptian dress, attributes, and physical characteristics was probably a conciliatory measure to encourage acceptance of their authority the Egyptian populace; it does not necessarily mean that total integration had been achieved. There are, in fact, several indications that the Libyans retained a large measure of their ethnic identity. Their distinctive and very un-Egyptian names—Osorkon, Sheshonq, Takelot, and others—survived for centuries after the arrival of the Libyans in Egypt, whereas in earlier periods foreigners usually adopted or

The Amduat papyrus of Ankhefenkhons described part of the journey of the sun-god through the twelve hours of the night. Such funerary papyri continued to be placed in private burials in Thebes during the 21st Dynasty, but the steep decline in the use of such documents by the 22nd Dynasty is one of the likely indications that the Libyan rulers of the 22nd–24th Dynasties encouraged major changes in funerary beliefs.

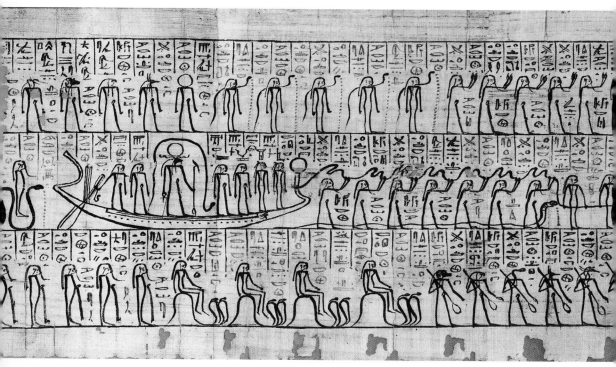

were given Egyptian names within one or two generations. In the same way, Libyan chiefdom titles were retained long after settlement in Egypt, and a feather worn in the hair survived as a distinguishing mark of chiefs of the Meshwesh and Libu. Long genealogies on statues and funerary objects are one of the most characteristic features of Libyan-Period texts, yet are not usual in Egyptian inscriptions before the late 21st Dynasty. The increase in such records apparently reflects a new importance attached to kinship and the preservation of extensive lines of descent—it is a class of evidence very much based on oral tradition, and tends to be an important feature of non-literate societies such as that of the Libyans.

The Libyans and the Egyptians had very different cultural backgrounds—the Libyans non-literate and semi-nomadic with no tradition of permanent building; the Egyptians literate, sedentary, and with a long tradition of formal institutions and monumental construction. Kings and dynasts of Libyan origin controlled all or most of Egypt for about 400 years, and some continued to hold power under the Kushites. It is, therefore, very likely that several of the major changes in the administration, society, and culture of Egypt that occurred during this period may have had their origins in this mixing of societies.

Power structures and political geography

The most characteristic feature of Egypt during the Third Intermediate Period is the political fragmentation of the country. This decentralization was a consequence of major changes in the government of Egypt, which distinguish the

Third Intermediate Period from the New Kingdom. Important factors are the long-term survival of Libyan chiefs in powerful positions, and the weakening of the authority of the king. Particularly significant was the king's policy of granting exceptional powers to kinsmen and provincial rulers, which created an impetus towards regional independence and a tension over access to and control of economic resources.

In the New Kingdom, the majority of royal relatives had been carefully excluded from effective administrative and military power, thereby neutralizing a potential threat to the authority of the king. But in the Third Intermediate Period kings' sons were given unprecedented administrative powers and were placed in charge of major settlements that enjoyed considerable autonomy—chief among these being Memphis, Herakleopolis, and Thebes. Until the pontificate of Harsiese (c.860 BC) all 22nd Dynasty high priests at Thebes were sons of the reigning king, and since many of these local

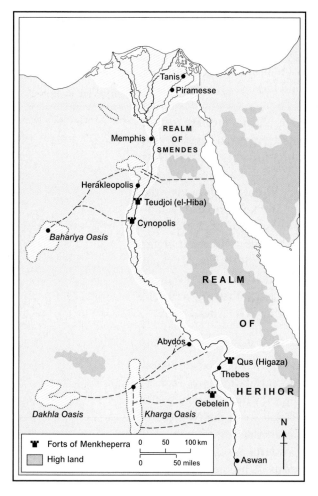

princes also had military power at their disposal, this had major implications for the political course of events.

Equally telling was the royal policy of permitting offices in the bureaucracy, clergy, and military to become hereditary benefices of provincial families. High office had sometimes been passed from father to son in the New Kingdom, but the process was by no means automatic. In the Third Intermediate Period the practice became endemic; already under the 21st Dynasty the posts of high priest of Amun and chief general were controlled by a single family. An attempt by the early rulers of the 22nd Dynasty to circumvent the debilitating effects of this monopoly by appointing king's sons as high priests at Thebes and other king's men to other high offices did not halt the trend; the former actually promoted decentralization, and in the case of the latter the hereditary principle soon reasserted itself. The effects of the practice are clear at Thebes, where genealogical inscriptions on funerary objects and temple statues show the descent of important posts in the administration and priesthood through many generations of local families. The appearance in genealogies at this period of the phrase *mi nen* ('the like-titled') before the names of ancestors is an indication that the passing of offices to successive generations had become commonplace. These families strengthened their own positions by intermarriage with other office-holding clans, creating powerful local élites who controlled provincial centres. Officials of traditional centralized government, such as the vizier and overseers of the treasury and granaries—who in the New Kingdom had constituted a check on the independence of the provinces—now wielded only local influence, or, as in the case of the southern viziers, were themselves members of the dominant provincial aristocracy.

Under these conditions, the independence of regional centres and the rise of collateral dynasties was virtually inevitable. The process of decentralization was most marked in the Delta. Here several provincial centres came under the control of Libyan chiefs, and some of these—notably Sais and Leontopolis—eventually eclipsed the pre-eminence of the 22nd Dynasty, whose sphere of influence was ultimately reduced to a small area focused around Tanis and Bubastis. The situation in Upper Egypt was analogous, althought this part of

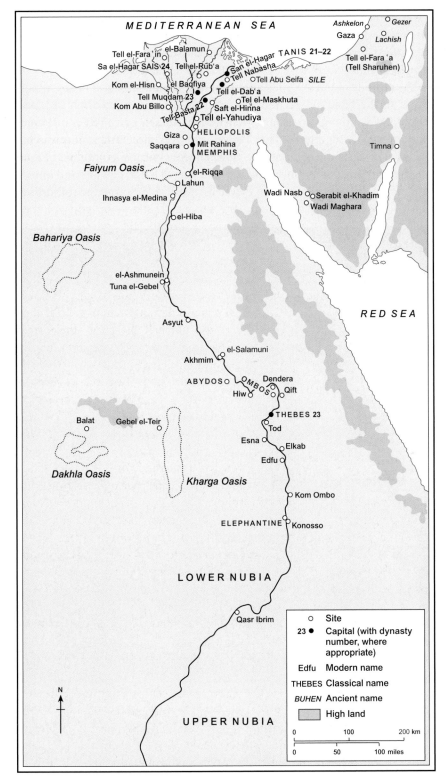

Two maps of Egypt, (*one facing*) showing the principal sites and political divisions at the beginning of the Third Intermediate Period (*c.*1069 BC), (*this page*) showing the major cities and dynastic centres in the late Third Intermediate Period (*c.*730 BC).

Map labels:

MEDITERRANEAN SEA

Ashkelon
Gezer
Gaza
Lachish

Tell el-Fara'in
el-Balamun
San el-Hagar TANIS 21–22
Sa el-Hagar SAIS 24 Tell el-Rub'a
Tell Nabasha
Tell el-Fara'a
(Tell Sharuhen)
Kom el-Hisn
el-Baqfiya
Tell Abu Seifa SILE
Tell Muqdam 23
Tell el-Dab'a
Kom Abu Billo
Saft el-Hinna
Tell-Basta 22
Tel el-Maskhuta
Tell el-Yahudiya
Giza
HELIOPOLIS
Timna
Saqqara
Mit Rahina
MEMPHIS

Faiyum Oasis
el-Riqqa
Lahun
Ihnasya el-Medina

Wadi Nasb
Serabit el-Khadim
Wadi Maghara

el-Hiba

Bahariya Oasis

el-Ashmunein
Tuna el-Gebel

RED SEA

Asyut

el-Salamuni
Akhmim

ABYDOS
Dendera
OMBOS
Qift
Hiw

Balat
Gebel el-Teir

THEBES 23
Tod
Esna
Elkab
Edfu

Dakhla Oasis

Kharga Oasis

Kom Ombo

ELEPHANTINE
Konosso

LOWER NUBIA

Qasr Ibrim

N

UPPER NUBIA

Legend:
○ Site
23 ● Capital (with dynasty number, where appropriate)
Edfu Modern name
THEBES Classical name
BUHEN Ancient name
▨ High land

0   100   200 km
0   50   100 miles

the country retained greater territorial cohesion than the north. Thebes was predominant throughout this entire period, its importance founded on its status as the main cult centre of Amun, and on its being the focus of the most powerful local élite.

The attitude of the kings to this progressive fragmentation is of key importance. In the First and Second Intermediate periods the division of power within Egypt among two or more rulers was definitely perceived as unacceptable; in the Third Intermediate Period, however, decentralization was not regarded consistently in a negative light. The long-term appointment of royal relatives to positions of power and the marrying of kings' daughters to important provincial governors may be viewed as measures to bolster the authority of

The distribution of Third Intermediate Period 'donation stelae', such as this example bearing a depiction of a Libu chief, may be an indication of the increasing exploitation of fresh areas of cultivable land as the Libyans gradually gained economic control of the Delta region.

the king; yet both produced the opposite effect, promoting decentralization by strengthening the power base of local rulers. It has been suggested that King Sheshonq III (825–773 BC), concerned at the waning authority of the 22nd Dynasty, intentionally established a collateral royal line, the 23rd Dynasty, as a means of retaining a measure of control over provincial élites. This is highly questionable, particularly in view of the debatable status of the 23rd Dynasty. A clearer picture emerges if it is assumed that decentralization was not only accepted but institutionalized as a form of government. The political picture that emerges as the Third Intermediate Period progresses is one of a federation of semi-autonomous rulers, nominally subject (and often related) to an over-lord–king. This is perhaps an example of the impact of the Libyan presence on the administration, since such a system can be seen as consistent with the patterns of rule in a semi-nomadic society such as theirs. In favour of this interpretation it should be noted that—despite the prominence of military titles and fortified settlements during this period—explicit references to internal conflict are limited and should not be interpreted as signs of a slide into anarchy.

Consideration of the political geography of Egypt in the Third Intermediate Period reveals indications of a north–south divide. Control of the north was almost entirely in the hands of the Libyans. Their influx was in fact crucial in the settlement and cultivation of the Delta: the Meshwesh occupied the principal towns of the eastern and central zones (Mendes, Bubastis, Tanis). The main influx of the Libu perhaps occurred later than that of the Meshwesh, and hence they settled on the less profitable western edge, around Imau. They ultimately founded the dynasty of Sais. Another group, the Mahasun, are found towards the south. The chronological and spatial distribution of 'donation stelae' perhaps reflects the progressive utilization of cultivable land, proceeding from the eastern and western edges of the Delta towards the centre, as areas previously unoccupied or uncultivated were taken over. The semi-autonomous status of centres such as Bubastis, Mendes, Sebennytos, and Diospolis was probably established during the early phase of Libyan settlement, and was retained throughout the succeeding centuries.

Upper Egypt was less fragmented than the Delta. While centres such as Hermopolis, Herakleopolis, el-Hiba, and Abydos were important, Thebes retained its pre-eminent status throughout the Third Intermediate Period. Southern resistance to the imposition of control from the north was a recurring feature of the tenth to the eighth centuries BC, with Thebes and its officials playing the leading role. There are signs of this already at the outset of the 22nd Dynasty; in inscriptions carved early in his reign, Sheshonq I holds the title 'chief of the Ma' rather than 'king'. Subsequently, entitlement to the post of high priest of Amun became a major source of contention. The claims of Prince Osorkon, son of Takelot II, to the pontificate provoked fierce resistance, the Thebans preferring to recognize the authority of the 23rd Dynasty kings Pedubastis I and Iuput I, and subsequently Osorkon III and his successors, rather than that of the Tanite pharaohs. Still later, the southern rulers made an alliance with Kush and continued to date inscriptions by the reigns of the Kushite monarchs even after their expulsion, indeed as late as the first years of Psamtek I (664–610 BC) of Sais.

Underlying the political north–south divide was an ethnic division. The evidence of names, titles, and genealogies reveals the population of the north as predominantly Libyan and that of the south as Egyptian. Reflections of this can also be detected in material culture. After the New Kingdom the evolution of the hieratic script used in business documents produced two divergent forms, demotic in the north and 'abnormal' hieratic at Thebes—an indication that the administration of the north had no appreciable impact on Thebes. Other linguistic changes confirm the indications of a breakdown of New Kingdom traditions; scribes of the Libyan period employed grammatical constructions and phonetic spellings that reflected current usage rather than tradition, and hieratic script was increasingly used in place of hieroglyphs in monumental inscriptions. These developments, particularly the last, are more common in the north and may reflect a lack of concern for tradition on the part of Libyans grappling with an unfamiliar idiom.

The ideology of kingship

The subordination of the temporal ruler to Amun, which was a key aspect of the theocracy, may have recommended itself to the Libyan rulers of the 21st Dynasty as a politically expedient means of securing divine sanction for their new regime. As noted in Chapter 10, the relationship between Amun and the king changed during the late New Kingdom. With the establishment of the theocracy in the 21st Dynasty, the political independence of the king reached its lowest point, and his executive authority scarcely exceeded that of the high priests. Indeed, while three of the Theban pontiffs adopted kingly titles, the pharaoh Psusennes I also appears as high priest of Amun, indications that the offices were closer to equality than ever before. The Thebans' assumption of royal attributes was restricted, for, although Herihor and Pinudjem I were depicted with kingly prerogatives (equal in stature to the gods, adorned with royal costume, and with names in cartouches), Herihor was shown so only in temple reliefs and on the funerary papyrus of his wife Nodjmet, while his royal prenomen is merely the title 'high priest of Amun'. The commander Menkheperra, son of Pinudjem I, merely used cartouches occasionally and was once depicted in kingly costume. Only Pinudjem I displayed fuller pretensions to pharaonic status and was buried with royal honours. This sporadic kingship may have been assumed mainly for cult purposes: since it was the king who was the point of contact between the world of men and that of the gods, a practically independent state such as that of Upper Egypt required someone to fulfil that role. By the beginning of the 22nd Dynasty, the Libyans were firmly entrenched in power, and hence the theocratic character of government was toned down. Sheshonq I and his successors re-emphasized the political authority of the king, but, when this weakened after c.850 BC, it was first the high priests at Thebes, and subsequently the 'god's wives of Amun' and their officials, rather than Amun himself, who wielded power.

Throughout the eleventh to eighth centuries BC the Libyan rulers made use of many of the outward manifestations of traditional pharaonic rule to assert their status as true Egyptian kings. They were depicted in pharaonic costume, with full fivefold titularies; the scene of the king smiting enemies before Amun (attested for Siamun and Sheshonq I) symbolized the traditional role of preserving *maat* (the ordered universe) by defeating Egypt's foes, and the holding of the *sed*-festival linked them to past generations of rulers. The *sed*-festival held at Bubastis in year 22 of Osorkon II (874–850 BC) was commemorated in reliefs on a specially built red granite gateway that show great adherence to ancient tradition in the forms of the ceremonies depicted. To lend greater legitimacy to the rule of foreigners, the royal ideology was developed along carefully selected lines. One of these developments is the more frequent assimilation of the king to the child Horus, son of Osiris and Isis, which is alluded to in the titularies of several Libyan kings from Sheshonq I onwards and finds a parallel in depictions of the pharaoh as a child suckled by a goddess. These phenomena were doubtless intended to reconcile the indigenous population to foreign rule; the Hyksos, Persians, and Ptolemies all found such assimilation politically useful. But, as noted above, the Libyans were never fully Egyptianized and, in spite of their pharaonic trappings, the kings preferred different patterns of rule to those of their New Kingdom precursors.

A clear instance of this is the Libyans' apparent tolerance of two or more 'kings' simultaneously, each entitled 'king of Upper and Lower Egypt', irrespective of their actual spheres of influence. This is not the only sign that the Libyans had adopted the trappings of Egyptian kingship without fully understanding it; in the New Kingdom great importance was attached to the composition of the royal titulary, which was different for each king and reflected a carefully devised programme for the reign. The titularies of the Libyan rulers, however, are characterized by a monotonous repetition of prenomina and royal epithets that frequently hinders the correct attribution of royal monuments of this period.

Not only is it more difficult to distinguish king from king; there is also a blurring of the distinction between the king and his subjects. The power structure in Egypt around 730 BC, as revealed by the 'victory stele' of Piy, shows chiefs of the Meshwesh on a footing of equality with kings, although without royal titles. A few decades later, at the end of Kushite rule, Assyrian records (the Rassam Cylinder) reveal a comparable situation, with all local governors grouped together irrespective of their titles. These include a 'king' (Nekau I (672–664 BC)), a 'great chief', a governor, and a vizier. The loss of the unique status of the king is manifested in numerous ways. In art, non-royal persons are depicted performing acts previously reserved for the king: a Libyan chief is depicted in a statuette kneeling and offering to a god; a relief shows another chief consecrating 'choice cuts' of meat on the altar to the gods of Mendes; a high priest of

Faience plaque showing a king (perhaps Iuput II) as a child-god emerging from a lotus.

Amun and a priest of lower rank offer the image of *maat* on stelae. The same phenomenon is reflected in economic sources, notably 'donation stelae'. In the New Kingdom such donations were undertaken only by the king; in the Third Intermediate Period numerous stelae record temple donations, and, while the donor is occasionally a king, in the majority of cases it is a Libyan chief or private individual. Even personal names can be revealing: Ankh-Pediese, named on a Serapeum stele as grandson of the Great Chief of the Meshwesh Pediese, bears a name that means 'May Pediese live', a commemoration of a Libyan chief in a context where usually only a royal person (king or 'god's wife of Amun') is named. Perhaps most remarkable of all is the intrusion of members of the king's retinue into their masters' burial place; the interment of General Wendjebauendjed in a chamber of the tomb of Psusennes I at Tanis would have been unthinkable in the New Kingdom, but now the king had more the character of a feudal overlord, supported by a network of close kinsmen and retainers whose ties with their master are prominent even in the grave.

The military in the Libyan period

After the New Kingdom, military power rather than bureaucratic control was a major basis of authority in Egypt. The new order was founded by army commanders, and the rulers of the southern principality throughout the whole of the 21st Dynasty were primarily generals. The appointments of the 22nd Dynasty rulers ensured that most provincial governors were army commanders, and the fact that these titles were not purely honorific is demonstrated by references to fortresses and garrisons under their command.

The building of fortresses is one of the best-documented activities of this period. Few of these are attested archaeologically by more than a few traces, but the locations of many are known from finds of bricks stamped with the names of the dedicators. This evidence shows that a whole series of fortresses was built in Upper Egypt during the 21st Dynasty (notably under Pinudjem I and Menkheperra). There was a particular concentration of these installations on the east bank of the Nile in northern middle Egypt: at el-Hiba, Sheikh Mubarek, and Tehna (Akoris). From these strongholds a careful watch could be maintained over Nile river traffic, and any local insurrections quickly crushed.

El-Hiba was more than just a lookout point and garrison. It was a frontier fort and the northern headquarters of the Upper Egyptian rulers during the 21st Dynasty. Papyrus letters of the period, mentioning the generals Piankh and Masaharta, have been found there, and the papyri bearing the literary compositions *Wenamun* and the *Tale of Woe*, as well as the *Onomasticon of Amenemope*, are probably from the same vicinity. The site continued to function as an important military headquarters under the 22nd Dynasty; a temple was built there by Sheshonq I and added to by Osorkon I. Still later, the place was used as an operational base by Prince Osorkon in his conflict with his Theban opponents.

Civilian settlements also appear to have acquired the character of military strongholds in the Third Intermediate Period. The administration of the Theban west bank took refuge in the fortified temple enclosure of Medinet Habu during the troubles at the end of the New Kingdom, and this apparently remained the high priests' residence during the 21st Dynasty. Nor was this an isolated instance. The account of Piy's campaign in *c.*730 BC shows that cities such as Hermopolis and Memphis were fortified and sufficiently strong to withstand a siege. The lifestyle of the Egyptians had evidently become habitually defensive in outlook.

The heavy concentration of troops along the Nile may have had its origins in the Libyan chiefs' determination to enforce their rule over Egypt. This, together with Thebes' well-documented resistance to external control, probably accounts for the siting of 21st Dynasty fortresses at such southerly locations as Qus and Gebelein, where they could scarcely have served to guard against attack from outside the Nile Valley. A rebellion in the Theban area occurred during the reign of Pinudjem I, but its nature is obscure. Indeed, it is only known from the stele set up by the high priest Menkheperra to commemorate the pardoning of some of the miscreants and their recall from the oasis to which they had been exiled as punishment. The struggles of Prince Osorkon against Theban rebels over a century later demonstrated the continued need for military force to retain authority in this area.

The relatively unadventurous foreign policy of Egypt's rulers in the Third Intermediate Period can be seen as the logical counterpart to the internal situation. Under a progressively decentralized regime, and with a substantial part of the available military force required to keep order within Egypt, the concentration of military effort and economic resources necessary to pursue a consistent expansionist policy abroad probably could not be achieved.

Economy and control of resources in the 21st–24th Dynasties
The period covered by the 21st to 24th Dynasties is conspicuous for the sparsity of large-scale royal stone monuments of the kind erected during the New Kingdom. Except for those at Tanis, royal building works were mainly confined to minor additions and repairs to existing structures. This reduced level of activity coincides with the extensive recycling of monuments and materials, a phenomenon particularly obvious at Tanis, where much of the stonework—blocks, columns, obelisks, statues—was brought from Piramesse and other sites, and reinscribed or simply re-erected without modification. Judged against the productions of other periods, these factors could be considered as signs of a weak economy. There is indeed no doubt that the Third Intermediate Period began at a time of economic stress, and, as far as can be discerned, revenues from the Levant and the African interior were much reduced during this period by comparison with what had been available during the New Kingdom.

There are, however, a number of indications that Egypt's economy did not remain seriously weak throughout this entire period. The unambitious nature of royal building projects and the high dependence on reused materials in the

Third Intermediate Period can be plausibly explained by the politically fragmented state of the country. Without a centralized administration under a single ruler it was no longer possible to manage Egypt's resources efficiently or to mobilize huge labour forces of the kind that had built the Memphite pyramids or the temples of Karnak. It is significant that the relatively brief phase of strong centralized government (the reigns of Sheshonq I to Osorkon II) coincided with the erection of several of the most substantial royal monuments of the time: the Bubastite Portal at Karnak and the 'festival hall' of Osorkon II at Bubastis.

Concerning the state of the agricultural economy at this period, information is very limited. A few papyri (including Papyrus Reinhardt) and the donation stelae are the only sources. These latter, however, are very interesting; the majority date from the 22nd and 23rd Dynasties, and they record the assignation of land to temples in order to establish endowments for funerary cults. The large numbers of these stelae that have been found in the north indicate that the productivity of agricultural land remained sufficient to enable a surplus to be available for such purposes. As noted above, the distribution of these stelae also indicates that substantial areas of the western and central Delta were being newly brought under cultivation.

There is also evidence that other forms of wealth were not lacking. The burial goods of the 21st and 22nd Dynasty kings found in the royal tombs at Tanis included substantial quantities of gold and silver, while an inscription from Bubastis recording the dedication by Osorkon I of statues and cult utensils to the temples of Egypt lists the equivalent of over 391 tons of gold and silver objects—all apparently presented during the first four years of the king's reign. A proportion of this, it has been postulated, may represent the booty from Sheshonq I's Palestinian campaign of a few years earlier, while some of it was perhaps recycled material extracted from New Kingdom tombs. Nevertheless, an economy in which so much bullion could be economically neutralized through consecration to deities could only have been a healthy one.

The recycling of resources undoubtedly played a part in keeping the state's coffers full. This was probably the principal reason (rather than pious regard for the dead) for the dismantling of the New Kingdom royal burials at Thebes during the 21st Dynasty. The mummies of the kings and their wives and families were removed from their tombs, stripped of almost all their valuables, and reburied in groups in unobtrusive and easily guarded caches. The hieratic dockets on coffins and shrouds that record these actions show that they were carried out on the authority of the ruling generals, while hundreds of rock graffiti written by the necropolis scribe Butehamun and his colleagues testify to the systematic searching-out and clearing of old tombs. Much precious metal was doubtless melted down for reuse, but some items seem to have been appropriated for the burials of the Tanite kings; pectorals found on the mummy of Psusennes I bear a strong resemblance to New Kingdom examples such as those from the tomb of Tutankhamun, and there are traces of altered names in some of the cartouches. Items of substantial size were also recycled. A granite sarcophagus was extracted from the tomb of Merenptah and transported to Tanis to be reinscribed for the burial of Psusennes I. The wooden coffins of Thutmose I were refurbished and used again to house the mummy of Pinudjem I. In this instance mere thrift may have been of less import to Pinudjem than the opportunity offered to associate himself directly with one of the great kings of Egypt's past, thereby lending ideological support to his own somewhat unorthodox claim to pharaonic status. Curiously, what may have begun as a prerogative of the Theban rulers alone was soon widespread; in the 21st Dynasty a high proportion of coffins used for burials at Thebes were reinscribed and reused within a short time of the original burial—probably illicitly: a docket written on a coffin in the British Museum records its restoration to the true owner after necropolis workers had been caught in the act of usurping it.

Kushite Rule (the 25th Dynasty, 747–664 BC)

For events in Nubia between the end of the New Kingdom and the early eighth century BC, evidence is extremely meagre. Although the suggestion that Lower Nubia was depopulated during this period is probably an exaggeration, the population may have been less prosperous than in earlier times and perhaps reverted to a semi-nomadic economy or migrated to the more prosperous south. Sporadic references to viceroys of Kush during the 21st–23rd Dynasties indicate that some Egyptian pretensions to authority there were maintained, and elements of royal titularies and formal epithets from temple inscriptions in Egypt have been adduced as supportive evidence for an aggressive policy to regain Upper Nubia—but, if this were the case, there was no lasting effect.

The Rise of Kush

There is no evidence from Nubia itself for any provincial government or campaign at this time. In fact, inscriptions from Nubia suggest that, following the withdrawal of Egyptian authority at the end of the New Kingdom, several local power groups arose, perhaps maintaining a degree of continuity at the pharaonic administrative and religious installations. It was probably these groups that were responsible for a small number of hieroglyphic inscriptions and reliefs in the Egyptian iconographic tradition, apparently dating from this period; the reliefs of Queen Karimala in the New Kingdom temple at Semna are a case in point.

The most important of these indigenous polities arose in the area downstream of the fourth cataract. The earliest of their rulers were buried at el-Kurru. Although the exact sequence of the tombs is uncertain, a clear evolution in the arrangements for the burials is apparent. The earlier tombs are strongly Nubian in character, having a circular tumulus or *mastaba*-style superstructure over a burial pit, which contained the corpse laid on bed. Later tombs are characterized by more Egyptian-inspired features (*mastaba* superstructure accom-

panied by offering chapel, all within an enclosure wall). El-Kurru may have been the original power base of these rulers, since a settlement with defensive walls has been identified there, but by the late eighth century BC their political and religious focus had shifted to Napata, close to the great rocky outcrop of Gebel Barkal. During the New Kingdom, this had been the centre of the cult of Amun in Nubia, and the worship of the state god of Egypt became a defining feature of the Kushite ruling élite. By the mid-eighth century the chieftains of Napata had become overlords of Nubia and were already entertaining pretensions to rule Egypt as well.

Facing: faience statuette of King Osorkon II kneeling to present an offering.

Inset: this gold vessel inlaid with coloured paste belonged to the 21st Dynasty general Wendjebauendjed, who was one of the individuals buried in Tomb III at Tanis.

The Kushite takeover of Egypt

Direct contact with Egypt was renewed around 750 BC. Kashta, the first ruler of Kush of whom contemporary records survive, appears to have been recognized as king throughout Nubia and as far north as Aswan, where a stele was erected showing him as 'King of Upper and Lower Egypt'. The inward-looking nature of Egypt's government probably facilitated these advances. Under Piy, son of Kashta, some form of agreement was perhaps reached with the 23rd Dynasty rulers recognized in the Theban area. Piy's authority was acknowledged and his sister Amenirdis I was adopted by the 'god's wife of Amun' Shepenwepet I as her successor. These preliminary steps were followed around 730 BC by a more overt demonstration of power in the form of a Kushite military expedition. According to the vivid description provided by Piy's triumphal stele from Gebel Barkal, the campaign was prompted by the rapid territorial expansion of Tefnakht of Sais. Having taken control of the entire western Delta and the Memphite area, this powerful prince was extending his influence over the towns and cities of northern Upper Egypt. Nimlot, petty king of Hermopolis, joined forces with Tefnakht, but another 'king', Peftjauawybast, having declared loyalty to Piy, was besieged in his city of Herakleopolis. Piy's forces advanced down the Nile, pausing at Thebes to offer homage to Amun, before relieving Peftjauawybast and capturing Hermopolis. Most of the other towns and cities along the river capitulated, but Memphis offered stubborn resistance and had to be taken by storm. Piy, however, with conspicuous reverence for the religious traditions of Egypt, took care that the temples there should be protected from looting or desecration. Having adored the gods at Memphis and Heliopolis, Piy received the homage of the provincial rulers, who acknowledged his authority over Egypt as well as Kush.

Piy spent the remainder of his reign in Nubia and at his death was buried at

The upper part of the triumphal stele of the Kushite ruler Piy from Gebel Barkal shows the provincial rulers of Egypt standing and prostrating themselves before Piy (whose figure was later erased).

el-Kurru in a tomb of strongly Egyptian character, with a pyramid superstructure and a burial outfit including *shabti*-figures. Quite un-Egyptian, however, was the interment nearby of a team of chariot horses, a feature also associated with the burials of Piy's successors, and evidently a distinctively Kushite practice. In the years that followed, the situation in the Theban area probably remained stable. The installation of Amenirdis as 'god's wife of Amun'—doubtless with the support of a Kushite retinue—lent weight to the influence of the Nubian rulers in the area. In the north, however, the local dynasts were left in control of their provinces, and under Tefnakht of Sais and his successor Bakenrenef the 24th Dynasty resumed its territorial expansion. Thus provoked, the new Kushite ruler Shabaqo reconquered Egypt in about 716 BC, and forcibly imposed his authority over the provincial governors.

The rule of the Kushite monarchs

The fundamental basis of Kushite rule was military power. Close links between the king and his army are apparent throughout the 25th Dynasty. The devotion of Piy's troops to their master is constantly stressed in the text of his triumphal stele, and physical prowess and military training were held to be of importance both to the rulers themselves and to their soldiers. Hence the young Taharqo was present in person at the battle of Eltekeh (701 BC), while a stele from Dahshur recounts details of a gruelling military exercise organized by the same king in the desert between Memphis and the Faiyum. However, in spite of the strength of their armed forces, the Kushite kings perhaps felt unequal to the task of controlling both their native land and a unified Egypt. This may have influenced their toleration of a decentralized administration within Egypt, since the principalities that had enjoyed near-autonomy under the Libyan pharaohs retained their individuality throughout the rule of the Kushites. Hence in the early seventh century BC Tanis was still ruled by local princes, some of whom boasted royal titles, a situation that is reflected in the demotic cycle of stories centring on a King Pedubast of Tanis—what connection (if any) these Tanite rulers had with the old royal line of the 22nd Dynasty remains unknown. The Saite principality too survived, ultimately to reunite Egypt under Psamtek I. At Thebes the office of 'god's wife of Amun' steadily increased in importance, constituting a valuable support for the authority of the king; other traditionally powerful offices, such as that of vizier, continued but were deprived of effective power. The post of high priest of Amun, so often a source of tension in previous years, had apparently remained vacant during the later eighth century but was now reinstated, and assigned once more to a king's son. Significantly, however, the holder wielded little or no civil or military power. Local influence in Upper Egypt increasingly devolved on those who held the office of governor of Thebes or belonged to the retinue of the 'god's wife'. In the early phase of Kushite rule Nubian retainers of the royal house were appointed to some of these major posts in the civil and religious administration at Thebes—only to be replaced after a few years by scions of local families.

Under the Kushites, the ideology of kingship was modified. Small but significant changes were made to royal iconography: a double uraeus was regularly depicted on the king's headband; the blue crown ceased to be shown, while the cap crown became common in depictions, both in its basic form and with additional bands—a distinctively Kushite headgear. Innovations are also apparent in the mode of transmission of kingship; whereas in Egypt royal succession had been patrilinear, in Kush a king was not necessarily succeeded by his son, but sometimes by his brother. Such a system certainly operated during the 25th Dynasty, both Piy and Shabitqo (702–690 BC) being succeeded by brothers. In spite of these divergences from Egyptian norms, however, the Kushite rulers sought to strengthen their legitimacy by posing as champions of ancient tradition. Hence Memphis became their chief royal residence; a stele from Kawa records that Taharqo was crowned at Memphis, and Shabaqo, Shabitqo, and Taharqo are all known to have carried out building works there. This made excellent political sense (Tanis being too remote geographically to serve as the focus for a united Egypt), but there were also sound ideological reasons for boosting the importance of the Memphite area, for in this way the Kushite pharaohs could associate themselves directly with the great rulers of the Old Kingdom. Royal tombs in Kush were constructed in pyramid form. Scenes in temple T at Kawa were copied by Memphite artists from Old Kingdom royal mortuary temples at Saqqara and Abusir (the inclusion at Kawa of a scene of Taharqo as a sphinx defeating Libyan foes—although based on Old Kingdom models—may well have been intended to emphasize the Kushites' triumph over Egypt's former rulers).

The verbose and monotonous royal titularies of the Libyan Period were replaced by simpler ones recalling the style of the Old Kingdom—the prenomen of Taharqo (Khunefertemra) also assimilating the king to the Memphite god Nefertem. The high status of the god Ptah was also reaffirmed through the preservation of the cosmological text known as the *Memphite Theology of Creation*. This inscription, allegedly copied from a decayed papyrus on the orders of Shabaqo, was carved on a basalt slab now in the British Museum; the text gives primacy to Ptah as creator of the universe. At the same time, the devotion to Amun which was so conspicuous a feature of the Kushite monarchy continued to be emphasized, with extensive renovations and additions made to the temples of Thebes and promotion also of Amun's role as creator-god, as emphasized in the form and decoration of a remarkable structure erected by Taharqo close to the sacred lake at Karnak.

Cross-cultural links: Egypt and Kush
The Kushite rulers had already absorbed a measure of Egyptian culture before Piy, as is shown by the design of the later tombs at el-Kurru. The sources of this influence in the early stages of the kingdom are unknown, but commercial contacts, together with some survival of Egyptian cult practices at Gebel Barkal, may have been significant. These tendencies developed further after the

intensification of contacts during the eighth century, and by the time of Kashta a strong Egyptianization of the ruler is apparent in iconography. Throughout the 25th Dynasty the rulers and the élite were depicted in Egyptian dress, adopted Egyptian burial practices, and professed devotion to Egyptian gods. This acculturation remained a key component of Kushite culture for centuries after the Nubians had relinquished control of Egypt.

The Kushite absorption of Egyptian material culture is most apparent in royal monuments. Both in Egypt and Nubia, temples were constructed according to Egyptian architectural traditions, with careful observance of the appropriate artistic canons and use of hieroglyphic script and Egyptian language in inscriptions. Although buried in their homeland, the rulers constructed tombs in the Egyptian style, each with a pyramid superstructure, an offering chapel to the east, and a vaulted burial chamber adorned with scenes and texts from the New Kingdom repertoire of 'books of the netherworld'. Their bodies were mummified and provided with anthropoid coffins, canopic jars, and *shabti*-figures.

As was the case with the Libyans, the effects of acculturation probably conceal the origin of many Kushites living in Egypt at this period, yet they too retained features of their ethnic identity. The rulers retained their Kushite birth names, despite adopting Egyptian names for the remainder of their titulary. Distinctive un-Egyptian names (Irigadiganen, Kelbasken) also mark out several other officials of the period as Kushites, while some took Egyptian names and retained their original Nubian names as well. Kushite ethnic features, including distinctive southern physiognomies, dark skin-colouring, and 'bobbed' feminine hairstyles are sometimes depicted in sculpture, painting, and relief. The cultural exchange, however, was almost entirely a one-way process, for very little that was Kushite was taken over into Egyptian material culture, and even that little was not retained permanently. The characteristic regalia of the Kushite rulers disappeared after the 25th Dynasty, as did other innovations such as the occasional depiction of the goddesses Isis and Nephthys with a close-cropped 'Nubian' hairstyle on funerary monuments.

The 25th Dynasty as a period of renewal

As part of their drive to obtain legitimacy as pharaohs, the Kushite rulers evinced deep respect for Egyptian religious traditions. They remodelled the ideology of the king—drawing inspiration from the distant past, as seen in their royal titularies, their burial style, and their promotion of the city of Memphis—and they made deliberate reference to the Old Kingdom. These associations were part of a much wider and deep-rooted revival of things past that affected many aspects of Egypt's court culture, religion, script, literature, art, architecture, and burial practices during the first millennium BC. Such 'archaism'—a turning to classic ages of the past as a source of new creative energy—was not new; it is a recurrent feature in Egyptian culture. In this instance it had its origins in the later Libyan period, having begun during the first half of the eighth century BC. Already in the late 22nd and 23rd Dynasties royal titularies show a progressive simplification, and imitation of Old and Middle Kingdom models begins to be apparent in royal iconography and funerary practices. The Kushites (perhaps lacking suitable indigenous traditions in their homeland) took up this trend actively. Archaism thus accelerated during the late eighth and early seventh centuries, becoming fully synthesized in the 26th Dynasty, with which period the trend is more usually associated.

By the 25th Dynasty, artists had revived the Old Kingdom canon of proportions for representing two-dimensional figures, with a reduction in the size of the squares in the grid system used by draughtsmen. Statues, both royal and private, also imitated older models; hence, among the many sculptures commissioned for the Theban governor Mentuemhat are examples copying the striding-male figures of the Old Kingdom and the seated cloaked statuettes typical of the Middle Kingdom. In burial customs, the funerary assemblage, which had been simplified under the 21st and 22nd Dynasties (see below), was enriched in the second half of the eighth century, with the revival of older features, and notably the return—in a revised form—of the *Book of the Dead*, as well as the introduction of new iconographic features (often incorporating archaic elements) for coffins and tombs.

As noted above, the escalation of archaism in the eighth and seventh centuries probably owes something to the aim of foreign rulers to be accepted as Egyptians. An additional factor, however, was a desire to preserve the past through copying earlier monuments. The most explicit reference to this is the introduction to the *Memphite Theology of Creation*, on the 'Shabaqo Stone', which relates how the king found the text on a worm-eaten papyrus and ordered it to be transcribed for posterity. Whether or not this statement is literally true, the intention to preserve the integrity of an ancient text was reflected through conscious imitation of the format, wording, and spelling of early documents.

The widespread reuse of older material in the 21st and 22nd Dynasties had enabled craftsmen to study and copy earlier models, and the greater productivity in temple and tomb construction fostered throughout

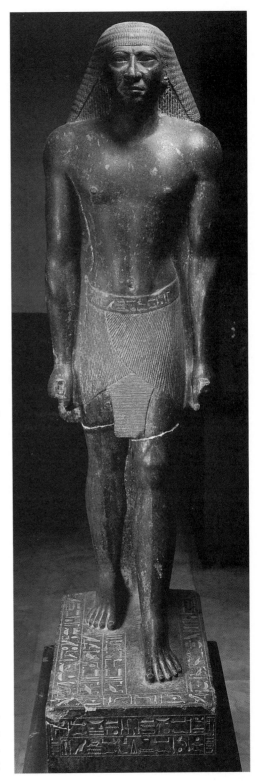

Egypt by the 25th Dynasty rulers provided an opportunity to express these new tendencies more fully. This was doubtless one of the main methods by which older models were transmitted, although the possibility exists that 'pattern books', copied repeatedly over the centuries, may also have played a part. Direct slavish copying was, however, rare. Even when a 25th Dynasty relief can be compared with an Old Kingdom model, as in the sphinx scene of Taharqo (mentioned above), there are some elements of innovation, and one cannot rule out the hypothetical role of lost intermediary copies in the transmission of such scenes over a long time span. As the example of Mentuemhat's statues demonstrates, the revivalism of the 25th Dynasty and later periods was characterized by an eclectic approach to sources. Many works of art mingle elements drawn from models of different periods, the 25th Dynasty showing a preference for the Old and Middle kingdoms, rather than New Kingdom models. This melding of different influences is apparent even within individual works: statues of Taharqo and Tanutamani (664–656 BC) from Gebel Barkal have the strongly modelled bodies and simple costumes typical of the Old Kingdom, while their torsos display the median line characteristic of sculptures created in the Middle Kingdom.

Kush and Assyria

Although centralized government had not been restored in Egypt by the Kushite monarchs, their authority as overlords enabled them to adopt a more active policy with regard to the Levant than had any of the Libyan kings since Sheshonq I. This led to conflict with Assyria, whose forces had taken over Babylonia and sections of the east Mediterranean coast during the eighth century BC. Although Kushite interference in Palestine was to lead ultimately to the Assyrian conquest of Egypt, a threat to the country's independence certainly existed. Fighting began when an army composed of Egyptians and Nubians advanced into southern Palestine in support of Hezekiah of Judah, and clashed with the forces of Sennacherib at Eltekeh in 701 BC. The Egyptian army was defeated, but this did not deter provincial rulers in Egypt from supporting other foreign princes in their resistance to Assyria. Thus provoked, the Assyrian king Esarhaddon turned his attention to the conquest of Egypt. A first invasion attempt in 674 BC was repulsed; a second, led by Esarhaddon in person, succeeded. Memphis was captured, and Taharqo fled to Nubia, leaving his wife and son as captives in the hands of the conquerors. Rather than attempt to govern Egypt themselves, the Assyrians withdrew, having first required the rulers of the Delta principalities to swear oaths to support Assyrian authority and to prevent any attempt by the Kushites to regain control of Egypt. Among these vassals was Nekau (Necho) of Sais, whose son Psamtek (the future Psamtek I) was conducted to Nineveh to receive instruction in Assyrian customs, before being returned to act as ruler of Athribis. None the less, Taharqo quickly recovered control of Egypt. A resurgence of Egypto-Kushite power (with the possibility of further interference in Palestine) could not be tolerated by the

Assyrians, and in 667 BC Ashurbanipal, son and successor of Esarhaddon, invaded Egypt. Taharqo again fled to Nubia, and the Egyptian dynasts submitted to the Assyrians. A subsequent plot to reinstate Taharqo failed and the Egyptian vassals who had been involved in it were executed. Nekau of Sais had abstained from supporting the Kushites, and his position was further strengthened by his appointment as governor of Memphis.

Taharqo died in Nubia in 664 BC and was buried beneath a pyramid tomb at Nuri, a new royal necropolis located opposite Gebel Barkal. His successor, Tanutamani, promptly invaded Egypt and defeated the Delta vassals who supported Assyria. This action brought very strong retaliation from Nineveh. A large army was dispatched to Egypt; the entire northern part of the country was quickly subdued, and the Assyrians advanced as far as Thebes, which they sacked and plundered. Tanutamani was expelled and returned to Nubia. The Kushite rulers, although maintaining nominal claims to authority over Egypt for several generations, were never afterwards able to put them into effect. However, the bloodshed and destruction that followed from the Kushite opposition to Assyria proved to be a cloud with a silver lining: it emphasized the necessity for military and civil cooperation by the rulers of the principalities, if independence was to be regained, and brought to power an exceptional individual who possessed the resources and abilities to liberate Egypt and lead it into a new phase.

Psamtek I of Sais, son of Necho, was among the vassal rulers left by the Assyrians to control the provinces. During his long reign he threw off the Assyrian yoke and succeeded, where the Kushites had failed, in reuniting the whole of Egypt under his sole command. It is only at this point that the Third Intermediate Period can be said to be at an end, with Egypt poised once more to reap the benefits of a centralized government controlled by a strong king.

Religion and Material Culture in the Third Intermediate Period

While there appears to have been considerable continuity in the practice of the temple cult throughout the pharaonic period, two factors distinguish its performance in the Third Intermediate Period—the diminished importance of the king and the prominence of women in cult activities. One aspect of the loss of the unique status of the king (see above) was that the performance of the temple ritual—essential to the preservation of the ordered universe—was no longer his sole prerogative; from the end of the New Kingdom it was increasingly the clergy who carried out this task. This, together with the hereditary character of priestly office throughout this period, contributed greatly to the solidarity of this section of society. Full-time priests were now usual, and pluralism enabled them to amass lucrative offices. The culmination of this trend was the unprecedented prominence of the high priest of Amun during the 21st–23rd Dynasties, at which period his power was augmented by civil and military authority. However, as has been noted above, the excessive influence of this individual had a destabilizing effect on the country, and the primacy of the post was eclipsed in the eighth century BC—religious authority at Thebes becoming increasingly centred on the 'god's wife of Amun', while civil and military powers were distributed to others.

Temple cult and personnel

The prominence of women in the temple cult was already well established in the 21st Dynasty, when several important religious offices were fulfilled by the wives and daughters of the high priests at Thebes. The most important of these posts was that of 'first great chief of the musical troupe of Amun'. While the precise religious significance of this office is unclear, it is not a coincidence that these high-ranking women also held titles relating to the importance of goddesses such as Mut and Hathor, each of whom were held to be instrumental in Amun's perpetuating the creative process, and hence in ensuring the continuation of the cosmos.

The post of 'chief of the musical troupe' disappeared during the 22nd Dynasty, and in its place there was a major development of the office of 'god's wife of Amun' (or divine adoratrice). Her principal religious function was to stimulate the god's procreative urges, and thereby to ensure the fertility of the land and the cyclical repetition of creation. In the Third Intermediate Period this post was usually filled by the daughter of a king or high priest, who was installed at Thebes. In contrast to the situation in the New Kingdom, when the office could be held by the king's wife, the 'god's wives' of the Third Intermediate Period were expected to be celibate, an innovation perhaps associated with the establishment of the theocratic state. As noted above, there was undoubtedly a political dimension to this. The rise of the 'god's wife' coincided with the decline of the power of the high priest of Amun, and may have been promoted as a measure to solve the 'problem' of Theban secessionism, for, while the 'god's wife' enabled the distant royal house to be represented at Thebes, her celibacy meant that no subdynasty could arise (successors being adopted). Consequently, the status of the 'god's wife' continued to rise and the adoption system persisted until the end of the 26th Dynasty.

The increase in importance of the 'god's wife' during the Third Intermediate Period is clear: from the 23rd Dynasty her status begins to approach that of the king, and in the 25th Dynasty she appears with greater prominence on monuments. The iconography extends beyond the traditional depiction of the 'god's wife' as shaking sistra. In the reliefs at the Karnak Osiris chapels and those of the 'god's wives' themselves at Medinet Habu they are seen in roles previously reserved for the king: offering to deities (including presenting *maat*), being embraced by gods, libating the image of the god, conducting foundation ceremonies, and receiving attributes of kingship from the gods. Thus Amenirdis I receives jubilee symbols from Thoth, while Shepenwepet I has her headdress adjusted by Amun, is suckled by a goddess, and is even shown wearing two double crowns simultaneously, a unique depiction. As fragmentary reliefs from

North Karnak show, the 'god's wife' could even celebrate the *sed*-festival, otherwise only attested for the king.

The 'god's wife' was the head of a 'domain of the divine adoratrice'. This employed a substantial personnel, including 'singers of the interior [chambers] of Amun' (celibate priestesses who were sometimes of high rank); inscriptions mention one who was a daughter of Takelot II and another whose father was a Delta Libyan chief. The domain also included priests and scribes and was headed by a 'chief steward'. Through the escalating importance of the 'god's wife' and her entourage, these stewards became powerful and influential figures at Thebes towards the end of the 25th Dynasty (as their elaborate tombs in the Asasif testify), and they were to play a key role in the reintegration of the south into a fully unified Egypt under the 26th Dynasty.

It is no coincidence that the prominent role played by high-ranking women in religious cults in the 21st Dynasty was often in connection with child-gods such as Horpakhered or Khons. Among their many titles these ladies were 'nurses' or 'divine mothers' of these gods, and the Third Intermediate Period

Scene of offerings being made to the 'god's wife of Amun' Amenirdis I in her funerary chapel at Medinet Habu. When Shepenwepet I adopted Amenirdis I as her successor, the Kushite ruler Piy was able to increase his influence over Upper Egypt. Both 25th and 26th Dynasty rulers preserved this crucial hold over Thebes by ensuring that Kushite and Saite princesses continued to be adopted as 'god's wives'.

marks the early stages in the growth of emphasis on the mother–child relationship in Egyptian religion, which was to become one of the pervading aspects of life in Egypt during the remainder of the first millennium BC. A major manifestation of this 'mammisiac' religion is the importance increasingly attached to divine triads, with the child-god (identifiable with the king) as offspring of two other deities. Two of the most prominent of these triads were those composed of Isis, Osiris, and Horus; and of Amun, Mut, and Khons, both already important in the Third Intermediate Period. The rise in importance of Osiris at this time is clear from the development of cult places dedicated to him at Thebes. Among the most familiar images from ancient Egypt which first come to prominence in the Third Intermediate Period are those of Isis nursing Horus, and the child Horus standing on crocodiles, triumphing over harmful forces (found chiefly on the magical stelae known as *cippi*). The rise in the importance of these deities—and particularly myths about the childhood of Horus in the marshes of the Delta—may be due in part to the dominant influence of Delta-based rulers at this period. Indeed, close links between mammisiac religion and the kingship are apparent; several rulers from Sheshonq I to Taharqo were depicted in temple reliefs and on small objects as nude children suckled by a goddess (such as Hathor or Bastet)—a scene that symbolized the transfer of kingship to a new ruler, rebirth being considered an appropriate metaphor for this rite of passage.

Throughout the Third Intermediate Period the cult of the Apis bull of Memphis was maintained irrespective of the repeated changes in authority over the city, as the burials in the Serapeum at Saqqara, with their abundant votive stelae, testify. It is at this time, too, that the association of certain animals with other deities first becomes marked—a trend that was to culminate in the animal cults of the Late Period with their legacy of vast numbers of bronze votive statuettes, and catacombs filled with millions of animal and bird mummies.

Burial practices

The political and cultural developments occurring in Egypt during this period are amply reflected in the manner of treatment accorded to the dead. Particularly noticeable are changes in the location of burials and in the types of tombs. For the élite, the old physical isolation of the necropolis was replaced by burial within the enclosure of a cult temple. Since the royal tombs at Tanis are the earliest (and best-documented) examples, this trend may have been an innovation by the 21st Dynasty kings, and was perhaps motivated partly by the intention to make Tanis a northern counterpart to Thebes. While the practice is most conspicuous for kings, it also extended to persons of high rank—the high priests at Memphis, whose tombs were constructed on the edge of the precinct of the temple of Ptah; Queen Kama, buried at Leontopolis near Bubastis; a high official buried adjacent to the enclosure wall of the temple at Tell Balamun. Whether or not the tendency had a Delta origin, it was soon manifested at Thebes, where high officials began to be buried within the precincts of Medinet

Habu and the Ramesseum. These locations, besides offering greater security from robbery, were a means of establishing closer proximity to the gods. The siting of the burials of 'King' Harsiese and the later 'god's wives' at Medinet Habu may also have been influenced by local cult activities: during the Third Intermediate Period, the Small Temple there became closely associated with the 'Mound of Djeme', where rituals relating to the creative powers of Amun took place.

The tombs themselves were much simpler structures than those of the New Kingdom. The period witnessed an interruption of the tradition of expending substantial resources on elaborate superstructures and labyrinthine rock-cut sepulchres. Both royal and élite tombs were reduced to small subterranean burial chambers with modest chapels directly above. Private tomb chapels are not well documented archaeologically, and seem to have been rare. Some have doubtless disappeared through poor preservation, yet there is little evidence for their existence outside the principal centres of Tanis, Memphis, and Thebes. The rarity of individual chapels coincides with a rise in the number and scale of communal burials, usually situated in older tombs or disused religious structures. The gathering of the New Kingdom royal mummies and the 21st Dynasty priests of Amun into caches in older tombs during the eleventh and tenth centuries BC seems to mark the beginning of this pattern. Throughout the period, persons of all ranks were buried in groups at sites throughout Egypt (there are examples at Saqqara, Herakleopolis, Akhmim, Thebes, and Aswan), and, where prosopographical data exist, as at Thebes, such grouping can often be shown to be family orientated.

There was a significant reduction in the quantity and range of burial paraphernalia. The fittings of the tomb chapel (such as statues and offering tables) all but disappeared, as did household furniture; clothing; tools and weapons and occupational equipment; musical instruments; games; and stone and pottery vessels. Apart from a small stele, usually of painted wood, the burial equipment was generally confined to a narrow range of purely funerary items—coffins, canopic containers (usually dummies), amulets, *shabtis*, and funerary papyri (one usually secreted within an Osirian statuette). The period is also marked by a steady decline and, eventually, a break in the tradition of providing funerary texts. While élite burials at Thebes in the 21st Dynasty continued to use the *Book of the Dead*, and even added the *Amduat* and *Litany of Ra* to the non-royal repertoire, these traditions were allowed to atrophy in the 22nd Dynasty. Funerary papyri ceased to be produced and texts on coffins were reduced to little more than repetitive offering formulas and speeches of gods, with a corresponding simplification of the iconographic repertoire.

These factors seem to reflect major changes in attitudes to death and burial in the Libyan Period. The lack of imposing tomb superstructures (even the most elaborate could have been built quickly) indicates that burial was no longer so carefully anticipated and prepared for. The *ad hoc* nature of tomb construction (roughly pieced together, often from reused blocks) supports this, and, significantly, this description applies especially to tombs in the Libyan-dominated north and in middle Egypt: at Tanis, Memphis, Leonto-polis, and Herakleopolis. Substantial items of burial equipment such as stone sarcophagi were almost confined to royalty, and even these few examples were mostly reused from earlier periods. This recycling of funerary objects extended to less costly items—notably in the 21st Dynasty, when extensive reuse of coffins occurred at Thebes. Yet Egypt did not lack material wealth, and the decentralization of the land in no way brought a decline in the skills of sculp-tors, painters, and metalworkers (see below). The changed attitude to the dead that these factors suggest may perhaps be more directly associated with the presence of the Libyans in society. Constructing an elaborate physical environ-ment for the dead and a focus for mortuary cults was doubtless not a major fea-ture of semi-nomadic societies such as theirs. Significantly, it was only with the imposition of authority by the Kushite rulers—whose devotion to the ancient traditions of Egypt was of a rather purist kind—that a revitalization of burial practices along traditional lines occurred.

This shift of emphasis away from the physical housing of the dead brought with it a greater concentration on the body itself and its immediate trappings. Mummification reached its peak in the 21st Dynasty and high standards of preparation were maintained throughout the succeeding period. Among the innovations were the use of subcutaneous packing to restore the shrunken fea-tures to lifelike form, more elaborate cosmetic treatments, with hair carefully arranged and finger nails meticulously preserved, and a more careful preserva-tion of the viscera, which were individually wrapped and returned to the body cavity (canopic jars continued to be provided but were often mere dummies). These techniques manifest a desire to make the body as complete and perfect as possible. Its status as an idealized image of the transfigured deceased was devel-oped, and its security further ensured by an increase in the number of coffins per burial—at least two and sometimes as many as four.

The decline in the production of individual tomb chapels with elaborate wall decoration led to a relocation of essential funerary images and texts on the sur-faces of the coffin and on papyri. Hence 21st Dynasty coffins were covered inside and out with a densely packed profusion of images. The priests of Thebes created a rich new repertoire of funerary iconography promoting the concept of rebirth through the combined mythologies of Osiris and the sun-god, and the images were devised with a view to concentrating multiple levels of mean-ing in a single complex scene. In keeping with the caching of burials and the general impermanence of the resting place at this time, the coffin took on the religious functions of the tomb, as it had under similar circumstances in the First Intermediate Period. By the end of the Third Intermediate Period the evo-lution of the surface imagery had given still greater prominence to the concept of the coffin as a miniature universe, with the deceased at the centre, identified (through the texts and imagery of the coffin) as the creator-god, and hence the source of his own resurrection.

Burial practices also lend support to the notion of a north–south division in the population and material culture of Egypt during this period. Although Delta sites (apart from Tanis) have yielded few burials datable to these centuries, evidence from the Memphite and Faiyum areas may be usefully compared with the more abundant material from the south. Of the limited range of burial goods provided in Third Intermediate Period graves, only coffins were used consistently throughout. Study of these hints at interaction between north and south, notably at the beginning of the 22nd Dynasty, when a major change in coffin style is attested at Thebes. This is apparent in the abandonment of the style in vogue in the 21st Dynasty, with its *horror vacui* and multi-level images, and the rapid establishment in its place of a new range of types—polychrome cartonnage cases enclosed in wooden coffins of much simpler design. These show an impoverishment of the iconographic repertoire, with greater concentration on symmetrical arrangements of gods, yet with a bolder use of colour. There are indications that these features derived from the north, as burials from the Memphite necropolis and from cemeteries around the entrance to the Faiyum testify. The evident importation of northern burial practices into Upper Egypt seems to coincide with the imposition of stronger royal authority over the south during the reigns of Sheshonq I and his successors. Yet during the succeeding period, distinctively northern and southern styles of coffin seem to emerge, probably reflecting the progressive decentralization of Egypt and perhaps also the social division hinted at by other evidence.

Towards the end of the Third Intermediate Period there was a marked return to older established traditions, coupled with innovations. Elaborate tombs for the élite began once more to be constructed. The Theban necropolis shows an evolution from tombs with modest superstructures in the late eighth century to the gigantic complexes built for Mentuemhat and his contemporaries at the end of the 25th Dynasty. These have free-standing superstructures and elaborate subterranean apartments, and the scale and craftsmanship of the monuments indicate that preparations for death were once again being taken seriously. The range of burial equipment increased; the development of coffin styles produced new types, combining the revival of old features with innovations—rectangular outer cases represent a shrine or the tomb of Osiris, inner coffins project a new image of the transfigured deceased, closely resembling a statue, with back pillar and pedestal. *Shabtis* followed a parallel course of development and statuettes of the composite deity Ptah–Sokar–Osiris (also in this shape) entered the funerary assemblage, ultimately to become one of the commonest features of Late Period burials. Functional canopic jars also returned and, more importantly, funerary literature enjoyed a revival. A revised *Book of the Dead* in the new so-called Saite recension (actually an achievement of the 25th Dynasty) was inscribed on papyri and coffins, while the archaizing fervour of the period led to the copying of passages from the Pyramid Texts and their addition to the current repertoire. This last excepted, Thebes seems to have been a major centre for these innovations, which spread northwards during the seventh century BC. This is not to deny that comparable developments may have been occurring in other areas, but the local chronology at sites such as Memphis is less clear.

Artistic developments and technology

Despite the decentralization of Egypt, the products of the craftsmen show no appreciable reduction in skill or expertise. It is true that stone sculpture on a large scale remained rare throughout, but work of unparalleled excellence was produced on a more modest scale, as new emphasis was given to craftsmanship in the old but underdeveloped media of metal and faience. All media reflect the progressive archaizing tendencies alluded to above, with the consequence that the influence of Old, Middle, and New kingdom models becomes increasingly apparent with the passage of time.

There was a reduction in the range of sculptural types. Royal statues in stone are particularly rare—those of the 21st Dynasty kings were usurped from earlier rulers, and, although original works were produced in the 22nd and 23rd Dynasties most of the surviving examples are of modest size. It was only under the Kushites that substantial and powerful royal sculpture returned: the granite head of Taharqo in Cairo, and the sphinx from Kawa in the British Museum, are among the most striking examples. However, during the 22nd to 25th Dynasties large numbers of statues of officials were dedicated in temples, some of which are of exceptionally fine work. Among these the block statue was notably popular, as were those forms in which the subject is represented supporting a shrine, stele, or image of a deity (naophorous and stelophorous statues). The fine reliefs of Sheshonq I from el-Hiba and of Osorkon II from

The silver coffin of Sheshonq 'II' was one of the items of funerary equipment found in the Third Intermediate Period royal tombs in the precinct of the temple of Amun at Tanis, which were discovered by the French archaeologist Pierre Montet just before the outbreak of the Second World War. The falcon-head, perhaps associating the king with the funerary god Sokar, was a characteristic feature of royal coffins of the 22nd Dynasty.

Bubastis show that two-dimensional work of high quality was still being produced, although the subject matter of the scenes was largely derivative. Painting also flourished, and at Thebes the rich New Kingdom tradition of tomb decoration was replaced by work of high standard on coffins, stelae, and funerary papyri.

Perhaps the most lasting contribution of the Third Intermediate Period to the arts and crafts lay in the field of metalworking. The silver coffins of kings Psusennes I and Sheshonq II and the wide range of gold and silver vessels and jewellery from the Tanite royal tombs testify to the continued expertise of Egyptian metalworkers, although foreign influence is occasionally apparent in the shapes and decoration of vessels. Of greater significance was the huge expansion of the range and technical excellence of metal sculpture that occurred during this period, some of it in gold and silver, but the major part in bronze. These pieces were often exquisitely finished, and brilliant effects were achieved through the embellishment of the surfaces with strands of precious metal hammered into channels in the bronze. Solid-cast statuettes were frequent, and now began the tradition of small bronze deity figures that led to the production of thousands of examples during the succeeding centuries. More important were the large bronze statues, hollow-cast using the lost-wax technique, which were dedicated as votive offerings or mounted on the portable barques of the gods. The figure of the 'god's wife' Karomama in the Louvre is the supreme example of the type, although a series of bronze Osiris statues, now represented only by decayed and incomplete specimens, may originally have been equally imposing. These statues, made in the ninth to seventh centuries BC, represent the earliest known attempts to create large bronze figures by the hollow-cast process, and were to serve as important influences on early Greek bronzeworking. Classical authors state that Samian craftsmen used Egyptian techniques in creating the earliest large hollow-cast metal sculptures in the Greek world, and this view is vindicated by the discovery of Egyptian bronzes of this period on Samos itself.

Scarcely less vigorous was the production of faience. While glass technology declined after the New Kingdom, that of faience boomed. The majority of *shabti*s of the period were made of this material, but a great many were crudely fashioned. Much finer were the lotiform chalices with relief scenes showing country life or the king in battle. The shape of these chalices evokes the notion of rebirth, and the scenes on them and on a related series of faience openwork spacer beads reflect aspects of the mythology of creation. Equally typical of the period are magical figurines designed to provide protection during childbirth and nourishment for the young—these are of blue-green faience, often with spots and details added in brown, and typically show the household god Bes, a monkey, or a nude female holding a vase or musical instrument, or sometimes suckling. Although they occur as far south as el-Kurru in Nubia, the concentration of finds of these figures at north-east Delta sites indicates that this was their main area of production.

Conclusion

As noted at the beginning of this chapter, the pejorative implications of the term 'intermediate' do little justice to the developments that took place in Egypt between 1069 and 664 BC. Although the power structure within the country was very different from that which obtained in the New Kingdom the towns and cities of Egypt flourished and the economy of the country was generally healthy. Though decentralization of the government led to occasional power struggles, the system adopted by the Libyan pharaohs and modified by the Kushites was generally effective. Large-scale royal constructions may have been restricted, but artistic continuity was maintained via other media (small sculpture, metalwork, faience).

In a large degree, the Third Intermediate Period constitutes a distinct cycle in Egypt's history, defined by a passage from the loss of unity at the end of the New Kingdom to the restoration of centralized authority under Psamtek I. Valuable lessons were learned from the fragmented politics of the period (particularly from the Assyrian invasions). These provided the impetus needed to restore centralized authority, and proved the ideological worth of archaism and the political value of institutions such as that of the 'god's wife of Amun' in fostering a stable and less turbulent state. The related changes in the status of the king and the prominence given to new trends in religion were also adumbrations of the future. Thus this period laid the foundations for the last great phase of ancient Egypt's prosperity.

13 THE LATE PERIOD

(664–332 BC)

ALAN B. LLOYD

Egyptologists have generally been dismissive of the Late Period, regarding it all too often as the last gasp of a once great culture. Such views seriously devalue the historical achievement of these centuries as well as the remarkable vitality that pharaonic civilization continued to display. The student of this age has also a unique advantage. In earlier periods we have to rely largely or exclusively on Egyptian evidence, with all its inherent distortions, but the historian of the Late Period disposes of a much broader range of written evidence, which offers unparalleled potential for cross-reference and thereby provides insights into the workings of Egyptian political and military institutions stripped of the propagandist veneer invariably applied to historical narrative by native Egyptian scribes.

The centuries under discussion break down into four clearly defined phases: the Saite Dynasty (664–525 BC); the First Persian Occupation (525–404 BC); a period of independence (404–343 BC); and the Second Persian Occupation (343-332 BC).

The Saite Dynasty: The Resurgence of Egypt's Power

The Saite reunification of Egypt in the mid-650s BC reversed a long-running trend in the country's history in that all recent precedents pointed imperiously to continued fragmentation punctuated by bouts of foreign domination. The years following the end of the 20th Dynasty had brought the disintegration of the kingdom under a variety of pressures: the weakness of the last Ramesside rulers provoked the collapse of centralized government; the development of the power of the priesthood of Amun-Ra at Thebes created a formidable rival

to royal authority; and the infiltration of the country by Libyans rapidly led to their ascendancy in the social and political hierarchy. Not surprisingly, vigorous Libyan princelings had experienced little difficulty in getting their hands on the royal office, thus creating a sequence of dynasties of varying efficiency. Later, the tangled web of the 25th Dynasty—characterized by intermittent Nubian domination—covered the best part of 100 years. Although the 25th Dynasty started well, it ended with the country suffering severely from the Assyrian invasions of 671 and 663 BC.

The founder of the 26th Dynasty, heir to this legacy, was, therefore, confronted by several problems: the ancient ideal of Egypt as a unified kingdom had been severely eroded by the rivalry of opposing power blocks in the form of the priesthood of Thebes and Libyan dynasts; this diffusion of power generated economic weakness and was, at the same time, aggravated by it; finally, the ambitions of Asiatic enemies and Nubian kings to regain control of Egypt posed a recurrent external threat. Any attempt to recreate a powerful and united Egyptian state was dependent on the eradication, or at least neutralization, of these factors. In this the 26th Dynasty achieved spectacular success, which was to be crowned with nothing less than the resurgence of Egypt as a major international power.

The credit for reunifying Egypt falls to Psamtek I (664–610 BC), whose father Nekau I (672–664 BC) had previously ruled at Sais under Assyrian protection and had been killed for his pains by the Nubian King Tanutamani (664–656 BC) in 664 BC. Psamtek succeeded to his father's position with Assyrian support, initially controlling about half the Delta with his main centres of power at Sais, Memphis, and Athribis, as well as close religious links with Buto. The Assyrians evidently saw this development as a continuation of the old system of rule through local princes, but the sands were swiftly running out for such power as Nineveh had in Egypt. Given their pressing commitments elsewhere in the Empire, the Assyrians simply did not have the military strength to maintain their position indefinitely so far west. With typical Saite strategic acumen, it did not take Psamtek long to exploit this situation, so that relations with Assyria quickly took a very different turn, and in about 658 BC we find him receiving support from Gyges of Lydia in emancipating himself from Assyrian control, an episode that may well be linked with Herodotus' tradition that Psamtek employed Carian and Ionian mercenaries in his efforts to strengthen and extend his authority. In addition to military power, our sources highlight a further dimension to his strategy: strengthening his economic base by developing trade links with Greeks and Phoenicians. It was evidently firmly grasped by this formidable ruler that all power must be based on a sound exchequer.

By 660 BC Psamtek had control of the entire Delta, and from this potent military base he was able to gain mastery of the rest of the country by 656 BC, mainly, it would seem, by diplomatic means, although the wheels of diplomacy were certainly oiled by the obvious availability of a substantial well-equipped military force of none-too-scrupulous foreign mercenaries. He also benefited

Facing: relief of Psamtek I engaged in ritual activity, probably from Heliopolis. The style is realistic, without necessarily being a portrait, and the treatment of the head and uraeus recalls the royal iconography of the 25th Dynasty.

substantially from the well-honed pliability of local princes such as the Shipmasters of Herakleopolis Magna and Mentuemhat of Thebes, who quickly saw the advantages of coming to an accommodation. At least equally pressing was the problem of gaining control of the powerful priesthood of Amun-Ra at Thebes, which had been a significant factor in weakening royal authority since the late New Kingdom. Here a major step in resolving the difficulty was taken when Psamtek arranged for his daughter Nitiqret to be appointed as heiress to the 'god's wife of Amun', thereby initiating a process intended to place the major southern repository of ecclesiastical power firmly in the hands of the dynasty.

Power gained is one thing; power maintained is quite another, but the process of consolidation was carried out with triumphant success. A major contribution was made by the mercenaries who had played such a significant role in the conquest of the country. Our documentation lays much emphasis on those of Greek and Carian extraction, but we also hear of Jews, Phoenicians, and possibly Shasu Bedouin. These troops had two functions. In the first place, they were intended to guarantee Egypt's security from external attack in the face of a series of enemies, initially Assyrians and subsequently Chaldaeans (Babylonians) and Persians. However, they also undoubtedly provided a counterweight within the country to the power of the *machimoi*, the native Egyptian warrior class, who were, in origin, Libyans and posed a significant potential internal threat to royal authority.

Herodotus informs us that *stratopeda* ('camps') were established between Bubastis and the sea on the Pelusiac branch of the Nile. He claims that these camps were occupied without a break for over a century until the mercenaries were moved to Memphis at the beginning of the reign of Ahmose II (570–526 BC), but the archaeological evidence presents a rather more complex picture. At Tell Defenna (Greek Daphnae) the earliest king exemplified is certainly Psamtek I, but the vast majority of the material dates to the time of Ahmose II—that is, the distribution contradicts the Herodotean tradition. We also know of another camp 20 km. from Daphnae, a little to the south of Pelusium, where sixth-century Greek pottery has been found in quantity. The most plausible explanation for the contradiction between our literary and archaeological evidence is that the troops were pulled out of the camps at the beginning of Ahmose's reign as the result of an anti-Greek backlash (see below), but reintroduced at a later stage to counter the growing menace of Persia. As for their integration into the Egyptian army, the famous Greek inscription on the leg of one of the colossi at Abu Simbel, as well as later practice, indicates that the mercenaries, under Egyptian command, formed one of the two corps in the army whose supreme commander was also Egyptian. It has to be said that these troops were not consistently reliable, and we do have evidence of a revolt of mercenaries at Elephantine during the reign of Apries (589–570 BC).

Petrie's work at Tell Defenna has provided a vivid and probably typical picture of the character of the permanent bases of such troops in the Saite period. The site is located on a large plain covered with pottery and dominated by the

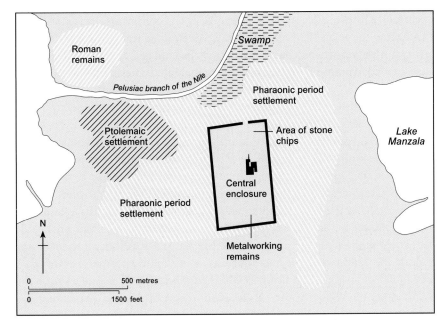

Plan of Tell Defenna. The casemate platform now called El-Kasr el-Bint el-Yehudi is dated by foundation deposits to the reign of Psamtek I. The remains of the settlement outside the fortress wall are clearly demarcated by fragments of late pottery.

remains of a mud-brick platform constructed on the standard honeycomb principle consisting of casemates many of which were filled with sand. Its original height was estimated by Petrie to have been about 30 feet (*c.*10 m.), and he believed that it had been surmounted by a fort. This structure, which was certainly built by Psamtek I, seems to have functioned as a keep within an enclosure demarcated by a massive oblong mud-brick wall, but this had been eroded to ground level by Petrie's time. Outside the wall lay the civilian settlement, mainly to the east. Excavation yielded a substantial quantity of Greek infantry equipment, but the site was also a naval base from which Greek-style war galleys could operate, a situation reflecting the important role played by the mercenaries in the Egyptian navy.

Not surprisingly, the preference shown to these foreign troops was far from welcome to the *machimoi*. According to Herodotus, a group of them mutinied and withdrew from Egypt to a site that may well have lain somewhere in the vicinity of the Blue Nile and Gezira area near Omdurman, if we can trust his topographical data. By the time of Apries, things had got far worse and eventually reached a disastrous level when we find the king being swept from the throne by a *machimoi* backlash against the privileged position of Greeks and Carians in the military establishment. The spark that lit this powder keg was a disastrous defeat sustained by a force of *machimoi* sent against the Greek city of Cyrene, which provided the opportunity for Ahmose to use these troops to defeat Apries' mercenaries at Momemphis in 570 BC and usurp the throne of Egypt.

The economy was an equally important focus of Saite policy in reconstructing Egypt. The foundation of a sound economy in the country was, and always has been, sound agriculture, and by Ahmose's time this had been raised to a spectacular level of success. Herodotus (II. 177, 1) comments, 'It is said that it was during the reign of Ahmose II that Egypt attained its highest level of prosperity both in respect of what the river gave the land and in respect of what the land yielded to men and that the number of inhabited cities at that time reached in total 20,000.'

Trade was also greatly encouraged. In our textual sources, Greek relations play a major role, although it would be as well to remember that most of the sources are themselves Greek. Within Egypt itself we hear of trading stations such as 'The Wall of the Milesians' and 'Islands' bearing such names as Ephesus, Chios, Lesbos, Cyprus, and Samos, but their precise relationship to the Crown or other Greek centres in the country is quite unclear for the earliest period. However, by far the best-documented trading centre is Naukratis, established on the Canopic branch of the Nile not far from the capital, Sais, and with excellent communications for internal and external trade. Although the city was founded by Milesians in the mid- or late-seventh century BC, members of other east Greek cities were also firmly established there, as well as traders from the island state of Aegina in the Saronic Gulf south of Athens. Excavation has revealed a series of sacred enclosures dedicated to Greek cults, a scarab factory producing material for export, and a typical Late Period honeycomb platform comparable to that at Tell Defenna, which may have been military in purpose but could equally well have had civilian, administrative functions.

It is difficult to determine to what extent trade was regulated in the early years of the foundation. It may be that from the very beginning the model of Mirgissa in Nubia during the Middle Kingdom applied. This system is summarily described in the stele of the eighth year of the reign of Senusret III as follows:

The palace-fort of Apries at Memphis which parallels El-Kasr el-Bint el-Yehudi. The mound, 12.5 m. high and defended by a ditch *c*.6 m. deep, is a classic late casement platform on top of which the palace proper was built. Remains of limestone column capitals can still be seen, some bearing the name of Apries.

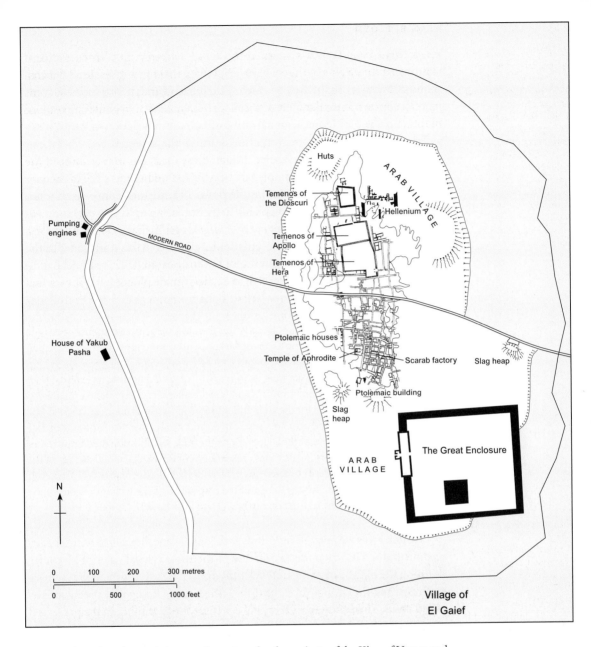

Huts

ARAB VILLAGE

Temenos of
the Dioscuri

Hellenium

Temenos of
Apollo

Temenos of
Hera

Pumping
engines

MODERN ROAD

House of Yakub
Pasha

Ptolemaic houses

Temple of Aphrodite

Scarab factory

Slag heap

Ptolemaic building

Slag
heap

ARAB
VILLAGE

The Great Enclosure

N

| 0 | 100 | 200 | 300 metres |

| 0 | | 500 | 1000 feet |

Village of
El Gaief

The southern frontier made in regnal year 8 under the majesty of the King of Upper and Lower Egypt Khakaure (may he live for ever and ever) in order to prevent it being passed by any Nubian journeying north by land or in a *kai*-boat as well as any livestock belonging to Nubians, with the exception of a Nubian who shall come to traffic at Mirgissa or on an embassy, or on any matter which may lawfully be done with them; but it shall be forbidden for any *kai*-boat of the Nubians to pass northwards beyond Semna for ever.

Be that as it may, there is no doubt that Naukratis became the channel through which *all* Greek trade was required by law to flow from *c.*570 BC. However, there is evidence of even more strenuous efforts to promote trade; we know that Nekau II (610–595 BC) at the very least began to construct a canal running from the Nile to the Red Sea, an activity that must indicate a revival of economic activity in the Red Sea area, which had been a major focus of commercial concern in earlier dynasties. It is also reasonable to regard the existence of the implausible Herodotean narrative of a circumnavigation of Africa instigated by Nekau II as a further reflection of interest in this quarter.

Impressive and even spectacular though these measures may have been, we must never lose sight of the simple fact that big battalions and a full exchequer can never be a sufficient basis for lasting power. There must always be an ideological underpinning that is acceptable to the subject people. In Egypt the basis for this had always been the concept of divine kingship that gave the pharaoh a clearly defined and universally accepted role, not only in the governance of the kingdom but in the very maintenance of the cosmos itself. This agenda had to be accepted and rigorously observed; to *be* a legitimate pharaoh it was essential to *act* legitimately. I have summarized this pharaonic ideal elsewhere as follows:

The basic elements are: pharaoh ascends the throne as Horus, champion of cosmic order (*maat*) and vanquishes the forces of darkness; in continuation of this role he then ensures the well-being of Egypt in economic terms by organizing the irrigation system and in military terms by maintaining its military forces and defeating its external foes; the *pax deorum* is ensured by supplying temples with all their requirements and by constructing monuments both for the gods and for himself (statues and mortuary installations); expeditions will be sent to Punt, Sinai, and other canonical sources of raw materials and in the course of these operations the gods will indicate their approval of the king by *biayt*, 'marvels', which may consist both of the conspicuous success of the enterprise and of any signs or omens which the gods may choose to provide. The result of all this will be long life for the king and the realization of the will of the gods in the establishment of the cosmic order on earth.   (*Herodotus Book II. Commentary* 2. 16–17)

Psamtek I was well placed here, but, at the same time, burdened with a heavy responsibility. He was undertaking one of the most critical roles of kingship, donning the mantle of Menes and Mentuhotep II: he was unifying the country and restoring the proper order of things, the state of being that the Egyptians called *maat*. This emerges with crystal clarity at the beginning of the preserved section of the Nitiqret Adoption Stele, the longest surviving royal inscription of his reign:

I [Psamtek] have acted for him as should be done for my father. (2) I am his first-born son, one made prosperous by the father of the gods, one who carries out the rituals of the gods; he begat him for himself so as to satisfy his heart. To be 'god's wife' have I given him my daughter, and I have endowed her more generously than those who were before her. Surely he will be satisfied with her adoration and protect the land of (3) him who gave her to him . . . I will not do that very thing which ought not to be done and drive out an heir from his seat inasmuch as I am a king who loves (4) truth—my special abomination is lying—the son and protector of his father, taking the inheritance of Geb, and uniting the two portions while still a youth.   (ll. 1–4)

This devotion to the gods could not be confined to statements of intent. Both Psamtek and his successors engaged in architectural work on sacred installations to express their devotion and maintain the goodwill and support of the gods. Saite buildings are poorly preserved in the archaeological record, to a considerable extent because they were constructed in the Delta, where conditions for survival are much less favourable than in Upper Egypt. Nevertheless, enough information is preserved in Herodotus, inscriptions, and the building fragments to demonstrate that the Saite rulers did everything they could to fulfil this part of the agenda of kingship. It is claimed that Psamtek I constructed the south pylon of the temple of Ptah at Memphis and also built on behalf of the Apis bull in the same shrine; his successor Nekau II is known to have been responsible for monuments in honour of Apis in the same city, and there is inscriptional evidence of his endeavours in the limestone quarries in the Mokattam Hills, where Psamtek II (595–589 BC) has also left signs of quarrying work. Ahmose II was also extremely active in Sais, the home of the dynasty, where he erected a pylon for the temple of Neith, set up colossal statues, and manufactured human-headed sphinxes for a processional way. Indeed, the evidence leaves us with a powerful impression of the ecclesiastical splendours of

Mourning scene from the tomb of the vizier Nesipaka-shuty, now in the Brooklyn Museum. Dating to the end of the reign of Psamtek I, this and related scenes were set up in a usurped tomb of the 11th Dynasty at Deir el-Bahri, Thebes. It shows the influence of New Kingdom prototypes, but other reliefs in the tomb show Old Kingdom traits as well as an interest in female anatomy typical of Late Period and Graeco-Roman art.

this city in the Late Period that must have owed much to the work of these Saite kings. The chief focus was the sacred enclosure of Neith, which contained the main cult centre (the 'Mansion of Neith') and provision for a host of associated gods (Osiris, Horus, Sobek, Atum, Amun, Bastet, Isis, Nekhbet, Wadjet, and Hathor). There was, in particular, a burial place of Osiris and a sacred lake on which the rituals of the Festival of the Resurrection of Osiris were celebrated, and the site was richly embellished with features such as obelisks of which the sad ruins of Sais give little hint today.

The city of Sais was, however, just one recipient of 26th Dynasty largesse. We also hear, for instance, of Ahmose setting up colossi at Memphis (two of granite), building a temple of Isis in the same city, and working at Philae, Elephantine, Nebesha, Abydos, and the oases, while he also made contributions to earlier structures on many other sites, including Karnak, Mendes, the Tanta area, Tell el-Maskhuta, Benha, Sohag, el-Mansha, and Edfu. This intense building activity is in turn reflected in quarry inscriptions at Tura and Elephantine.

The ideology of kingship not only encompasses the world of the living but also gives the king a critical function beyond the grave: the living king is the embodiment of Horus and rules the living; the deceased king is Osiris, king of the dead, but, at the same time, since Osiris in this context was assimilated to Ra, the king expected to participate in the cycle of cosmic action. In order to propel the king into his life beyond the grave and maintain him there, an elaborate programme of ritual was devised, the most spectacular surviving illustrations of which are the pyramids of the Old and Middle kingdoms and the New Kingdom tombs in the Valley of the Kings with their attendant cult temples. The rulers of the 26th Dynasty built no funerary monuments as spectacular as these but operated firmly within Late Period tradition. From the end of the New Kingdom, kings had been buried in chapel tombs in temple courtyards, partly, no doubt, for security reasons, but also possibly as a reflection of a sense of dependence on and devotion to the deities in question. Following this practice, the kings of the 26th Dynasty were interred in chapel tombs in the courtyard of the temple of Neith at Sais. None of these structures has survived, but there is no difficulty in reconstructing them from the description of Herodotus and obvious earlier parallels at Medinet Habu and Tanis. They consisted of two elements: above ground a mortuary chapel was constructed that was entered by way of a double door from a columned portico. The walls of this structure were probably decorated with painted relief sculpture relating to the mortuary cult of the deceased king that was celebrated in the chapel. Beneath was the burial vault containing the royal sarcophagus, and this too was probably decorated. Grave goods, to judge from Tanite precedents, would have been relatively restricted, but certainly included the traditional royal *shabtis* and canopic jars.

To date in this chapter we have concentrated largely on Saite policies and actions within Egypt, but, given the grim history of recurrent invasion in the 25th Dynasty, we cannot be far wrong in assuming that the major issue for the rulers of this period was the task of keeping the frontiers of Egypt free from

Bronze figure of Nekau II. This small figure of the king offering to a deity is one of only two known representations of this ruler in the round.

foreign invaders. The most critical area was Asia, where initially the problem was the defence of Egypt's border against a possible renewal of Assyrian attempts to gain control of Egypt, but difficulties much closer to their homeland made this impossible for the Assyrians to achieve. While evidence of Egyptian military activity in Asia at this stage is far from plentiful, Psamtek's operations clearly met with considerable success, despite the setback of a horde invasion of the Near East by Cimmerian barbarians in c.630 BC, which he countered with the eminently sensible expedient of buying them off. We hear of a successful, if protracted, siege of Ashdod (probably c.655–630 BC), and late in his reign we encounter Egyptian forces operating in Asia even further afield than in the heady days of the 18th Dynasty rulers Thutmose I and III. This startling phenomenon was the consequence of the double threat to Assyria's very existence posed, on the one hand, by the rise of the Chaldaeans in southern Iraq and, on the other, by the growing menace of Media to the east in Iran. This speedily led to an abrupt Assyrian volte-face in relation to Egypt, in the form of an alliance between the two nations as a result of which we find Egyptian forces operating against the Chaldaeans inside Iraq itself in 616 BC. Henceforth, until the last decades of the 26th Dynasty, it was the Chaldaeans who were the major enemy of Egypt.

Head of a black basalt statue of Apries. The damage is typical of statues of this king and may reflect his forceful deposition by Ahmose II. The blue crown was much favoured by 26th Dynasty kings, and the air of benign calm pervading the face is typical of Saite royal sculptures after the time of Psamtek I.

Psamtek's successor, Nekau II, continued his father's policy in the north. Initially things went well, and again we are confronted with the spectacle of Egyptian forces campaigning east of the Euphrates against the Chaldaeans, defeating *en passant* Josiah of Judah in 609 BC. The result was that the Egyptians were able to establish themselves on the Euphrates for a short while, but this position was soon lost in 605 BC as a result of their catastophic reverse at Carchemish, which was followed by a brusque retreat to the eastern frontier of Egypt. The Egyptians kept the Chaldaeans at bay, and on this occasion the border was not breached. A small recovery seems to have been made in the reign of Psamtek II, who was certainly able to mount some sort of expedition into Palestine during the fourth year of his reign. In addition, his diplomacy helped foment a general Levantine revolt against the Babylonians that involved, amongst others, Zedekiah of Judah. Herodotus makes it clear that the Near Eastern operations of these rulers were by no means entirely land orientated, indicating that Nekau constructed a fleet of ramming war galleys that may have been an early type of trireme and some of which were used in the Mediterranean and others in the Red Sea. Indeed, it may be that the abortive Red Sea canal was intended, in part, to facilitate the transfer of naval forces from the Red Sea to the Mediterranean as circumstances required.

Apries addressed himself vigorously to the Chaldaean problem. Initially he undertook large-scale operations against the Chaldaeans in conjunction with Phoenician cities and Zedekiah of Judah. These activities led to disaster and possibly invasion of Egypt in the late 580s BC. Subsequently a strategically well-conceived series of campaigns was directed against Cyprus and Phoenicia (*c.*574–570 BC) in which good use was made of the fleet. Ahmose II, who succeeded Apries, was nothing if not lucky. He was able to defeat a Chaldaean inva-

Facing: Naophorous statue of Psamteksineith from Memphis. He held office under the 27th (Persian) Dynasty as 'Director of all Workmen of the King in Silver and Gold'. This outstanding example of Egyptian portrait sculpture depicts the subject wearing an elaborate overgarment typical of the Persian Period. Statues of figures offering a shrine containing a divine image (in this case Osiris) are a major genre of Late Period sculpture and bear witness to the strong sense of proximity to and dependence on divine beings which is typical of this age.

sion of Egypt in the fourth year of his reign, and after that the Chaldaeans had sufficient problems within the empire to keep them fully occupied for the early part of his reign. In due course, however, he was faced with a much more dangerous enemy created by the rise of Persia under Cyrus the Great, who ascended the throne in 559 BC. To deal with this menace a grand alliance of threatened nations was created, which consisted of Egypt, Croesus of Lydia, Sparta, and the Chaldaeans. With consummate strategic skill Cyrus knocked out the link between the scattered allies by destroying Lydia in 546 BC. He then turned on the Chaldaeans and took their capital Babylon in 538 BC, leaving Ahmose with no major Near Eastern allies. Ahmose reacted by developing a policy of cultivating close relations with Greek states to strengthen his hand against the impending onslaught, and again he was lucky. He died in 526 BC before the storm broke, leaving his son Psamtek III (526–525 BC) to face the Achaemenid assault.

The south was not such an acute threat as the north, but the Nubians could not be ignored, not least because they had certainly not given up their ambitions to rule Egypt. There is no firm evidence of military action against them in the reign of Psamtek I—indeed, the introduction to the Nitiqret Adoption Stele suggests that he was prepared to forget his differences with the Nubians, which included the death of his father in battle against them, and that he adopted a conciliatory policy. This stance may well have persisted to the end of his reign, but we should be wary of assuming too much, given the highly defective nature of our evidence. The situation was certainly different in the reign of Nekau, who at some undefinable date was forced to turn his attention to what a fragmentary text indicates was a rebellion in Nubia; but the best-known Saite military commitment by far is that of Psamtek II, who dispatched a great expedition in the third year of his reign. This operation, which was designed to forestall a Nubian assault on Egypt, seems to have taken the Egyptian army at least to the fourth Nile cataract. It appears to have been successful, and we hear nothing more in the dynasty of major military operations to the south, although a demotic papyrus of the reign of Ahmose II describes the king as sending into Nubia a small expedition, the character of which is quite unclear, and there is archaeological evidence of an Egyptian garrison at Dorginarti in Lower Nubia during the Saite and Persian periods.

Relations with the Libyans were not consistently good during the Saite Dynasty. The Saqqara Stele of the eleventh year of the reign of Psamtek I, despite its damaged state, provides evidence of problems with Libyan tribes to the west. These he seems to have defeated, and they do not appear to have been a problem subsequently—quite the contrary! About 571 BC we find the Libyans asking for Egyptian assistance in dealing with the expansionist policy of Cyrene, a Greek colony that had been founded in their territory about 630 BC. At the end of the reign of Apries this city embarked on a programme of expansion that brought them into collision with Egyptian interests, and in the ensuing war Egypt was catastrophically defeated. Ahmose II adopted a totally different approach to the Cyrene problem. As early as 567 BC we find him forming an alliance with them against the Chaldaeans, and this diplomatic link was cemented by marriage to a Cyrenean woman who was alleged by some of Herodotus' sources, with considerable plausibility, to have been a princess. This alliance stood the test of time surprisingly well and was still in place at the time of the Persian invasion in 525 BC.

The First Persian Period

Egypt's confrontation with Persia came to a head with the invasion of Egypt in 525 BC, which led to the defeat and capture of Psamtek III by Cambyses (525–522 BC) at the Battle of Pelusium. Cambyses' activities in Egypt present a totally contradictory image in our sources, the comments in classical authors being extremely unfavourable, whereas the Egyptian evidence depicts a ruler anxious to avoid offending Egyptian susceptibilities and presenting himself as an Egyptian king in all respects. This aspect comes through particularly strongly in the inscriptions on the statue of Udjahorresnet, where at least three major points emerge: in the first place, Cambyses had assumed at least the forms of Egyptian kingship; second, he was perfectly prepared to work with and promote native Egyptians to assist in government; and, third, he showed a deep respect for native Egyptian religion. This latter point also emerges in his burial of an Apis bull with all the ancient rituals.

None of this prevented the outbreak of a revolt in Egypt when Cambyses died in 522 BC, but the independence gained was short lived, since Darius (522–486 BC) was able to regain complete control of the country in 519/18 BC. With this reign, Egypt settled into a pattern the beginnings of which are already clearly visible in the reign of Cambyses. The head of the government was the Great King whose position was legitimized for Egyptian purposes by the only means possible—that is, by defining him as pharaoh on the same terms as a native Egyptian ruler. Cambyses' policy of massaging Egyptian ideological susceptibilities also continued under Darius both in religious matters and administration: the building or restoration of temples was a prominent feature—the medical school at Sais was restored, the building (or rebuilding) of the temple of Amun of Hibis in the Kharga Oasis was begun, and work

was carried out at Busiris and the Serapeum at Saqqara, and possibly also at Elkab. Darius is also credited with a programme of law reform.

However, not all Persian kings showed the same delicate touch, and Xerxes (486-465 BC) received a particularly bad press for his impious disregard of temple privilege. As for administration, the Persians, like the Ptolemies after them, had the good sense to realize that the Egyptian system for running the country was the best that could be devised, and maintained it with only the minimum of Persian administrative overlay needed to integrate the province into the Achaemenid imperial organization. This primarily amounted to the insertion of a satrap at the top. The satrap, who was effectively a viceroy, was drawn from the cream of the Persian aristocracy, but his activities were none the less carefully monitored by the imperial network of inspectors or informers holding titles such as 'king's eye' or 'listeners'. He ran the central administration through a chancellory that was controlled by a chancellor assisted by a 'scribe'. The language used in the chancellory was Aramaic, a situation that required the employment of a staff of Egyptian translators. Below this level, the Persians showed a marked disinclination to innovate. The legal system remained Egyptian, and we can identify a series of Egyptians occupying positions of importance, if not power, throughout the period.

At the same time, we can see an uncompromising determination to keep firm control of the province, a policy that did not stop short of inserting non-Egyptians into Egypt and Egyptian institutions, as and when the Persians thought fit. They also ensured a substantial military presence for the maintenance of external and internal security, and Egypt was also expected to play its full part as a satrapy of the Persian empire. Between *c.*510 and 497 BC Darius completed the construction of a canal begun under Nekau II running from the Pelusiac branch of the Nile through the Wadi Tumilat to the Bitter Lakes and the Red Sea, a project that was clearly part of a policy of locking Egypt into the imperial network of communication. Not only were Egyptian craftsmen used for building operations as far afield as Persia, but also the military resources of the country were exploited to the full to advance Persian imperial expansion—Egyptians were involved in the naval assault on Miletus that brought the Ionian Revolt to an end in 494 BC, and Egyptian military and naval resources played a major role in the great assaults of Darius and Xerxes on Greece in 490 and 480 BC. The Egyptians supplied ropes for Xerxes' bridge of boats across the Hellespont and assisted in its construction, while the fleet Xerxes used against the mainland Greek states in 480/79 BC contained 200 Egyptian triremes under the command of Achaemenes, the brother of Xerxes himself, as against the 300 supplied by the Phoenicians, indicating that Egypt was no mean naval power at this period. This contingent performed particularly well at Artemisium, where it captured five Greek ships with their crews, although this record does not seem to have been maintained at Salamis. Finally, we should note that the fiscal obligations of a satrapy were also laid upon Egypt, but these were not unduly oppressive.

Overall, the impression created by such sources as we have is that the Persian regime in Egypt was far from oppressive, and more than a few Egyptians found it perfectly possible to come to terms with it. Indeed there is indisputable evidence of a slow Egyptianization of the conquerors themselves. Nevertheless, there are obvious areas where tensions might arise. While the Great King might be presented for ideological purposes as pharaoh, he was an absentee landlord based in Iran and could not fail to appear to many as a token pharaoh only. Secondly, the conquest by the Persians did not allay the ambitions of native dynasts to rule the country, and they would have watched carefully for any opportunity to assert Egyptian independence and realize their own ambitions. Furthermore, Egyptian xenophobia, highlighted by Herodotus in the fifth century BC, will hardly have promoted integration between Persians and Egyptians, and this could be aggravated by religious considerations, as illustrated by an episode in the reign of Darius II (424–405 BC) involving mercenaries settled at Elephantine and the local population. Here we find the priests of the ram-headed god Khnum locked in a conflict with Jewish mercenaries that ended in the destruction of the temple of Iao (Yahweh). Given such flashpoints, it is hardly surprising that the history of the First Persian Period is punctuated by revolts. However, all these efforts came ultimately to nought until, c.404 BC, the younger Amyrtaios successfully raised the flag of insurrection to inaugurate the last extended period of independence under native rulers that pharaonic civilization was to enjoy.

Egyptian Independence (404–343 BC)

Most of the detailed evidence for the political and military history of this period derives from Greek sources, which inevitably means that they reflect the interests of classical observers and readers. They paint a convincing picture of a period dominated by two recurrent issues: instability at home and the ever-present spectre of aggressive Persian power abroad. The grizzly panorama of intra- and inter-familial strife between aspirants to the throne emerges with stark clarity in the case of the 29th and 30th Dynasties. In the murky history of these two families we are confronted with a situation that we can only suspect for earlier Egyptian history but that, we can be confident, was not infrequently lurking behind the ideological mirage projected by pharaonic inscriptional evidence. Classical commentators, writing from quite a different perspective, reveal without compunction the complex interaction of individual ambition untrammelled by loyalty or ideological factors whereby ambitious political figures seize any opportunity for advancement provided by the sectional interests of the native Egyptian warrior class, Greek mercenary captains, and, less obviously, the Egyptian priesthood. For the 29th Dynasty our evidence is far from full, but it demonstrates unequivocally that almost every ruler had a short reign and suggests that all of them, with the exception of Hakor (393–380 BC), may have been deposed, sometimes probably worse. The classical sources are

Facing, top left: an avenue of 30th Dynasty sphinxes of Nectanebo I stretching northwards from the pylon of the Luxor temple towards the temple of Amun at Karnak. 30th Dynasty activity in this temple-complex asserted continuity with the long tradition of architectural work on the site and also with the many great kings in whose names these structures were erected.

Top right: detail of a cartouche of Nectanebo I in the oldest standing section of the temple of Isis at Philae. The prenomen (first cartouche) reading *Ḥprˁ-k₃-r* is identical to that of Senwosret I, one of the greatest pharaohs of the 12th Dynasty, doubtless intentionally. The earliest cult buildings at Philae were 26th Dynasty, but Nectanebo I's architectural work greatly enhanced the cult site and was clearly intended to promote the shrine as a major centre of Isiac worship.

Below: the inner coffin of Petosiris from the burial chamber of his tomb at Tuna el-Gebel, probably dating to the second Persian Period. Almost 2 m. long and made of highly valuable pine inlaid with well-formed coloured glass hierglyphs, this piece is unequivocally Egyptian in character, unlike some of the decoration in the tomb chapel. The text consists of a version of Ch. 42 of the *Book of the Dead*. The language, like that of the *Book of the Dead* as a whole, is the long obsolete classical Egyptian which would only have been intelligible to the learned at this period.

385

particularly revealing for the succeeding dynasty. The founder, Nectanebo I (380–362 BC), a general and apparently a member of a military family, almost certainly came to the throne as the result of a military *coup*, and we are unlikely to be guessing badly if we suspect that this experience motivated him in establishing his successor Teos (362–360 BC) as co-regent before his own death in order to strengthen the chances of a smooth family succession. Ultimately, this availed him nothing, because Teos was deposed in circumstances of which we are graphically informed. Indeed, nothing could give us the flavour of the politics of this period better than Plutarch's version of these events:

> Then, having joined Tachos [i.e. Teos], who was making preparations for his campaign [against Persia], he [Agesilaus] was not appointed commander of the entire force, as he was hoping, but only given command of the mercenaries, whilst Chabrias the Athenian was put in charge of the fleet. Tachos himself was commander-in-chief. This was the first thing which vexed Agesilaus; then, whilst he found the prince's arrogance and empty pretensions hard to bear, he was compelled to put up with them. He even sailed with him against the Phoenicians, and, setting aside his sense of dignity and his natural instincts, he showed deference and subservience, until he found his opportunity. For Tachos' cousin Nectanabis [i.e. the future Nectanebo II], who commanded part of the forces, rebelled, and, having been proclaimed king by the Egyptians and having sent to Agesilaus begging him for help, he made the same appeal to Chabrias, offering both men great rewards. Tachos presently learned of this and begged them to stand by him, whereupon Chabrias tried by persuasion and exhortation to keep Agesilaus on good terms with Tachos. . . . The Spartans sent a secret dispatch to Agesilaus ordering him to see to it that he did what was in Sparta's best interests, so Agesilaus took his mercenaries and transferred his allegiance to Nectanabis. . . . Tachos, deserted by his mercenaries, took to flight, but meanwhile another pretender rose up against Nectanabis in the province of Mendes and was declared king.   (Plutarch, *Life of Agesilaus* 36-9)

Egyptian evidence, though far from copious, provides intriguing insights into the self-perception of these last native rulers. If we consider the titularies of the rulers of the 29th Dynasty, we find that Nepherites I bears a Horus name borrowed from Psamtek I and a Golden Horus name taken from Ahmose II, while Hakor uses the Horus and *nebty* names of Psamtek I and the Golden Horus name of Ahmose II. These phenomena demonstrate unequivocally that both of these pharaohs were determined to associate themselves with the great rulers of the 26th Dynasty, the most recent 'golden age' in Egypt's history.

Service to the gods is also a recurrent feature: Nepherites I has left evidence of work at Mendes, Saqqara, Sohag, Akhmim, and Karnak (where his son Psammuthis was also active), and Hakor's building operations can be identified throughout the country. In the 30th Dynasty, efforts were particularly spectacular: Nectanebo I built at Damanhur, Sais, Philae, Karnak, Hermopolis (where he significantly set up a stele before a pylon of Ramesses II), and Edfu, and we have evidence of Nectanebo II's personal participation in the burial of an Apis at Saqqara, as also of his role in raising the status of the Buchis bull of Armant to that of the Apis bull of Memphis; there is also inscriptional evidence

of acts of piety to Isis of Behbeit el-Hagar, for whom he began the construction of an enormous temple. The cynicism of modern scholars has frequently led them to argue that these activities were very much the result of a determination to keep the support of the priests, and there is probably some truth in this, but it would be a mistake to deny that there was also genuine religious fervour. In the Hermopolis stele of Nectanebo I the traditional reciprocal relationship between gods and the king is asserted: the king makes offerings to Thoth and Nehmetawy in return for the support that he believes they gave him in gaining control of the kingdom; the king also makes the traditional claim that his work in the temple restored what he found in ruins—in other words, he is reaffirming the old doctrine of the 'cosmicizing' role of pharaoh. In the Naukratis stele of this same ruler we find him attributing his success to Neith, the great goddess of Sais (again an affinity with the 26th Dynasty), insisting that wealth is the gift of the goddess, and emphasizing that he is preserving what his ancestors had done. There is surely no reason to argue that these ancient concepts had lost any of their force to motivate a ruler or to deny the sincerity of the gratitude expressed by reciprocating the beneficence of the gods.

When we turn to foreign policy, the dominant consideration is Persia, for which the loss of Egypt was never—and could not be—an accomplished fact. Fortunately for these last native pharaohs, pressing Persian concerns nearer home meant that the recovery of Egypt made it difficult for the Great King to give such a distant province his undivided attention until 374/3 BC, when Artaxerxes II (405–359 BC) embarked on the first major attempt to recover the

Relief of Nectanebo I offering to the gods. This piece forms part of a monument that also contains representations of Psamtek I and II (cf. figure on p. 370), a clear case of the determination of the 30th Dynasty to associate itself with Saite rulers. Note the sense of individuality in the treatment of the face and the plasticity of the modelling of the anatomy, which anticipates Ptolemaic relief sculpture.

country. The Egyptian approach to the Achaemenid threat oscillated between using diplomatic means to keep the Persians at bay and having recourse to large-scale military operations. Since Egypt's preferred role was generally that of paymaster, direct military intervention by units of the army or navy is infrequent and occurs only when prompted by necessity or invincible ambition. The ease with which this policy could be conducted is explained by the fact that it unfolded as part of a much greater game, since all this Egyptian activity took place against the backdrop of the struggle for independence of other western provinces of the Achaemenid empire and the long-standing rivalry between Sparta and Persia to define their respective spheres of influence in the Aegean, Asia Minor, and the eastern Mediterranean. This created a lethal interplay of move and counter-move in which Egypt never had any difficulty in finding enthusiastic support. Indeed, its prominence in these operations was such that, even if the Persians had been prepared to let sleeping dogs lie, they could not have done so, since an independent Egypt would always have been a threat to the strategic equilibrium of the western empire. It is, therefore, hardly surprising that Artaxerxes III (343–338 BC) organized no fewer than three major assaults to recover this lost but highly dangerous province.

We are fortunate in knowing a great deal of the organization and character of the military operations of these sixty years of confrontation. At this time Egyptian military resources were made up of three main elements. In the first place, we frequently encounter Greek mercenaries, Egypt's rulers having, in the main, a keen perception of reality marked, amongst other things, by the firm conviction that Egypt's interests were best served by paying others to do its fighting for it. We therefore find Hakor putting together a large force of such troops in the 380s BC and Teos employing 10,000 picked mercenaries in 361/0 BC, while Nectanebo II is said to have had 20,000 when Artaxerxes III invaded the country in 343/2 BC. These troops showed a clear superiority over the native Egyptian *machimoi* (militia) in the civil war between Nectanebo II and Teos, but proved unreliable during the successful Persian invasion of Egypt in 343/2 BC. In addition to these troops we hear on a number of occasions of large forces of *machimoi*. Plutarch describes them at one point in somewhat disparaging terms as 'a rabble of artisans whose inexperience made them worthy of nothing but contempt', but they were certainly capable of effective military action: Diodorus comments on the effectiveness of their skirmishing tactics against the forces of Artaxerxes in 374/3 BC, while in the civil war of 360 BC they initially performed well against Agesilaus and Nectanebo II, even if they were ultimately both outgeneralled and outfought by their Greek opponents. On the negative side, that conflict also clearly demonstrates that they were of unpredictable loyalty and far from averse to playing the kingmaker, particularly if the promised rewards were right.

The third ingredient in Egyptian military resources was allied troops: the assets of the rebel Persian admiral Glo (in fact an Egyptian) brought a significant increment to the forces of Hakor in 380 BC; the Spartans were allies of Teos in 361/0 BC and sent 1,000 heavy infantry with Agesilaus to Egypt, though they subsequently switched their support to Nectanebo; the Phoenicians appear as allies of Nectanebo II in his struggle against Artaxerxes III; and Nectanebo availed himself of the services of c.20,000 Libyans in the same context. The troops featured in our Greek sources are generally infantry, but cavalry are also mentioned explicitly on one occasion. As we should expect, we have evidence of considerable Egyptian skill at military engineering in exploiting the defensive possibilities of the terrain. Nectanebo I is described as fortifying the coast and the north-east Delta very elaborately in 374/3 BC. All entrances were blocked off by land and sea: at each of the seven mouths there was a town with large towers and a wooden bridge dominating the entrance; Pelusium had a ditch around it with fortified points of access by water that were blocked by moles, and all the land approaches were flooded, whilst the town at the Mendesian mouth had both a surrounding wall and a fort inside. The Egyptians' expertise in this area also emerges in their operations against Agesilaus and Nectanebo in 360 BC, and in the measures taken by Nectanebo II to counter the assault of Artaxerxes III in 343/2 BC. Too often, however, it was the high command of the Egyptian army that proved the Achilles' heel, jealousy between Egyptian and foreign generals easily becoming a flashpoint. Whilst Hakor hired the Athenian Chabrias as general c.385 BC without untoward results, Teos' undiplomatic arrangements in 360 BC were not so happy, in that Agesilaus was given command of the Greeks only whilst Teos controlled the Egyptian troops and also retained overall command of the army. Martial failings on the part of the pharaoh could also be critical and eventually lost Egypt its freedom, for our sources make it clear that the major factor here was the ineptitude and cowardice of Nectanebo II himself.

These military confrontations were not confined to operations by land. Naval activity features prominently, as indeed it was bound to do, since one of the classic strategic techniques used by the Persians was, where possible, to shadow the movements of their armies by fleet movements along their flank. The best-known example of this is the invasion of Greece by Xerxes in 480 BC, but any large-scale attack on Egypt would present a perfect opportunity for such two-pronged operations. The Egyptians, therefore, needed to be able to counter Persian fleet movements as well as those of forces coming south by land. However, even beyond this specific context it should be remembered that the possession of effective naval units greatly strengthened the strategic and tactical mobility of Egyptian forces in the east Mediterranean theatre. Fleets are, therefore, a frequent matter of comment in our sources: for example, in 400 BC we find a rebel Persian admiral called Tamos (certainly Egyptian!) taking refuge in Egypt with his fleet and promptly being murdered by an enigmatic Egyptian ruler (probably Amyrtaios) specifically to gain possession of his naval assets, and in 361/0 a substantial fleet is prepared alongside the army to participate in the general revolt of the western provinces of the Persian empire. The technical sophistication of these forces was evidently high. Whenever Egyptian warships are mentioned they are called triremes: ramming war galleys propelled by three superimposed banks of oars, the classic first-rate battleship of the Mediterranean world at this period. In 396 BC we find Nepherites sending Agesilaus of Sparta the equipment for 100 triremes—clearly he had enough and to spare in his arsenals. We are told that the Cypriot rebel Evagoras acquired fifty triremes from Hakor in 381 BC; and in 361–360 BC we are told that Teos prepared a fleet of 200 such warships which were very well equipped. Although the Egyptian ships are always described as triremes, we should note that the Persian fleet collected for operations against Egypt in 374 BC consisted of 300 triremes and 200 triakontors (single-banked galleys with thirty oarsmen), and the Egyptian navy must also have contained such lighter units. That native Egyptian commanders could achieve the rank of admiral in the Persian fleet is a sufficient testimony to their quality, but the Egyptian navy at this time could recognize ability wherever it lay, and Teos had no hesitation in appointing the superb Athenian admiral Chabrias to command his naval units in 361 BC.

The re-establishment of Persian control in Egypt, which was completed no later than 341 BC, was attended by plundering of temples and a policy of consolidation that took the form of demolishing the defences of major cities and setting up once more a Persian provincial administration staffed in part by local Egyptian officials such as Somtutefnakht. Evidently the intention was a return to the arrangements of the previous occupation, but the outcome was a regime of recurrent viciousness and incompetence that soon raised the level of disaffection to the point of armed rebellion. It is surely here, perhaps about 339/8 BC, that the uprising of the much-discussed Khababash must be placed, a rebellion so successful that it gave him at least partial control of the country and a claim to the pharaonic office. In 333 BC there is an equally signal example of disaffection in the enthusiasm with which the appearance of the Macedonian rebel Amyntas was welcomed in the country. It comes as no surprise, therefore, that, when Alexander the Great invaded the country late in 332 BC, he had no difficulty in quickly terminating the hated rule of Persia.

Culture in Continuum

Up to this point our discussion has been dominated by the political, military, and economic vicissitudes of Egypt from the beginning of the Saite period to the Macedonian conquest. Although it is impossible to deny the vigour and skill with which the Egyptians met these challenges, our survey might easily create the impression of a nation subjected for generations to considerable discontinuity. When, however, we turn to cultural phenomena, a very different picture emerges. The visual arts are paradigmatic. While, on the one hand, they show a determination to draw on the traditions of the Old, Middle, and New kingdoms, as well as the Kushite Period, they display anything but the arid archaism of which they are still too often accused. On the contrary, the assertion of continuity with older tradition is combined with the exercise of considerable invention and originality both in materials and iconography, producing some of the most remarkable sculpture in the entire pharaonic corpus. For other spheres of cultural activity there is sometimes an unnerving lacuna in extant material—there are, for example, no literary texts securely dated to this period. For all that, close analysis of such evidence as we do possess confirms that Egyptian society and civilization as a whole were characterized by the same traits as the visual arts. We routinely encounter features with which the student of earlier periods will be completely familiar.

Mortuary contexts continue to reveal the intense importance of family ties, sometimes in a spectacular form: the tomb of the vizier Bakenrenef at Saqqara of the reign of Psamtek I appears to have been used for the burial of members of the family for the best part of 300 years, and the tomb of Petosiris at Tuna el-Gebel contained burials of five generations of his family running from the 30th Dynasty into the Ptolemaic Period. Non-mortuary epigraphy points in the same direction: the Wadi Hammamat inscription of Khnumibra shows a comparable awareness of family lineage in the 27th Dynasty, purporting to record his genealogy for over twenty generations as far back as the 19th Dynasty, though we must be cautious about the historical precision of this document. Such material also demonstrates the continued importance of continuity of office within the family: Petosiris' family occupied the office of High Priest of Thoth at Hermopolis over five generations, whilst Khnumibra's ancestors are alleged to have had something approaching a stranglehold over the offices of vizier and overseer of works for centuries.

Local loyalties are, if anything, even stronger than of old: Udjahorresnet insisted at the beginning of the 27th Dynasty on the sterling service that he had done for his native city, while the fourth-century inscription of Somtutefnakht, set up in the temple of Harsaphes in his home town of Herakleopolis Magna, indicates that such service was transmuted into devotion to the local god, an easy and natural formulation that was commonplace at this time. Such devotion to local gods is easily paralleled earlier, but its prominence in the Late Period is very marked, originating, no doubt, in the political fragmentation that was endemic after the collapse of the New Kingdom. A corollary of this situation is the marked tendency for the main focus of personal devotion to become the main city deity, who thus acquires the omnipotence and omniscience of the traditional great gods of the pantheon. This phenomenon generated, in turn, an intense sense of the imminence of the divine presence, which is probably a major factor in the development of animal cults, one of the distinctive religious features of the Late Period. Devotion to this immediately present deity was naturally accompanied by a powerful conviction of the dependence of man on divine favour, which is frequently expressed in sculpture through statues of individuals supporting and offering images of their local god.

Biographical inscriptions further reveal that the factors leading to success in life were perceived in essentially traditional terms: royal favour was still regarded as a prerequisite of success; it was also considered essential to lead one's life on the basis of *maat*, the order of the universe, both physical and moral, which came into existence at the creation of the world and is definitive—that is, incapable of improvement. Living in accordance with *maat* is described in the tomb of Petosiris as 'The Way of Life', and a frequently mentioned stimulus to follow this path is divine influence operating on the heart of the individual—that is, on the source of his moral being. Once again, this concept is not difficult to parallel earlier (for example, the old concept of the *netjer imy.k*, 'the god who is in you'), but it is much more systematically developed in the texts of the Late Period. To follow 'The Way of Life' under the guidance of god brought success in this world and also beyond the grave, where yet another sanction lay in wait. The day of judgement in the Hall of the Two Truths was set for all, and no distinction was made between rich and poor. However, this strong conviction that justice would ultimately be done did not prevent the expression of a *carpe diem* philosophy, revealing that the Egyptians had lost little of their love of life, and it is not surprising to find the appearance of the occasional protest at the unfairness of an early death that has prevented the enjoyment of all that life has to offer. Here again, however, we are not confronted with a complete novelty; for the fragility of Egyptian certainties about life after death is eloquently expressed in such earlier texts as the *Song of the Blind Harper* and Chapter 175 of the *Book of the Dead*. As for the principles of the mortuary cult, they remained the same in the Late Period, if less elaborately developed in practice, and old convictions such as the benefits to be gained by the recitation of formulas and the performance of funerary rituals retained much of their strength.

The concept of the prerequisites of the afterlife presented a somewhat contradictory picture, but again it was a question of working with and developing older ideas. Much effort was again spent by those who could afford it on the production of tombs, some of which are spectacular instances of conspicuous display. The mortuary complex of Mentuemhat at Thebes is the most impressive non-royal site in that or any area, and many a New Kingdom vizier would

Plan of the tomb of Mentuemhat. It shows the arrangement of the structures below ground-level which are entered by a descending passage to the east. This gives access via two columned halls to a great sun-court excavated in the rock but open to the sky which is flanked by chapels to north and south. This leads to another open court giving on to the subterranean part of the tomb which ends with the sarcophagus chamber at the extreme west of the installation. The walls were richly decorated with relief which shows a mixture of traditional elements, from such sites as the tombs of Menna and Rekhmira and the Deir el-Bahri complex, as well as contemporary features.

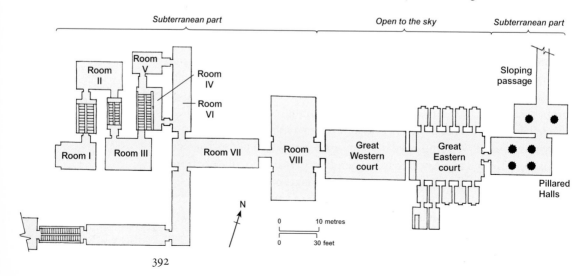

Subterranean part • Open to the sky • Subterranean part

Room II • Room V • Room IV • Room VI • Sloping passage • Room I • Room III • Room VII • Room VIII • Great Western court • Great Eastern court • Pillared Halls

N

0 — 10 metres
0 — 30 feet

have envied the tomb constructed for Bakenrenef looking out over the valley from the east escarpment at Saqqara.

In the Saite Period, particular ingenuity was expended on building unrobbable tombs that were filled solid with sand after interment, and had precisely the desired effect, but grave goods were no longer as plentiful or as rich as they had been in the New Kingdom, even though gold or gilt-silver masks and jewellery could still be buried with the deceased. This paucity of grave goods means that vaults are small—often little larger than the sarcophagi themselves. As far as low-status burials are concerned, we are better informed for this period than most others, particularly at Saqqara, where excavations have revealed bodies with little or no mummification interred in the poorest of coffins, frequently no more elaborate than palm-leaf mats, and deposited in a pit in the sand distinguished above ground, if at all, by nothing more than a simple marker to guide the poor attentions of a relative anxious to perform whatever minimal service could be afforded for the deceased. All this chimes well enough with indications from earlier periods to prove that at this level too the Late Period was continuing the ancient ways.

Biographical inscriptions reveal yet another shift of emphasis in the clear narrowing of the gap between the pharaoh and his subjects, and this is echoed by the ease with which non-royal persons were able to requisition ancient royal funerary literature: in several Saite tombs at Saqqara (including those of the vizier Bakenrenef, the commander of the royal fleet Tjanenhebu, and the physician Psamtek), the *Pyramid Texts* were employed, and fourth-century coffins also exemplified this development. The tomb of Petosiris shows a parallel phenomenon in that Petosiris himself claims at one point in his biographical inscription to have performed the old royal foundation ritual of stretching the cord. In all this, however, we are again not confronted with something totally new, given that the 12th Dynasty, for example, already provides ample demonstration of a willingness to concede the humanity of the supposed god-king. It is all too easy to ignore the fact that in every period of Egyptian history the

Painted relief from the east wall of the pronaos of the tomb of Petosiris at Tuna el-Gebel. A striking example of an attempt to reconcile old and new, this scene is based on the traditional tomb-chapel motif of harvesting grain, but the treatment of the subject departs radically from pharaonic iconography in dress, pose, the detailed treatment of the figures, and the attempt to create a sense of volume, all of which betray clear Greek influence.

393

relationship between the ideology of kingship and the practicalities of life was ultimately defined by historical experience, and the narrowing of the gap in these late sources reflects nothing less than the realities of the distribution of power in Late Period Egypt.

To conclude: the three centuries preceding the invasion of Egypt by Alexander the Great (332–323 BC) were centuries of no mean achievement. Although the country was twice subjected to Persian domination, it still succeeded in maintaining its independence for long periods against powerful enemies, and made a major impact on the course of the interminable Near Eastern power struggle as well as reasserting its interests on the Upper Nile. In the Saite Period several factors interacted to create the basis for success. In the first place, a family of rulers appeared who were both ideologically acceptable, politically streetwise, and militarily highly astute.

However, the Saites were also lucky in that for most of the dynasty the dynamics of imperialism in the Near East ran very much in their favour. Empires expand as long as their institutional structures and the will of their leaders can support such expansion. When the Assyrians and Chaldaeans attempted to incorporate Egypt into their empires, they were both operating at the outer limits of their capacity. Even a slight deterioration within their territory inevitably meant a diminution of resources that could be brought to bear against Egypt, to the extent that effective action and control became quite impossible. It is hardly surprising, therefore, that Assyrian rule was intermittent and very low key, whilst all the Chaldaeans could achieve was to threaten, invade, and withdraw.

The danger posed by the Persians was of a different order, since they possessed much greater assets in wealth and manpower, and initially a much more vigorous impetus to conquest derived ultimately from Cyrus. However able a pharaoh might be, if the Persians operated at the peak of their potential, the land of Egypt must fall. Yet the laws of grand strategy were the same for the Persians as their predecessors, and the marginal geographical position of Egypt in relation to the Achaemenid empire meant that it would inevitably be difficult to maintain permanent control and that the potential for successful revolt would always be there.

Against this background, the panorama presented by the fifth and fourth centuries BC of oscillation between rebellion, independence, and occupation becomes immediately intelligible. Yet none of this furious endeavour leads to any abatement in the vitality of Egyptian cultural life. Certainly we suffer badly from the severe loss of the art, architecture, and literary work of these years, but more than enough survives to reveal a society that was powerfully aware of its past while exploring new ways or, at least, insisting on finding its own points of cultural emphasis. Wherever we look, we are confronted by a powerful current of continuity united with a vital evolutionary dynamic that provides the obvious underpinning for and explanation of the very considerable achievements of the age of the Ptolemies that followed.

14 THE PTOLEMAIC PERIOD

(332–30 BC)

ALAN B. LLOYD

Ptolemaic Egypt is a tale of two cultures. Differing in ethos, focus, and aspiration, these cultures initially maintained a wary coexistence, in which convenience and the balance of power generated a viable degree of cooperation usually sufficiently effective to mask their mutual distaste. From the end of the third century BC, even this collaboration was increasingly eroded by the divisive pressures exerted by dynastic schism, maladministration, economic crisis, and Egyptian resentments. Not the least fascinating aspect of this complex relationship is the fact that, despite all its inner tensions, Egypt of the Ptolemies was in many ways spectacularly successful, whether we consider the achievements of the Graeco-Macedonian élite or those of the Egyptian cultural milieu.

Prelude

It is most appropriate to begin the study of Ptolemaic Egypt with the arrival of Alexander the Great in 332 BC, thus bringing to an end the second Persian Period, the passing of which was lamented by no one. Before Alexander resumed his conquests in 331 BC, he was obliged to address the problem of how to administer his new province.

The foundation of Alexandria was clearly an innovation intended to create a new base for governing the country, but in other respects Egypt's ancient ways prevailed. If we can trust the *Alexander Romance* (a semi-mythicizing biography written anonymously under the pseudonym of Callisthenes in about the second century AD or earlier), Alexander had himself crowned in the temple of Ptah at Memphis, thereby firmly asserting that he was assuming the mantle of an Egyptian pharaoh, but there is no doubt at all that he was conceptualized in those terms by the Egyptians, who gave him a standard royal titulary, and that he showed great respect for Egyptian religious susceptibilities. Keenly aware of the intrinsic strategic dangers latent in Egypt's wealth and geographical position, he evidently fought shy of concentration of power: the administration of the country was committed to an Egyptian called Doloaspis; the collection of tribute was entrusted to Kleomenes of Naukratis; the army was placed under the command of two officers, Peukestas and Balakros; and the navy was allotted a separate commander in the form of Polemon. Kleomenes was subsequently appointed governor of the entire province, which he administered with a high degree of corruption.

On Alexander's death in Babylon in June 323 BC, his mentally unpredictable half-brother Arrhidaeus (323–317 BC) was declared king, with Perdiccas as regent, on the understanding that, if the child yet to be born to Alexander's Bactrian wife Roxane were male, that child should be joint king. Major sections of the empire were at this point allocated by Perdiccas to Alexander's marshals, and in this division Ptolemy, son of Lagos, acquired Egypt, Libya, and 'those parts of Arabia that lie close to Egypt' with Kleomenes as his second in command.

The settlement of Perdiccas could not hold. It merely set the scene for the Wars of the Successors, which inevitably broke out to determine whether Alexander's empire would survive intact. This complex series of operations falls into two phases: the first, which ran from 321 to 301 BC, was fought out between the 'unitarians' (above all Perdiccas himself, Antigonus 'the one-eyed', and his son Demetrius 'the besieger'), who attempted to preserve the unity of the empire, and the 'separatists' (pre-eminently Ptolemy, Seleucos, and Lysimachos), who were determined to carve out their own kingdoms. Ptolemy's ambition speedily brought him to the fore as the major headache for the unitarians, who paid him the compliment of two invasions of Egypt, the first by Perdiccas in 321 BC and the second by Antigonus in 306 BC, both of which were defeated by Egypt's geography rather than by Ptolemy himself. The unity issue was resolved by the defeat and death of Antigonus at Ipsus in 301 BC, which decided this phase of the conflict in favour of the separatists. By that time all the major protagonists, including Ptolemy, had already anticipated this outcome by declaring themselves kings.

High Summer of a Kingdom

The second phase of the Wars of the Successors ran from 301 to 280 BC and is characterized by struggles between the separatists to establish, maintain, or increase their kingdoms. It came to an end with the death of Lysimachos at Corupedium in 281 BC, and the subsequent assassination of his conqueror, Seleucus, later in the same year. The outcome of these events was critical for the subsequent history of the Hellenistic world in that it yielded three great kingdoms: Macedon, with pretensions to rule neighbouring states that were sometimes realized, sometimes not; the Seleucid empire, based on Syria and

Mesopotamia; and the empire of the Ptolemies, the core of which was Egypt and Cyrenaica. With these kingdoms we are confronted with the protagonists in a power game that was to dominate the eastern Mediterranean and the Levant until Egypt was brought under Roman control in 30 BC.

It is important to grasp that the rivalry between these kingdoms was not confined to matters of political or military control, important though these issues were. The underlying psychological motivation lay where we should expect it to lie in any Graeco-Macedonian context—that is, in an invincible impetus to self-assertion that would, in turn, generate prestige. Cutting a fine figure in the great arena of Graeco-Macedonian activity—even beyond—and placing the opposition firmly in the shade were ultimately the most important issues. Certainly, military conquest was a major means of achieving this, but the creation of a kingdom of unequalled splendour was equally important and could absorb an enormous amount of effort and resources. In this battle for power and prestige the Ptolemies were beyond doubt the outright winners, in the third century at least.

To all three kingdoms the key issue of high politics and grand strategy was to expand their empires at the expense of their rivals by whatever means they could, but the history of their conflicts is far from simple. It is clear that the ambitions of the early Ptolemies were such that they posed a serious threat to the aspirations of both the other major players, who found it convenient to pool their resources against the common enemy. Not surprisingly, therefore, in the early 270s BC we find a peace being concluded between Macedon and the Seleucids, which was to become one of the very few constants in the history of the third century BC.

For the Ptolemies there were two main areas of expansionist activity: (1) the ancient centres of Greek culture in the eastern Mediterranean, and (2) Syria–Palestine. As for the first, it is important to grasp that the rulers of all these Hellenistic kingdoms felt themselves to be Macedonians with Macedonian traditions and a close and deep affinity with Greek culture. Therefore, the arena in which they above all wished to make their mark was the mainland of Greece, the Aegean, and the Greek cities on the coast of Asia Minor. For the Ptolemies of the third century BC this meant in political and military terms a long struggle for the hegemony of Greece against Macedon, which had acquired control of a large part of the area in the time of Philip II and regarded it unequivocally as Macedonian by right of conquest. This struggle, in turn, enmeshed the Ptolemies in supporting the major political forces in the Greek world, above all Epirus, the Aetolian and Achaean leagues, Athens, and Sparta, who inevitably looked to Egypt for help against the common enemy, but it also entailed efforts to maintain bases on and in the Aegean and along the south coast of Asia Minor, control of Cyprus, and a requirement to maintain an alliance with the strategically and economically important island of Rhodes. Inevitably, Ptolemaic ambitions in Asia Minor brought them into stark conflict with Seleucid interests in that area.

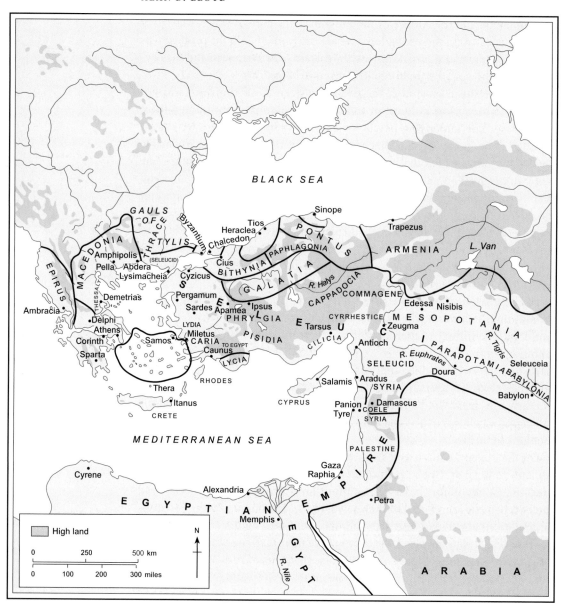

Map of the Mediterranean region during the Ptolemaic Period (332–30 BC).

Despite the challenge of two great kingdoms, the first three Ptolemies were initially highly successful in realizing their ambitions in the Aegean. Reviewing their achievements in that quarter, Polybius writes as follows:

their sphere of control included the dynasts in Asia and also the islands, as they were masters of the most important cities, strongholds, and harbours along the whole coast from Pamphylia to the Hellespont and the region of Lysimachia. They kept watch on affairs in Thrace and Macedonia through their control of Aenus and Maronea and of even more distant cities, and, in this way, having extended their reach so far and having shielded themselves at a great distance with these client kings, they never worried about

398

the safety of Egypt. That was why they rightly devoted much attention to external affairs . . . (Polybius, 5. 34).

However, we should read these words with care. Polybius does not say that these kings held an empire with clearly defined frontiers and a coherent imperial administration. The passage reveals—and this is confirmed by other evidence—that this 'empire' was, in truth, a thing of nuances, an amalgam of bases, alliances, protectorates, and friendly factions or individuals, frequently bought with Egyptian gold, forming a network of nodes through which the Ptolemies were able to exert political and military power. Nor, indeed, was the sphere a static one even in these early years. In the struggles generated by these ambitions, the early Ptolemies enjoyed mixed fortunes, but ultimately the Macedonians and Seleucids prevailed. By the end of the third century BC, Ptolemaic influence in Greece was gone as a significant force, although a garrison was maintained on Thera in the south Aegean until 145 BC. As for Asia Minor, the triumphs of Antiochus III in that area during the Fifth Syrian War precipitated the end of Ptolemaic hegemony on the west and south coast by c.195 BC.

The pattern of initial expansion giving way to severe recession by the early second century BC was repeated in Syria–Palestine. The determination to bring Coele-Syria and the Phoenician cities into the Ptolemaic kingdom surfaced early. The area had, of course, been a traditional focus of concern in pharaonic times, but there were better reasons than precedent for the Ptolemies to wish to hold it: strategically, its occupation facilitated the defence of Egypt as well as the Ptolemaic province of Cyprus; control of Phoenicia gave the Ptolemies access to Phoenician naval resources; finally, the occupation also yielded major economic benefits both in fiscal terms, and with regard to access to major trade routes (including the great commercial centre of Petra), and, in particular, the ability to exploit the timber resources of the Lebanon, which was a significant source of shipbuilding timber for the Ptolemaic fleet. Not surprisingly, therefore, Ptolemy I (305–285 BC) made repeated efforts to gain control of this area: he held it in the period 320–315 BC and briefly after the Battle of Gaza in 312, but in 301 BC he occupied Syria–Palestine probably as far as the Eleutherus River, despite the fact that this territory had been allocated to Seleucus after Ipsus. The determination of the Seleucids to maintain their claims gave rise to no fewer than six Syrian Wars beginning in the reign of Ptolemy II (285–246 BC) and ending with that of Ptolemy VI (180–145 BC), although the issue was decided to all intents and purposes by the Egyptian defeat at Panion in 200 BC, as a result of which Ptolemy V (205–180 BC) conceded the claims of the Seleucids to Syria and Phoenicia in c.195 BC.

These Ptolemaic military successes and ultimate failure were linked to a number of prerequisites: an effective army and navy; an administrative system at home that provided the basis, above all the economic infrastructure, to fund expansion; conditions within the kingdom that made it possible to concentrate such efforts on foreign enterprises; and rulers with the vision and capacity to carry them forward.

Military Might

The Ptolemaic army, like all its Hellenistic counterparts, was the army of Alexander, modified in the light of experience and necessity. Alexander's forces consisted of a variety of complementary units that reflected a tactical concept based on pinning the enemy down by infantry pressure along much of the line and delivering the crucial assault at a selected point by means of heavy cavalry. This meant that the major tactical elements were a phalanx of heavy infantry armed with pikes of considerable length (5.5 m., later increased) and a strike force of heavy cavalry made up of squadrons of Macedonians, Thessalians, and allies. The gap inevitably arising in action between these elements was plugged by élite light infantry called *hypaspists*, 3,000 strong. These field forces, on which victory in general actions depended, were supplemented by a wide range of light troops, both horse and foot, and largely mercenary, and complemented by a highly sophisticated siege train.

When we turn to the armies of the Ptolemies, we encounter much that Alexander would have found immediately recognizable. At Gaza in 312 BC the Ptolemaic assault was delivered by a force of 3,000 cavalry armed with swords and the traditional Macedonian cavalry pike or *xyston*. This succeeded in turning the flank of the opposing cavalry force, which broke and fled the field, exposing the enemy phalanx to an assault on its left flank. Faced with this threat, they quickly turned tail and fled in confusion. Almost a century later the tactical thinking at Raphia (217 BC) was very similar: Ptolemy IV's cavalry on the left wing was driven from the field by its Seleucid opposite numbers, whilst the Ptolemaic cavalry on the right wing reciprocated by defeating the Seleucid horsemen facing them. In this battle, however, victory was decided by Ptolemy's phalanx, which, on the king's personal encouragement, levelled pikes and charged the opposing phalanx which quickly collapsed. In 200 BC, Panion provides yet another example of cavalry as the striking wing, here very much to the disadvantage of the Ptolemaic army, since the Seleucid cavalry was able to demolish its left wing, drive it from the field, and then return to threaten the rear of the Ptolemaic phalanx, which had no alternative but to withdraw.

Despite the underlying tactical similarity to the armies of Philip II and Alexander, there was one crucial innovation that featured in all three actions: the use of war elephants, which was a tactic learned from the Indians. The elephants were employed as an ancient equivalent of the tank, in order to assault and disrupt the enemy line. One solution to such an assault was to prevent them reaching the line in the first place, and this was achieved brilliantly by Ptolemy I at Gaza by throwing out in front of his army a screen of men armed with iron-covered stakes that were fixed into the ground to block the advancing elephants of Demetrius. Another remedy, clearly generally adopted, was to attack the elephants and their drivers with highly mobile light troops armed with javelins or bows. This meant, in turn, that any force using elephants could not advance without its own light-armed troops in attendance to neutralize those of the opposition. The major problem of the Ptolemies in using the elephant was that of getting an adequate supply of good-quality animals—that is, Indian elephants. We hear of none in the army of Ptolemy I at Gaza, but after the defeat of Demetrius' elephant force he captured the survivors. The Ptolemaic attempt to solve the problem in the long term was to use African elephants, and hunts for these animals are mentioned on several occasions in our sources. Unfortunately, the only trainable elephants in Africa are the forest variety which is smaller than the Indian, so that it is not surprising to find that Ptolemy IV's elephants at Raphia quickly turned tail and fell back on his lines, with serious, though not disastrous, consequences for the army as a whole. We hear of no Ptolemaic elephants at Panion, though our one surviving source on this action is highly defective, but it is interesting to note that Seleucid elephants are claimed to have panicked the Aetolian cavalry on the crucial Egyptian left wing, and elephants are also mentioned as participating in the final encircling movement against the Ptolemaic phalanx that sealed the defeat of the entire army.

One of the most notable changes in the Ptolemaic army in the fourth and third centuries BC is the progressive dilution of its Macedonian element, initially in favour of mercenaries but ultimately leading to the incorporation of the Egyptian *machimoi*, or warrior class. As early as Gaza in 312 BC Diodorus describes the army as containing 18,000 infantry and 4,000 cavalry, partly Macedonian, partly mercenary, but we are also informed that there were numerous Egyptians in it, some employed as baggage-carriers, others as soldiers, presumably auxiliaries. By the time we get to Raphia these trends have gone much further. Here Ptolemy IV disposed of an élite cavalry force 3,000 strong, of which over 2,000 were Libyans or Egyptians. Similarly, in a phalanx of probably 45,000 men no fewer than 20,000 were Egyptian. Ptolemy fielded, in addition, 2,000 mercenary cavalry, both Greek and non-Greek, 3,000 Cretans, 3,000 Libyans, and 4,000 Thracians and Galatians. Indeed, it is highly improbable that Macedonians and their descendants formed more than a small proportion of this army.

The cost of funding such a large mercenary force was clearly a heavy drain on the resources of the Crown, which could be met only if the economy of the country was functioning properly, but the internal disruptions that rose thick and fast after the death of Ptolemy IV were bound to impair the ability of the rulers of Egypt to maintain such troops. The problem of guaranteeing an adequate supply of soldiers drawn from ethnic groups traditionally exploited by Macedon was addressed at an early stage by the Ptolemies through the creation of a large military reserve stationed in settlements throughout the country. In these places they were given land allotments whose size was determined both by rank and type of unit. These plots they often did not farm themselves but simply used as a source of income, but they received them on the understanding that, whenever they were needed, they would be called up for service, as in the case of the 4,000 Thracians and Galatians mentioned in the build-up to the Raphia campaign. It is, however, intriguing that this is the only contingent in this category mentioned by Polybius at that juncture, and the fact that it formed a relatively small part of the army fielded for this operation indicates that *cleruchs* (military settlers to whom the king gave allotments of land called *kleroi*) were not regarded as the ideal source for the bulk of the army.

Another obvious solution to the military manpower problem was the Egyptian militia or *machimoi*, a remedy first tried apparently at Gaza that fell into abeyance for many years, probably through a keen awareness of its possible political disadvantages. Ultimately, short-term necessity swept long-term considerations imperiously away, and we find this group being exploited with spectacular success at Raphia, where the bulk of the phalanx which gave Ptolemy the victory consisted of Egyptian soldiers. The growing reliance on this class created by the increasing difficulty in acquiring troops from traditional Ptolemaic sources led to a critical shift in the balance of power within the country, which is sharply highlighted by Polybius:

As for Ptolemy, his war against the Egyptians followed immediately on these events. For the aforementioned king, by arming the Egyptians for his war against Antiochus, decided on a course of action which was appropriate to the immediate circumstances, but ignored the future consequences. For the soldiers, exalted by their victory of Raphia, were no longer inclined to obey orders, but were casting around for a leader and figurehead, thinking themselves capable of looking after themselves. In this they finally succeeded, not long afterwards.   (Polybius 5. 107)

The army, however, was not the only requirement. The realization of Ptolemaic ambitions in the Aegean and Eastern Mediterranean was also dependent on the maintenance of a powerful battle fleet. This force was not only a means of establishing and maintaining a Ptolemaic presence in the area but also served as a weapon in the propaganda battle for prestige and status. As in more modern times, large and powerful naval units could be used to generate a sense of power even when direct armed confrontation was not at issue. The critical strategic importance of the fleet was grasped from the very beginning of the Ptolemaic period, and its rise and decline are an unfailing barometer of Lagid imperial and political fortunes in the Greek world.

Tactically, naval warfare developed to a marked degree in the late fourth century BC. The trends emerge clearly in the best recorded of Ptolemaic sea fights, the Battle of Salamis, which was fought off the east coast of Cyprus in 306 BC and ended in the catastrophic defeat of the Egyptian fleet. The action arose from an attempt by Ptolemy to relieve his brother Menelaos, who was being besieged in Salamis on land and sea by Demetrius, son of Antigonus. Ptolemy had approximately 140 warships, facing perhaps 180 of the enemy. Diodorus, our fullest source, unfortunately for our purposes, gives more information on the fleet of Demetrius than that of Ptolemy, but there can be little doubt that these details apply equally well to the opposition. A number of points emerge: in the first place, we hear of *soldiers* being embarked and of much action involving them; second, Demetrius equipped his ships with ballistae and catapults capable of firing bolts three spans (*c*.0.5 m.) in length, which were used to good effect; third, ships of various rates were engaged—for example, Demetrius' powerful left wing contained 30 'fours', 10 'fives', 10 'sixes', and 7 'sevens', though the bulk of his fleet consisted of 'fives'. The Ptolemaic fleet, on the other hand, was made up entirely of 'fives' and 'fours'; furthermore, both fleets appear to have drawn up for battle as three blocks of ships—a centre with a wing on either side—but Demetrius made his seaward wing particularly powerful while Ptolemy did likewise on the landward side; finally, we should note that the fleets employed a primitive system of signalling.

This summary reveals several important features. In the first place, naval warfare has clearly been powerfully influenced by warfare on land. While ramming manœuvres were still being executed, the emphasis has shifted from fighting battles of manœuvre to conducting land battles at sea,

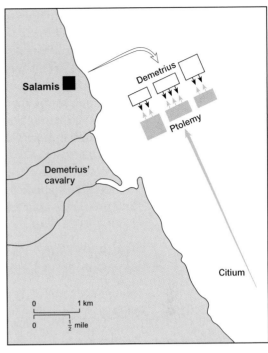

which placed a heavy premium on developing ever bigger units capable of carrying large forces of marines who force a decision by slogging it out toe-to-toe with the enemy. Athenaeus' description of Philadelphus' fleet demonstrates the point perfectly: not only does he state that it contained 2 'thirties', 1 'twenty', 4 'thirteens', 2 'twelves', 14 'elevens', 30 'nines', 37 'sevens', 5 'sixes', 17 'fives' (as well as a force of ships rated as 'fours' to 'one-and-a-halfs' which was numerically double the rest), but he also describes a monstrous 'forty' of Ptolemy IV that he makes a point of saying was capable of carrying no fewer than 2,850 marines. The structure of these heavy ships has been much misunderstood, older literature interpreting the terms used to designate them as referring to banks of oars. This is quite impossible. These vessels were propelled mainly, if not completely, by multiple-rower sweeps and would never have had more than three banks of oars, and the 'rating' must refer to the number of oarsmen in a *unit* of rowers. The largest ships are now known to have had a catamaran structure that would obviously greatly increase the deck space available for marines, making such ships a particularly formidable proposition in a land-battle-at-sea. The militarization of naval warfare is also illustrated by the mounting of artillery aboard ship, a practice that obviously reflects the greatly enhanced importance of artillery for both siege warfare and field use in the army of Philip II and Alexander. The use of a heavy wing as a strike force by both protagonists is another case of adapting land warfare to the sea, since the employment of that principle was a fundamental tactical device in the Macedonian army. The use of signals will also emanate from the same source.

Powerful and effective though the Ptolemaic fleet was in the first half century

Fleet dispositions at the Battle of Salamis exemplify the principle of a concentrated heavy assault on part of the enemy line much used in land warfare after the Battle of Leuctra in 371 BC. Demetrius' left wing, which he led personally, was the heavy wing on which he relied to shatter its opposite number and roll up the line against the shore, the centre and the right wing were relatively lightly held. Ptolemy placed the weight of his attack on the left wing. Ptolemy's left was victorious, but Demetrius' heavy contingent routed the opposing right wing and then induced the collapse of the Ptolemaic centre.

of the dynasty, their shipbuilding efforts in themselves could not guarantee consistent success, and in the mid-third century BC their fleets suffered three hammer blows that presaged the gradual unravelling of Ptolemaic sea power in the area: at Ephesus (probably in 258 BC) a Ptolemaic fleet suffered a reverse at the hands of the Rhodian admiral Agathostratus, probably, in this case, being outmanœuvred by superior seamanship rather than outfought in a struggle between marines; apparently about the same time the Ptolemies suffered a second major reverse off Cos at the hands of Antigonus Gonatas, king of Macedon, in which a powerful three-banked ship played a critical role in bringing the Macedonians victory; subsequently, apparently c.245 BC, Antigonus, although outnumbered, inflicted another defeat on the Ptolemaic navy at Andros, this time probably by outfighting the Ptolemaic marines.

The Land of Egypt

The Ptolemies' intense competitive spirit of self-assertion did not confine itself to military conflict. There were other weapons in the struggle for status and prestige in the cockpit of the Hellenistic world, which included their capital city of Alexandria. Founded by Alexander in 331 BC, this city became the Ptolemaic capital and was vigorously exploited from the beginning of the period as the major showcase for Ptolemaic wealth and splendour and by the same token as the most significant non-military means by which the Ptolemies could vie with and surpass their rivals. It quickly became the most spectacular city in the Hellenistic world. Strabo, who visited the city just after the demise of the Ptolemaic dynasty, had no doubt of the importance of conspicuous display in Ptolemaic building on the site: he describes the palace quarter in the northern part of the city as follows:

The city has most beautiful public enclosures and the palaces, which cover a fourth or even a third of its entire area. For just as each of the kings from love of splendour used to add some ornament to the public monuments, so also would he invest himself at his own expense with a residence in addition to those already in existence so that now, to quote the Poet [Homer], 'there is building after building'. All, however, are connected both with each other and with the harbour, even those that lie outside the harbour. (Strabo, *Geography* 17. 1. 8)

But there was much more than that. Closely associated with these installations was the *Sema*, the burial place of the Ptolemaic kings, also containing the body of Alexander the Great himself, which had originally been enclosed in a gold sarcophagus, though this was subsequently replaced by one of glass. The possession of this body was, in itself, one of the greatest propaganda assets that the Ptolemies enjoyed and was the result of an astute hijacking operation carried out by Ptolemy, son of Lagus, when the corpse was being transferred to Macedon for burial in the royal necropolis at Aegae. The most spectacular of all Alexandria's buildings was, of course, the lighthouse on the east end of Pharos

Head of an unidentified Ptolemy in grey schist; probably end of the 3rd century BC. This sculpture attempts to combine Egyptian and Hellenistic features with limited success. Based on traditional Egyptian royal iconography, it shows the king wearing the *nemes* headdress with uraeus and is executed in a medium much used in pharaonic times. On the other hand, the rendering of the face and the coiffure are entirely Hellenistic in character.

island. Yet another renowned feature of the city was the Mouseion, of which the world-famous library formed part. This institution was founded by Ptolemy I as part of a policy of making Alexandria the centre of Greek culture. The Mouseion was modelled on the schools of Plato and Aristotle at Athens and, like them, was a centre of research and instruction. Great efforts were expended to get volumes for this library, and Ptolemy I's agent Demetrius of Phalerum dispatched searchers all over the Greek world to obtain the required texts. So successful were the efforts of the Ptolemies in this respect that by the end of the period the library appears to have held no fewer than 700,000 volumes, and the entire installation provided a superb context for the pursuit of scholarship and scientific enquiry, so that Alexandria quickly became the major centre for these activities, boasting such figures as Eratosthenes of Cyrene (*c*.285–194) in science, Herophilus of Chalcedon (*c.*330–260 BC) in medicine, Zenodotus of Ephesus (born *c.*325 BC) and Aristarchus of Samothrace (*c.*217–145 BC) in literary scholarship, and Apollonius of Rhodes and Callimachus of Cyrene (both third century BC) in creative writing.

Alexandria also offered potential as a venue for great panhellenic events that attracted participants from the entire Greek world, who were thus able to marvel at the city that became the Ptolemies' masterpiece. Ptolemy II went so far as to establish a four-yearly festival called the Ptolemaieia (probably in 279/8 BC), which was intended to honour his father and, at the same time, the dynasty that he founded. Our sources are quite clear that this festival was intended to be equal in status to the Olympic Games themselves. We are particularly well informed on a spectacular piece of grand theatre organized on behalf of Ptolemy II, which illustrates the lengths and expense to which these rulers would go

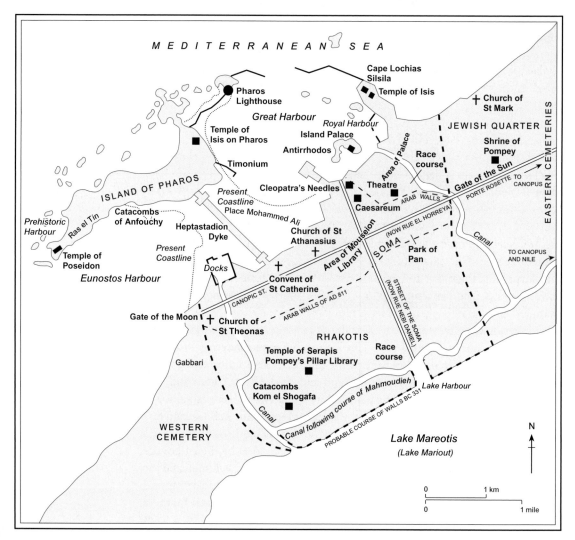

to impress their Graeco-Macedonian audience. Callixeinus of Rhodes describes in very great detail a *pompe*, 'procession', performed in the city's stadium and, as a preamble, tells of a remarkable pavilion constructed in the palace area that was intended to house a great *symposion*, 'drinking party', for the most distinguished guests. This structure was remarkable for its size and splendour and contained many extraordinary features: enormously expensive and lavish fittings and equipment, a remarkable variety of animal pelts of unusual size, rich floral embellishment that would not have been possible anywhere else in the world, and sculptures and paintings of the highest quality and value. In addition, this structure was designed to make statements about Ptolemaic kingship: it combined at several points Greek and Egyptian motifs, gave prominence to the Ptolemaic heraldic eagle linking the family with Zeus, insisted on the military aspects of Ptolemaic kingship, and asserted links with Dionysus and Apollo. The procession of Dionysus, which this remarkable structure was meant to service, continues the same propaganda line: the dynastic agenda emerges strongly in the association of Ptolemy I, Berenice, and Alexander the Great himself; the marked Dionysiac dimension to the procession asserts the dynasty's affinities with the god; the wealth of the kingdom is heavily emphasized in the copious references to the valuable commodities to which it had access such as frankincense, myrrh, saffron, and gold, as well as to Egypt's agricultural productivity. Access to remarkable animals in great quantities is also a major feature; we have a foreign-policy reference in the symbol representing the strategically critical city of Corinth in the procession; and the military might of Egypt is powerfully impressed on the spectator by the participation of a force of no fewer than 57,600 infantry and 23,200 cavalry. In all this activity at Alexandria, architectural and otherwise, the overwhelming cultural emphasis is on things Graeco-Macedonian, but the Ptolemies were strongly aware of the fascination that pharaonic civilization had long held for the Greek world and were far from averse to adding a touch of exotic spice drawn from that quarter. It is not surprising, therefore, to find evidence of the large-scale removal of Egyptian monuments to Alexandria or to identify examples in the city of colossal statues of Ptolemaic kings and queens represented in traditional Egyptian style.

The expense of maintaining these military operations and dynastic pretensions was enormous and presupposed a highly effective infrastructure capable of maximizing the potential of the Egyptian economy both internally and externally. The most effective methods for running the land of Egypt had been devised by the ancient Egyptians themselves. This the Ptolemies knew full well and contented themselves essentially with refining this ancient system in the interest of maximum economic return. The key principle of government was kingship, but a kingship rather more complex than that of the Ptolemies' Egyptian predecessors: the Ptolemies were not simply pharaohs but also Macedonian kings ruling a Graeco-Macedonian élite within the country, as well as subject peoples beyond. In the eyes of the Macedonians the king's claim to Egypt and its dependent provinces lay in the fact that it was 'spear-won'

Facing: the city of Alexandria. Its commercial pre-eminence was based on three main harbours: the deep Great Harbour formed by Cape Lochias and Pharos Island which was joined to the mainland by the artificial Heptastadium (also an aqueduct) and capable of taking the largest ships; Eunostos Harbour to the west; and the harbour on Lake Mareotis which received cargoes from inland which fed the export trade. The city's streets were designed on a chessboard pattern with the main thoroughfare (30 m. wide) running east-west from the Canobic Gate to the Gate of the Moon. The main quarters of the city were (from west to east) the Necropolis (famed for its gardens), Rhakotis (the Egyptian area), the Royal Quarter, and the Jewish Quarter.

Facing: limestone bust of Ptolemy II. This portrait is in Egyptian style following the traditions of the 30th Dynasty and shows the king wearing the *nemes* headdress with uraeus serpent.

territory—that is, his right to rule was the right of conquest, and by that right the kingdom became his estate to administer as he thought fit. Initially, this kingship was exercised by Alexander the Great, then Arrhidaeus, his brother, and Alexander IV (317–310 BC), Alexander's son, while Ptolemy, son of Lagus, was technically only the governor of the province, but in 305 BC Ptolemy himself assumed the crown, and a crown that had to be held fully within Macedonian tradition. In Macedon, to make good a claim to the throne two things were traditionally necessary: that Argead blood should flow through the veins of the claimant and that the army should formally approve the accession. The problem of satisfying the first condition was neatly solved by the claim that Ptolemy I was not the son of his historical father Lagus at all but of Philip II himself, who had already impregnated Ptolemy's mother before she was given to Lagus. As for acclamation by the army at Alexandria, it is not conspicuous in our sources but it was clearly long a recognized principle.

The process of validating Ptolemaic kingship in non-Egyptian contexts did not stop at such traditional Macedonian principles, as indeed it could not, because very quickly Macedonians lost their importance in the kingdom to the myriad Greeks who offered their services to Egypt or simply featured as subjects in the far-flung foreign domains that fell initially under Ptolemaic authority. From the time of Ptolemy II we find the claim being made that the king and his wife were themselves gods, a notion that quickly developed into the concept that the king belonged to a *hiera oikia* or 'sacred family' consisting of the living king and all dead rulers of the dynasty, including Alexander, through whom Ptolemies could derive their ancestry from Zeus himself (if the claim of direct descent from Philip was not accepted). These concepts also brought with them a claim of descent from Heracles and Dionysus that played a prominent role in the Ptolemaic propaganda of kingship. This body of concepts was associated with an offering cult in honour of the king and his consort that was essentially a ruler cult providing an opportunity to Greek subjects for the corporate acknowledgement and reaffirmation of the Ptolemies' political position—that is, we are confronted with a clear case of the use of cult activity as a support for a political system, a mechanism whose merits were subsequently not lost on Roman emperors. This development has frequently been claimed to have been inspired by Egyptian concepts, but anyone familiar with the development of fourth-century Greek thought on the relationship between human and divine and the clear blurring of the dividing line between man and god will have no difficulty in identifying the hellenic antecedents of this notion.

A very remarkable development within this royal house was the establishment of full brother–sister marriage as a recurrent, though not consistent, practice. This usage, initiated by Ptolemy II, who married his full-sister Arsinoe II, has frequently been claimed to have evolved on the basis of Egyptian historical precedent, a notion that has persisted into recent literature, despite the total lack of reliable pharaonic evidence that full brother–sister marriage was ever practised by Egyptian kings. It is possible that the *mythological* brother–sister

Limestone head of Queen Arsinoe II, sister and wife of Ptolemy II Philadelphus; *c*.270 BC. The piece shows workmanship of a very high quality and is an excellent example of the use of traditional Egyptian art to portray a Ptolemaic ruler. The queen is depicted wearing a heavy wig with lappets and the double uraeus. The stone dowel on top was almost certainly intended to receive the sun disc and cow horns which would identify the queen with Isis. The triangular face is well modelled and shows a slight smile.

marriage between Isis and Osiris had some influence in moving the Ptolemies in this direction, and a parallel was certainly drawn, but brother–sister marriage has an obvious Greek mythological prototype in the marriage of Zeus and Hera, which was easy to invoke for a family that claimed Zeus as an ancestor. Be that as it may, the underlying rationale for introducing the practice is likely to have had a severely practical dimension. Arsinoe II was a woman of formidable ability and strength of character, like so many Graeco-Macedonian women of rank—it is no coincidence that the best-known Ptolemy is Cleopatra VII (51–30 BC)—and the marriage guaranteed, or helped to guarantee, that she worked for, not against, him. Furthermore, it ensured that she did not marry a possible rival whose position would thereby have been powerfully enhanced. Above all, the union ensured Ptolemaic control of the major assets at her disposal from her previous marriage. The precedent, once set, was followed by many Ptolemaic rulers and was far from an unalloyed asset. Most obviously, by giving an institutional basis for the exercise of royal power by royal women at the very highest level, the Ptolemies impaired the position of the monarchy itself and contributed significantly to the long history of dynastic instability that crippled the family. The inherent dangers of the practice were further aggravated by the Ptolemaic taste for polygamy, which could not but create disastrous rivalries for the succession.

As for the Egyptians, they cast the Ptolemies in the role of pharaoh, the only form of legitimization of supreme political power that they knew. The first Ptolemy *known* to have been crowned pharaoh in the traditional manner was Ptolemy V, but there is a tradition that Alexander underwent this ceremony, and the balance of probability must lie heavily in favour of the assumption that it was standard practice. Certainly they were all *treated* as pharaohs on Egyptian monuments from the Macedonian conquest itself.

Below the king we find an administrative structure that has all the hallmarks of the pharaonic system made sharper. The overriding concern of the Ptolemaic system at all levels was fiscal, a fact that is reflected in the activities of the *dioiketes*, 'manager', the major officer of state whose chief concern was the financial administration of the kingdom. He was assisted by a veritable army of subordinates, including the *eklogistes*, 'accountant', and, at a later stage, the *idios logos*, 'privy purse', who was responsible for the private resources of the king. This economic focus is also in evidence when we turn to local government, which was based on the traditional system of 'nomoi' (the Greek term for ancient Egyptian *sepatu*), comprising about forty administrative districts comparable to modern British counties. Within these provinces agricultural production was the key focus. All land technically belonged to the Crown, but for practical purposes it was carefully divided into two categories: *basilike ge*, 'royal land', worked by 'royal farmers' holding their land on lease and paying a yearly rent, and *ge en aphesei*, 'remitted land', which fell into a number of categories: *hiera ge*, 'temple land', allocated to temples as their economic base; *klerouchike ge*, 'land held by cleruchs', parcels of which could be found throughout the country and consisted of *kleroi*, 'allotments', assigned to soldiers in return for military service as required; *ge en doreai*, 'land held in gift', assigned to servants of the Crown as a stipend for exercising government office and tied to that function; *idioktetos ge*, 'private land'—that is, land which was *de facto*, if not *de iure*, held by private individuals; and, finally, *politike ge*, 'city land', assigned to the very small number of Greek-style cities in Egypt. However, whatever the land title, agricultural activity was meticulously controlled by central government down to the smallest detail with the simple aim of maximizing the return to the royal treasury. The following extract from an administrative papyrus is typical of the uncompromising and pervasive rigour of this system:

Audit the revenue accounts, if possible, village by village—and we think it not to be impossible, if you devote yourself zealously to the matter. If this is not possible, [do it] by toparchies, approving in the audit nothing but payments to the bank in the case of money taxes, and in the case of corn dues or oil-bearing produce only deliveries to the corn-collectors. If there is any deficit in these, compel the toparchs and the tax-farmers to pay into the banks, for the arrears in corn, the values assigned in the ordinance, for those in oil-bearing produce, liquid produce according to each kind.   (*Papyri Tebtunis* 703. 117–34)

The same level of state control is equally visible in all other forms of economic activity—the exploitation of mines and quarries, the production of papyrus, the operation of the novel banking system, currency control, and also foreign commerce, in which Philadelphus was conspicuously active, not only opening or maintaining lucrative foreign trading connections but facilitating it by large-scale engineering enterprises such as the completion of the Pharos lighthouse, the improvement of the Koptos road joining the Nile Valley to the Red Sea, and the reopening of the old Persian canal joining the Pelusiac branch of the Nile to the Gulf of Suez.

The relationship between the Graeco-Macedonian élite and their Egyptian subjects in the earlier phase of Ptolemaic rule is not always clear and, where it is, it shows some inconsistency. An inscription at Akhmim appears to refer to a

Ptolemaic princess who had married a prince of the 30th Dynasty, and the old Egyptian aristocracy was certainly not relegated to impotence: members of the 30th Dynasty royal line seem to have retained high military office into the Macedonian Period; in the reign of Ptolemy II we find a man called Sennush-epes as overseer of the royal harem and holding high office in the Koptite nome; evidence from the same reign also places Egyptians in high administrative and military positions within the Mendesian nome. These and other cases justify the strong suspicion that the Egyptian Dionysius Petosarapis, who appears with high court rank in Alexandria in the 160s BC, had more precedents in the early Ptolemaic Period than we are often inclined at present to concede.

Evidence is much fuller for the large class of priests and temple scribes, although we should not fall into the trap of regarding them as a closed group. Priestly office was compatible with secular office, so that we cannot maintain a firm distinction between a secular aristocracy of rank and office, on the one

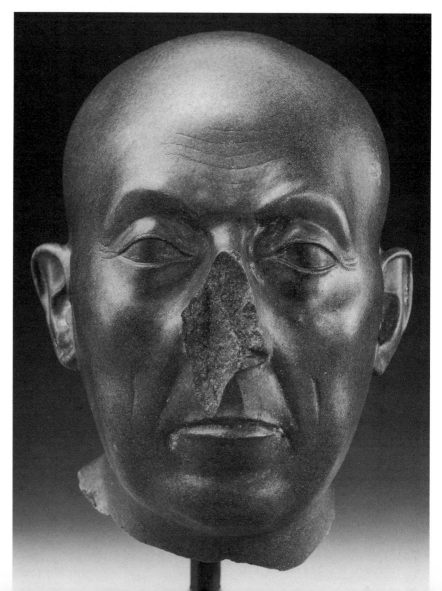

The Boston Green Head; probably late 3rd–early 2nd century BC. This piece from the Memphite Serapeum, with its high polish, superb craftsmanship, and its interest in the individual exemplifies
all that is best in Late Period sculpture and is one of the pinnacles of Egyptian artistic genius. The extraordinary sense of the underlying bone structure, the furrowed brow, the crow's feet in the corners of the eyes, and the highly unusual facial wart all create a powerful sense of personality which leaves no doubt that the head is a portrait.

hand, and ecclesiastical status, on the other. The priests were based at numerous temples, which were frequently rebuilt or embellished in Ptolemaic times and still constitute some of the most spectacular and complete remains of pharaonic culture. One of the best examples is the temple of Horus the Behdetite at Edfu, which is virtually completely Ptolemaic, being a focus of building activity from 237 until 57 BC, although it is highly significant that the Ptolemies chose to retain for the holy-of-holies the shrine of Nectanebo II, thus affirming their continuity with Egypt's past. Another major focus of Ptolemaic temple-building activity was Philae, where again we see close links affirmed with the last native Egyptian Dynasty. These and all other temples in the land continued to perform their ancient function as the power houses of Egypt, the interface between the human and divine in which pharaoh, through his proxy, the local high priest, conducted the critical rituals of maintenance for the gods, and the gods, in turn, channelled their life-giving power through pharaoh into Egypt.

Basalt head; 1st century BC. Here the gradual erosion of Egyptian culture in the later Ptolemaic period is clearly exemplified. The hair-line is Hellenistic, and the Hellenistic tradition of portraiture is also evident in the treatment of the face, particularly the nose and mouth. On the other hand, an Egyptian artistic vision is easily identifiable in the schematic treatment of the curls and the idealized and simplified rendering of the face.

One of the distinctive features of major state temples in the Ptolemaic and Roman periods was the provision of a small peripteral temple, invariably placed at right angles to the main temple, for which Champollion coined the term *mammisi* (an invented Coptic word meaning 'birth house'). The Ptolemaic *mammisis* were usually surrounded by colonnades with intercolumnar screen walls, and they were used to celebrate the rituals of the marriage of the goddess (Isis or Hathor) and the birth of the child-god. There appear to have been earlier counterparts of the *mammisi* in the form of 18th Dynasty reliefs describing the divine birth of the king at Deir el-Bahri and Luxor. The temple of Hathor at Dendera includes two *mammisis*, one dating to the Roman Period and the other to the time of Nectanebo I (380–362 BC), the latter evidently being used for the enactment of thirteen-act 'mystery plays' concerning the births both of the god Ihy and of the pharaoh.

However, the temples were far from being simply cult centres. They were also important foci of economic activity whose resources were provided by the produce from land ceded to them by the Crown, although this land did not become their absolute property, and they also benefited from dues such as tithes and state grants. They produced manufactured goods for secular purposes, particularly cloth, and were major sponsors of artistic works such as sculptures, which would be created in their *hut-nebu* or 'houses of gold', or through their building programmes, which generated an enormous market for the skills of sculptors and painters. The work of these artists is of very great interest, since it provides the clearest Ptolemaic evidence of an attempt at cultural accommodation between Greek and Egyptian in that their work was patently taking them in two different directions. In the first place their determination to continue the traditions of Late Period Egypt is particularly evident in the relief sculpture that survives in enormous quantities in Ptolemaic temples, but it also shows through in numerous examples of sculpture in the round, some of it quite unsurpassed in the entire canon of Egyptian sculpture. There is, however, an increasing tendency for the influence of classical sculpture to make an impact, so that works in a rather incongruous mixed style become more and more common, a trend that was destined ultimately to have serious consequences for traditional Egyptian art.

The priests enjoyed considerable political power, not least because their good will was evidently seen by the Ptolemies as the key to the acquiescence of the Egyptian population, and some of them, like Manetho of Sebennytus, played a major role in Ptolemaic cultural politics. The High Priests of Memphis were particularly important from this point of view, both because they were the most significant figures in the second city in the kingdom and because they were the supreme pontiffs of Egypt at the time, with wide-ranging contacts and influence in the country as a whole. The Ptolemies did everything they could to ensure this support, but they spread their blandishments much more widely than that, as is indicated in such well-known expressions of priestly gratitude as the Canopus and Rosetta decrees. Indeed, a sensitive reading of such texts

The Rosetta Stone, which records a decree of 196 BC made by a synod of Egyptian priests at Memphis conferring honours on Ptolemy V Epiphanes which reciprocate his many benefactions to Egyptian temples. Written in hieroglyphic (classical Egyptian), demotic (a much later form of the language), and Classical Greek, it is one of a large number of copies set up in temples throughout the country, and formed the basis for the decipherment of the hieroglyphic and demotic scripts. The text illustrates the Ptolemies' growing need to court the support of the priestly class, and even the Greek version shows the marked influence of the Egyptian concept of kingship.

reveals an ever greater care on the part of the Ptolemies to keep the priests on the side of the government as the political and military power of the state declined.

The priests and scribes were the pre-eminent repositories and exponents of traditional Egyptian culture, a role in which they were clearly spectacularly successful in Ptolemaic times. If we consider textual material produced for use in the temple cult, such as *The Legend of Horus of Behdet and the Winged Disc* carved on the inside of the west enclosure wall at Edfu, we encounter a profound knowledge of ancient tradition combined with an impressive capacity for narrative and an ability to write surprisingly good classical Egyptian, despite some contamination from Late Egyptian and Demotic stages of the language, and an exuberant development of the potential of the hieroglyphic script that would have made the text frequently unintelligible to any reader of the high

Facing, above: the Pharos lighthouse. It was probably begun by Ptolemy I to facilitate navigation into the eastern harbour of Alexandria. According to Strabo it was built of 'white stone', presumably limestone, but recent archaeological work in the area has revealed large granite blocks averaging 75 tons which probably formed part of the structure. It stood *c.*135 m. high and had three storeys, each narrower than the one below, the lowest being square and the second octagonal. The top storey was circular and supported the lantern.

Facing, below: this print by David Roberts (1796–1864) offers a superb view of the great temple of Isis on the island of Philae, probably the most beautiful of all Egyptian temples. The earliest extant structures are 30th Dynasty, but most of the building is Ptolemaic, beginning with work of the reign of Ptolemy II and ending with Ptolemy XII, though construction was resumed during the Roman Empire. In addition to Isis and Isiac deities, the temple also served cults of the first cataract region as well as Imhotep and the Nubian gods Arensnuphis and Mandulis.

A scene in sunk relief from the inner west side of the enclosure wall of the Ptolemaic temple at Edfu illustrating the myth of Horus, a sequence of texts dealing with the defeat of Seth, an embodiment of the forces of chaos. The cluttered hieroglyphs, which are typical of the Ptolemaic period, are used to write traditional material in classical Egyptian, and the highly plastic and often sensuous treatment of the human body owes much to Late Pharaonic artistic development.

Middle or New kingdoms. In other contexts we find the old genres continuing to flourish—for example, tomb biographies and cognate mortuary texts, pseudepigrapha, ritual texts, stories, and wisdom texts. The old compositional principles retain their currency, and the conceptual world is unequivocally that of late pharaonic culture.

In the Ptolemaic concept of the afterlife, the judgement of the dead was still central, as was the conviction that the verdict of the tribunal (before which all must come in the underworld) depended on a virtuous life. Negative attitudes to death could certainly emerge, in that there was a willingness to complain of the injustice of an untimely end to life and the helplessness of man in the face of death, and this could lead, in turn, to a conviction that man should make the most of life while it was possible to do so. However, in relation to both death and life, there was the overriding conviction that the gods were maintaining a moral order and that it was of critical importance to determine their will and abide by it. This order was clearly seen as a definitive framework of long standing that could not be changed, the structure and workings of which could be determined by looking to the past, and in particular to the ancient texts described in one passage as 'the Souls of Re'. There was a very strong sense of

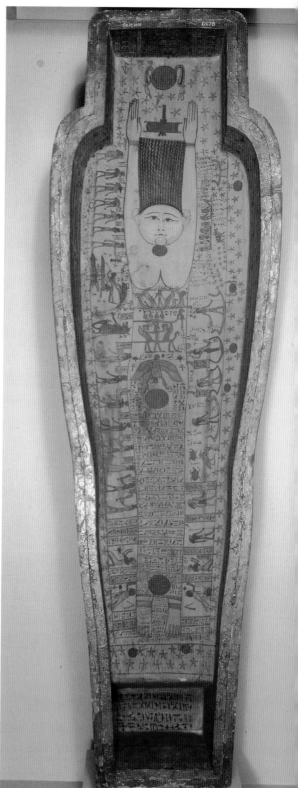

dependence on the will of the gods and a conviction that they would exact retribution for unacceptable behaviour. There was much talk of something that we translate as 'Fate', but it is evident that this could become coterminous with the will of the gods. However, the Egyptians were not left completely in the dark as to what that will might be, for they were convinced that the gods frequently communicated with man, particularly by means of dreams.

There was also an increased taste in Ptolemaic times for apocalyptic literature, which was believed to give a direct insight into the workings of the divine order. There continued to be a strong conviction that there were experts who could break outside the normal range of human capacity through their knowledge of words and actions of power (*heka*) that could create changes, often spectacular, in the physical world. As for the concept of the make-up of man, this had not changed, and the view of his social relations contains nothing surprising. Thus the Egyptians continued to see themselves in a social context that transcended the present to embrace both ancestors and descendants whose good report was a significant part of the immortality which Egyptians craved. There was also a clear sense of social hierarchy and a recognition that a person's position within that structure determined his authority. In day-to-day living, family solidarity and the interests of the local town were emphasized, as was the time-honoured paternalistic principle and active concern for those less well-off than oneself. On the other hand, the wisdom literature could express a hard-headed practicality and circumspection that left little room for trusting one's fellow man; it could also betray a misogyny that had much to do with the recognition of the sexual power of woman.

As of old, much weight was placed on self-control and restraint as cardinal virtues, and in political relations the pharaoh could still be seen as a divine benefactor whose support was essential to success, although there was a greater willingness to concede even his dependence on the gods and the possibility that he could act in a manner unacceptable to them that would bring retribution on him and the kingdom. Finally, we should not ignore the important point that there was one aspect of this vital culture that made a deep and lasting impression on Egypt's Hellenic masters—religion, where the success, in particular, of Isis and the Egyptianizing cult of Serapis constitute a remarkable example of cultural syncretism.

Below the large group of Egyptian scribes engaged in temple duties was a significant number of scribes who functioned as civil servants and secretaries. Indeed, there were ample opportunities in local and provincial government if they were prepared to learn enough Greek to act as intermediaries between Egyptians and the Graeco-Macedonian élite. Lower in the social hierarchy were the artisans and craftsmen who might express their talents in the temples, but there was certainly scope in Ptolemaic Egypt for the independent entrepreneur, particularly in the larger centres of population where we encounter numerous small businessmen and even businesswomen producing for the retail trade. Below them again we encounter the *machimoi* or militia who were largely

Facing: this Ptolemaic coffin in the British Museum illustrates the vitality of traditional pharaonic mortuary art before the onset of contamination by Hellenistic motifs which characterized the later Ptolemaic period.

417

Egyptian and functioned as soldiers or policemen (see Chapter 13). Having their origins in pharaonic times, the *machimoi* continued into the Ptolemaic period, and, after their success at Raphia in 217 BC, their importance in the military establishment increased. Their economic and social status was not, however, high, since the land allotments that they received were significantly smaller than those of their non-Egyptian counterparts, typically 5 or 7 *arourai* (1 *aroura* = 0.7 acre) as against the 20, 30, 70, or even more allocated to Greek *cleruchs*. The productivity of these allotments was such that there was no margin to employ assistant labour, so that, if *machimoi* were called away for military service, they could run into severe economic difficulties.

Not much lower than the *machimoi* was the great mass of the Egyptian peasantry engaged in the agricultural production that formed the basis of the economy. This involved the back-breaking task of creating and maintaining the irrigation system in addition to the normal agricultural activities of cereal and fodder production, arboriculture, and stock rearing. The peasantry might carry out these tasks as labourers or tenants on Crown and temple land or on great estates, and the more enterprising and successful might rent additional acreage from landholders such as *cleruchs* who had no taste for the agricultural life themselves. Some of them were also perfectly capable of making the most of any additional opportunities for supplementing their income—for example, acting as transport agents as required by government or local centres of economic production. Indeed, it is clear that some tenants of Crown land were in quite a good line of business, but in most cases the peasantry was evidently operating at the level of marginal subsistence, and its lot could easily become intolerable, particularly in times of internal political disruption, which were increasingly common from the end of the third century BC.

A Long Decline

The erosion of the Aegean and Syrian possessions of the Ptolemies in the late third and early second centuries BC was to leave them with only two foreign provinces: Cyrenaica and Cyprus. Polybius blames the rot squarely on the character deficiencies of Ptolemy IV himself, but the decline of Ptolemaic power lay deeper than the iniquities of a single ruler. In the first place, dynastic schism, which had its roots in the very institutional character of the monarchy itself, became a recurrent feature of Ptolemaic history, generating murderous bouts of internecine strife that at best were enervating and at worst raised instability in the kingdom to a disastrous level. These problems were often aggravated by the fury of the Alexandrian mob, which first surfaced at the death of Ptolemy IV in the lynching of his minister Agathocles—indeed, nothing gives a better picture of their unbridled and vicious temper than Polybius' description of the murder of Agathocles' relatives and associates:

All of them were then handed over together to the mob, and some began to bite them, others to stab them, others to gouge out their eyes. As soon as any of them fell, the body was torn limb from limb until they had mutilated them all; for the savagery of the Egyptians is truly appalling when their passions are aroused.   (Polybius, 15. 33)

Their predilections as king-makers are subsequently demonstrated in numerous episodes. Thus the long conflict between Ptolemy VI and VIII frequently involved the actions of the mob, and in 80 BC they excelled themselves by assassinating Ptolemy X himself. Finally in 48/7 BC their anarchic propensities reached a crescendo that culminated in the summary destruction of their power by none other than Julius Caesar. The effects of these inherent weaknesses at the centre of the kingdom were compounded on many occasions by the self-seeking ambition of high-ranking Greeks, military and civilian, who were determined to do anything to further their personal interests.

In Egypt outside Alexandria the political situation rapidly deteriorated from the late third century BC onwards, as the country seethed with internal discord. These circumstances certainly facilitated the elevation of some of the more able and enterprising Egyptians, and there is clear evidence that they were succeeding in closing or even eliminating the gap that normally existed between Greek and Egyptian, gaining estates of some considerable size and even attaining the rank of provincial governor (*strategos*) or governor-general (*epistrategos*). The recurrent civil unrest has often been seen as a nationalistic, ethnically motivated reaction by Egyptians against the hated Greek, but the situation was clearly much more complex than that and is probably better read as the natural outcome of the weakening of royal authority that created a context where ancient rivalries and aspirations of various kinds were no longer contained by central authority. These might be hostilities between Egyptian cities, as when Hermonthis (Armant) and Theban Crocodilopolis went to war against each other in the time of Ptolemy VIII (170–116 BC). Again, when, between 205 and 186 BC, an independent state was established in the Thebaid, governed in succession by two native kings called Haronnophris and Chaonnophris, we may well be seeing a resurgence of the ancient political ambitions of the priesthood of Amun, and it is worth noting that, in the final battle in 186 BC, Nubian troops fought in Chaonnophris' army—that is, we may also have evidence of a resurgence of the ancient interest in Thebes by Nubian devotees of the god. However, since religiously determined xenophobia is a soundly documented phenomenon in the Late Period, it would be extremely suprising if it were totally absent from Egyptian motives in this move to independence.

There are many other signs, large scale and otherwise, of disaffection among the Egyptian population—strikes, flight (sometimes to the point where whole settlements were abandoned), brigandage, attacks by desperadoes on villages, despoliation of temples, and frequent recourse to the temples' right of asylum. These are indisputably the reactions of people pushed beyond the limits of endurance by famine, rampant inflation, and an oppressive and vicious administrative system operated by officials who were all too often corrupt and beyond the effective control of central government. Against such men, the lower strata of society, who were largely Egyptian, were, in reality, defenceless and, therefore, easy targets. Uprisings by these people might easily be construed as nationalistic, given the close congruence between economic status and ethnic origin, and we can be confident that they acquired that dimension explicitly from time to time, but at the most fundamental level the uprisings were those of the oppressed against the establishment regarded as responsible for that oppression, and that establishment could just as easily be perceived as the Egyptian priesthood and their temples as Graeco-Macedonian officialdom. Whatever the motivation, however, the corrosive economic effects of these disruptions struck a deadly blow at the economic infrastructure at precisely the time when alternative sources of wealth had largely dried up.

All these internal events were played out against the backdrop of growing interventionism by Rome in the eastern Mediterranean. Sometimes solicited, sometimes not, this process led progressively to the elimination of the kingdom of Macedon (167 BC), the acquisition of the kingdom of Pergamum in 133 BC, the gradual erosion of Seleucid power culminating in the annexation of the rump of the kingdom in 64 BC, and eventually the demise of the kingdom of the Ptolemies itself. The last event was long in coming and was the last episode in Ptolemaic relations with Rome that went back to the early years of the dynasty

One of two sunk-relief scenes on the exterior rear wall of the sanctuary of the Hathor temple at Dendera. It shows Cleopatra VII and her son Ptolemy XV Caesarion engaged in cult activity for the benefit of the deities of the shrine. The main officiant is Ptolemy, whilst his mother, wearing the headdress of Isis, assists him as priestess. Caesarion, the alleged son of Julius Caesar, was associated with his mother in 42/1 BC, become joint ruler in 36, and was murdered on Octavian's orders in 30 BC at the age of 17.

and evolved through several phases. Starting on a basis of equality in the reign of Ptolemy II with diplomatic courtesies between equals expressed in an embassy to Rome in 273 BC, we move in the early second century BC to a situation where Rome became the guarantor of Egyptian independence.

Polybius' description of C. Popilius Laenas' removal of Antiochus IV from Egyptian territory in 168 BC perfectly illustrates the ensuing shift in power. On handing the king the Senate's decree:

> Popilius did something which seemed insolent and arrogant to the highest degree. With a vine stick which he had in his hand he drew a circle around Antiochus and told him to give his reply to the message before he stepped out of that circle. The king was astounded by the arrogance of this action and hesitated for a short time and said he would do everything the Romans asked.   (Polybius, 29. 27).

From this it was a natural progression to become the mediator in dynastic disputes: during the long-drawn-out quarrel between the brothers Ptolemy VI and VIII, Rome was the arbitrator; Ptolemy XI (80 BC) owed his kingdom to Rome and allegedly left it to his benefactor by will; in the dispute between the Alexandrians and Ptolemy XII (80–51 BC), Rome played a decisive role; and Rome's involvement in the murderous conflicts between Cleopatra VII and her brothers Ptolemy XIII and XIV ushered in the last phase of Ptolemaic kingship.

In this maelstrom, and improbably, Cleopatra was able briefly to resurrect past glories c.36 BC when, through the largesse of Mark Antony, we see the fleeting resurgence of Ptolemaic control in southern Asia Minor and Syria–Palestine, but this ran counter to the general trend that featured Rome as the sole beneficiary of the long decline of the dynasty: Cyrenaica was acquired in 96 BC, Cyprus in 58. Finally, it was Egypt's turn. In 30 BC, through a struggle as spectacular and dramatic as anything that antiquity can offer, this brilliant and ancient kingdom fell to Rome, thereby initiating the final long-drawn-out chapter in the history of pharaonic culture.

Cleopatra and Mark Anthony. Silver coin, c.34 BC, bearing both.

15 THE ROMAN PERIOD

(30 BC–AD 311)

DAVID PEACOCK

There can be few historical events better known than the love affair between Mark Antony, triumvir of Rome, and the beautiful and talented Queen Cleopatra VII of Egypt. His association with Cleopatra may not have been without political motives, for there was much to be gained by Rome fostering good relations with Egypt, the wealth of which was proverbial. Ultimately, however, his relationship brought him into conflict with his astute, single-minded, brother-in-law, Octavian. The issue was finally settled in the battle of Actium, fought in September 31 BC, and a year later Octavian, who in 27 BC changed his name to Augustus, entered Egypt for the first and last time. Egypt, the land of the pharaohs and their Hellenistic successors, the Ptolemies, was now part of the Roman empire.

Egypt was a land apart—an exotic and distant part of the empire, perhaps more bizarre than any other province. Here, pharaonic culture thrived and a visitor to Roman Egypt would have found himself in a time capsule, for the sights, sounds, and customs of Roman Egypt would have had more in common with pharaonic civilization than with contemporary Rome. Temples were still built in traditional style. The hieroglyphic script continued to be used, and Egyptian was spoken by the common people, although the lingua franca was Greek. Cleopatra was, as far as we know, the only Graeco-Roman ruler of Egypt to learn Egyptian, and then it was one of a multitude of languages in which she was proficient. Further indications of the depth of the all-pervading pharaonic culture is the persistence of mummification as a burial rite and continuing reverence for Egyptian gods. The special nature of Roman Egypt is undeniable, although there is a growing body of scholars who consider the 'Romanity' of Egypt to be a more significant aspect.

Whether this is the case or not, cultural differences existed and it is hardly surprising that Rome adopted a somewhat hostile and suspicious attitude to Egypt. Roman senators were forbidden to enter the country and native Egyptians were excluded from the administration. It is significant that the only Egyptian town founded by Rome was Antinoopolis, on the Nile in Middle Egypt. The force behind this establishment was Hadrian, one of the few emperors ever to visit the country. His own love affair with Egypt is reflected in his great villa at Tivoli, where he attempted to recreate a Nilotic landscape in the Canopus garden.

Despite its unique aspect, Egypt has a special role to play in our understanding of the Roman empire as a whole. The dry climate has led to the preservation of a wealth of evidence that is lacking in more temperate regions. It is, for example, a repository of written evidence that is seldom preserved elsewhere. Best known are the papyri, which give an unrivalled insight into the business affairs and daily life of Roman Egypt. One of the most famous and productive sites is the town of Oxyrhynchus near the Nile, about 200 km. south of Cairo. In 1897 two Oxford scholars, Grenfell and Hunt, began to quarry the rubbish of the ancient town (*sebakh* in Arabic) for papyri. Their work proved to be a windfall for papyrology, for the documents so far published occupy nearly sixty volumes and there is almost the same quantity awaiting study.

Egypt is also the most important country for ostraca, documents written on potsherds in place of papyrus. Between 1987 and 1993 excavations at the Mons Claudianus fort in the Eastern Desert yielded over 9,000 ostraca, the largest collection from anywhere in the ancient world. For the first time they document quarry operations and give us a unique insight into the provisioning and logistics of a major Roman enterprise in the desert.

Documentary evidence apart, Egyptian town sites and tombs often yield organic matter that is seldom available elsewhere. Textiles are often beautifully preserved, as are basketry, leather, or food remains. Unfortunately the potential of this material has yet to be fully explored, as all too often it has been discarded in favour of the written evidence. Thus, Grenfell and Hunt seem to have thrown this material aside to be used as fertilizer by the fellahin. Recent excavations, such as those at Mons Claudianus, are beginning to rectify this imbalance.

Administration

Roman Egypt was divided into about thirty administrative units called 'nomes', a system inherited from the preceding Ptolemaic era. Each had a governor or *strategos*, appointed by and answerable to the Prefect or governor of Egypt, via one of four *epistrategoi*, the regional administrators. The Prefect was assisted by procurators responsible for finance and by other officials.

Each of the nomes had a capital town or *metropolis*, where the seat of local government was located. Unfortunately we do not know very much about

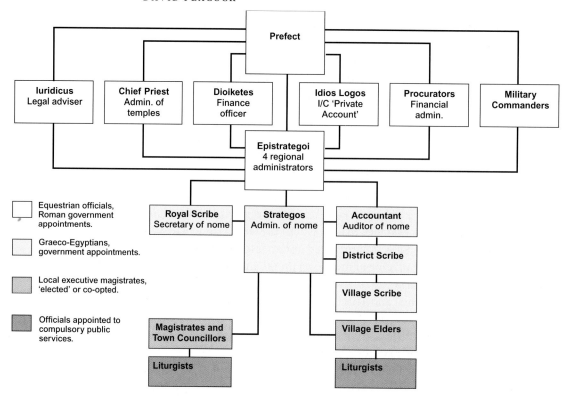

Diagram showing the bureaucratic structure of Roman Egypt.

these, as the urban topography of Roman Egypt has been little studied. The two best understood are Oxyrhynchus and Arsinoe, whence the evidence is derived from papyri. It appears that they were places of some sophistication and wealth. Thus, Oxyrhynchus had a gymnasium, public baths, a theatre, and about twenty temples, while Arsinoe had running water supplied by two reservoirs into which water was pumped from an arm of the Nile.

During the first two centuries AD, the nomes and their metropolises enjoyed little in the way of self-government, but in AD 200 Septimius Severus ordered the creation of town councils in each nome, a step towards upgrading the metropolises to *municipia* (a *municipium* being, in essence, a self-governing borough). This, however, led to considerable resentment, for with increased responsibility came increased financial burdens to the holders of office.

Under Roman rule, all males between the ages of 14 and 60 were obliged to pay a poll tax annually. Roman citizens were exempt, but these probably only formed a minor part of the population. The upper classes, the 'metropolites', paid at a reduced level. Class was, thus, a subject of some consequence and at the age of 14 a metropolite boy would be required to present his credentials.

The Army

As in other provinces, the main agent of control was the army. The epigraphic and papyrological evidence that Egypt provides furnishes an unrivalled picture of the functioning of a provincial army, to which can be added the archaeological evidence of the forts from which the army operated. Many of these, preserved by the desert, still stand to their wall tops.

One of the major early historical sources on the disposition of troops was Strabo (17. 1. 12), who, in a much-cited passage, states:

There are three legions of soldiers, one in the city and the others in the chora. In addition there are nine Roman cohorts, three in the city, three on the border with Ethiopia at Syene, as guard for those places and three elsewhere in the chora. There are three horse units which are likewise positioned in important places.

The city is, of course, Alexandria, where the fort of Nikopolis, about 5 km. east of the centre, stood until the late nineteenth century. Today a few fragments remain in the Khedival palace that was built on the site and all but obliterated it. Another legion seems to have been stationed in the fortress of Babylon (fragments of which can still be seen in the grounds of the Coptic museum in Cairo), while the third had the task of guarding the Thebaid. The legions deployed include the XXII Deiotariana, the III Cyrenaica, the II Traiana, and the XV Apollinaris.

Strabo is much less specific about the auxiliary units, but here it is possible to fill in the detail from a variety of sources within and outside Egypt. The evidence includes dedications, diplomas, tombstones, and other inscriptions, as well as papyri and ostraca, the latter two more or less restricted to Egypt itself. During the first three centuries AD there seem to have been, on average, three to four *alae* (cavalry units) stationed in the country, as well as about eight cohorts, which accords remarkably well with Strabo's claims.

The units changed and moved from one part of the empire to another, and between different places within Egypt, and in some cases it is possible to reconstruct their history. Thus, the *ala* Vocontorium is one of the earliest and best-attested auxiliary units in Egypt. Prior to AD 60 it seems to have been based in the Koptos area and there is also evidence for its presence in the fort at Babylon in AD 59. During the Flavian period it may have served on the German frontier, returning to Egypt by AD 105. It was later deployed in the Eastern Desert at Mons Porphyrites (AD 116), then again in the Nile Valley, until it disappeared from the records in AD 179.

Another example is the cohors II Ituraeorum, which is attested in Syene (Aswan) in AD 28 and AD 75 and later at various other places in the Syene area, before ending up at Mons Claudianus in AD 223–5.

The tasks that the army had to perform were multifarious. Defence of the empire was obviously important. According to Strabo, the areas to the south and east of Egypt were peopled by tribes largely identified to the Romans by their eating habits. There is little doubt that the troops stationed at Syene (Aswan) would have been charged with securing the southern limits of the state. Equally, desert security might have been, in some measure, the responsibility of units based along the Nile in Upper and Middle Egypt. There were certainly forts in parts of both the Eastern and Western Deserts, but they seem as much related to mineral exploitation and the promotion of trade as to security.

However, the army based in Egypt played a major role in most of the eastern military campaigns, such as the annexation of Arabia in AD 106 and Trajan's Parthian War. It was also called on to quell the Jewish revolts of the first and second centuries AD. Here the legions at Nikopolis and the units stationed at Pelusium in northern Sinai would have played a significant part, as they could have moved with relative rapidity to eastern trouble spots. Alexandria was undoubtedly the key military base. The legions based nearby would have been charged with controlling the unruly Alexandrian mob, securing this jewel of a city against attack, policing the countryside, and playing a part in the wider problems of the empire.

In fact, a major role of the army everywhere was to act as a police force. There is a substantial number of ostraca, principally referring to the Eastern Desert, that specify guard duties and the manning of *skopeloi* or watch towers. It appears that the guards were organized into *dekanoi*, which were controlled by *curatores*, who in turn were responsible to centurions. Movement along desert roads seems to have been very strictly controlled, with need for permits, written on an ostracon, or perhaps sometimes papyrus. Undoubtedly this was a measure to limit the banditry for which Egypt was notorious. This enduring problem must have been a major preoccupation of the army, with units of soldiers under the command of the *strategos* hunting down both the bandits and their sympathizers in the general population. Banditry would have been particularly prevalent in the mountainous parts of the Eastern Desert, where there would have been ample opportunity to hide, and rich picking to be had from the caravans of oriental luxuries travelling from Berenice or Myos Hormos (Quseir el-Qadim) on the Red Sea coast to the Nile. This undoubtedly accounts for the string of forts between Berenice and Koptos and particularly for the forts and numerous watchtowers on the road between Quseir el-Qadim and Koptos.

The army seems to have been involved in many other activities, such as the supervision of grain boats travelling down the Nile to Alexandria, guarding the ever unpopular tax collectors while executing their duties, and supplying and supervising quarrying and mining enterprises in the desert. Here, the evidence from Mons Claudianus suggests that they lived alongside civilians and were an integral part of the extractive system. They were charged, amongst other things, with supervising the *skopeloi*, with guarding valuables such as iron tools, and perhaps with the maintenance of structures.

The Economy

There are three interrelated aspects of the economy of Roman Egypt. The most important is the agricultural production of the Nile Valley and the Delta. The fecundity of Egypt was well known and the city of Rome relied heavily on the Alexandrian grain ships to feed its teeming population. A second facet is the mineral extraction focused largely, but by no means exclusively, on the Eastern Desert. Here gold had been exploited since pharaonic times, but during the Roman period it was also a source of exotic stones such as the *granito del foro* and imperial porphyry. The red granite of Aswan has a long history of exploitation and it is not surprising that it was also one of the most important decorative stones used by the Romans.

The third aspect of the economy is the role that Egypt played in articulating Roman trade. Alexandria was, of course, one of the great trading cities of the ancient world, but Egypt is uniquely placed, with access to both the Mediterranean and the Red Sea, which itself leads to the Indian Ocean and beyond. The country thus played a major role in Rome's trade with the Orient: with India in particular, but through it contact was made with Malaysia and possibly even China.

To many people today Egypt is a long thin ribbon of land expanding to a triangle in the form of the Delta. This is where the population lives and works and this is where the food is grown. Today, as in the past, the fertile land produces a surplus. The cause of this fertility is not, of course, the climate, for rainfall is negligible, but the river Nile. Before the building of the first Aswan dam, the river would burst its banks annually, depositing a fresh layer of rich silt on the surface of the fields. So important were these floods that their height was measured with specially constructed Nilometers, Roman examples of which can be seen at, for example, Aswan and Luxor, with a fine medieval one at Cairo. The level of taxation was adjusted to the height of the water: a good flood would mean a good crop, and the populace would be able to stand higher taxes. Pliny (*Historia Naturalis*, 5. 58) is quite specific about the importance of flooding:

The Nilometer at Aswan; gradations mark the height of the river on the right of the steps.

An average rise is one of seven metres. A smaller volume of water does not irrigate all localities and a larger one, by retiring too slowly, retards agriculture; and the latter uses up the time for sowing because of the moisture of the soil while the former gives no time for sowing because the soil is parched. The province takes careful note of both extremes: in a rise of five-and-a-half metres it senses famine and even at one of six metres it begins to feel hungry, but six-and-a-half metres brings cheerfulness, six-and-three-quarters complete confidence and seven metres delight.   (Trans A. Bowman).

Rome's reliance on Egyptian grain has a long history, stretching back to the Ptolemies, when, as early as 211 or 210 BC, Rome requested a consignment of grain from Ptolemy IV. The arrival of the Alexandrian grain ships was to become an important element in the economy of Rome, upon which the fates of emperors might hang. Under Augustus it may have reached 20 million *modii* (well over 1 million tons). The corn trade was part of the *annona*, the tax in kind levied by Rome on the producing provinces. There is some evidence to suggest that even the cost of transport from the estate to the Nile had to be met by the producers.

The supply of grain from the growing areas to the warehouses of Alexandria was a carefully regulated operation. The shipment was carried out by the *sitologos* (corn official), aided by the *antigrapheus* (clerk), and a financial assistant.

A sealed sample or *deigma* would be entrusted to the boat's captain for delivery with the consignment. This would be a check against adulteration or substitution of the cargo with one of lower quality during the voyage. In any case, it seems to have been normal practice for a soldier to be present on board during the journey. On arrival at the great granaries in Alexandria, the corn would be in the care of special Roman procurators who, with their staff, were responsible for its safe-keeping and condition.

The corn ships generally left Alexandria in May or June and the journey to Rome, against the prevailing northerly winds, could take a month or perhaps even two. The route would be along the North African coast or north to Cyprus, then hugging the south coast of Turkey. The return with a tail wind took about a fortnight, the ships travelling 'with the speed of racehorses', as the emperor Gaius claimed. Either way, the journey was not without its hazards, as St Paul's shipwreck on Malta vividly illustrates.

Archaeologically, we know very little about the estates that produced this corn, but the papyri known as the Heroninos archive permit the detailed reconstruction of the working of one of them operating during the third century AD, the Appianus estate in the Faiyum. It appears that the owner of the estate, Aurelius Appianus, was a landowner of some standing with holdings comparable with those of Roman senators. His central administrators, bound by patronage, were recruited from the town councillors and landowners of the nome, and below them were the *phrontistai* or production managers, probably recruited from wealthy rural families, who perhaps worked for several estates simultaneously. The labour was provided by a nucleus of full-time workers supplemented by extra labourers when needed. It seems that the supply of paid labour from the poorer classes in rural Egypt made it unnecessary and uneconomic to seek slave labour.

There were three categories of full-time labourers: the *paidaria*, *oiketai*, and *metrematiaioi*. The first two categories seem to have been employed for life and perhaps provided with free accommodation, while the *metrematiaioi* were independent villagers contracted to work for a varying set number of years. Casual labourers came from many different backgrounds sometimes outside the village.

The primary aim of the unit was the production of wine for external sale. The other crops were grown to provide food for the employees, fodder for the estate draught animals, and grain for tax. All of these were necessary to permit the economic functioning of the estate. It is thus apparent that the grain for which Egypt was renowned was produced as part of a complex and sophisticated system of farming, which made profits in other ways.

The mineral resources of the Eastern Desert were known and exploited during pharaonic times. For example, the amethyst mines of Wadi el-Hudi have yielded a stele recording the use of the army in mines operated under Senusret I of the Middle Kingdom. Furthermore, the New Kingdom temple of Sety I at Abydos was granted rights at the gold mines in the Eastern Desert, a gang of workmen to bring back the gold, and a settlement at the mines themselves. These may well be the mines at Umm el-Fawakhir in the Wadi Hammamat, which are still in use at the end of the twentieth century. A remarkable papyrus map in the Turin Egyptian museum is thought to depict this area.

Interest in the mineral resources, particularly gold, persisted through the Ptolemaic period into Roman times. Finds of black gloss pottery at sites such as

A lever or 'Olynthian' mill from Mons Porphyrites, introduced by the Greeks but still used in Egypt in the Roman Period, see p. 443–4.

Abu Zawal, about 20 km. west of Mons Claudianus, suggest that it, and probably other mines, were established before the Roman conquest, although they
undoubtedly continued to operate after it.

Gold working sites have been little studied, but their appearance is distinctive. There is usually a cluster of small huts surrounded by stone heaps, and
everywhere there is evidence of the apparatus used to crush the quartzite from
which the ore would be extracted. The principal tool seems to be a well-made
type of curved saddle quern with a heavy upper stone shaped like Napoleon's
hat, the 'brim' of which formed the handles. Water would be needed in considerable quantity to separate the pay dirt from the gangue, and some sites, of
which Abu Zawal is characteristic, have a substantial well forming the core of
the complex. In other cases the crushed rock would have been taken away and
separated elsewhere.

The method of extracting the gold was observed by the Greek geographer
Agatharchides, who visited the mines in the second century BC. His original
work has been lost, but fortunately his description has been preserved in the
writings of Diodorus Siculus. He tells us that the rock was broken by fire setting
and the use of hammers. It was then crushed in large stone mortars to the size
of a pea, after which it would be ground to a fine powder in hand mills before
being washed with water on a sloping surface to separate the gold and country
rock. Presumably, the saddle querns, now so much in evidence on these sites,
were used in the final grinding.

Stone quarrying also has a long ancestry in Egypt. The most celebrated example must be the great complex at Aswan, now unfortunately much disturbed
and built over by the expansion of the modern town. Aswan produced a variety
of granitic rocks, the most celebrated of which was the red- or rose-coloured
granite. During the pharaonic period it was used for sarcophagi, for obelisks,
and as capping for the great pyramids of Giza, perhaps because its reddish
colour suggests the sun. During the Roman period, the quarries continued
unabated, and columns carved from Aswan granite are found in quantity
around the shores of the Mediterranean. It is, in fact, one of the 'big three' decorative rocks of the Roman world, on a par with the *granito violetto* from the
Troad and *Cipollino* from Greece.

The success of Aswan clearly results from its location on the banks of the
Nile. The products could easily be loaded onto barges and floated to Alexandria, where they would be transferred to the *lapidariae naves*, the special stone
ships used for transporting heavy loads across the Mediterranean. Other successful quarries such as those for sandstone at Gebel el-Silsila or those for
'Egyptian alabaster' (or 'calcite alabaster') in Middle Egypt, were also situated
within easy reach of the Nile (although the principal calcite-alabaster quarries
at Hatnub were at least half a day's journey away, and presumably somewhat
longer when hauling large blocks). At Aswan, the quarries seem to have had a
long life, the Romans continuing a tradition of quarrying of several thousand
years.

For obvious logistical reasons, the large-scale quarrying of remote desert stone (for use in buildings or sculpture) was eschewed by the pharaohs, with the exception of *bekhen*, a greywacke sandstone from Wadi Hammamat, and even more remarkably, the so-called 'Chephren diorite', an anorthosite-gneiss from Gebel el-Asr in the Western Desert about 200 km. south-west of Aswan. During the Roman Period, however, an attempt was made to exploit the very considerable lithic resources of the desert more thoroughly, and the focus was the Eastern Desert, where a range of hard basement rocks was exploited, comprising mainly porphyry and varieties of diorite.

The centre that articulated most of this activity seems to have been Mons Porphyrites (Gebel Dokhan), about 70 km. north-west of Hurghada. Ostraca from Mons Claudianus state that the men working there were part of the *numerus* of Porphyrites and the *arithmos* of Claudianus. Similarly, the workers at nearby Tiberiane (Barud), the source of the *granito bianco e nero*, seem to have been of the *numerus* of Porphyrites and the *arithmos* of Tiberiane. To this can be added the scatter of tiny chips of porphyry found on most quarry sites in the Eastern Desert, suggesting that men who had worked the porphyry were being sent to other quarries.

A recently discovered inscription documents the discovery of this area in a remarkable way. It tells us that the resources were found by Gaius Cominius Leugas, who must have been the Roman equivalent of a field geologist, on 23 July AD 18. He appears to have discovered porphyry, black porphyry, multi-coloured stones, and *knekites* ('safflower stone'), which has yet to be geologically defined.

The dating of the earliest quarrying at Mons Porphyrites to the reign of Tiberius (AD 14–37) is confirmed by a further inscription, and it appears to have persisted until the late fourth or possibly even the early fifth century AD, if the pottery dating is correct. Purple had been worn as a mark of nobility in the Mediterranean region for many thousands of years and no doubt the discovery of a purple rock would have been a major event of considerable interest to the emperor personally. The operation itself has been described, with some justification, as the most remarkable manifestation of Roman activity to be seen anywhere in the empire. It was necessary to supply the quarries with food, to dig wells tapping the fossil water (which, contrary to popular belief, abounds in the desert), and to construct forts for the military and villages for the workers. While the two might have cohabited to some extent, the quarries are on the

The Pan-Min inscription from the Mons Porphyrites quarries in the Eastern Desert, which identifies the ancient discoverer of the porphyry (and several other stones) as Gaius Cominius Leugas; it also gives the date of this event as 23 July, AD 18.

tops of mountains and it was convenient to post workers nearer to their place of labour. The site seems to have begun as a series of scattered mountain villages, which were later, in the second century AD, to be controlled by a fort at wadi level. In the late Roman period convicts may have been used, and a passage in the writings of Eusebius refers to a group of Christians (almost certainly quarry-workers) who had their eyes gouged out and their hamstrings cut before being deported to Palestine—presumably for trying to proselytize the garrison. However, for much of the time the operation was probably manned by civilians and soldiers working together, which was certainly the case at Mons Claudianus. Even Christianity was generally tolerated, as a number of inscriptions attest.

This ostracon from Mons Claudianus, bearing a letter from Apollos to his sister Mikkalous, is one piece of evidence for the presence of women in the fort.

Mons Claudianus, some 50 km. to the south of Mons Porphyrites, was the source of a grey granodiorite used mainly for columns. This is now the most intensively studied of the Roman quarry sites in the Eastern Desert. The complex comprises a fort of Domitianic date, and an earlier one that has produced an ostracon of Nero, with 130 small quarries scattered within a radius of about 1 km. around; each was connected to the main wadi bed by a slipway, which terminated in a loading ramp—the place where the products would be transferred from rollers or sledges to carts for the 120-km. journey across the desert to the Nile. Some of these carts must have been very large, for a 20 m. column would weigh over 200 tonnes. Here, it is pertinent to note that an ostracon refers to a twelve-wheeled cart and, in the Naq el-Teir plain, tracks have been observed with a span of 3 m.

It used to be thought that the rock of Mons Claudianus, also known as the *granito del foro*, from its frequent occurrence in the Roman forum, had a pan-Mediterranean distribution. However, a programme of chemical and petrographic analysis during the 1990s has shown that its distribution is virtually restricted to some of the finer monuments in Rome. It appears that Mons Claudianus lay outside the normal orbit of Roman trade and may have been more or less the personal property of the emperor. It is interesting to note that other grey rocks of similar appearance were exploited in more accessible outcrops on the islands of Elba and Giglio, and also in western Turkey. The rock of Mons Claudianus was special, not because of its properties, but because of where it came from. It was a product from the utmost end of the empire and could be won only by extraordinary efforts. This could be the secret of the whole quarrying enterprise in the Eastern Desert, which makes little sense in rational economic terms.

The importance of Egypt to the Roman economy went beyond production. Perhaps one of the strangest and most bizarre aspects of taste among the Roman nobility was the predilection for oriental luxuries: pearls, pepper, silks, frankincense, and myrrh, as well as various other spices and exotic medicines.

Facing, left: mummy portrait of a young lady from Hawara, wood, encaustic, and paint. Roman Period, 2nd century AD.

Facing, right: mummy of a young boy with inserted portrait in encaustic on wood, Roman Period, early 2nd century AD.

An 18 m. broken column in a granodiorite (*granito del foro*) quarry at Mons Claudianus.

Egypt articulated this trade, for these goods were brought by ship across the Indian Ocean and thence to the western shores of the Red Sea. Here they were offloaded and dragged across 150 km. of desert to the Nile, whence they were floated to Alexandria and then on to Rome. India benefited from this trade, for in return it received glass, textiles, wine, grain, fine pottery, and precious metals as well as human cargoes, such as singing boys and maidens for the pleasure of Indian potentates.

It might be thought advantageous for the ships to sail up the Red Sea and to cross the isthmus now occupied by the Suez Canal. Indeed, there was a project, begun under Ptolemy II and improved by various successors, particularly Trajan and Hadrian, that connected the Nile with the Bitter Lakes. However, it was not extensively used, at least in the first centuries BC and AD, largely because of the severe northerly wind that blows down the Red Sea for 80 per cent of the year. This would have been a major hazard to Roman shipping and it was preferable to make a more southerly landfall and to take goods overland to the Nile. The two ports established by Ptolemy II Philadephus (285–246 BC) to facilitate this trade were Berenice, named after his wife, and Myos Hormos. It appears that Myos Hormos was pre-eminent during the second century BC and that Berenice began to rise in importance during the first century BC and became dominant in the first century AD, although Myos Hormos continued in use. The India trade was thus developed in Ptolemaic times and the Romans merely took over and perhaps expanded a well-established concern. The Red Sea would also have been known to pharaonic traders, for it undoubtedly gave access to the mysterious East African land of Punt (see Chapter 11), from whence came exotic plants and animals.

The site of Berenice is well established and has been equated with the ruins near Ras Banas in southern Egypt, since its discovery by Belzoni in 1818. Myos Hormos has been the subject of extended debate, most writers siting it at Abu Shaʿar, 20 km. north of Hurghada, because this accords with the latitude and longitude given in Ptolemy's *Geography*. However, the 1990s excavations of the little fort on the site demonstrated that it is a late Roman and Byzantine foundation, with no evidence of earlier settlement. However, the site of Myos Hormos is described in some detail in Classical literature, and study of satellite images suggests that the closest correspondence is with the site of Quseir el-Qadim at the end of the fortified road from Koptos on the Nile. This diagnosis has recently been confirmed by excavations at el-Zerqa about halfway along the route, for these have produced ostraca demonstrating beyond reasonable doubt, that the port at the end of the road was indeed Myos Hormos.

The nature of this trade can be filled out from both literary and archaeological sources. The main document is the *Periplus Maris Erythraei*, a sailing guide to the Red Sea, the Gulf of Aden, and the western Indian Ocean, compiled in the first century AD. It is supplemented with references in Tamil poems to 'cool fragrant wines brought by the Yavana in their ships' or again 'the thriving town of Muziris, whither the beautiful large ships of the Yavana come bearing gold, making the waters white with foam and return laden with pepper'. It appears that the best time to leave Egypt was July, when the south-western monsoons would drive the ships across the Gulf of Aden and the Indian Ocean, while the return would be delayed until November to take advantage of the north-eastern monsoons.

The south-western monsoons are some of the most ferocious winds on earth, and the ships must have been immensely large and strong to withstand such a voyage, perhaps akin to those on the Alexandria–Rome run, which were up to 60 m. long and had a displacement of around 1,000 tons. Certainly the profits would have made the risks worthwhile: a recently published papyrus describes a shipment of nard (aromatic plants), ivory, and textiles from Muziris in India to Alexandria; this consignment had a value of 131 talents, enough to buy 2,400 acres of the best farmland in Egypt.

Archaeology can also help in understanding this trade. Sir Mortimer Wheeler excavated the Roman settlement of Arikamedu on the Coromandel coast of India, where he found amphorae that would have contained the best wine of Campania, and fine red pottery of Tiberian date, produced in the workshops of Lyons, Pozzuoli, and Pisa. In Egypt, an excavation project during the 1990s at Berenice promises to furnish equivalent information on the Egyptian end. In the late 1970s and early 1980s small-scale excavations at Quseir el-Qadim, then thought to be the port of Leucos Limen, produced interesting material, including a sherd with a Tamil inscription on it. A new programme of excavation began in 1999.

The overland routes from Berenice and Myos Hormos across the desert have been thoroughly studied. The one from Berenice runs in a north-westerly direction for over 350 km. and is equipped with *hydreumata* (watering places)

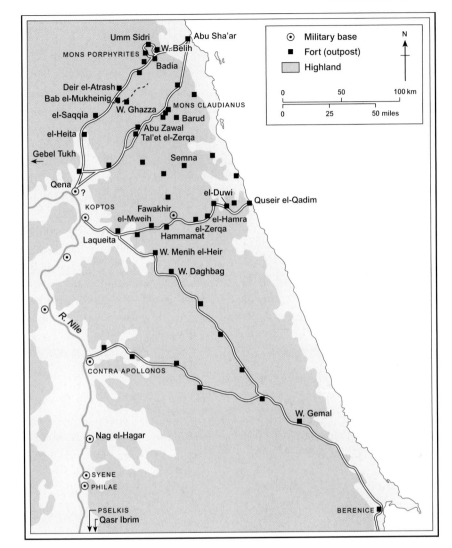

Map of forts in the Eastern Desert and the routes from the Red Sea ports Berenice and Myos Hormos (Quseir el-Qadim) to the Nile in the Roman Period (30 BC–AD 395).

every 20–30 km. Its destination is Koptos, but about halfway along there is a branch to the west that leads to Apollinopolis Magna (Edfu). The route from Myos Hormos again leads to Koptos, and Strabo tells us that the journey took six or seven days, the route being furnished with *hydreumata* dug to a great depth. Two of these (el-Mweih and el-Zerqa) were excavated in the 1990s, producing new documentary evidence in the form of ostraca, the publication of which is awaited.

The final leg of the trade, from Alexandria to Rome, may well have been intimately connected with the *annona* (the tax in kind, mentioned above), since shippers who served the state were able to carry some of their own goods free of tolls. However, this is by no means the whole story. Alexandria has produced many more examples of Baetican oil amphorae than any other major city in the eastern Mediterranean, a single example that serves to emphasize its role as a

Bronze figure of the
Egyptian hawk-god
Horus dressed in
Roman armour, of
unknown provenance.

major port for inter-regional trade of all sorts and in all directions. To Strabo it was the greatest port in the world, and, of course, its Pharos or lighthouse was one of the wonders of the ancient world.

Religion

There can be no aspect of Roman Egypt more complex or more difficult to understand than religion. In effect, Rome inherited pharaonic religion, on which a classical gloss had been superimposed, largely during the preceding Ptolemaic period. Visitors to the ancient temples of Egypt usually think that they are looking at masterpieces of the Dynastic era, but in many cases— Dendera, Edfu, Kom Ombo, Esna, and Philae, for example—the extant structures are substantially Ptolemaic and Roman.

Although the first and most striking aspect of Egyptian religion is polytheism, there were a number of overriding beliefs (for further discussion, see the section on New Kingdom religion at the beginning of Chapter 10). Thus, such gods as Ra, the sun; Geb, the earth; and Nut, the sky, seem to have been worshipped almost everywhere in Egypt. There was, however, also a tendency towards monotheism. Ra was the source of everything, Ptah is described as 'the heart and tongue of the gods', and in the mid-fourteenth century BC Akhenaten decreed that Aten was the one god that should be worshipped. Another readily observed feature of Egyptian religion is the partiality for animal cults. For example, Horus is represented by a falcon and Hathor by a cow. It was not, however, the animals themselves that were the focus of the worship, but the gods that chose to take on their forms. From this arose the custom of mummifying animals, often by the thousand: crocodiles, baboons, cats, the Oxyrhynchus fish, and so on.

Each of this plethora of gods had his or her own role to play, but the situation is far from simple, because their roles changed through time, and gods could merge together so as to become all but indistinguishable from one another. Thus Horus, the falcon, shown with a sun disc, is often indistinguishable from the sun-god Ra. Amun was originally the god of water and air, but later became the god of physical reproduction, the giver of life.

After Alexander's conquest in 332 BC, Greek culture became implanted, not only in the Greek cities of Alexandria, Naukratis, and Ptolemaïs, but also in the Greek communities scattered throughout the land. The Greeks identified their own gods within the Egyptian spectrum. Thus, Horus was equated with Apollo, Thoth with Hermes, Amun with Zeus, Hathor with Aphrodite, and so on. How the beautiful Athene would have reacted to being equated with the hippopotamus-goddess Taweret, we do not know.

A good example of this process of hellenization is the god Pan. He was equated with Amun-Min, the god of sexual reproduction, who had an important sanctuary at Koptos. The city is at the end of desert roads leading to the east. Amun-Min thus became the god of the east and was shown with an

437

Facing: marble bust of the bearded Zeus-like god Serapis, whose cult emerged out of that of Osirapis during the Ptolemaic Period, eventually spreading outside Egypt to many other parts of the Roman empire.

incense burner, perhaps symbolizing the spices and perfumes of the orient. From these beginnings, during the Roman period, Pan became the god of the Eastern Desert, the capricious guardian of the desert routes. He is shown not as the Pan of Greek mythology, but as the ithyphallic Min, his erection clearly inherited from his previous life.

During Ptolemaic times, a new god called Serapis was invented with the object of giving a greater degree of political and religious unity. Unlike the traditional pharaonic-period deity Osirapis, from whom he derived, he is shown not as an animal but as a bearded man, not unlike Zeus: of all the Egyptian gods, he is the most similar to a Graeco-Roman god. Serapis became immensely popular at Memphis, the old capital of Egypt, and then at Alexandria, when the seat of government was moved there. Eventually the cult gained adherents in Sabratha and Lepcis, Rome, and later Ephesus and the Danube provinces.

Another very popular god in Roman Egypt was Isis, sometimes identified with Hathor. She was both wife and sister to Osiris, who was judge and ruler of the dead and supreme god of the funerary cult. Her role was that of a prototype for motherhood and the faithful wife. She was much adored by women, to whom she was queen of heaven and earth, of life and death. She looked favourably on all women's activities to such an extent that she was at one time the goddess of prostitutes as well. As in the case of Serapis, Isis' worshippers were to be found all over the empire, particularly in Spain. The rituals associated with her cult changed little from pharaonic times: at dawn her statue would be uncovered and adorned with jewels while the sacred fire was lit—all to the accompaniment of sacred music.

Just as the gods of Roman Egypt were essentially Egyptian gods, so temple architecture forms a continuum with Dynastic and Ptolemaic temples. The exception is the Paneion, which because of Pan's special role in the desert may be situated away from habitation in remote spots. Often they were no more than a rock on which travellers would write their dedications. A fine example of this is to be seen in the Wadi Hammamat.

The temple of Hathor at Dendera provides a good idea of the appearance of a late Ptolemaic–Roman temple. The propylon (north gate) is the work of Domitian and Trajan, but the main focus of the complex, the beautifully preserved temple of Hathor, was constructed between 125 BC and AD 60. The front of the building has a massive façade marked by six columns with Hathor-headed capitals surmounted by a cornice. The entrance leads to a hypostyle hall, built in the twenty-first year of Tiberius by Aulus Evilius Flaccus, with the aid of the inhabitants of the town and district, and its roof is supported by Hathor-headed columns. The hall leads through to an inner hypostyle hall and two 'vestibules', the inner of which contains the sanctuary, surrounded by a number of chapels. The ornament is characteristically Egyptian, but many of the subjects are Roman emperors. Thus we see Tiberius before the gods, Claudius making an offering to Hathor and Ihy, and representations of Augustus and

439

Plan of the Graeco-Roman
temple of Hathor at
Dendera.

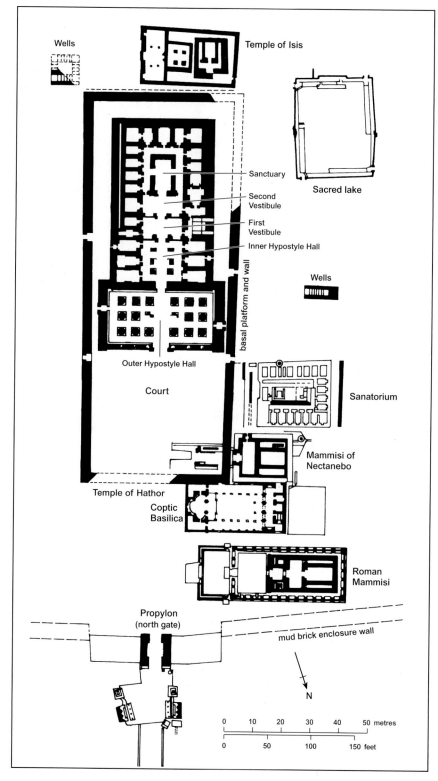

Wells

Temple of Isis

Sacred lake

Sanctuary

Second
Vestibule

First
Vestibule

Inner Hypostyle Hall

basal platform and wall

Wells

Outer Hypostyle Hall

Court

Sanatorium

Mammisi of
Nectanebo

Temple of Hathor

Coptic
Basilica

Roman
Mammisi

Propylon
(north gate)

mud brick enclosure wall

N

| 0 | 10 | 20 | 30 | 40 | 50 metres |

| 0 | 50 | 100 | 150 feet |

Nero. The whole complex is a strange experience for a student brought up on classical scholarship.

Another fine example of a Roman temple is Trajan's kiosk at Philae, preserved on an island between Aswan and the High Dam. This elegant and finely proportioned building has fourteen columns with bell capitals and screen walls, two of which are decorated with scenes representing Trajan making offerings to Isis, Osiris, and Horus. The symbolism of all these temples must have had a very special message to the population of Roman Egypt. Here there is no question of the emperor as god; he is seen as a supplicant to the great gods of old Egypt.

However, from the mid-first century AD onwards a new phenomenon appeared on the religious scene: Christianity. It seems to have taken root in Alexandria, whence it spread to the rest of the country. No doubt, with so many cults in existence, one more could be accepted and absorbed. However, Christianity was an uncompromising religion that did not see itself on a par with the others and actively sought to win converts from paganism. The old order was threatened, and from the mid-third century onwards persecution began in a sporadic way until its culmination in the great purges of Diocletian, begun in AD 303.

In the third century AD there emerged a new trend in religious practice that was to sweep the world. The desert is a religious testing ground, away from the hurly-burly of ordinary life where survival depends on reliance on God. Christ had already set the scene when he spent forty days and forty nights in the desert undergoing the temptations of the devil. In the late third century, according to tradition, two rich young men, Paul, the first hermit, and Anthony, the first monk, each separately left their homes in the Nile Valley to live in the solitude of the wilderness. How they survived is not really a mystery, because holy men everywhere are treated with respect and fed by people they encounter. Since they both settled by springs, no doubt they would have been visited by Bedouin who would have known of the water source and had rights there. Eventually, despite his isolation, the fame of Anthony spread and even the emperor Constantine wrote to him asking for prayers. He was visited by his old disciples, various dignitaries, pilgrims, and, of course, curious sightseers. The coming and going of visitors led to the establishment of a caravanserai, which eventually developed into a monastery—the most significant monastery in Christendom, from which all others derived.

Burial customs are, of course, intimately connected with religious practices. It is not surprising, therefore, that the practice of mummification persisted alongside paganism—in some cases as late as the fourth century AD. The poor might receive the simplest burial as plainly bandaged mummies, but the rich would be given an elaborate mummy case, as pharaonic tradition dictated. During the Roman Period encaustic portraits painted on board were set into the head of the mummy case. These minor works of art are some of the most vivid and realistic to be seen anywhere in the Roman world. No doubt they

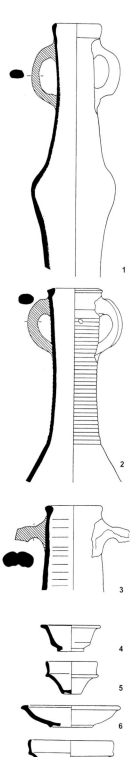

would be commissioned from a highly skilled artist and, as they have an almost photographic degree of realism, they appear to have been executed while the individual was still alive. It has been suggested that they were painted during the prime of life and success, and were then kept for their eventual funerary use.

In Alexandria, there is evidence for an alternative style of burial, perhaps reflecting a different taste amongst the wealthy inhabitants of Greek origin. In the Kom el-Shugafa (the hill of the potsherds) is a complex of catacombs dating to the second century AD. It comprises a circular stairwell leading to a complex of burial chambers and a banqueting hall where mourners visiting the tombs could dine in close proximity to the deceased. While it was originally designed for the wealthy, it seems to have been extended to the poorer classes, for there are many small niches to accommodate unpretentious burials. Artistically the decoration is of some interest, deriving elements from both the Greek and the Egyptian canons. There are false sarcophagi decorated with masks, ox skulls, and festoons, but elsewhere are reliefs depicting deities such as Anubis or Thoth.

Crafts and Trades

Minor arts and crafts are in abundant evidence in Roman Egypt. Almost every site of this period is littered with pottery, glass, and faience as well as organic materials, which are not normally seen in more temperate climates, such as basketry, textiles, and leather. Because of the architectural *richesse* of Egypt and the wealth of written evidence, everyday crafts have received less attention than they merit. Their potential for the analysis of trade, chronology, and technology has yet to be realized, but since the 1980s particularly the systematic study has commenced and is beginning to show interesting results.

Pottery is widely acknowledged to play a vital role in many aspects of archaeological enquiry. Imports to Roman Egypt such as wine jars from Italy and France, oil jars from Spain, fine red wares from North Africa, or lamps from Italy can be recognized and dated. Their importance is undeniable and they are beginning to throw light on trading contacts with the rest of the Mediterranean. However, our knowledge of the local Egyptian wares is still relatively limited. Most assemblages are dominated by jars made from 'Nile silt', a dull dark-brown clay characteristic of the Nile floodplain. There is every reason to believe that these were being produced at many potteries along the Nile Valley and in the Delta, but there is a marked archaeological *lacuna* and we know of only a few kiln sites—all of them situated on the southern shore of Lake Mareotis near Alexandria and all discovered through the researches of one man, Jean-Yves Empereur. These Alexandria kilns appear to have been producing a type of amphora that is not closely datable and that appears on a majority of Roman sites in Egypt. In the third century, the kilns may have been producing imitations of Koan amphorae, presumably because they were destined to contain Koan-style wine, which was a medicinal variety made with sea water.

At the other end of Egypt, pottery with a red slip or wash was made at Aswan, and it is again found widely throughout the country, particularly in first- and second-century contexts. However, this is most certainly only part of the story and there must have been many other establishments along the Nile Valley producing jars or fine table wares such as the Egyptian 'red slip ware' first defined by John Hayes. Among the papyri from Oxyrhynchus are three that are leases for potteries. It appears that production was closely linked to the estate. The lessor, presumably the estate-owner, agrees to provide the pottery building, the storeroom, the wheel, the kiln, the clay, and the fuel for firing, in return for which the lessee must provide his own workforce and supply the lessor with a very large number of jars, in one case in excess of 15,000, which must have been destined to contain the produce of the estate. It is unfortunate that it is not possible to link this fascinating documentary evidence of estate production to the actual pottery or even to the type of pots produced.

Throughout most of the Roman world, fine table wares take the form of red gloss wares, produced in Gaul, Italy, or the East. While these are also found in Egypt, their place is taken by brilliant blue or green faience vessels. Faience is not pottery but a glazed quartz frit formed by grinding quartz and mixing it with an alkali salt and a colourant such as a copper salt. There are several ways of making faience, all of which produce much the same end result: for example, a core of fine quartz cemented with alkali can be packed into a glazing mixture of plant ash, copper oxide, and lime, or the frit can be prepared and painted onto the fashioned core. Alternatively, as the quartz dries, the colourant is drawn to the surface so that, on firing, it fuses to produce the characteristic glaze. Faience cannot be thrown and was usually formed by moulding: it is thus more suited to the production of beads and figurines, but in the Roman period it was used for plates, dishes, and drinking cups. We know little about the production of Roman faience and it is unfortunate that the one kiln site known, at Memphis, was excavated early this century before modern techniques of observation and recording had been developed.

Glass is another common component of Roman rubbish deposits. Much of it is of surprisingly fine quality, often thin walled and clearly very accomplished. Even on desert sites the vessels may be blown, mould-blown, or with multicoloured ornament or cut decoration. At present it is unclear how much of this was imported from the great glasshouses of Syria or how much was locally produced. Alexandria is described by Strabo and other later writers as a great centre for glass-making, perhaps making some of the finest polychrome vessels, but archaeologically we know very little about it. There were certainly other glasshouses, judging from the guild of glass workers mentioned in the Oxyrhynchus papyri.

The production of flour was an important trade closely connected with subsistence. Rotary querns were certainly in use, but the type of mill most commonly encountered is the lever or 'Olynthian' mill. It comprises a slab of stone about 50 sq. cm. with a slot, which forms the hopper, in the middle. A lever is

Facing: some of the main pottery types made in Roman Egypt (1–3 = local amphorae, 4–6 = Egyptian red slip ware, 7 = Aswan ware).

443

fixed across the top of the stone, which is oscillated to and fro around a pivot. Examples have been found in the Greek settlement of Naukratis, but also at Tanis, in the Faiyum, at Quseir el-Qadim, and in the forts of Tiberiane (Barud) and Mons Porphyrites. It is almost certain that this type of mill was introduced by the Greeks, where the type continued in use until at least the third century BC. However, in Egypt they certainly persisted into the Roman period and the example from Quseir belongs to the first century AD, while those from the forts are certainly of first- or second-century AD date. The fort at Badia, in the Mons Porphyrites complex, has produced the components of segmented mills in lava probably from the Greek island of Nisyros. The type is known from Delos, although the examples from Badia could be of late Roman date.

In the ancient world it seems that Egypt was renowned for its textiles, and significant collections, largely of the later Roman period, have been recovered from the towns of Antinoopolis and Panopolis, where there may have been woollen mills. Again Alexandria seems to have been important, supporting a linen trade and the reworking of oriental silks.

Other crafts that might be mentioned are the growing and manufacture of papyrus, the manufacture of drugs and medicines, the production of jewellery, leather working and metalworking, all of which are still inadequately studied.

Demography

The demography of Roman Egypt during the first three centuries AD is well documented, for we have about 300 papyri recording census returns. These returns detail not only members of families living in the Nile Valley, but also their lodgers and slaves.

Estimates of the population of Roman Egypt are fraught with difficulty, not least because the two principal historical sources contradict one another. Diodorus Siculus puts the population in the first century BC at 3 million, while Josephus, writing in the first century AD, gives a figure of 7.5 million exclusive of Alexandria. On the whole, modern scholars find the figure given by Diodorus to be the more credible.

Alexandria, one of the most populous cities in the ancient Mediterranean, is said by Diodorus to have a population of 300,000, which is not so far removed from the modern estimates of around 500,000. It can also be argued that the rural population was distributed over 2,000–3,000 villages, each with an average population of around 1,000–1,500, giving a total figure of 3 million, which accords well with the probable rural population before the nineteenth century. Such calculations by modern scholars give a total population of 4.75 million, of which 1.75 million lived in the towns.

The census returns enable us to flesh out these bare figures. It seems that around two-thirds of households comprised conjugal families (with their siblings) or multiple families linked by kinship, while most of the remaining households were occupied by solitary persons or by families extended by the presence of co-resident kin. Lodgers seem to have been comparatively rare. Slaves, on the other hand, constitute about 11 per cent of the total population. Since the returns give ages, it is possible to estimate death rates. Among women, it seems that very few lived to their sixties, and female life expectancy at birth was probably in the mid to low twenties. Male life expectancy, on the other hand, was at least twenty-five years. The sex ratio of the 1,022 persons whose sex can be adduced was 540 males to 482 females, but among slaves it is reversed (thirty-four males to sixty-eight females).

Marriage in Roman Egypt was a legal status that had consequences for the offspring, but weddings and divorces were private matters in which the state did not intervene. The wife would nearly always live in the husband's household, often with his extended family. About a sixth of all marriages were those between brothers and sisters. Most women would have married by their late teens and virtually all by their late twenties, but only half of all men had married by the age of 25. The average age of women at maternity was around 27 years. The demographic picture of Roman Egypt thus corresponds closely with that of a typical pre-industrial Mediterranean population.

The Nature of Roman Egypt

All Roman provinces were an amalgam between the influence of Rome and indigenous culture. In most cases, the former more or less subsumed the latter. Thus, in Roman Britain or Gaul, for example, traces of the pre-existing Iron Age persist, but the most marked aspect is the change to a Mediterranean style of life. Only in Egypt, and perhaps to some extent in the Greek lands of the north-eastern Mediterranean, is the Roman period an essay in continuity with what went before. At least one of the reasons for this must lie in pharaonic architecture. The creation of a landscape dominated by buildings made of massive blocks of stone, which were not easily swept away, must have been a major factor. They served exactly their intended purpose: to remind people of the greatness of pharaonic civilization and to be a constant witness to the beliefs and values of that period of Egyptian greatness. This may not be the only reason, but it must have been a contributory factor.

It would be wrong to suggest that the Roman era was one of stagnation or that there was no change at all during the seven centuries that lay between the death of Cleopatra on 12th August 30 BC and the Arab conquest of AD 642. However, the major cultural change took root in the third century AD, when Christianity gained widespread acceptance, as it did throughout the empire generally. Monasticism had its roots in the Egyptian desert led by people such as St Paul and St Anthony. Even here pharaonic culture was not without its influence, for Anthony started his religious life living in an old tomb near his village on the Nile and it is here that he wrestled with demons and wild animals, before making his journey into the wilderness.

EPILOGUE

In the *Book of Gates* (a series of funerary texts and images used to decorate late New Kingdom tombs), the Egyptians represented the infinity of time with an apparently endless snake or with a doubly twisted rope being spun from the mouth of a deity (stars above the twists in the rope serving as indications of the passage of units of time). In this image, time is evidently conceived as a phenomenon emerging from the original depths of creation and eventually falling back into the same depths. It is the universal, cyclical nature of time that pervades the ancient Egyptians' sense of their own history. In this history we have untangled some of the twists and caught glimpses of events as they vanish back into the mouth of the snake, but we can ultimately reach a true understanding of Egyptian history only if we combine archaeological and textual evidence into a complete patchwork of material culture and politics, as the contributors to this volume have attempted to do. All ancient history tends to be more or less fragmentary and elusive but the sheer diversity of Egyptian sources occasionally allows certain historical episodes or ways of life to spring very sharply and vividly into focus.

FURTHER READING

Abbreviations

AAR	*African Archaeological Review*
AJA	*American Journal of Anthropology*
ASAE	*Annales du Service des Antiquités de l'Égypte*
BASOR	*Bulletin of the American Schools of Oriental Research*
BIFAO	*Bulletin de l'Institut Français d'Archéologie Oriental*
BiOr	*Bibliotheca Orientalia*
BSEG	*Bulletin de la Société d'Égyptologie de Genève*
BSFE	*Bulletin de la Société Française d'Égyptologie*
CdE	*Chronique d'Égypte*
GM	*Göttinger Miszellen*
JAI	*Journal of the Anthropological Institute*
JARCE	*Journal of the American Research Center in Egypt*
JAS	*Journal of African Studies*
JEA	*Journal of Egyptian Archaeology*
JFA	*Journal of Field Archaeology*
JNES	*Journal of Near Eastern Studies*
JRA	*Journal of Roman Archaeology*
JRS	*Journal of Roman Studies*
JSSEA	*Journal of the Society for the Study of Egyptian Antiquities*
JWP	*Journal of World Prehistory*
LÄ	*Lexikon der Ägyptologie,* ed. W. Helck *et al.* (Wiesbaden, 1975–86)
MDAIK	*Mitteilungen des Deutschen Archäologischen Instituts, Abteilung Kairo*
MIFAO	*Mémoires de l'Institut Français d'Archéologie Oriental*
MMJ	*Metropolitan Museum Journal*
OLP	*Orientalia Lovaniensa Periodica*
PPS	*Proceedings of the Prehistoric Society*
RdE	*Revue d'Égyptologie*
SAK	*Studien der altägyptischen Kultur*
VA	*Varia Aegyptiaca*
WA	*World Archaeology*
ZfS	*Zeitschrift der für ägyptische Sprache und Altertumskunde*

General

As far as histories and general reference works are concerned, the following are well worth consulting: I. E. S. Edwards *et al.* (eds.), *Cambridge Ancient History*, vols. 1–4, 3rd edn. (Cambridge, 1971–3); Bruce Trigger *et al.*, *Ancient Egypt: A Social History*

(Cambridge, 1983); Barry Kemp, *Ancient Egypt: Anatomy of a Civilization* (London, 1989); Nicolas Grimal, *A History of Ancient Egypt* (Oxford, 1992); Donald Redford, *Egypt, Canaan and Israel in Ancient Times* (Princeton, 1992); Jean Vercoutter, *L'Égypte et la vallée du Nil*, i. *Des origines à la fin de l'ancien empire* (Paris, 1992); Claude Vandersleyen, *L'Égypte et la vallée du Nil*, ii. *De la fin de l'ancien empire à la fin du nouvel empire* (Paris, 1995); Ian Shaw and Paul Nicholson, *The British Museum Dictionary of Ancient Egypt* (London, 1995); Serge Donadoni (ed.), *The Egyptians* (Chicago, 1997); Judith Lustig (ed.), *Anthropology and Egyptology: A Developing Dialogue* (Sheffield, 1997), and Regina Schulz and Matthias Seidel (eds.), *Egypt: The World of the Pharaohs*, English edn. ed. Peter Der Manuelian (Cologne, 1998).

There are numerous general works on the art and literature of Egypt and the following are only a small selection: Cyril Aldred, *Egyptian Art in the Days of the Pharaohs* (London, 1980); Bernard Bothmer *et al.*, *Egyptian Sculpture of the Late Period 700 BC to AD. 100* (New York, 1960); Raymond Faulkner, *The Ancient Egyptian Pyramid Texts* (Oxford, 1969); Miriam Lichtheim, *Ancient Egyptian Literature*, 3 vols. (Berkeley and Los Angeles, 1973–80); Antonio Loprieno (ed.), *Ancient Egyptian Literature: History and Forms* (Leiden, 1996); Jaromir Malek, *Egyptian Art* (London, 1999); Richard Parkinson, *Voices from Ancient Egypt* (London, 1991); William Peck, *Egyptian Drawings* (New York, 1978); Georges Posener, *Littérature et politique dans l'Égypte de la XII dynastie* (Paris, 1956); Gay Robins, *The Art of Ancient Egypt* (London, 1997); Heinrich Schäfer, *Principles of Egyptian Art* (Oxford, 1978); Donald Spanel, *Through Ancient Eyes: Egyptian Portraiture* (Birmingham, Ala., 1988), and William Stevenson Smith, *The Art and Architecture of Ancient Egypt*, rev. W. Kelly Simpson (Harmondsworth, 1981).

Many articles in periodicals have tackled various aspects of Egyptian religion and ideology, but only a few monographs have dealt with this crucial area of Egyptian culture. Some earlier works still have a great deal to offer, e.g. Henri Frankfort, *Kingship and the Gods* (Chicago, 1948), and Siegfried Morenz, *Egyptian Religion* (London, 1973), but the best of the works published over the last twenty years are: Jan Assmann, *Egyptian Solar Religion in the New Kingdom: Re, Amun and the Crisis of Polytheism* (London, 1995); Erik Hornung, *Conceptions of God in Ancient Egypt* (Ithaca, NY, 1982), and *Idea into Image: Essays on Ancient Egyptian Thought* (New York, 1992); Stephen Quirke, *Ancient Egyptian Religion* (London, 1992); John Romer, *Valley of the Kings* (London, 1981); A. I. Sadek, *Popular Religion in Ancient Egypt during the New Kingdom* (Hildesheim, 1988); Byron E. Shafer (ed.), *Religion in Ancient Egypt: Gods, Myths and Personal Practice* (London, 1991), and W. Kelly Simpson (ed.), *Religion and Philosophy in Ancient Egypt* (New Haven, 1989).

There is no shortage of books on Egyptian funerary practices, but the following are probably the most up-to-date and widely available recent publications: Sue D'Auria *et al.*, *Mummies and Magic: The Funerary Arts of Ancient Egypt* (Boston, 1988); I. E. S. Edwards, *The Pyramids of Egypt* (Harmondsworth, 1985); Erik Hornung, *The Valley of the Kings* (New York 1990); M. Lehner, *The Complete Pyramids* (London, 1997); Nicholas Reeves, *The Valley of the Kings: The Decline of a Royal Necropolis* (London, 1990); Nicholas Reeves and Richard Wilkinson, *The Complete Valley of the Kings* (London, 1996), and Jeffrey Spencer, *Death in Ancient Egypt* (Harmondsworth, 1982).

Apart from the books on funerary practices mentioned above, a surprisingly small number of works deal with the overall development of Egyptian architecture. Somers Clarke and Reginald Engelbach, *Ancient Egyptian Masonry: The Building Craft* (Oxford, 1930; repr. New York, 1990, as *Ancient Egyptian Construction and Architecture*), is still useful but has been very much replaced by Dieter Arnold, *Building in Egypt: Pharaonic Stone Masonry* (Oxford, 1991). Alexander Badawy, *A History of Egyptian Architecture* (Berkeley and Los Angeles, 1968), and Stevenson Smith, *Art and Architecture* (see above under the topic of art), are both useful on the more religious and aesthetic aspects of the topic, respectively.

Settlements, society, and material culture are discussed by the following: Manfred Bietak, 'Urban archaeology and the "Town Problem" in ancient Egypt', in Kent Weeks (ed.), *Egyptology and the Social Sciences* (Cairo, 1979), 95–144; Morris Bierbrier, *Tomb-Builders of the Pharaohs* (London, 1982); Barry Kemp, 'The Early Development of Towns in Egypt', *Antiquity*, 51 (1977), 185–200, and *Ancient Egypt: Anatomy of a Civilization* (London, 1989); Dominique Valbelle, *Les Ouvriers de la tombe: Deir el-Médineh à l'époque ramesside* (Cairo, 1985), 261–317; Gay Robins, *Women in Ancient Egypt* (London, 1993), and Paul Nicholson and Ian Shaw (eds.), *Ancient Egyptian Materials and Technology* (Cambridge, 2000).

Major books and articles on ancient Nubia include Bruce Trigger, *History and Settlement in Lower Nubia* (New Haven, 1965); Fred Wendorf (ed.), *The Prehistory of Nubia*, 2 vols. (Dallas, Tex., 1968); William Adams, *Nubia: Corridor to Africa* (London, 1977); Brigitte Gratien, *Les Cultures Kerma: Essai de classification* (Lille, 1978); Steffen Wenig, *Africa in Antiquity: The Arts of Ancient Nubia and Sudan*, 2 vols. (New York, 1978); Charles Bonnet, *Kerma, royaume de Nubie* (Vienna, 1992), and 'Excavations at the Nubian Royal Town of Kerma: 1975–91', *Antiquity*, 66 (1992) 611 ff.; Stuart Tyson Smith, *Askut in Nubia* (London, 1995); Peter Shinnie, *Ancient Nubia* (London, 1996); Derek Welsby, *The Kingdom of Kush: The Napatan and Meroitic Empires* (London, 1996), and Dieter Wildung (ed.), *Sudan: Ancient Kingdoms of the Nile* (Paris, 1997), the latter being a well-illustrated exhibition catalogue.

1. Introduction

As far as the chronology of ancient Egypt is concerned, there are many different sources, but three that provide very different perspectives on the way in which the dating system has been constructed from an elaborate combination of astronomical observations, king-lists, and genealogies are Richard Parker, *The Calendars of Ancient Egypt* (Chicago, 1950); Kenneth Kitchen, 'The Chronology of Ancient Egypt', *WA* 23 (1991), 201–8, and Donald Redford, *Pharaonic King-Lists, Annals and Day-Books: A Contribution to the Egyptian Sense of History* (Mississauga, 1986). For the idea of the study of cultural and social change during various periods, as opposed to conventional political history, see David O'Connor, 'Political Systems and Archaeological Data in Egypt: 2600–1780 BC', *WA* 6 (1974), 15–38; Stephan Seidlmayer, 'Wirtschaftliche und gesellschaftliche Entwicklung im Übergang von alten zum mittleren Reich', in J. Assmann and W. V. Davies (eds.), *Problems and Priorities in Egyptian Archaeology* (London, 1987), 175–217; Barry Kemp, *Ancient Egypt: Anatomy of a Civilization* (London, 1989); Kathryn Bard, 'Toward an Interpretation of the Role of Ideology in the Evolution of Complex Society in Egypt', *Journal of Anthropological Archaeology*, 11 (1992), 1–24, and Robert Wenke, 'Anthropology, Egyptology and the Concept of Cultural Change', in J. Lustig (ed.), *Anthropology and Egyptology* (Sheffield, 1997), 117–36.

For Manetho, see *Manetho, Aegyptiaca*, ed. and trans. W. G. Wadell (London, 1940); for the Royal Turin Canon, see Alan Gardiner, *The Royal Canon of Turin* (Oxford, 1959), and Jaromir Malek, 'The Original Version of the Royal Canon of Turin', *JEA* 68 (1982),

93–106; and, for the Palermo Stone, see Heinrich Schäfer, *Ein Bruchstück altägyptischer Annalen* (Berlin, 1902), and Georges Daressy, 'La Pierre de Palerme et la chronologie de l'ancien empire', *BIFAO* 12 (1916), 161-214.

The complex question of the links between Sothic heliacal risings and Egyptian chronology is discussed in numerous books and articles, including the following: Parker, 'Sothic Dates and Calendar "Adjustment" ', *RdE* 9 (1952), 101–8; Jacques Vandier, *Manuel d'archéologie égyptienne*, I (Paris, 1952), 842–3; Jaroslav Černy, 'Note on the Supposed Beginning of a Sothic Period under Sethos I', *JEA* 47 (1961), 150–2; M. F. Ingham, 'The Length of the Sothic Cycle', *JEA* 55 (1969), 36–40; Laszlo Kakosy, 'Die Mannweibliche Natur des Sirius in Ägypten', *Studia Aegyptiaca*, 2 (Budapest, 1976), 41–6; G. Clerc, 'Isi-Sothis dans le monde romain', *Hommages à Maarten J. Vermaseren* (Leiden, 1978), 247–81; Christiane Desroche-Noblecourt, 'Isis Sothis—le chien, la vigne—et la tradition millénaire', *Livre du Centenaire, IFAO 1880–1980* (Cairo, 1980), 15–24, and Rolf Krauss, *Sothis- und Mondaten: Studien zur astronomischen und technischen Chronologie Altägyptens* (Hildesheim, 1985).

For Flinders Petrie's system of seriation for the Predynastic, see his own expositions of the technique: 'Sequences in prehistoric remains', *JAI*, NS 29 (1899), 295–301, and *Diospolis Parva* (London, 1901), but, for more recent approaches, see D. G. Kendall: 'A Statistical Approach to Flinders Petrie's Sequence-Dating', *Bulletin of the International Statistics Institute*, 40 (1963), 657–80; Barry Kemp, 'Automatic Analysis of Predynastic Cemeteries: A New Method for an Old Problem', *JEA* 68 (1982), 5–15, and Toby Wilkinson, *State Formation in Ancient Egypt: Chronology and Society* (Oxford, 1996).

The ongoing debate concerning co-regencies can be explored by consulting W. Kelly Simpson, 'Studies in the Twelfth Egyptian Dynasty: I–II', *JARCE* 2 (1963), 53–63; William Murnane, *Ancient Egyptian Coregencies* (Chicago, 1977), and David Lorton, 'Terms of Coregency in the Middle Kingdom', *VA* 2 (1986), 113–20.

A number of problems relating to the social and political history of Egypt (many relating to the nature of the 'intermediate periods') are discussed in the following: Barbara Bell, 'The Dark Ages in Ancient History: I. The First Dark Age in Egypt', *AJA* 75 (1971), 1–26, and 'Climate and the History of Egypt: the Middle Kingdom', *AJA* 79 (1975), 223–69; Kenneth Kitchen, 'The Basics of Egyptian Chronology in Relation to the Bronze Age', in Paul Astrom (ed.), *High, Middle or Low: Acts of an International Colloquium in Absolute Chronology Held at the University of Gothenburg 20–22 August 1987* (Gothenburg, 1987), 37–55; P. James *et al.*, *Centuries of Darkness: A Challenge to the Conventional Chronology of Old World Archaeology* (London, 1991); Manfred Bietak (ed.), *Ägypten und Levante III: Acts of the Second International Colloquium on Absolute Chronology* (Vienna, 1992); William Ward, 'The Present Status of Egyptian Chronology', *BASOR* 288 (1992), 53–66, and Leo Depuydt, 'On the Consistency of the Wandering Year as Backbone of Egyptian Chronology', *JARCE* 32 (1995), 43–58.

2. Prehistory

Full bibliographic references for this period, with topographic and thematic indexes, as well as maps locating prehistoric sites, can be found in Stan Hendrickx, *Analytical Bibliography of the Prehistory and the Early Dynastic Period of Egypt and Northern Sudan* (Leuven, 1995), to which yearly additions appear in the journal *Archéo-Nil*. Most of the recent synthetic works are part of general works on Egypt's early history, such as Béatrix Midant-Reynes, *The Prehistory of Egypt: From the First Egyptians to the First Pharaohs*

(Oxford, 2000), and Michael A. Hoffman, *Egypt before the Pharaohs* (London, 1980), the revised edition of which (Austin, Tex., 1991) includes an extra chapter summarizing recent discoveries.

An excellent recapitulation of the state of research is provided by Frank Klees and Rudolph Kuper (eds.), *New Light on the Northeast African Past* (Cologne, 1992), which includes contributions by leading specialists. The work is particularly important with regard to the syntheses of the different stages of the Palaeolithic and discussion of the Neolithic of the Western Desert.

The basic publications for the work of the Combined Prehistoric Expedition on the Nubian and Egyptian prehistory, are Wendorf (ed.), *The Prehistory of Nubia*, 2 vols. (Dallas, Tex., 1968), and Wendorf and Schild (eds.), *The Prehistory of the Nile Valley* (New York, 1976).

For the prehistory of the Western Desert, the first systematic study is that on the Kharga Oasis, by Gertrude Caton-Thompson, *The Kharga Oasis in Prehistory* (London, 1952). More recent studies related to particular regions are those by Schild and Wendorf: for Dakhla, *The Prehistory of Dakhla Oasis and Adjacent Desert* (Wroclaw, 1977), and for Bir Sahara, *The Prehistory of an Egyptian Oasis: A Report of the Combined Prehistoric Expedition to Bir Sahara, Western Desert, Egypt* (Warsaw, 1981). The evidence concerning the so-called radar channels is summarized in two articles in *JFA* 14 (1987) and 15 (1988), by respectively William P. McHugh and Wendorf and their associates.

The Middle Palaeolithic of Bir Tarfawi and Bir Sahara is presented at large in Wendorf, Schild, Close, *et al.*, *Egypt during the Last Interglacial: The Middle Paleolithic of Bir Tafawi and Bir Sahara East* (New York, 1993). For an extensive study on the Levallois technique, using mainly examples from Egypt and Nubia, there is Philip Van Peer, *The Levallois Reduction Strategy* (Madison, 1992).

The most recent overview of Middle and especially Late Palaeolithic chert mining in Egypt is given by Vermeersch, Paulissen, and Van Peer, in *Archaeologia Polona*, 33 (1995), while Vermeersch *et al.*, 'Une minière de silex et un squelette du paléolithique supérieure à Nazlet Khater', *L'Anthropologie*, 88 (1984), 231–44, consists of a summary of the finds at Nazlet Khater, including the Late Palaeolithic burial. The even older burial from Taramsa Hill can be found in Vermeersch *et al.*, 'A Middle Palaeolithic Burial of a Modern Human at Taramsa Hill, Egypt', *Antiquity* 72 (1988), 475–84. Egypt's earliest rock art is presented by Dirk Huyge, 'Hilltops, Silts and Petroglyphs: The Fish Hunters of El-Hosh', *Bulletin des Musées royaux d'Art et d'Histoire* 69 (1998), 1–17.

The Late Palaeolithic site E 71K12 near Esna is described in Wendorf, Schild, Baker, Gautier, Longo, and Mohammed in *A Late Paleolithic Kill-Butchery Camp in Upper Egypt* (Dallas, Tex., and Warsaw, 1997). The sites from the same period at Wadi Kubbaniya are published as Wendorf, Schild, and Close (eds.), *The Prehistory of Wadi Kubbaniya I: The Kubbaniya Skeleton* (Dallas, Tex., 1986), and Wendorf, Schild, and Close (eds.), *The Prehistory of Wadi Kubbaniya II: Stratigraphy, Palaeoeconomy and Environment* (Dallas, Tex., 1989), and Wendorf, Schild and Close (eds.), *The Prehistory of Wadi Kubbaniya III: Late Palaeolithic Archaeology* (Dallas, Tex., 1989). The same authors are also responsible for the excavation report on the Early Neolithic at Bir Kiseiba in the Western Desert: *Cattle-Keepers of the Eastern Sahara: The Neolithic of Bir Kiseiba* (Dallas, Tex., 1984). A first summary of the megaliths found at Nabta Playa is given by Wendorf and Schild in *Sahara*, 5 (1992–3).

The work by the *Besiedlungsgeschichte der Ost-Sahara* project is summarized by Rudolf Kuper in *CRIPEL* 17 (1995). The full results of the work in the Wadi el-Akhdar can be found in Werner Schön, *Ausgraburgen im Wadi el-Akhdar; Gilf Kebir (SW-Ägypten)* (Cologne, 1996). A summary of the Neolithic in the Dakhla Oasis is provided in Mary M. A. McDonald, 'Early African Pastoralism: View from Dakhleh Oasis (South Central Egypt)', *Journal of Anthropological Archaeology* 17 (1998), 124–42.

The Epipalaeolithic Elkabian was published as Vermeersch, *Elkab II: L'Elkabien, Epipaléolithique de la Vallée du Nil Egyptien* (Leuven, 1978).

Interpretations of the Faiyum cultures are given in Fekri Hassan, 'Holocene Lakes and Prehistoric Settlements in the Western Fayum, Egypt', *JAS* 13 (1986), 483–501, and Boleslaw Ginter and Janusz K. Kozlowski, 'Kulturelle und paläoklimatische Sequenz in der Fayum-Depression: Eine zusammensetzende Darstellung der Forschungsarbeiten in den Jahren 1977–1981', *MDAIK* 42 (1986). Ginter, Kozlowski, and Barbara Drobniewicz published the evidence on the Tarifian in *Silexindustrien von El Târif* (1979).

The different stages of cultural development at Merimda have been published as Josef Eiwanger, *Merimde—Benisalâme I–III*, 3 vols. (1984–92). For the culture of el-Omari, see Fernand Debono and Bodil Mortensen, *El-Omari* (Mainz am Rhein, 1990).

The three principal excavation reports for the Badarian are: Guy Brunton and Caton-Thompson, *The Badarian Civilisation and Prehistoric Remains near Badari* (London, 1928), and two volumes by Brunton, *Mostagedda and the Tasian Culture* (London, 1937), and *Matmar* (London, 1948). Among the studies dealing with various aspects of the Badari culture, Renée F. Friedman, *Predynastic Settlement Ceramics of Upper Egypt: A Comparative Study of the Ceramics of Hemamieh, Naqada and Hierakonpolis* (1994), presents a most important study regarding the settlement ceramics of both the Badari and Naqada culture. An equally important study for the lithic industries has been made by Diane L. Holmes, *The Predynastic Lithic Industries of Upper Egypt: A Comparative Study of the Lithic Traditions of Badari, Naqada and Hierakonpolis* (Oxford, 1989). For Badarian social stratification, see W. Anderson, 'Badarian Burials: Evidence of Social Inequality in Middle Egypt during the Early Predynastic Era', *JARCE* 29 (1992), 51–66. Recent work on Badarian sites in the Badari area and at Mahgar Dendera is presented respectively by Holmes and Friedman in *PPS* 60 (1994), and Hendrickx and Midant-Reynes, 'Preliminary Report on the Predynastic Living Site: Maghara 2 (Upper Egypt)', *OLP* 19 (1988), 5–16. For an alternative view on the links between the Neolithic cultures in the Delta and the Badarian culture, see the article by Werner Kaiser, 'Zur Südausdehnung des vorgeschichtlichen Deltakulturen und zur frühen Entwicklung Oberägyptens', *MDAIK* 41 (1985), 61–88.

3. The Naqada Period

These suggestions for further reading are by no means exhaustive; Stan Hendrickx, *Analytical Bibliography of the Prehistory and the Early Dynastic Period of Egypt and Northern Sudan* (Leuven, 1995), gives some idea of the wealth of published material concerning the Predynastic Period, and the list below is intended to give only the fundamental works, which should allow the reader to gain a deeper knowledge of the various topics.

Apart from the pioneering work of Flinders Petrie and James Quibell (e.g. Petrie and Quibell, *Naqada and Ballas* (London, 1896), and Petrie, *Prehistoric Egypt* (London, 1920)), there are more recent syntheses of the Predynastic cultures by Lech Krzyzaniak, *Early Farming Cultures on the Lower Nile: The Predynastic Period in Egypt* (Warsaw, 1977); Michael Hoffman, *Egypt before the Pharaohs: The Prehistoric Foundations of*

Egyptian Civilization (Austin, Tex., 1991), and Béatrix Midant-Reynes, *The Prehistory of Egypt: From the First Egyptians to the First Pharaohs* (Oxford, 2000). Jean Vercoutter, *L'Égypte et la vallée du Nil*, i: *Des origines à la fin de l'ancien empire* (Paris, 1992), devotes over 200 pages to the question of the beginnings of Egyptian culture. Also recommended are the excellent articles by Fekri Hassan, 'The Predynastic of Egypt', *JWP* 2 (1988), 135–86, and Kathryn Bard, 'The Egyptian Predynastic: A Review of the Evidence', *JFA* 21/3 (1994), 265–88.

For Predynastic chronology since Petrie, the crucial work undertaken by Werner Kaiser (e.g. 'Zur inneren Chronologie der Naqada-Kultur', *Archeologia Geographica* 6 (1957), 69–77) has been continued by Hendrickx in his doctoral thesis, a clear summary of which was published as one of the papers in Jeffrey Spencer (ed.), *Aspects of Early Egypt* (London, 1996). For discussion of the radiocarbon dates from Predynastic sites, see Fekri Hassan, 'Radiocarbon Chronology of Neolithic and Predynastic Sites in Upper Egypt and the Delta', *AAR* 3 (1985), 95–16.

Comparatively little recent work has dealt with the Naqada culture, but the available funerary data are thoroughly exploited in J. J. Castillos, *A Reappraisal of the Published Evidence on Egyptian Predynastic and Early Dynastic Cemeteries* (Toronto, 1982), and Kathryn Bard, *From Farmers to Pharaohs: Mortuary Evidence for the Rise of Complex Society in Egypt* (Sheffield, 1994). For the French excavations at el-Adaïma, which have begun to clarify many aspects of Naqada funerary practices, see the preliminary reports published by Midant-Reynes *et al.* in *BIFAO* from 1990 onwards. The American work at Hierakonpolis is discussed in Hoffman, *The Predynastic of Hierakonpolis: An Interim Monograph* (Giza-Macomb, Ill., 1982), and Renée Friedman and Barbara Adams (eds.), *The Followers of Horus: Studies Dedicated to Michael Hoffman* (Oxford, 1992).

With regard to the northward expansion of the Naqada culture into the Delta, see Alexander Scharff, *Das vorgeschichtliche Gräberfeld von Abusir el Meleq* (Leipzig, 1926), concerning the excavation of the cemetery of Abusir el-Melek, and, for the recent German work at the eastern Delta site of Minshat Abu Omar, see Karla Kroeper and Dietrich Wildung, *Minshat Abu Omar: Ein vor- und frühgeschichtliche Friedhof im Nildelta, I, Gräber 1–114* (Mainz, 1994), as well as Kroeper, 'Tombs of the Élite in Minshat Abu Omar', in Edwin van den Brink (ed.), *The Nile Delta in Transition: 4th–3rd Millennium BC*, (Jerusalem, 1992), 127–50, which includes precious information relating to the northward expansion of Upper Egyptian cultures.

With regard to the south, and contacts with the Nubian A Group, the results of the Scandinavian expeditions are reported in H. Nordström, *Neolithic and A-Group Sites* (Uppsala, 1972), and the American work has been published by Bruce Williams, *Excavations between Abu Simbel and the Sudan Frontier: Part I : A Group Royal Cemetery at Qustul: Cemetery L* (Chicago, 1986). The latter includes important funerary remains at Qustul, which Williams, 'The Lost Pharaohs of Nubia', *Archaeology* 33 (1980), 13–21, has claimed as proof of Nubian roots for the Egyptian pharaonic civilization. William Adams's opposition to this suggestion, in 'Doubts about Lost Pharaohs', *JNES* 44 (1985), 185–92, and Williams's subsequent response ('The Forebears of Menes in Nubia: Myth or Reality?', *JNES* 46/1 (1987), 15–26) give some idea of the fierce debates that can sometimes rage in the Egyptological world.

For the Maadi/Buto culture, see the German publications of I. Rizkana and Jürgen Seeher, *Maadi*, 3 vols. (Mainz, 1987–9), and the synthetic article published by Seeher: 'Maadi—eine prädynastische Kulturgruppe zwischen Oberägypten und Palästina', *Prähistorische Zeitschrift*, 65/2 (1990), 123–56. In addition there is a description of current Italian research by Isabela Caneva, 'Recent Excavations in Maadi', in L. Krzyzaniak and M. Kobuciewicz (eds.), *Late Prehistory of the Nile Basin and the Sahara* (Poznan, 1989). K. Köhler, 'The State of Research on Late Predynastic Egypt: New Evidence for the Development of the Pharaonic State?', *GM* 147 (1995), 79–92, puts forward a modification to the usual view of the two cultural groupings, Naqada and Maadi, which she suggests are too schematic, arguing instead that there were a number of regional differences. See Diana Holmes, *The Predynastic Lithic Industries of Upper Egypt: A Comparative Study of the Lithic Traditions of Badari, Nagada and Hierakonpolis* (Oxford, 1989), for evidence of such regional distinctions in the lithic industries of Upper Egypt. Köhler's hypothesis, however, is vehemently contested by Werner Kaiser, 'Trial and Error', *GM* 149 (1995), 5–14.

Finally, it is worth stressing the importance of the proceedings of a colloquium held in Cairo: Edwin van den Brink (ed.), *The Nile Delta in Transition: 4th–3rd Millennium BC* (Jerusalem, 1992), which provides a good summary of current research concerning this part of the Nile Valley, which was long considered hostile and uninhabited during the Predynastic Period, including a number of papers dealing with early contacts between the Delta and the Near East.

4. The Emergence of the Egyptian State

The most complete listing of bibliographical material for this period can be found in Stan Hendrickx, *Analytical Bibliography of the Prehistory and the Early Dynastic Period of Egypt and Northern Sudan* (Leuven, 1995), which also has detailed maps of early sites in Egypt, the Eastern and Western Deserts, Nubia, Sinai, and southern Palestine. Although somewhat outdated in terms of tomb identifications, Bryan Emery, *Archaic Egypt* (Harmondsworth, 1967), is an important contribution to these studies, and he published several volumes on his excavations at North Saqqara (Cairo, 1938, 1939, 1949, London, 1954, 1958). More recent synthetic works include Jeffrey Spencer, *Early Egypt* (London, 1993), Toby Wilkinson, *Early Dynastic Egypt* (London, 1999), and Michael Rice's somewhat controversial study, *Egypt's Making* (London, 1991).

A major contribution concerning the intellectual foundations of the early state in Egypt and early cults is found in Barry Kemp, *Ancient Egypt: Anatomy of a Civilization* (London, 1989). The early state in Egypt is also discussed in Jac. Janssen, 'The Early Egyptian State', in J. M. Claessen and P. Shalnik (eds.) *The Early State* (The Hague, 1978). The environmental parameters are discussed in Karl Butzer, *Early Hydraulic Civilization in Egypt* (Chicago, 1976). For an overview of Predynastic cultures, see Kathryn Bard, 'The Egyptian Predynastic: A Review of the Evidence,' *JFA* 21 (1994), 268–88. For a study of the late Predynastic and Early Dynastic periods, including a list of cemeteries, see Bodil Mortensen, 'Change in the Settlement Pattern and Population in the Beginning of the Historical Period', *Ägypten und Levante*, 2 (1991), 11–37.

The Followers of Horus (Oxford, 1992), is an excellent collection of articles compiled by Renée Friedman and Barbara Adams in memory of the late Michael Hoffman, who directed excavations at Hierakonpolis. See especially the articles by David O'Connor on Early Dynastic temples, Thomas von der Way on architecture at Buto, and Harry Smith on connections between Egypt, Susa, and Sumer.

On Egyptian state formation, see Bruce Trigger, 'Egypt: A Fledgling Nation', *JSSEA* 17 (1990), 58–66, and 'The Rise of Egyptian Civilisation', in Trigger *et al.*, *Ancient Egypt: A Social History* (Cambridge, 1983), 1–70. See also Jürgen Seeher, 'Gedanken zur Rolle

Unterägyptens bei der Herausbildung des Pharaonenreiches', *MDAIK*, 47 (1991), 313–18, and E. Christiana Köhler, 'The State of Research on Late Predynastic Egypt: New Evidence for the Development of the Pharaonic State?', *GM* 147 (1995), 79–92. For a theoretical perspective, see Robert Wenke, 'Egypt: Origins of Complex Societies', *Annual Review of Anthropology*, 18 (1989), 129–55, and 'The Evolution of Early Egyptian Civilization: Issues and Evidence', *JWP* 5/3 (1991), 279–329. Werner Kaiser has written a number of important articles on the subject in *MDAIK* (1958, 1985, 1990), and in *ZÄS* (1956, 1959, 1960, 1961, 1964). Another important reference is Wolfgang Helck, *Untersuchungen zur Thinitenzeit* (Wiesbaden, 1987). The question of the location of the Early Dynastic city of Memphis is discussed by David Jeffreys and Anna Tavares in 'The Historic Landscape of Early Dynastic Memphis', *MDAIK* 50 (1994), 143–74.

The origins and initial form of writing in late Predynastic and Early Dynastic Egypt are considered by John Ray in 'The Emergence of Writing in Egypt', *WA* 17/3 (1986), 390–8, while the social implications of the use of writing are discussed by John Baines in 'Literacy and Ancient Egyptian Society', *Man*, 18 (1983), 572–99. Baines also provides a stimulating analysis of the relationship between early Egyptian art and writing: 'Communication and Display: The Integration of Early Egyptian Art and Writing', *Antiquity*, 63 (1989), 471–82. The social and economic context from which hieroglyphs emerged is discussed in comparison with early Mesopotamian, Chinese, and Mesoamerican languages by Nicholas Postgate, Tao Wang, and Toby Wilkinson in 'The Evidence for Early Writing: Utilitarian or Ceremonial?', *Antiquity*, 69 (1995), 459–80.

The ceremonial palettes and maceheads of the late Predynastic Period have been the subject of numerous books and articles. Nicholas Millet seeks to understand their decorative schemes and cultural significance by comparing them with other items such as the labels attached to funerary equipment ('The Narmer Macehead and Related Objects', *JARCE* 27 (1990) 53-9), while others adopt more speculative historical and art-historical approaches (e.g. W. A. Fairservis Jr., 'A Revised View of the Naʿrmr Palette', *JARCE* 28 (1991), 1–20, and W. Davis, *Masking the Blow: The Scene of Representation in Late Prehistoric Egyptian Art* (Berkeley and Los Angeles, 1992)).

For the early temple on Elephantine Island, see Kaiser's articles in *MDAIK*, 32 (1976) and 33 (1977), and Kaiser *et al.* in *MDAIK* 51 (1995). Günter Dreyer, *Elephantine VIII: Der Tempel der Satet* (Mainz, 1986), is a very thorough publication of these excavations. Excavations at Hierakonpolis were reported for the Egyptian Research Account in J. E. Quibell and Flinders Petrie, *Hierakonpolis I* (London, 1900), and Quibell and F. W. Green, *Hierakonpolis II* (London, 1902). Barbara Adams has published studies of the early excavations, *Ancient Hierakonpolis* (Warminster, 1974), and a *Supplement* (Warminster, 1974), to this, as well as *The Fort Cemetery at Hierakonpolis* (Warminster, 1987). Michael Hoffman published numerous articles on his fieldwork there, and two important books, *The Predynastic of Hierakonpolis: An Interim Monograph* (Cairo, 1982), and *Egypt before the Pharaohs*, 2nd edn. (Austin, Tex., 1991). Three reports on excavations at Hierakonpolis were published: Walter Fairservis, *Occasional Papers in Anthropology* (Poughkeepsie, 1983, 1983, 1986).

Petrie published his Egypt Exploration Fund excavations at the royal cemetery at Abydos in two volumes: *The Royal Tombs of the First Dynasty I–II* (London, 1900–1). For a discussion of the debate concerning the location of the royal and non-royal tombs at Abydos and Saqqara, see Kemp's articles in *JEA* 52 (1966), and *Antiquity*, 41 (1967). For David O'Connor's recent work at Abydos, see 'The Earliest Pharaohs and the University Museum', *Expedition*, 29/1 (1987), 27–39, and 'New Funerary Enclosures (Talbezirke) of the Early Dynastic Period at Abydos', *JARCE* 26 (1989), 51–86; 'Boat Graves and Pyramid Origins: New Discoveries at Abydos', *Expedition,* 33/3 (1991), 5–17, and 'The Earliest Royal Boat Graves', *Egyptian Archaeology* 6 (1995), 3–7. For the recent excavations of the German Archaeological Institute at Umm el-Qaʿab, see articles in *MDAIK* by Kaiser (1981, 1987), Kaiser and Dreyer (1982), Kaiser and Grossman (1979), and Dreyer (1987, 1990, 1991, 1993).

An overview of Egyptian relations with Palestine is given in Donald Redford, *Egypt, Canaan, and Israel in Ancient Times* (Princeton, 1992). For more specific archaeological information, see Edwin van den Brink (ed.), *The Nile Delta in Transition: 4th–3rd Millennium BC* (Jerusalem, 1992), including articles on recent excavations in the Delta at Mendes, Minshat Abu Omar, Tell el-Faraʿin/Buto, Tell el-Farkha, and Tell Ibrahim Awad. Also in this volume are important articles by Israeli archaeologists on Egyptian evidence in southern Palestine.

5. The Old Kingdom

No specialized history of the Old Kingdom has yet been written, therefore it is necessary to resort to the relevant sections of the more general histories of Egypt. W. Helck, *Geschichte des Alten Ägypten* (Leiden, 1981), may be beginning to show its age, but remains by far the best concise history of ancient Egypt published in the past two or three decades. For an update on some latest ideas, it is useful to consult more recent publications of the same type, such as Nicolas Grimal, *A History of Ancient Egypt* (Oxford, 1992), and especially Jean Vercoutter, *L'Égypte et la vallée du Nil,* i: *Des origines à la fin de l'Ancien Empire* (Paris, 1992). For more general background information, read Barry Kemp, *Ancient Egypt: Anatomy of a Civilization* (London, 1989). Jaromir Malek's more popularly oriented *In the Shadow of the Pyramids* (London, 1986) provides information on Old Kingdom economy, administration, religion, and arts and contains a spectacular collection of photographs of Old Kingdom monuments by Werner Forman. Dietrich Wildung, *Die Rolle ägyptischer Könige im Bewußtsein ihrer Nachwelt* (Berlin, 1969), gives a more unusual view of the history of the Old Kingdom.

Aspects of Old Kingdom economy, administration, and foreign policy have been discussed by W. Helck in a number of books and articles. The originality of his contribution surpasses that of any other scholar, and at least his *Wirtschaftsgeschichte des Alten Ägypten im 3. und 2. Jahrtausend vor Chr.* (Leiden, 1975), *Untersuchungen zu den Beamtentiteln des ägyptischen Alten Reiches* (Glückstadt, 1954), and *Die Beziehungen Ägyptens zu Vorderasien im 3. und 2. Jahrtausend v. Chr,* 2nd edn. (Wiesbaden, 1971), must be mentioned. K. Baer, *Rank and Title in the Old Kingdom: The Structure of the Egyptian Administration in the Fifth and Sixth Dynasties* (Chicago, 1960), is another classic that has lost little of its interest. Hans Goedicke introduced many new ideas in his *Königliche Dokumente aus dem Alten Reich* (Wiesbaden, 1967) and *Die privaten Rechtsinschriften aus dem Alten Reich* (Vienna, 1970).

More recent specialized studies include Naguib Kanawati, *The Egyptian Administration in The Old Kingdom: Evidence on its Economic Decline* (Warminster, 1977), and *Governmental Reforms in Old Kingdom Egypt* (Warminster, 1980), although they are not entirely uncontroversial. See also Nigel Strudwick, *The Administration of Egypt in the Old Kingdom: The Highest Titles and their Holders* (London, 1985). E. Martin-Pardey, *Untersuchungen zur ägyptischen Provinzialverwaltung bis zum Ende des Alten Reiches* (Hildesheim, 1976), deals with a difficult but very important topic. P. Posener-Kriéger,

Les Archives du temple funéraire de Néferirkarê-Kakaï (Les Papyrus d'Abousir): Traduction et commentaire, 2 vols. (Cairo, 1976), is of fundamental importance. R. Müller-Wollermann, *Krisenfaktoren im ägyptischen Staat des ausgehenden Alten Reichs* (Tübingen, 1986), is an extremely thought-provoking publication. K. Zibelius, *Ägyptische Siedlungen nach Texten des Alten Reiches* (Wiesbaden, 1978), is a very useful survey of the problem. B. L. Begelsbacher-Fischer, *Untersuchungen zur Götterwelt des Alten Reiches im Spiegel der Privatgräber der IV. und V. Dynastie* (Freiburg, 1981), sets out the main parameters for the study of Old Kingdom religion.

Old Kingdom monuments and art have been discussed in many publications. The best are: I. E. S. Edwards, *The Pyramids of Egypt*, 5th edn. (Harmondsworth, 1993); R. Stadelmann, *Die ägyptischen Pyramiden: vom Ziegelbau zum Weltwunder* (Darmstadt, 1991), and W. Stevenson Smith, *A History of Egyptian Sculpture and Painting in the Old Kingdom*, 2nd edn. (Boston, 1949). Others include Yvonne Harpur, *Decoration in Egyptian Tombs of the Old Kingdom: Studies in Orientation and Scene Content* (London, 1987), noteworthy for its thoroughness, while Nadine Cherpion, *Mastabas et hypogées d'Ancien Empire: Le Problème de la datation* (Brussels, 1989), presents an admirably audacious challenge to current thinking. Problems that currently preoccupy art historians of the Old Kingdom can be found in *Kunst des Alten Reiches. Symposium in Deutschen Archäologischen Instituts Kairo am 29 und 30. Oktober 1991* (Mainz, 1995). N. Grimal (ed.), *Les Critères de datation stylistiques à l'Ancien Empire* (Cairo, 1998), and the exhibition catalogue *Egyptian Art in the Age of the Pyramids* (New York, 1999). For recent developments in archaeology, one may consult Miroslav Verner, *Forgotten Pharaohs, Lost Pyramids: Abusir* (Prague, 1994).

Alessandro Roccati, *La Littérature historique sous l'Ancien Empire égyptien* (Paris, 1982), is an excellent survey of textual sources. Elmar Edel's contribution to our knowledge of Old Kingdom texts has been remarkable—for example, in his *Hieroglyphische Inschriften des Alten Reiches* (Opladen, 1981). Raymond Faulkner's translation of *The Ancient Egyptian Pyramid Texts* (Warminster, 1986) is a rich seam that will be mined for many years to come. Henry Fischer's contribution to the study of the Old Kingdom has been outstanding, and at least his *Dendera in the Third Millennium BC* (Locust Valley, 1968) must be pointed out. These books will provide references to primary publications of material and to articles in specialized periodicals that cannot be listed here because of lack of space.

6. The First Intermediate Period

As a general survey of the political history of the First Intermediate Period based mainly on contemporary epigraphic sources, W. C. Hayes, 'The Middle Kingdom in Egypt: Internal History from the Rise of the Heracleopolitans to the Death of Ammenemenes III', in I. E. S. Edwards *et al.* (eds.), *Cambridge Ancient History*, I.2 (Cambridge, 1971), 464–531, is still useful. Translations of nearly all of the relevant texts are to be found in W. Schenkel's invaluable volume, *Memphis, Herakleopolis, Theben: Die epigraphischen Zeugnisse der 7.-11. Dynastie Ägyptens* (Wiesbaden, 1965). The chronological problems are summarized in Stephan Seidlmayer, 'Zwei Anmerkungen zur Dynastie der Herakleopoliten', *GM* 157 (1997), 81–90, while R. Müller-Wollermann provides a multifaceted discussion of possible reasons for the collapse of the Old Kingdom in her *Krisenfaktoren im ägyptischen Staat des ausgehenden Alten Reiches* (Tübingen, 1986).

The archaeology of the First Intermediate Period is surveyed by Seidlmayer, *Gräber-*

felder aus dem Übergang vom Alten zum Mittleren Reich, Studien zur Archäologie der Ersten Zwischenzeit (Heidelberg, 1990), and 'Wirtschaftliche und gesellschaftliche Entwicklung im Übergang vom Alten zum Mittleren Reich', in W. V. Davies *et al.* (eds.), *Problems and Priorities in Egyptian Archaeology* (London, 1987), 175–218. Information on decorated coffins and the early history of the Coffin Texts is to be found in Harco Willems, *Chests of Life* (Leiden, 1988). The early history of button seals and their implications for First Intermediate Period popular culture and popular religion are studied in A. Wiese, *Die Anfänge der ägyptischen Stempelsiegel-Amulette* (Freiburg, 1996). For the importance of Egyptian popular traditions in general, see Barry Kemp, *Ancient Egypt: Anatomy of a Civilization* (London, 1989), 64–107.

First Intermediate Period prosopography and the development of provincial administration in the individual regions of Upper Egypt are treated in Henry Fischer's admirable works *Dendera in the First Millennium BC* (Locust Valley, 1968) and *Inscriptions from the Coptite Nome* (Rome, 1964), as well as in a series of excellent articles by Edward Brovarski, including 'Ahanakht of Bersheh and the Hare Nome in the First Intermediate Period', in W. Kelly Simpson and W. Davies (eds.), *Studies in Ancient Egypt, the Aegean, and the Sudan (Festschrift D. Dunham)* (Boston, 1981), 14–30; 'The Inscribed Material of the First Intermediate Period from Naga-ed-Dêr', *AJA* 89 (1985), 581–4; 'Akhmim in the Old Kingdom and First Intermediate Period', in P. Posener-Kriéger (ed.), *Mélanges Gamal eddin Mokhtar* (Cairo, 1985), 117–53; 'Abydos in the Old Kingdom and First Intermediate Period: part 1', in C. Berger *et al.* (eds.), *Hommages à Jean Leclant*, i (Cairo, 1994), 99–121, and 'Abydos in the Old Kingdom and First Intermediate Period: part 2', in D. Silverman (ed.), *For his Ka, Essays Offered in Memory of Klaus Baer* (Chicago, 1994), 15–44. These questions are further addressed in F. Gomaà, *Ägypten während der Ersten Zwischenzeit* (Wiesbaden, 1980), and Naguib Kanawati, *Akhmim in the Old Kingdom* (Sydney, 1992).

The tomb of Ankhtifi at el-Mo'alla, with its famous inscription, was published by Jacques Vandier in *Mo'alla* (Cairo, 1950). In Vandier, *La Famine dans l'Égypte ancienne* (Cairo, 1936), the evidence for famines from ancient Egyptian historical sources is assembled. Barbara Bell, 'The Dark Ages in History I: The First Dark Age in Egypt', *AJA* 75 (1971), 1–26, provides an interpretation of the reasons for the First Intermediate Period referring to climatic change (although, from a historian's point of view, the methodological basis of this exceedingly influential article seems questionable). The development of irrigation during the First Intermediate Period is studied in W. Schenkel, *Die Bewässerungsrevolution im Alten Ägypten* (Mainz, 1978).

The royal tombs of the 11th Dynasty were re-excavated and studied by Dieter Arnold, *Gräber des Alten und Mittleren Reiches in el-Târif* (Mainz, 1976). For the excavations at the Kôm Dâra, it is still necessary to refer to R. Weill, *Dara, Campagnes de 1946–1948* (Cairo, 1958).

For the small amount of evidence on Herakleopolitan dynastic history, see J. von Beckerath, 'Die Dynastie der Herakleopoliten', *ZÄS* 93 (1966), 13–20. The important inscriptions of the Asyut nomarchs were restudied by Elmar Edel in *Die Inschriften der Grabfronten der Siut Gräber* (Opladen, 1984) and by Detlef Franke in 'Zwischen Herakleopolis und Theben: Neues zu den Gräbern von Assjut', *SAK* 14 (1987), 49–60. Recent studies (including translations) of the literary works that have been dated to the Herakleopolitan Period are Richard Parkinson, *The Tale of the Eloquent Peasant* (Oxford, 1991), and J. F. Quack, *Studien zur Lehre für Merikare* (Wiesbaden, 1992).

The problem of using later literary texts as historical sources for the First Intermediate Period was addressed by G. Björkman in 'Egyptology and Historical Method', *Orientalia Suecana*, 13 (1964), 9–33, and by F. Junge in 'Die Welt der Klagen', in J. Assmann (ed.), *Fragen an die altägyptische Literatur, Gedenkschrift E. Otto* (Wiesbaden, 1977), 275–84. The lasting impact that the experience of the First Intermediate Period had on Egyptian thought was set out by J. Assmann in his outstanding book *Ägypten: eine Sinngeschichte* (Munich, 1996), 122–34.

7. The Middle Kingdom Renaissance

To understand the major difficulties of Middle Kingdom chronology, a start can be made with the 'standard chronology' given both by W. F. Edgerton, 'Chronology of the Twelfth Dynasty', *JNES* 1 (1942), 307–14, and by R. A. Parker, *The Calendars of Ancient Egypt* (Chicago, Ill., 1950), and 'The Sothic Dating of the Twelfth and Eighteenth Dynasties', in J. H. Johnson and E. F. Wente (eds.), *Studies in Honor of G. R. Hughes* (Chicago, Ill., 1976), 177–89). A clear account of the problems involved with any chronology and with the co-regency theory is presented in W. Kelly Simpson, 'Studies in the Twelfth Egyptian Dynasty: I–II', *JARCE* 2 (1963), 53–63. For 'revised chronologies' modifying this mainstream view, see, for example, Rolf Krauss, *Sothis und Monddaten* (Hildesheim, 1985), and Detlef Franke, 'Zur Chronologie des Mittleren Reiches I and II', *Orientalia*, NS 57 (1988), 113–38.

In *Die chronologische Fixierung des ägyptischen Mittleren Reiches nach dem Tempelarchiv von Illahun* (Vienna, 1992), I. Luft has proposed fixed dates for the Middle Kingdom based on the el-Lahun papyri. In *Sésostris Ier, étude chronologique et historique du règne* (Brussels, 1995), Claude Obsomer re-examines the previous theories and the evidence (translations and line drawings of texts) and offers a number of cogent reasons why the co-regency theory should be questioned in regard to Amenemhat I, II, and Senusret I. Josef Wegner, 'The Nature and Chronology of the Senusret III–Amenemhat III Regnal Succession: Some Considerations Based on New Evidence from the Mortuary Temple of Senusret III at Abydos', *JNES* 55 (1996), 249–79, conveniently reviews the chronology debate (although he virtually ignores the arguments mounted by Obsomer) and produces new and vital evidence for the reign of Senusret III. In 'Amenemhat I and the Early Twelfth Dynasty', *MMJ* 26 (1991), 5–48, Dorothea Arnold has strongly questioned the dating of tombs normally attributed to the period of Mentuhotep III, her views setting the transfer of government to Lisht in about year 20 of the reign of Amenemhat I.

Herbert Winlock, *The Rise and Fall of the Middle Kingdom* (New York, 1947), still deserves to be read, not least because Winlock did so much of the original investigation for this period. Edouard Naville, *The XIth Dynasty Temple at Deir el-Bahari*, 3 vols. (London, 1907–13), is indispensable. Dieter, Dorothea, and Felix Arnold's reinvestigations are more important for insights into the meaning and purpose of the architecture and pottery of this period: *Mentuhotep Tempel des Königs Mentuhotep von Deir el Bahari* (Mainz, 1974), *Der Pyramidenbezirk des Königs Amenemhet III* (Mainz, 1987), and *The South Cemeteries of Lisht, i: The Pyramid of Senwosret I* (New York, 1988). Györö Vörös's interesting discovery of the 11th Dynasty temple of Mentuhotep III, as well as another building, and his probable tomb, on Thoth Hill at Luxor, is published in *Temple of the Pyramid of Thebes* (Budapest, 1998).

A number of very detailed and thoughtful studies of individual reigns have been published, beginning with Labib Habachi's study of Mentuhotep II: 'King Nebhepetre

Mentuhotpe: His Monuments, Place in History, Deification and Unusual Representations in the Form of Gods', *MDAIK* 19 (1963), 16–52. Winlock, *The Slain Soldiers of Nebhepet-Re Mentu-hotpe* (New York, 1945), looks at warfare in Mentuhotep II's time; Alan Gardiner, 'The First King Mentuhotpe of the Eleventh Dynasty', *MDAIK* 14 (1956), 42–51, solves the problem of the various names of the king. For the 12th Dynasty there is Ronald Leprohon, *The Reign of Amenemhat I* (Toronto, 1980), and Robert Delia, *A Study of the Reign of Senusert III* (New York, 1980). Obsomer's quite splendid *Sésostris Ier* (cited above), which, among other things, puts forward a persuasive argument for discounting the theory of co-regencies for the 12th Dynasty, has set new standards for such works. For the 'Tod treasure', see Fernand Bisson de la Roque *et al.*, *Le Trésor de Tod* (Cairo, 1953). Dietrich Wildung, *Sesostris und Amenemhet, Ägypten im Mittleren Reich* (Freiburg, 1984; French trans., *L'Âge d'or*) offers a penetrating artistic analysis for the entire Middle Kingdom. Two chapters of Gay Robins' *The Art of Ancient Egypt* (London, 1997) survey Middle Kingdom art and architecture at a more general level, but offer more insights than the earlier studies of Edward Terrace, *Egyptian Paintings of the Middle Kingdom* (New York, 1967).

Essential reading on administration during the 13th Dynasty is Stephen Quirke's pithy monograph *The Administration of Egypt in the Late Middle Kingdom* (New Malden, 1990), while his *Middle Kingdom Studies* (New Malden, 1991) includes some useful discussions concerning various processes of change in both the the 12th and 13th dynasties. Miriam Lichtheim, *Ancient Egyptian Autobiographies chiefly of the Middle Kingdom* (Freiburg, 1988), provides vital source material.

Torgny Säve-Söderbergh, *Aegypten und Nubien* (Lund, 1941), is the basic volume for Middle Kingdom activities in Nubia, supplemented by Paul Smither, 'The Semnah Dispatches', *JEA* 31 (1945), 3–10, which provides fascinating insights into life in the Nubian forts. Bryan Emery, *Lost Land Emerging* (New York, 1967), gives a popular account of the excavation of Nubia in more recent times. Extremely helpful information on the workings of the Egyptian administration in Nubia are provided by Stuart Tyson Smith in various articles, as well as in *Askut in Nubia* (London, 1995).

For information on life within the palace during the Middle Kingdom, see Alexander Scharff's article on Papyrus Bulaq 18: 'Ein Rechnungsbuch des königlichen Hofes aus de 13. Dynastie (Papyrus Boulaq Nr. 18)', *ZÄS* 56 (1920), 51–68, as well as Quirke's *Administration* volume (mentioned above), and Manfred Bietak (ed.), *Haus und Palast im Alten Ägypten* (Vienna, 1996), which contains a wealth of information on Middle Kingdom houses and palaces (most articles in English). The second part of Barry Kemp, *Ancient Egypt: Anatomy of a Civilization* (London, 1989), provides an informative, lively account of the organization and daily lives of bureaucrats and townspeople who lived at this time.

The letters of Hekanakhte were translated by T. G. H. James in *The Hekanakhte Papers and other Early Middle Kingdom Documents* (New York, 1962). Middle Kingdom literature has been made available in many texts, such as Miriam Lichtheim, *Ancient Egyptian Literature*, i (Los Angeles, 1973), and Richard Parkinson, *Voices from Ancient Egypt* (London, 1991), while the classic interpretation of links between Middle Kingdom literature and politics is Georges Posener, *Littérature et politique dans l'Égypte de la XIIe dynastie* (Paris, 1956).

Numerous articles and monographs have been written on Egyptian religion, such as Stephen Quirke, *Ancient Egyptian Religion* (London, 1992), but no single book has yet been written on the religion of the Middle Kingdom in particular. In the meantime,

Quirke's essay on Middle Kingdom religion in W. Forman and S. Quirke, *Hieroglyphs and the Afterlife* (London, 1996), has gone some way towards addressing this deficiency. Raymond Faulkner, *The Ancient Egyptian Coffin Texts*, 3 vols. (London, 1972–8), contains essential primary source material, while two books by Harco Willems, *Chests of Life* (Leiden, 1988), and *The Coffin of Heqata* (Groningen, 1994), discuss the evidence for religious beliefs and practices of the Middle Kingdom.

8. The Second Intermediate Period

New evidence concerning the Second Intermediate Period is emerging so quickly that many publications are out of date before they are printed, but a few of them contain sufficient basic documentation to ensure that they will remain important for a long time. Others are useful for the fresh eye they cast upon well-worn facts. I have limited the Further Reading to these categories.

I have used the Kamose texts as a guide through the maze of evidence relating to the Second Intermediate Period. The best translation of them is that given by H. S. Smith and A. Smith, 'A Reconsideration of the Kamose Texts', *ZÄS* 103 (1976), 48–76. The most wide-ranging discussion of the period is provided by the contributors to Eliezer D. Oren (ed.), *The Hyksos: New Historical and Archaeological Perspectives* (Philadelphia, 1997).

J. von Beckerath, *Untersuchungen zur politischen Geschichte der zweiten Zwischenzeit in Ägypten* (Glückstadt, 1965), is still the best introduction to chronological questions, but it needs to be updated with D. Franke, 'Zur Chronologie des Mittleren Reiches Teil II: Die sogenannte "Zweite Zwischenzeit" Ältägyptens', *Orientalia*, 57 (1988), 245–74. Further discussions can be picked up from his bibliography. A fresh and highly speculative review of the written sources is given by D. Redford, *Egypt, Canaan and Israel in Ancient Times* (Princeton, 1992). The most up-to-date and comprehensive study of the contemporary written sources is Kim Ryholt, *The Political Situation in Egypt during the Second Intermediate Period* (Copenhagen, 1997). Ryholt's reconstruction of the Turin Canon papyrus, the most important source for the period, has been followed in the writing of Chapter 8 but his chronology and his integration of those kings who are known only from scarabs into the Dynastic series has not been accepted. For an important review of Ryholt, see Daphne Ben-Tor, Susan Allen, and James Allen, 'Seals and Kings' *BASOR* 315 (1999), 47–74.

The evidence for Asiatics in Egypt during the Second Intermediate Period is discussed by Georges Posener, 'Les Asiatiques en Égypte sous les XII et XIII Dynasties', *Syria*, 34 (1957), 145–63; D. Arnold, F. Arnold, and S. Allen, 'Canaanite Imports at Lisht, the Middle Kingdom Capital of Egypt', *Ägypten und Levante*, 5 (1994), 13–32; Kenneth Kitchen in 'Non-Egyptians Recorded on Middle Kingdom Stelae in Rio de Janeiro', in Stephen Quirke (ed.), *Middle Kingdom Studies* (New Malden, 1991), 87–90; Daphne Ben-Tor, 'The Historical Implications of Middle Kingdom Scarabs found in Palestine bearing Private Names and Titles of Officials' *BASOR* 294 (1994), 7–22 and 'The Relations between Egypt and Palestine in the Middle Kingdom as reflected by contemporary Canaanite Scarabs, *IEJ* 47 (1997) 162–89; Rolf Krauss, 'An examination of Khyan's place in W. A. Ward's seriation of royal Hyksos scarabs' *Ägypten und Levante* VII (1998), 39–42.

As far as the Delta-site of Avaris (Tell el-Dab'a) is concerned, everything which M. Bietak writes is 'work in progress', so that every publication contains new information. The most recent information will be found in the journal *Ägypten und Levante* edited by Bietak. Comprehensive summaries of the Tell el-Dab'a finds are M. Bietak, *Avaris: The Capital of the Hyksos* (London, 1996), and 'Egypt and Canaan during the Middle Bronze Age', *BASOR* 281 (1991), 27–72. A more detailed report of the final phase of Hyksos power is Perla Fuscaldo, *Tell el-Dab'a X. The Palace District of Avaris. The Pottery of the Hyksos Period and the New Kingdom (Areas H/III and H/VI). Part I : Locus 66.* Vienna, 2000. For different perspectives on Tell el-Dab'a, see Oren (ed.), *The Hyksos* (cited above), and W. Vivian Davies and Louise Schofield (eds.), *Egypt, the Aegean and the Levant* (London, 1995); Patrick McGovern, *The Foreign Relations of the 'Hyksos'. A neutron activation study of Middle Bronze Age pottery from the Eastern Mediterranean.* (Oxford, 2000).

For the Delta in general, see Bietak, 'Zum Königreich des '3-zh-R' Nehesi', *SAK* 11 (1984), 59–75; Jean Yoyotte, 'Le Roi Mer-djefa-Re et le dieu Sopdu: Un monument de la XIV Dynastie', *BSFE* 114 (1989), 17–63, and J. S. Holladay, Jr., *Tell el-Maskhuta* (Malibu, 1982), and Mohamed Abd El-Maksoud, *Tell Heboua (1981–1991) Enquête archéologique sur la Deuxième Période Intermédiaire et le Nouvel Empire à l'extrémité orientale du Delta* (Paris, 1998).

For the study of the Memphis region in the Second Intermediate Period, see Dorothea Arnold, 'Keramikbearbeitung in Dahschur 1976–1981', *MDAIK* 38 (1982), 25–65; Dieter Arnold, *The South Cemeteries of Lisht I: The Pyramid of Senwosret I* (New York, 1988); Janine Bourriau, 'Beyond Avaris: The Second Intermediate Period in Egypt outside the Eastern Delta', in Oren (ed.), *The Hyksos* (cited above); W. C. Hayes, 'Horemkhauef of Nekhen and his trip to It-Towe', *JEA* 33 (1947), 3–11; and Quirke, 'Royal Power in the 13th Dynasty', in Quirke (ed.), *Middle Kingdom Studies* (cited above), 123–39.

On administrative titles, see Quirke, 'The Regular Titles of the Late Middle Kingdom', *RdE* 37 (1986), 107–30.

For a discussion of the boundary between the Asiatic and Egyptian Nile, see J. Bourriau, 'Some Archaeological Notes on the Kamose Texts', in A. Leahy and J. Tait. (eds.), *Studies on Ancient Egypt in Honour of H. S. Smith*, (London, 1999), 43–48.

For Thebes, see Herbert Winlock, 'The Tombs of the Kings of the Seventeenth Dynasty at Thebes', *JEA* 10 (1924), 217–77 which is now complemented by new evidence discussed by Michel Dewachter, 'Nouvelles Informations relatives à l'exploitation de la Nécropole Royale de Drah Aboul Neggah', *RdE* 36 (1985), 43–66 and Daniel Polz, 'The Ramsesnakht Dynasty and the Fall of the New Kingdom. A New Monument in Thebes', *SAK* 25 (1998), 257–93; P. Vernus, 'La Stèle du roi Sekhemsanktaowyre Neferhotep Iykernofret et la domination Hyksos', *ASAE* 68 (1982), 129–35, and 'À propos de la stèle du pharaon Mntw-htpi', *RdE* 41 (1990), 22.

For funerary texts, see P. Vernus, 'Sur les graphies de la formule "L'offrande que donne le roi" au Moyen Empire et à la Deuxième Periode Intermédiaire', in Quirke (ed.), *Middle Kingdom Studies* (cited above), 141–52, and Parkinson and Quirke, 'The Coffin of Prince Herunefer and the Early History of the Book of the Dead', in A. B. Lloyd (ed.), *Studies in Pharaonic Religion and Society* (London, 1992), 37–51.

For Sobekemsaf's expedition to the Wadi Hammamat, see Annie Gasse, 'Une expédition au Ouadi Hammamat sous le règne de Sebekemsaf I', *BIFAO* 87 (1987), 207–18.

With regard to the remains at Elephantine and the Second Cataract Forts, see Detlef Franke, *Das Heligtum des Heqaib auf Elephantine* (Heidelberg, 1994); Cornelius von Pilgrim, *Elephantine XVIII. Untersuchungen in der Stadt des Mittleren Reiches und der*

Zweiten Zwischenzeit (Mainz, 1996); Stuart Tyson Smith, *Askut in Nubia* (London, 1995), and Janine Bourriau, 'Relations between Egypt and Kerma during the Middle and New Kingdoms', in W. V. Davies (ed.), *Egypt and Africa: Nubia from Prehistory to Islam* (London, 1991), 129–44.

For the principal excavations relating to the Kingdom of Kush, see Charles Bonnet, *Kerma, Royaume de Nubie* (Geneva, 1990) and *Edifices et rites funéraires à Kerma* (Paris, 2000).

For the history of the war against the Hyksos and subsequent reunification of Egypt, see Claude Vandersleyen, *Les Guerres d'Amosis, Fondateur de la XVIII Dynastie* (Brussels, 1971); Peter Lacovara, *Deir el Ballas: Preliminary Report on the Deir el Ballas Expedition 1980–1986* (Winona Lake, 1990); M. C. Wiener and James Allen, 'Separate Lives: the Ahmose Tempest Stela and the Theran eruption', *JNES* 57/1 (1998), 1–28, and W. J. Eastwood, N. J. Pearce, J. A. Westgate, and W. T. Perkins, 'Recognition of Santorini (Minoan) Tephra in Lake Sediments from Gölhisar Gölü, Southwest Turkey by Laser Ablation ICP-MS', *Journal of Archaeological Science*, 25/7 (July 1998), 677–87.

9. The 18th Dynasty before the Amarna Period

For the 18th Dynasty generally, see the excellent volume by Claude Vandersleyen, *L'Égypte et la vallée du Nil*, ii: *De la fin de l'ancient empire à la fin du nouvel empire* (Paris, 1995) [see p. 284 n. 1 for a detailed bibliography for the temples of Hatshepsut and Thutmose III at Deir el-Bahri]. See also two volumes by Donald Redford: *History and Chronology of the Eighteenth Dynasty, Seven Studies* (Toronto, 1967), and *Egypt, Canaan, and Israel in Ancient Times* (Princeton, 1992). On Karnak, see Jean-Claude Golvin and Jean-Claude Goyon, *Les Bâtisseurs de Karnak* (London, 1987).

For the reign of Ahmose, see Manfred Bietak, *Avaris: The Capital of the Hyksos: Recent Excavations at Tell el-Dab'a* (London, 1996), and W. V. Davies and Louise Schofield (eds.), *Egypt, the Aegean, and the Levant. Interconnections in the Second Millennium BC* (London, 1995); particularly important are the stelae published by Claude Vandersleyen, 'Une tempête sous le règne d'Amosis: Deux nouveaux fragments de la stèle d'Amosis relatant une tempête', *RdE* 19 (1967), 123–59, *RdE* 20 (1968), 127–34. On the Donation Stela, see Michel Gitton, in, for example, *Les Divines Épouses de la 18e dynastie* (Paris, 1984). For discussion of the confusion of royal coffins and grave goods, see Marianne Eaton-Krauss, 'The Coffins of Queen Ahhotep, Consort of Seqeni-en-Re and Mother of Ahmose', *CdE* 65 (1990), 195–205.

For the reigns of Amenhotep I, Thutmose I, and Thutmose II, see Franz-Jürgen Schmitz, *Amenophis I* (Hildesheim, 1978); Catherine Graindorge and Philippe Martinez, 'Karnak avant Karnak: Les Constructions d'Aménophis Ier et les premières liturgies amoniennes', *BSFE* 115 (1989) 36–64; James Romano, 'Observations on Early Eighteenth Dynasty Royal Sculpture', *JARCE* 13 (1976), 97–111; Ingegerd Lindblad, *Royal Sculpture of the Early Eighteenth Dynasty in Egypt* (Stockholm, 1984), and Helen Jacquet-Gordon, *Le Trésor de Thoutmosis Ier: La Décoration*, 2 vols. (Cairo, 1988). Anthony Spalinger, *Three Studies of Egyptian Feasts and their Chronological Implications* (Baltimore, 1992), includes discussion of the jambs from the Third Pylon at Karnak bearing inscriptions concerning Amenhotep I's religious festivals. For detailed discussion of the reign of Thutmose II, see two articles by Luc Gabolde: 'La Chronologie du règne de Thoutmosis II, ses conséquences sur la datation des momies royales et leurs répercutions sur l'histoire du développement de la Vallée des Rois', *SAK* 14 (1987),

61–87, and 'La "Cour des fêtes" de Thoutmosis II à Karnak', *Karnak*, 9 (1993), 1–82.

For Hatshepsut and Thutmose III, see Peter Dorman, *The Monuments of Senenmut* (London, 1988), and *The Tombs of Senenmut: The Architecture and Decoration of Tombs 71 and 353* (New York, 1991); Suzanne Ratié, *La Reine Hatchepsout* (Leiden, 1979); Donald Redford, in *LÄ* vi (Wiesbaden, 1988), and Guido P. F. van den Boorn, *The Duties of the Vizier: Civil Administration in the Early New Kingdom* (London, 1988). For discussion of the implications of the texts from the tombs of User in terms of the royal prerogatives assumed by members of the court of Hatshepsut and Thutmose III, see Erik Hornung, 'Die königliche Dekoration der Sargkammer', in Eberhard Diziobek (ed.), *Die Gräber des Vezir User-Amun Theben Nr. 61 und 131* (Mainz, 1994), 42–7.

For Amenhotep II and Thutmose IV, see Peter der Manuelian, *Studies in the Reign of Amenophis II* (Hildesheim, 1987); Charles Van Siclen III, *Two Monuments from the Reign of Amenhotep II* (San Antonio, 1982), *The Alabaster Shrine of King Amenhotep II* (San Antonio, 1986), and 'The Building History of the Tuthmosid temple at Amada and the Jubilees of Tuthmosis IV', *VA* 3 (1987), 53–66; Hourig Sourouzian, 'A Bust of Amenophis II at the Kimbell Art Museum', *JARCE* 28 (1991), 55–74; Betsy M. Bryan, *The Reign of Thutmose IV* (Baltimore, 1991), and 'Portrait sculpture of Thutmose IV', *JARCE* 24 (1987), 3–20, as well as Bernadette Letellier, 'La Cour à peristyle de Thoutmosis IV à Karnak', *BSFE* 84 (1979), 33–49, and 'Thoutmosis IV à Karnak', *BSFE* 122 (1991), 36–52.

For Amenhotep III, see Eric Cline and David O'Connor (eds.), *Amenhotep III: Perspectives on His Reign* (Ann Arbor, 1998), with chapters referred to above by David O'Connor and William J. Murnane; Arielle Kozloff and Betsy M. Bryan, *Egypt's Dazzling Sun: Amenhotep III and his World* (Cleveland, Oh., 1992); Lawrence Berman (ed.), *The Art of Amenhotep III: Art Historical Analysis* (Cleveland, 1990) [including W. Raymond Johnson, 'Images of Amenhotep III in Thebes: Styles and Intentions'], and 'The Deified Amenhotep III as the Living Re-Horakhty: Stylistic and Iconographic Considerations', *International Association of Egyptologists, Congress 6: Atti*, ii (Turin, 1993), 231–6; Claude Vandersleyen, 'Les Deux Jeunesses d'Amenhotep III', *BSFE* 111 (1988), 9–30; Dorothea Arnold, *The Royal Women of Amarna* (New York, 1996); William L. Moran, *The Amarna Letters* (Baltimore, 1992); William Murnane, *Ancient Egyptian Coregencies* (Chicago, 1977), and *The Road to Kadesh: A Historical Interpretation of the Battle Reliefs of King Sety I at Karnak*, 2nd edn. (Chicago, 1990), and Mario Liverani, *Prestige and Interest: International Relations in the Near East, ca. 1600–1100 BC* (Padua, 1990).

10. The Amarna Period and the Later New Kingdom

There is a vast literature on all aspects of the Amarna Period; over 2,000 titles are listed in Geoffrey Martin, *A Bibliography of the Amarna Period and its Aftermath: The Reigns of Akhenaten, Smenkhkare, Tutankhamun and Ay (c.1350–1321 BC)* (London, 1991). There is also a journal devoted entirely to the period: *Amarna Letters: Essays on Ancient Egypt ca. 1390–1310 BC*, i (San Francisco, 1991). Translations of all the relevant texts are now available in William Murnane, *Texts from the Amarna Period in Egypt* (Atlanta, 1995). Two classic studies are Cyril Aldred, *Akhenaten, King of Egypt* (London, 1988), and Donald Redford, *Akhenaten: The Heretic King* (Princeton, 1984); both have been compared and contrasted in a highly informative review by Marianne Eaton-Krauss, 'Akhenaten versus Akhenaten', *BiOr* 47 (1990), 541–59. A recent book on Akhenaten and his new religion is Erik Hornung, *Echnaton: Die Religion des Lichtes* (Zürich, 1995).

The city of el-Amarna is brilliantly treated by Barry Kemp, *Ancient Egypt: Anatomy of a Civilization* (London, 1989), 261–317.

For the political developments at the end of the dynasty, the pre-royal career of Horemheb, and the role of Maya, see Jacobus van Dijk, *The New Kingdom Necropolis of Memphis: Historical and Iconographical Studies* (Gröningen, 1993), 10–83. Egypt's foreign policy during the Amarna Period and the early 19th Dynasty is admirably treated in William Murnane, *The Road to Kadesh: A Historical Interpretation of the Battle Reliefs of King Sety I at Karnak* (Chicago 1985; 2nd rev. edn., 1990). For the Memphite necropolis, see Geoffrey Martin, *The Hidden Tombs of Memphis: New Discoveries from the Time of Tutankhamun and Ramesses the Great* (London, 1991), and Jacobus van Dijk, 'The Development of the Memphite Necropolis in the Post-Amarna Period', in A.-P. Zivie (ed.), *Memphis et ses nécropoles au Nouvel Empire: Nouvelles Données, nouvelles questions* (Paris, 1988), 37–46. On the Delta residence of the Ramessid pharaohs, see Manfred Bietak, *Avaris and Piramesse: Archaeological Exploration in the Eastern Nile Delta.* (London, 1979).

Studies on the dynastic history of the Ramessid Period include Murnane, 'The Kingship of the Nineteenth Dynasty: A Study in the Resilience of an Institution', in David O'Connor and David Silverman (eds.), *Ancient Egyptian Kingship* (Leiden, 1995), 185–217; Kenneth Kitchen, *Pharaoh Triumphant: The Life and Times of Ramesses II, King of Egypt*, 3rd edn. (Warminster, 1985); Labib Habachi, *Features of the Deification of Ramesses II* (Glückstadt, 1969); Hourig Sourouzian, *Les Monuments du roi Merenptah* (Mainz, 1989); Rosemarie Drenkhahn, *Die Elephantine-Stele des Sethnacht und ihr historischer Hintergrund* (Wiesbaden, 1980); Pierre Grandet, *Ramses III: Histoire d'un règne* (Paris, 1993); A. J. Peden, *The Reign of Ramesses IV* (Warminster, 1994), and Kitchen, 'Ramesses VII and the Twentieth Dynasty', *JEA* 58 (1972), 182–94. For the role played by the Libyans in Later New Kingdom Egypt, see the essays collected in M. Anthony Leahy (ed.), *Libya and Egypt c.1300–750 BC* (London, 1990). A new and highly attractive reconstruction of the events at the end of the Twentieth Dynasty is given by Karl Jansen-Winkeln, 'Das Ende des Neuen Reiches', *ZÄS* 119 (1992), 22–37, and 'Die Plünderung der Königsgräber des Neuen Reiches', *ZÄS* 122 (1995), 62–78.

For the economic history of the New Kingdom, see the fundamental studies by Jac Janssen, 'Prolegomena to the Study of Egypt's Economic History during the New Kingdom', *SAK* 3 (1975), 127–85, and *Commodity Prices from the Ramessid Period* (Leiden, 1975); see also Kemp, *Ancient Egypt: Anatomy of a Civilization* (cited above), 232–60. Three recent studies by Jan Assmann on the social and religious history of the New Kingdom are *Egyptian Solar Religion in the New Kingdom: Re, Amun and the Crisis of Polytheism*, trans. A. Alcock (London, 1995), *Ägypten: Theologie und Frömmigkeit einer frühen Hochkultur* (Stuttgart, 1984), 221–85, and *Ägypten: Eine Sinngeschichte* (Munich, 1996), 223–315; see also P. Vernus, 'La Grande Mutation idéologique du Nouvel Empire: Une nouvelle théorie du pouvoir politique: Du démiurge face à sa création', *BSEG* 19 (1995), 69–95; A. M. Gnirs, *Militär und Gesellschaft. Ein Beitrag zur Sozialgeschichte des Neuen Reiches* (Heidelberg, 1996), and M. Römer, *Gottes- und Priesterherrschaft in Ägypten am Ende des Neuen Reiches: Ein religionsgeschichtliches Phänomen und seine sozialen Grundlagen* (Wiesbaden, 1994).

11. Egypt and the Outside World

For general discussions of Egyptian contacts with the outside world, see Dominique

Valbelle, *Les Neuf Arcs* (Paris, 1990); Donald Redford, *Egypt, Canaan, and Israel in Ancient Times* (Princeton, 1992); Edda Bresciani, 'Foreigners', in S. Donadoni (ed.), *The Egyptians* (Chicago, 1997), and E. Uphill, 'The Nine Bows', *Jaarbericht van het Voorazi-atische–Egyptisch Genootschap Ex Oriente Lux*, 19 (1965–6), 393–420.

With regard to textual and visual sources for Egyptian racial caricatures and ethnic designations, see J. Osing, 'Ächtungstexte aus dem Alten Reich', *MDAIK* 32 (1976), 133–85; Georges Posener, 'Ächtungstexte', in *LÄ* i (Wiesbaden, 1975), 67–9; G. Posener, *Cinq figures d'envoûtement* (Cairo, 1987), and Martin Bernal, *Black Athena: The Afro-Asiatic Roots of Classical Civilization*, 2 vols. (London, 1987–91).

For views of the problem of ethnicity with regard to ancient Egyptians and their neighbours, see John Baines, 'Contextualizing Egyptian Representations of Society and Ethnicity', in J. S. Cooper and G. M. Schwartz (eds.), *The Study of the Ancient Near East in the Twenty-First Century: The William Foxwell Albright Centennial Conference* (Winona Lake, 1996), 339–84; Henry Fischer, 'Varia Aegyptiaca', *JARCE* 2 (1963), 17–51; Anthony Leahy, 'Ethnic Diversity in Ancient Egypt', in J. M. Sasson (ed.), *Civilizations of the Ancient Near East* (New York, 1995), 225–34, and F. M. Snowden, Jr., 'Ancient Views of Nubia and the Nubians', *Expedition*, 35 (1993), 40–50 [and for Ptolemaic ethnicity, see the further reading for Chapter 14].

For the history of Egyptian contacts with Nubia, see W. B. Emery, *Egypt in Nubia* (London, 1965); Bruce Trigger, *Nubia under the Pharaohs* (London, 1976); William Adams, *Nubia: Corridor to Africa*, 2nd edn. (London, 1984); W. Vivian Davies (ed.), *Egypt and Africa: Nubia from Prehistory to Islam* (London, 1991); David O'Connor, *Ancient Nubia: Egypt's Rival in Africa* (Philadelphia, 1993); T. Celenko (ed.), *Egypt in Africa* (Indianapolis, 1996), and (especially from a visual point of view) Dieter Wildung (ed.), *Sudan: Ancient Kingdoms of the Nile* (Paris, 1997).

For the people and cultures of pre-Greek Libya, see W. Hölscher, *Libyer und Ägypten* (Glückstadt, 1937); Kenneth Kitchen, *The Third Intermediate Period in Egypt* (Warminster, 1986), 287-361; M. A. Leahy, 'The Libyan Period in Egypt: An Essay in Interpretation', *Libyan Studies*, 16 (1985), 51–65, and (ed.) *Libya and Egypt, c.1300–750 BC* (London, 1990), and Anthony Spalinger, 'Some Notes on the Libyans of the Old Kingdom and Later Historical Reflexes', *JSSEA* 9 (1979), 125–60.

For the much-debated question of the location of the kingdom of Punt, the means by which Egyptians travelled there, and the products that they were seeking, see Louise Bradbury, 'Kpn-Boats, Punt Trade and a Lost Emporium', *JARCE* 33 (1996); David Dixon, 'The Transplantation of Punt Incense Trees in Egypt', *JEA* 55 (1969), 55–65; R. Fattovich, 'The Problem of Punt in the Light of Recent Fieldwork in the Eastern Sudan', in S. Schoske (ed.), *Akten München 1985*, iv (Hamburg, 1991), 257–72; R. Herzog, *Pount* (Glückstadt, 1968); Kitchen, 'The Land of Punt', in Thurstan Shaw *et al.* (eds.), *The Archaeology of Africa: Food, Metals and Towns* (London, 1993), 587–608; 'Further thoughts on Punt and its neighbours', in A. Leahy and J. Tait (eds.), *Studies on Ancient Egypt in Honour of H. S. Smith* (London, 1999), 173–8, and William Stevenson Smith, 'The Land of Punt', *JARCE* 1 (1962), 59–60.

For Egyptian social, political, and economic involvement in Syria–Palestine, Turkey, and Mesopotamia, see Raphael Giveon, *The Impact of Egypt on Canaan* (Göttingen, 1978); W. Helck, *Die Beziehungen Ägyptens zu Vorderasien im 3. und 2. Jahrtausend v. Chr.* (Wiesbaden, 1962); Barry Kemp, 'Imperialism and Empire in New Kingdom Egypt', in P. Garnsey and C. R. Whittaker (eds.), *Imperialism in the Ancient World* (Cambridge, 1978), 7–58; Jean Leclant, *Les Relations entre l'Égypte et la Phénicie du voyage d'Ounamon à l'expédition d'Alexandre* (Beirut, 1968), and William Ward, *Egypt and the East Mediterranean World* (Beirut, 1971).

For the contacts between Egyptians and the inhabitants of the north Mediterranean islands (and the Greek mainland), see Jean Vercoutter, *L'Égypte et le monde égéen préhellénique* (Cairo, 1956); John Barns, *Egyptians and Greeks* (Oxford, 1966); John Boardman, *The Greeks Overseas* (Harmondsworth, 1964); H.-J. Thissen, 'Griechen in Ägypten', in *LÄ* iii (Wiesbaden, 1977), 898–903; Barry Kemp and Robert Merrilees, *Minoan Pottery from Second Millennium Egypt* (Mainz, 1981); Naphthali Lewis, *Greeks in Ptolemaic Egypt* (Oxford, 1986), and W. Vivian Davies (ed.), *Egypt, the Aegean and the Levant* (London, 1995).

For the Sea Peoples, see T. and M. Dothan, *People of the Sea: The Search for the Philistines* (New York, 1992); Redford, *Egypt, Canaan and Israel* (cited above), 285–394, and Nancy Sandars, *The Sea Peoples* (New York, 1985).

12. The Third Intermediate Period

For the period as a whole the basic source is still Kenneth Kitchen, *The Third Intermediate Period in Egypt (1100–650 BC)* (Warminster, 1973; 2nd edn. with *Supplement*, 1986; 3rd edn., with new preface, 1995). The Supplement and 1995 preface summarize and criticize studies on chronology and political geography published since 1973. Textual sources for the period are scattered, and up-to-date studies of many key texts are still awaited. Translations of some basic texts are provided by Miriam Lichtheim, *Ancient Egyptian Literature*, iii (Berkeley and Los Angeles, 1980). For a brief but well-chosen selection of texts, see Pascal Vernus, 'Choix de textes illustrant le temps des rois tanites et libyens', in J. Yoyotte (ed.) *Tanis, l'or des Pharaons* (Paris, 1987), 102–111.

Genealogies and prosopography of official families are discussed in M. L. Bierbrier, *The Late New Kingdom in Egypt (c. 1300–664 BC)* (Warminster, 1975); P.-M. Chevereau, *Prosopographie des cadres militaires égyptiens de la Basse Époque* (Antony, 1985), and G. Vittmann, *Priester und Beamte im Theben der Spätzeit* (Vienna, 1978).

Papers discussing the royal and official families and the chronology of the period are numerous; among the most significant modifications to the structure outlined by Kitchen are (1) a reappraisal of events at the beginning of the Third Intermediate Period: K. Jansen-Winkeln, 'Das Ende des Neuen Reiches', *ZÄS* 119 (1992), 22–37; 'Die Plünderung der Königsgräber des Neuen Reiches', *ZÄS* 122 (1995), 62–78; (2) the historical status and sphere of influence of the 23rd Dynasty: D. A. Aston, 'Takeloth II—A King of the "Theban Twenty-Third Dynasty"?', *JEA* 75 (1989), 139–53; M. A. Leahy, 'Abydos in the Libyan Period', in M. A. Leahy (ed.), *Libya and Egypt, c.1300–750 BC* (London, 1990), 155–200. Revisionist theories by various authors, proposing major contraction of the chronology of the Third Intermediate Period, have not been generally accepted.

On ideological aspects of kingship in the Third Intermediate Period, see M.-A. Bonhème, *Les Noms Royaux dans l'Égypte de la Troisième Période Intermédiaire* (Cairo, 1987). For a well-documented study of the society, administration, and culture of the period, see David O'Connor, 'New Kingdom and Third Intermediate Period, 1552–664 BC', in B. Trigger *et al.*, *Ancient Egypt: A Social History* (Cambridge, 1983), 183–278. For a general summary of the period with emphasis on Tanis, see J. Yoyotte (ed.), *Tanis, l'or des pharaons* (Paris, 1987).

The chronology, culture, and society of the Libyan Period are discussed in M. A. Leahy (ed.), *Libya and Egypt, c.1300–750 BC* (London, 1990), while the Libyan character of the 21st Dynasty is covered in K. Jansen-Winkeln, 'Der Beginn der Libyschen Herrschaft in Ägypten', *Biblische Notizen*, 71 (1994), 78–97. For the impact of Libyan immigration on Egyptian culture and society, see M. A. Leahy, 'The Libyan Period in Egypt: An Essay in Interpretation', *Libyan Studies*, 16 (1985), 51–65. For Libyan Period historical and biographical inscriptions, see R. A. Caminos, *The Chronicle of Prince Osorkon* (Rome, 1958), and K. Jansen-Winkeln, *Ägyptische Biographien der 22. und 23. Dynastie* (Wiesbaden, 1985). For discussion of the Delta principalities, see J. Yoyotte, 'Les Principautés du Delta au temps de l'anarchie libyenne (études d'histoire politique)', *MIFAO* 66 (1961), 121–81, pls. I–III, and F. Gomaa, *Die libyschen Fürstentümer des Deltas* (Wiesbaden, 1974). For donation stelae, see D. Meeks, 'Les Donations aux temples dans l'Égypte du Ier millénaire avant J.-C.', in E. Lipinski (ed.), *State and Temple Economy in the Ancient Near East*, ii (Leuven, 1979), 605–87.

The Kushite Period (25th Dynasty) is dealt with in Laszlo Török, *The Birth of an Ancient African Kingdom: Kush and her Myth of the State in the First Millennium* BC (Lille, 1995), and Jean Leclant, 'Kuschitenherrschaft', in *LÄ* iii (Wiesbaden, 1980), 893–901. For the campaign of King Piye, see N. Grimal, *Le Stèle triomphale de Pi-(ankh)y au Musée du Caire* (Cairo, 1981), and E. R. Russmann, *The Representation of the King in the XXVth Dynasty* (Brussels, 1974).

A number of articles and monographs discuss the religion and material culture of the Third Intermediate Period. H. Kees, *Die Hohenpriester des Amun von Karnak von Herihor bis zum Ende des Äthiopienzeit* (Leiden, 1964), still contains useful material though now superseded on specific issues of identification and genealogy of the priests of Amun during the Third Intermediate Period; see also J.-M. Kruchten, *Les Annales des prêtres de Karnak (XXI–XXIIIèmes dynasties) et autres textes contemporains relatifs à l'initiation des prêtres d'Amon* (Leuven, 1989). For oracles, see J.-M. Kruchten, *Le Grand Texte oraculaire de Djéhoutymose, intendant du Domaine d'Amon sous le pontificat de Pinedjem II* (Brussels, 1986); for the role of women in temple cult, see S.-A. Naguib, *Le Clergé Féminin d'Amon thébain à la 21ᵉ Dynastie* (Leuven, 1990); for the God's Wife of Amun, see E. Graefe, *Untersuchungen zur Verwaltung und Geschichte der Institution der Gottesgemahlin des Amun vom Beginn des Neuen Reiches bis zur Spätzeit* (Wiesbaden, 1981); for religious iconography, see Richard Fazzini, *Egypt: Dynasty XXII–XXV* (Iconography of Religions xvi(10); Leiden, 1988).

Burial customs are described in Pierre Montet, *La Nécropole royale de Tanis*, i–iii (Paris, 1947–60), and coffins are discussed in A. Niwinski, *21st Dynasty Coffins from Thebes: Chronological and Typological Studies* (Mainz am Rhein, 1988), and R. van Walsem, *The Coffin of Djedmonthuiufankh in the National Museum of Antiquities at Leiden* (Leiden, 1997). Funerary papyri are covered in A. Niwinski, *Studies on the Illustrated Theban Funerary Papyri of the 11th and 10th Centuries* BC (Freiburg, 1989).

The sculpture of the Third Intermediate Period is discussed in Karol Mysliwiec, *Royal Portraiture of the Dynasties XXI–XXX* (Mainz am Rhein, 1988). Pottery is described by David Aston, *Egyptian Pottery of the Late New Kingdom and Third Intermediate Period (Twelfth–Seventh Centuries* BC) (SAGA 13) (Heidelberg, 1996); faience figurines are described by J. Bulté, *Talismans Égyptiens d'heureuse maternité* (Paris, 1991); and metalworking is discussed by Christiane Ziegler, 'Les Arts du métal à la Troisieme Période Intermédiaire', in J. Yoyotte (ed.), *Tanis, l'or des pharaons* (Paris, 1987), 85–101; R. S. Bianchi, 'Egyptian Metal Statuary of the Third Intermediate Period (Circa 1070–656 BC), from its Egyptian Antecedents to its Samian Examples', in M. True and J. Podany (eds.), *Small Bronze Sculpture from the Ancient World* (Malibu, 1990), 61–84.

Theban tombs of the later Third Intermediate Period are described in D. Eigner, *Die Monumentalen Grabbauten der Spätzeit in der Thebanischen Nekropole* (Vienna, 1984).

13. The Late Period

Studies of the Late Period as a whole feature in all general Egyptian histories, such as Émile Drioton and Jacques Vandier, *L'Égypte*, 5th edn. (Paris, 1975); Alan Gardiner, *Egypt of the Pharaohs* (Oxford, 1961), Bruce Trigger *et al.*, *Ancient Egypt: A Social History* (Cambridge, 1983), and Nicolas Grimal, *A History of Ancient Egypt* (Oxford, 1992), but the best book dedicated to this period is F. K. Kienitz, *Die politische Geschichte Ägyptens vom 7. bis zum 4. Jahrhundert vor der Zeitwende* (Berlin, 1953).

For the Saite Period in particular, consult Kenneth Kitchen, *The Third Intermediate Period in Egypt (1100–650 BC)* (Warminster, 1973); T. G. H. James, 'Egypt: The Twenty-Fifth and Twenty-Sixth Dynasties', in J. Boardman *et al.* (eds.), *The Cambridge Ancient History*, iii(2), 2nd edn. (Cambridge, 1991), 677–750, and Anthony Leahy, 'The Earliest Dated Monument of Amasis and the End of the Reign of Amasis', *JEA* 74 (1988), 183–99.

For the First Persian Occupation, see Georges Posener, *La Première Domination perse en Égypte* (Cairo, 1936); Edda Bresciani, 'La satrapia d'Egitto', *Studi classici e orientali*, 7 (1958), 153–87, and John Ray, 'Egypt: 525–404 BC', in Boardman *et al.* (eds.), *The Cambridge Ancient History*, iv, 2nd edn. (Cambridge, 1988), 254–86. For the independence period and the Second Persian Occupation, see Alan Lloyd in Boardman *et al.* (eds.), *The Cambridge Ancient History*, vi (Cambridge, 1994), 337 ff.

For discussions of kingship in the 26th–30th dynasties, see Eberhard Otto, *Die biographischen Inschriften der ägyptischen Spätzeit* (Probleme der Ägyptologie 2, Leiden, 1954); Peter Kaplony, 'Bemerkungen zum ägyptischen Königtum, vor allem in der Spätzeit', *CdE* 46 (1971), 250–74; Janet Johnson, 'The Demotic Chronicle as an Historical Source', *Enchoria* 4 (1974), 1–17, and Leahy, 'Royal Iconography and Dynastic Change, 750–525 BC: The Blue and Cap Crowns', *JEA* 78 (1992), 223–40.

With regard to social structure during the Late Period, see E. Meyer, 'Gottestaat, Militärherrschaft und Ständewesen in Ägypten', *Sitzungsberichte der preussischen Akademie der Wissenschaften und Philosophische-historiche Klasse*, 28 (1928), 495–532, and Alan Lloyd, in Trigger *et al.*, *Ancient Egypt* (cited above), 299–301. For discussion of the economy and systems of administration, see Lloyd, in Trigger *et al.*, *Ancient Egypt* (cited above), 325–37. The *machimoi* and their Libyan ancestors are discussed by Kitchen, *The Third Intermediate Period* (cited above), F. Gomaà, *Die libyschen Fürstentümer des Deltas vom Tod Osorkons II. bis zur Wiedervereinigung Ägyptens dur Psametik I* (Wiesbaden, 1974), and Lloyd, *Herodotus Book II*, 3. 184 ff. For commercial and military contacts between the Greeks and the Egyptians during the Late Period, see John Boardman, *The Greeks Overseas* (Harmondsworth, 1964); Whitney Davis, 'The Cypriotes at Naukratis', *GM* 41 (1980), 7–19; William Coulson and A. Leonard, Jr., *Cities of the Delta*, i. *Naukratis: Preliminary Report on the 1977–1978 and 1980 Seasons* (Malibu, 1981); Lloyd, 'Triremes and the Saïte Navy', *JEA* 58 (1972), 268–79, and Boardman, 'Settlement for Trade and Land in North Africa: Problems of Identity', in G. R. Tzetskhladze and F. Angelis (eds.), *The Archaeology of Greek Colonization: Essays Dedicated to Sir John Boardman* (Oxford, 1984), 137–49.

For discussion of the priesthood during the Late Period, see Hermann Kees, *Das Priestertum im ägyptischen Staat* (Leiden, 1953); Serge Sauneron, *Les Prêtres de l'ancienne Égypte* (Bourges, 1957), and G. Vittmann, *Priester und Beamte im Theben der Spätzeit*

(Vienna, 1978). For religion in general during this period, see Otto, *Die biographischen Inschriften* (cited above), *passim*.

For Late Period art, see Bernard Bothmer *et al.*, *Egyptian Sculpture of the Late Period 700 BC to AD 100* (New York, 1960); Richard Fazzini, *Images for Eternity: Egyptian Art from Berkeley and Brooklyn* (New York, 1975); Cyril Aldred, *Egyptian Art in the Days of the Pharaohs* (London, 1980), chs. 16–17, and William Stevenson Smith, *The Art and Architecture of Ancient Egypt*, rev. W. Kelly Simpson (Harmondsworth, 1981), ch. 21. For detailed study of archaism in Late Period art and literature, see H. Brunner, 'Archaismus', in *LÄ* i (Wiesbaden, 1975), 386–95; John Cooney, 'Three Early Saïte Tomb Reliefs', *JNES* 9 (1950), 193–203, and Peter Der Manuelian, *Living in the Past: Studies in Archaism of the Egyptian Twenty-Sixth Dynasty* (London, 1994).

A comprehensive study of Late Period mortuary archaeology is lacking, but relevant material appears in Jeffrey Spencer, *Death in Ancient Egypt* (Harmondsworth, 1982). See also David Aston, 'Dynasty 26, Dynasty 30, or Dynasty 27? In search of the Funerary Archaeology of the Persian Period', in A. Leahy and J. Tait (eds.), *Studies on Ancient Egypt in Honour H. S. Smith* (London, 1999), 17–22.

14. The Ptolemaic Period

Useful general studies of the period are C. Préaux, *Les Grecs en Égypte d'après les archives de Zénon* (Brussels, 1947); W. Tarn and G. T. Griffith, *Hellenistic Civilisation*, 3rd edn. (London, 1952); E. Will, *Histoire politique du monde hellénistique*, 2 vols. (Nancy, 1966–7); C. Préaux, *Le Monde hellénistique*, 2 vols. (Paris, 1978); Hartwig Maehler and V. M. Strocka, *Das ptolemäische Ägypten: Akten des Internationalen Symposion 27.–29. Sept 1976 in Berlin* (Mainz am Rhein, 1978); F. W. Walbank, *The Hellenistic World* (Glasgow, 1981); J. Boardman *et al.* (eds.) *The Cambridge Ancient History*, vii(1), 2nd edn. (Cambridge, 1984), viii, 2nd edn. (Cambridge, 1989), ix, 2nd edn. (Cambridge, 1993), x, 2nd edn. (Cambridge, 1996); N. G. L. Hammond, *The Macedonian State* (Oxford, 1989); G. Hölbl, *Geschichte des Ptolemäerreiches* (Darmstadt, 1994); J. Whitehorne, *Cleopatras* (London, 1994), and S. Vleeming (ed.), *Hundred-Gated Thebes* (Papyrologica Lugduno-Batava 27; Leiden, 1995). For discussion of Alexandria, see P. M. Fraser, *Ptolemaic Alexandria*, 3 vols. (Oxford, 1972).

For the military history of the Ptolemies, see F. Adcock, *The Greek and Macedonian Art of War* (Berkeley and Los Angeles, 1957), and Leo Casson, *Ships and Seamanship in the Ancient World* (Princeton, 1971).

For Ptolemaic kingship, see Janet Johnson, 'The Demotic Chronicle as an Historical Source', *Enchoria*, 4 (1974), 1–17; E. E. Rice, *The Grand Procession of Ptolemy Philadelphus* (Oxford, 1983); K. Bringmann, 'The King as Benefactor: Some Remarks on Ideal Kingship in the Age of Hellenism', in A. Bulloch *et al.* (eds.), *Images and Ideologies: Self-definition in the Hellenistic World* (Berkeley and Los Angeles, 1993) [including the article by L. Koenen, 'The Ptolemaic King as a Religious Figure']; W. Huss, 'Das Haus des Nektanebis und das Haus des Ptolemaios', *Ancient History*, 25 (1994), 111–17; J. K. Winnicki, 'Carrying Off and Bringing Home the Statues of the Gods: On an Aspect of the Religious Policy of the Ptolemies towards the Egyptians', *Journal of Juristic Papyrology*, 24 (1994), 149–90. On brother–sister marriage, see R. S. Bagnall and B. W. Frier, *The Demography of Roman Egypt* (Cambridge, 1994).

For the economic and social history of the Ptolemaic period, see J. N. Svoronos, *Die Münzen der Ptolemäer* (Athens, 1908); M. Rostovtzeff, *A Large Estate in Egypt in the*

Third Century BC: *A Study in Economic History* (Rome, 1967; repr. of 1922 edn.), and *The Social and Economic History of the Hellenistic World*, 3 vols. (Oxford, 1953); D. J. Crawford, *Kerkeosiris: An Egyptian Village in the Ptolemaic Period* (Cambridge, 1971); N. Davies and C. M. Kraay, *The Hellenistic Kingdoms: Portrait Coins and History* (London, 1973); S. B. Pomeroy, *Women in Hellenistic Egypt from Alexander to Cleopatra* (Detroit, 1984); Dorothy Thompson, *Memphis under the Ptolemies* (Princeton, 1988); R. A. Hazzard, *Ptolemaic Coins: An Introduction for Collectors* (Toronto, 1995), and Dominic Montserrat, *Sex and Society in Graeco-Roman Egypt* (London, 1996).

On Ptolemaic priests, temples, and religion, see Serge Sauneron, *Les Prêtres de l'ancienne Égypte* (Bourges, 1957); F. Dunand, 'La Classe sacerdotale et sa fonction dans la société égyptienne à l'époque hellénistique', in J. Margueron *et al.* (eds.), *Sanctuaires et Clergés* (Paris, 1985), 41–59; Eleni Vassilika, *Ptolemaic Philae* (Leuven, 1989); W. Huss, *Der makedonische König und die ägyptischen Priester: Studien zur Geschichte des ptolemäischen Ägypten* (Stuttgart, 1994), and R. Merkelbach, *Isis Regina, Zeus Serapis. Die griechisch-ägyptische Religion nach den Quellen dargestellt* (Stuttgart, 1995).

On ethnicity during the Ptolemaic Period, see C. Préaux, 'Esquisse d'une histoire des révolutions égyptiennes sous les Lagides', *CdE* 11 (1936), 522–52; Naphthali Lewis, *Greeks in Ptolemaic Egypt* (Oxford, 1986); K. Goudriaan, *Ethnicity in Ptolemaic Egypt* (Amsterdam, 1988), and P. Bilde *et al.*, *Ethnicity in Hellenistic Egypt* (Aarhus, 1992).

On the art and literature of the period, see Bernard Bothmer *et al.*, *Egyptian Sculpture of the Late Period 700 BC to AD 100* (New York, 1960); Richard Fazzini, *Images for Eternity: Egyptian Art from Berkeley and Brooklyn* (New York, 1975); Fazzini and Robert Bianchi, *Cleopatra's Egypt* (New York, 1981), and Miriam Lichtheim, *Ancient Egyptian Literature*, iii. *The Late Period* (Berkeley and Los Angeles, 1980).

15. The Roman Period

Until recently there was a dearth of books on Roman Egypt, a situation that is rapidly being rectified. The best overall introduction is undoubtedly Alan Bowman, *Egypt after the Pharaohs* (London, 1986). Other general works worth reading include Naphthali Lewis, *Life in Egypt under Roman Rule* (Oxford, 1983), and J. G. Milne, *A History of Egypt under Roman Rule* (London, 1924). On the Romanization of Egypt, see Lewis 'The Romanity of Egypt: A Growing Consensus', *Atti del XVII Congresso Internazionale di Papirologia* (Naples, 1984), 1077–84. The special place of papyri and ostraca is now discussed by Roger S. Bagnall, *Reading Papyri, Writing Ancient History* (London, 1995). The administration of Roman Egypt is a complex issue, but good summaries will be found in the books by Bowman and Lewis cited above.

The role of the army is evaluated by R. Alston in *Soldier and Society in Roman Egypt* (London, 1995), but for a recent review of the army in the Eastern Desert see Valerie Maxfield, 'Eastern Desert Forts and the Army in Egypt during the Principate', in Donald Bailey (ed.), *Proceedings of the British Museum Conference on Roman Egypt*, published as *JRA* supplement 19 (1996), 9–19. Much of J. Lesquier, *L'Armée romaine de l'Égypte d'Auguste à Dioclétian* (Cairo, 1918), is still valid.

The grain trade has been the subject of much debate, but a fundamental work is G. Rickman, 'The Grain Supply under the Roman Empire', in J. H. D'Arms and E. C. Kopff (eds.), *The Seaborne Commerce of Ancient Rome: Studies in Archaeology and History* (Rome, 1980), 261–76. For the Appianus estate, see Dominic Rathbone, *Economic Rationalism and Rural Society in Third Century AD Egypt* (Cambridge, 1991).

The stone resources of the Eastern Desert are discussed by David Peacock, *Rome in the Desert: A Symbol of Power* (Southampton, 1992), and in Peacock and Maxfield, *Survey and Excavation at Mons Claudianus 1987–1993*, i. *The Topography and Quarries* (Cairo, 1996). The distribution of Mons Claudianus rock is discussed in Peacock *et al.*, 'Mons Claudianus and the Problem of the *granito del foro*: A Geological and Geochemical Approach', *Antiquity*, 68 (1994), 209–30. For the site of Myos Hormos, see Peacock, 'The Site of Myos Hormos: A View from Space', *JRA* 6 (1993), 226–32. Desert routes are discussed by J.-C. Golvin and M. Reddé, 'Du Nil à la Mer Rouge: Documents anciens et nouveaux sur les routes du désert oriental d'Égypte', *Karthago*, 21 (1987), 5–64; Steven Sidebotham *et al.*, 'Survey of the Abu Sha'ar–Nile Road', *AJA* 95 (1991), 571–622, and R. Zitterkopf and S. Sidebotham, 'Stations and Towers on the Quseir-Nile Road', *JEA* 75 (1989), 155–89. On trade, see also L. Casson, *The Periplus Maris Erythraei* (Princeton, 1989), and Sidebotham, *Roman Economic Policy in the Erythra Thalassa* (Leiden, 1986).

Aspects of religion in Roman Egypt are covered in H. I. Bell, *Cults and Creeds in Graeco-Roman Egypt* (1953); David Frankfurter, *Religion in Roman Egypt: Assimilation and Resistance* (Princeton, 1998), and R. Witt, *Isis in the Graeco-Roman World* (London, 1971). For Christianity and monasticism, see Colin Walters, *Monastic Archaeology in Egypt* (Warminster, 1974), and Bagnall, *Egypt in Late Antiquity* (Princeton, 1993). For mummy portraits, see Euphrosyne Doxiadis, *The Mysterious Fayum Portraits* (London, 1995); Susan Walker and Morris Bierbrier (eds.), *Ancient Faces: Mummy Portraits from Roman Egypt* (London, 1997), and Bierbrier (ed.), *Portraits and Masks in Roman Egypt* (London, 1997).

For pottery, see Jean-Yves Empereur, 'Un atelier de Dressel 2–4 en Égypte au IIIe siècle de notre ère', *Bulletin de Correspondence Hellénique*, suppl. 13 (1986), 599–608, and Empereur and M. Picon, 'À la recherche des fours d'amphores', *Bulletin de Correspondence Hellénique*, suppl. 13 (1986), 103–24. For papyrological evidence, see H. Cockle, 'Pottery Manufacture in Roman Egypt', *JRS* 71 (1981), 87–97. For faience and glass manufacture, see Paul T. Nicholson, *Egyptian Faience and Glass* (Princes Risborough, 1993), and D. B. Harden, *Roman Glass from Karanis* (Ann Arbor, 1936).

The nature of society in Roman Egypt is discussed in both R. S. Bagnall and B. W. Frier, *The Demography of Roman Egypt* (Cambridge, 1994), and Dominic Montserrat, *Sex and Society in Graeco-Roman Egypt* (London, 1996).

GLOSSARY

Acheulean stone tool industry, characterized by roughly symmetrical bifacial hand-axes and cleavers, which is linked with the appearance of *Homo erectus* and also early *Homo sapiens*

akh one of the five principal elements that the Egyptians considered necessary to make up a complete personality (the other four being the *ka*, *ba*, name, and shadow); it was believed to be both the form in which the blessed dead inhabited the underworld, and also the result of the successful reunion of the *ba* with its *ka*

Amarna Letters set of cuneiform tablets from the city at Amarna, most of which derive from the 'Place of the Letters of Pharaoh', a building identified as the official 'records office' in the central city at Amarna; all but thirty-two of the 382 documents are items of diplomatic correspondence between Egypt and many of the rulers of Western Asia

'anatomically modern' humans The first hominids (*a*) to resemble modern humans (in anatomical terms) and (*b*) to belong to the subspecies *homo sapiens sapiens*; the term is in fact rather misleading, since the early examples (who have brow ridges and larger teeth) are quite different from genuinely modern humans such as ourselves

ankh hieroglyphic sign denoting 'life', which takes the form of a cross surmounted by a loop; the sign was adopted by the Coptic church as its unique form of cross

Apis bull sacred bull who served as the *ba* (physical manifestation) of the god Ptah, the cult of which dates back to the beginning of Egyptian history; the bulls were buried in the Serapeum at Saqqara

Aten deity represented in the form of the disc or orb of the sun, the cult of which was particularly promoted during the reign of Akhenaten

Aterian Palaeolithic industry (named after the site of Bir el-Ater in eastern Algeria) that was characterized by a distinctive type of tanged stone point (implying the use of hafting)

ba, *ba*-**bird** aspect of human beings that resembles our concept of 'personality', comprising the non-physical attributes that made each person unique; it was often depicted as a bird with a human head and arms, and was also used to refer to the physical manifestations of certain gods

bark, bark shrine type of boat used to transport the cult images of Egyptian gods from one shrine to another. As well as the principal shrines in the temples, there were also small 'bark shrines' (also described as 'resting places', or 'way stations') along the routes of ritual processions

benben **stone** sacred stone (perhaps a lump of meteoric iron) at Heliopolis, which symbolized the primeval mound and perhaps also the petrified semen of the sun-god Atum-Ra; it served as the earliest prototype for the obelisk and possibly even the pyramid

block statue type of sculpture representing an individual in a very compressed squatting position, with the knees drawn up to the chin, thus reducing the human body to a schematic blocklike shape

Book of the Dead funerary text known to the Egyptians as the 'spell for coming forth by day', which was introduced at the end of the Second Intermediate Period and consisted of about 200 spells (or 'chapters'), over half of which were derived directly from the earlier Pyramid Texts and Coffin Texts; the text was usually written on papyrus and placed in the coffin, alongside the body of the deceased

BP abbreviation for 'before present', which is most commonly used for uncalibrated radiocarbon dates or thermoluminescence dates; 'present' is conventionally taken to be AD 1950

canopic jars four stone or ceramic vessels used for the burial of the viscera (liver, lungs, stomach, and intestines) removed during mummification; specific elements of the viscera were placed under the protection of four anthropomorphic genii known as the Sons of Horus

cartonnage material consisting of layers of linen or papyrus stiffened with plaster and often decorated with paint or gilding; it was most commonly used for making mummy masks, mummy cases, anthropoid coffins, and other funerary items

cartouche (*shenu*) elliptical outline representing a length of knotted rope with which certain elements of the Egyptian royal titulary were surrounded from the 4th Dynasty onwards

cataracts, Nile the six rocky areas of rapids in the middle Nile Valley between Aswan and Khartoum

cippus type of protective stele or amulet on which the naked child-god Horus was portrayed standing on a crocodile and holding snakes, lions, or other animals. It was probably used to heal snake bites or scorpion stings, but probably also had a more general prophylactic purpose

Coffin Texts group of over 1,000 spells, selections from which were inscribed on coffins during the Middle Kingdom

demotic (Greek: 'popular (script)') cursive script known to the Egyptians as *sekh shat*, which replaced the hieratic script by the 26th Dynasty; initially used only in commercial and bureaucratic documents, by the Ptolemaic Period it was also being used for religious, scientific, and literary texts

divine adoratrice (*duat-netjer*) religious title held by women, which was originally adopted by the daughter of the chief priest of the god Amun in the reign of Hatshepsut; from the reign of Rameses VI onwards it was held together with the title 'god's wife of Amun'

donation stele slab of inscribed stone recording the granting of areas of cultivable land to the gods of local temples

dromos processional way interconnecting different temples

encaustic painting technique, employing a heated mixture of wax and pigment, which was particularly used for the Faiyum mummy portraits of Roman Egypt

Epipalaeolithic chronological term usually applied to the last phase of the Palaeolithic period in North Africa and the Ancient Near East; the Egyptian and Lower Nubian Epipalaeolithic is characterized mainly by its innovative lithic technology (microlithic flake tools (see below)) and its chronological position between the Nilotic Upper Palaeolithic and Neolithic (i.e. *c.*10,000–5200 BC)

faience glazed non-clay ceramic material widely used in Egypt for the production of such items as jewellery, *shabti*s, and vessels

false door stone or wooden architectural element comprising a rectangular imitation door placed inside Egyptian private tomb chapels, in front of which funerary offerings were usually placed

foundation deposits buried caches of ritual objects placed at crucial points under important structures such as pyramid complexes and temples; the offering of model tools and materials was believed to maintain the building magically for eternity

'god's wife of Amun' (*hemet-netjer nt Imen*) religious title first attested in the early New Kingdom that later became closely associated with the 'divine adoratrice'. She played the part of the consort of Amun in religious ceremonies at Thebes. From the late 20th Dynasty onwards, she was barred from marriage and adopted the daughter of the next king as heiress to her office. In the 25th and 26th Dynasties, the 'god's wife' and her adopted successor played an important role in the transference of royal power

hieratic (**Greek:** *hieratika*, **'sacred'**) cursive script used from at least the end of the Early Dynastic Period onwards, enabling scribes to write more rapidly on papyri and ostraca, making it the preferred medium for scribal tuition. An even more cursive form of the script, known as 'abnormal hieratic', began to be used for business texts in Upper Egypt during the Third Intermediate Period

hieroglyphics (**Greek: 'sacred carved (letters)'**) script consisting of pictograms, ideograms, and phonograms arranged in horizontal and vertical lines, which was in use from the late Gerzean Period (*c.*3200 BC) to the late fourth century AD

Horus name the first royal name in the sequence of five names making up the Egyptian royal titulary, usually written inside a *serekh* (see below)

hypostyle hall (**Greek: 'bearing pillars'**) large temple court filled with columns and lit by clerestory windows in the roof; the columns were often of varying diameter and height, but those along the axial route of the temple were usually tallest and thickest

instruction (**Egyptian:** *sebayt*; **wisdom texts, didactic literature**) type of literary text (e.g. *The Instruction of Amenemhat I*) consisting of aphorisms and ethical advice, the earliest surviving example of which is said to have been composed by the 4th Dynasty sage, Hardjedef

ka the creative life force of any individual, whether human or divine; represented by a hieroglyph consisting of a pair of arms, it was considered to be the essential ingredient that differentiated a living person from a dead one

kiosk small chapel without a roof, which was used to contain cult statues of deities during festivals

Maat Goddess symbolizing justice, truth, and universal harmony, usually depicted either as an ostrich feather or as a seated woman wearing such a feather on her head. Small figurines depicting Maat were frequently offered to deities by Egyptian rulers, thus indicating the king's role as guarantor of justice and harmony on behalf of the gods

mammisi (**'birth place', 'birth house'**) Coptic term invented by Champollion to describe a building in major temple complexes of the Late Period and Graeco-Roman Period, in which the rituals of the marriage of the goddess (Isis or Hathor) and the birth of the child-god were celebrated; it was placed at right angles to the main temple axis

mastaba-**tomb** (**Arabic: 'bench'**) type of Egyptian tomb, the rectangular superstructure of which resembles the low mud-brick benches outside Egyptian houses; it was used for both royal and private burials in the Early Dynastic Period but only for private burials from the Old Kingdom onwards

Medjay Nubian nomadic group from the eastern deserts of Nubia, who were often employed as scouts and light infantry from the Second Intermediate Period onwards; they have been identified with the archaeological remains of the so-called pan-grave people (see below)

microlith type of stone tool, comprising a small blade or fraction of blade, usually less than 5 mm. long and 4 mm. thick, which is regarded as the archetypal tool of the Mesolithic Period, although it is now also recognized in some Palaeolithic industries. Single microliths were sometimes used as the tip of an implement, weapon, or arrow, while multiple examples were evidently hafted together to form composite cutting edges on tools

Mousterian one of the key stone tool industries of the Middle Palaeolithic, based on flakes produced from carefully prepared cores using the Levallois technique, which gradually replaced the heavier handaxes of the Acheulean industry (see above)

Mnevis bull sacred animal regarded as the *ba* (physical manifestation) of the sun-god at Heliopolis. Each Mnevis bull was required to be totally black and was usually represented with a sun-disc and uraeus between its horns. Because of his close connections with the sun-god, the Mnevis was one of the few divine entities recognized by Akhenaten

Nilometer device for measuring the height of the Nile, usually consisting of a series of steps against which the increasing height of the annual indundation, as well as the general level of the river, could be measured

nome, nome symbols Greek term used to refer to the forty-two traditional provinces of Egypt, which the ancient Egyptians themselves called *sepat*; for most of the Dynastic Period, there were twenty-two Upper Egyptian and twenty Lower Egyptian nomes

nomen (birth name) royal name introduced by the epithet *sa-Ra* ('son of Ra'), which was usually the last one in the sequence of the royal titulary; it was the only one to be given to the pharaoh as soon as he was born

offering formula (*hetep-di-nesu,* 'a gift which the king gives') prayer asking for offerings to be brought to the deceased, which formed the focus of food offerings in private tombs; the formula is often accompanied by a depiction of the deceased sitting in front of an offering table heaped with food

Opening of the Mouth ceremony funerary ritual by which the deceased and his funerary statuary were brought to life

ostracon (Greek: *ostrakon;* pl. *ostraka;* 'potsherd') sherds of pottery or flakes of limestone bearing texts and drawings, commonly consisting of personal jottings, letters, sketches, or scribal exercises, but also often inscribed with literary texts, usually in the hieratic script (see above)

palace façade architectural style comprising a sequence of recessed niches, which was particularly characteristic of the external walls of Early Dynastic funerary buildings at Abydos and Saqqara

pan-grave culture material culture of a group of semi-nomadic Nubian cattle-herders who entered Egypt in the late Middle Kingdom and Second Intermediate Period; well attested in the Eastern Desert, their characteristic feature being the shallow circular pit grave in which they buried their dead

peret ('coming forth') Egyptian term for the spring season. The Egyptians divided the year into twelve months and three seasons: *akhet* (the inundation itself), *peret* (when the crops began to emerge), and *shemu* (harvest-time). Each season consisted of four 30-day months, and each month comprised three 10-day weeks

playa plain characterized by a hard clayey surface and intermittently submerged beneath a shallow lake

prenomen (throne name) one of the five names in the Egyptian royal titulary, which was introduced by the title *nesu-bit*: 'he of the sedge and the bee', which is a reference both to the individual mortal king and the eternal kingship (not 'king of Upper and Lower Egypt', as it is sometimes erroneously translated)

pylon (Greek: 'gate') massive ceremonial gateway, called *bekhenet* by the Egyptians, which consisted of two tapering towers linked by a bridge of masonry and surmounted by a cornice; it was used in temples from at least the Middle Kingdom to the Roman Period

Pyramid Texts the earliest Egyptian funerary texts, comprising some 800 spells or 'utterances' written in columns on the walls of the corridors and burial chambers of nine pyramids of the late Old Kingdom and First Intermediate Period

rekhyt-**bird** Egyptian term for the lapwing (*Vanellus vanellus*), a type of plover with a characteristic crested head, often used as a symbol for foreigners or subject peoples

'reserve head' type of Memphite 4th Dynasty funerary sculpture, consisting of a limestone human head, usually with excised (or unsculpted) ears and enigmatic lines carved around the neck and down the back of the cranium

royal titulary classic sequence of names and titles held by each of the pharaohs consisting of five names (the so-called fivefold titulary), which was not fully established until the Middle Kingdom; it consisted of the Horus name, the Golden Horus name, the Two Ladies name (*nebty*), the birth name (nomen; *sa-Ra*), and the throne name (prenomen; *nesu-bit*)

sacred lake artificial pool in the precincts of many Egyptian temples from the Old Kingdom to the Roman Period

saff-**tomb** type of rock-cut tomb used in the el-Tarif area of western Thebes by the local rulers of the Theban 11th Dynasty

satrapy province in the Achaemenid empire

scarab type of seal found in Egypt, Nubia, and Syria–Palestine from the 11th Dynasty until the Ptolemaic Period; its name derives from the fact that it was carved in the shape of the sacred scarab beetle (*Scarabaeus sacer*)

sed-**festival** (*heb-sed*; **royal jubilee**) royal ritual of renewal and regeneration, which was intended to be celebrated by the king only after a reign of thirty years had elapsed

Serapeum term usually applied to buildings associated with the cults of the Apis bull or the syncretic god Serapis. The Memphite Serapeum at Saqqara, the burial place of the Apis bull, consists of a series of catacombs to the north-west of the Step Pyramid of Djoser

serdab (**Arabic: 'cellar'; Egyptian:** *per-twt*, **'statue-house')** room in *mastaba*-tombs of the Old Kingdom, where statues of the *ka* of the deceased were usually placed

serekh rectangular panel (perhaps representing a palace gateway) surmounted by the Horus falcon, within which the king's 'Horus name' was written

shabti (*ushabti*, *shawabti*) funerary figurine, usually mummiform in appearance, which developed during the Middle Kingdom out of the funerary statuettes and models provided in the tombs of the Old Kingdom; the purpose of the statuettes was to perform menial labour for their owners in the afterlife

shaduf irrigation tool comprising a long wooden pole with a vessel at one end and a weight at the other, by means of which water could be transferred between rivers and canals

sistrum (Egyptian: *seshesht*; Greek: *seistron*) musical rattling instrument played mainly by women, except when the pharaoh was making offerings to the goddess Hathor

solar boat (**solar bark**) boat in which the sun-god and the deceased pharaoh travelled through the netherworld; there were two different types of bark: that of the day (*mandet*), and that of the night (*mesektet*)

speos (Greek: 'cave') type of small rock-cut temple

sphinx mythical beast usually portrayed with the body of a lion and the head of a man, often wearing the royal *nemes* headcloth, as in the case of the Great Sphinx at Giza; statues of sphinxes were also sometimes given the heads of rams (criosphinxes) or hawks (hierakosphinxes)

talatat **blocks** small sandstone relief blocks dating to the Amarna Period, the name for which probably derives from the Arabic word meaning 'three hand-breadths', describing their dimensions (although the word may also have stemmed from the Italian word *tagliata*: 'cut masonry'

throne name see prenomen

triad group of three gods, usually consisting of a divine family of father, mother, and child worshipped at particular cult centres

Two Ladies name (*nebty*) one of the royal names in the 'fivefold titulary'; the term derives from the fact that this name was under the protection of two goddesses: Nekhbet and Wadjet

uraeus serpent-image that protruded just above the forehead in most royal crowns and headdresses; the original meaning of the Greek word uraeus may have been 'she who rears up'

viceroy of Kush (**King's son of Kush**) the Egyptian official governing the whole of Nubia (Wawat and Kush) in the New Kingdom

vizier term used to refer to the holders of the Egyptian title *tjaty*, whose position is considered to have been roughly comparable with that of the vizier (or chief minister) in the Ottoman empire; the vizier was therefore usually the next most powerful person after the king

CHRONOLOGY

This chronology has been compiled on the basis of a number of different criteria, ranging from the interpretation of ancient texts to the radiocarbon dating of excavated materials. The dates from 664 BC to AD 394 are precise (deriving primarily from Classical sources), whereas those for prehistory (c.700,000–3000 BC) are approximations based on a combination of stratigraphic information, seriation of artefacts, radiocarbon dates, and thermoluminescence dates.

The dates for the majority of the Pharaonic Period (i.e. c.3000–664 BC) are based mainly on ancient king-lists, dated inscriptions, and astronomical records. In the New Kingdom and Third Intermediate Period the margin of likely error is about a decade, but this tends to increase as we move further back in time, so that in the Old Kingdom it might be about fifty years, and in the 1st Dynasty it might be as high as 150 years.

When the dates for two or more dynasties overlap (principally in the Second and Third Intermediate periods), this is because their rule was accepted in different parts of the country. Overlapping dates for reigns within dynasties usually indicate co-regencies (i.e. periods when a king and his successor ruled simultaneously). When there are apparent gaps in the chronology (particularly at the end of dynasties), this is usually because there are one or two extremely poorly documented rulers, whose regnal dates are unknown or difficult to assess.

By the beginning of the Old Kingdom, Egyptian rulers had five names; the oldest of these was the so-called Horus name, and this is the one that we have usually cited for kings of the 1st–3rd dynasties (except in the case of Djoser, whose Horus name, Netjerikhet, is given in parentheses). From the 4th Dynasty onwards, we have usually given one or both of the so-called cartouche names (i.e. the 'nesu-bit' and 'son of Ra' names), and we have also sometimes added the Greek form of the name, especially when this is the name by which a ruler is better known to modern readers (e.g. Cheops for Khufu). Note that the existence and chronological position of the 3rd Dynasty ruler Nebka are currently a matter of debate.

PALAEOLITHIC PERIOD[1]	c.700,000–7000 BP
Lower Palaeolithic	c.700/500,000–250,000 BP
Middle Palaeolithic	c.250,000–70,000 BP
Transitional Group	70,000–50,000 BP
Upper Palaeolithic	c.50,000–24,000 BP
Late Palaeolithic	c.24,000–10,000 BP
Epipalaeolithic	c.10,000–7000 BP

SAHARAN NEOLITHIC PERIOD	c.8800–4700 BC
Early Neolithic	c.8800–6800 BC
Middle Neolithic	c.6600–5100 BC
Late Neolithic	c.5100–4700 BC

PREDYNASTIC PERIOD	c.5300–3000 BC
Lower Egypt[2]	
Neolithic	c.5300–4000 BC
	(or c.6400–5200 BP)
Maadi Cultural Complex	c.4000–3200 BC
Upper Egypt	
Badarian Period[3]	c.4400–4000 BC
Amratian (Naqada I) Period	c.4000–3500 BC
Gerzean (Naqada II) Period	c.3500–3200 BC
After c.3200 BC the same chronological sequence applies to the whole of Egypt	
Naqada III/'Dynasty 0'	c.3200–3000 BC

EARLY DYNASTIC PERIOD	c.3000–2686 BC

1st Dynasty	c.3000–2890
Aha	
Djer	
Djet	
Den	
Queen Merneith	
Anedjib	
Semerkhet	
Qaʿa	

2nd Dynasty	2890–2686
Hetepsekhemwy	
Raneb	
Nynetjer	
Weneg	
Sened	
Peribsen	
Khasekhemwy	

OLD KINGDOM	2686–2160 BC

3rd Dynasty	2686–2613
Nebka	2686–2667
Djoser (Netjerikhet)	2667–2648
Sekhemkhet	2648–2640
Khaba	2640–2637
Sanakht?	
Huni	2637–2613

4th Dynasty	2613–2494
Sneferu	2613–2589
Khufu (Cheops)	2589–2566
Djedefra (Radjedef)	2566–2558
Khafra (Chephren)	2558–2532
Menkaura (Mycerinus)	2532–2503
Shepseskaf	2503–2498

5th Dynasty	2494–2345
Userkaf	2494–2487
Sahura	2487–2475
Neferirkara	2475–2455
Shepseskara	2455–2448
Raneferef	2448–2445
Nyuserra	2445–2421
Menkauhor	2421–2414
Djedkara	2414–2375
Unas	2375–2345

6th Dynasty	2345–2181
Teti	2345–2323
Userkara [a usurper]	2323–2321
Pepy I (Meryra)	2321–2287
Merenra	2287–2278
Pepy II (Neferkara)	2278–2184
Nitiqret	2184–2181

7th and 8th Dynasties	2181–2160

Numerous kings, called Neferkara, presumably in imitation of Pepy II.

FIRST INTERMEDIATE PERIOD	2160–2055 BC

9th and 10th Dynasties	2160–2025
(Herakleopolitan)	
Khety (Meryibra)	
Khety (Nebkaura)	
Khety (Wahkara)	
Merykara	

11th Dynasty (Thebes only)	2125–2055
[Mentuhotep I (Tepy-a: 'the ancestor')]	
Intef I (Sehertawy)	2125–2112
Intef II (Wahankh)	2112–2063
Intef III (Nakhtnebtepnefer)	2063–2055

MIDDLE KINGDOM	2055–1650 BC

11th Dynasty (all Egypt)	2055–1985
Mentuhotep II (Nebhepetra)	2055–2004
Mentuhotep III (Sankhkara)	2004–1992
Mentuhotep IV (Nebtawyra)	1992–1985

12th Dynasty	1985–1773
Amenemhat I (Sehetepibra)	1985–1956
Senusret I (Kheperkara)	1956–1911
Amenemhat II (Nubkaura)	1911–1877
Senusret II (Khakheperra)	1877–1870
Senusret III (Khakaura)	1870–1831
Amenemhat III (Nimaatra)	1831–1786
Amenemhat IV (Maakherura)	1786–1777
Queen Sobekneferu (Sobekkara)	1777–1773

13th Dynasty	1773–after 1650
Wegaf (Khutawyra)	
Sobekhotep II (Sekhemra-khutawy)	
Iykhernefert Neferhotep (Sankhtawy-sekhemra)	
Ameny-intef-amenemhat (Sankhibra)	
Hor (Awibra)	
Khendjer (Userkara)	
Sobekhotep III (Sekhemra-sewadjtawy)	

Neferhotep I (Khasekhemra)
Sahathor
Sobekhotep IV (Khaneferra)
Sobekhotep V
Ay (Merneferra)

14th Dynasty	1773–1650

Minor rulers probably contemporary with the 13th or 15th Dynasty

SECOND INTERMEDIATE PERIOD	1650–1550 BC

15th Dynasty (Hyksos)	1650–1550
Salitis/Sekerher	
Khyan (Seuserenra)	*c.*1600
Apepi (Aauserra)	*c.*1555
Khamudi	

16th Dynasty	1650–1580

Theban early rulers contemporary with the 15th Dynasty

17th Dynasty	*c.*1580–1550
Rahotep	
Sobekemsaf I	
Intef VI (Sekhemra)	
Intef VII (Nubkheperra)	
Intef VIII (Sekhemraherhermaat)	
Sobekemsaf II	
Siamun (?)	
Taa (Senakhtenra/Seqenenra)	*c.*1560
Kamose (Wadjkheperra)	1555–1550

NEW KINGDOM	1550–1069 BC

18th Dynasty	1550–1295
Ahmose (Nebpehtyra)	1550–1525
Amenhotep I (Djeserkara)	1525–1504
Thutmose I (Aakheperkara)	1504–1492
Thutmose II (Aakheperenra)	1492–1479
Thutmose III (Menkheperra)	1479–1425
Queen Hatshepsut (Maatkara)	1473–1458
Amenhotep II (Aakheperura)	1427–1400
Thutmose IV (Menkheperura)	1400–1390
Amenhotep III (Nebmaatra)	1390–1352
Amenhotep IV/Akhenaten	
(Neferkheperurawaenra)	1352–1336
Neferneferuaten (Smenkhkara)	1338–1336
Tutankhamun (Nebkheperura)	1336–1327
Ay (Kheperkheperura)	1327–1323
Horemheb (Djeserkheperura)	1323–1295

RAMESSID PERIOD	1295–1069 BC

19th Dynasty	1295–1186
Rameses I (Menpehtyra)	1295–1294
Sety I (Menmaatra)	1294–1279
Rameses II (Usermaatra Setepenra)	1279–1213
Merenptah (Baenra)	1213–1203
Amenmessu (Menmira)	1203–1200?
Sety II (Userkheperura Setepenra)	1200–1194
Saptah (Akehnrasetepenra)	1194–1188
Queen Tausret (Sitrameritamun)	1188–1186

20th Dynasty	1186–1069
Sethnakht (Userkhaura Meryamun)	1186–1184
Rameses III (Usermaatra Meryamun)	1184–1153
Rameses IV (Heqamaatra Setepenamun)	1153–1147
Rameses V (Usermaatra Sekheperenra)	1147–1143
Rameses VI (Nebmaatra Meryamun)	1143–1136
Rameses VII (Usermaatra Setepenra	
Meryamun)	1136–1129
Rameses VIII (Usermaatra Akhenamun)	1129–1126
Rameses IX (Neferkara Setepenra)	1126–1108
Rameses X (Khepermaatra Setepenra)	1108–1099
Rameses XI (Menmaatra Setepenptah)	1099–1069

THIRD INTERMEDIATE PERIOD	1069–664 BC

21st Dynasty	1069–945
Smendes (Hedjkheperra Setepenra)	1069–1043
Amenemnisu (Neferkara)	1043–1039
Psusennes I [Pasebakhaenniut]	
(Akheperra Setepenamun)	1039–991
Amenemope (Usermaatra Setepenamun)	993–984
Osorkon the Elder (Akheperra setepenra)	984–978
Siamun (Netjerkheperra Setepenamun)	978–959
Psusennes II [Pasebakhaenniut]	
(Titkheperura Setepenra)	959–945

22nd Dynasty	945–715
Sheshonq I (Hedjkheperra)	945–924
Osorkon I (Sekhemkheperra)	924–889
Sheshonq II (Heqakheperra)	*c.*890
Takelot I	889–874
Osorkon II (Usermaatra)	874–850
Takelot II (Hedjkheperra)	850–825
Sheshonq III (Usermaatra)	825–773
Pimay (Usermaatra)	773–767
Sheshonq V (Aakheperra)	767–730
Osorkon IV (Aakheperra)	730–715

23rd Dynasty	818–715

Kings in various centres, contemporary with the later 22nd, 24th, and early 25th dynasties, including:

Pedubastis I (Usermaatra)
Iuput I
Sheshonq IV
Osorkon III (Usermaatra)
Takelot III (Usermaatra)
Rudamon (Usermaatra)
Peftjauawybast
Iuput II (Usermaatra)

24th Dynasty	727–715
Bakenrenef (Bocchoris)	720–715
25th Dynasty	747–656
Piy (Menkheperra)	747–716
Shabaqo (Neferkara)	716–702
Shabitqo (Djedkaura)	702–690
Taharqo (Khunefertemra)	690–664
Tanutamani (Bakara)	664–656

LATE PERIOD	**664–332 BC**
26th Dynasty	664–525
[Nekau I	672–664]
Psamtek I (Wahibra)	664–610
Nekau II (Wehemibra)	610–595
Psamtek II (Neferibra)	595–589
Apries (Haaibra)	589–570
Ahmose II [Amasis] (Khnemibra)	570–526
Psamtek III (Ankhkaenra)	526–525
27th Dynasty (1st Persian Period)	525–404
Cambyses	525–522
Darius I	522–486
Xerxes I	486–465
Artaxerxes I	465–424
Darius II	424–405
Artaxerxes II	405–359
28th Dynasty	404–399
Amyrtaios	404–399
29th Dynasty	399–380
Nepherites I [Nefaarud]	399–393
Hakor [Achoris] (Khnemmaatra)	393–380
Nepherites II	c.380
30th Dynasty	380–343
Nectanebo I (Kheperkara)	380–362

Teos (Irma atenra)	362–360
Nectanebo II (Senedjemibra setepenanhur)	360–343
2nd Persian Period	343–332
Artaxerxes III Ochus	343–338
Arses	338–336
Darius III Codoman	336–332

PTOLEMAIC PERIOD	**332–30 BC**
Macedonian Dynasty	332–305
Alexander the Great	332–323
Philip Arrhidaeus	323–317
Alexander IV [4]	317–310
Ptolemaic Dynasty	
Ptolemy I Soter I	305–285
Ptolemy II Philadelphus	285–246
Ptolemy III Euergetes I	246–221
Ptolemy IV Philopator	221–205
Ptolemy V Epiphanes	205–180
Ptolemy VI Philometor	180–145
Ptolemy VII Neos Philopator	145
Ptolemy VIII Euergetes II	170–116
Ptolemy IX Soter II	116–107
Ptolemy X Alexander I	107–88
Ptolemy IX Soter II (restored)	88–80
Ptolemy XI Alexander II	80
Ptolemy XII Neos Dionysos (Auletes)	80–51
Cleopatra VII Philopator	51–30
Ptolemy XIII	51–47
Ptolemy XIV	47–44
Ptolemy XV Caesarion	44–30

ROMAN PERIOD [5]	**30 BC–AD 395**
Augustus	30 BC–AD 14
Tiberius	AD 14–37
Gaius (Caligula)	37–41
Claudius	41–54
Nero	54–68
Galba	68–69
Otho	69
Vespasian	69–79
Titus	79–81
Domitian	81–96
Nerva	96–98
Trajan	98–117
Hadrian	117–138
Antoninus Pius	138–161

Marcus Aurelius	161–180	Maximian	286–305
Lucius Verus	161–169	Galerius	293–311
Commodus	180–192	Constantius	293–306
Septimius Severus	193–211	Constantine I	306–337
Caracalla	198–217	Maxentius	306–312
Geta	209–212	Maximinus Daia	307–324
Macrinus	217–218	Licinius	308–324
Didumenianus	218	Constantine II	337–340
Severus Alexander	222–235	Constans (co-ruler)	337–350
Gordian III	238–242	Constantius II (co-ruler)	337–361
Philip	244–249	Magnetius (co-ruler)	350–353
Decius	249–251	Julian the Apostate	361–363
Gallus and Volusianus	251–253	Jovian	363–364
Valerian	253–260	Valentinian I (west)	364–375
Gallienus	253–268	Valens (co-ruler, east)	364–378
Macrianus and Quietus	260–261	Gratian (co-ruler, west)	375–383
Aurelian	270–275	Theodosius (co-ruler)	379–395
Probus	276–282	Valentinian II (co-ruler, west)	383–392
Diocletian	284–305	Eugenius (co-ruler)	392–394

[1] The dates for the Palaeolithic Period are primarily based on uncalibrated radiocarbon dates, therefore they are given as radiocarbon years BP (before present) rather than as BC dates. In order to establish a secure link between the BP and BC dates, the overall range for the Neolithic is cited in terms of both BP and BC. All other dates are BC or AD.

[2] The term 'Lower Egypt' here denotes the Delta, the Faiyum, and an area stretching as far as 100 km. south of Cairo.

[3] The Badarian may have been a culture restricted to the Badari region near Asyut in Middle Egypt, rather than being a chronological phase throughout the whole of southern Egypt.

[4] Alexander IV was only the nominal ruler in 310–305 BC.

[5] The overall dates given here for the Roman Period begin with the official establishment of Egypt as a Roman province (on 31 August 30 BC) and end with the final division of the empire into western and eastern sections in AD 395 (i.e. the beginning of the Byzantine Period, which is usually described as the Coptic or Christian Period in Egypt).

ILLUSTRATION SOURCES

The editor and publishers wish to thank the following for their kind permission to reproduce the illustrations on the following pages:

Frontispiece © The British Museum
1   The Griffith Institute, Ashmolean Museum, Oxford
3   After Gordon Pearson
4   Barbara Ibronyi
5   Museo Archeologico, Palermo
6–7 *top* The Griffith Institute, Ashmolean Museum, Oxford
6–7 *bottom* Bibliothèque Nationale de France
8   Scala, Florence
15 © BPK, Berlin/Ägyptisches Museum/ Jürgen Liepe
17 The Griffith Institute, Ashmolean Museum, Oxford
19 Belgian Middle Egypt Prehistoric Project of Leuven University/ P. M. Vermeersch, E. Paulissen, and P. Van Peer, *Le Paléolithique de la vallée du Nil égyptien: L'Egypte des millénaires obscurs* (Marseille, 1990)
20 drawing by P. Van Peer, *The Levallois Reduction Strategy* (Monographs in World Archaeology, 13; Madison, 1992)
25 Belgian Middle Egypt Prehistoric Project of Leuven University
26–7 Belgian Middle Egypt Prehistoric Project of Leuven University/drawings by Marc Van Meenen/P. M. Vermeersch, E. Paulissen, P. Van Peer, *Le Paléolithique de la vallée du Nil égyptien: L'Egypte des millénaires obscurs.* (Marseille, 1990); P. M. Vermeersch, E. Paulissen, and P. Van Peer,

'Palaeolithic Chert Mining in Egypt', *Archaeologia Polona*, 33 (1995), 27
28 drawing by Nancy Brill; F. Wendorf, R. Schild, and A. E. Close, *The Prehistory of Wadi Kubbaniya, ii. Stratigraphy, Palaeoeconomy and Environment* (Dallas, 1989)
30 Prof. Fred Wendorf
31 Committee of the Egypt Exploration Society/Winkler 1938
33 Prof. Fred Wendorf
37 British Library/G. Caton-Thompson and E. W. Gardner, *The Desert Fayum* (1934)
40 Fitzwilliam Museum, Cambridge
41 © The British Museum
44 The Griffith Institute, Ashmolean Museum, Oxford
48 © The British Museum
50 Petrie Museum of Egyptian Archaeology
51 *top* Petrie Museum of Egytian Archaeology
51 *bottom* Béatrix Midant-Reynes
52–3 University College London Library/ Quibell and Green, *Hierakonopolis II* (1902)
55 © BPK, Berlin/Ägyptisches Museum
56 © The British Museum
60 © The British Museum
61 The Griffith Institute, Ashmolean Museum, Oxford
63 University College London Library/ W. B. Emery, *Archaic Egypt* (Penguin Books)

381 H: 40 cm. Museo Civico Archeologico, Bologna

383 H: 44.5 cm. Cairo Museum

387 © The British Museum

392 Asasif tomb no. 34; Leclant, *Montou-emhat;* Institut Français d'Archéolgie Orientale, Cairo

393 G. Lefebvre, *Petosiris* (1924)

395 Graham Harrison

405 H: 37 cm. © Peabody Museum of Natural History, Yale University Art Gallery, photo by Michael Agee

409 H: 45 cm. Courtesy of the Brooklyn Museum of Art, Charles Edwin Wilbour Fund (37, 37E)

410 H: 12.2 cm. The Metropolitan Museum of Art, Gift of Mrs John D. Rockefeller, Jr., 1938 (38.10)

412 H: 10.8 cm. Henry Lillie Pierce Fund Courtesy Museum of Fine Arts, Boston © 1997 Museum of Fine Arts, Boston. All Rights Reserved

413 H: 31.8 cm. Courtesy of Phoebe Apperson Hearst Museum of Anthropology and the Regents of the University of California

415 © The British Museum

416 Ian Shaw

420 Ian Shaw

422 Graham Harrison

424 A. Bowman, *Egypt after the Pharaohs* (British Museum Press, 1986)

427 David Peacock

429 David Peacock

431 David Peacock

432 David Peacock

433 David Peacock

436 © The British Museum

439 Graham Harrison

Picture research by Sandra Assersohn and Kathy Lockley

INDEX

Note: Page references in *italics* refer to black and white illustrations and their captions. Colour plates (which are unpaginated) are located by reference to the nearest page of text, printed in **bold**. Dynasties are indexed by word rather than number (e.g First Dynasty, not 1st Dynasty).